THE INCLUSIVE CLASSROOM

STRATEGIES FOR EFFECTIVE DIFFERENTIATED INSTRUCTION

Director and Portfolio Manager: Kevin M. Davis
Content Producer: Janelle Rogers
Development Editor: Bryce Bell/Carolyn Schweitzer
Content Project Manager: Pamela D. Bennett
Media Project Manager: Lauren Carlson
Portfolio Management Assistant: Anne McAlpine
Executive Field Marketing Manager: Krista Clark
Executive Product Marketing Manager: Christopher Barry
Procurement Specialist: Carol Melville

Cover Designer: Carie Keller
Cover Photo: Erstin Bittner/Westend61/Offset.com
Full-Service Project Management: Norine Strang,
  Cenveo® Publisher Services
Composition: Cenveo® Publisher Services
Printer/Binder: LSC Communications
Cover Printer: Phoenix Color
Text Font: Garamond 3 LT Pro

Cataloging-in-Publication Data is available on file at the Library of Congress.

1   18

ISBN 10:   0-13-489502-9
ISBN 13: 978-0-13-489502-4

SIXTH EDITION

THE INCLUSIVE CLASSROOM

STRATEGIES FOR EFFECTIVE DIFFERENTIATED INSTRUCTION

Margo A. Mastropieri
George Mason University

Thomas E. Scruggs
George Mason University

 Pearson

330 Hudson Street, NY, NY 10013

MARGO A. MASTROPIERI, Ph.D., is University Professor Emerita and past coordinator of the Special Education Program, College of Education and Human Development, George Mason University. She has served as a diagnostic remediator for the Learning Center at Mount Holyoke College and as a classroom teacher for students with special needs, from preschool to secondary levels, in Massachusetts and Arizona. Prior to working at George Mason University, she served as Professor of Special Education at Purdue University and as Assistant Professor of Special Education at Utah State University, where she also worked as a researcher at the Early Intervention Research Institute. She earned her Ph.D. from Arizona State University. She has codirected federally funded research projects in mnemonic strategy instruction, inclusive science and social studies education, and writing instruction at the elementary, middle school, and high school levels, in addition to directing undergraduate and doctoral-level training grants. From 1991 to 1997 she served as coeditor of *Learning Disabilities Research & Practice,* the journal of the Division for Learning Disabilities of the Council for Exceptional Children. From 1992 to 2011 she served as coeditor of the research annual *Advances in Learning and Behavioral Disabilities* (Emerald), and from 2009 to 2015 she served as coeditor of *Exceptional Children.* Among her publications are over 200 journal articles, 67 chapters in books, and 31 coauthored or coedited books. In 2007, she was awarded the Distinguished University Professor title from George Mason University. In 2008, she was the recipient of a Teaching Excellence Award at George Mason University. In 2010, she was the recipient of the Virginia Outstanding Faculty Award, which is the Commonwealth's highest honor for faculty at Virginia's public and private colleges and universities.

THOMAS E. SCRUGGS, Ph.D., is University Professor Emeritus, College of Education and Human Development, George Mason University. He served as a classroom teacher for students with a variety of special needs, including gifted students, from preschool to secondary levels in Massachusetts and Arizona. Prior to working at George Mason, he served as Professor of Special Education at Purdue University, where he also had served as the director of the Purdue Achievement Center, and as a research/evaluation specialist at Utah State University. He earned his Ph.D. from Arizona State University. He has directed or codirected externally funded research projects in peer tutoring, test-taking skills, mnemonic strategy instruction, and inclusive science and social studies education at the elementary, middle school, and high school levels. From 1991 to 1997 he served as coeditor of *Learning Disabilities Research & Practice,* the journal of the Division for Learning Disabilities of the Council for Exceptional Children. From 1992 to 2011 he served as coeditor of the research annual *Advances in Learning and Behavioral Disabilities* (Emerald), and from 2009 to 2015 he served as coeditor of *Exceptional Children.* Among his publications (mostly in collaboration with Margo Mastropieri) are over 200 journal articles, 62 chapters in books, and 31 coauthored or coedited books. In 2010, he received the Scholarly Achievement Award from the College of Education and Human Development, George Mason University.

Both authors are the recipients of the 2006 Council for Exceptional Children Special Education Research Award and the 2011 Distinguished Research Award from the American Educational Research Association: Special Education Special Interest Group for their research efforts in working with and advocating on behalf of individuals with exceptionalities.

One of the major features that characterize our classrooms today is student diversity. Not only have classrooms become more diverse with respect to race, religion, language, and ethnicity, but also more students with disabilities than ever are being included in general education classrooms. Data reported by the U.S. Department of Education indicate that over three-fourths of students with disabilities are now being served largely within the general education classroom setting.

Unfortunately, today's teachers consistently report that they do not feel prepared to teach students with disabilities in their general education classrooms. Only about one-fourth believe that they possess the skills necessary for effective inclusive teaching. We have written this book in order to place before teachers a wide variety of effective, evidence-based practices that can be successfully applied in today's inclusive classrooms.

Text Philosophy

There are numerous high-quality textbooks on inclusive education available today. This in itself is a notable advance from just a few years ago and indicates an increasing awareness of the important role of inclusive education in today's schools. We wrote *The Inclusive Classroom: Strategies for Effective Differentiated Instruction* to add our own perspective on inclusive education. We believe that teachers certainly should be provided with necessary information regarding legal issues and the characteristics of students with disabilities and other special needs. In addition, we describe and emphasize a wide variety of practical teaching and learning strategies that are directly relevant to the tasks and academic demands required of teachers in inclusive classrooms in today's schools.

However, we do not believe that "inclusion strategies" can be effectively implemented in the absence of overall effective teaching skills. That is, we believe that effective overall teaching and classroom management skills are necessary prerequisites for working with students with disabilities who attend inclusive classrooms. Therefore, we have described inclusion strategies within the overall framework of effective instruction and management of general education classrooms. The organization of this book reflects our perspective.

New to the Sixth Edition

For the sixth edition, we made a number of changes as a result of helpful suggestions from editors and reviewers that we believe have greatly improved the text.

- We have reorganized and combined the previous edition's chapter on motivation and affect with the chapter on classroom behavior and social skills to improve the overall coherence of the text.
- We have expanded our discussions of response to intervention (RTI) or multi-tiered systems of support (MTSS) and provided additional relevant examples.
- We have included additional information relevant to universal design for learning (UDL) and its applications to inclusive differentiated teaching.
- We have added additional discussion of differentiated instruction throughout the text.
- We have expanded our discussion of the Common Core State Standards (CCSS) and their relevance for inclusive education throughout the text.
- We have updated our coverage of technology applications in the *Apps for Education* feature.
- We have provided additional coverage and updated references in each chapter to reflect the latest research.

TEXT ORGANIZATION

PART 1: THE FUNDAMENTALS   The first part of this book presents the fundamentals of inclusive teaching, including information on the history of special education, the legal and political background of legislation for individuals with disabilities, and relevant, practical information on the individualized education program (IEP) and the changes brought about by the Individuals with Disabilities Education Improvement Act of 2004 (IDEA) and the Every Student Succeeds Act (ESSA) of 2015. Chapter 2 provides specific information on strategies for consultation and collaboration with students, parents, and other school personnel, including special education teachers, paraprofessionals, and other specialized school personnel. Chapters 3 and 4 provide information on the various characteristics of specific disability areas identified in IDEA (as well as attention deficit hyperactivity disorder), the federal special education law, and general adaptations that can be made for each of these disability areas. Chapter 5 describes other special needs areas not specifically covered under IDEA, including cultural diversity, students at risk, and students with special "gifts" and talents.

PART 2: DEVELOPING EFFECTIVE TEACHING SKILLS   The second part of this book describes a range of strategies that can be applied across curriculum areas and grade levels to address special needs and particular problems. Chapter 6 describes effective strategies for the general education teacher that have been demonstrated to be very helpful in promoting learning in inclusive settings. This chapter covers the variables most closely associated with student achievement, including engaged time on task, teacher questioning and feedback, and the most effective uses of praise, with specific reference to students with special needs. Chapter 7 describes response to intervention (RTI) or multi-tiered systems of support (MTSS) procedures that are presently implemented in many schools throughout the country and are intended to be helpful for individuals with learning difficulties. Chapter 8 describes strategies for improving motivation and affect, as well as behavior management strategies, and also describes strategies for improving social skills. Chapter 9 provides strategies for the effective use of peers to help accommodate diversity in classroom learning and behavior, including peer assistance, peer tutoring, and cooperative learning. These strategies can be used to transform classrooms into effective collaborative learning environments.

Chapter 10 describes strategies for enhancing attention and memory for entire classrooms as well as for individual students with special needs. Chapter 11 discusses strategies for teaching study skills, including organizational strategies, highlighting and outlining skills, listening and note-taking skills, and research and reference skills. Finally, Chapter 12 describes assessment and how adaptations can be made to accommodate the special needs of individual students as well as the classroom in general. These chapters in Part 2 are intended to provide teachers with effective general strategies for maximizing the potential of all learners.

PART 3: TEACHING IN THE CONTENT AREAS   The third part of this book describes targeted strategies that can promote learning in specific academic areas for a wide variety of students. Chapter 13 describes learning in basic literacy areas, including reading, writing, and spelling, and how special problems in learning in these areas can best be addressed. Chapter 14 presents effective strategies for promoting learning in mathematics, from early number concepts to algebra. Finally, Chapter 15 covers strategies for inclusive instruction of science and social studies and for facilitating transitions to a number of different settings, including postsecondary, vocational, and community environments.

Practical and effective teaching and learning strategies

In writing the sixth edition, as in previous editions, we wanted to emphasize the practical, research-based teaching and learning strategies essential in inclusive environments. For this reason, we focus on the basic tools educators need and directly relate this content to the academic and professional demands of teachers in inclusive settings.

Strategies Featured in the Text

Chapters 2 through 15 contain strategies that teachers can use in their inclusive classrooms with all students. The strategy sections are designated with a special design treatment to make them easy to find for the reader.

STRATEGIES FOR

COMMUNICATING EFFECTIVELY

USE ACTIVE LISTENING TECHNIQUES   Active listening is demonstrated through both nonverbal and verbal actions. Nonverbally, you demonstrate active listening by maintaining direct eye contact, leaning toward the speaker, nodding your head in agreement or understanding, and demonstrating that you are devoting all of your attention to the speaker. Verbal components of active listening involve responding with affirmative words, such as "Yes," "Yes,

---

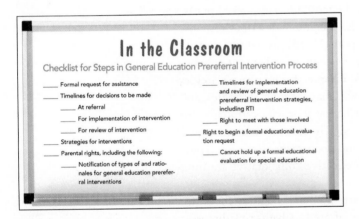

In the Classroom features offer tips, strategies, and resources that address very specific need areas and may be used directly in classroom situations. These features include effective resource materials that can be practically applied in inclusive classrooms.

CLASSROOM SCENARIO

Debbie

Debbie is a 10th grader with physical disabilities and communication difficulties who has been experiencing problems completing her work within a typical school day. This morning, six of Debbie's teachers—her math teacher, Ms. Juarez; her English teacher, Mr. Mantizi; her science teacher, Mr. Stubbs; her history teacher, Ms. Blackman; her speech and language therapist, Ms. Ramirez; and her special education teacher, Mr. Graetz—are meeting with Ms. Meyer, Debbie's paraprofessional, in the small conference room near the front office. They are trying to determine what they can do to help Debbie be more successful in high school. Everyone at the meeting is sincere in their desire to brainstorm ways to arrange the school day so that Debbie can learn successfully.

Mr. Graetz, the special education teacher, began the conversation by saying, "Thanks for agreeing to meet this morning to look at what's been happening with Debbie and try to come up with some solutions together. Recently, Debbie appears to be having a hard time keeping up with all of her work. Her grades have started slipping. Maybe if we share some ideas, we might be able to help her."

Classroom Scenarios provide context for the specific teaching strategies featured in the text. These cases model how to identify students who would benefit from specific teaching strategies.

Inclusion Checklists at the end of each chapter summarize the strategies described in the chapter and are helpful for finding immediate references for specific strategies, pinpointing difficulties teachers might be having, or planning specific interventions. Teachers may wish to consider the suggestions contained in the appropriate checklists prior to referring students for special education services. For example, if a teacher is considering referring a student for special education based on observed problems with attention or memory, the teacher could first consult the Inclusion Checklist in Chapter 10 for a list of possible interventions in these areas.

IMPROVING ATTENTION AND MEMORY

If students are having problems with attention, have you considered the following? If not, see the pages listed here.

STRATEGIES FOR IMPROVING ATTENTION

☐ Address the preconditions of attention with teacher effectiveness, 230
☐ Provide assistance with basic skills problems, 230–231
☐ Use direct appeal, 231
☐ Use proximity, 231
☐ Break up activities, 231–232
☐ Allow sufficient movement to reduce restlessness, 232
☐ Provide student activities, 232
☐ Use classroom peers to promote attention, 232
☐ Provide direct consequences for attention, 232–234
☐ Teach self-recording strategies, 234

STRATEGIES FOR ADDRESSING EXTREME CASES OF ATTENTION DEFICITS

☐ Provide intensive teacher-led instruction, 235
☐ Consider strengths and weaknesses of stimulant medication, 235
☐ Provide behavioral techniques, 235
☐ Promote joint attention, 235

If students are having problems with memory, have you considered the following? If not, see the pages listed here.

STRATEGIES FOR IMPROVING MEMORY

☐ Address memory preconditions, 236
☐ Develop "metamemory," 236–237
☐ Use external memory, 237
☐ Enhance meaningfulness, 237
☐ Use concrete examples, pictures, or imagery, 237–239
☐ Minimize interfering information, 239
☐ Use enactments and manipulation, 239
☐ Promote active reasoning, 239–240
☐ Increase practice, 240
☐ Use clustering and organization, 240
☐ Promote elaboration, 241

STRATEGIES FOR IMPROVING MEMORY WITH MNEMONIC TECHNIQUES

☐ Use the keyword method for verbal associations, 242–245
☐ Use the pegword method for numbered or ordered information, 245–248
☐ Use letter strategies for lists, 248–249
☐ Create mnemonic pictures, 249–250
☐ Combine mnemonic strategies with other classroom activities, 250–251

Research and resources that support practice and professionalism

A Tier 2 Reading Intervention for Fourth-Grade Students

Ritchey, Silverman, Montanaro, Speece, and Schatschneider (2012) developed and implemented a multicomponent Tier 2 intervention in reading for fourth-grade students identified as being at risk for reading failure. They implemented this intervention with two cohorts of students over a 2-year period. The intervention employed science content-area texts to increase motivation and to ease scheduling demands when supplemental intervention required students to miss content-area instruction.

The intervention included 24 scripted lessons provided over 12- to 15-week periods and focused on expository text comprehension.

It included repeated reading to promote fluency, comprehension instruction, vocabulary instruction, and text instruction. Student choice and four hands-on science activities were included in the lessons to incorporate motivational components. After a 2-year implementation period, the performance scores of students in the Tier 2 intervention were compared with the scores of a no-treatment control condition. Intervention students performed significantly better on science knowledge as well as knowledge and use of comprehension strategies. However, students in the intervention did not perform better as a whole on word reading, fluency, or comprehension. Although some components of

this Tier 2 intervention were very successful, the limitations suggest that additional instructional time may be needed at the upper-elementary level and that further research is needed on RTI interventions at this level.

QUESTIONS FOR REFLECTION

1. Why do you think the researchers did not find performance differences on word reading, fluency, or comprehension?
2. What might you implement to obtain performance differences on word reading, fluency, and comprehension?
3. After training, what could you do to help students to continue to use the intervention independently or to generalize the intervention to social studies?

Research Highlights explain the research behind certain teaching strategies developed for use with students with special needs, provide resources for further information and explanation, and tie chapter content to the research with reflection questions. The descriptive nature of the Research Highlights allows readers to see the need to verify strategies teachers use. Each Research Highlight contains Questions for Reflection.

Diversity in the Classroom

Working with Families from Diverse Backgrounds

Family involvement is a critical component of the special education process but is particularly critical for children from diverse backgrounds. Families representing diverse cultural and linguistic backgrounds can provide

- Maintain open and good lines of communication with families from the start of the school year.
- Ask families how they can help participate in their child's educational program at home and school.
- When families speak a language other than English, have interpret-

- Arrange for child care during family school visits when necessary.
- Determine whether families require transportation assistance to attend school functions.
- Arrange tutoring programs to assist both students and family members who may require additional

Diversity in the Classroom addresses the fact that classrooms are more diverse not only in respect to students with disabilities but also with respect to race, gender, religion, language, and ethnicity.

Apps for Education

IEP Software

Special education paperwork can be reduced by using efficient systems for recording data, for maintaining records, and for communications. Advances in technology can help teachers save valuable time. For example, teachers can use basic templates in word-processing programs with school stationery for communications, as well as databases containing frequently

having a facilitator at IEP meetings. *Schedule My IEP* (CME Apps, Inc.) contains a calendar with built-in reminders for meetings and important due dates.

There are numerous software programs commercially available to assist with writing IEPs and other aspects of special education in general. Many of these programs share common features in that they work easily on both PC and

will provide numerous commercially available programs.

Commercially available programs are usually advertised as highly relevant, timesaving devices that help teachers produce high-quality IEPs. Although this may be true in many cases, teachers should use caution to ensure that students' IEP objectives are not limited simply to what is available within individual software programs.

Apps for Education features provide information on technological applications relevant to the content of the chapter. These features provide up-to-date information on new technologies and how they can be employed to improve the academic or social functioning of students with special needs.

Professional Standards (including CEC and INTASC) are listed at the end of each chapter where relevant.

Support materials for instructors

The following resources are available for instructors to download at www.pearson-highered.com/educators. Instructors enter the author or title of this book, select this particular edition of the book, and then click on the "Resources" tab to log in and download textbook supplements.

Instructor's Resource Manual and Test Bank (ISBN 0-13-445038-8)

The Instructor's Resource Manual and Test Bank includes numerous recommendations for presenting and extending text content. It is organized by chapter and contains chapter objectives, chapter summaries, key terms, presentation outlines, discussion questions, application activities, suggested readings, and test items. The test bank contains more than 800 questions. These multiple-choice, short-answer, and essay questions can be used to assess students' recognition, recall, and synthesis of factual content and conceptual topics from each chapter.

PowerPoint® Slides (ISBN: 0-13-445047-7)

The PowerPoint® slides include key concept summarizations, diagrams, and other graphic aids to enhance learning. They are designed to help students understand, organize, and remember core concepts and theories.

TestGen (ISBN: 0-13-445039-6)

TestGen is a powerful test generator that instructors install on a computer and use in conjunction with the TestGen test bank file for the text. Assessments, including equations, graphs, and scientific notation, may be created for both print and online testing.

TestGen is available exclusively from Pearson Education publishers. Instructors install TestGen on a personal computer (Windows or Macintosh) and create tests for classroom testing and for other specialized delivery options, such as over a local area network or on the web. A test bank, which is also called a Test Item File (TIF), typically contains a large set of test items, organized by chapter and ready for use in creating a test, based on the associated textbook material.

The tests can be downloaded in the following formats:

TestGen Test Bank file—PC
TestGen Test Bank file—MAC
TestGen Test Bank—Blackboard 9 TIF
TestGen Test Bank—Blackboard CE/Vista (WebCT)
TIF Angel Test Bank (.zip)
D2L Test Bank (.zip)
Moodle Test Bank
Sakai Test Bank (.zip)

MyEducationLab

MyEducationLab is an online homework, tutorial, and assessment program designed to work with the text to engage learners and improve learning. Within its structured environment, learners see key concepts demonstrated through real classroom video footage, practice what they learn, test their understanding, and receive feedback to guide their learning and ensure their mastery of key learning outcomes. Designed to bring learners more directly into the world of inclusive classrooms and to help them see the real and powerful impact of the concepts covered in this book, the online resources in MyEducationLab with the Enhanced eText include the following:

- *Video Examples.* Each chapter has embedded videos that provide an illustration of an inclusive classroom principle or concept in action. These video examples most often show students and teachers working in classrooms. Sometimes they show students or teachers describing their thinking or experiences.
- *Self-Checks.* In each chapter, self-check quizzes help assess how well learners have mastered the content. The self-checks are made up of self-grading multiple-choice items that not only provide feedback on whether questions are answered correctly or incorrectly but also provide rationales for both correct and incorrect answers.
- *Application Exercises.* These scaffolded analysis exercises challenge learners to use chapter content to reflect on teaching and learning in real classrooms. The questions in these exercises are usually constructed-response items. Once learners provide their own answers to the questions, they receive feedback in the form of model answers written by experts.

Acknowledgments

There are many individuals who contributed to the production of this book and to whom we are indebted. For the sixth edition, we would like to thank our editor, Kevin Davis; Development Editor, Bryce Bell; and Project Manager, Norine Strang for their continuous support for the project. We would also like to thank Ann Davis for her assistance with this edition, as well as with all the previous editions of this book. We feel the sixth edition of this text has been greatly improved by their imaginative and helpful ideas, suggestions, and support. We also thank the technical editors and production staff at Pearson.

The external reviewers also delivered much useful feedback and provided commentaries on earlier versions of this book that were thoughtful, thorough, and professionally delivered. Reviewers who provided valuable input for this edition include Morgan Chitiyo, Duquesne University; Yun-Ching Chung, Illinois State University; Beth Jones, Texas A&M University–Commerce; and Sararose Lynch, Westminster College. Most of all, we thank the numerous individuals with whom we have had contact throughout our lives who have taught us about individuals with disabilities and teaching. Also included in our thanks are the numerous special education professionals whose research and publications form the core of substance for this book, without whose contributions this book would not be possible. Finally, we would like to remember and thank our parents, Francis and Dorothy Mastropieri and Edward and Janet Scruggs, who provided us with a continual source of support and a love for learning and curiosity throughout our lives.

M. A. M.
T. E. S.

3

CHAPTER 3

Teaching Students with Higher-Incidence Disabilities 53

4

CHAPTER 4

Teaching Students with Autism and Lower-Incidence Disabilities 79

7

CHAPTER 7

Response to Intervention and Multi-Tiered Systems of Support 153

8

CHAPTER 8

Improving Motivation and Social Behavior 175

9

CHAPTER 9

Promoting Inclusion with Classroom Peers 207

10

CHAPTER 10

Improving Attention and Memory 229

11

CHAPTER 11

Teaching Study Skills 255

14

CHAPTER 14

Mathematics 343

15

CHAPTER 15

Science, Social Studies, and Transitions 375

1

Introduction to Inclusive Teaching

2

Collaboration: Partnerships and Procedures

3

Teaching Students with Higher-Incidence Disabilities

4

Teaching Students with Autism and Lower-Incidence Disabilities

5
Teaching Students with Other Special Learning Needs

1

Introduction to Inclusive Teaching

LEARNING OUTCOMES

After studying this chapter, you should be able to:

1.1 Understand and describe educational rights for individuals with disabilities.

1.2 Describe the concept of *least restrictive environment*, and explain where students with disabilities are served.

1.3 Summarize and describe the legal foundations, litigation, and legislation concerning students with disabilities, such as IDEA (Individuals with Disabilities Education Act), Section 504 (Vocational Rehabilitation Act), and ADA (Americans with Disabilities Act).

1.4 Describe the models of service delivery and the continuum of services available to students with special needs.

In 1975, Congress passed a law that would change the face of public education in the United States. The Education for All Handicapped Children Act (now known as the Individuals with Disabilities Education Act, or IDEA) specified that all children—including those with disabilities formerly excluded from school—were entitled to a free, appropriate public education (FAPE). This law went far beyond any previous legislation in specifying that, to the greatest extent possible, this "special" education was to be provided in the least restrictive environment (LRE). In other words, students with disabilities were to be educated to the greatest extent possible in the general education classroom. This book is dedicated to describing the means by which this "least restrictive environment" can become a reality.

The passage of IDEA and its subsequent amendments has largely achieved its purpose. More than ever, students with disabilities now receive FAPE. Furthermore, this education is being provided more often in the general education classroom.

Before the passage of IDEA, students with disabilities were often denied access to public education (Yell, 2016). In some cases, they were placed in institutions. In other cases, the parents were forced to pay for private schools, often in inappropriate settings. Today, all students with disabilities are legally entitled to a free, appropriate education suited to their needs. The following scenarios compare a case from many years ago with a similar case from today. As a result of IDEA and related legislation, society has an increased understanding of individuals with disabilities and is much better able to accommodate individual differences in schools, in workplaces, and in social settings.

HISTORICAL SCENARIOS

Mr. and Mrs. Patterson

In 1960, Mr. and Mrs. Patterson had a brand-new baby girl, Hope. The initial excitement about the successful pregnancy and delivery was soon shrouded by a dark cloud. They were informed by the doctors that their precious infant was "retarded." Mrs. Patterson tells their story:

"We felt horrible when the physician informed us that our beautiful baby girl was retarded. I can still hear his words: 'You probably don't want to keep her. The state institution is the best place for infants like her. The staff at the institution will be able to take care of her better than you.' I immediately hated the doctor. How could he be saying this to me about my brand-new baby girl? I felt as if I was having a nightmare and that at any moment I would awake and find that everything was okay.

"At first we were so angry and couldn't help thinking thoughts like, *Why did this happen to us? We didn't do anything wrong; this is unfair!* We looked for someone to blame. We blamed the doctors and the staff at the hospital. It must be their fault—it couldn't be ours! Then, gradually, we both felt so guilty. We racked our brains for things that we might have done incorrectly during pregnancy. Did I fall? Was I exposed to any harmful substances? We didn't know whom to turn to for help. We felt overwhelmed and lost. The only individuals we knew we could speak with were the doctors and staff at the hospital, who had already expressed their opinions to us.

"We loved our baby and decided to keep her. She was very slow at developing. We were always searching for effective ways to help her. Everything was so hard. Each little thing we did seemed like an enormous journey. When Hope reached kindergarten age, she had passed some important developmental milestones. We knew she wasn't developmentally the same as other children her age, but we hoped that she might begin to catch up once she was in school.

"Unfortunately, however, within the first week of kindergarten, we were contacted by the school and asked to remove Hope from the school. We were told that she wasn't ready for school and that she took too much time away from the other children in the class. If we wanted Hope exposed to any educational program, the only solution available to us was to place Hope in the state institution's school.

"We were again devastated with this horrible decision. We felt as if we had no educational option. We went through the same grieving process as we did when Hope was born. We were angry and felt guilty for sending her away, but we sincerely believed we had no other options available to us. Although we made the best decision for us at the time, we still feel guilty."

Mr. and Mrs. Baxter

Now imagine a family in circumstances similar to those of the Pattersons over 55 years later. Mr. and Mrs. Baxter have a brand-new baby girl, Holly. The excitement turns to dismay when they are informed by the doctors that their precious infant is severely developmentally delayed. This time, however, the Baxters have additional legal guarantees in place that will provide a free and appropriate education for their child in the LRE beginning with early intervention services and continuing through supported employment options into adulthood. Some early intervention programs are available in their own community. Some of the program options are center-based, in which the intervention occurs at the school; some are home-based, in which the intervention takes place in the home; and others are a combination of center- and home-based programs. This means that Holly can participate daily in relevant educational programs in a variety of setting options.

Additionally, established networks of organizations provide support to parents and families of children with disabilities. Although the Baxters will still have some of the same painful experiences that the Pattersons had, at least the federal government has mandated services for families with children with severe special needs. Mrs. Baxter tells her story:

"We felt horrible when the physician informed us that our beautiful baby girl was developmentally delayed. Her words still ring in my ears: 'Your baby has a serious disability.' We barely heard the rest of her statement: 'We have a staff of early childhood specialists and nurses who will be in contact with you later today.' We couldn't believe our ears. The doctor must have us mixed up with someone else. There must be a horrible mistake. How could anything be wrong with our brand-new baby girl? I felt as if I was having a nightmare and that at any moment I would wake up and find that everything was okay."

The Baxters, like the Pattersons, went through the same questions of "Why us?" and "What happened?" and the associated feelings of denial, anger, guilt, and aloneness. Later on the same day, however, the Baxters felt the support from an early childhood specialist and a nurse. As Mrs. Baxter reported:

"They explained the types of intervention services that were available for our baby and for us. At first, everything seemed like a blur, but as reality sank in, we realized that we had hope for Holly again. Specialized services were available, she would receive assistance, and we would receive educational support. Although we still felt the anger and wanted to blame someone, we began to realize there were individuals and support services that would help us begin to adapt and provide appropriate services for our baby with special needs."

QUESTIONS FOR REFLECTION

1. Describe the various feelings experienced by the Pattersons. In what way were they similar to the feelings expressed by the Baxters? How do you think you would feel as a parent facing these issues?

2. Which of the Baxters' program options do you think you would have chosen? Why?

What Are the Educational Rights for Individuals with Disabilities?

Before the passage of federal legislation mandating services for students with disabilities, these individuals were routinely and legally excluded from school. Johnson (1986, pp. 1–2) documented several instances from years past across the United States, including the following examples:

- In Massachusetts in 1893, a child with disabilities was excluded by a school committee because "he was so weak in mind as to not derive any marked benefit from instruction and further, that he is troublesome to other children . . ." (*Watson v. City of Cambridge*, 1893).

- In Wisconsin in 1919, a 13-year-old with normal intelligence but physical disabilities was excluded for the following reasons:

    His physical condition and ailment produces a depressing and nauseating effect upon the teachers and school children; . . . he takes up an undue proportion of the teacher's time and attention, distracts attention of other pupils, and interferes generally with discipline and progress of the school. (*Beattie v. Board of Education of City of Antigo*, 1919).

- In 1963, Nevada excluded any student whose "physical or mental conditions or attitude is such as to prevent or render inadvisable his attendance at school or his application to study" (Nevada Revised Statutes, 1963).

- In 1971, Alaska excluded students with "bodily or mental conditions rendering attendance inadvisable" from school (Alaska Statutes, 1971).

- Virginia law in 1973 allowed school exclusion for "children physically or mentally incapacitated for school work" (Code of Virginia, 1973).

Today, these laws are no longer applicable. According to federal law, all students, regardless of disability, are entitled to a free and appropriate public education, including access to the general education curriculum. Since 1975, public education has truly become "education for all."

Along with increased rights of individuals with disabilities from legislation such as IDEA come increased responsibilities for teachers. General education teachers today have more students with disabilities in their classrooms than ever. In fact, only a small proportion of students with disabilities currently receives more than 60% of their education outside the general education classroom (see Table 1.1). Today, therefore, teachers must be especially aware of their responsibilities in providing appropriate instruction for students with disabilities.

Although more responsibilities are placed on the general education teacher, they should not be considered a burden. On the contrary, classroom diversity—whether in the form of gender, race, ethnicity, or ability—is something to be valued in its own right. Diversity provides a more exciting, dynamic classroom and the opportunity for students to learn that all people are not the same. Diversity provides opportunities for students to understand, respect, and value others for their differences. Finally, diversity provides the opportunity for you to use all of your imagination, skills, and resources to be the best teacher you can be. In the end, effective inclusive teaching is about being the most effective teacher possible and supporting all students to learn in the LRE.

TABLE 1.1 Percentage of Students Ages 6 Through 21 with Disabilities Receiving Services in Different Educational Environments

	Served Inside the Regular Class			
Disabilities	**80% or more of the Day (%)**	**40% to 79% of the Day (%)**	**Less than 40% of the Day (%)**	**Separate Environments (e.g., Residential, Separate Facilities, Correctional, Home-Bound/ Hospital Environments) (%)**
Specific learning disabilities	68.2	24.1	6.0	1.8
Speech or language impairments	87.1	5.5	4.3	3.2
Intellectual disabilities	16.7	26.6	49.1	7.6
Emotional disturbance	45.2	17.7	19.7	17.4
Multiple disabilities	13.4	16.3	46.2	24.1
Hearing impairments	59.4	16.0	12.2	12.4
Orthopedic impairments	55.2	16.0	21.4	7.4
Other health impairments	64.7	21.8	9.5	4.0
Visual impairments	65.2	12.9	10.7	11.3
Autism	39.7	18.2	33.3	8.8
Deaf-blindness	23.6	12.0	34.9	29.5
Traumatic brain injury	49.6	22.1	20.1	8.2
Developmental delay	63.0	19.3	16.1	1.5
All disabilities	**62.1**	**19.2**	**13.7**	**5.0**

Source: Thirty-Seventh Annual Report to Congress on the Implementation of Individuals with Disabilities Act (Section I, p. 48), 2015, Washington, DC: U.S. Department of Education.

MyEdLab: **Self-Check 1.1**

MyEdLab: **Application Exercise 1.1: Educational Rights: Education for All**

The Least Restrictive Environment

WHERE ARE STUDENTS WITH DISABILITIES SERVED?

Critical to IDEA legislation is the concept of *least restrictive environment* (LRE; Rozalski, Miller, & Stewart, 2011). This phrase means that students with disabilities must be educated in the setting least removed from the general education classroom. To the greatest extent possible, students with disabilities are not to be restricted to education in special schools or special classrooms but rather should have access to the same settings to which students without disabilities have access. When students with disabilities are educated, to any extent, in a different setting, there must be a compelling reason that this setting is in the student's best interest.

MAINSTREAMING AND INCLUSION

Mainstreaming was the first movement devoted to the placement of students with disabilities within the general education classroom. Advocates of **mainstreaming** three or four decades ago did not necessarily want to see students with disabilities placed in special classes for the entire school day, but they argued that more exposure to the general classroom would be in everyone's best interest (e.g., Blankenship, 1981). Often, mainstreaming was thought to be something individual special education students could "earn" by demonstrating that their skills were adequate to function independently in general education settings. Since then, the term **inclusion** has been used to describe the education of students with disabilities in general education settings. Although many definitions have been used to describe *inclusion*, the term is generally taken to mean that students with disabilities are served primarily in the general education classroom, under the responsibility of the general classroom teacher. When necessary and justifiable, students with disabilities may also receive some of their instruction in another setting, such as a resource room. Additional support can also be provided within the general education classroom by paraprofessionals or special education teachers. Although this is a similar concept to mainstreaming, a critical difference of inclusion is the view of the general classroom as the primary placement for the student with disabilities, with other special services regarded as ancillary (Lipsky & Gartner, 1997).

In addition to mainstreaming and inclusion, the term *full inclusion* is also used, referring to the practice of serving students with disabilities and other special needs entirely within the general classroom. In full-inclusion settings, all students with disabilities are served for the entire day in the general classroom, although special education teachers and other personnel may also be present in the general classroom at times (Kauffman, Nelson, Simpson, & Mock, 2011; Zigmond, 2015).

WHO IS SERVED UNDER IDEA?

IDEA is intended to provide necessary support services to students with disabilities. To accomplish this goal, students with disabilities are categorized in particular disability groups. It is important to remember, however, that all students served by IDEA are first human beings and individuals, capable of achievement, accomplishment, friendship, affection, and all other attributes of any other individual. Disability status may not be a permanent characteristic of all individuals; in fact, most people can expect to be considered "disabled" at one time or another in their lives. This in no way detracts from their fundamental worth as human beings. In fact, it is this principle of individual worth that has inspired much of today's special education legislation.

In short, although students served under IDEA have been given a disability "label," it is important to consider the individual first, and then consider the label as a secondary factor, along with other characteristics that help identify the unique aspects of the individual. For this reason, it has been recommended that "person-first" language be adopted (Russell, 2008). For example, we speak of "students with hearing impairments," rather than "hearing-impaired students." It is also important to remember that we use these descriptions only when it is directly relevant to a situation. When it is not relevant to list hearing impairment as a characteristic, for example, we speak simply of "Amy," or "Richard," or "Ana." For example, Margo, as a high school student, was best friends with Carol, a student 1 year older. They played on the basketball team together and spent much of their after-school time together. After several years of close friendship, Margo expressed surprise that Carol had not gotten her driver's license, even a year after her 16th birthday. Further, Carol went to a separate setting to take the SAT. When she asked Carol about these things, Carol revealed that she was legally blind. Margo was astonished to hear this—and this situation demonstrated clearly to her that many characteristics of individuals, such as warmth, caring, sincerity, and understanding, can be much more important than disability status. It also demonstrated that important relationships can be developed and maintained that have little or nothing to do with disability status.

GENERAL CHARACTERISTICS   Students served by IDEA are distributed among 13 disability categories. Following is a brief description of each category (see IDEA, 2004; Assistance to States for the Education of Children with Disabilities and Preschool Grants for Children with Disabilities; Final Rule, No, 156, Vol. 71, C.F.R. Parts 300 and 301, 2006). Individual states may use different terminology.

- *Autism.* Autism is a developmental disability generally manifested within the first 3 years of life. Major characteristics can include impairments in communication and reciprocal social interaction, resistance to change, engagement in repetitive activities, and unusual responses to sensory stimuli.

- *Deaf-blindness.* Individuals in this category have moderate to severe impairments in both vision and hearing, causing such severe communication and educational needs that programming solely for children with deafness or children with blindness is not appropriate.

- *Deafness.* Individuals with deafness have hearing impairments so severe that processing linguistic information through hearing is severely limited, with or without amplification, and educational performance is negatively impacted.

- *Emotional disturbance (or serious emotional disturbance).* This category includes individuals with a condition in one or more of the following areas over an extended period of time: (a) inability to learn, not due to intellectual, sensory, or health problems; (b) inability to build and maintain social relationships with peers and teachers; (c) inappropriate behavior and affect; (d) general pervasive depression or unhappiness; (e) tendency to develop fears or physical symptoms associated with school and personal problems; and (f) schizophrenia (a disorder in perception of reality). According to the federal definition, emotional disturbance is not intended to apply to socially maladjusted children unless they are also characterized as having serious emotional disturbance.

- *Hearing impairments.* Hearing impairments, with or without amplification, affect educational performance and developmental progress. The impairment may be permanent or fluctuating, mild to profound, unilateral or bilateral, but this category includes impairments not included under the definition of deafness.

- *Intellectual disabilities.* Intellectual disabilities (referred to as *mental retardation* in IDEA) describes significantly below-average intellectual functioning, as well as concurrent deficits in "adaptive behavior" (age-appropriate personal independence and social responsibility). It is manifested between birth and age 18 and negatively affects educational performance.

- *Multiple disabilities.* This category includes any individuals with two or more disabling conditions. However, this category often includes intellectual disability as one of the categories and is usually used when disorders are serious and interrelated to such an extent that it is difficult to identify the primary area of disability. It does not include deaf-blindness.

- *Orthopedic impairments.* Orthopedic impairments are associated with physical conditions that seriously impair mobility or motor activity. This category includes individuals with cerebral palsy, individuals with diseases of the skeleton or muscles (such as poliomyelitis), and accident victims.

- *Other health impairments.* This category includes chronic or acute health-related difficulties that adversely affect educational performance and are manifested by limited strength, vitality, or alertness. It can include such health problems as heart conditions, sickle-cell anemia, lead poisoning, diabetes, and epilepsy. It can also include attention deficit hyperactivity disorder (ADHD).

- *Specific learning disabilities.* This category refers to a disorder in one or more of the basic psychological processes involved in understanding or using spoken or written language, which can result in difficulties in reading, writing, listening, speaking, thinking, spelling, or mathematics. The term *learning disabilities* does not apply to children with learning problems that are primarily the result of visual, hearing, or physical disabilities; intellectual disability; emotional disturbance; or environmental, cultural, or economic disadvantage.

- *Speech or language impairments.* This category includes disorders of articulation, fluency, voice, or language that adversely affect educational performance.

- *Traumatic brain injury.* Traumatic brain injury is an acquired injury to the brain due to external force resulting in a total or partial disability, psychosocial impairment, or both, which negatively affects educational performance (does not apply to congenital or degenerative injuries or to brain injuries acquired during birth).

- *Visual impairments, including blindness.* A visual impairment is a loss of vision that, even when corrected, affects educational performance. It may be mild to moderate to severe in nature. Students who are blind are unable to read print and usually learn to read and write using braille. Students with low vision can usually read when the print is enlarged sufficiently.

In addition, children aged 3 to 9 can be classified as experiencing developmental delay if they have developmental delays in one or more of the following areas: physical, cognitive, communication, social or emotional, or adaptive development. Such children may need special education and related services.

OTHER INSTANCES OF CLASSROOM DIVERSITY

IDEA mandates services for most of the recognized disability areas. However, there are other sources of classroom diversity, not associated with disabilities, that you need to consider when planning and implementing classroom instruction. These areas include the following:

- *Culturally and linguistically diverse groups.* These students are culturally or linguistically different from the majority U.S. culture or different from the teacher. Teachers should plan and implement instruction that is considerate of and sensitive to students' linguistic or cultural differences (Gollnick & Chinn, 2013).

- *At-risk students.* Students characterized as "at risk" exhibit characteristics, live in an environment, or have experiences that make them more likely to fail in school, drop out, or experience a lack of success in future life. These factors are many and varied, but they include "slow learners" not served by IDEA categories and individuals who have sociocultural disadvantages, are at risk for suicide, or come from dysfunctional home environments (e.g., marred by drug or alcohol abuse, domestic violence, or child abuse). Such learners may require any of a variety of adaptations to help them succeed in school and later life (Frieman, 2001).

- *Gifted and talented.* These students exhibit skills or abilities substantially above those of their age in areas such as academic achievement in one or more subject areas, visual or performing arts, or athletics. If the abilities of such students greatly exceed classroom standards or curriculum, special adaptations or accommodations may be appropriate. Although many states have passed laws providing for the identification and education of gifted and talented students, in many cases, funding for gifted programs is not provided (Davis & Rimm, 2011).

MyEdLab: **Self-Check 1.2**

MyEdLab: **Application Exercise 1.2: Least Restrictive Environment**

Legal Foundations

In the years following World War II, political change, litigation, and resulting legislation began to emerge that increased the inclusion of all groups of people in U.S. society. Most significant was the civil rights movement, which primarily addressed the rights of African Americans in U.S. society. This movement influenced the ideas on which much litigation and legislation involving individuals with disabilities are based. In the *Brown v. Board of Education* (1954) decision, the Supreme Court ruled that it was unlawful to discriminate against any group of people. With respect to schoolchildren, the Court ruled that the concept of "separate-but-equal" educational facilities for children of different races was inherently unequal. The justification for this ruling was found in the 14th Amendment to the U.S. Constitution, which states that individuals cannot be deprived of life, liberty, or property without due process of law.

LEGAL PROCEEDINGS AND LEGISLATION

People with disabilities also began to be identified as a group whose rights had been denied. In the years following *Brown v. Board of Education*, court cases were decided that underlined the rights of individuals with disabilities to a free, appropriate education. Other cases supported nondiscriminatory special education placement of individuals from minority groups in the United States. Some of the important court cases relating to individuals with disabilities demonstrate a progression of increasing rights for individuals with disabilities (see also Murdick, Gartin, & Crabtree, 2014; Wright & Wright, 2007; Yell, 2016):

- *1954: Brown v. Board of Education* (Kansas). The Supreme Court determined that "separate-but-equal" education is illegal.

- *1970: Diana v. State Board of Education* (California). The court ruled that children cannot be placed in special education based on culturally biased tests.

- *1972: Pennsylvania Association for Retarded Children (PARC) v. Commonwealth of Pennsylvania* and *Mills v. Board of Education* (District of Columbia). These cases established the right to education for students with disabilities and found that denial of education violates the 14th Amendment.

- *1977: Larry P. v. Riles* (California). The court ruled that the use of standardized IQ tests for placement into special education classes for students with "educable mental retardation" was discriminatory.

- *1982: Board of Education v. Rowley* (New York). The Supreme Court defined "free and appropriate education" and directed that public schools must provide appropriate special education services.

- *1988: Honig v. Doe* (California). This decision was concerned with extensive suspensions of students with emotional disturbances from school for aggressive behavior that the court determined was disability related. The court ruled that a suspension of longer than 10 days was effectively a change in placement, requiring all the necessary procedures governing a change in placement.

- *1992: Oberti v. Board of Education of the Borough of Clementon School District* (New Jersey). A federal district court ruled that a self-contained special education class was not the LRE for a student with Down syndrome. The court ruled that school districts were obligated to consider regular class placement first, with supplementary aids and services, before considering alternative placements.

Along with this litigation, laws began to be passed that provided further support for the rights of students with disabilities. Some of these laws are summarized in Figure 1.1. In the following text, some of the most significant legislation involving individuals with disabilities is described (see also Murdick et al., 2014; Rothstein & Johnson, 2014; Yell, 2016). This legislation includes Section 504 of the Vocational Rehabilitation Act, the Americans with Disabilities Act, and the most significant law for special education, the Individuals with Disabilities Education Act (Public Law [PL] 94-142).

SECTION 504

Section 504 of the Vocational Rehabilitation Act of 1973 (reauthorized as the Carl D. Perkins Career and Technical Education Act of 2006; U.S. Department of Education, Office of Special Education and Rehabilitative Services, 2006) is a civil rights law that prevents discrimination against individuals with disabilities by any institution that receives federal funds and provides for a FAPE. Some private schools that do not receive federal funding may be exempt from Section 504. This law applies both to schools and to the workforce. Section 504 provides for equal opportunities in all aspects of education. Students may not be classified as disabled according to the IDEA guidelines, but they must demonstrate a significant learning problem that affects their ability to function in school. Under Section 504, disability is considered to be an impairment, physical or mental, that substantially limits a major life activity (Lazarus, Thurlow, Lail, & Christensen, 2009; U.S. Department of Education, Office of Special Education and Rehabilitative Services, 2006). Some students who may not be served under IDEA because they do not meet the definitional requirements of one of the IDEA disability categories can still obtain services under Section 504 (deBettencourt, 2002). For example, some students with ADHD, as well as some students who require modifications for their severe allergies or asthma, may be covered under this law. Other types of disabilities likely covered under Section 504, but not IDEA, might include the following (Smith, 2002):

- Students who had been placed in special education programs but have transitioned out

- Students thought to be socially maladjusted, or who have a history of alcohol or drug abuse

- Students who carry infectious diseases such as AIDS

Students can be referred for Section 504 services by anyone but are usually referred by teachers or parents. If a group of knowledgeable school personnel believes the child is eligible, the school must then conduct an evaluation to determine eligibility and the nature of services needed to ensure a FAPE. The decision is based on professional judgment rather than test scores

1973	Section 504–Rehabilitation Act of 1973, U.S.C. Section 794: Recipients of federal funds cannot discriminate on the basis of disability.
1975	Education for All Handicapped Children Act (PL 94-142), 20 U.S.C. Sections 1400–1461: This law requires, and provides support to, states to implement a plan to provide free education and appropriate related services (on an individualized basis) to students with disabilities, including due-process provisions. It requires Individualized Education Programs (IEPs) for each student served under this law. This law was amended in 1983, 1986, 1990, 1997, and 2004. The 1990 amendments also renamed this law the Individuals with Disabilities Education Act (IDEA).
1977	Final regulations of Education for All Handicapped Children Act are passed.
1978	Gifted and Talented Children's Education Act: This act provides financial incentives for state and local educational agencies to develop programs for gifted and talented students.
1983	Amendments to the Education of the Handicapped Act (PL 98-199): These amendments mandate states to collect data on students with disabilities exiting systems and to address transition needs of secondary students with disabilities. In addition, they provide incentives to states to provide services to infants and preschoolers with disabilities.
1984	Developmental Disabilities Assistance and Bill of Rights Acts (PL 98-527): These acts provide for the development of employment-related training activities for adults with disabilities.
1984	Perkins Act, 20 U.S.C. 2301, 233–234: This act mandates that 10% of all vocational education funding must be for students with disabilities. Vocational education should be provided in the LRE secondary support is provided for students with disabilities.
1986	Education for All Handicapped Children Act Amendments (PL 99-457): These amendments encourage states to develop comprehensive services for infants and toddlers (birth through age 2) with disabilities and to expand services for preschool children (ages 3–5). After the 1990–91 school year, all states must provide free and appropriate education to all 3- to 5-year-olds with disabilities or forfeit federal assistance for preschool funding.
1986	Rehabilitation Act Amendments (PL 99-506): These amendments provide for the development of supported employment programs for adults with disabilities.

Figure 1.1 History of Relevant Legislation

and numerical indicators. If a student is considered eligible, the law does not provide funding; however, it does require that school personnel create a written plan that will help accommodate these special needs and provide an accessible environment. Accommodation plans can include a statement of student strengths and weaknesses, a list of accommodations to be implemented, and designation of the person(s) responsible for implementation. Accommodations are usually inexpensive, commonsense modifications intended to provide nondiscrimination and FAPE (Smith, 2002).

AMERICANS WITH DISABILITIES ACT

The Americans with Disabilities Act (ADA) was signed into law in 1990 and mandated that individuals with disabilities should be provided with "reasonable accommodations" in the workplace and that such individuals could not be discriminated against. ADA also included protections for individuals enrolled in colleges and universities. Adults with disabilities attending universities are also entitled to appropriate modifications in classes. These modifications, in many ways, parallel those made in public schools in compliance with IDEA. Major components of the ADA are given in Figure 1.2.

- Employers may not discriminate on the basis of disability.
- Employers may not ask if applicant has a disability.
- "Reasonable accommodations" must be provided in the workplace.
- New buses must be made accessible.
- Most communities must provide transportation.
- Rail service must accommodate individuals with disabilities within 20 years.
- Public locations—hotels, stores, and restaurants—are accessible.
- State and local governments may not discriminate.
- Telephone companies must provide adapted communication options for the deaf.

Figure 1.2 Major Components of ADA
Note: From U.S. Department of Justice, 1990.

The ADA is of particular significance because of its aim to maximize the employment potential of millions of Americans with disabilities. It can be considered an important extension of IDEA because it provides for reasonable accommodations and nondiscriminatory treatment of individuals with disabilities beyond the high school years.

INDIVIDUALS WITH DISABILITIES EDUCATION ACT (IDEA)

IDEA is the major special education law. Originally signed in 1975 as the Education for All Handicapped Children Act, IDEA has been amended several times since then, most recently in 2004 (IDEA, 2004) as the Individuals with Disabilities Education Improvement Act (referred to here as IDEA), as summarized in Figure 1.3. The most important provision in IDEA is that all children, from 3 through 21 years of age, regardless of type or severity of disability, are entitled to a FAPE (see Yell & Crockett, 2011). Discretionary assistance is also provided to develop interagency programs for all young children with disabilities from birth to 3 years of age. This provision overrides previous legislation and decisions that limit the attendance of students with disabilities in public schools. Overall, six major principles have remained in the law throughout its amendments (Murdick et al., 2014; Yell, Katsiyannis, & Bradley, 2011). These principles are as follows:

1. *Zero reject.* This principle requires that no child with a disability can be excluded from public education.

2. *Nondiscriminatory testing.* Schools are required to use a variety of nondiscriminatory methods to determine whether a student has a disability and, if so, whether special education is required. Testing must not discriminate on the basis of race, culture, or ethnicity, and it must be administered in the student's native language. A variety of measures is required so that placement decisions are not made on the basis of a single test score. Further, the law is intended to address multicultural issues, as described in the *Diversity in the Classroom* feature.

3. *Free and appropriate education.* Students who have been referred to special education must have an individualized education program (IEP) that details their special learning needs and mandates appropriate services. Short- and long-term goals and objectives for students are listed explicitly in their IEPs.

4. *Least restrictive environment.* Students with disabilities are entitled to be educated with their nondisabled peers to the greatest extent possible.

5. *Due process.* Due process must be followed in all placement decisions and changes in placement. Records are to be kept confidential, and parents are to be involved in all aspects of the planning and placement process.

6. *Parent participation.* Schools must collaborate with parents in the design and implementation of special education services (see also Staples & Diliberto, 2010).

Content of IEPs
- Present level of performance must include the "child's academic achievement and functional performance."
- Annual goals must be measurable.
- Short-term objectives are required only for children who take alternative assessments.
- IEPs must describe how progress will be measured and when reports will be issued.

Research-based practice
- Statements supporting special education services must be based on peer-reviewed research.

Accommodations and alternative assessments
- Statements indicating the need for individual accommodations for testing and alternative statewide assessments must be provided.
- Justification for participation in alternative assessments must be provided.

IEP meetings
- The teacher's attendance may be waived (1) if the teacher's curriculum area is not addressed, or (2) if a report based on the curriculum area is submitted prior to the meeting and is approved by the student's parents and the local education agency (LEA).
- Fifteen states may apply for an optional multi-year IEP pilot program. This means that, in some cases, annual IEP meetings may not be required and may be conducted no less than every 3 years.

Discipline
- If students violate a code of conduct at school, they may be suspended for up to 10 days.
- If the behavior was related to the disability, a functional behavior assessment and behavior intervention plan must be completed for the child.
- If the behavior was unrelated to the disability, students may be suspended for more than 10 days, like any other student in the school.
- If students are suspended for more than 10 days, they must be provided with a free and appropriate education, and the IEP team must identify alternative placements.

Identification of learning disabilities
- Schools can use a *Response to Intervention* (see Chapter 3) model to determine eligibility for learning disabilities.

Early intervention funding
- LEAs may apply some of its special education funding to develop coordinated early intervention services, which may include students not identified for special education, but in need of academic or behavioral support.

Special education teacher licensure
- A highly qualified teacher is one who holds full teaching credentials required by a state in conformance with the *No Child Left Behind Act*. Special education teachers who teach in core subject areas must also hold the full teaching credentials in those subject areas.

Figure 1.3 IDEA 2004 Amendments
Sources: IDEA (2004), Mandlawitz (2006), and Wright and Wright (2005).

Along with these six common principles, several additions have been made to the original law:

1. *Transition services.* All 16-year-old students with disabilities must be provided with a statement of transition-services needs in their IEPs. These services, which must be included in the IEP by age 16, are intended to facilitate the student's transition from school to community, vocational programs, college, or employment. The transition plan can involve professionals from other agencies, such as social or vocational services. Transition planning conferences are also specified for the transition from infant and toddler programs to preschool programs.

1. A current statement of the child's functioning levels
2. A current statement of the family's needs and strengths in relation to the child with special needs
3. A statement of the major expected outcomes, including a timeline
4. A statement of the specific services to be provided to meet the special needs of the child and the family
5. The initiation and anticipated duration dates for services
6. Designation of a case manager
7. A statement of the transition steps from infant early intervention services to preschool services

2. *Early childhood education.* Amendments to the Education for All Handicapped Children Act (now IDEA) in 1986 and 1990 provided for services to infants, toddlers, and preschoolers with disabilities. Very young children (younger than 3) are entitled to an individualized family service plan (IFSP), which replaces the IEP and takes family needs and responsibilities into account. Necessary components of the IFSP are listed in Table 1.2. States are required to take action to locate as many young children as possible who may require special education services.

3. *Assessments.* Students with disabilities must participate in general state- and district-wide assessment programs. If students cannot participate in state- and district-wide assessments, justification must be provided, and these students must participate in alternative assessments.

4. *Early intervention services.* The 2004 amendments to IDEA specify that not more than 15% of the funding that the local education authority receives from the federal government can be allocated to programming for students (K–12, with an emphasis on K–3) not currently identified for special education but who need additional academic and behavioral support to succeed in the general education environment (U.S. Department of Education, Office of Special Education and Rehabilitative Services, 2006). These services can include those referred to as response-to-intervention (RTI) or multi-tiered systems of support (MTSS) services.

NO CHILD LEFT BEHIND ACT (NCLB) OF 2001 AND EVERY STUDENT SUCCEEDS ACT (ESSA) OF 2015

The No Child Left Behind Act (NCLB), a reauthorization of the 1965 Elementary and Secondary Education Act (ESEA), was not written specifically for students with disabilities. However, many aspects of the legislation had important implications for students with disabilities (Chrismer, Hodge, & Saintil, 2006).

The law required that all children be tested in grades 3 through 8, in reading and math, through tests developed by the states. Schools must demonstrate adequate yearly progress (AYP) toward the goal of 100% proficiency in reading, math, and science for all students. Schools must demonstrate that students make progress in equal increments toward this goal, that is, that they are making steady, equivalent gains from year to year. Schools that fail to make AYP for 2 consecutive years must offer parents of the students the option to transfer to another public school, and the districts must pay the cost of transportation (if allowed under state law). The school district must provide technical assistance to the school. If schools fail to make AYP for more than 2 consecutive years, further corrective measures can be taken (Council for Exceptional Children, 2002). Other aspects of the law include compensatory education grants (Title I), bilingual and immigrant education programs, and standards and provisions for teacher training and recruitment of "highly qualified" teachers who hold full state certification or licensure (Wright, Wright, & Heath, 2004). IDEA has aligned itself with features of the NCLB, including AYP, highly qualified personnel, and evidence-based practices (Crockett, 2011; Yell, Shriner, & Katsiyannis, 2006).

In 2015, another reauthorization of ESEA referred to as the Every Student Succeeds Act (ESSA) replaced NCLB. According to this new legislation, states can choose their own academic standards and can develop their own accountability systems to identify and support struggling schools, not necessarily based solely on federally mandated testing. The federal

Multicultural Considerations for the Identification of Individuals with Disabilities

Legal Assistance

 Federal legislation has provided protections and guidance for the proper identification of individuals with disabilities. These assurances are to guarantee that only the correct individuals become identified as having disabilities. It is especially important that individuals from culturally and linguistically diverse backgrounds are not overrepresented in special education programs. The following protections are part of IDEA:

- *Disproportionality requirement:* States must devise plans to prevent overidentification and provide data to document whether disproportionality by race is occurring with respect to identification and placement of individuals with disabilities.
- *Development, review, and revisions of IEPs:* Consider the language needs as related to the IEP for individuals with limited English proficiency.
- *Evaluation procedures:*
  - Test materials are not to be discriminatory against races or cultures.
  - Tests must be administered in the individual's native language.
  - Test materials for individuals with limited English proficiency must be used to measure a disability and not the individual's English skills.
  - Tests must be valid and reliable and administered by trained professionals.
  - No single procedure can be used as a sole criterion for determining whether a disability exists.
- *Eligibility determination:* An individual may not be eligible if the only difficulty appears to be limited English proficiency.

The U.S. Office of Civil Rights also provides guidance and protections and is the compliance monitor for prereferral practices that may also influence overrepresentation of individuals from culturally and linguistically diverse backgrounds. These protections include the following:

- *Section 504 of the Rehabilitation Act of 1973 and Title II of the Americans with Disabilities Act:* Provide protection against discrimination for individuals with disabilities and those perceived as having disabilities or those who have been misclassified.
- *Title VI of the Civil Rights Act:* Provides protection from discrimination based on national origin, color, or race.

When districts are out of compliance with these federal laws and have an overrepresentation of individuals from culturally or linguistically diverse backgrounds, they may become involved in legal actions and asked to provide a plan to correct the problems.

---

government provides support for struggling schools but may not prescribe specific interventions that schools must use (National School Boards Association, 2016). The act also places a statewide cap of 1% for students with the most significant cognitive disabilities to participate in alternate assessments, aligned to alternate academic achievement standards.

One important feature of federal legislation is that it is constantly changing. Some technological approaches for keeping abreast of federal legislation are described in the *Apps for Education* feature.

COMMON CORE STATE STANDARDS Both NCLB and ESSA made reference to high standards for student achievement. State education standards have been employed since the early 1990s. By the early 2000s, each state had developed and adopted its own academic standards that identified specifically what students in grades 3–8 and high school should be able to do, in compliance with federal regulations. However, each state also had its own definition of proficiency, which led to disparities in standards across states. Because of this, many states joined in the effort to develop the Common Core State Standards (CCSS) in 2009 (National Governors Association Center for Best Practices, Council of Chief State School Officers, 2016). Over time, most states have adopted these standards, which address achievement in English language arts and mathematics from kindergarten through high school. The CCSS note that students with disabilities are expected to meet the same high standards, although with needed supports such as instructional supports based on universal design for learning (UDL) principles

Federal Government Updates

One way to keep abreast of the changes in federal legislation is to check regularly the U.S. Department of Education website (www.ed.gov). This website contains a wealth of frequently updated information as well as links to relevant research and legislation sites. For example, a link to the Every Student Succeeds Act (formerly No Child Left Behind Act) provides an overview of the act, which was signed in December 2015, as well as commonly asked questions and answers that are presented in an easy-to-understand format, links to specific state-level contacts, information on how states can apply for waivers in the law, links for parents and for educators and policymakers, newsletters, and even slide presentations that emphasize key points.

Additional helpful websites linked to the U.S. Department of Education (U.S. DOE) page are directly relevant to special education initiatives. These sites are the Office of Special Education and Rehabilitative Services website and the Office of Special

Education Programs website. These sites contain information such as current special education initiatives, including the recent IDEA legislation; possible changes in the procedures for identification of learning disabilities; recent research findings from projects funded by the U.S. DOE; model programs and personnel preparation; and the annual reports to Congress indicating the status of special education programs across the country with respect to numbers of children served, aged birth through 21. The Library of Congress website (https://congress.gov) allows individuals to research federal legislative information such as the Congressional Record, bills, and congressional activities. Information about sponsored special education research can also be found on the websites of the Institute of Education Sciences (http://ies.ed.gov) and the What Works Clearinghouse (WWC). The WWC site also contains a database of research revealing evidence-based practices, practice guides, intervention reports, single-study reviews, and other reviews.

The Council for Exceptional Children (CEC) website (www.cec.sped.org) has numerous updates and interpretations of federal legislation relevant to special education. Check the CEC website for updates to this information and the CEC's journals *Exceptional Children* and *Teaching Exceptional Children* for the most recent research and teaching articles. The CEC has numerous disability-specific and area-specific divisions, such as the Division for Learning Disabilities, that have their own journals (e.g., *Learning Disability Research and Practice*) and websites (e.g., http://teachingld.org/) that contain a wealth of disability-specific information, from research to practice to advocacy.

Apps are available that describe relevant legislation or funding opportunities. The *Americans with Disabilities Act Reference* app (Connecting People Software) provides the actual bill in sections and is easy to use. The *Federal Register* (Allogy Interactive) and *Federal Register Mag* (PressPad Sp) apps provide regular listings of all federal funding opportunities and notices.

(see Chapter 6), assistive technology, and instructional accommodations, as described throughout this book. The CCSS are described with respect to specific topics in subsequent chapters; for a complete listing of the standards, see http://corestandards.org.

> MyEdLab: **Self-Check 1.3**
>
> MyEdLab: **Application Exercise 1.3: IDEA and Legal Foundations**

Models of Service Delivery

THE CONTINUUM OF SERVICES

The initial emphasis of legal actions was to provide access to educational services for students with disabilities. Once access was obtained, the focus shifted to the setting and placement of students with disabilities during education. Most placement guidelines emphasized the availability of a range of services and programs, commonly referred to as a **continuum of services,** within the LRE for students with disabilities. *LRE* is defined in IDEA as meaning that students with disabilities should be educated in a setting that resembles the general education program as closely as possible while simultaneously meeting the unique special needs of each individual with disabilities (Rozalski et al., 2011; Zigmond, 2015). The basic model of a continuum of services ranges from full-time placement in the general education classroom to full-time placement in a nonpublic school facility, on a day or residential basis, based on student need. As the needs of the individual with a disability increase, the LRE may be further removed from the general education class on the continuum of services. Figure 1.4 presents a sample of the range of placement options.

WHERE ARE MOST STUDENTS WITH DISABILITIES SERVED?

Most students with disabilities are served in public schools with their nondisabled peers in Levels 1 through 5. In other words, these students receive their education in their local public schools. Most students with mild disabilities, including those with learning disabilities, mild intellectual disabilities, speech and language disabilities, and serious emotional disturbance, are currently served in Levels 1 through 4. That is, these students spend some, if not all, of the day in the general education classroom along with students without disabilities. The general education teacher is responsible for their education for some, if not all, of the day, depending on the amount of time spent in that general education class. Table 1.1 provides a listing of disability categories and the corresponding proportion of students currently served outside general education classrooms.

WHAT ARE GENERAL EDUCATION CLASSROOM AND CONSULTATION SERVICES?

In some cases, students may be served in general education classes by general education teachers. Some special services may be provided by a **consultant** who works with individuals as needed. Special education teachers frequently provide consultative services to general education teachers. This consultation is intended to provide assistance and ideas for how to teach and work with the students with disabilities who are placed in general education classes. Although

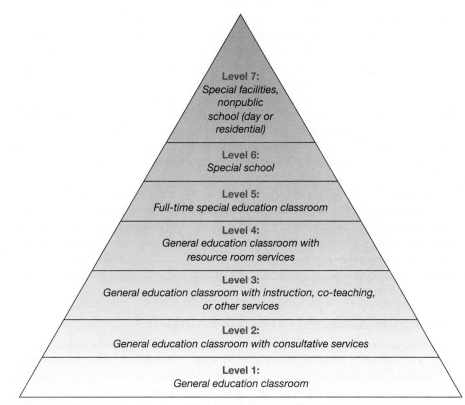

Figure 1.4 Sample Continuum of Services, from Least Restrictive to Most Restrictive

special education teachers may not work directly with identified students, they may meet regularly with general education teachers, review assessment and progress data, and make specific recommendations for addressing special learning needs. These students would be receiving services at Levels 1 or 2 of the continuum-of-services model.

In other cases, special education teachers and classroom assistants (or paraprofessionals) may deliver instruction to students with special needs in the general education classroom. In these cases, students with disabilities still receive all their instruction in the general education classroom, but it may be delivered by different teachers or paraprofessionals. Teachers collaborate and share instructional responsibilities in one of several **co-teaching** models (Dettmer, Knackendoffel, & Thurston, 2013). For example, a special education teacher may lead instruction for small groups of elementary students with special needs during classroom reading instruction. At the secondary level, the special education teacher may co-teach with a general education teacher in a high school biology class. The two teachers share teaching responsibilities, with the special education teacher focusing on strategies for addressing special learning needs. These students would be receiving services at Level 3 of the continuum-of-services model.

In any of these circumstances teachers adapt instruction and classroom procedures to meet the special learning needs of individual students. This approach to teaching is referred to as differentiated instruction (Tomlinson, 2014), and could be employed in any level of service delivery.

WHAT ARE RESOURCE AND SELF-CONTAINED SERVICES?

Special education teachers also provide instruction in resource and self-contained classrooms within the public schools. In a resource-room model, students with disabilities leave the general education class for a designated time period to visit the resource room and receive specialized instruction in areas such as language, reading, and math. For example, Kathi is a sixth grader who has been classified as having learning disabilities. Kathi is functioning intellectually within the average ability range, but she has reading, spelling, and written language skills at an upper-third-grade level. The multidisciplinary team recommended that Kathi should receive specialized instruction in reading, written communication, and spelling with a special education teacher for 1.5 hours per day in her school's resource room. This means that Kathi would be receiving services at Level 4 of the continuum-of-services model.

Most of her school day will be spent in the LRE of her general education class with Mrs. Gomez. Mrs. Gomez will be responsible for Kathi's instruction for the entire time that she is in the general education class. This might even include making some adaptations in instructional procedures and assignments to accommodate Kathi's special learning needs in the general education sixth-grade classroom. For example, during content-area classes, Mrs. Gomez will need to provide adapted reading and study materials appropriate to Kathi's skill levels. During her 1.5 hours in the resource room, Kathi will receive instruction from Mr. Halleran, the special education teacher in the same school. This resource-room arrangement represents the LRE to meet Kathi's special needs in reading, written communication, and spelling while maintaining her placement in her general education class for the majority of the school day.

The resource model is sometimes referred to as a *pull-out* model, indicating that students with disabilities are pulled out of the general education class for special education instruction. In a self-contained model of instruction (Level 5 of the continuum-of-services model), students with disabilities receive all or most of their classroom instruction from special education teachers. Even in these models, however, students with disabilities often have opportunities to interact with their nondisabled peers during such activities as art, music, physical education, recess, lunch, and assemblies.

SPECIAL SCHOOLS AND SPECIAL FACILITIES

In some cases, the need for specialized instruction is considered so significant that a special school or other facility is considered necessary. In some cases, special public schools are established to focus specifically on the special needs of the students. In other cases, students are sent to nonpublic schools, either as special day schools or as residential schools. These students would be receiving services at Level 6 or 7 of the continuum-of-services model. The numbers of special schools or other facilities have declined since the early years of IDEA, as traditional public schools have accommodated more students with disabilities and other special needs within their educational programs.

Charter schools receive government funding but function independently of the public school systems in which they are located. In some cases, charter schools are privately owned. In some states charter schools are linked to local education agencies (LEAs) while in other states they may be considered separate LEAs (National Center for Technology Innovation, 2011).

WHAT OTHER RELATED SERVICES ARE AVAILABLE?

Students with disabilities are also eligible to receive related services if it is determined that the students require these services to benefit from special education. According to IDEA, related services may include parent counseling and training, physical therapy, occupational therapy, school health services, or special transportation. This means that in addition to receiving special services along the continuum of services for a primary disability area, some students may also be eligible to receive additional related services. Related services may be delivered to individuals with disabilities in any of the setting options. Although described as "related" services, in many cases, these services may be of critical importance in attending to the special needs of individual students (Downing, 2004). For example, Michael, a student with intellectual disabilities, receives physical therapy in addition to his educational program to meet his special needs. Janice requires special transportation services to accommodate her wheelchair and adaptive physical education (PE), which are provided as related services.

The continuum-of-services and related-services models have been effectively applied throughout the history of IDEA. However, over this same time period, there have been recommendations regarding how all or most students with disabilities could be more easily served entirely within the general education classroom, often referred to as the full-inclusion movement.

FULL INCLUSION

Over the past decades, the full-inclusion movement came to the forefront (Fuchs & Fuchs, 1994). Full inclusion has been referred to as placing and serving all students with disabilities, regardless of severity or type of disability, entirely within the general education classroom for the entire school day.

Consider the case of Kathi, our sixth grader with learning disabilities. If Kathi were placed in a full-inclusion classroom, Mrs. Gomez, her general education teacher, would have Kathi in her room all day, every day with all of the other sixth-grade students. Mrs. Gomez would be primarily responsible for all of Kathi's instruction and for making adaptations appropriate for addressing Kathi's learning disabilities. In some full-inclusion models, Mr. Halleran, the special education teacher, would consult with Mrs. Gomez and provide ideas for her to use in teaching Kathi in her IEP need areas. In other full-inclusion models, Mr. Halleran might go into Mrs. Gomez's room and teach Kathi reading, spelling, and writing in that room. In this model, instruction with Mr. Halleran and Kathi may occur at a small table, perhaps with other students with special needs, while other groups of students meet for literacy activities. In still other full-inclusion models, Mr. Halleran may co-teach with Mrs. Gomez for part or all of the school day. During co-teaching, Mr. Halleran and Mrs. Gomez would work collaboratively on planning and implementing instruction for the entire class. In any of these full-inclusion models, however, Kathi remains in the general education class with her nondisabled peers all day.

As might be expected, debate surrounds the issue of full inclusion. It is important to remember that virtually all educational professionals recommend placement in general education classes for students with disabilities and other special needs; the disagreement usually centers on the extent to which students should be placed in general education settings. Both proponents of full inclusion and proponents of a continuum of services have articulated their positions, which are summarized in Figure 1.5 (see also Fuchs & Fuchs, 1994; Huefner, 2015; Kauffman et al., 2011; Lipsky & Gartner, 1997, 2008; Zigmond, 2015; Zigmond & Kloo, 2011).

As can be seen, the issue of full inclusion versus a continuum of services is still debated. Professional organizations and advocates do not always agree on the best service options (e.g., Andrews, Shaw, & Lomas, 2011). General education students have expressed various opinions

Proponents of Full Inclusion	Proponents of a Continuum of Services
1. *Full inclusion is a civil right.* Students with disabilities have a right to be educated alongside their nondisabled peers. Separate educational settings are inherently not equal.	1. *A continuum of service options is necessary.* Many services needed by students with disabilities are not usually available in the general education classroom. Court decisions have usually placed more emphasis on "appropriate education" than "least-restrictive" components.
2. *Full inclusion reduces stigma.* Harmful stigmatizing effects may be associated with students attending special schools or special classrooms.	2. *The regular classrooms may also be stigmatizing.* Special services, such as speech therapy, physical therapy, or specialized reading instruction, may be stigmatizing when undertaken in the company of general education peers.
3. *Full inclusion is beneficial.* Students in full-inclusion classrooms improve their interactions with others, learn to communicate better, develop better social skills, and increase their friendships.	3. *General education teachers are not prepared for full inclusion.* Many general education teachers lack the necessary time and training to make full inclusion a success.
4. *Full inclusion is more efficient.* Fully included students avoid the disruptive and time-consuming effects of being "pulled out" of the general education class to receive special services. Full inclusion guarantees access to the general education curriculum.	4. *General education classrooms may lack appropriate resources.* Students with special needs may require materials at lower reading levels, braillers, speech synthesizers, specialized computers, or specialized training materials that general education classrooms lack.
5. *Full inclusion promotes equality.* Including all students in the same classroom is simply the most fair and equitable solution to the problem of placement. Including all students in the same classroom actively promotes the idea of equality.	5. *Research evidence does not support the superiority of full inclusion.* Although research data are to some extent equivocal, clear evidence of the superiority of full-inclusion placements is presently lacking.

Figure 1.5 Arguments of Proponents of Full Inclusion and Proponents of a Continuum of Services

(e.g., Siperstein, Parker, Norns Bardon, & Widerman, 2007); parents also seem to be divided between those who favor specialized placement and services and those who favor integration in the general education class (Palmer, Fuller, Arora, & Nelson, 2001).

WHAT DOES THIS DEBATE MEAN FOR TEACHERS?

Teachers need to be aware of the arguments for and against full inclusion. As a teacher, you also must become familiar with your own legal responsibilities. For example, what are general education classroom teachers' legal responsibilities with respect to the IEP when all instruction is implemented in the general education classroom? Other questions, although not necessarily legal in nature, may be relevant to the spirit of the law.

Teachers should approach the issue in a practical way, with respect to their own school and district. Specific questions to ask about full inclusion include the following:

- What are the school- and district-wide policies and procedures regarding full inclusion?
- What are my obligations as a general educator with respect to the IEP, IEP meetings, case conferences, assessment procedures, annual review meetings, and meetings with parents?
- What types of modifications are expected, and is there a "reasonableness" standard associated with the number and types of modifications expected?
- Is this the best placement option for the particular student with special needs?

- How will we evaluate whether or not this placement and this set of accommodations are successful?
- What resources are available to assist me in working with the student with special needs?
- How can I receive necessary training for working with students in specific disability areas?
- What kinds of records and documentation should I maintain?

Answers to questions such as these can help determine the best placement options for students with disabilities and other special needs.

MyEdLab:
Video Example 1.1.

Listen to the teacher in this video describe what needs to be present for effective inclusive practices to occur.

TEACHER ATTITUDES

One of the most important determinants of inclusion success is the attitude of the general education teacher toward accommodating students with disabilities. Although most teachers are positive about inclusion, general education teachers report a need for additional planning time, additional training for inclusive teaching, and additional resources, in the form of personnel and specialized instructional materials (Cook, Tankersley, Cook, & Landrum, 2000; Scruggs, 2012; see also the *Research Highlight*). Teacher and administrator support for collaborative efforts in schools can also affect attitudes. The two scenarios that follow help illustrate the initial implementation of inclusion in two different schools under very different circumstances.

CLASSROOM SCENARIOS

Volunteerism

In a small rural school, Mrs. Ghardisi, the fourth-grade teacher, volunteered to take all of the fourth-grade students with disabilities into her classroom. Because she worked well with Mrs. Rana, the special education teacher, she went to her principal and said, "Next year, I would like to have all five of the fourth graders who have disabilities in my room. They can still go to the resource room for part of the day, but during science class and other content classes, I would like to have all of them. Also, Mrs. Rana and I would like to team-teach during science class when all five children are included."

That summer, Mrs. Ghardisi and Mrs. Rana met and discussed curriculum and planning issues for their science class. Mrs. Ghardisi was considered the "content expert," whereas Mrs. Rana was the "adaptation expert." When the school year began, they met at least once a week after school to co-plan the activities for each science class. Mrs. Ghardisi and Mrs. Rana had a good working relationship that enabled them to solve problems as they arose. Because they planned together, they took turns presenting information and monitoring students during class. They were both enthusiastic and worked hard to design adaptations so that the five students with disabilities could be active participants. They viewed science as an opportunity to have fun, and their students appeared to really enjoy science.

Mandated Inclusion

In a suburban middle school, Ms. Irby, the special education teacher, was told by her building principal 2 days before school began that she was going to implement inclusive instruction for one period per day during the coming year. She was told she would be working with six students with learning disabilities in Mrs. Toro's sixth-period, seventh-grade history class on a daily basis.

Unfortunately, Mrs. Toro, the history teacher, had not been informed by the principal that Ms. Irby was going to be team-teaching with her. When Ms. Irby went to see Mrs. Toro and explained the situation, Mrs. Toro appeared visibly shaken.

It is clear that many aspects must be considered in order for inclusive placements to be successful. These involve careful planning and attention to the multiple perspectives of general education teachers, special education teachers, parents of students with and without disabilities, and, of course, the students themselves. However, with careful planning and appropriate programming, inclusive instruction can prove to be a successful and rewarding experience for everyone.

Teacher Attitudes Toward Inclusion

Teacher attitudes have been considered fundamental to successful inclusion (Cullen, Gregory, & Noto, 2010). But what are teacher attitudes, and have they changed over time? Scruggs, Leins, and Mastropieri (2011) and Scruggs (2012) summarized the results of 61 survey, comparative, and qualitative investigations of teacher attitudes published between 1996 and 2010, and they compared these with the results of a previous investigation (Scruggs & Mastropieri, 1996) that studied attitudes from 1958 through 1995. For the survey research, it was reported that 62.8% of teachers (vs. 65.0% from the 1996 investigation) overall supported the concept of inclusion, and 61.4% (vs. 54.4%, 1996) expressed willingness to teach students with disabilities. These numbers were remarkably similar over the years. Further, it was found that there was higher agreement for more generally worded items of less intensity. That is, whereas 70.8% voiced general support for inclusion, only 40.5%

supported inclusion for all students with disabilities for most or all of the school day. Again, these percentages were very similar to data from earlier decades. Across all years of surveys, teachers generally expressed a wish for additional time and training, as well as personnel and administrative support for implementing inclusion in their classrooms. Analysis of comparative studies revealed that, similar to previous years, more positive attitudes were reported by elementary teachers (vs. secondary teachers), special education teachers (vs. general education teachers), female teachers (vs. male teachers), and teachers who had taken more (vs. less) coursework relevant to inclusion. Qualitative studies generally confirmed other types of research, especially with reference to both the benefits and challenges of inclusion. Reported benefits include social benefits, support from the special education teacher, and the general enrichment provided by a more diverse classroom. Reported challenges included class size, student skill levels, and making

accommodations. More recent studies have reported similar findings (Majoko, 2016).

Scruggs (2012) concluded that teacher attitudes are generally positive and have changed very little over the past several decades. Teacher attitudes seemed to be less influenced by prejudice toward students with disabilities and more oriented toward practical classroom concerns, including appropriate class size, time to prepare for inclusive instruction, and training appropriate to teaching inclusive classes. Appropriately supported teachers are more likely to have positive attitudes toward including students with disabilities.

QUESTIONS FOR REFLECTION

1. Why do you think attitudes toward inclusion have changed so little over the years?
2. How might overall attitudes toward inclusion be improved?
3. Why do you think elementary-grade teachers report more positive attitudes than secondary-grade teachers?

MyEdLab: **Self-Check 1.4**

MyEdLab: **Application Exercise 1.4: Continuum of Services**

1 Summary

- Before the passage of federal law, students with special needs were routinely excluded from public school. Public Law 94-142 (IDEA) and its subsequent amendments established the rights of students with disabilities to a free, appropriate public education (FAPE).

- Six important principles in IDEA are (1) zero reject, (2) nondiscriminatory testing, (3) free and appropriate education, (4) least restrictive environment, (5) due process, and (6) parent participation.

  - LRE refers to the environment that is least removed from the general education classroom and can meet a student's special needs.

- Other court rulings and federal laws, such as Section 504 and the Americans with Disabilities Act, have provided for nondiscriminatory treatment of individuals with disabilities.

- Current educational practice provides for a continuum of services for students with disabilities, from full-time placement in the regular education classroom to special residential schools. Currently, most students with disabilities are served in regular education classrooms.

  - "Full inclusion" is the full-time placement of students with disabilities in regular classrooms. Important points

have been raised by concerned individuals on both sides of this issue.

- Most teachers favor some form of inclusion for their own classes. However, teachers report a need for sufficient time, training, and resources to teach effectively in inclusive classrooms. When these supports are provided, attitudes toward inclusive teaching improve.

PROFESSIONAL STANDARDS LINK:
Introduction to Inclusive Teaching

Information in this chapter links most directly to:

- CEC Standards: 1 (Learner Development and Individual Learning Differences), 2 (Learning Environments), 6 (Professional Learning and Practice), 7 (Collaboration)

- INTASC Standards: 2 (Learning Differences), 3 (Learning Environments), 4 (Content Knowledge)

Note: **CEC** is the Council for Exceptional Children, an organization dedicated to improving educational outcomes for students with disabilities and gifted students. **INTASC** is the Interstate New Teacher Assessment and Support Consortium, which created standards for licensing new teachers to be compatible with the National Board for Professional Teaching Standards.

2

Collaboration: Partnerships and Procedures

LEARNING OUTCOMES

After studying this chapter, you should be able to:

2.1 Describe collaboration and how it can be used to meet students' needs.

2.2 List and describe six major steps involved in effective interpersonal communication.

2.3 Describe procedures for collaboration and communication for intervention, including prereferral procedures employing response-to-intervention (RTI) and multi-tiered systems of support (MTSS) models.

2.4 Describe the process of collaboration for referrals and placements.

2.5 Describe strategies for establishing partnerships between general education teachers and special education teachers, paraprofessionals, and families.

The Individuals with Disabilities Education Act (IDEA, 2004) provides the legal right for individuals with disabilities to receive free, appropriate public education. However, for the law to be effective, constructive and collaborative partnerships must be established among parents, teachers, school specialists, school administrators, and community agencies. The school and parents must accept certain basic responsibilities for the system to work effectively. Table 2.1 lists some of these responsibilities. To meet these responsibilities, parents and school personnel must engage in problem-solving strategies, working together to devise procedures necessary for identification, referral, assessment, and placement processes to differentiate instruction to accommodate students with exceptionalities and other at-risk students.

Collaboration—involving cooperation, effective communication, shared problem solving, planning, and finding solutions—is the process for ensuring that all students receive the free, appropriate public education mandated by IDEA. The establishment of excellent partnerships among all involved in working with students with disabilities is essential for constructive collaboration.

TABLE 2.1 School and Parent Responsibilities

School Responsibilities	Parent Responsibilities
Provide free and appropriate education through age 21.	Provide consent for educational evaluation and placement.
Provide an individualized education program (IEP) for each student who requires special education and related services.	Participate in the case conference committee, including development of the IEP.
Assure testing, evaluation materials, procedures, and interpretations are nonbiased.	Cooperate with the school and teachers.
Educate students with disabilities in the least restrictive environment.	Attend case reviews and provide input to ensure the IEP remains appropriate.
Assure confidentiality of records for individuals with disabilities.	Reinforce procedures and policies (e.g., help with homework routines).
Conduct searches to identify and evaluate students with disabilities from birth through age 21.	Assist with any home–school behavioral contracting efforts.
Provide procedural due-process rights for students and parents.	Help maintain open communication with the school and teachers.

CLASSROOM SCENARIO

Debbie

Debbie is a 10th grader with physical disabilities and communication difficulties who has been experiencing problems completing her work within a typical school day. This morning, six of Debbie's teachers—her math teacher, Ms. Juarez; her English teacher, Mr. Mantizi; her science teacher, Mr. Stubbs; her history teacher, Ms. Blackman; her speech and language therapist, Ms. Ramirez; and her special education teacher, Mr. Graetz—are meeting with Ms. Meyer, Debbie's paraprofessional, in the small conference room near the front office. They are trying to determine what they can do to help Debbie be more successful in high school. Everyone at the meeting is sincere in their desire to brainstorm ways to arrange the school day so that Debbie can learn successfully.

Mr. Graetz, the special education teacher, began the conversation by saying, "Thanks for agreeing to meet this morning to look at what's been happening with Debbie and try to come up with some solutions together. Recently, Debbie appears to be having a hard time keeping up with all of her work. Her grades have started slipping. Maybe if we share some ideas, we might be able to help her."

Ms. Blackman, the history teacher, says, "I know that Debbie is interested in the topics we are studying because her eyes become animated during class. But I'm not sure how I can tap into that enthusiasm. Maybe if I could get her to participate more actively, she would feel better about school."

The speech therapist, Ms. Ramirez, suggests, "Have you tried allowing Debbie to type out responses to questions on her iPad and then asking Ms. Meyer to read her answers to the class or having the iPad speak her answers?"

"Hey, that's a good idea. I have time to do that while students are completing their lab work in science class," says the science teacher, Mr. Stubbs.

Ms. Juarez, the math teacher, adds, "I sometimes stop the discussion and allow extra time for Debbie to type her responses, and I have found that this provides additional thinking time for everyone in my math class. . . ."

And so the discussion continues. These teachers are collaborating by sharing suggestions in instructional modifications with the intention of trying something that will promote school success for Debbie.

QUESTIONS FOR REFLECTION

1. How could any disagreements that arise be handled in this meeting?
2. If you were Mr. Graetz, how could you determine that the suggestions made in this meeting would be carried out?
3. What do you think would be some of the challenges in arranging a meeting such as this?

Collaboration to Meet Students' Needs

Collaboration to decide how to best meet students' needs can occur among teachers and other school specialists during informal meetings, co-teaching, and formal meetings of professionals to recommend interventions or consider the appropriateness of special education services. Collaboration also takes place with parents, siblings, guardians, and families—during parent conferences as well as during day-to-day communication with parents regarding the progress of their children.

SHARED GOALS

Collaboration means working jointly with others, willingly cooperating with others, and sharing in goal setting, problem solving, and goal achievement. For example, a special education teacher might have Marilyn, who is classified as having mild intellectual disabilities, for three periods a day, while the general education seventh-grade content-area teachers teach her the remainder of the school day. General and special education teachers must collaborate effectively to implement the goals and objectives on Marilyn's IEP. For example, Marilyn's IEP specifies that general education teachers prioritize objectives, use positive reinforcement, adapt learning activities to reduce the amount of reading and writing required, adapt testing situations, and provide Marilyn with additional support as necessary. For these goals to be implemented consistently throughout the day for Marilyn, this team of teachers must work collaboratively and share ideas for best meeting Marilyn's needs. For effective collaboration to happen, teachers must communicate effectively. This is best achieved when collaborators hone their interpersonal skills and interject a positive attitude into the collaboration efforts.

MyEdLab: **Self-Check 2.1**

MyEdLab: **Application Exercise 2.1: Collaboration to Meet Students' Needs**

Effective Communication

Interpersonal interactions revolve around communication. When communication is effective, several common elements are in place: active listening, depersonalizing situations, identifying common goals and solutions, and monitoring progress to achieve those goals (Gordon, 2003; see also Ginott, 1998; Ginott, Ginott, & Goddard, 2003; Vostal, McNaughton, Benedik-Wood, & Hoffman, 2015).

STRATEGIES FOR
COMMUNICATING EFFECTIVELY

USE ACTIVE LISTENING TECHNIQUES   Active listening is demonstrated through both nonverbal and verbal actions. Nonverbally, you demonstrate active listening by maintaining direct eye contact, leaning toward the speaker, nodding your head in agreement or understanding, and demonstrating that you are devoting all of your attention to the speaker. Verbal components of active listening involve responding with affirmative words, such as "Yes," "Yes, I see," "I understand," and, "Can you tell me more?" An active listener is able to restate or summarize the major points of the conversation and may do this during the course of the conversation with statements such as, "So, what you are telling me is... ." Teachers who use active listening techniques are more likely to maintain open communication and to avoid misunderstandings (see the *Research Highlight*). Active listening is a way of informing the speaker that his or her views are important to you, and it can be helpful in keeping interactions positive.

DEPERSONALIZE SITUATIONS   Depersonalized conversations avoid negative comments that may be offensive and instead emphasize a goal. For example, if a student, Lisa, has not been turning in homework assignments, a "depersonalized" statement is, "Lisa, 7 out of the last 10 homework assignments are missing; what can we do to improve that?" A negative statement that might hinder finding a solution is, "Lisa, you obviously do not care enough about science to turn in your homework."

In the Classroom

Communication Summary Sheet

For: _____ On: _____
    (Student's Name)   (Date)

Conversation Among (list participants):

_____ _____

_____ _____

Goals Identified:

1.

2.

3.

Solution Steps to Be Implemented (and by whom):   *Person Responsible*

Solution Step

   1.

   2.

   3.

Progress Toward Goals Will Be Reviewed On:

_____ _____

(Date) (By Whom)

Depersonalized conversations are beneficial when communicating with everyone, including students, other teachers, school specialists, administrators, parents, and professionals from community organizations.

FIND COMMON GOALS It is important to restate and summarize conversations to identify common goals. Once common goals are found, conversations can be more positive and productive. Questions such as "Lisa, what do you want to do in science?" and "What are the barriers currently preventing Lisa from turning in her homework?" can help direct the conversations toward the identification of common goals. A positive and productive common goal among all teachers, the parents, and Lisa could be the following:

> We all want Lisa to succeed, and one way to help her succeed is to find ways to assist her in turning in her homework.

Once common goals are stated positively, it is easier to turn the entire conversation into productive problem solving geared toward goal attainment.

BRAINSTORM POSSIBLE SOLUTIONS Effective communicators can use brainstorming techniques during meetings to help identify ways to achieve any common goals. During brainstorming, suggestions for solutions are compiled by participants, without passing judgment on any of them. The list of possible solutions can then be prioritized from those offering the most potential for success to the least. When all participants join in the creation of possible alternatives for helping Lisa succeed, they are more invested in reaching their goal. In Lisa's case, a brainstormed list created by her, her teachers, and her parents might include the following: serving detention for a month; quitting her job; keeping an assignment notebook; eliminating or restricting her television-watching time; staying after school once a week for homework assistance; and rewarding Lisa if she meets a certain criterion by the end of the quarter.

An Active Listening Strategy for Teachers

 Effective parent–teacher communication is critically important to effective collaboration and building cooperative relationships. McNaughton, Hamlin, McCarthy, Head-Reeves, and Schreiner (2007) developed and implemented an active-listening strategy for preservice teachers, and Vostal et al. (2015) replicated and extended the strategy. They refer to this strategy as "LAFF" and list the following components:

L = Listen, empathize, and communicate respect.
A = Ask questions, and ask permission to take notes at the meeting.
F = Focus on the problem, or issues, and summarize issues as described by the parent.
F = Find a first step by identifying and agreeing upon appropriate procedures and how they will be implemented.

Empathetic listening allows the teacher to understand clearly the problems or issues as perceived by the parent. Asking questions and taking notes helps clarify issues and provides information to be considered for future meetings. By focusing on the problem at hand, attention is directed away from ancillary issues, which helps lead to the exploration of relevant first steps to undertake for resolving the problem.

McNaughton et al. (2007) taught this strategy to a group of preservice teachers and applied it to a series of role-play scenarios with parents, including one pretest scenario, six training scenarios, and one posttest scenario. After training, it was found that the trained preservice teachers exhibited a significantly higher number of effective communication skills compared with their pretest scores and the scores of control preservice teachers. Further, a diverse panel of parents overwhelmingly identified the trained teachers as exhibiting stronger communication skills. All trained participants agreed, or strongly agreed, that the training would be helpful to them professionally. For example, one participant said, "This strategy has helped me to communicate more effectively in situations dealing with problems" (2007, p. 229).

Vostal et al. (2015) extended the strategy to applications with preservice special educators for use with general education teachers when addressing a student issue. In addition to the previous training, preservice students were taught to think about asking questions using the mnemonic "What When Who—4, 3, 2" (p. 8), which represented asking four "what" questions to define the problem, three "when" questions to pinpoint when the problem happened, and two "who" questions to identify individuals associated with the problem. Findings revealed that preservice students improved significantly following training. Participants reported that the strategy was very helpful. For example, one person said that it provided "some structure to an otherwise stressful and unpredictable situation." Another candidate wrote, "Pointing out these ways to communicate seemed obvious, but they are quite necessary!" (Vostal et al., 2015, p. 10).

More recently, McNaughton and Vostal (2010) noted some things to avoid when communicating with parents and suggested a "LAFF, don't CRY" strategy, where C = criticize others not present at the meeting; R = react hastily, promising something that can't be delivered; and Y = "yakety-yak-yak," or unnecessary talk that is not related to the issues. Considering things to avoid as well as things to implement may help solidify active-listening techniques.

QUESTIONS FOR REFLECTION

1. What mistakes do you think teachers may make when conferring with parents or other teachers?
2. Why do you think this particular strategy is helpful?
3. What do you think is most important about active listening?
4. What does "don't CRY" add to the LAFF strategy?

SUMMARIZE GOALS AND SOLUTIONS Summarizing the statement of goals and proposed solutions verbally (and perhaps in writing), before the end of the meeting, is beneficial for all participants. This prevents any misunderstandings and provides an opportunity for clarification. In our example, the teacher summarizes the meeting by stating, "Let me summarize what we all agreed on. We all want Lisa to succeed in science. One way to have Lisa be more successful is to help her turn in all of her homework assignments. One thing Lisa will do is keep an assignment notebook in which she records her assignments and due dates, which she will show daily to her parents and teachers. Another step will be for Lisa and her parents to find a place at home for her to complete her homework. Her parents will assist her by asking regularly if she has completed her homework assignments. Finally, Lisa will attend after-school help sessions if she does not understand what to do to complete the assignments. We will meet and review Lisa's progress toward her goals within 1 month, at which time we will determine whether we need to modify any of the possible solutions."

FOLLOW UP TO MONITOR PROGRESS Summarization makes the entire conversation positive and concrete. A goal statement is made, possible solutions are listed, one is selected for implementation and evaluation, and follow-up target dates are set for monitoring progress toward goal attainment.

All steps promote communication with everyone involved in educating students with disabilities. Review the *In the Classroom* feature, which can be used to ensure decisions made by the group during problem solving are more easily executed. Whatever model of communication you use, note that practicing good communication skills enables you to be effective in the many roles associated with collaboration.

MyEdLab: **Self-Check 2.2**

MyEdLab: **Application Exercise 2.2: Parent-Teacher Communication**

Collaboration and Communication for Intervention

Many types of collaboration occur in larger groups or "teams" within schools. One type of schoolwide team is the general education **prereferral assistance team.** Depending on the school district, these teams may also be referred to as multidisciplinary teams, student study teams, general education assistance teams, prereferral intervention teams, problem-solving teams, or teacher assistance teams and may vary in the way they are implemented (Bennett, Erchul, Young, & Bartel, 2012). Many schools today have employed teams implementing *response to intervention* (RTI) or *multi-tiered systems of support* (MTSS) to support prereferral procedures. These programs employ schoolwide screening and progress monitoring to help identify students in need of supports, and they employ multiple levels, or tiers, of instructional intensity to meet student needs, as described later in this chapter (Division for Learning Disabilities, 2007). No matter what the team is called, its function is to determine the need for educational interventions to assist individual students who are struggling to succeed at school. In addition, the teams' intervention strategies assist teachers who, after careful observation, are unsure whether a student needs special education services. Hence, the team's first purpose is to determine whether intervention strategies can make a difference for the student so that special education placement is prevented. The team usually convenes after a formal request is made to the building principal or other designated individual within a school.

GENERAL EDUCATION PREREFERRAL REQUEST

A formal prereferral request can be made by a teacher, school specialist, parent, school administrator, or the student at any time. For example, a request might be made by a general education teacher who has worked with a student for a period of time and finds that all her efforts have not made the differences they should have in that child's educational success. In the case of schools implementing RTI procedures, this request may be based on general education classroom screening and progress-monitoring measures.

Documentation of observations, student work samples, test scores, and other relevant data often are submitted with a formal intervention request. It is important to reiterate that before Mrs. Mayer requested help from the intervention team, she had taken a number of steps to address the problem (see *Classroom Scenario*). Often, these steps are sequential, in that each item checked should be undertaken before the next concern. Mrs. Mayer first reviewed Omar's records to verify that vision and hearing screenings had taken place. Parent conferences and student interviews were conducted to discuss the problem areas and consider possible solutions.

MyEdLab:
Video Example 2.1.
This video provides an overview of the prereferral process. Pay attention to how the teachers collaborate.

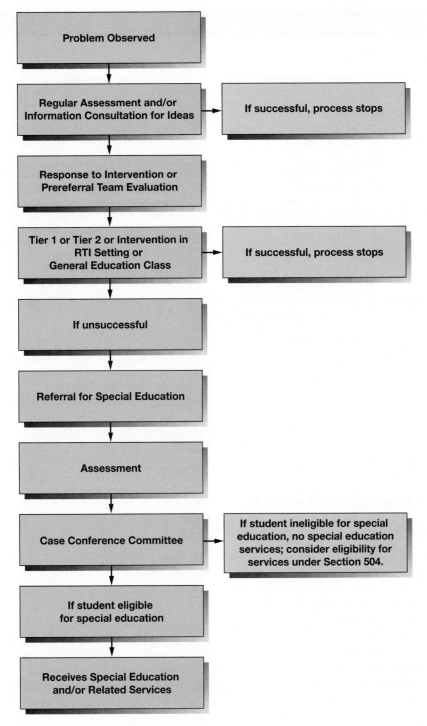

Figure 2.1 Steps in the Referral Process

She collected, analyzed, and filed samples of Omar's recent academic classwork and evidence of disciplinary actions. She informally asked for advice from other teachers, school counselors, special education teachers, and the prereferral assistance teams. Mrs. Mayer made documentation available to the team of specific intervention strategies she had tried before asking the team for help. All of this information was useful to team members in deciding what other modifications, adaptations, or interventions might be tried to find the best educational program for Omar. For an illustration of all the steps in the referral process in a 3-tier RTI model, see Figure 2.1.

Table 2.2 presents a comparison of the sequence of steps that might be implemented with a second-grade student who starts to experience reading challenges in schools using a prereferral assistance team approach with an RTI or MTSS approach. Notice the similarities and differences. Both systems intend to help struggling students, but they use slightly different approaches.

TABLE 2.2 Prereferral Assistance Team Versus Multi-Tiered System of Support

	Typical Steps in Process to Referral to Special Education*	Prereferral Assistance Team	Multi-Tiered System of Support (MTSS) or Response to Intervention (RTI)
Starts School	Child starts third grade	Teacher teaches reading using the school- and district-adopted curriculum materials and approaches	Teacher teaches reading using Tier 1 procedures, which are scientifically based instructional techniques, and collects regular performance data as part of the program
Experiences Challenges	Third-grade child experiences challenges in reading and reading comprehension	Teacher talks to parents, checks all data on child's performance, documents additional instructional procedures that he or she has implemented, and may talk to other teachers for suggestions and assistance	Teacher teaches using Tier 1 procedures, which are scientifically based instructional techniques, and collects regular performance data as part of the program; teacher may have noticed this child struggling and spoken with parents and MTSS team members
Challenges Persist	Third grader still experiences challenges in reading	Teacher brings all data collected on various adaptations made in reading to the prereferral assistance team, which evaluates the data and makes recommendations to be implemented	Teacher makes a decision based on student's Tier 1 performance data to have the child enter Tier 2 reading program
Special Education Referral Process Initiated	Still experiencing challenges	Referral to special education begins; possible special education placement	Teacher makes a recommendation for Tier 3, which in many districts is also a referral for special education
Special Education Placement	Still experiencing challenges	More intensive interventions	More intensive interventions, which may be Tier 3

*At any time, a parent or teacher can make an immediate referral to special education.

CLASSROOM SCENARIO

Omar

Mrs. Mayer is a second-grade teacher. At the beginning of the school year, Mrs. Mayer noticed that Omar seemed to be behind his classmates on schoolwide screening measures and was not progressing well academically. In spite of additional review of first-grade material, Omar continued to have problems with reading and writing tasks and had a hard time maintaining attention to tasks.

When Omar continued to struggle, Mrs. Mayer decided that she and Omar needed some assistance. She contacted her school's prereferral assistance team. The team members included a first-, third-, fourth-, and fifth-grade teacher; a school psychologist; the principal; and a special education teacher. The team scheduled a meeting to discuss the nature and severity of Omar's difficulties and designed intervention strategies that Mrs. Mayer could implement and review within a specified timeline.

QUESTIONS FOR REFLECTION

1. How would you determine whether a problem was serious enough to contact the prereferral intervention assistance team?

2. How would you determine whether your assessment of Omar's problem was objective and unbiased?

THE INTERVENTION PROCESS

The strategies addressed in the intervention process are designed, implemented, and evaluated before any formal referral for special education services. These are not special education procedures but are part of the general education system required by some state special education legislation (schools implementing RTI procedures may allocate up to 15% of federal special education funds to these procedures). The *In the Classroom* feature identifies a checklist of steps in a prereferral process.

All prereferral procedures, including RTI and MTSS, are preventative in nature; they are intended to reduce inappropriate referrals and decrease the likelihood of future problems. These procedures provide general education teachers and students with immediate assistance with classroom-related problems, including disciplinary issues. To determine whether the general education intervention is appropriate, team members may observe the student before the prereferral intervention takes place. It is wise to try to involve the parents whenever possible; however, before any general education intervention plan is implemented, parents must be notified in writing of the team's recommendation for intervention strategies and the rationale for implementing them. Finally, the intervention is implemented.

ESTABLISHING TIMELINES   Once intervention strategies are developed, timelines are set to accompany the implementation and review of those strategies. In Mrs. Mayer's case, a strategy was designed to be implemented with Omar. In some cases, the prereferral assistance team could recommend strategies Mrs. Mayer could implement in her class to help Omar. In a schoolwide RTI system, Omar could be referred to a Tier 2 RTI program (possibly a more intensive small-group supplemental instruction several times a week) if he had not responded sufficiently to Tier 1, that is, interventions employing evidence-based practice in the general education classroom. Omar's parents will be contacted and asked to give permission for an educational evaluation for possible special education services. Omar's parents can request an educational evaluation for special education at any time during this process, and their request will be honored and not delayed due to the implementation of the general education intervention.

INTERVENTION STRATEGIES   Intervention strategies vary depending on the specific needs of the student but may include adaptations in (a) the curriculum, (b) instructional procedures, (c) classroom management, or (d) the classroom environment. Curriculum adaptations involve altering the curriculum, such as using universal design for learning (UDL) materials that allow students to change text to larger fonts and have text-to-voice features. Adaptations in instructional procedures include providing additional instruction or using different presentation formats; varying the types of practice activities; altering testing procedures, such as having tests read aloud; and regrouping students within instructional activities. Adapting classroom management procedures involves intensifying behavioral monitoring for increasing attention to task, providing individual student behavioral contracts, or increasing reinforcement. Environmental changes consist of rearranging the classroom desks, making the classroom more accessible, or changing seating positions. Finally, other resources available within the school and community may be used to assist in implementing general education interventions. Tier 2 interventions, usually consisting of intensive small-group instruction, could be employed for students who do not benefit from evidence-based general education classroom (Tier 1) instruction.

RESEARCH ON PREREFERRAL INTERVENTIONS   Truscott, Celinae, Sams, Sanborn, and Frank (2005) surveyed state departments of education regarding their prereferral intervention practices and found that there was considerable variability from state to state in whether prereferral interventions were required, the terminology used to describe them, and how they were carried out (see also Buck, Polloway, Smith-Thomas, & Cook, 2003). Similar variability has been observed in the implementation of RTI (Berkeley, Bender, Peaster, & Saunders, 2009; Prewett et al., 2012). Although prereferral intervention practices are not always successful (Rock & Zigmond, 2001), they may be effective in preventing special education placement (Burns & Symington, 2002). Some evidence suggests that RTI procedures may reduce the placement of students in special education programs (Wanzek & Vaughn, 2011).

RESPONSE-TO-INTERVENTION (RTI) PROCEDURES   As described previously, since the passage of the IDEA 2004, schools have been allowed to use federal funds to provide *early intervention services* for students experiencing difficulty in school but not yet referred for special education. These services may be delivered in *tiers* of increasing intensity, where, for example, Tier 1 interventions may be research-validated teaching practices, with targeted adaptations implemented in the classroom when needed. Tier 2 interventions can be planned for students who fail to respond to Tier 1 interventions (National Center on Response to Intervention,

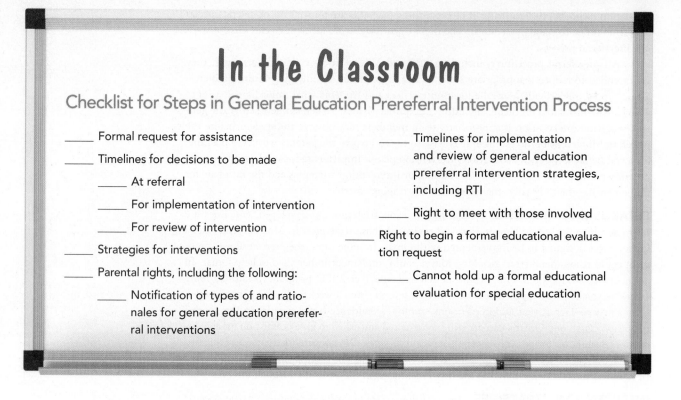

In the Classroom

Checklist for Steps in General Education Prereferral Intervention Process

_____ Formal request for assistance

_____ Timelines for decisions to be made

    _____ At referral

    _____ For implementation of intervention

    _____ For review of intervention

_____ Strategies for interventions

_____ Parental rights, including the following:

    _____ Notification of types of and rationales for general education prereferral interventions

_____ Timelines for implementation and review of general education prereferral intervention strategies, including RTI

_____ Right to meet with those involved

_____ Right to begin a formal educational evaluation request

_____ Cannot hold up a formal educational evaluation for special education

2011). These second-tier interventions can take place with small groups of students who have not responded well to Tier 1 interventions and may be considered an intensive and systematic type of prereferral intervention. Tier 2 interventions may include, for example, 20 or 30 minutes of intensive small-group instruction in reading. The goal is to help students acquire needed classroom skills within a specific time period (e.g., 10–20 weeks; Vaughn & Roberts, 2007). If students still do not make acceptable progress, they may be provided with even more intensive (Tier 3) services, including referral for evaluation for special education placement (see Hoover, 2010). Research suggests that Tier 2 interventions in reading can help many students gain important skills (Kamps et al., 2008; National Center on Response to Intervention, 2011; Solis, Vaughn, & Scammacca, 2015) and may lead to a reduced rate of referral for special education services (Wanzek & Vaughn, 2011). Additional information on RTI and MTSS is provided in Chapter 7.

MyEdLab: **Self-Check 2.3**

MyEdLab: **Application Exercise 2.3: Response to Intervention**

Collaboration for Referrals and Placements

The special education referral process is usually initiated by the student's teachers or parents but can also be initiated by others, including the student. Each school has written referral procedures, designated staff for the various positions within the referral process, and accompanying forms.

Once the prereferral team determined that the strategies Mrs. Mayer had implemented on her own (or Tier 1 and Tier 2 interventions in schools implementing RTI) were insufficient to help Omar successfully perform in second grade, the referral process for educational evaluation began. Mrs. Mayer completed the school's "Referral Evaluation Form" (see Figure 2.2 for a sample referral form). Once the referral form was completed, Omar's parents were contacted and asked to meet with school personnel. They were told that their son had been referred for an educational evaluation. They were told why he was referred and were asked to

Date Received _____

Student's Name _____ Gender _____ Birthdate _____

School _____ Grade _____ Teacher _____

Parent/Guardian _____ Primary Language _____

Address _____ Home Phone _____ Work Phone _____

Current Educational Program _____

Referring Person _____
                (signature)   (title)   (date)

Principal/Designee _____
                    (signature)   (date)

1. Please describe briefly the reason(s) for this referral.

2. Documentation of the general education intervention (attach copy of the general education intervention plan): What are the effects of the intervention?

   Comments from the remedial reading instructor, if applicable:

3. Documentation of support services such as counseling or psychological (nontesting) services provided by school or other agency.

   Comments and observations from the school counselor:

   Has a previous psychological evaluation been conducted?

   Yes _____ No _____ Date _____ Agency _____

4. Documentation of conferences, or attempts to conference, with the parent and appropriate school personnel concerning the student's specific problem(s).

5. Which of the disabilities/handicaps do you suspect?

   _____ Autism _____ Communication disorders _____ Emotional disability

   _____ Hearing impairment _____ Learning disability _____ Mental disability

   _____ Orthopedic impairment _____ Other health impairment

   _____ Traumatic brain injury _____ Visual impairment

6. In what subjects are the student's problems most apparent?

7. List schools previously attended and dates:

(continued)

Figure 2.2 Sample Referral Form

Figure 2.2

(*Continued*)

8. Comments from school nurse:

   Current general health _____

   Previous medical problems _____

   Is the student taking medication? ___ If yes, specify _____

   Vision: L _____ R _____ Correction _____

   Date of vision screening _____ (must be done within a year)

9. Comments from speech, hearing, and language clinician:

   Hearing: L _____ R _____ Correction _____

   Date of hearing screening _____ (must be done within a year)

   Is the student receiving speech and language therapy? In the past?

10. Copy and attach information from the student's education record:

    1. Previous achievement test results
    2. Grades earned since school entry
    3. Attendance record
    4. Summary of disciplinary actions

Complete and send all referral information to Special Services.

Eligibility and Evaluations

   Parents can:

   - Request special education evaluations
   - Provide or revoke consent for evaluations
   - Consent to or deny special education and related services
   - Have access to written records, including copies of evaluations and IEPs

   Schools must:

   - Explain evaluation results to parents

Independent Education Evaluations (IEEs)

   - If parents disagree with school evaluations, then parents can request independent education evaluations (IEEs) at public expense
   - Parents can privately pay for IEEs and present them to IEP teams for non-binding consideration

IEP Participation

   Parents:

   - Have the right to participate in IEP meetings
   - Must receive written documentation stating parental legal rights
   - Can invite individuals or advocates familiar with their child to IEP meetings

   Local Education Agency:

   - Must appoint a surrogate parent when a child is a ward of the state or parental identification is impossible

Changes in Placement or Denial of Services

   - Parents have rights to request prior written notice regarding any changes in placement, or refusal of services.
   - After requesting prior written notice, schools must document rationale behind placement changes or service refusals.
   - Parents can use this documentation in any mediation or due process proceeding.

Figure 2.3 Parental Rights Under IDEA

Note: Contributed by Catherine Creighton Thompson. Reprinted with permission.

General Education Teachers teach any grade level, any subject area, K–12; may be responsible for implementing part or all of a student's IEP.

Special Education Teachers teach any grade level, any disability area, K–12; may teach in any of the settings described for general education teachers; usually have primary responsibility for the implementation of the IEP.

School Psychologists or Diagnosticians take the lead on the educational evaluations, have major responsibilities in administering, scoring, and interpreting tests; sometimes serve as behavioral consultants to teachers.

Counselors advise students; may conduct some social and emotional assessment; may deliver counseling sessions or advise teachers on how to deal with social-emotional needs for their students.

Speech/Language Therapists work with students who require assistance with any speech and/or language needs.

Physical Therapists provide assessment and interventions in gross motor areas.

Occupational Therapists provide assessment and interventions for students in the fine motor areas.

School Nurses often provide medical histories, distribute medications to students; provide a link between families and other school personnel.

School Administrators provide administrative assistance among all involved; may include school principals, vice principals, directors of special education, directors of special services, and special education coordinators.

Social Workers provide the link between families and schools; have similar roles to that of counselors.

Paraprofessionals provide assistance to teachers, special education teachers, and students with disabilities.

Other School Specialists provide assistance in specialized ways, including adaptive physical education; sign language interpreting; bilingual special education; mobility specialists, psychometrists (complete educational testing), probation officers, and other consultants as necessary.

Figure 2.4 School Personnel as Team Members and Their Roles

provide written permission to proceed. Omar's parents were informed about the evaluation procedures and told that a case conference committee meeting would be scheduled within 65 school days of the parents' signing the permission for testing. They were also told about how the school had already attempted to help Omar through the general education program (or Tier 1 and Tier 2 programs in schools implementing RTI).

All information should be presented verbally and in writing for the parents, in the parents' native language. If parents speak Spanish, for example, then school personnel must communicate with the parents using Spanish. Figure 2.3 contains a listing of parental rights.

THE EDUCATIONAL EVALUATION OR ASSESSMENT STEP The educational evaluation for a referral to special education is much more comprehensive than the evaluation described for prereferrals by the general education teams. This evaluation provides extensive information on how the student learns best and the student's level of performance, and it identifies strengths and potential need areas. The evaluation team includes a school psychologist and other school specialists as needed (see Figure 2.4). For example, if a child is suspected of having a problem involving speech or language, then a speech and language therapist would be a member of that evaluation team. In the case of Omar, who is suspected of having reading and writing problems that may be associated with learning disabilities, a teacher of students with learning disabilities will be a member of that team.

The education evaluation includes various activities, procedures, and tests. A physical examination, developmental history, and vision and hearing tests may be required. A battery of academic, intellectual, adaptive, and social-emotional tests will be administered, depending on the specific referral reason. Observations of the student throughout the school day may be completed. The classroom teacher is asked to evaluate the student's classroom strengths and need areas. If the school is using an RTI model, data showing inadequate progress in Tier 2 settings are also presented.

MyEdLab:
Video Example 2.2.
This video features a case conference committee. Who are the members of the committee? Pay attention to everyone's role in the process.

All testing must be culturally unbiased, be completed in the student's native language, and consider cultural background and presumed disability to provide the most accurate picture of the student's current level of functioning. This means, for example, that if a student's native language is Spanish, then it may be important to administer tests in Spanish; otherwise, an inaccurate picture of the student's abilities may be obtained. Parents, teachers, or other school personnel can request a reevaluation whenever one is deemed necessary.

THE CASE CONFERENCE COMMITTEE A case conference committee or multidisciplinary team is composed of all individuals concerned with a particular student. The amendments to IDEA require that general education teachers participate in the development, review, and revision of IEPs. Moreover, the amendments require that parents be included as members of any group that makes educational decisions about their child. The members include the parents, their child, and parent advocates, if desired; general and special education teachers; the school psychologist; school administrators, such as the building principal or special education director; and any other related personnel, such as the school nurse, counselor, and social worker, or specialists such as speech and language, physical, or occupational therapists.

A case conference committee meeting is convened after the educational evaluation is finished. The meeting is intended to determine whether the student is eligible for special education and related services. If so, then the IEP is developed, and appropriate educational services decisions are made. Case conference committee meetings also take place during each annual review.

EASE THE CONCERN OF PARENTS AND STUDENTS During these meetings, all members of the committee should be made to feel welcome and comfortable. Parents and students may feel overwhelmed, intimidated, or frightened by attending a meeting with so many school personnel. Prepare for meetings by thinking about how to present information in comprehensible ways for parents and students. It may be beneficial to practice with another teacher when describing classroom routines. For example, parents may be unfamiliar with terminology that is used so commonly among teachers (e.g., *decoding* is a term frequently used by teachers but not necessarily by parents and children). Try to describe class activities, student performance, and behaviors using concrete, simple, direct language. Teachers frequently use abbreviations or acronyms when speaking with each other (e.g., saying "LD" instead of "learning disabilities"), but they should avoid doing so when speaking at case conference committees so that parents do not become lost in the educational jargon. Secure brochures describing common disabilities in ways suitable for parents and for students. Brochures, important phone numbers, e-mail addresses, and websites can be printed on handouts for parents.

Martin et al. (2006) reported that special education teachers spoke 51% of the time at IEP meetings, whereas family members spoke only 15% of the time. These findings suggest that input from parents and other family members should be more actively solicited in order to gather all relevant information. Parents are also allowed to invite a parent advocate to the IEP meeting but should notify the school in writing ahead of time.

When parents feel comfortable at the meeting, they will be more likely to share important information about their child. Parental input at the meeting can be invaluable. Parents have insight into their child's behaviors that no one at the school may have considered. They can provide input regarding the student's study habits at home and any difficulties encountered during homework. During the case conference committee, one member records the information on the case conference summary form. A copy of this is distributed to the parents at the end of the meeting. Figure 2.5 displays a sample case conference summary form. If the student does not qualify for special education, the student may still qualify for services under Section 504 of the Vocational Rehabilitation Act.

RELATED SERVICES Related services are other services that are necessary to help students with disabilities benefit from special education services. Related services may include physical therapy, occupational therapy, audiological services, counseling, rehabilitation counseling, social work services, parent counseling, psychological services, school health services, medical services, early identification, transportation, recreation services, adaptive physical education, or other services identified by the case conference committee. If a situation requires substantial

CASE REVIEW CONFERENCE SUMMARY

Student's Name _____ DOB _____ School _____

Parents/Guardian _____ Address _____

Phone _____ Surrogate Parent _____

Committee Meeting: _____

                    (date)   (time)   (location)

The Case Review Committee was composed of the following:

_____

Chairperson   Administrator

_____

Teacher   Teacher   Teacher

_____

Evaluation Team Member(s)

_____

Parent(s)   Student

_____

Others

The eligibility decision has been _____

Least restrictive placement has been _____

Purpose of conference   _____ initial evaluation   _____ re-evaluation   _____ review of IEP

                               _____ transition planning   _____ new to district

Multidisciplinary report of present level of performance:

_____

_____

_____

_____

Based on the data presented, the following eligibility decision was made:
The student is

_____

Placement recommendation:

_____

     Harmful effect considered: _____ yes

Options considered: _____

Reasons options were rejected: _____

Other factors relevant to the proposed placement _____

_____

Signatures of committee members with dissenting opinions:

      _____

      _____

      _____

Figure 2.5   Summary from Case Conference Committee Meeting

mobility adaptations, the case conference committee might recommend bus routes with special or adapted vehicles, assign an aide as an assistant, or acquire special equipment such as oxygen, ramps, or lifts.

THE INDIVIDUALIZED EDUCATION PROGRAM (IEP)   An IEP is written by the case conference committee when it is determined that a student is eligible for special education services (Bateman, 2011). The IEP has several major components, including the following:

- Student's current level of academic achievement and functional performance
- Statement of measurable annual goals, including academic and functional goals
- Statement of short-term objectives for children who take alternative assessments
- Statement of special and related services, based on peer-reviewed research and any program modifications to be provided for support for the child
- Statement of any individual modifications in state- or district-wide assessment procedures
- Statement of why a child cannot participate in state- or district-wide assessment procedures if an alternative assessment is recommended
- Initiation dates of service delivery and the duration and frequency of services
- Statement of transition services for all students 16 years of age and older, including appropriate postsecondary goals and transition services needed to meet those goals
- Statement of how annual goals will be measured, how parents will be informed, and how progress will be monitored

Moreover, when a special education student is placed in a general education setting, the IEP will contain modifications needed, including curriculum, instructional procedures, staffing, classroom organization, and special equipment, materials, or aides.

Although IEP formats used by school districts vary across the country, all must contain the required components. Some computerized IEP programs are available commercially and are used to assist in developing the basic format of the IEPs (see the *Apps for Education* feature).

School districts provide the parents with a written summary of the case conference committee meeting (see Figure 2.5), a copy of the IEP, and a copy of parental rights (see Figure 2.3), and parents must provide written consent agreeing to the IEP before any services can begin.

WRITING GOALS AND OBJECTIVES   A critical component of the IEP is the specification of the long-term annual goals and short-term objectives. Short-term objectives are required only for students who take alternative assessments. Long-term annual goals are based on the case conference committee's judgment of what the individual student should accomplish within a year. Annual goals can refer to academic functioning, such as reading grade-level textbooks at specific skill levels, or social behavior, such as exhibiting appropriate behavior in the cafeteria. In some cases, annual goals can refer to adaptive behavior or life skills, such as ordering independently in a restaurant or managing a personal bank account.

Annual goals are measurable, positive, student-oriented, and relevant (Capizzi, 2008). Goals that are measurable can be more easily evaluated later. For example, "[Student] will read and comprehend grade-level reading materials" is much easier to measure at the end of the year than "[Student] will improve reading." Positively written goals (e.g., "[Student] will use appropriate language in the classroom at all times") provide better implications for instruction than negatively written goals (e.g., "[Student] will stop swearing"). Student-oriented goals describe what the student will do (as in the previous examples) rather than what others will do (e.g., "[Student] will be given spelling worksheets"). Finally, relevant goals are not always limited to academic goals but also provide for the student's current and future needs, including social-emotional functioning, communication, and career/vocational areas, when appropriate (Gartin & Murdick, 2005).

Short-term objectives are more limited and precise, and they specify the steps to be taken to achieve long-term annual goals. For example, short-term objectives relevant to a long-term annual goal in reading should specify the subskills (e.g., letter identification, word recognition) that students will acquire on the way to meeting the long-term goal. Short-term objectives should also be measurable, positive, student-oriented, and relevant. In addition, short-term

IEP Software

Special education paperwork can be reduced by using efficient systems for recording data, for maintaining records, and for communications. Advances in technology can help teachers save valuable time. For example, teachers can use basic templates in word-processing programs with school stationery for communications, as well as databases containing frequently used names and addresses. Such timesaving programs are common features on most computers.

Numerous apps are available to assist with understanding IEPs, developing IEPs, and running and scheduling IEP meetings. *IEP Goals & Objectives with Common Core State Standards* (NASET) contains sections on annual goals, objectives, common core standards, activities, and measuring progress designed to assist in preparing IEPs. The *IEP Checklist* (Nurvee; PEATC.org) app provides a checklist in English and Spanish for parents and teachers to consider as they develop IEPs. *IEP Facilitation* (Region 10 Education Service Center) describes the roles, responsibilities, and purpose of

having a facilitator at IEP meetings. *Schedule My IEP* (CME Apps, Inc.) contains a calendar with built-in reminders for meetings and important due dates.

There are numerous software programs commercially available to assist with writing IEPs and other aspects of special education in general. Many of these programs share common features in that they work easily on both PC and Mac computer platforms. Many contain general templates for information that is required by law to be included in the IEP. Some also contain banks of possible IEP objectives. Some of the available programs include the following: *Goalview* by Public Consulting Group, *Genesea* by Edupoint, *IEP Planner* by AbleData, and *IEP Online* by PCG Education. Spectrum K12 School Solutions provides software for RTI implementation as well as IEP development. Interventioncentral .org contains a wealth of resources, including academic and behavior intervention planners, chart construction tools, and test construction ideas. A simple search using a search engine such as Google

will provide numerous commercially available programs.

Commercially available programs are usually advertised as highly relevant, timesaving devices that help teachers produce high-quality IEPs. Although this may be true in many cases, teachers should use caution to ensure that students' IEP objectives are not limited simply to what is available within individual software programs.

The Common Core Standards (Mastery Connect) presents all the reading and math standards, which can be used as a reference and when preparing for IEP meetings and can be helpful for educators and parents.

Finally, there are numerous apps available for monitoring behavior at home and school that can be linked to IEP objectives. For example, the *IRewardChart* (Gotclues) app allows parents to monitor behaviors and implement rewards for chore completion, homework completion, or other good behaviors. Progress is charted, and rewards are awarded when prespecified standards are met. Coordination between home and school management programs is also possible.

objectives are usually best when they specify conditions, behavior, and criteria. As an example, consider the following objective: "In the lunchroom, [Student] will use appropriate tone of voice at all times." In this case, "lunchroom" specifies the conditions, "appropriate tone of voice" specifies the behavior, and "at all times" (i.e., 100% of the time) specifies the criteria. When objectives are specified in this way, they can be easily evaluated on the way toward meeting long-term goals.

TRANSITION SERVICES Transition services are required to be written into IEPs when students turn 16 but, in fact, may be appropriate at younger ages (Magdalena, Kopechanski, Cameron, & Hughs, 2008). IDEA and its amendments also require transitioning for preschoolers.

Often, transition services can be implemented the year before students begin to accumulate credits toward high school graduation. At the annual review meeting, when the student is 16, the case conference committee may determine student educational, vocational, or employment training needs. Specific interagency linkages and responsibilities must be explicated in the individualized transition plan (ITP), which is a supplement to the IEP. The committee also determines whether students may require continual adult services upon completion of high school.

MONITORING IEPS Legal safeguards are provided to ensure IEPs are monitored to reflect accurately the needs of individuals with disabilities. Regular reviews and evaluations of progress are required. Due-process procedures are always available to resolve any disputes between the parents and the school district regarding the student's education.

Due Process Due process is how conflicts are resolved between parents and schools regarding the student's education. Disagreements can arise in several areas: whether a student is eligible for special education, the outcome of an educational evaluation, the educational placement, the IEP, or some aspect of the "free, appropriate public education" (FAPE) guaranteed by IDEA.

Several alternatives exist for resolving these disagreements, some of which take place before a formal due-process hearing. The simplest procedure for resolving conflicts is through informal meetings with parents and school personnel.

If conflicts remain unresolved during informal meetings, mediation can be used to try to resolve the dispute. Mediation is a voluntary process that must be requested by both parties. After a formal mediation request is signed by both parties, the state selects a mediator and schedules a hearing within 10 working days. Mediators should be trained in special education and mediation, possess excellent interpersonal skills, and serve as neutral facilitators. If mediation is successful, a written agreement is completed and forwarded to the case conference committee for its approval. Many conflicts can be resolved through mediation (Mueller, 2009).

A request for a due-process hearing is a formal request by either the parents or the school district to have the dispute arbitrated by an independent hearing officer. This process is more formal than mediation and must take place within timelines as specified in the law. The case is presented to the independent hearing officer, who makes a decision based on the evidence presented by both parties. Both parents and the school district may be represented by legal counsel, present information pertaining to the case, and bring forth relevant witnesses, and both are entitled to see, at least 5 days before the hearing, any evidence the other party plans to introduce. Due-process hearings can be open or closed to the public, and the student may or may not be present. After listening to all the evidence, hearing officers produce a written decision. After the hearing decision but within a specified number of days, the decision must be either executed or appealed to the appropriate state board of special education by either party.

The appeal of the due-process-hearing decision must describe the parts of the decision that are objectionable and the associated rationale. The state board of special education is required to schedule another impartial review of the hearing and report on its decision. Its decision is considered final unless either party appeals to the civil court within 30 calendar days. Throughout this process, the students remain in their current placement unless both parties agree to something else.

Special education departments in each school district have policies and procedures outlining teachers' roles and responsibilities should they become involved in these processes. The intent of the law is to best serve the student with disabilities, and these safeguards are in place to ensure that both parents and school district personnel are afforded due-process rights.

Annual Reviews Annual review meetings are conducted to monitor progress. During these meetings, teachers, parents, and other team members discuss the student's progress and make recommendations to amend, modify, or adjust the IEP as necessary. Changes in a student's educational placement to a more or less restrictive environment might be made based on the review.

MyEdLab: **Self-Check 2.4**

MyEdLab: **Application Exercise 2.4: Referral Procedures**

Collaboration as Partnerships

Relationships develop among the many individuals working together to design optimal educational programs for students with disabilities. Relationships of special education and general education teachers may develop into collaborative consultation for shared decision making and planning, as well as co-teaching relationships. Collaborative partnerships can also develop with paraprofessionals and with parents and families. These partnerships can substantially improve the school and life functioning of students with disabilities.

CONSULTATION BETWEEN SPECIAL AND GENERAL EDUCATORS

Consultation exists when two individuals, such as special and general educators, work together to decide on intervention strategies for a specific student. During these meetings, which can be formal or informal and verbal or in writing, effective communication procedures are critical.

For example, special education teachers may send weekly notes or e-mails to general education teachers to ask about the progress of specific students with disabilities. Teachers then describe any potentially difficult assignments for which they expect students with disabilities will require additional assistance, as in the following examples:

- A biology teacher indicates that a science fair project is being assigned next week. It will be due in a month, and students with disabilities may benefit from extra assistance.

- A history teacher indicates that an important unit test is approaching, and students with disabilities may require additional studying assistance.

This information alerts special education teachers, who can then help decide whether additional assistance is needed and then work with teachers in developing appropriate interventions as needed for students with disabilities.

In other cases, teachers may ask for specific input from the special education teacher, for example, on how to deal with behavior problems. Kampwirth and Powers (2016) described how a special education teacher partnered with a general education teacher. After discussion, the general education teacher focused on two specific concerns: teasing and not turning in homework. The two teachers worked out specific plans for conferencing with the student, home–school notes with the parent, and peer mediation in class. These interventions were monitored and found to be effective in improving the student's behavior.

CO-TEACHING

Different models of collaboration and co-teaching are used to meet the needs of diverse learners within a single classroom setting. During co-teaching, two teachers are present in the inclusive classroom during instructional periods (Friend & Cook, 2013).

There are several different ways co-teaching can be carried out. In **interactive teaching** (or **team-teaching**), teachers take turns presenting and leading classroom activities and share responsibilities equally. In other cases, one teacher assumes more responsibility for delivering instruction, and the other teacher assists individual students (**one teach, one drift**) or observes individual students to improve instructional decision making (**one teach, one observe**). In **station teaching**, smaller groups of students move through several independent workstations for new information, review, or practice while the teachers monitor different stations. In **parallel teaching**, the class is divided into skill or ability groups, and each teacher leads one group. In **alternative teaching**, one teacher leads the larger group while the other teacher (often, the special education teacher) provides additional practice or strategies to students who may require additional support. In practice, however, the roles of the two teachers can deviate from these (Friend & Cook, 2013).

Co-teaching at the secondary level can present some unique challenges because of such factors as increased emphasis on content knowledge, the pace of instruction, scheduling constraints, the expectation for independent study skills, and high-stakes testing (Friend, Cook, Hurley-Chamberlain, & Shamberger, 2010). Murray (2004) suggested that general education

MyEdLab:
Video Example 2.3.
The teacher in this video discusses collaborative efforts in her middle school. Notice the different types of collaboration, including co-teaching, as they are explained.

teachers develop "dream lists" of what they would like most from the special education teachers with whom they would be collaborating. These teachers then meet with special education teachers to revise and discuss the lists and reflect on the outcome of the meetings. Similarly, Murawski and Dieker (2004) recommended systematically sharing hopes, attitudes, responsibilities, and expectations before proceeding with co-teaching. They provided a chart of teacher activities to help organize tasks. For example, if one teacher is lecturing, the other teacher could be modeling effective note-taking procedures or managing classroom behavior. While one teacher is passing out papers, the other teacher could be reviewing directions and demonstrating the first problem. As one teacher prepares lesson plans, the other teacher could provide suggestions for accommodations and adaptations for diverse learners. Establishing a chart such as this could help maximize efficiency during co-teaching. Murawski (2006) underlined the importance of common planning for inclusive teaching, parity in teacher roles, and the use of varied instructional models.

Sufficient planning time for the two teachers to work cooperatively to develop lessons to co-teach is very important (Conderman, 2011). Ask for assistance from school administrators to include as much co-planning time as possible. Consider using the following guidelines when establishing co-teaching:

- Decide goals and objectives for co-teaching.
- Inform parents and request their support and permission, especially if co-teaching alters any IEP placement decisions that were made with parental consent.
- Determine student and teacher attitudes toward the co-teaching.
- Determine how instructional responsibilities will be shared during co-teaching, what co-teaching models will be implemented, how parity of co-teaching roles will be established, what instructional adaptations will be made for students with disabilities, and how the effectiveness of co-teaching arrangements will be evaluated.

RESEARCH SUPPORT Generally, teachers and students have reported positive attitudes toward co-teaching. Reported benefits of co-teaching include improved instruction, increased enthusiasm for teaching, more communication, and more opportunities to generalize learned skills to the general education class environment (Cook, McDuffie-Landrum, Oshita, & Cook, 2011).

Challenges to effective co-teaching have also been described (Murawski & Swanson, 2001; Murray, 2004; Weiss & Lloyd, 2003) that include budgetary constraints, lack of sufficient planning time, lack of cooperation, personality conflicts, and increased teacher workloads. Other concerns include maintaining the full continuum of services for students, fear of losing necessary services, confronting negative attitudes, and confidentiality issues. Finally, the diminished role of the special education teacher and the frequent use of a whole-class approach to instruction has sometimes been a concern. Use of the effective communication strategies discussed earlier, and the effective teaching strategies described throughout this book, can help ensure that the co-teaching experience is pleasant and productive.

Scruggs, Mastropieri, and McDuffie (2007) summarized 32 qualitative studies of co-teaching, describing over 400 co-teachers using interviews, observations, and classroom products. They found that teachers generally appreciated co-teaching and felt it was beneficial to teachers as well as students with and without disabilities. However, they also identified a number of challenges, including the need for more administrative support, more time to plan for co-teaching, and additional training. The most common model was "one teach, one assist," with the general education teacher presenting traditional, whole-class teaching, and the special education teacher often assuming a subordinate role. Several observed classrooms, however, demonstrated special and general education teachers in true partnerships, actively collaborating on the best instruction for all students.

Conners (2008) observed and interviewed 30 special education middle school teachers during co-taught and self-contained classes. All teachers were previously identified as expert special education teachers by district personnel. Based on the observations and interviews, Conners concluded that these expert special education teachers demonstrated excellent co-teaching behaviors. These behaviors included those described in Table 2.3.

TABLE 2.3 Expert Co-Teaching Characteristics and Behaviors

Collaborative Co-Teachers

- *Capitalize* on each other's strengths
- *Complement* each other's teaching styles
- *Negotiate* all practice
- *Respect* what each "brings to the table"
- *Exhibit* comfort and trust with each other's teaching style
- *Make* their personalities and teaching styles complement one another, and work to establish good rapport
- *Demonstrate* evidence of co-planning and personal commitment to the co-teaching relationship

Both Teachers Viewed as a "Teacher"

- *Share and value* all students and have high expectations for everyone
- *Share roles and all responsibilities* in an equal partnership
- *Demonstrate flexibility* within roles
- *Exhibit* smooth transitions between teachers during instruction
- *Alternate* roles continuously during instruction while both teachers exhibit a teaching mode at all times

Note: From Conners (2008). Adapted with permission from the author.

A considerable amount of research has described the process and characteristics of co-teaching. However, more research needs to be conducted on the overall effectiveness of co-teaching and the relative benefits of one model of co-teaching over another (Friend et al., 2010; Murawski, 2006). The limited efficacy research that has been conducted to date (e.g., Castro, 2007; McDuffie, Mastropieri, & Scruggs, 2009) has been effective in describing the benefits of co-teaching; however, teachers implementing co-teaching should collect evidence in their own classrooms to support the effectiveness of their practices.

STRATEGIES FOR
COLLABORATING WITH PARAPROFESSIONALS

CLARIFY ROLES AND RESPONSIBILITIES Paraprofessionals may be aides to special education teachers, specialized aides for students with disabilities, or general aides for teachers within a school. Within those roles, paraprofessionals assume a variety of responsibilities, including recordkeeping, supervising, monitoring seatwork and classroom behavior, assisting with feeding and toileting, and providing instruction. It is important that paraprofessionals are viewed as part of a team and that they receive appropriate role clarification, training, and supervision (Giangreco, Suter, & Doyle, 2010; Walker & Smith, 2015). To avoid communication problems, paraprofessionals need to be informed specifically of what their duties are (Carter, O'Rourke, & Sisco, 2009).

Develop schedules for paraprofessionals that include the person responsible and the date for completion of specific tasks. Also schedule where all people will be at different times of the day or week (Pickett & Gerlach, 2003).

Very specialized responsibilities may be assigned to a paraprofessional. In the case of Jamal, for example, a third grader who uses a motorized wheelchair and has difficulties communicating and using his hands, a paraprofessional accompanies him throughout the school day. The paraprofessional functions as Jamal's assistant and accompanies him before, during, and after school in any activities, including helping him eat at lunch and dress appropriately for physical education and recess. It may be a new experience for general education teachers to have another adult in their classrooms during instruction, but once teachers become familiar with the activities Jamal can accomplish independently, they will gain a better understanding of how to maximize the role of the paraprofessional. For example, activities the paraprofessional can help Jamal with include handling his class materials, reading tests out loud to him, writing down his responses, and assisting with mobility.

Paraprofessionals assist students in their tasks throughout the school day. However, it is possible for paraprofessionals to spend too much time in close proximity with their students. This can lead to a more limited sense of ownership by and less interaction with the teacher, separation from classmates and peer interaction, overdependence on adults, and a loss of personal control (Giangreco & Broer, 2007; Giangreco, Broer, & Suter, 2011). Students should receive all the assistance they need but not more than they require.

COMMUNICATE EFFECTIVELY WITH PARAPROFESSIONALS On occasion, teachers may feel overwhelmed with their responsibilities and find it difficult to know what to do with paraprofessionals. This may be especially true if paraprofessionals have strong personalities, are older, or have worked in schools longer than the teacher. If a touchy situation arises, such as disagreeing on the amount of assistance necessary for a student, relations may become strained. To defuse these situations, use effective communication and problem-solving strategies to identify the problem and brainstorm potential solutions. If you do not think you can handle the situation alone, seek the assistance of a more established teacher within your school. Often, simply discussing the situation makes everyone feel more comfortable.

STRATEGIES FOR
COLLABORATING EFFECTIVELY WITH PARENTS AND FAMILIES

Building positive partnerships with parents yields important benefits to your students' education and is a significant component of IDEA legislation (Kampwirth & Powers, 2016). Establish positive communication early in the school year, and aim toward strengthening home–school cooperation. You will learn a great deal about your students from the parents' perspective of how they learn and interact in the home and outside of school. Overall, parents and families can be important and powerful allies in the education of children with special learning needs (Singer, Maul, Wang, & Ethridge, 2011; Turnbull, Turnbull, Erwin, Soodak, & Shogren, 2015).

BE SENSITIVE TO VARIABILITY IN BACKGROUNDS AND FAMILY STRUCTURES

Parents represent the continuum of educational backgrounds, as well as racial or ethnic backgrounds and socioeconomic status. Be sensitive to all individual parental needs, and make all parents welcome in your classroom (see Zhang, Hsu, Kwok, Benz, & Bowman-Perrott, 2011). Many parents feel intimidated by teachers, so be sure to let them know you share their goal of wanting the best for their child.

State information in such a way that noneducators can understand what you are saying. If parents do not read or speak English, make the communications available in formats that are comprehensible to them. This may mean having native-language notes available for parents who do not read or speak English or having interpreters available for those with hearing impairments or who speak another language. Remember to have information read to parents who may not have the prerequisite literacy skills.

Families of today represent a wide array of configurations. The chances are good that the stereotypical family, consisting of a mother who stays at home taking care of children and a father who works outside of the home, may not be representative of many of your students' families. You may be working more closely with an individual who is not a parent but rather is the legal guardian of your student. Be sensitive to all family configurations. The *Diversity in the Classroom* feature provides some suggestions for interacting with diverse families.

MAINTAIN POSITIVE COMMUNICATION
A good way to initiate positive communication with parents is to send introductory notes home at the beginning of the school year. For example, Ms. Susan Chung, an eighth-grade English teacher, sends home a short note introducing herself and describing her class.

A positive first communication is especially important if a problem arises later and contact with home becomes necessary. Parents may be more likely to feel comfortable discussing sensitive issues concerning their child if you have contacted them earlier. If you only communicate when there is a problem, parents get the understandable impression that you only want to see them when something bad has happened, and they may become more reluctant to maintain communication with the school.

MyEdLab:
Video Example 2.4.
Parent communication is essential to work effectively with students. The principal in this video explains how parents may feel about the process. ∎

Many teachers also request parents' assistance regularly in their classes. This happens more frequently at the elementary level but also occurs at the secondary level. For example, letters may be sent home asking if any parents could volunteer in the class. Sometimes teachers specify what types of volunteer activity would be beneficial (e.g., making photocopies, organizing materials, or baking cookies for class parties). At other times, teachers might ask for help in obtaining specialized materials needed during specific units of instruction. But no matter what the request, it is important to emphasize that you realize it may be impossible for some parents to volunteer in class due to their other responsibilities or to contribute financially to class activities. Be sure parents understand that neither of these limitations undermines the value of their roles in supporting the education of their children.

Sending home "happy notes" is another way to maintain positive communication with parents. Happy notes communicate positive things from school events that day, week, or month. School-to-home notebooks also can be an effective means of maintaining communication with parents. Balance affirming messages with areas of concern, ask parents how they wish to communicate, and determine what information is most important to them (Davern, 2004). E-mail and text messages are also possible avenues for ongoing communication with parents; however, be aware that all parents might not be willing or able to communicate in this way (Turnbull et al., 2015).

COMMUNICATE ABOUT HOMEWORK Establish a "homework communication line" with parents. Some teachers have students maintain assignment notebooks in which daily homework assignments are recorded, including a listing of the materials necessary to complete assignments. When Mrs. Hesser, a fifth-grade teacher, assigned problem numbers 2 through 8 on page 27 in the math book, due Thursday, the students wrote down that information, along with the notation that they need to take home their math books to complete the assignment. If there is no assignment, students are required to write "No homework tonight" in the assignment book. Parents are shown the assignment books nightly and are asked to check and initial the book. This extra supervision keeps parents informed of assignments and provides opportunities for monitoring homework. In some schools, "homework hotlines" have been established, in which parents can call a phone number or check a website that informs them of their child's homework assignments.

RESOLVE DISAGREEMENTS On occasion, some parents may appear hostile toward teachers. In these cases, being prepared is an important step. Be sure you understand the problem and have developed, or are prepared to collaboratively develop, a plan of action (Turnbull et al., 2015). Use the strategies for communicating effectively discussed earlier in this chapter, especially active listening and depersonalizing situations. For significant or persistent problems, it is recommended that teachers obtain school or district assistance. Some districts may recommend that specific documentation procedures be implemented; others may recommend that parent conferences be scheduled and attended by several teachers, including the building administrators (Steedman, 2012). Understand that parent hostility might be attributable to a number of reasons, and assistance is available to help improve parental relations and ensure the best possible education for the student.

PARTNER WITH PARENT ADVISORY GROUPS Set up a parent advisory group in your school to meet every month or two. This group can function as a liaison between parents and the school regarding class projects, special curriculum areas, or regular school functions and as a disseminator of information. Teachers can share information about special class projects with all parents at regular parent advisory group meetings. For example, these meetings might be a nice time for Mrs. Hesser to let parents know about the assignment notebooks. Mrs. Hesser could make sure that all the parents knew that during the upcoming parent advisory meeting, she would be presenting that information and that she welcomed their comments regarding how they thought the process was working.

Other suitable topics include discussing the upcoming co-teaching planned by the sixth-grade and special education teachers or discussing special education referral information. Again, these meetings afford extra opportunities for positive communication and collaboration efforts among family members and school personnel. Finally, teachers can ask the group to assist in identifying topics of interest to parents, and specific presentations could be tailored to their needs.

Working with Families from Diverse Backgrounds

Family involvement is a critical component of the special education process but is particularly critical for children from diverse backgrounds. Families representing diverse cultural and linguistic backgrounds can provide important information on their child's culture, language spoken at home, beliefs, customs, and other relevant background information. Schools need to be sensitive to all cultural values, beliefs, and needs when working with families from culturally and linguistically diverse backgrounds. The following strategies can help build strong trust and collaboration with families:

- Maintain open and good lines of communication with families from the start of the school year.
- Ask families how they can help participate in their child's educational program at home and school.
- When families speak a language other than English, have interpreters present for parent conferences and other school events such as open house, school plays, concerts, and athletic events.
- Translate home announcements and other school-related documents that go home so that parents can access the content.
- Advertise locations of English as a second language (ESL) classes for interested families.

- Arrange for child care during family school visits when necessary.
- Determine whether families require transportation assistance to attend school functions.
- Arrange tutoring programs to assist both students and family members who may require additional assistance with understanding school assignments.
- Schedule multicultural events during which individuals from different backgrounds have opportunities to share information about their respective backgrounds, food, clothing, and culture.

HELP PARENTS AND FAMILIES COPE WITH DISABILITY ISSUES   It may be difficult for some parents to understand and accept that their child has a disability. In these cases, request assistance from the school social worker, counselor, or special education teacher. Parents may be frightened or feel overwhelmed when trying to understand why their child has a disability, what needs to be done, and how they can help. It may be beneficial for parents to attend support groups for parents of children with specific disabilities. Use the expertise of the specialists within your school district to gather as much information as possible for the parents (Turnbull et al., 2015).

Most schools have brochures and reference lists of sources suitable for parents to read concerning specific disability areas. Many parents appreciate knowing the names of books or articles that can provide additional information on their child's disability (e.g., Conroy, Yell, Katsiyannis, & Collins, 2010). Reference lists can identify where the materials can be located (e.g., the town library, the school library, the special library for parents). Professional organizations also maintain reference lists for specific disability areas. For example, the Council for Exceptional Children is a major special education organization that not only maintains reference lists but also has divisions specific to disability areas, such as the Division for Learning Disabilities and the Council for Children with Behavioral Disorders. Each division provides information pertaining to specific disability areas, including journals, newsletters, and websites.

MyEdLab: **Self-Check 2.5**

MyEdLab: **Application Exercise 2.5: Paraprofessionals**

2 Summary

- Collaboration—involving cooperation, effective communication, shared problem solving, planning, and finding solutions—is the process for ensuring that all students receive the free, appropriate public education mandated by IDEA.

- Effective communication is critical for successful collaboration. Effective communication involves active listening, depersonalizing situations, finding common goals, brainstorming steps for achieving common goals, identifying possible solutions, and summarizing the conversation. These steps can be very helpful in solving problems.

- General education prereferral interventions and response to intervention are steps taken by schools to promote success in the regular classroom before deciding on referral for special education. These actions can involve general and special education teachers, specialists, administrators, parents, and students, and they are often undertaken as part of a school response-to-intervention program.

- Building effective collaborative partnerships is one of the most significant tasks of a successful inclusive teacher. With effective teamwork, solutions can be found to any number of problems.

- Collaboration can take the form of consultation, in which teachers work together to decide on intervention strategies for a specific student. Collaboration can also take the form of co-teaching, in which a general education and special education teacher teach together in an inclusive classroom setting.

- Effective collaboration with paraprofessionals can improve communication and provide clarification of roles and responsibilities. Effective collaboration with parents is a key to effective inclusive teaching. Teachers should consider variability in family backgrounds and family structures and maintain close, positive contacts with parents.

PROFESSIONAL STANDARDS LINK:
Collaboration: Partnerships and Procedures

Information in this chapter links most directly to:

- CEC Standards: 2 (Learning Environments), 5 (Instructional Planning and Strategies), 6 (Professional Learning and Practice), 7 (Collaboration)

- INTASC Standards: 2 (Learning Differences), 3 (Learning Environments), 7 (Planning for Instruction), 8 (Instructional Strategies), 10 (Leadership and Collaboration).

COLLABORATION: PARTNERSHIPS AND PROCEDURES

If you would like to improve your communication and collaboration skills, have you employed effective communication strategies, including the following? If not, see the pages listed here.

STRATEGIES FOR COMMUNICATING EFFECTIVELY

STRATEGIES FOR COLLABORATING WITH PARAPROFESSIONALS

STRATEGIES FOR COLLABORATING EFFECTIVELY WITH PARENTS AND FAMILIES

3

Teaching Students with Higher-Incidence Disabilities

LEARNING OUTCOMES

After studying this chapter, you should be able to:

3.1 Describe and discuss the prevalence and characteristics of students with speech and language impairments, and explain strategies for classroom adaptations.

3.2 Describe and discuss the prevalence and characteristics of students with learning disabilities, and explain strategies for classroom adaptations.

3.3 Describe and discuss the prevalence and characteristics of students with intellectual disabilities, and explain strategies for classroom adaptations.

3.4 Describe and discuss the prevalence and characteristics of students with behavioral disorders and emotional disturbance, and explain strategies for classroom adaptations.

3.5 Describe and discuss the prevalence and characteristics of students with attention deficit disorder (ADD) and attention deficit hyperactivity disorder (ADHD), and explain strategies for classroom adaptations.

Individuals who have higher-incidence disabilities—the disabilities that are most commonly seen in schools—include a wide range of abilities and disabilities, from mild to severe in intensity. Some higher-incidence disabilities are temporary, whereas others are lifelong conditions. Higher-incidence disability areas include speech or language impairments, learning disabilities, mild or moderate intellectual disabilities, and emotional disturbance. Together these disability areas make up over 70% of the total population of students ages 6 to 21 with disabilities served under the Individuals with Disabilities Education Act (IDEA; U.S. Department of Education, 2015) and about 6% of the school-age population. Within the population of students with disabilities, percentages of students in each category in the United States are as follows:

> Speech or language impairment—17.9%
>
> Learning disabilities—39.5%
>
> Intellectual disabilities—7.1%
>
> Emotional disturbance—6.0%

In addition, about 3% to 7% or more of all school-age children have ADHD (Rooney, 2011), and ADHD may also be associated with other conditions. Although the intellectual disability figure includes those with severe intellectual disabilities, about 85% of the individuals would be characterized as having mild or moderate intellectual disabilities, as described in this chapter.

Speech or Language Impairments

PREVALENCE, DEFINITIONS, AND CHARACTERISTICS OF SPEECH OR LANGUAGE IMPAIRMENTS

Individuals classified as having speech or language impairments make up 17.9% of all students ages 6 to 21 served under IDEA and represent 1.5% of the school-age population. **Speech** is the system of forming and producing sounds that are the basis of language, whereas **language** is considered the system of communicating ideas. Most students receiving speech and language therapy work individually or in small groups with a specialist for brief sessions several times a week and usually spend the remainder of the day in general education classes. In some schools, speech and language teachers may conduct therapy sessions in the general education classroom (Owens, Farinella, & Metz, 2015).

Some students with speech and language disorders may have another primary disability area, such as a learning disability, cerebral palsy, traumatic brain injury, or other severe disabilities. The latter groups are more likely to be using **alternative and augmentative communication** (AAC) devices to help them communicate.

EXAMPLES AND CHARACTERISTICS OF SPEECH DISORDERS Speech disorders may exist as voice, articulation, or fluency disorders. Voice disorders affect the volume, pitch, flexibility, and quality of the voice and affect about 3% to 6% of school-age children (Owens et al., 2015). Examples of voice disorders include speech that is chronically strained, hoarse, breathy, or nasal. In the most severe instances, voice is not present at all.

Articulation disorders represent the largest subgroup of communication disorders (about 75%) and include difficulty pronouncing words, including omissions (e.g., "libary" for *library*), additions (e.g., "terribubble" for *terrible*), distortions (such as lisping), and substitutions (e.g., "tram" for *clam*). A child with articulation problems might say, "wabbits aw fuwwy animals."

Fluency disorders are interruptions in the natural flow or rhythm of speech. A common fluency disorder is **stuttering**, "a communication disorder that interferes with a person's ability to speak fluently. It involves the repetition, prolongation, or blockage of sounds, syllables, or words" (Scott, 2010, p. 1). Most people who stutter begin stuttering before age 5 but only after they have begun to speak in sentences.

EXAMPLES AND CHARACTERISTICS OF LANGUAGE DISORDERS Language disorders are problems in using or comprehending language, either expressive (using language) or receptive (understanding the language of others). Language disorders may involve difficulties with phonology, morphology, syntax, semantics, or pragmatics. **Phonology** involves the ability to blend and segment the sounds that individual letters or groups of letters make to form words. For example, it may be difficult for students to identify the final sound in the words *cap* and *cat* if they have a phonological problem. **Morphology** involves the meaningful structure of words, as expressed in **morphemes**, the smallest units of language that carry meaning or function. For example, the word *swimmer* contains two morphemes: a **free morpheme** (can stand alone as a word) (*swim*) and a **bound morpheme** (depends on other words) (*-er*). **Syntax** is the grammatical structure of language and is concerned with such things as word order and noun–verb agreement. **Semantics** refers to the meanings of words used in language. For example, the sentence "Walk can I take?" may convey a semantic meaning but is not syntactically correct. **Pragmatics** refers to the use of language in the context of social situations. For example, students typically speak to teachers in a different manner than they would speak to classmates (Owens et al., 2015).

One of the most severe language disorders is **aphasia**, which refers to difficulties speaking (expressive aphasia) or comprehending (receptive aphasia) language. Aphasia often accompanies brain injuries, and individuals may experience difficulty retrieving words that they knew before the injury (Owens et al., 2015).

In the most severe communication disorders, individuals cannot speak and must learn to rely on AAC devices (Beukelman & Mirenda, 2013).

CAUSES OF SPEECH OR LANGUAGE IMPAIRMENTS

In most cases, specific causes of speech and language disorders are unknown. Some children have severe language delays during early childhood development, but the reasons for the delay are unknown. Voice disorders can be caused by growths, infections, or trauma to the **larynx** (structure containing the vocal cords); infections of the tonsils, adenoid glands, or sinuses; or physical disorders such as **cleft palate**, in which the upper part of the oral cavity is split. The cause of stuttering is presently unknown (Scott, 2010).

IDENTIFICATION AND ASSESSMENT OF SPEECH OR LANGUAGE IMPAIRMENTS

Parents are usually the first to identify a potential speech or language problem, when, for example, their 2-year-old has not begun to develop language. Primary school teachers may be the first to refer a child for a speech and language evaluation when they notice problems with speech or language. Frequently administered tests include articulation tests, auditory discrimination tests, language development tests, vocabulary tests, and language samples taken from a variety of social contexts.

STRATEGIES FOR

MAKING ADAPTATIONS FOR STUDENTS WITH SPEECH OR LANGUAGE IMPAIRMENTS

Instruction is effectively differentiated when adaptations are made in the physical environment, instructional materials, instructional procedures, and assessment methods appropriate to the special needs of individual learners. Following are some adaptations that are generally appropriate for students with speech and language impairments. More specific techniques are provided in Parts 2 and 3 of this text.

ADAPT THE PHYSICAL ENVIRONMENT Place students with communication disorders near the front of the room for easier listening. This will also enable easier access if they need help or if you have devised a special cueing system with them for responding orally in class. The following *In the Classroom* feature provides a checklist for consideration of different types of adaptations in the physical environment.

ADAPT MATERIALS Allow students to use any technology that may help them with their disability area. Various alternative methods are now available to improve classroom communication.

Use Alternative or Augmentative Communication Adaptive communication methods are referred to as alternative and augmentative communication (AAC) techniques. AAC symbols and techniques fall into two broad categories: aided and unaided. Aided communication involves the use of some external device, such as simple handmade materials, a picture board, or more sophisticated computer-assisted devices. Unaided communication does not involve any apparatus other than the individual's own body. Examples include manual signing, making physical gestures, miming, pointing, and moving the eyes (Beukelman & Mirenda, 2013).

Alternative communication techniques involve the use of communication boards to assist communication. Communication boards contain pictures or words of commonly asked questions and responses to questions. When asking or responding to questions, students can point to the picture that communicates what they mean. Pointing devices that attach to the head can be used for students who have difficulty pointing with their hands or fingers. When the AAC user is unable to point, a communication partner can help identify the correct symbol. Some commercially available boards, such as the *Accent 1400* available from the Prentke Romich Company, produce speech output when the corresponding symbol or picture is touched. Communication devices including text-to-speech apps are also available on tablets such as the iPad.

ADAPT INSTRUCTIONAL PROCEDURES Effective teaching practices, including clear, well-organized presentations and activities, will help meet the needs of students with speech and language disorders in your classroom. Appropriate pace of instruction and maximized student engagement—including frequent questioning and feedback—can help ensure academic success.

MyEdLab:
Video Example 3.1.
Observe the interaction between a teacher and a little girl with language disabilities in this video as she uses her communication board to request a specific toy.

In the Classroom. . .

Sample Environmental Adaptation Considerations

Seating Position

_____ Near teacher

_____ Near peer assistant

_____ Near paraprofessional

_____ Near board

_____ Near front of room

_____ Alone

_____ Quiet space

_____ Other

Seating Planned for

_____ Lunchroom

_____ Assemblies

_____ Bus

_____ All classes

_____ Other

Rearrange Physical Space

_____ Move desks

_____ Move class displays

_____ Other

Reduce Distractions

_____ Visual

_____ Auditory

_____ Movement

_____ Other

Provide Daily Structure

_____ First thing to do when entering class

_____ Second thing

_____ Third thing

_____ Being prepared

_____ Other

Provide Designated Places

_____ Inboxes

_____ Outboxes

_____ Other

Provide Orderly Models

_____ Organized desks

_____ Organized lockers

_____ Other

Facilitate Verbal Responding　　Allow sufficient time for students with communication disorders to speak when responding. Do not impose time pressures on oral responses, and resist the temptation to finish words or talk for the student who stutters. When a student finishes, repeat the response for the entire class to hear when needed. For example, Mr. Lee allowed Natalie, a student with a speech and language disorder, sufficient time to respond, and then said, "Natalie, that was a good answer. Natalie said, 'The numbers 11 and 23 are both prime numbers.'" When referring to stuttering, talk about it like any other matter; do not treat it as something to be ashamed of.

At the beginning of the school year, Mrs. Stobey, a high school history teacher, met with Micky, a student who stuttered. Together they decided that if Micky raised his hand, then he felt comfortable trying to participate in the discussions, and only then would Mrs. Stobey call on him to talk.

Initially, ask a student who stutters questions that can be answered in just a few words. Talk with the student about a preferred time to be called on. If you are going to call on many students in class to answer questions, the student who stutters may prefer to be called on relatively early, to allow less time for anxiety to develop (Scott, 2010).

Monitor your pace of instruction, especially when introducing new vocabulary to students with receptive language disorders. Use language cards containing representational pictures and illustrations depicting the definitions. Whenever possible, use concrete examples, rather than lengthy verbal descriptions, to illustrate new concepts.

Practice Oral Presentations If oral presentations are mandatory, practice alone with students first and provide feedback. Consider allowing students to present with partners or in small groups, such that each group member has a different role during oral presentations.

Enlist Peer Assistance Sometimes students who stutter are teased or bullied by their peers. Speak privately to the student about teasing and brainstorm ways to respond. Speak to peers (particularly those suspected of teasing) and enlist their support in ensuring that all students are treated fairly (Scott, 2010).

ADAPT ASSESSMENT METHODS Some students may require extended time periods to complete class tests. Others may require the assistance of readers, scribes, or communication boards and communication partners while taking tests. If your testing parallels your classroom instruction, students should be able to use the same materials and procedures they normally do in class when taking tests.

MyEdLab: **Self-Check 3.1**

MyEdLab: **Application Exercise 3.1: Speech/Language Disability**

Learning Disabilities

PREVALENCE AND DEFINITIONS OF LEARNING DISABILITIES

Learning disabilities (LD; referred to as *specific learning disabilities*, or SLD, in IDEA) is a general term describing a group of learning problems. Students with LD are highly represented in general education classes, as LD is the largest single disability area. Approximately 3.4% of all school-age children are classified as having learning disabilities, or 39.5% of the children requiring special education services in the schools (U.S. Department of Education, 2015). About twice as many males as females are identified as having learning disabilities (Pullen, Lane, Ashworth, & Lovelace, 2011).

CLASSROOM SCENARIO

Maria

Maria is a 12-year-old girl of average intelligence who has a pleasant, cooperative disposition. She tries hard to succeed in school but has great difficulty reading independently. She writes slowly, using simple statements and words that are easy for her to spell. Her writing is labored and does not accurately reflect her thinking.

Maria receives assistance with her reading and writing in the resource room 4 days a week. Mr. Harrison, Maria's teacher, has prioritized Maria's class assignments. Mr. Harrison does not require that she read or write independently to participate in class activities. In social studies, for example, when the class is given an assignment to read parts of the textbook, Maria is allowed to read together with a classmate. The classmate reads questions from the assignments aloud, and Maria is allowed to write simple answers to the questions or dictate longer answers to her partner or into a tablet with a speech-to-text app. Mr. Harrison uses clear, structured presentations to maximize Maria's understanding of the lessons. Finally, Maria's performance is systematically monitored to ensure that she is learning adequately and that the need for further adaptations is examined. By the second semester, Maria's reading and writing skills have improved enough that she is encouraged to independently complete reading and writing assignments when possible but to ask a classmate or teacher for specific assistance when required.

Learning disabilities is used as an umbrella term to classify those individuals with average or above-average intelligence who nonetheless have difficulties with academic tasks. The federal definition is given as follows:

> "Specific learning disability" means a disorder in one or more of the basic psychological processes involved in understanding or using language, spoken or written, which may manifest itself in an imperfect ability to listen, think, speak, read, write, spell, or to do mathematical calculations. The term includes such conditions as perceptual handicaps, brain injury, minimal brain dysfunction, dyslexia, and developmental aphasia. The term does not include children who have learning problems that are primarily the result of visual, hearing, or motor handicaps, of mental retardation, of emotional disturbance, or of environmental, cultural, or economic disadvantage. (Assistance to states for education of handicapped children: Procedures for evaluating specific learning disabilities, No. 250, Vol. 42, part 121A, 1977)

The standard that learning problems are not the result of sensory, motor, intellectual, emotional, or sociocultural influences is sometimes referred to as an **exclusionary** clause. Over the years, many definitions of *learning disability* have been proposed by various task groups and professional organizations (Hallahan, Pullen, & Ward, 2014). Most definitions share components with the federal definition.

Most states previously required the presence of a *discrepancy* between ability and achievement to support the identification of a learning disability. For example, Edward had a full-scale IQ (intelligence quotient) score of 101 and a standard score of 85 on a test of reading achievement. This amounts to a discrepancy of 16 standard score points between ability (the IQ test) and achievement (the reading achievement test), where the full-scale IQ is average (about the 50th percentile), and the reading achievement score is substantially lower (about the 16th percentile). Other evidence in support of the presence of learning disabilities was also usually required (Raymond, 2017). According to the most recent IDEA amendments, states may no longer require schools to use discrepancy criteria for identification purposes. Instead, schools are encouraged to determine whether students respond sufficiently to research-based intervention, as described later in the chapter (Division for Learning Disabilities, 2012; Wright & Wright, 2005).

CAUSES OF LEARNING DISABILITIES

The specific causes of learning disabilities remain unknown but are generally believed to be associated with brain function. Three major factors—organic, genetic, and environmental—have been hypothesized as possible causes. Organic factors include indications of brain differences in size or functioning, perhaps due to differences during the development of the brain. Medical research in detecting brain dysfunctions has yielded evidence for a neurological basis that may be linked to possible causes of LD (Pullen et al., 2011). Possible genetic factors include heredity, in that students with reading problems often have other family members with similar problems, and that identical twins are more likely than fraternal twins to share learning disabilities (Astrom, Wadsworth, & DeFries, 2007; Kirkpatrick, Legrand, Iacono, & McGue, 2011). Finally, environmental factors such as poor diet and nutrition and exposure to toxins such as alcohol, smoke, and cocaine, either prenatally or postnatally, may contribute to learning disabilities (Raymond, 2017).

ISSUES IN IDENTIFICATION AND ASSESSMENT OF LEARNING DISABILITIES

One controversial issue involves whether students classified as learning disabled represent a truly specific category—that is, that they are distinguishable from students who are simply low achievers (e.g., the bottom 25% in achievement). Some researchers have maintained that there are few meaningful differences between the two groups of students (Fletcher et al., 2002). However, Fuchs, Fuchs, Mathes, Lipsey, and Roberts (2002) conducted a **meta-analysis** (research synthesis) of 86 studies comparing students with LD and low-achieving students in reading and found that students with LD generally scored considerably lower than low-achieving students. Debate on this issue continues.

Another related issue is the use of IQ–achievement discrepancy criteria. Lyon et al. (2001) argued that discrepancy criteria are not conceptually sound, are vulnerable to measurement error, and inhibit early identification of learning disabilities. In addition, MacMillan and Siperstein (2002) suggested that schools may not always apply discrepancy criteria correctly in identifying students with LD. Nevertheless, students with learning disabilities are generally thought to experience serious academic problems in spite of average or above-average general ability, and therefore they could be expected to demonstrate some type of discrepancy (Council for Exceptional Children [CEC], 2012; Mastropieri & Scruggs, 2002). Although discrepancy models are still used, schools are not required to use IQ–achievement discrepancy criteria for identification (Raymond, 2017).

As an alternative to discrepancy criteria, schools are now encouraged to employ a response-to-intervention (RTI) approach (also referred to as a *multi-tiered system of supports*), where general education teachers implement scientifically based practices and use curriculum-based measurement to document student progress on a regular basis. Students who prove to be "treatment resisters" (do not show adequate progress in spite of extra attention) may be eligible for more intensive interventions administered in different "tiers" or referral to special education (National Center on Intensive Interventions, 2016; National Center on Response to Intervention, 2011). Evidence of failure to respond appropriately to these interventions can be used in the referral process to identify learning disabilities. These standards are now specifically encouraged in the most recent IDEA amendments (Wright & Wright, 2005).

RTI approaches are also associated with some controversy. Consistent implementation procedures have not yet been developed, the degree to which RTI discriminates between learning disabilities and other disabilities such as intellectual disabilities is not known, and procedures for intervention and identification are less clear in areas other than early reading (Division for Learning Disabilities, 2012; Gerber, 2005; Mastropieri & Scruggs, 2005). However, these issues may continue to be addressed in the future as schools implement ongoing RTI procedures.

CHARACTERISTICS OF LEARNING DISABILITIES

Individuals with learning disabilities possess a variety of characteristics that distinguish them from other students. However, not all individuals with learning disabilities have all the characteristics described in this section.

LANGUAGE AND LITERACY Many students with learning disabilities experience difficulties with both expressive and receptive language, including the following:

- Discriminating between sounds (e.g., mistakes *cat* for *cap*)
- Misunderstanding grammar (including use of certain pronouns and prepositions)
- Understanding subtleties in language
- "Word-finding" abilities or retrieving appropriate words when needed (Schmitt, Justice, & Pentimonti, 2014)

Most students with learning disabilities have significant reading problems (Raymond, 2017). Many students with learning disabilities lack **phonemic awareness**—the awareness that words are made up of individual speech sounds (Siegel & Mazabel, 2014). Reading problems result when such students are unsuccessful in learning the sound codes represented by the letters in the alphabet and in applying those codes for successful reading ("decoding"). These individuals often have slow and labored oral reading abilities, are not inclined to read for pleasure, and lack effective strategies for fluent reading. Reading comprehension difficulties frequently accompany decoding problems (Fletcher, Lyon, Fuchs, & Barnes, 2007). Other literacy problems encountered by students with learning disabilities include handwriting, spelling, and written composition (e.g., Graham, 2004).

MATHEMATICS It is estimated that two-thirds of students with learning disabilities have mathematics disabilities (Montague, 2011). Students may exhibit difficulties in learning math facts, rules, procedures, or concepts and in personal math such as managing money (Geary, 2014).

ATTENTION AND MEMORY Many students with learning disabilities experience difficulties with sustaining attention to tasks. Some have more serious problems referred to as **attention deficit disorder** (ADD) or **attention deficit hyperactivity disorder** (ADHD) (American Psychiatric Association, 2013). Many students who have a primary disability area such as learning disabilities, emotional disabilities, or intellectual disabilities may also have ADD or ADHD (Denckla et al., 2014).

Many students with learning disabilities have deficits in both long- and short-term memory, memory for verbal information (**semantic memory**), and working memory, which provides the ability to hold information while simultaneously processing the same or other information (Swanson & Zheng, 2014). Memory problems can impede successful school performance unless students are provided with effective strategies to help compensate for such difficulties.

THINKING AND REASONING Thinking and reasoning difficulties are apparent in many individuals with learning disabilities. Abstract reasoning may be especially problematic (Mastropieri, Scruggs, Boon, & Carter, 2001; Raymond, 2017). Individuals may take longer than others to learn new tasks and information. Other problems may include difficulty in organizing thinking, difficulty in drawing conclusions, over-rigidity in thinking, and general lack of effective strategies for solving problems.

METACOGNITIVE ABILITIES, INCLUDING STUDY SKILLS, LEARNING STRATEGIES, AND ORGANIZATIONAL STRATEGIES **Metacognition** refers to knowledge about one's own learning and understanding. Students with well-developed metacognitive skills know how to study effectively, monitor their own understanding (**self-monitoring**), and wisely plan and budget their time. They are familiar with cognitive strategies that help them learn and remember more efficiently, and they regulate their own strategy use (**self-regulation**). In contrast, many students with learning disabilities lack the metacognitive skills necessary to become successful, self-sufficient learners (Grayson, Baird, Dearing, & Hamill, 2009). They may appear disorganized and lack an understanding of what to do or how to proceed with academic tasks or assignments.

SOCIAL-EMOTIONAL FUNCTIONING As many as one-third to one-half of students with learning disabilities may also exhibit problems with social or emotional functioning. Social-emotional problems include social skill difficulties, low self-esteem, low self-awareness and self-perception, low self-concept, weak self-confidence, anxiety, and depression (Al-Yagon & Margalit, 2014; Hutchinson, Freemen, & Berg, 2004). Individuals with learning disabilities are more susceptible to adjudication than the population as a whole (Zhang, Hsu, Katsiyannis, Barrett, & Ju, 2011).

GENERALIZATION AND APPLICATION Most students with learning disabilities—as well as those in other high-incidence disability areas—have difficulty generalizing learned information to novel situations. Some students may master content-area material in special education settings but fail to apply that information to the general education classroom or real-life settings (Raymond, 2017).

STRATEGIES FOR

MAKING CLASSROOM ADAPTATIONS FOR STUDENTS WITH LEARNING DISABILITIES

Following are adaptations that may be of use in differentiating instruction for students with learning disabilities. Adaptations can be made in the environment, instructional materials, instructional procedures, and assessment methods.

ADAPT THE PHYSICAL ENVIRONMENT Rearrange seating positions near students or personnel who can help students in the classroom and during school functions and who can help them focus their attention. Arrange desks so they face away from any obvious distraction. When needed, arrange for a special quiet space within your classroom. Model organization for

Inclusive Instruction for Common Core Math Standards

 Teachers are experiencing not only more students with math disabilities in their inclusive classes but also expectations for all students to meet the new Common Core Math Standards (CCMS). Anchored instruction research using a problem-solving approach delivered by video obtained generally favorable results (e.g., Bottge, Heinrichs, Chan, & Serlin, 2001; Bottge, Rueda, Grant, Stephens, & LaRoque, 2010); however, several unmet-need areas for students with disabilities were also identified. For example, many students required additional practice activities, and the anchored instruction did not teach or improve skills for solving fractions. In addition, supplemental instruction was required to teach sub-problem-solving skills using manipulatives, either delivered technologically or with hands-on activities. Bottge et al. (2015) designed the enhanced anchored instruction (EAI) to test whether features added to address previous shortcomings would improve the math learning of middle school inclusive classes containing students with and without disabilities. Students with and without disabilities from 25 inclusive middle school co-taught classes were assigned to either a business as usual (BAU) condition (N = 248) or the EAI condition (N = 223). Students with disabilities (N = 134) included those with specific learning disabilities, emotional and behavioral disorders, mild mental disabilities, autism, and other health impairments. Experimental condition students were provided training on five areas from the CCMS covering probability, ratios, fractions, geometry, and statistics in general education math classes over 66 instructional days. EAI employed author-developed computerized instruction, videos, and hands-on activities for each major unit designed to facilitate learning. For example, one unit required application of skills learned in previous units to design, build, determine costs, and test rollover cages for hovercrafts.

In the BAU condition, teachers and students completed instruction and activities complying with their assigned district and state math curriculum. Tests administered included a researcher-developed fractions computation test and a problem-solving test along with the Computation and Problem Solving and Data Interpretation subtests of the Iowa Tests of Basic Skills (ITBS) (Hoover, Dunbar, & Frisbie, 2008). Analysis of posttest scores indicated that students in the EAI condition significantly outperformed BAU-condition students on researcher-developed tests but not on the standardized subtests of the ITBS. It was also found that when special education teachers provided more instructional support to students with disabilities in inclusive classes, those students significantly outperformed students in the BAU condition. An analysis of the co-teaching revealed that the most frequently observed model of co-teaching was one teach and one assist (44%), during which the special educator assumed the assistant role. Team teaching was observed 17% of the time, no co-teaching model was observed 21% of the time, and any other co-teaching models were infrequently observed. When special educators provided explicit assistance and instruction to students with disabilities during co-taught classes, the performance of students with disabilities improved. These results suggest that the EAI approach can be effectively implemented in inclusive classrooms for the benefit of all students, but it will be more effective for students with disabilities when special educators provide more explicit instructional support.

QUESTIONS FOR REFLECTION

1. Why did general education students benefit as much from this EAI as the students with disabilities?
2. Why do you think more supportive classes were able to provide more explicit instruction for students with disabilities?
3. Can you think of some other ways to enhance the implementation of EAI? How would you implement it?

the physical environment by designating specific locations for books, coats, lunch boxes, and other personal materials. In addition, demonstrate how desks, lockers, and notebooks should be organized. Structure daily routines and schedules: clearly identify the first, second, and third thing to be done when entering the class, and provide clear schedules for students to follow.

ADAPT INSTRUCTIONAL MATERIALS For students with literacy problems, adapt materials to reduce literacy requirements whenever possible; for content-area learning, use hands-on learning activities, media presentations, computer simulations, and partner reading. High-interest, low-reading-level (or "hi-lo") books provide exciting, age-appropriate content for students who read below grade level (published by, e.g., High Noon Books or Patnor). Some assistive technology applications to reduce literacy requirements are described in the *Apps for Education* feature. Teach students to adapt their own materials as study skills for classroom learning. These adaptations could include keeping assignment notebooks, scheduling time, and developing prompts for using cognitive strategies when studying.

ADAPT INSTRUCTIONAL PROCEDURES   Instructional procedures can be modified to facilitate successful inclusion of students with learning disabilities (Vaughn & Bos, 2015). The use of the teacher effectiveness variables—including maximizing student engagement, providing structured and clearly presented lessons, and monitoring student progress toward goals—can help students with learning disabilities learn more effectively. For example, provide clear organization to your presentations, and make your expectations very explicit. Question students frequently (with a high probability of successful answers), and ask students to rephrase information in their own words to monitor their understanding; use their answers to monitor and adjust your instruction. Periodically review previously learned material to promote long-term learning, and use specific strategies to enhance memory. Use peer tutors when needed to support learning. Provide clear directions and frequent reminders for assignments. Use research-based literacy practices, and use explicit instruction of study skills.

ADAPT ASSESSMENT METHODS   Adapt test formats (e.g., multiple choice, matching) so that they are easy to understand. Practice taking tests with students and teach test-taking skills. Read test items to students with learning disabilities when this practice does not violate test standardization and reading is not being tested. Consider alternatives such as portfolio assessment and performance assessment, rather than relying entirely on traditional test formats. Use frequent formative evaluation so that you can evaluate regular progress toward meeting objectives. These adaptations will help ensure that you are obtaining a fair and accurate picture of what students with learning disabilities know and whether they are meeting their objectives. Formative evaluation techniques can also provide evidence that students with special learning needs are benefiting from differentiated instruction in the inclusive classroom environment (Tier 1) or whether a more intensive form of instruction (Tier 2) may be required.

MyEdLab: **Self-Check 3.2**

MyEdLab: **Application Exercise 3.2: Learning Disabilities**

Intellectual Disabilities

PREVALENCE AND DEFINITIONS OF INTELLECTUAL DISABILITIES

Individuals identified as having intellectual disabilities represent 7.1% of the students ages 6 to 21 served under IDEA (U.S. Department of Education, 2015) or about 0.6% of the population in general. Although this number includes all individuals with intellectual disabilities served under IDEA, 80% to 90% have mild or moderate intellectual disabilities, as opposed to severe disabilities (Polloway, Patton, & Nelson, 2011; Raymond, 2017).

Although *intellectual disabilities* (or *intellectual disability*) is commonly used, other terms are used to describe this condition, including *mental retardation, cognitive disability, mental deficiency, mental subnormality, mentally handicapped,* or *intellectually challenged*. Intellectual disability is also referred to as one type of the more general term *developmental disability* (Polloway et al., 2011). The American Association on Mental Retardation (AAMR) has changed its name to the American Association on Intellectual and Developmental Disabilities (AAIDD; Schalock et al., 2007). The AAIDD's definition of intellectual disability is as follows:

> Intellectual disability is a disability characterized by significant limitations both in intellectual functioning and in **adaptive behavior** as expressed in conceptual, social, and practical adaptive skills. This disability originates before age 18. (Schalock et al., 2010, p. 1)

Assistive Technology Ranges from Low Tech to High Tech

 Assistive technology (AT) refers to supports that help individuals maintain, increase, or improve their capabilities. AT, a critical component of individualized education programs (IEPs) for students with disabilities, is written into IDEA 2004. AT consists of devices and services. *AT devices* refer to any tools that range from low tech to high tech or represent the range of simple adaptations to more complex technological solutions. *AT services* refer to the supports and training an individual might require to learn and use the AT devices. The following table presents examples of low- and high-tech solutions.

Area	Low Technology	High Technology
Writing	Pencil grip; scribes take notes for individual, *Stage Write Raised Line Paper* (Therapro)	Notebook computers, tablet PCs, mobile devices, audio recorders, apps such as *SoundNote* (David Estes) to record notes, or *Dragon Dictation* (Nuance Communications, Inc.) to dictate notes, word-prediction software such as *Co:Writer Universal* (integrates across desktop, iPads, Google) (Don Johnston) or *WordQ and SpeakQ* (GoQ Software)
Reading	Picture cards to enhance meaning; peer assistants	Software such as *Boardmaker* or *Boardmaker Plus* (Mayer-Johnson) or use of text readers such as *Read: Outloud* (Don Johnston), *Aspire Reader* (Aequus Technologies), *IntelliTalk* (Intellitools), *Victor Reader Soft Bookshare Edition* (HumanWare) for blind or low vision; programs for beginning literacy such as *WiggleWorks* (Scholastic), *Let's Go Read* (Riverdeep Interactive Learning), or the free reader available from www.microsoft.com
Math	Lined or graph paper and pencil	Activities and virtual tools available on websites (e.g., the learning games available at http://illuminations.nctm.org, the unifix cubes available at didax.com, and the virtual manipulatives available at nlvm.usu.edu)
		Tools with web-based activities using interactive web-based components; software such as *Unifix Software* (Didax Inc.), *MatchTime* (Attainment Company Inc.), *Mighty Math Astro Algebra* (Edmark, Inc.)

Five assumptions should be used in applying the definition: (1) consideration of the context of community, peers, and culture; (2) consideration of cultural and linguistic diversity; (3) consideration of strengths as well as weaknesses; (4) the necessity of developing a profile of needed supports; (5) the expectation that the individual's functioning will improve over time with appropriate supports.

Within the general area of intellectual disability, different levels of severity are often noted. Previously, professional organizations such as the American Psychological Association (APA) described levels of functioning with corresponding IQ levels, including mild (IQ about 55 to 70), moderate (IQ about 35 to 54), severe (IQ about 20 to 34), and profound (IQ below about 20) (Jacobson & Mulick, 1996; in the general population, the average IQ is 100, and about two-thirds of the population score between 85 and 115). Today, the AAIDD (2010) does not employ a classification system based on IQ level; rather, the AAIDD definition suggests that individuals can be evaluated relative to a system of services and supports. These include support areas (e.g., human development, teaching and education, home and community living), relevant support activities (e.g., individual's interest, activities, and settings for participation), and levels and intensity of supports (intermittent, limited, extensive, or pervasive). These levels were intended to replace previous classification systems of mild to severe intellectual disabilities, although these latter terms are still widely used (Polloway et al., 2011; see also American Psychiatric Association, 2013). Similarly, the APA now emphasizes adaptive functioning in conceptual, social, and practical domains more than cutoffs in IQ scores.

Students under the age of 9 who are experiencing delay, or who are considered at risk for developing delay, may be characterized as having *developmental delay*, a classification provided by the federal government to provide early services to children without reference to the intellectual disability or mental retardation label (Polloway et al., 2011).

CAUSES OF INTELLECTUAL DISABILITIES

Although a variety of causes for intellectual disabilities have been identified, many, if not most, causes are unknown (Polloway et al., 2011; Raymond, 2017). Overall, the causes of mild intellectual disabilities are more difficult to determine than the causes for severe and profound intellectual disabilities. Known or suspected causes can be categorized as genetic factors, brain factors, and environmental factors.

GENETIC FACTORS Genetic disorders or damage to genetic matter can cause intellectual disabilities. Disorders can include chromosomal abnormalities and genetic transmission of traits through families. **Down syndrome** is an example of a genetic disorder based on a chromosomal anomaly. It is sometimes referred to as trisomy 21 because the 21st pair of chromosomes divides into three (trisomy) instead of a single pair of chromosomes. Down syndrome is associated with some specific characteristics, including intellectual functioning in the mild to moderate ranges, short stature, upward slanting of the eyes, and a susceptibility to heart defects or upper respiratory infections. Of course, as with any population with or without disabilities, individuals with Down syndrome also exhibit a wide variety of individual characteristics. The most common inherited cause of intellectual disabilities is **fragile X syndrome**, which is caused by a mutation on the X chromosome and affects only males (Polloway et al., 2011).

BRAIN FACTORS Brain factors refer to defects in the brain or central nervous system. These can occur during prenatal development, perinatally (during the birth process), or postnatally (after the baby is born). Brain factors may be congenital (present at birth) or may appear later in life. Prenatal factors include exposure to rubella (German measles) and syphilis. Exposure to alcohol during prenatal development can lead to fetal alcohol syndrome (FAS), which may result in intellectual disabilities (Harris, 2010). Infections such as meningitis and encephalitis, which cause inflammations to the brain, may result in brain damage. Some forms of intellectual disabilities are associated with cranial malformations that result in microcephaly or hydrocephaly. **Microcephaly** is associated with a very small skull, whereas **hydrocephaly** is often characterized by an enlarged head due to an interference in the flow of cerebral spinal fluid in the head. Finally, it is known that **anoxia**, or lack of oxygen to the brain, at any time, including during birth, causes brain damage and may result in intellectual disabilities, depending upon the extent of the damage (Harris, 2010).

ENVIRONMENTAL INFLUENCES Environmental influences refer to factors such as poor nutrition during prenatal development that can influence the development of the brain and result in intellectual disabilities (Raymond, 2017). Many premature and low-birth-weight babies may have intellectual disabilities. The ingestion of lead, often through lead-based paint, can also cause intellectual disabilities. Although factors such as poverty and lack of early sensory stimulation are associated, it is more difficult to prove that such environmental factors always lead to intellectual disabilities. Future research may uncover additional important factors related to causes and prevention of intellectual disabilities.

ISSUES IN IDENTIFICATION AND ASSESSMENT OF INTELLECTUAL DISABILITIES

Both intellectual functioning and adaptive behavior are assessed in making determinations regarding intellectual disability. Individually administered intelligence tests are used in most states to assess intellectual functioning and usually contain, for example, measures of vocabulary, common knowledge, short-term memory, and ability to solve mazes and jigsaw puzzles. Adaptive behavior scales assess how well individuals are able to perform daily living skills, self-help care, communication skills, and social skills. Although there is variability across states, in most states an individual should be functioning at least two standard deviations below average (approximately the second percentile) on both measures to be classified as having an intellectual disability. The level of services and supports thought to be required for an appropriate education is also frequently considered (Schalock et al., 2010).

CHARACTERISTICS OF INTELLECTUAL DISABILITIES

The most common features associated with intellectual disabilities include slower pace of learning, lack of age-appropriate adaptive behavior and social skills, and below-average language

In the Classroom . . .

Getting Classmates Ready for Students with Disabilities

_____ Prepare general education students for the arrival of students with disabilities by asking a special educator to talk about disabilities and explain strengths and limitations of individuals with disabilities.

_____ Encourage students to ask questions, and set a model of open acceptance.

_____ Tell students about their roles as possible peer tutors and helpers. Provide models of how peers can assist, but make it clear that they should also encourage independent functioning. They should not try to do everything for students with disabilities.

_____ Explain that all classmates, even if they are not peer tutors or helpers, can encourage students with disabilities to be active participants and members of the class.

and academic skills. Many individuals with intellectual disabilities exhibit poor motor coordination, which can be improved by working with occupational therapists, physical therapists, or adaptive physical educators (Wessendorp, Houwen, Hartman, & Visscher, 2011). However, most students with mild and moderate intellectual disabilities have the ability to learn to read, write, and do mathematics up to the sixth-grade level, or higher in some cases. Following is an autobiographical statement written by Kirstin Palson, an individual with intellectual disabilities who was institutionalized as a child many years ago, before IDEA legislation. Her statement was included in a book of poetry she wrote.

From "About the Author":

My name is Kirstin Ann Palson. I was born in Boston, Massachusetts, in 1952 with complications. My diagnosis was mental retardation plus cerebral palsy, due to brain damage at birth. It was difficult those early years. Because of my behavior problems, I was sent to the Wrentham State School when I was seven years old. Those were horrendous times. At the age of fourteen I came out of Wrentham. I have overcome my handicaps, graduated from High School at twenty-two, and worked as a volunteer library aid in two elementary schools. For two years after graduation, I had a struggle getting employment. Finally I got a full time job in a company and worked five years. The company moved out of town and I struggled with unemployment and job search for six and a half months. I have gained employment in another company full time. I got both jobs on my own.

I have a great love for words. When I was growing up, it was the reading of children's stories by Mom at bedtime which gave me the ability for reading and loving books. During the past years I have given books of my poetry to family members as gifts, especially at Christmas. My love for poetry is still with me and will remain forever more. K. A. P. (Palson, 1986)

INTELLECTUAL AND COGNITIVE FUNCTIONING Individuals with intellectual disabilities exhibit deficits in intellectual functioning. In addition, these individuals usually function substantially below their age peers in related areas, including metacognitive abilities, memory, attention, thinking, and problem-solving abilities. Like students with learning disabilities, individuals with intellectual disabilities often have difficulty generalizing learned information to novel situations (Polloway, Patton, & Nelson, 2011).

SOCIAL AND ADAPTIVE BEHAVIOR By most definitions, individuals with mild intellectual disabilities have less-well-developed adaptive behavior than their peer counterparts, including such behavior as using the telephone or dressing appropriately. They may appear socially immature, exhibit inappropriate social behavior, or have difficulty making and maintaining friendships. Some individuals may become easily frustrated when they experience difficulty and then may act inappropriately, drawing negative attention to themselves. On the other hand, some individuals with intellectual disabilities have particularly amiable dispositions and are well liked by others (Raymond, 2017).

Some individuals with intellectual disabilities tend to have an external "locus of control," meaning they see their lives as being controlled and influenced by factors outside of themselves (e.g., fate, chance, other people). This external locus of control may hinder their development of self-reliance. A related problem is "outerdirectedness"—that is, looking to external cues or modeling behavior of others rather than relying on their own judgments. These characteristics may sometimes contribute to a lower level of motivation (Polloway et al., 2011).

LANGUAGE Both receptive and expressive language are problem areas for individuals with intellectual disabilities. There is usually a direct relationship between the severity of intellectual disabilities and all aspects of language development (Vicari, Caselli, Gagliardi, Tonucci, & Volterra, 2002). Communication skills are typically less well developed, which can result in misunderstandings of directions (Cascella, 2004). Students may exhibit difficulties with comprehension of abstract vocabulary and concepts (McDuffie & Abbeduto, 2009).

ACADEMIC SKILLS Individuals with intellectual disabilities may have difficulty learning the basic skills of reading, writing, and mathematics. The rate of learning new information may be very slow, and students may require repetition and concrete, meaningful examples for all learning activities (Polloway et al., 2011).

STRATEGIES FOR

MAKING CLASSROOM ADAPTATIONS FOR STUDENTS WITH INTELLECTUAL DISABILITIES

MAKE PREPARATIONS Careful preparation can greatly enhance the successful inclusion of students with intellectual disabilities. First, have an open, accepting classroom environment so that students feel welcome as genuine class members. Provide students with the same materials—desks, lockers, mailboxes—as the other students. Involve students in daily activities. Meet with them privately and preteach the daily routine. Show them where materials are kept and how class activities proceed. This will help build their confidence before they come in for the first time in company with their general education peers. More information for preparing classmates is given in the *In the Classroom* feature.

MONITOR PEER RELATIONSHIPS Although peers can be good friends and strong supporters of students with intellectual disabilities, teachers also should be aware that some students may try to take advantage of students with intellectual disabilities. For example, in one sixth-grade class, several boys bullied a boy with an intellectual disability and consistently took away part of his lunch. In another example, high school students who had been smoking cigarettes in the girls' restroom handed their cigarettes to a girl with an intellectual disability when a teacher entered the restroom. Careful monitoring can decrease the likelihood of such negative situations occurring and increase the likelihood that peer relations will be positive and productive.

ADAPT INSTRUCTIONAL MATERIALS Reduce reading, writing, and language requirements, and simplify relevant worksheets. Use concrete examples, relevant experiences, and hands-on materials for activities whenever possible.

Use specialized curriculum when necessary. Some students with intellectual disabilities may benefit from an alternative, more functional curriculum. Such a curriculum may include language and communication, community living, domestic skills, socialization, self-help, and vocational and leisure skills. Additionally, some students may benefit from a life-skills curriculum that emphasizes transition to adulthood. This curriculum could include education in home and family skills, community involvement, seeking employment, emotional and physical health, and personal responsibility and relationships (see Cronin, Patton, & Wood, 2007).

Diversity in the Classroom

Culturally Responsive Instruction

The population in the United States has become increasingly diverse, and schools and individual classrooms reflect that diversity. The percentage of minority students, including Hispanic American, Native American, Asian American, and African American students, has increased to estimates of 45% to 48% (Ford, 2012; U.S. Department of Education, 2014). Students with higher-incidence disabilities may also represent diversity in ethnic and cultural backgrounds (Casteel & Ballantyne, 2006; Graves, 2010) and include many students who are considered English learners (ELs). With estimates of the numbers of children from immigrant families increasing, there are also growing numbers of languages spoken within a single school. For example, as many as 160 different languages have been reported within the Fairfax County, Virginia, public school system (Shapiro, 2012). Nationally, languages other than English are spoken at home by over 20% of the school-age population (Camarota & Zeigler, 2014). Fortunately, there is accumulating evidence to provide teachers with guidance for working more effectively within these diverse classrooms to meet the needs of the children and their families (Casteel & Ballantyne, 2006).

Aceves and Orosco (2014) described emerging evidence-based practices for delivering culturally responsive instruction. One important aspect is to consider the culture, language, and racial identity of all students when planning instruction and implement educational practices that connect to and reflect culture, race, language, values, customs, daily lives, and beliefs (see Aceves & Orosco, 2014, p. 33). Another consideration is to increase multicultural awareness by teaching about the various cultures, modeling and encouraging respect for and sensitivity to others, and using child-centered and problem-solving approaches while motivating all students to become engaged, active learners (see Aceves & Orosco, 2014; Echevarria & Graves, 2011, 2015; Harry, 2008).

ADAPT INSTRUCTIONAL PROCEDURES   Many of the modifications described in the learning disabilities section may also be helpful for students with intellectual disabilities. However, additional modifications probably will be required if the general education experience is to be successful, such as the following:

- *Prioritize objectives* for students with intellectual disabilities in general education classes by determining the most important things for students to learn from specific lessons, and teach directly to these prioritized objectives.

- *Adapt instruction* by employing clear, organized presentations; providing concrete, meaningful examples and activities; providing frequent reviews; and encouraging independent thinking. Use frequent feedback and reinforcement for longer or more difficult tasks.

- *Communicate with families* to further your understanding and obtain additional information on how students work and learn best. The *Diversity in the Classroom* feature describes practices for culturally responsive instruction.

ADAPT ASSESSMENT METHODS   Use alternative assessments for statewide assessments such as the Common Core State Standards, when appropriate. Individual testing, portfolio assessments, audio or video recordings, or other techniques may also be appropriate.

MyEdLab: **Self-Check 3.3**

MyEdLab: **Application Exercise 3.3: Intellectual Disabilities**

Emotional Disturbance

PREVALENCE AND DEFINITIONS OF EMOTIONAL DISTURBANCE

Individuals classified as having emotional disturbance (or behavioral disorders) represent 6.0% of all students ages 6 to 21 served under IDEA, or about 0.5% of the school population (U.S. Department of Education, 2015). However, prevalence studies have suggested that the actual percentage of students requiring some type of intervention may be much higher, perhaps as high as 6% to 10% of the school-age population (Kauffman & Landrum, 2013). Boys outnumber girls in this category by about 3.5 to 1 (Oswald, Best, Coutinho, & Nagle, 2003).

Although *emotional disturbance* (or emotional disability) is commonly used, other terms are used to describe this condition, including *emotional handicap, behavioral disorder, emotional/behavioral disorder,* or *social and emotional disorder* (Raymond, 2017).

Emotional disturbance refers to a number of different, but related, social-emotional disabilities. Individuals classified as emotionally disturbed meet at least one of several characteristics that persist over time and that negatively affect school performance, including the following:

a. An inability to learn that cannot be explained by intellectual, sensory, or health factors.

b. An inability to build or maintain satisfactory interpersonal relationships with peers and teachers.

c. Inappropriate types of behavior or feelings under normal circumstances.

d. A general pervasive mood of unhappiness or depression.

e. A tendency to develop physical symptoms or fears associated with personal or school problems. (Assistance to States for the Education of Children with Disabilities: A Child with a Disability, 34 C.F.R. Part 300.7, 2002; Child with a Disability, 2002).

Individuals classified as emotionally disturbed represent a range of severity, and the disability itself may be temporary or permanent. Specific emotional disturbance areas include childhood-onset **schizophrenia**; **selective mutism** (failure to speak in selected circumstances); seriously aggressive or acting-out behavior; conduct disorders; inappropriate affective disorders, such as depression, social withdrawal, psychosomatic disorders, anxiety disorders, and self-mutilating behaviors; and excessive fears (or phobias). Individuals characterized as socially maladjusted (e.g., juvenile delinquency) are not considered emotionally disturbed according to IDEA unless they also exhibit other evidence of emotional disturbance (Kauffman & Landrum, 2013).

CAUSES OF EMOTIONAL DISTURBANCE

Most behavioral disorders or emotional disturbances have no known cause. However, possible causes include biological, family, school, and cultural factors (e.g., Landrum, 2011).

Biological factors are genetic, biochemical, and neurological influences that interact and result in emotional disabilities. Schizophrenia and **Tourette syndrome**—a tic disorder characterized by involuntary muscular movements, vocalizations, and/or inappropriate verbal outbursts—appear to have biological bases that interact with other factors and may contribute to emotional disturbances. However, Tourette syndrome is not necessarily associated with emotional disturbance. Family factors (such as domestic violence) are also considered to be strong contributing factors to emotional disturbance. School factors (such as failure to accommodate for individual needs, inappropriate expectations, or inconsistency) can also contribute to an emotional disability. Finally, certain cultural and environmental factors (including peer group, urbanization, bullying, and neighborhood factors) interact with the individual, the home, and the school and may also contribute to emotional disabilities (Kauffman & Landrum, 2013).

ISSUES IN IDENTIFICATION AND ASSESSMENT OF EMOTIONAL DISTURBANCE

Individuals with emotional disabilities are difficult to identify and classify objectively. Moreover, there appears to be reluctance on the part of school personnel to label a child "emotionally disturbed." Traditional measures to identify emotional or behavioral disabilities come from a variety of sources and include teacher checklists; parental checklists; classroom behavioral observations; and tests of intelligence, achievement, and psychological status (Raymond, 2017). Checklists are listings of frequently observed behaviors. Behavior rating scales used for identification and assessment include the Behavioral and Emotional Rating Scale (BERS-2; Epstein, 2004) and the Behavior Assessment System for Children (BASC-2; Reynolds & Kamphaus, 2004). Teachers and parents complete checklists by indicating the types and severity of problem behaviors. Direct observations are conducted during classes, on the playground, at lunch, and in other parts of the school (Kauffman & Landrum, 2013).

CHARACTERISTICS OF EMOTIONAL DISTURBANCE

As with other categories of exceptionality, not all individuals with emotional disturbance will exhibit all the characteristics described in this section.

SOCIAL BEHAVIOR Most students with emotional disturbance have problems with their social behavior, often manifested as less mature or inappropriate social skills (Kauffman & Landrum, 2013). Some students may be particularly aggressive with peers and adults and cause harm when playing or interacting with others. These students act out in class, do not appear to respond appropriately to discipline from teachers, and may seem oblivious to class and school rules (Furlong, Morrison, & Jimerson, 2004). Students with behavioral disorders are at higher risk for substance abuse (Swendsen et al., 2011).

Other students may exhibit social behavior similar to that of younger children and act socially immature. Some students may withdraw from others and appear socially isolated. Although withdrawn students may not call as much attention to themselves as students with conduct disorders, they nonetheless may require intensive interventions (Gresham & Kern, 2004). These students may exhibit symptoms of depression. Social isolates do not interact with any peers or adults, and in the most severe cases, they may exhibit selective (or elective) mutism. Individuals with selective mutism have the physical ability to talk but nevertheless do not speak in appropriate situations (Carbone et al., 2010). All of these emotional or behavioral disorders share the characteristic of an inability to interact appropriately with others, including peers, teachers, siblings, and parents, which negatively affects school performance (Raymond, 2017).

Students with emotional disturbance may also inappropriately attribute their behavioral or social problems to causes outside of themselves, saying things such as, "Teachers are out to get me," or "Other kids always get me into trouble." By doing this, these students are able to avoid acknowledging or evaluating their own behavior and their own role in behavior problems.

AFFECTIVE CHARACTERISTICS Some students with emotional disturbances have serious affective disorders. Affective disorders can take many forms, but the most commonly recognized forms include depression, severe anxiety disorders, phobias, and psychosomatic disorders (Kauffman & Landrum, 2013). Individuals with many of these disorders may be treated with different medications.

ACADEMIC CHARACTERISTICS Research has indicated that students with emotional disturbances may function 2 or more years below grade level in reading, math, writing, and spelling (Algozzine, Wang, & Violette, 2011; Lane, 2004). These deficiencies may be related to the emotional disabilities. For example, if students have severe anxieties or feelings of anger, they may be unable to attend, listen, and learn in school. Some students lack social skills that are necessary for school success. Others may exhibit severe deficiencies in metacognitive skills, memory skills, and attention, which may in turn lead to academic underachievement (e.g., Scruggs, Mastropieri, Berkeley, & Marshak, 2010). Students with emotional disturbance are at risk for dropping out of school, hindering their future life possibilities. Nevertheless, some students with emotional or behavioral disabilities attain average, or even above-average, academic achievement.

STRATEGIES FOR
MAKING CLASSROOM ADAPTATIONS FOR STUDENTS WITH EMOTIONAL DISTURBANCE

General adaptations can facilitate the inclusion of students with emotional and behavioral disorders into inclusive classes. The *In the Classroom* feature lists some examples. Some specific adaptations for differentiating instruction to promote successful inclusion are presented next.

PREPARE THE CLASS Prepare your class for students with emotional disabilities by describing any relevant special needs the students might have. Set up models for tolerance and acceptance. Provide opportunities for students with emotional disabilities to assume class responsibilities, such as distributing papers. Give examples of ways general education peers can help students with emotional disabilities, such as how to ignore inappropriate behaviors. Some students may be able to serve as peer tutors or assistants to help support and reinforce appropriate behaviors from students with emotional disabilities. However, select peers carefully; not all peers would be good choices. Remember that sometimes students with emotional disabilities will do better working alone even when the rest of the class is working in small groups.

ADAPT THE PHYSICAL ENVIRONMENT Adjust seating arrangements where needed to help prevent challenging behavior. Consider increasing the degree of proximity to good peer models and positive teacher and teacher aide attention. Conversely, arrange seating to avoid proximity to other students with whom the target student interacts negatively. Keep all potentially harmful objects or substances away from easy access.

ADAPT INSTRUCTIONAL MATERIALS When appropriate, use the suggestions listed for students with learning disabilities and intellectual disabilities. Devise self-monitoring checklists that students can use to check off activities as they complete them (e.g., Mastropieri, Scruggs, Cerar, et al., 2012). Break assignments into short segments to avoid overwhelming students. Teach the classroom social skills necessary for success.

ADAPT INSTRUCTIONAL PROCEDURES Use the teacher effectiveness variables and teacher presentation variables to ensure that content is covered adequately. *Help students focus* by teaching clearly and enthusiastically, providing additional review, and teaching self-monitoring for attention.

You can help prevent challenging behavior through effective planning and scheduling, by implementing rules and procedures, and through effective instruction (Scheuermann & Hall, 2016). Illustrate rules with clear examples and specify rewards for following rules as well as consequences when rules are disobeyed. Be consistent when enforcing rules, but make sure the overall classroom atmosphere is positive, not punitive. Provide models of acceptable behaviors to avoid confusion or misinterpretation on the part of students:

> "Here's one thing you can say if you think another student is sitting too close to you. . . ." "Here is something you should *not* say. . . ."

Maintain a positive relationship with students with emotional disabilities by responding to them as human beings, rather than responding simply to their overt behavior, which may sometimes be unpleasant. Use positive comments frequently to reinforce good behavior when you see it. Say things like the following:

- "Jeff, I appreciate the way you tried hard in class today. I know that math is not your favorite subject."
- "Leslie, I am glad that you volunteered an answer in class today. Thank you for doing that."

Positive comments can be varied so that they are suitable for either elementary-, middle-, or secondary-level students.

Before reprimanding negative social behavior, say, "Stop and think about what you just did. What should you have done? Now, try to do it more appropriately."

Be tolerant, and use judgment in allocating times for enforcing compliance, times for cooling off, and times for allowing divergent responding. For example, one fifth-grade teacher, Mrs. Bahs, allowed a student with emotional disabilities to remain at his desk even though she had asked all students to move to the floor in the front of the room to view a new class iguana. In this way, she was able to prevent a confrontation and allow the student to participate in his own way.

Some students may have specific fears and anxieties, such as fear of the dark, water, or getting dirty; in some cases, they may not acknowledge these fears (e.g., "I'm not afraid of snakes; I just don't like them!"). Be aware of those fears by communicating with special education teachers, parents, and the students themselves. If class activities seem to bring out those fears in some students, have alternative activities available that they can work on independently.

In the Classroom . . .

General Accommodations for Students with Emotional Disabilities

_____ Establish an open, accepting environment.

_____ Clearly state class rules and consequences.

_____ Emphasize positive behaviors, and program for success.

_____ Reinforce positive behavior.

_____ Supply extra opportunities for success.

_____ Be tolerant.

_____ Use good judgment.

_____ Teach social skills.

_____ Teach self-control, self-monitoring, and conflict resolution.

_____ Teach academic survival skills.

_____ Teach positive attributions.

_____ Carefully select partners.

_____ Have alternative activities available.

_____ Design activity checklists.

_____ Use carefully selected peers as assistants.

_____ Allow students to work alone rather than in small groups when appropriate.

_____ Use behavioral contracts.

Many students in your classes, especially students with emotional disturbance, can benefit from general social skills instruction. For example, review more acceptable ways of asking and answering questions and more suitable ways of resolving conflicts at appropriate times.

Teach students to monitor their own behavior and to make positive attributions. Teach students how to attribute their successes to positive strategies and effort on their part, rather than to luck or other external forces. Likewise, teach them to attribute their failures to things under their control, such as their own behavior, and not to external factors, such as, "The teacher hates me." Model effective positive attributions by saying, for example: "I used the 'stop and think' strategy before acting, so I stayed out of trouble!" (see Polsgrove & Smith, 2004).

Use behavioral contracts with students with emotional disabilities. Behavioral contracts are individually negotiated contracts between the teacher and student. Specific behaviors students are expected to complete are listed, along with designated rewards for the positively accomplished goals.

ADAPT ASSESSMENT METHODS   Maximize student potential on exams by providing distraction-free environments, providing extended time allocations during testing periods, and ensuring that students have the skills to take tests efficiently (Scruggs & Marsing, 1988; Shriner & Wehby, 2004). In some cases, individual testing, where this does not violate standardization, can lead to more accurate and valid test results.

SUPPORT MULTI-TIERED INTERVENTIONS   Many schools now promote a schoolwide system of positive behavior interventions and supports (PBIS) to promote positive social behavior. Like other multi-tiered systems, PBIS can be implemented at different levels, or tiers, of increasing intensity; it is used to provide increasing behavioral support as needed and, ultimately, referral to special education where necessary (Sailor, Doolittle, Bradley, & Danielson, 2009).

MyEdLab: **Self-Check 3.4**

MyEdLab: **Application Exercise 3.4: Emotional Disturbances**

TABLE 3.1 Elementary School Report Cards and Commonly Observed Statements Describing Students with ADHD

	Typical Behaviors on Report Cards	Observed Statements Describing Students with ADHD
Compliance	• Follows directions • Obeys rules	• Frequently ignores directions • Talks continuously
Self-Control	• Waits turn • Tolerates frustration	• Impatient • Gives up easily
Social	• Polite, courteous	• Often interrupts
Development	• Keeps hands to self	• Touches everything
Attention	• Stays on task • Makes efficient use of time	• Rarely finishes work • Frequently fidgeting

Note: Adapted from *Rethinking Attention Deficit Disorders* (p. 126), by M. Cherkes-Julkowski, S. Sharp, and J. Stolzenberg, 1997, Cambridge, MA: Brookline Books. Copyright 1997 by Brookline Books. Adapted with permission.

Attention Deficit Hyperactivity Disorder (ADHD)

DEFINITIONS, PREVALENCE, AND CHARACTERISTICS OF ADHD

Robert has an attention deficit hyperactivity disorder; his family and teacher could benefit from suggestions as to how to best work with him. Robert's disruptive behaviors and his inability to sustain attention could put Robert at risk for failing in school (Rooney, 2011). Attention deficit hyperactivity disorder (ADHD) refers to a "neurological condition that involves problems with inattention and hyperactivity that are developmentally inconsistent with the age of the child" (U.S. Department of Education, 2008, p. 1). Observations made in the classroom will identify these students as those who often say "Huh, what?" immediately following directions; often appear to be daydreaming; act before they think; blurt out answers; interrupt; and constantly fidget, wiggle, and move around. Table 3.1 compares the sharp contrast between commonly noted behaviors on elementary school report cards and those noted for students with ADHD.

From 3% to 7% or more of all school-age children may have ADHD. Most students with ADHD are served full time in general education classrooms, with some individuals qualifying for special education services under the Other Health Impairments category in IDEA (Rooney, 2011).

The *Diagnostic and Statistical Manual* (DSM-5) of the American Psychiatric Association (APA, 2013) describes criteria for the classification of ADHD. The symptomatic behaviors must be maladaptive and must be present for a minimum of 6 months to warrant a classification as either inattentive ADHD or hyperactivity-impulsivity ADHD. Several symptoms should have been present before 12 years of age. Furthermore, a child must display a minimum number of identifying characteristics before ADHD is diagnosed. For example, students must meet six of nine characteristics under "Inattention" (e.g., fails to give close attention, often easily distracted, is often forgetful) or six of nine characteristics under "Hyperactivity/Impulsivity" (e.g., often fidgets, often leaves seat, often interrupts or intrudes on others). There also must be evidence of impairment in social, occupational, or academic functioning, and some impairment from the symptoms must be present in at least two settings.

Any inattentiveness, impulsivity, and hyperactivity must be observed across settings (APA, 2013). Or, as in the case of Robert, the teacher and parents must observe similar behavior patterns at school and at home. Although some symptoms change over time, ADHD is now considered potentially a lifelong disorder. Males outnumber females in this disorder (Rooney, 2011). Students with ADHD are thought to be more likely to have a learning disability than other children (McGillivray & Baker, 2009).

MyEdLab:
Video Example 3.2.

In this video, the clinical director and therapists of a day treatment setting for children discuss the characteristics of ADHD and the possible causes of ADHD. Notice the strategies used with this student.

CAUSES OF ADHD

Precise causes of ADHD are unknown; however, it is thought that many factors contribute to it. These factors include genetic, nongenetic, psychosocial, and neurobiological bases. Genetic evidence is based on research with families whose members have ADHD. Some researchers estimate that as many as 40% of children with ADHD have parents with ADHD, and concordance of ADHD has been seen to be much higher in identical (monozygotic) twins than in fraternal (dizygotic) twins, suggesting a genetic component (Rooney, 2011). Many children with ADHD exhibit attention and self-control difficulties at a very early age (Kauffman & Landrum, 2013). Nongenetic factors include prenatal and perinatal factors, allergies, and thyroid disorders. Although both food additives (Feingold, 1975) and sugar (Smith, 1975) have been proposed as direct causes of ADHD, research has not substantiated these as plausible (Rooney, 2011); however, they may play a role in some individual cases. Other research has investigated the psychosocial and neurological correlates associated with ADHD, with evidence growing in support of neurological indicators. To date, however, as with many disorders, no definitive single etiological factor has been uncovered. At present, it seems that ADHD appears to be more influenced by neurological and genetic factors than by social or environmental factors (Barkley, 2014).

CLASSROOM SCENARIO

Robert Black

Robert Black had so much energy that he drove everyone around him crazy, including his parents; his teacher, Ms. Moore; and his classmates. When he arrived at school, everything around him appeared to get caught in a whirlwind of activity: Papers flew to the floor, books were dropped, toys were broken, classmates were annoyed, and teachers threw their hands up in dismay. Robert was a nice 8-year-old boy, but he could not focus on one thing at a time. He seemed mesmerized by everything, moving from activity to activity with limitless energy. When someone spoke, he would interrupt and start talking about something that popped into his head. If he saw something that interested him, he would immediately take it in his hands. His feet, hands, and eyes seemed to be moving constantly. He seemed unable to sit still. Ms. Moore was frustrated and unsure of how to handle Robert in the classroom, so she called Mr. and Mrs. Black and asked them to come in for a conference. What became immediately evident at the parent conference was that Mr. and Mrs. Black were experiencing similar problems and frustrations at home with Robert—and had been since he was 2 years old.

QUESTIONS FOR REFLECTION

1. Why do you think Mr. and Mrs. Black were experiencing similar challenges with Robert at home?
2. What types of strategies might be helpful for Robert and his parents to use at home?
3. What behavioral and instructional supports are available for working with Robert in school?

ISSUES IN IDENTIFICATION AND ASSESSMENT OF ADHD

There is no individual test to identify ADHD. Most experts recommend a multidisciplinary assessment (Rooney, 2011). A first step is to determine whether ADHD exists, and a second step could attempt to determine whether the student's educational progress is adversely affected by it. During the first step, information is collected on observations of the individual's behavior throughout the day, medical history, family information, school information, social-emotional functioning, and cognitive-academic functioning. A medical exam, clinical interview, and rating scales of the individual's behavior completed by parents and teachers can be part of this evaluation process (Kauffman & Landrum, 2013).

There is no IDEA category representing ADHD, so identified students do not necessarily qualify for services. To qualify for special education services in the "other health impairment" category of IDEA, it must be documented that the ADHD has an adverse effect on educational performance. To qualify for special services under Section 504 of the Vocational Rehabilitation Act, it must be documented that the ADHD substantially limits learning. If either of these requirements is met, an intervention plan is designed and implemented as either part of the IEP in compliance with IDEA or the accommodation plan for compliance with Section 504. In the event that students with ADHD do not meet criteria for either IDEA or Section 504, no special accommodations are designed as part of any legally mandated system. However, these students with ADHD also frequently benefit from some of the general classroom adaptations described in this text and listed in the following section.

STRATEGIES FOR

MAKING CLASSROOM ADAPTATIONS FOR STUDENTS WITH ATTENTION DEFICIT HYPERACTIVITY DISORDER

Many strategies described earlier in this chapter for differentiating instruction by adapting the physical environment, materials, instruction, and assessments for students with higher-incidence disabilities are appropriate for students with ADHD. The following *In the Classroom* feature provides some suggestions for accommodations that can add to classroom success (see also Kauffman & Landrum, 2013; Wolraich, DuPaul, & Stevens, 2010).

ADAPT INSTRUCTION WITH BEHAVIORAL INTERVENTIONS   Behavioral interventions are strategies used to analyze and modify behavior. Students' behaviors are first analyzed with respect to **antecedent** and **consequent** events (that is, what happened before and after the undesirable behavior occurred). Strategies are then implemented systematically based on that analysis (Duhaney, 2003). For example, a teacher observed that every time a worksheet was distributed in class, Max got out of his seat to sharpen his pencils and get a drink of water, bothering several classmates in the process. After this, the teacher would reprimand Max, which would make Max feel sullen and resentful. After analyzing this behavior, it seemed likely that Max was reacting to the difficulty or interest level of the task and his own predisposition toward physical activity. The teacher decided to have Max sharpen his pencils and get a drink of water before class every day. In addition, the teacher would praise Max for remaining in his seat and leaving classmates alone after the worksheets were passed out. The teacher also monitored the content of the academic activities to make sure they were of the appropriate difficulty level and held some interest for Max. She provided alternative opportunities for Max to leave his seat under teacher supervision so that he could engage in some physical movement when needed. Such strategies can be effective when they are designed to meet the specific needs underlying problem behaviors.

ADAPT INSTRUCTION WITH COGNITIVE-BEHAVIORAL INTERVENTIONS
Cognitive-behavioral interventions use the same principles of behavior management just described, but in addition, they add a **self-instruction and self-monitoring** component to the intervention. For example, Max could be taught to keep daily records of (1) how often he remembered to sharpen his pencils and get a drink of water before class, and (2) whether he was able to stay in his seat once the worksheet was handed out. Specific rewards might even be paired with how well he monitored his own behavior. Other commonly used cognitive-behavioral interventions involve the use of self-monitoring for on-task behavior and task completion. Strategies such as these have been particularly successful with students with ADHD.

MONITOR USE OF MEDICATIONS   As many as 2 million students with ADHD take psychostimulant medications, such as Ritalin (methylphenidate) or Adderall (dextroamphetamine and amphetamine), to help control their attention and hyperactivity (Rooney, 2011). The number of children taking medications for ADHD has risen considerably over the years. If students are taking medications, teachers must keep thorough records of behavior to help monitor their effects. Reviews of research on the effects of stimulant medication generally indicate positive benefits, in that attention to task increases, and hyperactivity decreases (Barkley, 2014). However, the practice of administering medications has remained controversial. Some educators and physicians argue that the side effects of medications can be harmful and that no students should be given medications to control their classroom behavior. When medication is prescribed, however, concomitant behavior therapy, such as the cognitive and behavioral interventions described previously, is generally also recommended (Rooney, 2011).

In the Classroom . . .

Accommodation Suggestions for Students with ADHD

For Beginning Activities

_____ Give small amounts of work.

_____ Provide signals to begin.

_____ Use timers and encourage self-monitoring.

_____ Use verbal and written directions.

_____ Provide additional structure (e.g., large-lined paper).

_____ Highlight directions using larger fonts or colors.

For Keeping on Task

_____ Increase the frequency of positive reinforcement.

_____ Use peer assistants.

_____ Make tasks interesting.

_____ Break tasks into smaller "manageable" units.

_____ Allow breaks.

_____ Use hands-on activities.

For Listening

_____ Teach note taking and encourage the use of notebook organizers.

_____ Use positive reinforcement.

_____ Allow doodling.

_____ Allow standing.

For Excessive Activity

_____ Use activity as a reward (run errands, wash boards, move desks).

_____ Allow standing during class.

_____ Encourage active participation.

_____ Reward sitting.

For Impulsive Behavior

_____ Provide acceptable alternatives.

_____ Encourage trying to continue with another part of the assignment before interrupting the teacher.

_____ Recommend note taking during lectures.

_____ Recommend writing down questions and answers before blurting out.

_____ Teach acceptable social behavior for conversations, for class behavior, and for interacting with peers.

_____ Reward listening and appropriate behaviors.

For Working Independently

_____ Ensure tasks match ability levels.

_____ Provide brief directions.

_____ Use brief tasks.

_____ Use checklists for self-monitoring.

_____ Use positive reinforcement.

For Following Class Rules

_____ Keep rules simple.

_____ Post and review class rules.

_____ Model and role-play following rules.

_____ Be consistent with enforcement of rules.

_____ Provide students with copies of rules.

MyEdLab: **Self-Check 3.5**

MyEdLab: **Application Exercise 3.5: Attention Deficit Hyperactivity Disorder (ADHD)**

3 Summary

- Students with communication disorders may exhibit problems with speech or language. Speech disorders may involve voice, articulation, or fluency; language disorders may involve difficulties with phonology, morphology, syntax, semantics, or the pragmatics of language use.

- Students with learning disabilities make up about half of students with higher-incidence disabilities. These students may exhibit specific problems in basic academic skill areas, as well as areas such as language, attention, memory, social skills, and metacognition.

- Students with intellectual disabilities exhibit deficiencies in intellectual functioning and corresponding levels of adaptive behavior. These students also may exhibit learning problems related to language, social behavior, attention, reasoning, academics, comprehension, and problem solving.

- Students with behavioral disorders or emotional disturbance may exhibit problems in classroom behavior and social relations or may exhibit disorders of affect, such as anxiety or depression.

- Students with attention deficit disorder or attention deficit hyperactivity disorder may be served under Section 504 or IDEA. Adaptations for this group of individuals may include behavioral approaches, cognitive-behavioral training, medication, or a combination of the three.

PROFESSIONAL STANDARDS LINK:
Teaching Students with Higher-Incidence Disabilities

Information in this chapter links most directly to:

- CEC Standards: 1 (Learner Development and Individual Learning Differences), 2 (Learning Environments), 5 (Instructional Planning and Strategies)

- INTASC Standards: 2 (Learning Differences), 3 (Learning Environments), 7 (Planning for Instruction), 8 (Instructional Strategies)

TEACHING STUDENTS WITH HIGHER-INCIDENCE DISABILITIES

If a student with higher-incidence disabilities is having difficulties in your classroom, have you tried the following general modifications? If not, see the pages listed here.

STRATEGIES FOR MAKING CLASSROOM ADAPTATIONS FOR STUDENTS WITH SPEECH OR LANGUAGE IMPAIRMENTS

- ☐ Adapt the physical environment, 55
- ☐ Adapt materials, 55
- ☐ Adapt instructional procedures, 55–57
- ☐ Adapt assessment methods, 57

STRATEGIES FOR MAKING CLASSROOM ADAPTATIONS FOR STUDENTS WITH LEARNING DISABILITIES

- ☐ Adapt the physical environment, 60–61
- ☐ Adapt instructional materials, 61–62
- ☐ Adapt instructional procedures, 62
- ☐ Adapt assessment methods, 62

STRATEGIES FOR MAKING CLASSROOM ADAPTATIONS FOR STUDENTS WITH INTELLECTUAL DISABILITIES

- ☐ Make preparations, 66
- ☐ Monitor peer relationships, 66
- ☐ Adapt instructional materials, 66
- ☐ Adapt instructional procedures, 67
- ☐ Adapt assessment methods, 67

STRATEGIES FOR MAKING CLASSROOM ADAPTATIONS FOR STUDENTS WITH EMOTIONAL DISTURBANCE

- ☐ Prepare the class, 70
- ☐ Adapt the physical environment, 70
- ☐ Adapt instructional materials, 70
- ☐ Adapt instruction, 70–71
- ☐ Adapt assessment methods, 71
- ☐ Support multi-tiered interventions, 71

STRATEGIES FOR MAKING CLASSROOM ADAPTATIONS FOR STUDENTS WITH ATTENTION DEFICIT HYPERACTIVITY DISORDER

- ☐ Adapt instruction with behavioral interventions, 74
- ☐ Adapt instruction with cognitive-behavioral interventions, 74
- ☐ Monitor use of medications, 74

4

Teaching Students with Autism and Lower-Incidence Disabilities

LEARNING OUTCOMES

After studying this chapter, you should be able to:

4.1 Describe and discuss the prevalence and characteristics of students with autism, and explain strategies for classroom adaptations.

4.2 Describe and discuss the prevalence and characteristics of students with physical disabilities and other health impairments, and explain strategies for classroom adaptations.

4.3 Describe and discuss the prevalence and characteristics of students with severe and multiple disabilities, and explain strategies for classroom adaptations.

4.4 Describe and discuss the prevalence and characteristics of students with visual impairments, and explain strategies for classroom adaptations.

4.5 Describe and discuss the prevalence and characteristics of students with hearing impairments, and explain strategies for classroom adaptations.

Individuals who have lower-incidence disabilities are far less commonly represented in schools than individuals with higher-incidence disabilities. Lower-incidence disabilities cover a wide range of disabilities, which can be present at birth (**congenital**) or acquired later in life (**adventitious**). Some lower-incidence disabilities are associated with very severe impairments; others involve only mild impairments. Some lower-incidence disabilities are temporary; others are permanent or even life-threatening. Lower-incidence disabilities include physical and other health impairments, severe and multiple disabilities, visual impairments, and hearing impairments. It is exciting to see some of the creative adaptations that have been developed to help students with lower-incidence disabilities become more successful in inclusive classes.

In this chapter, we also include autism spectrum disorder. Formerly a low-incidence disability, autism is as commonly identified in schools today as one of the higher-incidence disabilities. We include it with lower-incidence disabilities because of its historical connection with lower-incidence disabilities and because many students with autism are more severely involved.

Autism

PREVALENCE, DEFINITIONS, AND CHARACTERISTICS OF AUTISM

Autism is a disorder characterized by impairments in social, emotional, and intellectual functioning. Children with autism are often described as having great difficulty communicating and interacting with and responding to other people. Many individuals with autism also exhibit stereotypic behavior such as self-stimulating behaviors (e.g., rocking, hand flapping); bizarre speech patterns, such as repeating the words of other people over and over again (echolalia); and disruptive behavior, sometimes including self-injury (Hall, 2013). Children with autism are typically identified before the age of 3. Frequently, parents are the first ones to become concerned when their infants do not respond positively to being touched and held closely and when language does not develop along the common developmental milestones.

The causes of autism are unknown, although genetic, neurological, and environmental factors have been proposed (Hall, 2013). Individuals with autism make up approximately 0.7% of the school-age population, or 8.2% of the students served under IDEA (U.S. Department of Education, 2015). The prevalence of autism appears to be increasing in recent years, although the reasons for this are not completely clear. For instance, in 2004, students with autism represented only 0.2% of the school-age population, more similar to the rates of other low-incidence disabilities (U.S. Department of Education, 2015). One possibility is that changes in diagnostic criteria, along with more public awareness of autism, have led to increased rates of identification (Hill, Zuckerman, & Fombonne, 2015).

Related diagnostic categories include autistic disorder, Rett syndrome, childhood disintegrative disorder, Asperger's disorder, early infantile autism, and pervasive developmental disorder. These categories are now collected under the broader term **autism spectrum disorders** (ASD; Conroy, Stichter, & Gage, 2011). The American Psychiatric Association (2013) no longer considers Asperger's disorder—thought to be a milder form of autism—to be distinct from autism spectrum disorder. The current diagnoses indicate that individuals with autism may function along a continuum of severe to mild disabilities and that educational accommodations vary according to an individual's functioning level. Individuals with severe autism may have limited to no expressive and receptive language, whereas individuals with milder forms of autism may have developed more sophisticated communication. Although symptoms and severity level can vary greatly among individuals with autism, communication and social competence are typically the two greatest challenges. Many individuals with autism have cognitive deficits similar to those of individuals with intellectual disabilities. Individuals with Asperger's disorder, however, can be highly intelligent (Conroy et al., 2011).

STRATEGIES FOR

MAKING CLASSROOM ADAPTATIONS FOR STUDENTS WITH AUTISM

Classroom adaptations for individuals with autism can be classified into adaptations for those with severe autism and those with mild autism. Individuals with severe forms of autism may function similarly to individuals with severe disabilities, and it is recommended that you employ the suggested adaptations for individuals with severe disabilities. Conversely, for individuals with milder forms of autism, you may wish to consider using modifications recommended for students with mild disabilities, including learning disabilities and behavior disorders. In both cases, work closely with special education teachers and parents. This collaboration ensures that individualized education program (IEP) goals and objectives are being addressed and that you have assistance in interacting with students. The National Professional Development Center on Autism Spectrum Disorder (2014) at the Frank Porter Graham Center of the University of North Carolina identified 27 evidence-based practices (EBPs) demonstrated to have effectiveness with students with autism spectrum disorder (Wong et al., 2013). The EBPs include social behavior, social skills, communication, applied behavior analysis, self-management, and peer-mediated interventions, among others. The following adaptations may also be generally helpful for differentiating instruction for students with autism in general education classes.

ESTABLISH EFFECTIVE COMMUNICATION Discuss optimal communication patterns and design communication strategies with special education teachers, parents, and peers. Strategies might include sign language or augmentative and alternative communication (AAC) methods. For example, in the following scenario, Tony is a young boy with autism who does not have language but communicates with an AAC procedure referred to as the Picture Exchange Communication System (PECS). PECS teaches students to use pictures and symbols to initiate communication and respond to communication from others (Bondy & Frost, 2011). Apps have been developed for tablets such as the iPad to assist with communication. Figure 4.1 presents examples of commonly used symbols in different communication systems.

Figure 4.1 Sample Communication Board Symbols (PCS = Picture Communication Symbols; PIC = Pictogram Ideogram Communication)

Note: Reprinted with permission from "Non-speech modes and systems," by G. C. Vanderheiden and L. L. Lloyd, 1986, in S. W. Blackstone (Ed.), *Augmentative communication* (pp. 48–161), Rockville, MD: American Speech–Language Hearing Association.

USE DIRECT INSTRUCTION AND APPLIED BEHAVIOR ANALYSIS Many students with autism (and many other students as well) benefit from direct instruction, including small-group or one-to-one structured, teacher-directed lessons, with lots of direct questioning, student responding, teacher feedback and praise, and careful recording and monitoring of progress toward predetermined objectives. Instruction is carefully sequenced according to student needs (e.g., Wheeler, Mayton, & Carter, 2015). For example, if a student had no expressive language, training might begin with the teacher providing reinforcement for imitating sounds, such as "aaa," followed by imitating words (e.g., *hat*), followed by responding to simple directions ("Point to the hat"), followed by word production ("What is this?" [teacher points to a hat]). Throughout this progression, the teacher would provide explicit feedback and reinforcement for attending and for correct

Tony

Tony had a difficult first day in his inclusive kindergarten. His teachers saw his crying, tantrum-throwing, and acts of aggression, and, fortunately, realized that much of his behavior reflected not simply the fact that he had autism, but rather his inability to communicate in a new environment. His teachers used the Picture Exchange Communication System (PECS) to train him in socially appropriate ways to obtain what he wanted, using the six phases of the training program (Scott, Clark, & Brady, 2000). In the first phases, they determined that Tony enjoyed playing with a particular toy truck. When he reached for it, they placed the picture card of a truck in his hand, then guided him to give the picture to his teacher. The teacher immediately gave him the truck. In later phases, Tony was encouraged to go to a touch board for the picture, then discriminate the truck from other pictures, and then build sentence structure by choosing first the "I want" card, followed by the picture of the desired object. In the fifth phase, Tony responds to "What do you want?" questions, and in the sixth phase, Tony uses the PECS cards to answer teacher questions, such as "What do you have?" or "What do you see?"

As Tony learns the PECS program, his tantrum-throwing and inappropriate behavior diminishes, and he learns socially appropriate ways of interacting with others. Other students use the PECS materials to interact with Tony. The PECS training continues to include additional language concepts, such as adjectives, verbs, and yes–no responses. Tony is learning important lessons for communicating and socializing with teachers and classmates.

QUESTIONS FOR REFLECTION

1. Why do you think using the PECS system is easier for Tony than using spoken language?
2. Why would a language training program help to improve Tony's social behavior?
3. How could Tony's classroom peers assist in developing Tony's communication skills?

MyEdLab:
Video Example 4.1.
While watching this video of a teacher using direct instruction, notice the carefully sequenced structure, the simple directions, and the explicit feedback and reinforcement she uses. Notice also her use of lots of direct questioning and recording and monitoring of progress.

responding. Applied behavior analysis (ABA) involves the use of reinforcement (e.g., praise, tokens, edible reinforcers) for displaying appropriate behaviors (e.g., sitting, attending, responding) and carefully recording student behaviors on charts that are used in decision making (Hall, 2013; Martin & Pear, 2015). These practices may also employ functional behavioral assessments and Positive Behavioral Interventions and Supports (PBIS) (see Chapter 8 for additional information on behavioral supports). Teachers may document the antecedents as well as observed consequences of specific behaviors (e.g., screaming, tantrums) and then arrange the environment and environmental consequences to minimize inappropriate behaviors.

DEVELOP SOCIAL COMPETENCE Unless you design behavior plans with the student's IEP team and implement these plans systematically, you may find it easy to become overwhelmed by the student's challenging behaviors. Teach students to wait their turn, to share materials, and to know when they need to be quiet and when they can talk. Teach them to use socially appropriate behaviors throughout the school day to help promote generalization of appropriate social behavior. Reward successive approximations (as students come closer to their goals), and work toward having students become more independent. Develop behavior management plans based on an analysis of student preferences and classroom dynamics. Direct-instruction and ABA techniques can be helpful in these areas (Wheeler et al., 2015).

Create a learning environment in which the student with autism feels comfortable, including a predictable schedule of daily activities, a pattern of events, and class routines. Use pictures to list the sequence of activities if the student is a nonreader, and allow the student to order the sequence if possible. If you change the class routine, prepare the student in advance to avoid undue stress.

Goldstein, Lackey, and Schneider (2014) reviewed available research on social skills interventions for preschoolers with autism and concluded that these treatments had been generally effective in improving social functioning. Treatments included modeling, peer mediation, self-monitoring, and other interventions. Similarly, Carr, Moore, and Anderson (2014) reviewed research on self-management interventions for students with autism, across age levels, and concluded that these interventions also were effective.

One promising technique for improving social behavior is the use of social stories (Barry & Burlew, 2004; Wheeler et al., 2015). Social stories use simple sentences and pictures to demonstrate the anticipated sequence of desired social behaviors (e.g., when eating lunch at the school cafeteria) and the feelings and reactions of others. In this instance, the student could be shown a photo of himself returning his tray with the teacher smiling at him, with a caption such as, "When I return my tray after I have finished eating, my teacher is happy." Social stories have been seen to improve the social functioning of students with autism in a variety of school settings (e.g., Graetz, Mastropieri, & Scruggs, 2009).

Technological advances, now and in the future, may prove helpful in improving social competence in students with ASD. For example, the Autism Glass Project at Stanford University has been working with a Google Glass device that has been modified to interpret facial expressions to describe how the person facing the individual wearing the Google Glass is feeling, for example, "happy" if the individual is smiling (Cardon, 2016).

Enlist the help of peers to reinforce socially appropriate behavior. Group students with autism with higher-functioning students. Students with autism can be included successfully in cooperative learning groups when paired with partners who have been taught to communicate effectively with them (Zhang & Wheeler, 2011).

Watch for signs that the student is becoming stressed. Students with autism may react aggressively or withdraw completely under novel or stressful situations. Try to predict when the class demands might become stressful, and attempt to eliminate the sources of stress.

Finally, establish and maintain effective communication with all individuals who are in contact with students with autism. Communicate regularly with parents. Send home weekly or daily notes, short recorded messages, or a journal that travels back and forth between you and parents.

MyEdLab:
Video Example 4.2.

Watch this video to see an example of peers who have been taught to interact with a classmate with autism.

MyEdLab: **Self-Check 4.1**

MyEdLab: **Application Exercise 4.1: Autism**

Physical Disabilities and Other Health Impairments

PREVALENCE, DEFINITIONS, AND CHARACTERISTICS OF PHYSICAL DISABILITIES AND OTHER HEALTH IMPAIRMENTS

Physical disabilities (or orthopedic impairments, according to the Individuals with Disabilities Education Act [IDEA]) and other health impairments include many types of disabilities that range from mild to moderate to severe and from temporary to permanent or life-threatening. Approximately 1.3% of the school-age population has a physical (0.1%) or other health-related disability (1.2%), or 14.7% of the students served under IDEA (U.S. Department of Education, 2015). Physical disabilities are often described as either orthopedic or neuromotor impairments, and IDEA considers neuromotor impairments part of the orthopedic impairments category. **Orthopedic impairments** involve damage to the skeletal system, and **neuromotor impairments** involve damage to the nervous system (Best, 2010b). Frequently, physical disabilities are referred to by the affected parts of the body. For example, **quadriplegia** means that both arms and legs are impaired, **paraplegia** means that the legs are impaired, **hemiplegia** means that either the left or right side of the body is involved, and **diplegia** means that both legs are involved more than the arms (Best & Bigge, 2010). Common physical disabilities include cerebral palsy, epilepsy, spina bifida, muscular dystrophy, rheumatoid arthritis, scoliosis (curvature of the spine), osteogenesis imperfecta (brittle bone disease), and arthrogryposis (joint contractures; Best, 2010b).

Cystic fibrosis. Cystic fibrosis is an inherited disease in which upper respiratory and digestive problems are chronic due to the inability of the pancreas to produce digestive enzymes (Kelly, 2004). Glands in the bronchial tubes also malfunction and produce thick mucus that stagnates in the bronchial tubes. Treatments include special diets and intensive respiratory therapy (Kelly, 2004). Work closely with medical staff to monitor the condition.

Hemophilia. Hemophilia is an inherited sex-linked disorder in which the blood does not clot properly and excessive bleeding may occur with minor cuts or injuries (Kelly, 2004). Know relevant first aid information. Internal bleeding is very serious. Watch for falls at recess or during physical education classes. Avoid dangerous situations in which cuts are possible. Follow safety guidelines when using sharp objects or cutting tools.

Rheumatic fever. Rheumatic fever usually begins with a throat infection that may lead to painful swelling in the joints that can spread to the heart or brain and result in severe damage. Consult with medical personnel and your student's family to design optimal interventions.

Cancer. Cancer is a group of diseases in which the normal process of cell production malfunctions. Cell growth is uncontrolled, becomes malignant, and damages healthy tissues. Individuals with cancer may require special supports for both social-emotional well-being and for accommodating less energy and pain during school activities. Radiation treatments have been associated with learning disabilities, so additional instructional accommodations may be needed (Best, 2005).

Tuberculosis. Tuberculosis is a disease in which bacteria infect the lungs, and may spread to the brain, kidneys, or bones.

Nephrosis and nephritis. Nephrosis and nephritis are disorders of the kidneys. These disorders, if left untreated, can result in kidney failure.

Sickle-cell anemia. Sickle-cell anemia is an inherited disease in which an abnormal red hemoglobin is formed (Kelly, 2004). This results in less oxygen in the body, and the malformed cells may move improperly through the bloodstream, resulting in additional complications. Students with sickle-cell anemia may tire more easily and may need accommodations such as reduced assignments commensurate with their energy-ability levels.

Figure 4.2 Other Health-Related Disorders

Other health impairments include physical or medical conditions resulting from diseases or illnesses. Great variability exists in the severity level of impairment. Some health impairments improve over time, whereas others do not. Major health conditions include cancer, acquired immune deficiency syndrome (AIDS), allergies, asthma, and fetal alcohol syndrome (Heller, Forney, Alberto, Best, & Schwartzman, 2009) and are discussed next. Other conditions are presented in Figure 4.2.

School-related difficulties due to physical disabilities and other health impairments are covered by the provision of "special education services" under IDEA 2004. Sometimes physical disabilities or other health impairments do not lead to difficulties in academic or intellectual functioning. Some students with other health impairments, including asthma, AIDS, tuberculosis, diabetes, drug or alcohol addiction, or behavioral problems, might not qualify for services under IDEA, but they may qualify for services under Section 504 of the Vocational Rehabilitation Act (Zirkel, 2009).

PHYSICAL AND HEALTH-RELATED DISABILITIES

CEREBRAL PALSY Cerebral palsy is the most common physical disability, with approximately 1 to 2.4 occurrences in every 1,000 births and affecting approximately 15% of premature infants. It is a neurological disorder that causes permanent disorders of movement and positions. Cerebral palsy is not progressive in nature, which means it does not worsen over time. It does, however, range in impairment levels from mild to moderate to severe. Individuals with cerebral palsy may or may not have coexisting difficulties in language, communication, vision, hearing, psychosocial, self-help, and intellectual development. Between 25% and 50% of individuals with cerebral palsy may be subject to seizure disorders (Heller & Garrett, 2009).

The most common forms of cerebral palsy are spastic (characterized by increased muscle tone), athetosis (characterized by involuntary nonpurposeful movements), ataxic (characterized by lack of coordination in balance and equilibrium), and mixed (Heller & Garrett, 2009). Many individuals with cerebral palsy use wheelchairs or other motorized vehicles to assist with mobility or use other adaptive devices to assist with fine motor control and speech and language difficulties. **Alternative and augmentative communication** (AAC) techniques used with some individuals with cerebral palsy and other disabilities include communication boards containing pictures or words of commonly asked questions and responses to questions and computerized devices using synthesized speech. The *Apps for Education* feature describes uses of technology, *News-2-You* and *Boardmaker*, to improve communication.

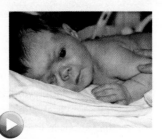

MyEdLab:
Video Example 4.3.
In this video, you will learn about Abigail, a little girl with spina bifida. Pay particular attention to the parental perspective.

SPINA BIFIDA Spina bifida is caused during fetal development when the vertebrae do not properly enclose the spinal cord, causing the nerves that control muscles in the lower body to develop incorrectly. Spina bifida occurs in approximately 1 in 2,000 births. Resulting motor impairment can range from mild to severe and include loss of sensation to paralysis in the lower body. Spina bifida is often associated with hydrocephalus, a condition in which cerebrospinal fluid collects in the brain tissues. If left untreated, swelling can cause severe brain damage and result in intellectual disability and attention and learning problems (Heller, 2009). Shunts, or one-way valves, are inserted surgically to drain the fluid from the brain to reduce the risk of pressure on the brain and possible resulting brain damage. Shunts need to be replaced as children grow. Be aware of warning signs or changes in a student's behavior, as sudden changes may indicate shunt blockage or infections. Alert parents immediately of any changes.

Individuals with spina bifida—and other physical disabilities—may lack bladder and bowel movement control due to paralysis of the lower body. Most children lacking bladder control use a catheter, attached to a bag, to collect their urine. Many children are taught to use a procedure called *clean intermittent catheterization* (CIC) or *intermittent self-catheterization* (ISC; Heller, Bigge, & Allgood, 2010). Request guidance from school nurses or other educational team members to learn how to assist a child with this procedure. Plan restroom breaks to accommodate these students' specialized toileting needs.

Many children with spina bifida walk with braces or crutches, relying on wheelchairs for longer distances. In these cases, maintain classroom space to ensure clear, wide, and open walkways for students with mobility difficulties. Arrange storage for crutches or removable braces near students for easy access.

MUSCULAR DYSTROPHY Muscular dystrophy refers to a group of diseases that weaken and progressively destroy muscle tissue. Muscular dystrophy occurs in approximately 1 in 3,500 births. No known cure exists. Some forms of muscular dystrophy are fatal, but other forms are not life-threatening. At birth, children appear to function normally; however, between the ages of 2 and 6 they may begin to experience motor difficulties, which increase with age. Often by the ages of 10 to 14, children lose the ability to walk. Children with muscular dystrophy should be lifted only by those with explicit training, as their limbs are easily dislocated. Because the disease is often progressive, it is important to learn what types of muscular difficulties may be expected throughout an academic year (Heller, Mezei, & Schwartzman, 2009).

TRAUMATIC BRAIN INJURY Traumatic brain injury (TBI), although now a separate category of exceptionality under IDEA, represents a type of physical and cognitive disability. Traumatic brain injury is the result of an external injury that impedes learning along the continuum from mild to severe disabilities and may result in physical, cognitive, attention, memory, problem-solving, sensory, and psychosocial difficulties. The resulting disabilities may be temporary or permanent. Often, traumatic brain injuries result from falls or motor vehicle accidents. Child abuse also can be a cause of brain injury (Grandinette & Best, 2009).

According to the U.S. Department of Education (2015), only 0.4% of students with disabilities and approximately 0.04% of the student population are characterized as having TBI. However, this number is considered to be a substantial underestimate of the entire population because over 1 million students per year are affected by TBI. Among elementary-age students, TBI is often the result of play or bicycling accidents, falls, and motor vehicle accidents. Adolescents most often acquire TBIs from motor vehicle accidents, intensive sports activities, assault, and risk-taking behaviors. TBI can also result from gunshot wounds, suicide

Alternative and Augmentative Communication: *News-2-You* and *Boardmaker*

 Many students with low-incidence disabilities require some adaptations in literacy materials that will aid their ability to communicate. Alternative and augmentative communication (ACC) devices are widely available and range from high-tech to low-tech options, including apps. This means that some use very little technology, whereas others are reliant on more complex technological systems for delivery. One alternative and augmentative version of a newspaper is *News-2-You* (AssistiveWare). *News-2-You* is published weekly during the school year and is available for a subscription fee. The newspaper features relevant, newsworthy stories printed using visual symbols that represent words. Each paper includes four to five pages of weekly current-event news stories, a recipe, a joke, a game page, a sports story, and a weekly quiz based on the paper and is available in printable, audio, and booklet formats. The paper also includes sample communication boards as downloads that can be used as part of *Boardmaker*, a software program that contains graphics that can be used to develop and design communication displays or Microsoft Word documents (for those who do not have access to *Boardmaker*). The newspaper provides an excellent vehicle for access to news for many students who might otherwise be unable to read a paper. Because the paper is available online on a weekly basis, a teacher can select to have students read it online, from a saved online version on a computer or tablet, or in a printed hard-copy format. There is also a speaking version, which reads text material. The newspaper provides an excellent tool for working on reading comprehension skills with the short quizzes that accompany the weekly papers. Teachers can also decide to make their own versions of newspapers and reading materials using similar formats.

For example, teachers who like the format of *News-2-You* will most likely want to obtain the software *Boardmaker* or the online version, which can be used to develop a wide range of displays using the over 3,000 graphic picture communication symbols and over 100 templates for calendars, schedules, and other formats. Pictures can be sized to meet your needs, and *Boardmaker* for Windows comes with 19 languages, including English, Spanish, German, Portuguese, Vietnamese, Russian, and Turkish, but has space for over 150 languages. The software is available from Mayer-Johnson (http://mayer-johnson.com). *Boardmaker* can also be combined with *Speaking Dynamically Pro* to include speech capabilities. With this combination, the symbols are used as overlays with the corresponding sounds spoken aloud, which is effective for students who require hearing the symbols in addition to looking at them. *Boardmaker Plus* adds sound, voice, animation, and video capabilities to the software.

Apps are also available for assistive technology and adaptive communications. *SpeakText FREE* (BorG Technology) converts keyed-in text and web pages to speech and also translates into more than 30 languages. *Speakall!* (Speak MODalities) can be used with a Picture Exchange Communication System (PECS), and developers can import custom pictures and record speech. *iCommunicate* (Grembe Apps) is costlier but allows the user to design and develop visual schedules, communication boards, storyboards, and flashcards. Developers can record their own voice or use the text-to-speech option. Finally, *My Pictures Talk—Video Modeling Tool* (Grembe Apps) enables uploading and editing of videos so that users can create their own social stories or video modeling sequences.

The following sample page from *News-2-You* shows a restaurant review questionnaire:

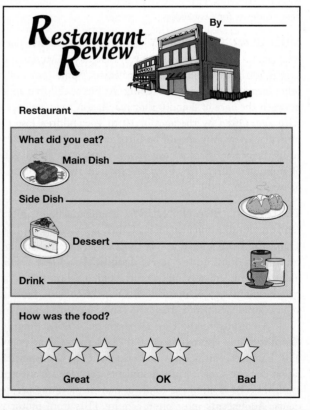

attempts, and abuse of drugs or alcohol (Grandinette & Best, 2009). Special education services often are provided for the resulting difficulties in school learning. Teachers can play an important preventative role by encouraging students to take safety precautions, such as wearing helmets when riding bicycles.

A significant role of the classroom teacher is in assisting with the reintegration and transitions the individual has to make from the hospital to rehabilitation to the classroom. Successful transition planning includes preparing peers for the changes in the behavior of the affected classmate. IEPs may need to be adjusted and modified more frequently due to changing conditions in students with TBI.

Students with TBI who recover adequate intellectual functioning but who continue to exhibit difficulties in learning may resemble students with learning disabilities in some respects. Students may continue to change neurologically, even months after their readmission to school. Achievement test scores may be misleading because they may reflect knowledge or skills acquired prior to the injury. Further, psychosocial problems may emerge as a consequence of coping with the challenges associated with TBI. Unpredictable difficulty could occur even years after the injury if parts of the brain were injured that are needed for later maturation (Best, 2010b).

EPILEPSY A seizure occurs when abnormal electrical energy is released in the brain that can cause a loss of consciousness and lack of motor control. The effects can be minimal or severe, depending on the amount of energy released and the number of brain cells affected. The precise cause of epilepsy is not well understood (Heller & Cohen, 2009), but some cases are due to brain damage from physical trauma or infections.

Any child may have a seizure. Individuals may experience a single seizure associated with a head injury or high fever and never have one again. Repeated seizures are indicative of epilepsy. About half of those with seizure disorders also have intellectual disabilities. No matter what the physical condition that leads to a seizure, be aware that seizures vary in duration, frequency, onset, associated movements, and causes, and individuals with seizures may have varying associated disabilities and levels of control during seizure events.

Seizure disorders can be treated with antiepileptic medications, special diets, vagus nerve stimulation, and surgery (Heller & Cohen, 2009). Because of the chance of body injury or brain damage, it is wise to learn about the correct handling of seizures and to educate all students about seizures and their treatment. Some suggestions are provided later in the chapter.

ARTHRITIS Arthritis is a disease in which the muscles and joints are affected. Juvenile rheumatoid arthritis is chronic arthritis present in an individual before the age of 16. Arthritis can be painful and can severely impede mobility. Treatments are directed toward relieving pain, increasing function, and avoiding further deterioration and include heat–cold therapy, massage, electrical stimulation, and exercise, such as aquatic movement, under the supervision of a physical or occupational therapist. However, at present, no known cause or cure exists (Heller & Avant, 2009). Because mobility may be hindered, some children with severe arthritis use canes or braces while walking. Be aware that these students will have good days and bad days, and build in extra rest periods during more painful days. Students may experience great difficulty trying to grip a pencil. Writing may be extremely tedious and painful. Reduce writing demands by allowing students to use audio recorders, speech-to-text features on electronic devices, or other students as scribes. Provide extended time for written assignments.

ASTHMA AND ALLERGIES Asthma is associated with breathing difficulties due to sensitivity to airborne particles and can be exacerbated during exercise. Children with severe asthma often require restricted athletic activities and may need to be reminded to take appropriate medication (Best, 2010a). Physicians can provide relevant information on particular adaptations for individual cases.

Allergies are conditions in which elements in the environment cause allergic reactions in some individuals. Exposure to pollens, molds, dusts, animal dander, and carpet fibers can cause reactions such as congestion in the nose, chest, and eyes. Allergic reactions to certain foods, such as milk, fish, or peanuts, can cause skin rashes and more serious mouth and throat reactions. Still other reactions are caused by insect bites, such as honeybee stings, and can result in anaphylactic shock, a condition that can be fatal if not treated immediately (Best, 2010a). Many individuals who know they have these conditions carry emergency kits with them.

Be sure to have plans in place for dealing with such medical emergencies, including the quickest ways to seek medical assistance.

Know which of your students have asthma and allergies, the associated allergens, the preventative medications, first aid, and the specific nature of the allergic reactions. In some cases, it may be necessary to maintain an environment that is free of dust and animal dander to avoid allergic reactions. In other cases, teachers or other school staff can monitor food consumption during lunchtime and class parties (Best, 2010a).

DIABETES   Diabetes is an inherited condition in which sugar is not metabolized correctly due to insufficient production of insulin in the pancreas (Heller, 2009). Individuals with diabetes have strict diets and special schedules for administering medication that need close monitoring. Learn the warning signs of diabetic shock, and be ready to administer first aid (Best, 2010a). The school nurse can usually provide relevant information for classroom teachers, who can then share the information with all students. Monitor dietary needs during the school day for students with diabetes (or create a plan for an aide to do so), especially if extra food or physical activities are added to the regular schedule. Careful planning with the family and other health-care providers is necessary to ensure safety during daily class activities, especially for special events such as field trips or overnight trips.

FETAL ALCOHOL SYNDROME   Fetal alcohol syndrome (FAS) results when pregnant mothers consume alcohol, which damages the developing fetus (Jones, Smith, Ulleland, & Streissguth, 1973). This places a child at risk for a variety of developmental disabilities, including intellectual disability, learning disabilities, and physical disabilities, in addition to problems with attention and impulsivity (Polloway, Patton, & Nelson, 2011). Exposure to substances during the first trimester is likely to cause neurological and structural damage to the developing fetus (Briggs, 2001). Effective service delivery for infants born under these conditions comes from personnel from health, social services, mental health, children's services, education, and drug and alcohol programs, who must collaborate to work effectively with the family.

ACQUIRED IMMUNE DEFICIENCY SYNDROME   Acquired immune deficiency syndrome (AIDS) is caused by the human immunodeficiency virus (HIV), which destroys a type of white blood cell, weakening the immune system. HIV can be transmitted to an unborn fetus during pregnancy, or during childbirth to an infant, or through infected breast milk during nursing. Other sources of transmission include sexual activity and blood exposure through, for example, shared needles in intravenous drug use or transfusions of contaminated blood (although this occurred most frequently prior to 1984, when blood screening was initiated). HIV is not spread by casual contact. Children with AIDS may have coexisting characteristics such as developmental delay, cognitive disabilities, and any of a number of physical or health conditions, including problems with respiratory, cardiovascular, motor, or kidney functioning (Best & Heller, 2009).

Recently developed combination therapies, known as highly active antiretroviral therapy (HAART), have proven very effective in reducing HIV/AIDS symptoms and have even restored the functioning of the immune system. However, HAART does not eliminate the infection. Improved preventative treatments have also significantly reduced the transmission of HIV from mother to child (Best & Heller, 2009).

STRATEGIES FOR

MAKING CLASSROOM ADAPTATIONS FOR STUDENTS WITH PHYSICAL DISABILITIES AND OTHER HEALTH IMPAIRMENTS

Although each individual and disability area may require specific adaptations, the following general guidelines can help you develop adaptations for differentiating instruction for individuals with physical and other health impairments (see also Best, Heller, & Bigge, 2010).

PREPARE THE CLASS   Prepare the class for students with disabilities who are about to enter the class. Describe the students' special needs and the roles of classroom peers in supporting the inclusive classroom. One way to enhance disability awareness in students is by using classroom simulation activities and providing demonstrations of adaptive devices. For example, allowing students to try out wheelchairs or use walkers, braces, or canes may enable them to appreciate the challenges encountered in simple tasks such as getting a drink from a water

MyEdLab:
Video Example 4.4.
In this video, you will meet Oscar, a student with a severe physical disability. Watch for the classroom modifications made for Oscar.

fountain or getting to and from the playground. Discussions with all students following simulation activities can help increase their awareness of the frustrations that may be encountered by students with disabilities. Although disability simulations are not without some controversy and may not always improve attitudes significantly (Flower, Burns, & Bottesford-Miller, 2007), such activities may provide students with some insights into the challenges faced by individuals with disabilities and the need for adaptations (Ison et al., 2010).

Puppet shows, such as "Kids on the Block" (http://kotbom.org), have also been used to educate younger children about different types of disabilities and to help dispel fears, myths, and misconceptions about persons with disabilities. Dunst (2014) reviewed research on use of such puppet shows and concluded that they had generally been effective in improving attitudes and knowledge toward individuals with disabilities.

MONITOR MEDICAL GUIDELINES Medical needs are of primary concern. Devise checklists containing reminder steps for general class and emergency procedures specific to the medical conditions of students. For example, a medical checklist could include items such as the following: check medication schedule, monitor medication effects and side effects, monitor first-aid and emergency procedures, and communicate with parents. Maintain careful records of student behavior (such as lethargy or fatigue), and communicate clearly any changes in your students' behavior.

Be Aware of Medications An awareness of the types of medications, specific uses, and potential side effects is necessary. Careful monitoring of students' behaviors while on and off medication (for example, with observational records) can provide valuable educational insights for teachers, parents, and prescribing physicians.

A school nurse or other designated school official distributes medications to students from a centralized location in the school, usually the nurse's office. Be sure that students obtain their medication at the scheduled times and that they ingest the medication when administered. Some students feign taking their medication and attempt to give or sell it to others. This is a serious problem that can become troublesome or dangerous if not monitored closely.

Plan for Fatigue Students with physical disabilities or other health impairments, such as traumatic brain injury and muscular dystrophy, may tire more easily than other students. If so, schedule frequent rest breaks throughout a day, prioritize daily schedules, and schedule break periods in the nurse's office if needed. If students lack the strength to carry necessary materials from class to class and to and from school, obtain duplicate sets of books and materials. Some students may require a shortened school day while they recuperate from illnesses. Reduce assignments, prioritize to ensure that students receive the most critical information, and assign peers to share class notes and materials.

Establish Emergency Procedures All classes containing students with physical and other health impairments may require specialized classroom procedures for emergencies such as fire or tornadoes. For example, assistance may be required to move adaptive equipment along with the student. Also, depending on the position of the individual in the class when the emergency alarm sounds, students may need assistance into their wheelchairs, braces, or other adaptive mobility devices. During fire drills, students often proceed to an athletic field adjacent to the school, and mobility across the uneven grass may be especially difficult for some students with physical disabilities. Others tire easily and cannot walk quickly enough to maintain the speed of evacuation with the rest of the class.

Pair students with and without disabilities for evacuation efforts during emergencies. It may be helpful to have more than one student assigned to assist each student with disabilities. You can add the names of peer assistants to the overall listing of procedures on your "emergency chart." Be prepared: outline emergency procedures in advance, and practice them many times so that if an actual emergency situation occurs, all students are well prepared for any evacuation procedures.

Plan for Seizures Know which of your students are likely to have seizures and what first-aid treatment is appropriate. Have an established emergency plan which includes contacting the school office immediately, implementing procedures for supporting the student with a seizure, and reassuring the rest of the class. Because seizures range in severity from very minor to very intense and severe, consult your student's family and physician for precise medical treatment. If a seizure does occur, stay calm. You are a model for your students, and if you stay calm, so will they. Help the student to the floor. Gently tilt the head to the side so that the child does not choke. In any seizure, do not attempt to restrain the movements of the individual or place anything in between the teeth or in the mouth of the affected person. Clear all harmful objects out of the way, and place a blanket or pillow under the student's head to minimize the potential for injury.

Try to remember all of the distinctive features associated with the seizure to record on monitoring sheets and share with parents and attending physicians later. Record the date and time of the seizure as well as the behavior exhibited before, during, and after the seizure. Note the student's and peer reactions to the seizure and any other information that seems relevant. If it is the student's first seizure, have the office or school nurse contact a physician and the parents immediately. Moreover, if seizures persist for more than 5 minutes, immediate medical attention should be sought. Notify parents when seizures have occurred (Best & Bigge, 2010).

Learn how to handle a student who has just recovered from a seizure. Some students may feel tired and disoriented after a seizure and may want to lie down and rest. Others may feel fine and simply want to continue with the class activity. Still others may feel embarrassed and may need time outside of the class to regain self-control and self-respect. It is also important to re-direct the attention of peers away from the student who had the seizure. The individual having a seizure should not be made to feel self-conscious. Do anything necessary to make the student feel comfortable. Provide all students with relevant information about seizures and proper ways of handling situations emotionally during and after seizures (Best & Bigge, 2010).

Moving and Positioning Students   Determine what special procedures are required for moving, lifting, or transferring body positions of students with special needs. Some students—for example, those with brittle bone disease (osteogenesis imperfecta)—should be lifted only by people with specialized knowledge about how to lift and position the individual. Physical therapists, who often work directly with these students, can provide valuable information to you and your students.

Find out whether students feel more comfortable in some positions than others. Periodically check their positions throughout the school day. Some types of positioning devices, such as braces and wedges, help improve personal comfort, control muscle movements, and position students to more easily communicate or complete schoolwork. Figure 4.3 shows examples of positioning devices.

Adapt for Chronic Medical Conditions   If students in your class have chronic medical conditions, you should know how to accommodate them. Consult with medical personnel to learn to recognize the signs and symptoms of relevant medical problems and any modifications you can make. Limiting physical activity, administering medications, providing diet and fluid supplements as needed, and providing easy access to bathrooms are common modifications, depending on the condition.

Dealing with Terminal Illness   Health-care and mental health professionals are good sources of information about dealing with terminally ill students, as are the students' parents. Ask how you should interact with the terminally ill student and the student's classmates.

1.   2.   3.

Figure 4.3   Alternatives to Allow Change of Position Throughout the Day: (1) Sidleyer, (2) Wedge, (3) Tricycle with Built-Up Back and Pedals (Adult Three-Wheeled Bikes Are Available for Older Children)
Note: From *Teaching individuals with physical or multiple disabilities* (p. 198), by S. J. Best, K. W. Heller, and J. L. Bigge, 2005, Upper Saddle River, NJ: Merrill/Prentice Hall. Reprinted by permission.

In many cases, school may be the most "normal" component of their lives, and students may appreciate the distraction provided by educational activities. If the student dies, request assistance from the school's crisis intervention team and mental health professionals. Different individuals may react to death in different ways; teachers should share their own personal feelings and reactions with the class (Best, 2009). Mental health professionals can sometimes provide extra guidance and counseling sessions to small groups of students to address their questions about interacting with a terminally ill student.

ADAPT THE PHYSICAL ENVIRONMENT Arrange the classroom to meet the mobility requirements of students with physical disabilities. Provide sufficiently wide aisles to accommodate wheelchairs, walkers, three-wheel motorized wheelchairs, crutches, canes, braces, or other adaptive devices. Most wheelchairs require passages at least 32 inches wide for one wheelchair to pass. Keep aisles clear of debris and monitor regularly to ensure that no books, book bags, backpacks, toys, or other objects impede mobility. Verify that the height of doorknobs, water fountains, sinks, and cabinets is accessible for students with physical disabilities. If not, perhaps minor adaptations can be made to ensure equal accessibility.

Examine the type of flooring in your classroom with respect to whether carpeting or tile is used and the extent to which surfaces either facilitate or impede the mobility of individuals with physical disabilities. For example, carpeted floors can decrease slippage, but they may also impede the mobility of some adaptive devices. Conversely, tile surfaces may be dangerously slippery, especially after washing and waxing.

ADAPT INSTRUCTIONAL MATERIALS Commercially available materials include communication boards, computers to assist with voice synthesizer production, specially designed hand grippers, head pointers, keyboards, touchscreens to assist with computer usage, and speech-reading or word-prediction software to minimize difficulty producing output for assignments. Other adaptive devices include flap switches and reaches that can be added to pencils or dowels to extend the grasp of individuals and are available from suppliers such as the Prentke Romich Company.

The pages of electronic books can be turned easily with a light touch on the edge of the page. Some teachers assist students with fine motor difficulties in turning book pages by placing double-sided foam tape or cardboard between the pages. Tongue depressors can also serve as handles for turning pages. A book stand can be designed to hold instructional materials at an appropriate height and distance for easy viewing for students with restricted mobility. Choose books that are larger and easier to manipulate. Anchor materials in place by using clipboards or magnets to help stabilize papers (see Best, Reed, & Bigge, 2010).

Enlarge the gripping area of pencils by attaching spongelike material, plastic tubing, or plastic golf balls around pencils and pens. Use felt-tip pens, which require less pressure than some other writing tools. Specialized rubber stamps with large handles that contain commonly written items, such as names, *yes, no, restroom,* and *hungry,* also can help students communicate, as can communication boards.

Larger paper with extra space between lines helps accommodate writing needs for some students. When class activities involve charting or graphing, provide larger graphs, stickers, or magnets for students to place on graphs rather than using smaller paper-and-pencil versions. Felt boards and pieces of felt are easier for some students to manipulate. Place vocabulary words or other content inside clear picture photograph cubes. Put clear plastic folders or sheet protectors on paper handouts. These are easier to grip than a single sheet of paper and can be held together with a clip. The coating also protects the papers from spills. Use calculators with large numbers that are easier to touch and read. Speech-recognition functions on tablets such as the iPad may also facilitate writing.

Stabilize instructional materials with Velcro. Slatted trays or trays with built-in dividers can be used to hold small objects that need to be manipulated during activities. Place a detachable bag or backpack onto the wheelchair for carrying books and other materials. Notes or recorded messages to parents can be placed in the bag before students leave school. Often, simple modifications such as these can allow students with physical disabilities to participate more independently (Best et al., 2010).

Some students with physical disabilities may also have the assistance of an animal, such as a service dog, that is specially trained to perform such actions as pulling a wheelchair, retrieving small objects, or opening doors, and that accompanies the students throughout the school day. Teachers need to know how they and their students in the class and throughout the school should interact with the animal. Usually, no one is allowed to pet or interact with the animal other than the individual with disabilities. The student's family can provide detailed information on how to interact appropriately with service animals (Best et al., 2010).

ADAPT INSTRUCTION   Schedule extra reading, studying, and instructional support time when needed. Students who have difficulty speaking require extra time to respond to teacher questions. When calling on an individual during class discussions, provide sufficient wait time, and make students feel comfortable and not rushed while responding.

Instruction can be adapted, with respect to individual needs, in all academic areas, including literacy, math, and academic content areas, as well as vocational education. Refer to the relevant chapters throughout this text when planning instruction for students with physical disabilities and other health impairments.

Consider assigning a peer assistant to work with individuals with physical disabilities or health impairments. Peer assistants can enable the student to be a more active participant during class activities. In some cases, paraprofessionals are assigned to accompany students throughout the school day. Work closely with paraprofessionals to design effective modifications.

ADAPT ASSESSMENT METHODS   Testing and assessment modifications are necessary for students with physical disabilities and other health impairments. Because many of these students have difficulty reading and writing independently, schedule their tests when a special education teacher, paraprofessional, aide, peer assistant, or tutor can read the test items and record responses. Students can use communication boards during testing situations, and helpers can record responses as students point to answers on response sheets. These individualized sessions may require more time than the regularly scheduled time slots for exams. See also the Assessment chapter 12 for additional suggestions.

MyEdLab: **Self-Check 4.2**

MyEdLab: **Application Exercise 4.2: Physical Disabilities and Other Health Impairments**

Severe and Multiple Disabilities

PREVALENCE, DEFINITIONS, AND CHARACTERISTICS OF SEVERE AND MULTIPLE DISABILITIES

Many individuals with severe disabilities have severe and profound mental retardation/intellectual disability. Some individuals with moderate intellectual disability may also be included in this group (Bruce, 2011). Individuals with severe impairments may have several coexisting disabilities (e.g., sensory or physical disabilities). Moderate intellectual disability has been classified according to an IQ test score continuum of 35 to 54, severe intellectual disability is represented by scores between 20 and 34, and profound intellectual disability is classified as any score less than 20 (Jacobson & Mulick, 1996). The American Association on Intellectual and Developmental Disabilities (AAIDD, 2010; Schalock et al., 2010) supports a classification system for intellectual disabilities based on the level of support needed, with severe and profound intellectual disability requiring more extensive and pervasive support. The American Psychiatric Association (2013) has similarly placed less emphasis on psychometric IQ and maintained that IQ scores are less valid at these lower levels. Individuals with moderate, severe, and profound intellectual disability represent approximately 15% of all individuals with intellectual disabilities, or approximately 0.09% of the school-age population and 1.1% of the students served under IDEA, as estimated from U.S. Department of Education (2015) data. Just as with other disability categories, individuals with severe disabilities are a heterogeneous group, with much variability in strengths and weaknesses, abilities, and personal characteristics (Westling et al., 2015).

Multiple disabilities refers to the presence of two or more impairments that significantly influence an individual's ability to learn and function without adaptations and that cannot be accommodated in special education programs devoted to only one of the impairments.

A major disability with minor impairments or secondary conditions is not considered multiple disabilities; at least two separate categories of impairment must be present (Best, 2010c). The only exception to this is deaf-blindness, which is a separate category of disability under IDEA. Students with multiple disabilities represent approximately 0.2% of the school-age population and approximately 2.1% of the students served under IDEA (U.S. Department of Education, 2015).

EDUCATIONAL PLACEMENT CONSIDERATIONS   The optimal educational placement and the design of effective instruction for students with severe and multiple disabilities are usually determined by the case conference team. The priorities vary depending on the age, severity level, and needs of the individual. Priorities come from family, medical, school, leisure, transitional, vocational, and peer-support concern areas and are designed to match each student's needs and strengths.

Students with severe and multiple disabilities generally have severe cognitive and adaptive behavior difficulties and require instruction in self-help skills, communication skills, functional academic skills, daily living skills, and community awareness, as well as recreation, social, and vocational education skills. These students benefit greatly from positive social interactions with their general education peers. The creation of peer-support networks, friendship circles, and social circles and participation in after-school activities are strongly advocated for individuals with severe disabilities (Westling, Fox, & Carter, 2015).

Some have suggested that instruction for students with severe disabilities should focus primarily on essential life skills (Ayres, Lowrey, Douglas, & Sievers, 2011). Conversely, Browder and colleagues described reasons for providing students with severe disabilities access to the general education curriculum and the Common Core State Standards (CCSS) (Browder, 2015; Courtade, Spooner, Browder, & Jimenez, 2012). Browder and her colleagues argued that students with severe disabilities have the right to full educational opportunities, including increased expectations. Since the adoption of the CCSS, all students have a right to preparation for the real-life demands of adulthood. Browder also argued that the potential of students with severe disabilities in this area is unknown because they have historically been denied access to the general education curriculum; therefore, it is appropriate that they are included in these new standards. Finally, she pointed out that life skills and academic skills are not mutually exclusive and can be taught concurrently, and as students learn, expectations will change.

STRATEGIES FOR
MAKING CLASSROOM ADAPTATIONS FOR STUDENTS WITH SEVERE AND MULTIPLE DISABILITIES

Because of the nature of severe and multiple disabilities, most students require special education and related services from many educational team members, including physical therapists, occupational therapists, speech and language therapists, adaptive physical education specialists, special educators, and paraprofessionals. Establish good working relationships with these partners, and arrange the classroom for easy access by these specialists. Specialists may include their activities along with general education instruction. For example, specialists can assist with positioning and grasping techniques during classes involving art activities or computer applications. Arrange a special place in the classroom for specialists to work with the students with severe disabilities within the general education classroom. This should be done in a way that neither draws unnecessary attention to students with severe disabilities nor distracts the rest of the class. The *Research Highlight* describes a peer-support project in secondary classes. The *Diversity in the Classroom* feature describes a comprehensive model for supporting diverse families.

ESTABLISH GOOD WORKING RELATIONSHIPS WITH PARAPROFESSIONALS
Paraprofessionals (or paraeducators) are often assigned to accompany students with severe disabilities for the entire school day. This means general education teachers would have another adult in the classroom whenever the student with severe disabilities is present. Because many teachers are used to being alone in their classrooms, having another adult in their room while teaching may require some adjustment. However, the benefits can outweigh the disadvantages because paraprofessionals can assist in many instructional and administrative responsibilities,

Peer Support for Adolescents with Disabilities

Carter, Moss, Hoffman, Chung, and Sisco (2011) examined how peers could assist in supporting students with severe disabilities in accessing social and academic experiences in inclusive classes. They hypothesized that students with severe disabilities and their general education peer assistants might profit from a peer-assistance arrangement in their general education classes. Findings revealed that social interactions involving both academic and social topics increased between students and their peer assistants. Carter and his colleagues (Hochman, Carter, Bottema-Beutel, Harvey, & Gustafson, 2015) extended that research to include peer networks to work with high school students with both autism spectrum disorders (ASD) and intellectual disabilities (ID) in order to increase their social connections in school.

Four high school students with ASD and ID ranging from 9th to 11th grade with a range of classes and functioning levels, 3 adult facilitators (one special educator and two paraprofessionals), and 11 general education peers participated. During the baseline preintervention condition, data were collected during the lunch period. Peer assistants and other general education students were present in the room but did not directly interact with the students with disabilities, although some interaction was observed (e.g., greetings).

Facilitators were given orientation meetings, a peer network manual, and a 10-item checklist to be used during weekly meetings that included questions such as, "Were focus students and partners present?" and "Were shared interests identified or suggestions for when social interactions might happen?" Selected peers—who were nominated by teachers based on dependability, good social skills, friendship skills, and expressed interest in students with disabilities—also participated in orientation meetings to (a) understand the goals of the peer networks, (b) learn about others in the program, (c) generate ways to improve social interactions, and (d) become familiar with the roles and responsibilities, including confidentiality and attendance at weekly meetings. More specific activities were included in weekly network meetings during which target students and peers had time to eat, play board games or engage in other shared activities, converse about upcoming school and sporting events and spring break, and report any social interactions that occurred outside of weekly meetings.

Findings revealed that peer interactions and social engagements for students with ASD and ID increased. Peers indicated that their partners interacted more socially both within the network meetings and outside of meetings, such as in the school lunch room and hallways. Students with disabilities described their network peers as their friends with whom they wanted to maintain contact. The authors concluded that a major barrier to social interactions between the two groups of students might have been the lack of opportunity during the school day.

QUESTIONS FOR REFLECTION

1. Why do you think students with disabilities increased in interactions and social engagement?
2. Why do you think the weekly peer network meetings facilitated social interactions with the students with disabilities?
3. What implications are associated with the results of this study?
4. What other extensions of this study could be conducted?

as well as self-help care (Carroll, 2001; Giangreco, Doyle, & Suter, 2014). Such assistance might include the following:

- Adapting materials under the direction of the teacher or special education teacher
- Administering tests individually to students with severe disabilities
- Reviewing and practicing materials already covered in class
- Presenting adapted materials to students
- Taking notes for students
- Assisting teachers during a class presentation
- Promoting peer cooperation during class
- Helping to arrange the classroom environment to accommodate activity needs
- Grading papers and assisting with recordkeeping

Diversity in the Classroom

Supporting Diverse Families: The Comprehensive Support Model

Students with disabilities and their families from diverse cultures are confronted with numerous challenges. Halgunseth, Peterson, Stark, and Moodie (2009) provide recommendations for increasing family involvement for all families, including diverse families. One model, the Comprehensive Support Model (CSM), is intended to provide better services for students with exceptionalities and their diverse families (Obiakor, Utley, Smith, & Harris-Obiakor, 2002). CSM is based on the model educational services used in the African village, which values all parts of society. That is, the student, family, school, community, and government work together to solve educational problems. Five interacting components are important for effective implementation of CSM.

First, CSM assumes students will have active roles in the planning, self-responsibility for, and implementation of their educational programs. Students are encouraged to be motivated and active participants in school. Second, CSM acknowledges that families are important members who provide critical linkages between home and school. Families are encouraged to participate in activities during and after school hours. Third, CSM recognizes that school personnel are important, as they can provide understanding and valuing of diverse cultures and help to infuse culturally responsive instruction in classes. Schools can be catalysts for organizing programs for all teachers on culturally responsive practices. Programs can provide assistance on using culturally appropriate assessments and promotion of self-concept for students from all cultures. Fourth, CSM acknowledges that the community contains numerous untapped resources to enhance the education of all students. Some of these resources of the entire community include clergy from all religions, community leaders, and members of the various neighborhoods. Community members can serve as mentors and role models for students. Finally, local, state, and federal governments play important roles in CSM. Governments provide funding for school programs and provide guidance to assure protection of rights for all students with disabilities from diverse cultures. When all components of CSM are working together, students with disabilities from diverse cultures and their families will have greater opportunities for success (see also Harry, 2008; Turnbull, Turnbull, Erwin, Soodak, & Shogren, 2015).

- Assisting with duplicating or laminating class materials
- Attending case conferences or team meetings as necessary
- Assisting with feeding and toileting
- Assisting with dressing before and after recess
- Supervising during recess
- Assisting with mobility during class-changing time periods, including going to lunch and before and after school

Use strategies to promote positive interactions with paraprofessionals. Also, be careful that paraprofessionals assist students with disabilities when needed without preventing their access to other students or teachers. Be certain the student is able to interact with the teacher and other students as much as possible (Giangreco & Broer, 2007; Giangreco, Broer, & Suter, 2011).

INCREASE DISABILITY AWARENESS   Prepare your students for the arrival of a student with severe or multiple disabilities. Information regarding the strengths and needs of the individuals can be conveyed using a variety of formats to promote students' awareness of disability-related issues. One method of presenting information is to have guest speakers present information on specific disability-related issues pertaining to the student who will be included within the class. Special education teachers, parents of students with disabilities, speech–language therapists, physicians, school psychologists, or local disability organizations such as the Council for Exceptional Children (CEC) or the ARC can present relevant information.

MyEdLab:
Video Example 4.5.

Watch this video with several examples of paraprofessionals working on a range of tasks with different students for an idea of the importance of their role in the classroom.

Paula, a first-grade teacher, described how her students began to express their natural curiosity about "Lisa," and she used their curiosity to provide a teaching moment:

> One of the advantages of teaching first grade is that the children are totally honest. After about a week of having Lisa with us and watching her communicate with sign language, and using her book with symbols, the children began to ask questions about how Lisa was learning. We seized the moment and began answering questions about Lisa. They were so concerned and interested in their fellow classmate. How did she learn, can she see them (she tends to hold her head sideways and be involved in her own world), would she ever go to college, could they help her learn, could they learn to talk with her, and where did she go when she was not with us? I listened to their questions with tears in my eyes as I realized they had a genuine interest in her and wanted to be a part of her learning experience. Aren't children wonderful with their nonjudgmental behavior!

CONCEPTUALIZE INCLUSIVE INSTRUCTION Several authors have suggested a variety of ways to begin to conceptualize the inclusion of students with severe disabilities into general education classes (Brown, McDonnell, & Snell, 2016; Westling et al., 2015). These include the following:

- Focus on activities that can be engaged in by all students, without modification, such as homeroom or music class.

- Use *multilevel curriculum instruction*, or **differentiated instruction**, such as having a student in a wheelchair work on control of different muscles while the rest of the class does exercises on floor mats during physical education class. Students' learning goals are within the same subject, but they differ in difficulty or specific application.

- Engage in *curriculum overlapping*, for example, having the student work on communication skills in the context of working on another academic area, such as mathematics. In curriculum overlapping, the subject area may differ, but students share similar activities.

MONITOR SPECIAL HEALTH-CARE NEEDS Many students with severe disabilities have coexisting medical needs and require special health-care adaptations and accommodations. Some students may be medically fragile, have infectious diseases, or simply have coexisting severe medical needs.

Consider writing daily health-care plans for individuals with severe medical needs. Health-care plans, written with input from the student's health-care provider, can detail information pertaining to the condition itself, restrictions in activities or precautions to be considered, the independence of the student in health care, medication schedules, whether students can recognize signs or symptoms of their own disorders, toileting schedules, and emergency plans for medical or other emergency situations (such as procedures for contacting medical assistance and parental notification).

Some students need assistance from medical technology, such as respirator support, intravenous or nutritional support, alternative bowel and bladder assistance, breathing support with the use of ventilators, suctioning to remove mucus (especially for those with tracheostomies), and continuous feedings provided by pumps. The establishment of good, open lines of communication with health-care professionals and parents will enable general education teachers to better accommodate individuals requiring such assistance in their classes (Best et al., 2010).

ADAPT MATERIALS AND THE PHYSICAL ENVIRONMENT Students with severe disabilities may have coexisting physical disabilities. In these cases, adaptations to the physical environment and instructional materials—such as those detailed earlier in the section on students with physical disabilities—will be required.

In addition, many of the adaptations described for use with students with intellectual disabilities in Chapter 3 may be beneficial. Prioritize the educational and social objectives for the time spent in the general education class. Once the goals are prioritized, you will be in a better position to design and implement any necessary adaptations.

Primary adaptations for students with severe and multiple disabilities may involve devising procedures for communication systems (including ACC devices), handling instructional materials, allowing additional time to complete activities, and devising activities that are instructionally relevant and meaningful for students.

Work closely with the special education teacher to develop an appropriate and effective manner of interacting with students with severe disabilities. Because many students with severe disabilities have limited language skills, make certain that all your communications are clear and understandable.

Students with severe disabilities may be learning different things than other students in the classroom and therefore will have different learning objectives. Make certain that you are familiar with all the IEP objectives for students with severe (or any other) disabilities. All objectives should be stated in a way that progress can be directly observed and recorded. For example, if one of a student's objectives involves interacting more positively with other students, be certain you know exactly what is meant by *positive interaction* (e.g., more direct eye contact, friendly expression, positive statements or gestures), and monitor progress on this objective (Brown et al., 2016).

ADAPT ASSESSMENT METHODS   Students with severe and multiple disabilities may require different assessment methods than other students. A variety of assessment methods may be appropriate to determine achievement and chart progress. Use curriculum-based assessment, monitor progress on specific personal objectives toward predetermined goals and objectives, use alternative state assessments, and utilize portfolio assessments, as described in Chapter 12.

MyEdLab: **Self-Check 4.3**

MyEdLab: **Application Exercise 4.3: Severe and Multiple Disabilities**

Visual Impairments

PREVALENCE, DEFINITIONS, AND CHARACTERISTICS OF VISUAL IMPAIRMENTS

Individuals with visual impairments make up one of the smallest disability areas, approximately 0.05% of the school-age population and 0.4% of the students served under IDEA (U.S. Department of Education, 2015). Visual impairments range from mild to moderate to severe, and both legal and educational definitions exist. The legal definition includes acuity assessment information, and the educational definition is linked to learning to read. Individuals are classified as legally blind if their **visual acuity** is 20/200 or less, even with corrective lenses, and partially sighted if their visual acuity is 20/70. This means that a person who is legally blind can see something at 20 feet that a person with normal vision can see at 200 feet, and a person who is partially sighted can see something at 20 feet that a person with normal vision can see at 70 feet. Legal classification qualifies individuals for tax advantages and some other legal benefits (Zimmerman & Zebehazy, 2011).

Educational definitions are based more on the method necessary for learning to read. For example, many individuals classified as legally blind have some vision and can learn to read using enlarged print. These students are often referred to as students with low vision. Other individuals have such limited vision that they are referred to as totally blind and learn to read using the **braille** system (raised dots that are read with fingertips) or by ear using audio recordings. The federal definition is "an impairment in vision that even with correction, adversely affects a child's educational performance. The term includes both partial sight and blindness" (Definitions; Child with a Disability; Specific Learning Disability, 2004; U.S. Department of Education, 2006).

Visual impairments can be present at birth or acquired later in life. Common causes of visual impairments include **glaucoma** (excessive pressure on the eyeball), **cataracts** (clouding of the lens), **diabetic retinopathy** (lack of blood to the retina), **coloboma** (parts of the retina are improperly formed), **retinitis pigmentosa** (degeneration of the retina), and **retinopathy of prematurity** (caused by excessive oxygen given to premature infants). Muscle-functioning disorders of the eye, such as strabismus (crossed eyes) and nystagmus (rapid involuntary eye movements), also may result in visual impairments.

Individuals with visual impairments can have one or more of a wide range of disabilities, from mild to severe. A common characteristic is delayed language development due to the restriction of visual experiences. Students with severe visual impairments may rely on the tactile and auditory senses rather than the visual sense (Zimmerman & Zebehazy, 2011). These students need to hold and feel three-dimensional objects to obtain a sense of their characteristics. Because these students may miss opportunities for learning incidentally from seeing everything in their environment, it is necessary to present this information in alternative formats.

Some students with visual impairments engage in such repetitive behavior as head weaving or body rocking. These are known as stereotypic behaviors and are not harmful, but they can attract unwanted or negative attention. Stereotypic behaviors are sometimes addressed by reinforcement, self-monitoring, or physical prompts (Zimmerman & Zebehazy, 2011).

Mobility skills vary among individuals with visual impairments depending on the age of onset, degree of severity, and the individual's spatial ability. Spatial ability appears to affect the mobility access of individuals with visual impairments. Some individuals with visual impairments learn to walk with canes, although the training can be lengthy and difficult. Some canes have light sensors near the tip that emit sounds when the amount of light changes, indicating shadows or objects in the path ahead. Some individuals walk with human guides and guide dogs, although the latter are not as often seen with children (Davis, 2003).

STRATEGIES FOR

MAKING CLASSROOM ADAPTATIONS FOR STUDENTS WITH VISUAL IMPAIRMENTS

First, ensure that your classroom has clear, open walkways. Devise and teach classroom procedures for responding to emergency situations, including fire and tornado drills. Assign peers to assist students with visual impairments during emergency evacuations. Develop safety guidelines for using objects that are potentially harmful to students with visual impairments.

Following are strategies you can use to differentiate instruction to make your classroom more inclusive for students with visual impairments (see also Best et al., 2010; Zimmerman & Zebehazy, 2011).

ADAPT THE PHYSICAL ENVIRONMENT Keep aisles clear, wide, and open. Familiarize students with the physical arrangement of the room, and notify students if any changes are made. Extra space will be necessary to accommodate equipment for braille and reading enlarged-print materials.

ADAPT INSTRUCTIONAL MATERIALS Enlarge and enhance printed materials, including dramatically increasing the size of fonts. Increase the visibility of materials, which might include the use of bold-lined paper, special lighting, and magnification lenses. Certain technology may be used, such as projection microscopes, closed-circuit television, scanners, and equipment to convert print and other images to tactile formats (Best et al., 2010). Convert print to braille formats with the Perkins brailler or specialized computer programs such as *Duxbury* (Duxbury Systems). Figure 4.4 shows examples of braille. Use oral-output devices, which produce speech, to enable students with visual impairments to participate in the same activities as their peers. These include the *Jaws* screen reader (Freedom Scientific) and *Kurzweil 1000* (Kurzweil Education). Use descriptive video services, provided on many public television broadcasts, to provide additional verbal descriptions of visual events. Use tactile and three-dimensional models to enhance conceptual understanding.

ADAPT INSTRUCTION Be explicit when giving oral presentations. Avoid vague phrases such as *over here, almost, this,* and *that*, and use specific language such as *above your head, on your right*, and *the beaker in my hand*. Teach and use time orientations such as, "The model is on my desk at 2 o'clock." When walking with students, describe upcoming barriers by saying, for

The six dots of the braille cell are arranged and numbered thus: 1●●4 2●●5 3●●6

The capital sign, dot 6, placed before a letter makes it a capital. The number sign, dots 3, 4, 5, 6, placed before a character, makes it a figure and not a letter.

Figure 4.4 Samples of Braille

Note: Reprinted with permission from the Division for the Blind and Physically Handicapped, Library of Congress, Washington, DC.

example, "We are approaching an uphill ramp." When addressing students with visual impairments, always state their names first, so they know you are speaking to them, and speak in a normal tone of voice.

However you adapt your instruction, provide sufficient time for students with visual impairments to complete class activities. Remember that reading enlarged print and braille takes longer than reading regular print. Check with students to determine the optimal pace at which they are capable of working.

ADAPT ASSESSMENT METHODS   When assessing students with visual impairments, allocate sufficient time for students to complete tests. Extra time is required to transcribe responses from braille to print formats or to use peer assistants. When standardization of the test is not violated, consider individual teacher or paraprofessional administration of tests.

MyEdLab: **Self-Check 4.4**

MyEdLab: **Application Exercise 4.4: Visual Impairments**

Hearing Impairments Including Deafness

PREVALENCE, DEFINITIONS, AND CHARACTERISTICS OF HEARING IMPAIRMENTS

Individuals with hearing impairments make up 0.1% of the school-age population and 1.2% of the students served under IDEA (U.S. Department of Education, 2015). Hearing impairments range in severity from mild to moderate to severe to profound, with the greatest educational distinctions occurring between those who are hard of hearing and those who are deaf. Individuals classified as hard of hearing can hear speech tones when wearing hearing aids, whereas persons who are deaf cannot hear even with hearing aids.

The age at which a child loses hearing affects the degree of language delay and development. Children who are born with deafness have congenital hearing losses (**prelingual**) and more difficulty with language development than those who acquire deafness after age 2 (**postlingual**).

Pure-tone audiometers are used to assess hearing ability. Tones with different pitches (or frequency, measured in Hertz [Hz]) and volume (measured in decibels [dB]) are presented via headphones, and individuals respond (by, e.g., raising their hands or pushing a button) when they hear a sound. Levels of hearing impairment are classified along a continuum, with 0 dB indicating the quietest sound a person with normal hearing can detect. Individuals with slight hearing losses (27–40 dB) may not have difficulty in most school situations. Individuals with mild losses (41–55 dB) may miss up to 50% of classroom discussion if voices are faint or faces cannot be seen. Individuals with moderate losses (56–70 dB) can understand only loud speech and may have limited vocabularies. Individuals with severe losses (71–90 dB) may be able to hear loud voices within 1 foot of the ear, and speech is likely to be impaired. Individuals with profound losses (>90 dB) may hear some loud sounds but are more likely to sense vibrations, and they may rely on vision rather than hearing as a primary vehicle for communication. Specialized tests are needed to accurately assess the cognitive and academic functioning of individuals with hearing impairments (Owens, Metz, & Farinella, 2011).

Causes of hearing impairments include heredity, prenatal infections such as maternal rubella, ear infections, meningitis, head trauma, prematurity, and oxygen deprivation during birth. Impairments can be **conductive**, meaning the outer or middle ear along the passageway is damaged; **sensorineural**, referring to inner-ear damage; or a combination of the two (Andrews, Shaw, & Lomas, 2011).

Many children with hearing impairments have academic and cognitive deficiencies or developmental lags due to difficulties processing language. For example, the average 18-year-old with a hearing impairment can comprehend text at only the fourth-grade level (although many exceptions exist). In many inclusive classes, there may be less interaction between students who are deaf and students who hear normally, perhaps increasing feelings of isolation and loneliness (Andrews et al., 2011).

EDUCATIONAL PROGRAMMING

An ongoing debate exists over what should be considered the best approach for teaching individuals with severe hearing impairments. Some advocate **total communication** (Owens et al., 2011), which involves using speech (lip) reading, gestures, and sign language or both oral and manual methods. Teachers using total communication rely on the structure of the English language and speak while signing during communications with students who are deaf. Some advocate the use of only oral approaches, eliminating any manual components used in total communication. Teachers using only oral approaches rely heavily on parental and family involvement as well as auditory, visual, and tactile methods of presentation. Finally, others advocate using only sign language or manual approaches. These individuals advocate the exclusive use of sign language because they maintain that a unique "culture of the deaf" exists among those who communicate with sign language. They believe that when individuals with hearing impairments are taught only to speech-read or use oral techniques, they are denied full participation in the culture of the deaf (Hamill & Stein, 2011; Owens et al., 2011). Individuals with this perspective argue that they are not disabled but are part of another cultural group composed of individuals who are deaf.

Cochlear implants have in some cases provided more access to sound for many students who are deaf, and many students with cochlear implants have shown progress in oral language and reading. However, family support, resources, maintenance, and speech therapy are needed over time for the success of the implants. Overall effectiveness varies widely among individuals (Andrews et al., 2011).

Several signing systems are in use today, including American Sign Language (ASL), Fingerspelling, and Signing Exact English. All systems use manual signs made with the hands and fingers to represent words, concepts, and ideas. However, they are based on different systems. **American Sign Language** (ASL) is a visual-spatial language and, unlike English, is not phonologically based. Each sign has three parts: hand shape, location, and movement. ASL has its own rules of semantics, syntax, and pragmatics and its own vocabulary (Owens et al., 2011). Fingerspelling involves a manual alphabet of 26 distinct hand positions used to represent each letter in the English alphabet. Fingerspelling is especially appropriate for unfamiliar words such as proper names. Several apps are available to teach Fingerspelling, such as *ASL Finger Spelling* (Michael Bartmess) and *Sign Language Alphabet Trainer* (BidBox, LLC). Some teachers use Fingerspelling while speaking to students with hearing impairments. Signing Exact English is a system that employs components of ASL but attempts to use correct English usage for facilitating the learning of reading and writing skills in English for students who are deaf. No clear research evidence exists to promote one approach over the other in teaching students who are deaf. Therefore, it is likely that this debate will continue into the future.

STRATEGIES FOR

MAKING CLASSROOM ADAPTATIONS FOR STUDENTS WITH HEARING IMPAIRMENTS

Students with hearing impairments can benefit from instruction in general education classes if specific adaptations are made. Specific accommodations vary depending upon the degree of hearing impairment and whether students have interpreters to accompany them throughout the school day. If you have a student with hearing impairments in your class, establish classroom emergency procedures for use during fire and tornado drills. Many fire alarms can be equipped with a light that flashes while the bell rings, alerting students with hearing impairments. Consider assigning a peer assistant who can pass along information that comes from the announcement system and who can be a buddy during any emergency situations. In addition to these guidelines, consider differentiating instruction with the following strategies (see also Marshark, Lang, & Albertini, 2002; Pakulski & Kaderavek, 2002; Stewart & Kluwin, 2001).

ADAPT THE PHYSICAL ENVIRONMENT   Seat students close enough to the front of the class to maximize their hearing and enable them to read speech. They should also be able to turn to face other students while they are speaking. Because hearing aids are especially sound-sensitive, loud or irritating noises should be avoided. Consider choosing a room with carpeting and located away from noisy school areas, such as the cafeteria and gym.

ADAPT INSTRUCTIONAL MATERIALS   Use technology, including hearing aids, television captioning, adapted telephone equipment (TTY), computer-assisted instruction, and the Internet. When appropriate, use frequency-modulation (FM) sound systems, which include cordless microphones for teachers and receivers that attach to hearing aids for students. Pass your microphone to classmates who are speaking in a class discussion so that they can also be heard. Audio enhancement systems using infrared microphones have also been installed in classrooms. Some teachers report that these devices improve the volume and clarity of their speech, for the benefit of all students (Mathews, 2008). Use visuals such as illustrations, diagrams, pictures, and three-dimensional models to introduce vocabulary and concepts and enhance comprehension. Use language cards that contain vocabulary and illustrations of concepts and definitions that can accompany verbal presentations and be used to preteach. Encourage students to maintain personal dictionaries of their language cards.

ADAPT INSTRUCTION   Create authentic experiences by connecting new language and knowledge to real-world experiences in a context relevant to the student's linguistic and experiential background. As you teach, reiterate major points, write out assignments, or write down questions on overhead transparencies or the chalkboard. Give students outlines or closing summaries as handouts. Repeat questions or answers that other students contribute to enable students with hearing impairments to participate fully in class. Sequence steps or procedures on written cards and place them in clear view.

Use hand signals or devise a signaling system to denote transitions, and allow students with hearing impairments or interpreters to review questions, answers, and concepts. Alert students as to when to look or listen, and position yourself so that students with hearing impairments can clearly see your face, without shadowing from backlighting or the reflection of glaring light.

Use a "listen, then look, then listen" sequence of instruction so that students can focus on your face as you speak, then focus on the other aspects of the lesson separately, then focus on your face again. Say, for example, "Now, I'm going to pour the oil in with this water" (listen); then pour the oil (look), then say, "I poured the oil into the water. Who can tell me what happened?" (listen).

Repeat information from the school public address system to ensure students have understood the announcements.

Be sure to plan for interpreters. Interpreters often assist students who are deaf by translating lecture information, tutoring, and assisting special and regular education teachers (Luckner, Slike, & Johnson, 2012). Extra space, including chairs or desks, may be required for interpreters to be near students with hearing impairments. Because interpreters are typically adults and taller than your students, check to see that all children have a clear view of important classroom information. Prepare your students for the interpreter, and clearly explain the roles and functions the interpreter will have while in your classroom. Schedule time alone with the interpreter to discuss your typical classroom procedures, materials, and routines. Remember that an interpreter cannot proceed at the same pace as your verbal presentation; you need to slow your rate of presentation accordingly.

Work with family members to maximize the educational experience of students. Parents and other family members have an important influence on students with hearing impairments, with respect to such activities as going out and interacting with people, joining sports and other recreational activities, and monitoring and assisting with homework (Stewart & Kluwin, 2001). Work with family members to help them prioritize and encourage important activities.

ADAPT ASSESSMENT METHODS Testing and evaluation modifications for students with hearing impairments might include providing individual testing times in separate rooms and extending the time limit as necessary. Remember to allow sufficient time for interpreters during oral testing situations. Allow students to draw illustrations of concepts. Use performance-based testing measures and identification formats whenever possible.

MyEdLab: **Self-Check 4.5**

MyEdLab: **Application Exercise 4.5: Hearing Impairments**

4 Summary

- Students with autism or autism spectrum disorder may have mild to severe difficulties but usually have serious difficulties with social behavior. Students with more severe autism have difficulties with language, communication, cognitive tasks, attention, memory, and basic skills.

- Students with physical disabilities may exhibit difficulties using their arms, legs, or both the arms and the legs. Some of these students may exhibit problems with communication. Specific adaptations for increasing mobility, assisting with fine motor control, and improving communication skills help students become more independent and successful. Students with other health impairments may have serious medical needs that require special attention and that restrict their learning in school. Coordination with medical professionals while monitoring health and educational needs helps these students with school success.

- Some students with severe disabilities have severe intellectual disabilities and exhibit difficulties in cognition and adaptive behavior, as well as academic, social, self-help, problem-solving, attention, and memory skills.

- Individuals with visual impairments represent the smallest category of exceptionality. Students may have very low vision to no vision. These students may have difficulty

learning unless adaptations are made, such as arranging the physical environment for easy accessibility; enhancing printed materials; using braille and oral formats; and using concrete, tactile, and three-dimensional examples.

- Students with hearing impairments have mild to severe hearing losses. Individuals with mild to moderate hearing impairments usually wear hearing aids, whereas individuals who are deaf use sign language, total communication, or other aural techniques for communication. Students may require specific language, communication, and social skills instruction.

PROFESSIONAL STANDARDS LINK:
Teaching Students with Autism and Lower-Incidence Disabilities

Information in this chapter links most directly to:

- CEC Standards: 1 (Learner Development and Individual Learning Differences), 2 (Learning Environments), 4 (Assessment), 5 (Instructional Planning and Strategies), 7 (Collaboration)

- INTASC Standards: 2 (Learning Differences), 3 (Learning Environments), 6 (Assessment), 7 (Planning for Instruction), 8 (Instructional Strategies), 10 (Leadership and Collaboration)

TEACHING STUDENTS WITH AUTISM AND LOWER-INCIDENCE DISABILITIES

If a student with autism or lower-incidence disabilities is having difficulties in your classroom, have you tried the following? If not, see the pages listed here.

STRATEGIES FOR MAKING CLASSROOM ADAPTATIONS FOR STUDENTS WITH AUTISM

- ☐ Establish effective communication, 80–81
- ☐ Use direct instruction and applied behavior analysis, 81
- ☐ Develop social competence, 81–83

STRATEGIES FOR MAKING CLASSROOM ADAPTATIONS FOR STUDENTS WITH PHYSICAL DISABILITIES AND OTHER HEALTH IMPAIRMENTS

- ☐ Prepare the class, 87–88
- ☐ Monitor medical guidelines, 88–91
- ☐ Adapt the physical environment, 91
- ☐ Adapt instructional materials, 91–92
- ☐ Adapt instruction, 92
- ☐ Adapt assessment methods, 92

STRATEGIES FOR MAKING CLASSROOM ADAPTATIONS FOR STUDENTS WITH SEVERE AND MULTIPLE DISABILITIES

- ☐ Establish good working relationships with paraprofessionals, 93–95
- ☐ Increase disability awareness, 95–96
- ☐ Conceptualize inclusive instruction, 96
- ☐ Monitor special health-care needs, 96
- ☐ Adapt materials and the physical environment, 96–97
- ☐ Adapt assessment methods, 97

STRATEGIES FOR MAKING CLASSROOM ADAPTATIONS FOR STUDENTS WITH VISUAL IMPAIRMENTS

- ☐ Adapt the physical environment, 98
- ☐ Adapt instructional materials, 98
- ☐ Adapt instruction, 98–99
- ☐ Adapt assessment methods, 99

STRATEGIES FOR MAKING CLASSROOM ADAPTATIONS FOR STUDENTS WITH HEARING IMPAIRMENTS

- ☐ Adapt the physical environment, 101
- ☐ Adapt instructional materials, 101
- ☐ Adapt instruction, 101–102
- ☐ Adapt assessment methods, 102

5

Teaching Students with Other Special Learning Needs

LEARNING OUTCOMES

After studying this chapter, you should be able to:

5.1 Describe and discuss the prevalence and characteristics of students who are gifted, creative, or talented, and explain strategies for classroom adaptations.

5.2 Describe and discuss the prevalence and characteristics of students from culturally and linguistically diverse backgrounds, and explain strategies for classroom adaptations.

5.3 Describe and discuss the prevalence and characteristics of students at risk for school failure, and explain strategies for classroom adaptations.

Not all individuals with diverse or special learning needs are classified as having disabilities. Students with other special learning needs represent a wide range of abilities and include (1) students who are gifted and talented, (2) students from different cultural and linguistic backgrounds, and (3) students who may be considered at risk for school failure. These students belong to an increasing population in schools and are served in general education classes.

Gifted, Creative, and Talented

DEFINITIONS, PREVALENCE, AND CHARACTERISTICS OF GIFTED, CREATIVE, AND TALENTED

Individuals with special gifts and talents may be extraordinary in intellectual ability, specialized academic areas, music, or the arts (Clark, 2013). Although gifted, creative, and talented individuals are not included in IDEA, these students have unique needs that require special attention and accommodations for them to succeed in school. Various definitions of *gifted*, *creative*, and *talented* exist in the literature, and there is little agreement on the best definition (Callahan, 2011). Earlier definitions relied heavily on the use of IQ scores for identifying gifted individuals. The Javits Gifted and Talented Act, passed in 1978 (Public Law [PL] 95-561, Title IX, § 902) and reauthorized in 1994, included creative capabilities or high performance in the performing arts and has been widely adopted by states and school districts:

> Children and youth with outstanding talent perform or show the potential for performing at remarkably high levels of accomplishment when compared with others [of] their age, experience, or environment. These children and youth exhibit high performance capability in intellectual, creative, and/or artistic areas, possess an

unusual leadership capacity, or excel in specific academic fields. They require services or activities not ordinarily provided in the schools. Outstanding talents are present in children and youth from all cultural groups, across all economic strata, and in all areas of human endeavor. (Definitions; Gifted, 1998; see also U.S. Department of Education, 1993, p. 5)

These federal definitions highlight the areas of giftedness, talent, and creativity and are more representative of trends in gifted education. Other conceptualizations of giftedness continue to broaden the single-intelligence notion (see Plucker & Callahan, 2008, 2014). The following are examples of broadened definitions for gifted, creative, and talented youth: (1) three-trait definition, including above-average ability, task commitment, and creativity (Renzulli, 2005); (2) especially high aptitude, potential, or ability (Feldhusen & Moon, 1995); (3) synthetic, analytic, and practical intelligence (Sternberg, 2005); and (4) multiple intelligences (Gardner, 2006). All proposed models include more than a single IQ score as criteria, most include talents as critical components, and many recommend advice on counseling gifted and talented youth. Although general intelligence is the most widely accepted consideration in state definitions of giftedness and talent, specific academic ability, creative thinking, talent in the visual or performing arts, and leadership are also considered by many states (Education Commission of the States, 2004). The Davidson Institute for Talent Development (http://www.davidsongifted.org) provides definitions and other relevant information for each of the 50 states.

Given the variety of definitions, it is not surprising that little consensus exists on the actual number of gifted and talented youth. Many reports indicate that 3% to 5% of the population is gifted and talented; others believe the figures are much higher. Great variability also exists in how individual states identify students with gifts and talents, with some states identifying fewer than 3% of students and other states identifying as many as 16% (Callahan, 2011).

INTELLECTUALLY GIFTED Intellectually gifted students are those who have scored very high on standardized tests and usually excel in school. They are frequently very highly skilled verbally and have outstanding memories and literacy abilities—especially in reading and writing—compared with their typical age peers. They also tend to have outstanding critical thinking and problem-solving abilities and insatiable curiosities (Bireley, 1995). Intellectually gifted youth acquire, retain, and manipulate large amounts of information and may appear to learn in intuitive leaps (Davis, Rimm, & Siegle, 2011).

CREATIVE AND TALENTED The definitions of *creative* and *talented* are widely varied, but consensus usually converges on the identification of individuals with exceptional talents in particular areas (Clark, 2013). Creatively gifted and talented youth often excel in the visual or performing arts. These individuals typically show outstanding abilities at young ages in particular areas. Davis et al. (2011) listed the following characteristics related to creativity: original, independent, takes risks, aware of creativeness, motivated, curious, sense of humor, attracted to complexity, artistic, open-minded, need for time alone, intuitive, and intelligent.

HIDDEN GIFTED, CREATIVE, AND TALENTED Many students who are gifted and talented remain unidentified or hidden. This may be due to a number of factors. First, they might be underachievers, and consequently, their scores fall below the cutoff scores for classifying gifted students. Second, intelligence tests and standardized tests may underidentify some students because of cultural or linguistic diversity (Ford, 2012). Third, girls who may be gifted and talented may be underidentified (Navan, 2008), although precise reasons for this are unknown. Finally, some students may not be identified because of existing disabilities in other areas (learning or physical disabilities). Special attention during classification and screening efforts aimed at identifying gifted and talented youth can help eliminate underidentification of these individuals. Specific suggestions for finding and nurturing potential giftedness among Hispanic and African American students have been provided by Ford (2011) Castellano and Frazier (2011), and Gregory, Starnes, and Blaylock, (1988), including the following:

- Develop a "belief system" in school that culturally and linguistically diverse students can be and are gifted and talented.
- Develop an identification process that reflects an appreciation of the culture, language, values, and worldviews of culturally and linguistically diverse students and their families.

- Employ a multidimensional assessment process that includes qualitative as well as quantitative measures.

- Develop programs to educate the public in ways that giftedness may be manifested (and sometimes concealed) in different cultures. Collaborate with people knowledgeable in the particular culture for assistance and support.

- Ensure that insights gained in the identification and assessment process are incorporated into the instructional program.

ISSUES IN IDENTIFICATION AND ASSESSMENT OF GIFTED, CREATIVE, AND TALENTED

Several approaches exist for identifying gifted and talented children and youth. Common approaches include nomination methods, standardized test scores, talent pool searches, and a multiple-measures/multiple-criteria approach. Nomination approaches consist of distributing nomination forms to teachers and parents. Schools often implement an approach by which parents, teachers, peers, and students are provided nomination forms in which they detail reasons for nominating a student (or self) for the gifted and talented program.

Standardized-test-score approaches include the use of intelligence and achievement test scores. These may be individually or group-administered tests. Cutoff scores to qualify students as gifted and talented are often designated to identify high-scoring students, for example, in the top 8% (Callahan, 2011). This approach is usually combined with some other approach, in that standardized test scores are seldom the only criteria considered.

A multiple-measures/multiple-criteria approach is implemented in many schools (Davis et al., 2011). This approach combines many of the pieces of evidence collected in the approaches discussed previously but may also include detailed family histories, student work samples and inventories of interests, and discussion of all evidence by a gifted-and-talented screening committee.

STRATEGIES FOR

MAKING ADAPTATIONS FOR STUDENTS WHO ARE GIFTED, CREATIVE, AND TALENTED

Several educational approaches exist for programming curriculum and classes for gifted and talented youth. These include acceleration and enrichment and are provided in regular classes, resource classes, self-contained classes, and university classes and through mentoring programs (Davis et al., 2011). Careful pretesting identifies skills and information that gifted students have and can be used to place them in a more appropriate curriculum. In the inclusive classroom, differentiated instruction can include a number of appropriate adaptions.

IMPLEMENT ACCELERATION OR ENRICHMENT PROGRAMS Acceleration refers to moving students through the curriculum at a faster pace than that of general education students (Davis et al., 2011). Acceleration can mean admitting a child to school early, skipping grades, providing level-appropriate curriculum, or testing out of classes. Advancing students refers to placing them in programs that match their achievement levels. For example, a fourth grader who is working at a sixth-grade level academically might be advanced to the sixth-grade class. Another example is maintaining students in the age-appropriate class but providing them with the appropriate-level curriculum (sixth-grade level, in this example). It might also mean advancing students several grade levels but only in specific academic classes. For example, if seventh-grade students were gifted mathematically, they might be placed with juniors in the algebra II class but remain with their age peers for other subjects. Universities also may allow students who are gifted or talented to enroll in college-level courses when prerequisite criteria are met. Students who are gifted or talented frequently take Advanced Placement tests for college, which enables them to skip college-level courses. Finally, many students are admitted early to colleges and universities.

Acceleration is controversial, with proponents arguing strenuously for and opponents arguing strenuously against acceleration programs. Proponents claim students need acceleration to maintain interest in school and to be challenged adequately. Opponents claim that acceleration harms the social-emotional development of gifted students. Unfortunately, research results are ambiguous and yield no clear, definitive answers (Davis et al., 2011).

Numerous models of enrichment exist (Clark, 2013). The common element across enrichment programs is the expansion of the existing curriculum. Students are allowed and encouraged to study topics in depth that extend beyond the scope of the general education curriculum. The goals behind enrichment activities are to allow opportunities for critical thinking and problem solving through in-depth analyses of specific content areas. This is often accomplished by having students work independently on projects within general education classes. However, enrichment may also take place in off-campus settings. For example, students may be assigned to work with mentors in business and industry or in university settings. In either case, general education teachers can facilitate coordination of programming for students who are gifted or talented.

ADAPT INSTRUCTIONAL MATERIALS   In the case of either acceleration or enrichment, it may be necessary for general educators to adapt curriculum materials to better meet the needs of students who are gifted or talented. When students have demonstrated mastery of content, be prepared to move them ahead in the curriculum or design suitable enrichment activities that enable them to study more in depth in that area. Survey student interests to help provide directions for instructional enhancements. Seek assistance from teachers who work with students who are gifted or talented, experts from specific content areas, and guidance counselors, as well as from the families of the students.

ADAPT INSTRUCTIONAL AND EVALUATION PROCEDURES   Be prepared to adapt your instructional procedures for students who are gifted or talented. They may not require intensive or explicit instruction on new content. You may be able to meet with them independently and briefly explain new concepts and content, thus allowing more time for either acceleration or enrichment activities. Students who are gifted or talented may also be able to provide tutorial assistance to age peers. Be aware that some gifted and talented youth may also require explicit instruction in study and organizational skills when work demands increase for them. Finally, evaluation methods can be modified to allow for assessment of enrichment and acceleration activities. More performance-based measures may need to be devised to obtain true indicators of students' abilities on such tasks.

MyEdLab: **Self-Check 5.1**

MyEdLab: **Application Exercise 5.1: Gifted, Creative, and Talented**

Students Who Are Culturally and Linguistically Diverse

PREVALENCE, DEFINITIONS, AND CHARACTERISTICS OF CULTURALLY AND LINGUISTICALLY DIVERSE STUDENTS

Evidence exists that many students from culturally and linguistically diverse backgrounds are at a higher risk for school failure than students from European American backgrounds (Gollnick & Chinn, 2013). Furthermore, the prevalence rates for students with disabilities are different from those expected in some culturally and linguistically diverse groups. Table 5.1 presents risk ratios provided by the U.S. Department of Education (2015) for each racial/ethnic group in each category of disability.

TABLE 5.1 Risk Ratios for 6- to 21-Year-Old Students with Disabilities, by Race/Ethnicity and Disability Category: Fall 2013

Disability	American Indian/ Alaskan	Asian	Black or African American	Hispanic/ Latino	Native Hawaiian or Other Pacific Islander	White	Two or More Races
Learning disabilities	1.8	0.3	1.5	1.3	1.9	0.7	0.7
Speech or language impairment	1.3	0.7	1.0	1.1	1.1	1.0	0.9
Intellectual disabilities	1.5	0.5	2.3	0.9	1.6	0.7	0.7
Emotional disturbance	1.6	0.2	2.1	0.6	1.4	1.0	1.1
Multiple disabilities	1.7	0.6	1.4	0.7	1.9	1.1	0.7
Hearing impairment	1.2	1.2	1.0	1.3	2.8	0.8	0.7
Orthopedic impairment	1.0	0.8	0.8	1.2	1.5	1.0	0.7
Other health impairment	1.3	0.3	1.4	0.6	1.4	1.3	0.9
Visual impairment	1.5	0.9	1.1	1.0	1.9	1.0	0.8
Autism	0.9	1.2	1.0	0.8	1.3	1.2	0.9
Deaf-blindness	1.6	0.9	0.8	1.0	4.2	1.1	0.7
Traumatic brain injury	1.5	0.5	1.1	0.7	1.6	1.3	0.8
All disabilities	1.6	0.5	1.4	1.0	1.6	0.9	0.8

Source: Data from U.S. Department of Education (2015).

This means, for example, that during the fall of 2013, Black or African American students were 2.1 times as likely to receive services for emotional disturbance as were their age peers from all the other racial/ethnic groups combined, and Asian students were 0.3 times as likely (i.e., less likely) to receive services for learning disabilities as students in other racial/ethnic groups.

Similar findings have been presented in the past (Chinn & Hughes, 1987; Harry, 1992, 1994). This indicates that little has changed with respect to over- and underrepresentation issues by racial or ethnic group in past decades. Disproportional representation by race/ethnicity has also been reported in a number of other countries (Anastasiou, Gardner, & Michail, 2011; Harry, Arnaiz, Klingner, & Sturges, 2008; Kalyanpur, 2008).

Although exact reasons for observed overrepresentation of some racial/ethnic backgrounds are uncertain, several reasons have been hypothesized (see Ford, 2012; Harry & Klingner, 2006). Some have suggested that there are insufficient successful role models in schools and society for students from culturally and linguistically diverse backgrounds. Others suggest that cultural and linguistic differences often are inaccurately perceived as detriments (Cartledge, Gardner, & Ford, 2008; Gollnick & Chinn, 2013; Harry & Klingner, 2006), whereas others have suggested that students from these underrepresented groups are discriminated against because educational methods, traditional assessments, and grading procedures do not accommodate students from various cultural and linguistic groups (Baca, Baca, & de Valenzuela, 2004a; Patton, 1998). Some have proposed that percentages of some minority populations in special education are relatively higher due in part to low income and resulting disabilities associated with poverty, such as higher rates of exposure to harmful toxins (such as lead, alcohol, and tobacco), low birth weight, poorer nutrition, and less effective schools (Donovan & Cross, 2002; Gollnick & Chinn, 2013). It has also been suggested that representation in special education reflects the larger issue of representation in other remedial or compensatory programs such as Title 1 (MacMillan & Reschly, 1998).

Whatever the theory, however, the fact of overrepresentation of students who are culturally and linguistically diverse in special education is evidence that schools must pay greater attention to issues of cultural diversity. It is of critical importance that assessment instruments and procedures be nondiscriminatory, free of bias, and administered in the student's native language (Gollnick & Chinn, 2013). The National Research Council has suggested that a student should be considered eligible for special education only when his or her performance differs markedly from typical performance in specific academic or social-emotional domains, and there is evidence that the student has not responded to high-quality interventions in these specific domains of functioning (Donovan & Cross, 2002). These standards are compatible with response-to-intervention (RTI) initiatives (Mellard & Johnson, 2008).

Salend and Duhaney (2005) listed a number of suggestions for reducing overrepresentation of culturally and linguistically diverse students, including the following:

- Help create a diverse and culturally sensitive multidisciplinary planning team for making educational decisions.

- Provide effective prereferral and other ancillary services that can make culturally sensitive recommendations for interventions.

- Use alternatives to standardized testing, such as portfolio assessment, curriculum-based measurement, rubrics, and performance-based assessment.

- Look for any cultural factors that might contribute to learning problems, and include these in intervention plans.

- Employ culturally sensitive curriculum of interest to diverse learners.

- Use behavior-management strategies that are sensitive to cultural differences in social behavior, and include such strategies as culturally relevant reinforcers and group-oriented behavior-management techniques.

- Employ culturally responsive teaching strategies, such as, for example, verbal interactions, cooperative learning, divergent thinking, small-group instruction, real-world tasks, and positive teacher–student interactions.

- Encourage family involvement by using positive and respectful language, encouraging face-to-face meetings, and planning creatively to interact with family members in a manner convenient to them.

CULTURAL DIVERSITY Assimilation and cultural pluralism are two prevalent philosophical approaches toward the education of culturally diverse populations. Assimilation refers to having students from diverse ethnic and cultural groups assimilate into the dominant cultural group and essentially leave their own culture behind. Conversely, cultural pluralism refers to encouraging students from diverse ethnic and cultural groups to retain their own culture while succeeding in school (Gollnick & Chinn, 2013).

The concept of cultural pluralism becomes increasingly important as the number of individuals from diverse cultural and ethnic groups increases. This means that greater attention is needed to increase respect for all cultural and ethnic diversity in U.S. schools (Banks, 2015). Many proactive approaches can be implemented in schools to increase appreciation and awareness of cultural and ethnic differences. This approach is sometimes referred to as **multicultural education** because cultural pluralism is endorsed, which means appreciation of all cultures is taught and fostered (Gollnick & Chinn, 2013).

It is difficult to increase respect for all cultural groups without having some knowledge about differences among groups. However, it must be remembered that it is dangerous to generalize from cultural groups to individuals. As Lynch (1992) stated:

> Culture is only one of the characteristics that determines individuals' and families' attitudes, values, beliefs, and ways of behaving. . . . Assuming that culture-specific information . . . applies to all individuals from the cultural group is not only inaccurate but also dangerous—it can lead to stereotyping that diminishes rather than enhances cross-cultural competence. When applying cultural-specific information to an individual or family, it is wise to proceed with caution. (p. 44)

Just as students with a particular disability may lack all of the characteristics associated with a disability area, the same is true of someone from a particular culture. An individual representing a particular ethnic or cultural group may not be "representative" of that cultural group. However, when teaching and learning about cultures, some general characteristics can serve as guidelines for learning about the various cultural groups. Suggestions for teaching toward a more proactive, culturally pluralistic approach and away from a biased, monocultural approach are as follows:

- *Reduce teacher bias.* Increase awareness of prejudices and decrease prejudices and stereotypes. Record yourself teaching (video or audio), and analyze the recording for instances of language or behaviors that do not promote culturally responsive teaching.

- *Eliminate curriculum bias.* Select curriculum to reflect the diversity of all cultural groups; avoid stereotyping and overgeneralizations of cultural groups.

- *Teach about prejudice.* Discuss racism and discrimination; have students examine news for instances of racism; invite guest speakers; eliminate stereotypes.

- *Improve group relations and help resolve conflicts.* Use case studies and teach problem-solving strategies.

RECOGNIZE THE NEEDS OF STUDENTS FROM MULTIRACIAL FAMILIES

There is also an increasing number of multiracial and multicultural families in the United States. In the 2010 census, 2.9% of the population identified themselves as being from more than one race (U.S. Census Bureau, 2011). Moreover, multiracial marriages have resulted in more than a million multiracial children being born in the United States. Many of these children cannot be classified by only one part of their heritage. For example, Dorothy Adams, a 36-year-old whose father is African American and mother is Japanese American, stated:

> I'm for the multiracial category. When I was a kid, the first time I paid attention to the race box was on a Social Security form. It was a problem to check one box, so I checked black and Japanese. The teacher said to check only one box, so I checked "Other," then wrote in "black and Japanese." I've never gone back to see how I'm listed with Social Security. (Grossman, 1997, p. 13)

Be aware that many people represent a variety of racial and ethnic backgrounds and wish to be treated with sensitivity with respect to their particular heritage.

DEVELOP A PLAN TO ADDRESS LINGUISTIC DIVERSITY
Linguistic diversity is also an increasing issue within public schools in the United States. Currently, as many as 4 million children in the United States have limited proficiency in English, or over 9% of all students in public schools. The U.S. Census Bureau (2010) revealed that nearly 20% of respondents reported speaking a language different from English at home. Further, this number has been tripled since 1998. Spanish is currently the second most commonly spoken language in the schools (Echevarria & Graves, 2015), but the Census Bureau uses a list of 39 languages in assessing language use in the United States, including the category of "other languages" (U.S. Census Bureau, 2010). The *Apps for Education* feature describes the use of multilingual translators.

MyEdLab:
Video Example 5.1.
The teacher in this video discusses techniques that can be used to work with linguistically diverse students. Note that this teacher uses the term *ESOL*, which is synonymous with *English language learners.*

These data indicate that difficulties with learning are likely because students may not have acquired the necessary English-language skills for success in English-speaking schools. In addition, it is more challenging to establish effective communication between families and the school when common languages are unknown. It is necessary to enlist the assistance of interpreters who can translate communications, schoolwork, notes, papers, and materials between school and home settings (Gollnick & Chinn, 2013).

Several approaches are available for teaching students with limited English proficiency, and some controversy exists regarding the best approach. It is a matter of debate whether children should be "immersed" in English-speaking classrooms (with English instruction also provided by teachers of English as a second language) or whether English and non-English languages should be combined in classroom instruction. Furthermore, even if different languages are used during instruction, there is disagreement concerning how this can best be done to optimize the performance and learning of all students. It has been suggested that students may acquire practical, conversational skills in English much sooner than skills in more formal English for academic areas, and that it may be useful to support students in academic learning in their native language for several years until English skills are maximized (Gollnick & Chinn, 2013; Ovando & Combs, 2012). It is important to note that virtually all

Multilingual Translators

 Students for whom English is a second language may benefit from the use of a multilingual pocket translator. Multilingual translators can be small, pocket-sized electronic devices that contain a keyboard and a small screen. Students can enter text in one language, press a key, and have the text translated into another language. The devices are small enough to be carried from class to class in an unobtrusive fashion. They can provide valuable assistance and allow students to participate in class more frequently and to perform more optimally on class assignments and tests. In some schools, students are allowed to use these during the school day and even during statewide competency testing situations. Such devices would also be beneficial for teachers to have to enhance their communication with students and families of individuals for whom English is a second language.

The functions of the various devices range from that of a dictionary to explanations of phrases and idioms, to calculator functions, to data storage functions, to speech output. Some devices, such as the Language Teacher Pocket Translator, have built-in synthesizers that produce voice output as well. Many models have software available that can be loaded onto notebook computers or other handheld devices. More information on these devices can be obtained from http://translation.net (Language Teacher Pocket Translator) and Franklin Electronic Publishers, which also produces the Franklin Language Masters and Spell Checkers. Smartphones, tablets, and computers also feature apps such as Google Translate and SpeakText Free, which may also include speech-recognition features and translate over 100 languages from speech or text. Google Translate also has a Snap feature that translates pictures or photos of text into different languages.

concerned professionals agree that some level of support is needed for students who are not fluent in English.

Linguistic diversity is not limited to different languages. Some students may speak a dialect of English rather than a different language. For example, many African American students may speak a Black dialect or Black English rather than Standard English. Using a dialect in school may present some communication difficulties, especially with respect to written language assignments (Gollnick & Chinn, 2013), if teachers are not familiar with the dialect.

BILINGUAL SPECIAL EDUCATION   Bilingual special education refers to services provided for students with limited English proficiency who also have a disability. It is estimated that 14% of students with disabilities do not primarily use English in their homes. These students must accommodate two languages and two cultures, as well as face the challenges posed by their disabilities. Students who are bilingual and are also referred to special education are in need of both types of services and may be particularly at risk for inappropriate classification because of difficulties communicating in English (Echevarria & Graves, 2015). Bilingual special education teachers deliver services to those students who require bilingual education and special education services (Ehlers-Zavala, 2011).

ISSUES IN IDENTIFICATION AND ASSESSMENT OF CULTURALLY AND LINGUISTICALLY DIVERSE STUDENTS

The Individuals with Disabilities Education Improvement Act of 2004 (IDEA) provides stipulations for evaluations and assessments that are free of cultural and linguistic bias. It is especially important to monitor testing and assessment procedures to ensure this right for students from culturally and linguistically diverse backgrounds. Special precautions should be taken to ensure that ethnicity or cultural differences are not misinterpreted. For example, students in some cultures may tend to avoid direct eye contact with adults, a practice that may be misinterpreted by some teachers unfamiliar with cultural differences.

Overrepresentation in many cases may be attributed to inappropriate identification and assessment procedures (Gollnick & Chinn, 2013; Harry & Klingner, 2006). For example, African American students may be mistakenly referred for classification as having emotional or behavioral disabilities because of cultural misunderstandings (Obiakor & Roratori, 2014; Taylor & Whittaker, 2008). Likewise, research has suggested that some students who are bilingual exhibit behaviors that may be interpreted as behaviors similar to those of students with learning disabilities or behavioral disabilities (Yates & Ortiz, 2004). When students cannot understand the spoken language in class, they may appear uninterested or confused, or they may act inappropriately. Because these are some of the distinguishing characteristics of students with higher-incidence disabilities, general education teachers may misinterpret such behaviors and overrefer these students for special education services. Baca, Baca, and de Valenzuela (2004b) described the use of prereferral intervention for preventing inappropriate referrals for students who are bilingual, including assessing students in their dominant language. See the *Diversity in the Classroom* feature for a discussion of the RTI model as a multiculturally responsive prereferral intervention strategy.

Evaluation procedures need to be closely monitored to ensure that appropriate tests, testing situations, and familiar examiners are provided for such individuals. For example, students who do not speak and understand English fluently should not be placed in special education classes based on their performance on tests administered in English. Because many parents of students from diverse cultural and linguistic backgrounds speak only their native language fluently, have translators available to help facilitate communication efforts between families and schools when language barriers exist (Echevarria & Graves, 2015).

English as second language (ESL) teachers can provide valuable information on students who are beginning to learn English. They can provide suggestions to facilitate comprehension during classes. Bilingual teachers may provide academic instruction in students' native language. They may also work with special education teachers to ensure that instruction is sufficiently adapted to meet any specific disability needs. Use these specialists to help understand how to better serve students from different linguistic backgrounds. Bilingual special education teachers assume responsibility for the implementation of individualized education programs (IEPs) and provide ESL and special education instruction for students with both types of needs (Echevarria & Graves, 2015). These specialists work closely with general educators in inclusive models and coordinate instruction and instructional approaches to ensure IEP goals are met. Finally, consider the following:

- Test scores are only a single indicator of performance.
- Include multiple observations of students' behaviors.
- Testing by itself is insufficient for special education classification.
- Obtain assistance from bilingual and cultural diversity experts.
- Work closely with the families of students who are culturally and linguistically diverse to obtain the most valid and relevant information. (Baca & Cervantes, 2004; Obiakor & Rotatori, 2014)

STRATEGIES FOR

MAKING ADAPTATIONS FOR STUDENTS FROM CULTURALLY AND LINGUISTICALLY DIVERSE BACKGROUNDS

Many of the adaptations described for students with disabilities may be beneficial for accommodating students from diverse cultural and linguistic backgrounds.

CREATE A CULTURALLY RESPONSIVE ENVIRONMENT Create an open, accepting classroom environment to ensure that students from all cultural and linguistic backgrounds feel comfortable in classes. Make all students and their families feel welcome in your class. Model acceptance and tolerance of individual differences. Teach students that we are all alike and different, and that immigrants from all parts of the world have historically settled in the United States and contributed to its development (Gollnick & Chinn, 2013). Keep expectations high: Expect the best from all students, and be sure your students are aware of your expectations.

Complete a needs assessment to determine the ethnic, cultural, and linguistic backgrounds of the school, students, and community. Learn how school knowledge is perceived in students' cultures and the types of knowledge and skills that are valued (Gollnick & Chinn,

Culturally Responsive Prereferral Strategies

 Concerns about the overrepresentation of individuals from minority groups in special education have increased in recent years (see Ford, 2012). A promising strategy for delivering appropriate instruction and potentially reducing referrals of culturally diverse students to special education is response to intervention (RTI; see Fuchs & Vaughn, 2012). RTI is a model designed to provide the very best research-based instruction (or evidence-based practice) in tiers of increasing intensity and to identify those students who do not respond appropriately to that instruction.

Although RTI is a promising procedure for addressing mild learning difficulties prior to referral to special education, there are several considerations needed when implementing RTI in multicultural contexts. Klingner and Edwards (2006) have concurred that all instructional practice should be culturally responsive, and this should be considered in implementing the different tiers of RTI and when considering different tiers of placement for students. Teachers should be familiar with cultural

contexts in individual relationships, classrooms, and schools, as well as the larger community. Teaching should reflect students' level of cultural awareness from their home environments, and without a reexamination of cultural contexts, teachers should not necessarily assume that individual students should move to a more restrictive tier if they are not successful in the current tier. Klingner and Edwards (2006) recommended the following for the different tiers of RTI instruction in reading:

Tier 1: *The General Education Classroom.* All general education teachers should employ evidence-based interventions delivered by teachers who have developed culturally responsive attributes. In addition, teachers should know if their practices are effective and how to adjust instruction when they are less effective.

Tier 2: *Intensive Small-Group Instruction.* Because research on Tier 2 instruction with culturally diverse samples is limited, continued progress

monitoring and careful attention to cultural contexts are important. As part of Tier 2 instruction, a teacher assistance team (TAT), including experts in multicultural instruction, can complete evaluations and make specific recommendations. In some cases, the use of TATs could be considered a separate, third tier.

Tier 3: *Special Education.* This tier (or Tier 4, if Tier 3 is a separate TAT intervention) involves the creation of an individual IEP and individualized, intensive instruction. Before referral to special education, students from culturally diverse backgrounds should be evaluated using culturally appropriate assessments, and sufficient evidence should be present that previous culturally responsive instruction was not effective. In this way, the overrepresentation of culturally diverse students may be reduced, and appropriate learning opportunities may be maximized.

2013). Assess students' prior knowledge of and experience with academic content. Conduct a needs assessment (Baca & Cervantes, 2004), which can include information about language use as well as culturally relevant information about the community, family, school, and classroom. Information obtained can be used to plan activities that address all cultural and linguistic backgrounds.

Accommodate culturally diverse families. Culturally diverse families may (or may not) differ from the majority culture in areas such as discipline practices, home–school communication, and school involvement (de Valenzuela, Baca, & Baca, 2004; Echevarria & Graves, 2015). Learn to avoid preconceptions and to recognize and respect differences as you develop appropriate interactions with families (Grassi & Barker, 2010).

Include books and stories to enhance understanding of other cultures. East and Thomas (2007) have developed annotated bibliographies of over 450 titles in multicultural literature (see also Norton, 2012; Taylor & Whittaker, 2008). Some recommended books are presented in Figure 5.1 (see also National Education Association, 2015).

Title	Subject (estimated reading level)
Who Are You? Voices of Mixed Race Young People (P. F. Gaskins, Holt, 1999)	Stories about multiracial children (8–12).
Teaching with Folk Stories of the Hmong (D. Cha & N. J. Livo, Libraries Unlimited, 2000)	Teaching resource on Hmong cultural traditions, companion to *Folk Stories of the Hmong* by the same authors (9–12).
Arab American Encyclopedia (A. Ameri & D. Ramey, Eds., Gale Group, 2000)	Information about Arab Americans (5–12).
Happy Birthday, Mr. Kang (S. Roth, National Geographic Society, 2001)	Americanization and cultural traditions (2–5).
Harvesting Hope: The Story of Cesar Chavez (K. Krull, Harcourt, 2003)	Biography of the Mexican American labor leader (6–12).
Ellis Island: New Hope in a New Land (W. Jacobs, Scribner's, 1990)	Describes the role of Ellis Island in immigration to America (3–5).
The Flute Player: An Apache Folktale (J. Lacapa, Northland, 1990)	Folktale of an Apache boy who learns to play the flute for a girl who has captured his heart (3–5).
Children of Promise: African-American Literature and Art for Young People (C. Sullivan, Ed., Harry N. Abrams, 1991)	Stories, poems, plays, speeches, and documents that describe the African American experience (6–8).
Look What We've Brought You from Mexico: Crafts, Games, Recipes, Stories, and Other Cultural Activities from Mexican-Americans (P. Shalant, Julian Messner, 1992)	Describes the many contributions to the United States from Mexican culture (6–8).

Figure 5.1 Books to Promote Multicultural Awareness

ADAPT MATERIALS AND INSTRUCTION Teach about sensitivity and acceptance issues. Role-play scenarios that are concrete and meaningful to students. Examine curriculum materials to ensure they eliminate stereotypes. Examine your teaching style and practices to ensure all students are treated equally and offered chances of success. Figure 5.2 provides suggestions to increase appreciation of others.

Monitor the pace of instruction to ensure students with limited English proficiency are succeeding. Use concrete and familiar examples as frequently as possible when describing new concepts. Provide hands-on activities to ensure active involvement and active learning for all students. By using many modalities when teaching, you will help clarify language and provide multiple examples for developing new vocabulary words. Help students relate any prior knowledge to new concepts you present (Grassi & Barker, 2010). Incorporate feedback from assessments and from solicited student opinions to maximize the effectiveness of your classroom and to make your classroom motivating, enjoyable, and productive. The *Research Highlight* feature presented later in this chapter, describes recent reading instruction research with English learners.

MyEdLab: **Self-Check 5.2**

MyEdLab: **Application Exercise 5.2: Students Who Are Culturally and Linguistically Diverse**

For Younger Students	For Older Students
Share children's literature and stories about many cultures.	Complete a class, school, and community cultural and linguistic diversity profile.
Make a classroom "quilt."	Teach about inequity and individuals who have fought to combat inequitable practices.
Develop a class family cookbook.	
Discuss foods eaten at meals by different cultural groups.	Teach about cultural contributions:
Prepare, cook, and eat ethnic foods.	The arts, folk art, music, dances, literature, and crafts.
Dress in ethnic clothing.	Traditions, holidays, festivals, myths.
Wear ethnic jewelry and accessories.	Distinguished individuals and their accomplishments.
Play ethnic music.	
Teach ethnic dances.	Prepare, cook, and eat ethnic foods.
Teach words and phrases from different languages.	Dress in ethnic clothing.
	Play ethnic music.
Invite parents in to share family traditions.	Teach ethnic dances.
	Teach words and phrases from different languages.
Make illustrated family histories and post them in the classroom.	Bring in international newspapers or newspapers written in a language other than English.

Figure 5.2 Classroom Practices to Increase Appreciation for Others

Students at Risk

DEFINITIONS, PREVALENCE, AND CHARACTERISTICS OF STUDENTS AT RISK

Students at risk for school failure come from diverse environments and represent all racial, ethnic, and linguistic backgrounds. They also span all socioeconomic classes, although students with backgrounds of severe poverty may tend to be at a higher risk than others. At-risk students may ultimately fail or drop out of school and experience difficulties later in life. These students are usually found in general education classes, may require additional assistance from teachers, and may benefit from classroom modifications similar to those suggested for students with higher-incidence disabilities. Many educators have identified factors associated with at-risk students (e.g., Beach, 2014; Frieman, 2001). These factors are listed in Figure 5.3 and describe a variety of situations.

ABUSED AND NEGLECTED CHILDREN   Child abuse and neglect can have devastating emotional, physical, cognitive, social, and intellectual effects on children, and reported cases have been increasing in the United States (Crosson-Tower, 2014). Federal legislation, the Child Abuse Prevention and Treatment Act of 1974 and its subsequent amendments, defined child abuse and neglect as maltreatment, sexual abuse or exploitation, mental or physical injury, withholding medical treatment for life-threatening conditions, or negligent treatment of children younger than 18 by persons responsible for the child (Child Welfare Information Gateway, 2011). In some cases, child abuse has been linked to causing disabilities in children (Shaahinfar, Whitelaw, & Mansour, 2015). For example, severe shaking of infants has been linked to brain injury (Klein & Stern, 1971), some cases of abuse have been related to cerebral palsy (Diamond & Jaudes, 1983), and other cases have been linked to intellectual disabilities and learning disabilities (Caplan & Dinardo, 1986). The best overall predictor of child abuse and neglect is poverty (Grandinette & Best, 2009; Sedlak et al., 2010). Table 5.2 presents behavioral and physical indicators of child abuse and neglect.

- Children with poor academic performance
- Children who are born exposed to alcohol and other narcotic substances
- Children who abuse alcohol and drugs
- Abused and neglected children
- Children living in poverty conditions
- Children suffering from depression and suicidal tendencies
- Students who are pregnant or parents
- Homeless children and children who move excessively
- Children with excessive absenteeism
- Students who have been suspended two times within a year
- Students who drop out of school
- Children who are slow learners
- Students who have experienced traumatic events such as death of someone close to them
- Children whose parents are alcoholics or drug abusers
- Students who are older than their grade-level peers due to retention
- Children who may be from urban, suburban, or rural settings
- Children who are angry or socially alienated

Figure 5.3 Major At-Risk Factors

TABLE 5.2 Some Physical and Behavioral Indicators of Child Abuse and Neglect

Type of Abuse or Neglect, Definition	Physical Indicators	Behavioral Indicators
Physical abuse: Any act that, regardless of intent, results in a nonaccidental physical injury to a child	Questionable injuries, such as the following: - Bruises, welts, or other injuries - Burns - Fractures - Lacerations or abrasions	- Being uncomfortable with physical contact - Being wary of adult contacts - Showing behavioral extremes, either aggression or withdrawal - Not wanting to go home - Reporting an injury by a parent - Complaining of soreness or moving uncomfortably - Wearing excessive clothing to cover the body - Chronically running away from home (adolescents) - Reluctance to change clothes for gym activities (attempt to hide physical injuries)
Neglect: A caregiver's failure to provide something that a child needs	- Undernourished appearance - Lethargic - Signs of inadequate food or sleep - Untreated injuries - Evidence of unattended illness	- Begging for or stealing food because of persistent hunger - Poor hygiene - Inappropriate dress for the weather - Accidents and injuries - Risky adolescent behavior - Promiscuity, drugs, and delinquency - Being shunned by peers - Clinging behavior
Sexual abuse: The misuse of adult authority by involving children in sexual activities	- Most physical indicators would be found during a physical exam by a medical practitioner	- Expressions of age-inappropriate knowledge of sex and sexually "pseudomature" behaviors - Sexually explicit drawings - Highly sexualized play - Statements of unexplained fear of a person or place - Stated desire to avoid a familiar adult - Expressions of excessive concern about gender identity (boys) - Nightmares - Sleep interruptions - Withdrawal - A child's statement of sexual abuse

Source: Virginia Institute for Social Services Training Activities (2016).

Schools and teachers have the responsibility to report any signs of child abuse or neglect as per state and local definitions and guidelines. Determine state definitions and local procedures for reporting any cases, and adhere to those policies and procedures upon noticing any cases of child abuse or neglect (Crosson-Tower, 2014).

HOMELESS CHILDREN   The term *homeless* refers to individuals who lack a nighttime home, cannot afford housing, or live in provided public or private shelters, cars, or elsewhere (Heflin & Rudy, 1991). The number of homeless individuals in the United States is rapidly growing and includes an increasing number of families with children, from infants to teenagers (Children's Defense Fund, 2005). Some estimates indicate that most of the homeless families consist of single mothers with an average of two to three children (National Coalition for the Homeless, 2007). The number of homeless children and youth has been estimated to be 1.35 million. Approximately 87% of homeless school-age children are enrolled in school, and approximately 77% attend school regularly (National Coalition for the Homeless, 2007). Homeless children are twice as likely to receive services for learning disabilities and are three times as likely to receive services for emotional disturbance (Taormina-Weiss, 2012).

It is important to realize that homeless children have to confront many barriers to succeed in school and in life. Issues for homeless children include transportation problems; social barriers due to transience; lack of money for food, clothing, and shelter; appearance; acceptance by peers; legal barriers; family problems; and excessive absenteeism. Even more important are issues surrounding their self-esteem, security, safety, and trust. Some schools with high rates of homeless children have modeled examples of safe, comfortable environments with the following actions:

- Assessing students' abilities and strengths directly rather than assuming they will be slow learners
- Arranging for toys and play time for younger children
- Adjusting expectations for homework for students who must live in homeless shelters, which typically do not provide a place to do homework
- Helping to identify funds for supplies and trips
- Maintaining an emphasis on building self-esteem (Frieman, 2001)

ALCOHOL AND SUBSTANCE ABUSE   Students who use alcohol and illegal drugs are at a higher risk of failing in school and in life. In a report on drug, alcohol, and tobacco use among teens in the United States, the National Center on Addiction and Substance Abuse at Columbia University (2011) reported that 75% of all high school students have used alcohol, tobacco, or either legal or illegal drugs, and that one in five of these adolescents is addicted. This figure is distressing, but even more alarming are the reports that indicate that children in elementary schools also are using drugs. These students are at a greater risk of failing. Students may become more withdrawn and act irrationally. Moreover, many may become involved in stealing and other illegal activities to maintain their drug habits.

Miksic (1987; see also Kauffman & Landrum, 2013) described elements of a successful substance-abuse education program. These elements include a clear, well-defined school policy regarding how teachers and administrators will deal with drug use and possession; a basic drug education classroom curriculum; increasing teacher awareness; a supportive atmosphere for teacher training in dealing with drug-abuse problems; involving families as well as students; teacher self-evaluation; use of peer-group approaches; and promoting understanding that emotional concerns, such as self-esteem, are often associated with substance abuse.

Drug abuse is not appropriately treated in the classroom (Frieman, 2001); however, teachers should know whom to contact if a drug-related emergency occurs. Watch for unusual behavior or sudden changes in mood or behavior. It is appropriate to make referrals when drug use has been identified, particularly when it is associated with disruptive classroom behavior or problems in academic functioning (Kauffman & Landrum, 2013).

FAMILY POVERTY   It has been well documented that children living in poverty are at high risk of failing in school and life (Frieman, 2001; Tornquist, Mastropieri, Scruggs, Berry, & Halloran, 2009). Poverty complicates life success and places children at risk for failure for a variety of complex reasons. First, prenatal care may be inadequate or nonexistent for those in low-income families. This alone may result in low-birth-weight infants who are at higher

Reading Interventions for English Learners

 The number of students for whom English is a second language has been increasing dramatically in America's schools (U.S. Department of Education, 2015). Teaching reading to English learners (ELs) can be challenging for teachers because students may be below their grade and age levels in understanding spoken English and reading and speaking English, and they may have lower English vocabulary levels than in their native languages. The need for improved reading instruction for ELs is even more important with emphasis that the Common Core State Standards (CCSS) place on academic vocabulary and language. The Institute of Education Sciences (IES) recommended EL reading teaching guidelines that included building academic language and vocabulary and using explicit instruction with small groups of students (Baker et al., 2014). Explicit instruction provides clear learning objectives with multiple opportunities for practice and feedback, and learning in supported small groups provides teachers with more opportunities to interact with and address individual students' needs.

Richards-Tutor, Baker, Gersten, Baker, and Smith (2016) reviewed and synthesized the findings from 12 studies that examined the effects of reading interventions for ELs who struggled with reading or also were diagnosed with learning disabilities. The majority of the studies were conducted with students in kindergarten through third grade; two studies were conducted with students in grades 2 through 8, and one study was conducted with students in middle school. ELs varied greatly in both age and ability levels in English. All studies covered comprehensive reading instruction, and most included many of the following essential reading elements: phonemic awareness, phonics, fluency, vocabulary, and comprehension. However, the seven studies that were conducted in kindergarten or first grade emphasized the beginning reading skills, such as decoding, phonemic awareness, and phonological awareness, whereas the studies involving older students also included more vocabulary and instruction in listening and reading comprehension. All studies employed elements of explicit instruction, such as scaffolding, modeling, practice, and feedback, which are recommended for students with high-incidence disabilities as well. Most studies taught students in small groups, although two studies taught students in one-on-one situations. Intervention sessions averaged a total of 120, 30-minute sessions. Findings revealed that kindergarten and first-grade students made significant gains in phonemic awareness and on phonics measures, and some studies reported significant gains in reading or listening comprehension.

QUESTIONS FOR REFLECTION

1. Why might ELs require intensive reading instruction?
2. What are the educational implications of these findings?
3. How might you adapt these intervention findings to EL reading instruction in your school?

---

risk for ill-health and disabilities. Second, children born of substance abusers are at a greater risk for health-related problems. Third, children born to teenage mothers are more likely to be impoverished. Fourth, continued poor nutrition, lack of health care, and the low educational achievement of parents are factors associated with poverty that can perpetuate failure in school (Frieman, 2001; Jensen, 2009). In addition, families in poverty are less able to provide the educational materials, computers, or travel experiences that can enrich students' backgrounds and provide support for school learning. Children from families in poverty are more likely to be obligated to work to contribute to family income; these responsibilities may detract from schoolwork. Teachers can help by developing trust and planning predictable, secure, and stable environments.

YOUNG, PREGNANT, AND PARENTS   Teenagers who are pregnant or become parents are at risk of failing in school and present a high at-risk factor for their unborn children. Teenage pregnancy is found across all racial, ethnic, and socioeconomic strata. Many teenagers lack appropriate educational backgrounds, have poor prenatal care, and have babies that are also at very high risk for failing in school and life. Educational programs providing information about pregnancy, abstinence, sexually transmitted diseases, and AIDS are needed on a widespread basis to inform youth about the consequences of teenage pregnancy. More programs are needed to provide child care for teenagers with babies to help them complete their high school requirements and pursue advanced-degree training (Hoffman & Maynard, 2008).

WARNING SIGNS FOR SUICIDE OR VIOLENCE Many students in today's schools are at risk for suicide or violence, so it is important to be alert for warning signs. On average, five children or teens commit suicide every day, and eight children or teens are killed by firearms each day (Children's Defense Fund, 2011). According to the Suicide Prevention Lifeline (2005), suicide warning signs include (1) making threats, talking, or writing about death or suicide; (2) feelings of hopelessness or uncontrolled anger; (3) engaging in risky behavior without thinking; (4) an increase in the use of drugs or alcohol; (5) withdrawing from friends and family; and (6) feeling anxious or displaying dramatic mood changes. In addition, students may give away prized personal possessions or make overt threats of suicide.

If you encounter a student who is threatening suicide, stay with the student, and speak directly in a calm and nonthreatening manner. Try to get the student to talk; listen to and acknowledge the student's feelings. Do not judge; reassure the student that there is help and that he or she will not always feel like this. Provide continuous supervision, and remove means for self-harm. Remind the student that others care and would like to help. Peers should be encouraged not to keep suicidal thoughts secret (National Association of School Psychologists, 2012). Teachers should take all threats of violence, to self or others, seriously and report them promptly to parents, co-teachers, counselors, and building administrators.

COORDINATING INSTRUCTION WITH COMPENSATORY EDUCATION PROGRAMS

Schools may qualify for federal funding for compensatory education under Title I of the Elementary and Secondary Education Act, or No Child Left Behind (NCLB) Act, if they have concentrations of students from low-income and/or immigrant families. Funds may be provided for additional teachers, paraprofessionals, and supplies so that additional remedial instruction can be applied. If students are receiving additional assistance in basic skills under Title I, it is important that these programs are well coordinated with other types of instruction the student may be receiving.

STRATEGIES FOR
MAKING ADAPTATIONS FOR STUDENTS AT RISK

Students at risk for failure represent a wide and varied range of problems and potential difficulties. Most important is to maintain an open, accepting classroom environment and let your students know they are welcome in your room. Seek assistance from other school support personnel and students' families. Be considerate of students' needs, maintain realistic but high expectations, and encourage them to succeed in class. Provide additional opportunities for them to be successful in school. Model enthusiasm toward learning, encourage active participation, make students feel comfortable, and be ready to provide for additional supports and adapt instruction, as described next.

PROVIDE FOR ADDITIONAL SUPPORTS Help to coordinate services among community social services agencies, school, and parents to maximize the effectiveness of service delivery. Find out about and inform parents of all available services, including free meals, education, health-care services, special education, and mental health services. Keep in contact with parents or guardians because they may be unaware of all the services available to them. Provide assistance in obtaining support services such as counseling and social services, when needed. Help arrange before- and after-school care and activities for students who may lack supervision outside of school hours. Arrange for awareness training for personnel in your school so that they can better identify children at risk and at-risk factors (Mizerek & Hinz, 2004).

ADAPT INSTRUCTION Remediate basic skills when needed by providing for additional instruction with paraprofessionals or tutors so that students can apply themselves on higher-order academic tasks. Consider using the instructional adaptations suggested for students with higher- and lower-incidence disabilities with students considered at risk for school failure. These include adapting the physical environment, instructional materials, instructional procedures, and evaluation procedures with respect to specific special needs. Many students at risk may have a more limited experiential background, so be sure that the necessary prerequisite knowledge is understood by all students. Make sure that your classroom environment is seen as welcoming and supportive to all students and that all students feel safe in your classroom. Do not hesitate to seek assistance from school administrators or other personnel when uncertain.

Students at risk for school failure present some unique and special challenges for educators. Nevertheless, successfully differentiating instructional practices to help a student succeed, who might otherwise have failed, can be one of the most rewarding experiences you can have as a teacher.

MyEdLab: **Self-Check 5.3**

MyEdLab: **Application Exercise 5.3: Students at Risk**

---

5 Summary

- Students who are gifted, talented, or creative may be identified by a variety of methods, including test scores, behavioral descriptions, and qualitative/descriptive methods. Students who are gifted, talented, or creative may be served by acceleration programs, enrichment programs, or a combination of approaches.

- Students who are culturally or linguistically diverse may also present some special learning needs. Teachers should adopt a culturally sensitive, pluralistic approach that incorporates an awareness of cultural differences and their implications for learning.

  — Because students who are culturally or linguistically diverse are often overrepresented in special education placements, teachers should be particularly careful when considering referral for special education. Unbiased testing, culturally sensitive behavioral expectations, and prereferral intervention strategies can help address this important issue.

- Factors that may place students at risk for school failure include poverty, drug use, homelessness, teenage pregnancy, and child abuse and neglect. Contact and communication with students in question, their families, relevant school personnel, and community agencies can help address risk factors.

PROFESSIONAL STANDARDS LINK:
Teaching Students with Other Special Learning Needs

Information in this chapter links most directly to:

- CEC Standards: 1 (Learner Development and Characteristics of Learners), 2 (Learning Environments), 4 (Assessment), 5 (Instructional Planning and Strategies), 7 (Collaboration)

- INTASC Standards: 2 (Learning Differences), 3 (Learning Environments), 6 (Assessment), 7 (Planning for Instruction), 8 (Instructional Strategies), 10 (Leadership and Collaboration)

TEACHING STUDENTS WITH OTHER SPECIAL LEARNING NEEDS

If a student with other diverse learning needs is having difficulties in your classroom, have you tried the following? If not, see the pages listed here.

STRATEGIES FOR MAKING ADAPTATIONS FOR STUDENTS WHO ARE GIFTED, CREATIVE, AND TALENTED

STRATEGIES FOR MAKING ADAPTATIONS FOR STUDENTS FROM CULTURALY AND LINGUISTICALLY DIVERSE BACKGROUNDS

STRATEGIES FOR MAKING ADAPTATIONS FOR STUDENTS AT RISK

PART 2

Developing Effective Teaching Skills

6

Effective Differentiated Instruction for All Students

LEARNING OUTCOMES

After studying this chapter, you should be able to:

6.1 Define and describe differentiated instruction.

6.2 Describe the PASS variables and their application to effective differentiated instruction in inclusive settings.

6.3 Describe how to **p**rioritize instruction.

6.4 Describe how to **a**dapt instruction.

6.5 Describe how to **s**ystematically teach in inclusive settings using the SCREAM variables.

6.6 Describe how to **s**ystematically evaluate the outcomes of inclusive instruction.

To be an effective inclusive classroom teacher, you must first be an effective teacher. You must employ the skills that enable you to expect, and receive, the very best in learning and achievement from your students. This chapter describes the variables most important for maximizing student learning and ways you can implement these variables in your classroom. As you learn to apply these strategies consistently and systematically, you will see the learning, achievement, and attitudes of all of your students, including those with special needs, increase dramatically.

Research over the past several decades, known as *teacher effectiveness research,* has identified the variables most strongly associated with student achievement (e.g., Archer & Hughes, 2011; Danielson, 2010; Good & Brophy, 2007; Mastropieri & Scruggs, 2004; Rosenshine & Stevens, 1986). Some of this research also has shown that teachers who are most effective at including students with disabilities and other diverse learning needs are also effective classroom teachers in general (Larrivee, 1985; Scruggs & Mastropieri, 1994b). Overall, this research has been critically important in identifying the things teachers should do and not do to maximize learning for all students. In this chapter, we summarize much of what has been learned from this research and its implications for effective differentiated instruction.

What Is Differentiated Instruction?

As described in previous chapters, differentiated instruction means making adjustments in order to meet the individual needs of all learners in an inclusive classroom. According to Tomlinson (2014b):

> Teachers who differentiate provide specific alternatives for individuals to learn as deeply as possible and as quickly as possible, without assuming one student's road map for learning is identical to anyone else's. (p. 4)

MyEdLab:
Video Example 6.1.
This video provides an overview of the concept of differentiation, with multiple illustrations of teachers working with students.

Throughout this book, we identify and discuss methods for adjusting general education classrooms to meet a variety of special needs, and these methods can be fairly characterized as differentiated instruction.

Years ago, "mainstreaming" often referred to students with special needs "earning" their right to placement in the general education classroom for some or all of the school day by demonstrating that they could function independently in that setting. The inclusion movement established the appropriateness of general education placement whenever the student could succeed with appropriate supports—that is, when the student's learning experience could be appropriately "differentiated" to meet their special needs.

In previous chapters, we have discussed how instruction can be differentiated to meet the special learning needs of students with specific disabilities and special needs areas. We refer to differentiating instruction by adapting the environment, instructional materials, instructional methods, and evaluation of instruction that are similar to the elements of learning environment, content, process, and product described by Tomlinson (2014a; 2014b).

DIFFERENTIATING THE LEARNING ENVIRONMENT   In many cases, environments must be modified to meet the needs of students with physical disabilities—for example, wider aisles for students using crutches or wheelchairs or appropriate seating options for science lab. But environments can also be modified to provide for other differential learning needs, such as the need for a quiet space in the classroom or adaptations to address the need of some students for movement. Moving a student away from a window or away from the pencil sharpener is also an example of differentiating the environment. Also, environments can be altered to reflect a variety of different cultures or different home environments to make the classroom more inviting for all learners.

DIFFERENTIATING INSTRUCTIONAL MATERIALS   Instructional materials can be differentiated in a number of ways to address the needs of individual learners. For example, differentiation could include the use of textbooks and reading materials with different fonts or differing difficulty levels, use of a text-to-speech reader, use of vocabulary guides, or use of physical manipulative materials. Likewise, worksheets or other student activities can be differentiated to meet different learner needs.

DIFFERENTIATING INSTRUCTIONAL METHODS   *Process* and instructional methods refer to the activities students participate in to learn the content. When process is differentiated, this means that students may be given different means by which they can meet learning objectives. Some students may learn better when paired with a partner, in small groups, or in a peer-tutoring arrangement. Another example is the use of tiered activities, where some students may receive more support, more challenge, or more complexity in order to meet the same objectives. Teachers may find opportunities to reteach essential concepts for particular learners in need of additional instruction. Additionally, some students may be given more time to complete a task they are having difficulty with or more time for a task because of a special interest or a desire to explore the topic in more depth.

DIFFERENTIATING EVALUATION   Evaluation of instruction can also be differentiated to address special needs, for example, by allowing verbal instead of written responses to test questions, allowing additional time to complete the test, reading questions aloud to individual students, or allowing the use of calculators when mastery of math facts is not a requirement. Remember that changes in evaluation procedures in standardized tests may limit the interpretability of test results; nevertheless, in many cases, differentiating evaluation methods can lead to more beneficial outcomes.

MyEdLab: **Self-Check 6.1**

Promoting Effective Differentiated Instruction: The PASS Variables

To maximize the success of students with special needs in inclusive settings, we recommend using the **PASS** variables (Mastropieri & Scruggs, 2002; Scruggs & Mastropieri, 1995). PASS represents a way of thinking and approaching differentiated, inclusive instruction. PASS stands for the following variables:

1. **P**rioritize instruction.
2. **A**dapt instructional methods, instructional materials, or the learning environment.
3. **S**ystematically teach with the "SCREAM" variables.
4. **S**ystematically evaluate the outcomes of your instruction.

The PASS variables can be used as a guideline for planning, delivering, and evaluating effective inclusive instruction for specific students with special needs. Using these variables and other information from this chapter, you can deliver effective instruction to all of your students.

P: PRIORITIZE INSTRUCTION

When planning instruction, it is very important that you determine the relative importance of what you will teach. There are elements of your instruction that are very important for every student to learn; others are of less importance. For example, a teacher found that some students spent a lot of time staining slides of onion cells; there was a lot of mess to clean up, and poorly stained slides could not be viewed easily. She determined that understanding cell structure was the most important element of this unit and that staining slides was less important, and she adjusted her instruction accordingly to spend the most time on the content with the highest priority.

Prioritizing instruction should not be thought of as something teachers can only apply to individual lessons; you should prioritize all of your instruction by planning for content coverage, basing your instruction on prioritized objectives, considering scope and sequence, selecting appropriate curriculum, and pacing instruction to maximize coverage of your prioritized objectives.

STRATEGIES FOR
PLANNING FOR CONTENT COVERAGE

The importance of content coverage is obvious, in that students almost certainly will not learn content that has not been covered. However, the amount of content covered must be appropriate to the skills and abilities of the students learning the content and must reflect your instructional priorities. Careful planning of content coverage can help ensure that learning will be maximized for all students. Several important considerations to make when planning content coverage include objectives, scope and sequence, curriculum, and pacing.

BASE INSTRUCTION ON SPECIFIC PRIORITIZED OBJECTIVES   All content to be covered should be based on specific instructional objectives. Objectives state the outcomes of instruction in ways that allow you to find out whether your instruction was successful. Objectives specify (1) the content of the objective (what is being taught), (2) the conditions under which a student's performance will be assessed (e.g., in writing, oral responding), and (3) the criteria for acceptable performance (level of achievement). For example, consider the following objective: "The student will write five precipitating causes of the Civil War with 100% accuracy." The content of the objective is the causes of the Civil War, the conditions specify that students will write, and the criterion for acceptable performance is five causes written with 100% accuracy. Another example of an objective is as follows: "The student will read 3 pages from the grade-level reading materials at a rate of 120 words per minute with 95% of words read correctly." This objective also specifies the content, the conditions, and the criteria to be achieved. Another objective could state, "After silent reading of a grade-level narrative reading assignment, the student will verbally restate the setting, main characters, problem, and resolution with 100% accuracy."

Because the content of instruction is based on objectives, it is important to include as many objectives as necessary to maximize content coverage. This is particularly important for students who receive special education services because their individualized education programs (IEPs) are based on objectives. An effective inclusive teacher specifies objectives and translates IEP objectives into relevant methods and materials, with the assistance of the special education teacher.

In order to ensure that all students are learning and engaged with the curriculum, teachers may need to select and prioritize objectives for some students with disabilities. This means examining all instructional objectives, determining which are the most important for students with disabilities who are included in general education classes, and eliminating objectives that are unnecessary for those students. For example, Cliff has severe arthritis and has a great deal of difficulty using a pencil and completing tasks that require much fine motor control. He uses canes to assist with mobility. His fifth-grade teacher, Mr. Masoodi, employs a hands-on approach to science instruction. To accommodate Cliff's needs, Mr. Masoodi prioritized his class objectives. He examined the content and selected the most important objectives for Cliff. He determined that understanding of critical scientific concepts and a positive attitude toward science had the highest priority as objectives. Handwriting and physical manipulation of instructional materials had a lower priority and were not always required in Cliff's case. By first examining all the class objectives and then reviewing Cliff's instructional needs, Mr. Masoodi was able to prioritize objectives for Cliff.

PLAN INSTRUCTION BASED ON SCOPE AND SEQUENCE Scope and sequence refer to the breadth and depth of content that will be presented in school (scope) and the order in which the content will be presented (sequence). All areas of instruction should be presented with respect to an overriding scope and sequence of prioritized instructional objectives. Scope and sequence allow for long-term planning and evaluation of instruction, provide implications for time allocations, and set the overall pace of instruction. Most states have published curriculum guidelines that contain scope and sequence for all subject areas across grade levels. Prioritized content should receive substantial attention within the scope and sequence of instruction.

The **Common Core State Standards Initiative** introduced in 2011 is a state-led effort to provide a clear and consistent framework in order to prepare students for college and the workforce by the time they graduate from high school. Many states are participating in this initiative, whereas other states are employing their own standards. Teachers in participating states should determine what these standards are and how they will be implemented in inclusive classrooms in their own schools (Scruggs, Mastropieri, & Brigham, 2013).

SELECT AN APPROPRIATE CURRICULUM The curriculum not only includes the instructional materials used for learning but also refers to the course of study for each discipline and the scope and sequence within each grade level necessary to build conceptual understanding. The curriculum serves as an interface between the student and the learning objectives and has been described as the overall experience provided to a student by the school (Gartin, Murdick, Imbeau, & Perner, 2002; Moore, 2011).

Curriculum decisions can play an important role in inclusive schooling. The accompanying *In the Classroom* feature shows a checklist of curriculum materials being considered to maximize learning for all students. When serving on curriculum adoption committees or making a choice from existing school materials, be certain to consider the points noted to maximize learning for all students. Curriculum materials that feature many of these characteristics should be given a higher priority than those with fewer of these characteristics.

The curriculum need not be the same for every student. In fact, the curriculum can be carefully selected to address specific learner needs, and individual curriculum decisions are an important component of differentiated instruction.

PACE INSTRUCTION EFFECTIVELY Pacing refers to the rate at which teachers and students proceed through the curriculum and is another way of prioritizing instruction. For example, Mr. Isaac teaches American history but has only gotten to World War II by the end of the school year. He has determined (intentionally or not) that events in American history from 1945 to the present have a lower priority, as he did not cover this content. Unless the content at the beginning of the text has a higher priority, and content at the end of the text is judged to be of less value, however, more efficient planning would have produced a pace of instruction that better reflected instructional priorities.

In the Classroom

Checklist for Curriculum Materials for Inclusive Environments

_____ Do the materials provide sufficient opportunity for active student involvement, or do they simply provide verbal information to be recalled?

_____ Are the materials written on a level that is most comprehensible to all students, or do they include unnecessary complexity or an overabundance of unnecessary vocabulary?

_____ Do the materials lend themselves to use by cooperative learning groups or other peer-interactive activities?

_____ Do the materials allow for sufficient practice of key concepts before moving on to other content?

_____ Do the materials provide simple means for frequent evaluation of learner progress toward prespecified goals and objectives?

_____ Do the materials include examples of individuals from culturally diverse backgrounds and people of diverse learning abilities?

_____ Do the materials provide recommendations for modifications for students with disabilities or other special needs?

_____ Do the materials provide evidence-based practice data that demonstrate that positive learning gains can be realized from use of the materials?

One of the most significant problems teachers encounter in inclusive settings is adjusting the pace of instruction to diverse learning needs. Whereas some students appear to master new content almost as soon as they are exposed to it, other students require substantially more instructional time to learn the same content. Students who have learned certain concepts should not be held back and instead could be engaged in learning more in-depth knowledge about a concept or learning about related concepts while other students receive additional practice.

Once objectives have been prioritized, instruction has been planned based upon scope and sequence of prioritized objectives, and curriculum has been selected and paced appropriately, it is necessary to implement appropriate adaptations.

MyEdLab: **Self-Check 6.2**

A: ADAPT INSTRUCTIONAL METHODS, INSTRUCTIONAL MATERIALS, OR THE LEARNING ENVIRONMENT

Once the instructional objectives have been prioritized, the instruction, materials, and/or the environment can be adapted to accommodate more completely the needs of the students with disabilities. These adaptations carefully link the characteristics of the curriculum with the characteristics of the learner and are at the heart of differentiated instruction. For example, students in Cliff's group often recorded Cliff's notes for him or carried out experiments according to Cliff's directions when needed. Mr. Masoodi provided extra time for Cliff to work on the science activities if necessary. Mr. Masoodi also adapted materials, for example, by acquiring handheld lenses that were larger and easier to handle. Mr. Masoodi also adapted the environment by rearranging desks to create more aisle space for Cliff and his two canes. Similar adaptations for differentiated instruction, for a wide variety of objectives, are described throughout this text.

MyEdLab:
Video Example 6.2.

Listen to the teacher in this video as she describes how she plans for differentiation of her lessons, including differentiation of methods, materials, and the learning environment.

According to the Individuals with Disabilities Education Improvement Act (IDEA, 2004), special education is "specially designed instruction," and IDEA defines specially designed instruction as follows:

> (3) *Specially designed instruction* means adapting, as appropriate to the needs of an eligible child under this part, the content, methodology, or delivery of instruction—
> (i) To address the unique needs of the child that result from the child's disability; and
> (ii) To ensure access of the child to the general curriculum, so that the child can meet the educational standards within the jurisdiction of the public agency that apply to all children. [§300.39(b)(3)]

IDEA does not specifically define adaptations with respect to "accommodations" and "modifications." However, accommodations are generally understood to mean those adaptations that do not involve changing the goals and objectives of instruction. For example, a student who is given a specially designed study guide to organize study skills may still take the same test, with the same evaluative criteria, as all other students. Modifications, on the other hand, generally refer to those adaptations that change to some degree the expectations or standards of instruction. For example, taking a specially designed spelling test for a student's individual target spelling words might constitute a modification (Fennell, 2007). In practice, the terms *accommodations* and *modifications* have been used interchangeably (Center for Parent Information and Resources, 2016). However, it is important to know whether a particular adaptation is intended to help a student meet an instructional objective or whether the level of expectation has been changed.

Appropriately developed adaptations allow students of different abilities to succeed within the same curriculum and constitute the core of differentiated instruction. When planning adaptations to improve student learning, consider specifically *what* will be taught and to *what level of proficiency*. These considerations have been referred to as **types and levels of learning** (Mastropieri & Scruggs, 2002). Knowing what types and levels of learning are desired provides guidelines for planning instructional adaptations for differentiated instruction.

STRATEGIES FOR
MAKING ADAPTATIONS

BASE ADAPTATIONS ON STUDENT CHARACTERISTICS All instruction is concerned with the interaction of characteristics of the learner with the characteristics of the instructional methods, materials, and environment. Appropriately adapted methods or materials take this interaction into account. Specific adaptations in a variety of academic and behavioral skills and content areas are described in detail throughout this text. Table 6.1 lists some examples of possible adaptations based on specific learning characteristics.

BASE INSTRUCTIONAL ADAPTATIONS ON TYPES OF LEARNING Different types of learning occur in school, across all different subject areas. These types include learning of discriminations, facts, rules, procedures, and concepts, as well as problem solving/critical thinking (Mastropieri & Scruggs, 2002). Although there can be much overlap on school tasks, it is helpful to examine some of the distinctions among the categories. Teachers who understand the different types of learning required of students are more able to plan effective instruction. They are also more able to plan effective instructional adaptations, focused specifically on the nature of the learning task. That is, when a student is demonstrating difficulty with a learning task, it is helpful to determine the type of learning the task represents (e.g., factual learning rather than math or social studies or English) when planning adaptations. Table 6.2 summarizes types of learning and example adaptations.

Discrimination Learning Discrimination often occurs early in learning and involves determining how one stimulus is either the same as or different from another stimulus. Making discriminations is important in early learning of such things as the alphabet, numbers, colors, shapes, and math concepts. For example, learning to discriminate between a triangle and a square may be difficult at first for students with disabilities. Careful attention to the relevant and irrelevant distinctions between various stimuli can help improve **discrimination learning**. For example, the critical feature that distinguishes p from q is the relative placement of the round part of the letter. The critical feature that distinguishes squares from triangles is the

TABLE 6.1 Adaptations Based on Student Characteristics

Learner Characteristics	Possible Adaptations
Physical	• Optimal location of student in classroom (preferential seating) • Rearrangement of classroom layout to promote mobility and accessibility for wheelchairs or braces • Adaptations to promote grasping (e.g., pencil grips, alligator clips, Velcro) • Peer assistance to support physical manipulation • Technological adaptations for computer use
Sensory	• Environmental adaptations to accommodate low vision (e.g., clear routes through the classroom) or hearing ability (e.g., carpets to reduce extraneous noise) • Adaptations to promote access to text (e.g., braille, Kurzweil readers) • Peer assistance to support access to visual or auditory stimuli • Sign language or frequency-modulation (FM) systems to provide support for hearing impairments
Language	• Language cards for specific vocabulary • *Boardmaker* or teacher-made communication boards • Targeted language instruction • Peer mediation/peer assistance • Sign language instruction
Literacy	• Direct teaching of literacy skills and strategies • Books on tape • Text-to-speech systems (e.g., Kurzweil readers) • Peer reading/writing assistance • Hands-on/activity-oriented instruction
Emotional/Behavioral	• "Safe" areas of classroom for target student to use when needed • Reduced interaction with peers if needed • Recording chart for monitoring target behaviors with token systems • Peer support • Class rewards for target student behavior • Parent involvement for social behavior

number of sides (and not, for example, size). For students exhibiting difficulty in discrimination learning tasks, additional repeated practice that emphasizes comprehension of the critical distinctions can provide a beneficial adaptation.

Factual Learning   Factual learning is a common aspect of school learning and includes vocabulary words and their definitions, names of famous people and their accomplishments, dates and causes of historical events, addition facts, and names of rivers and other geographical features. Some factual learning is in the form of **paired associates**, where one thing is paired with another (e.g., Ulan Bator = Capital of Mongolia; the Italian word *mela* = "apple"). Other factual learning is in the form of a **serial list** (e.g., "a–b–c–d–e–f–g . . ."; "2–4–6–8–10 . . ."), where information is learned with respect to a specific sequence. Appropriate strategies include redundancy, drill and practice, enhancing meaningfulness, and use of elaborations or other memory-enhancing techniques; all of these strategies can be useful in adapting instruction for special needs.

Rule Learning   Rules are also pervasive in school, and many students with disabilities and other special needs have difficulties learning these rules. Examples of **rule learning** include social behavior rules (e.g., "Always raise your hand before speaking in class") and math rules (e.g., "When dividing fractions, invert the divisor and multiply"). Rules often include discriminations, facts, and appropriate circumstances for the use of those rules. For example, students might need to know that the rules for speaking in class are different in Mr. Halleran's class

TABLE 6.2 Adaptations Based on Types of Learning

Type of Learning	Possible Adaptations
Discrimination	• Present examples and nonexamples (e.g., "This is purple; this is not purple. Is this purple?"). • Use models, prompts, and feedback. • Teach relevant dimensions (e.g., "This is an insect; notice it has six legs").
Factual	• Use repetition, rehearsal, and practice (e.g., "Cheyenne is the capital of Wyoming. What city is the capital of Wyoming? Cheyenne, yes, good."). • Present information in clusters or chunks. • Use overlearning (teaching beyond a criterion) and distributed practice with frequent review. • Use verbal elaboration and mnemonics ("A 'buoy' can help you remember the meaning of *buoyant*").
Rule	• Practice using rules, and provide feedback. • Use "sayings" for rules (e.g., "*I* before *e*, except after *c*"). • Model applications for rules. • Remind students of rules (e.g., "What is the rule for recess?").
Procedure	• Model use of procedures. • Write out steps of procedures as reminders. • Use drill and practice. • Practice applications of the procedure and recognizing, retrieving, and executing steps in the procedure. • Use acronyms for procedure steps (e.g., "What is the first step in answering an essay question using the SNOW strategy? 'S = Study the question,' good").
Concept	• Directly teach relevant rules and discriminations. • Use examples and nonexamples (e.g., "Is this an example of radial symmetry?"). • Enhance meaningfulness with multiple concrete examples.
Problem solving	• Use modeling and think-alouds ("Here's how I would try to solve this problem"), coaching, and prompting. • Reteach any relevant procedures; practice with similar, simpler problems. • Activate prior knowledge; help students learn more about the problem to be solved.

than they are in Ms. Butcher's class and that they need to learn to apply the rules appropriately in each class. Some individual students may have more difficulty assimilating these differences and may require additional practice as an adaptation.

Procedural Learning   Procedural learning involves the sequential execution of multiple steps and frequently is found in school tasks. Remembering and executing the steps involved in going through the cafeteria lunch line (e.g., take your place at the end of the line, take your tray, pick up your silverware) is an example of procedural learning. Academic examples include reading-comprehension strategies (e.g., determine the purpose, survey the material, read, recite, review), math algorithms (e.g., learning to execute the steps in solving long-division problems), and study strategies. This can involve describing or listing the steps in the procedure, modeling or demonstrating the application of the procedure, or prompting students to execute the steps of the procedure. Procedural learning requires that students (1) *recognize* when a specific procedure is called for (e.g., a strategy for learning a list of spelling words), (2) *retrieve* the steps in the procedure (e.g., C–C–C, or cover, copy, and compare), and (3) correctly *execute* the procedure (e.g., use the strategy correctly to learn the list). When students exhibit difficulty with procedural learning tasks, consider which of these three steps they have not mastered.

Conceptual Learning   Most tasks involve some conceptual learning, which can be taught using procedures similar to those for discrimination-, factual-, and rule-learning paradigms. **Concepts** are completely learned only when the concepts can be applied to a new instance. For example, students do not know the concept of "dog" if they can only identify their own household pet as a dog—they must be able to identify dogs they have never seen before.

Concepts can range from simple ("red") to more complex ("radial symmetry," "nonpolar covalent bonding"). Conceptual learning can be enhanced by the use of examples (e.g., of radial symmetry or of the color red), provision of noninstances ("this is *not* an example of a carnivore"), and statement and application of rules ("insects have six legs; how many legs does this specimen have?"). These enhancements can be helpful adaptations for any students who do not immediately master relevant concepts.

Problem Solving/Critical Thinking   **Problem solving** refers to determining solutions when no specific strategy for solving the problem is known. Similarly, **critical thinking** refers to the use of active reasoning to acquire novel concepts, ideas, or solutions or to evaluate or analyze information to reach a justifiable conclusion. These types of learning are commonly found in science and mathematics curricula (e.g., geometric proofs) but could also be found in any other area (e.g., understanding or solving a social problem in social studies). Problem solving and critical thinking are important goals in education, but they also present some of the greatest challenges for students with disabilities. They can be enhanced by the use of teacher "think-alouds" ("Here's how I think as I try to solve this problem . . .") and careful questioning or coaching techniques, as described elsewhere in this chapter.

BASE INSTRUCTIONAL ADAPTATIONS ON THE APPROPRIATE LEVEL OF LEARNING
Another important consideration for teachers when planning instructional adaptations is the level of proficiency to be attained by the student for any of the previously described types of learning. Levels of learning address *how well* something will be learned, and it may be possible to isolate learning problems within these parameters (Mastropieri & Scruggs, 2002; Scheuermann & Hall, 2016). For example, if we say that a student "has not learned" something, it may be that the student *has* learned at one level (e.g., initial acquisition) but not at the level necessary for success (e.g., fluency or application). These levels include—in order of complexity—initial acquisition, fluency, application, and generalization. Consideration of the appropriate level of learning can help when planning adaptations.

Acquisition and Fluency   **Acquisition** refers to simple accuracy-level criteria, such as 9 out of 10 correct responses to listing 10 letters of the alphabet. Accuracy criteria are important in the initial stages of learning. **Fluency** combines the accuracy criteria with specified amounts of time—for example, 90% accuracy within 2 minutes, or 90 out of 100 letters correct in 5 minutes. Fluency is particularly important when tasks need to become automatic, such as in basic literacy, math, and letter-formation skills. Many students, for example, have acquired the skills needed to read individual words but are not sufficiently fluent to comprehend what they are reading. Such students would benefit from fluency instruction.

Application and Generalization   **Application** refers to applying learned skills or content to relevant contexts, and **generalization** is the ability to transfer previous learning to novel situations. For example, applying a social skill learned in a lesson in the special education setting to a role-play activity is an example of the application level. An example of generalization is employing appropriately, in an inclusive classroom setting, a social skill previously learned in the special education classroom.

Application and generalization levels of learning can be difficult for some students with disabilities to attain (Sabornie & deBettencourt, 2009). Simply because a student has learned a particular skill (e.g., telling time or a social skill for greeting new people) in one situation, you should not assume the student will now apply or generalize that skill to every appropriate situation. In many cases, specific strategies to promote application and generalization are needed.

Application and generalization levels of learning can be promoted by training "loosely" and allowing flexibility in responding; by using "indiscriminable contingencies" (rewarding students when they do not know they are being observed); by using modeling and role-play; by employing classroom peers; by encouraging self-monitoring, where students evaluate their own performance; and by retraining the desired behavior in a variety of different circumstances (see also Alberto & Troutman, 2012; Scruggs & Mastropieri, 1994a).

TABLE 6.3 Instructional Strategies for Specific Levels of Learning

Levels of Learning	Instructional Strategies
Acquisition	• Slow the pace of instruction, and provide for additional practice. • Use modeling and demonstrations. • Provide lots of reinforcement for accurate responding.
Fluency	• Provide a faster pace of instruction. • Practice with timed responding (e.g., "How many words can you read in a minute this time?"). • Provide reinforcement for rapid, accurate responding.
Application	• Provide several instances of different application problems. • Model procedures and directions in different cases. • Provide meaningful demonstrations and examples. • Use active coaching with questioning to prompt correct responding (e.g., "Remember how we did . . .; this is just like it, only now. . .").
Generalization	• Ensure students have mastered relevant skills. • Train and retrain "loosely" in real-world settings. • Use multiple examples of stimuli. • Use peer assistance and indiscriminable contingencies. • Train students to use self-monitoring; use modeling and role-play. • Reinforce appropriate generalization. • Practice skills to be generalized (e.g., "When we go to the store, we are going to use the *polite behaviors* that we practiced before. Now, if you need help, how will you ask?").

Identification Versus Production For any of the levels of learning, students can be asked to identify or produce relevant responses. **Identification** includes such responses as pointing to the correct answer (e.g., on a communication board) and responding to matching, multiple-choice, or true/false test formats and is usually learned more readily. **Production** is more difficult and includes such responses as writing, saying, computing, orally spelling, and exhibiting appropriate behavior. When planning instruction, consider whether students will be required to identify or produce correct responses. For example, if students are required to produce correct responses (such as spelling words), it is important that they practice producing, rather than simply identifying, correctly spelled words during instruction.

Consider Types and Levels of Learning to Address Specific Learning Problems
To best address special learning needs, first determine where the problems lie. For example, Janine cannot remember the correct sequence of steps in multiplying an algebraic expression. Mario can identify but not produce correctly spelled words from his weekly list. Shawna can control her impulsivity in the classroom but not the cafeteria. Once these are identified as problems of procedural learning, identification/production, and generalization, respectively, they can be specifically addressed. As such, your instruction can be much more precise (and much more effective) than if these problems are simply considered to be problems with math, spelling, or social behavior. Tables 6.2 and 6.3 present some examples of adaptations to address problems in specific levels and types of learning. Remember that many different strategies may be successful and that identification and production formats can be considered with any of the other levels and types of learning.

USE PRINCIPLES OF UNIVERSAL DESIGN FOR LEARNING Universal design for learning (UDL) principles involve developing materials or structuring the environment to improve accessibility for all learners (CAST, 2011, 2012; Hall, Meyer, & Rose, 2012); thus, it is very compatible with the principles of differentiated instruction. For many years, the CAST organization has been developing software intended to address a diversity of learner needs. For example, in reading text, students with physical disabilities may benefit from page-turning technology, students with limited vision or reading disabilities may benefit from text-to-speech technology, and students with limited vocabulary may benefit from links to definitions. These and other options could potentially be embedded within a single digital book (Meyer, Rose, & Gordon, 2014). Whenever possible, UDL seeks to present highly similar curricula to all students that can be accessed by all in ways that address individual learning needs.

Three guiding principles for UDL proposed by CAST and its National Center for UDL are (1) multiple means of engagement (e.g., recruiting interest, sustaining effort and persistence), (2) multiple means of representation (e.g., perception, language, expressions, symbols), and (3) multiple means of action and expression (e.g., physical action, expression, and communication) in order to design curricula that address the needs of all types of learners (see also CAST.org). These are each described as follows.

Multiple Means of Engagement   Providing multiple means of engagement is intended to develop purposeful, motivated learners. This is accomplished by providing options for self-regulation, which include promoting positive expectations and beliefs, facilitating coping skills, and teaching self-assessment and reflection. Additionally, multiple means are needed for sustaining persistence of effort, for example, by encouraging collaboration with others, varying demands and resources, and increasing feedback toward personal mastery. Finally, it is important to promote interest on the part of individual learners by providing personal choice, enhancing task relevance and value, and minimizing interfering or distracting stimuli. In supplying and promoting multiple means of engagement, UDL seeks to address the affective component of learning.

Multiple Means of Representation   Providing multiple means of representation is intended to develop resourceful, knowledgeable learners. In order to achieve this, a variety of options should be provided for comprehension, including activating background knowledge, highlighting significant features and ideas, guiding the multiple ways the information can be processed, and directly focusing on generalization and transfer of learned information and skills. In addition, options should be provided for different uses of language as well as mathematical and symbolic communication, by clarifying vocabulary and syntax, and use of a variety of means for enhancing comprehension. It is also of significant importance to provide options for how information is perceived, including alternatives for auditory or visual information, and customizing how information is displayed. These multiple means of representation provide options for all learners to access information.

Multiple Means for Action and Expression   Providing multiple means for action and expression is intended to develop strategic, goal-directed learners. These means are concerned with how students respond to instructional stimuli. They include options for executive functioning, including goal-setting, planning, strategy development, and progress monitoring. Options are also provided for expression and communication, including the use of multimedia, multiple tools for composition, and fluency-building activities. Physical activity is also considered, including providing various methods to respond to instructional materials and navigate the curricula and providing optimal access to tools and assistive technologies. In planning instruction, it is important to consider how students will respond to instructional curriculum and to ensure that multiple options are available for different learning needs.

CAST provides specific guidelines for the development of new materials to promote accessibility for diverse learners, rather than adapting existing materials. One example of a curriculum material designed with UDL principles is *WiggleWorks* (produced and distributed by Scholastic), which provides a blend of technology, literature, and teacher support to help students develop reading and writing skills. However, because many materials were developed without the principles of UDL, those existing materials may be adapted or differentiated more successfully by using the UDL guidelines.

Rao, Ok, and Bryant (2014) summarized research studies evaluating UDL principles and reported that research generally supported the effectiveness of these applications. However, the number of studies identified was limited, terminology was used in widely varying ways, and many of these studies were qualitative or descriptive, rather than experimental. Rao et al. recommended that in the future, researchers should (a) use terminology related to UDL consistently, (b) identify specifically the relations between their own intervention components and UDL principles, and (c) conduct more empirically based research that directly examines the efficacy of applications of UDL principles.

As can be seen, many of the strategies recommended in this book chapter are consistent with the principles of UDL. Essentially, when instruction considers the needs of all learners and provides multiple alternative means for engagement with curricula, representation of information, and action and expression in response to the curriculum, principles of UDL are being employed.

MyEdLab: **Self-Check 6.3**

MyEdLab: **Application Exercise 6.1: Prioritize Instruction**

S: SYSTEMATICALLY TEACH WITH THE SCREAM VARIABLES

Systematic teaching is the third component of the PASS variables and builds on the previous ones; indeed, in order to systematically teach, you need to incorporate planning for content and prioritizing objectives as well as adapting instruction, materials, and/or the environment. Systematic teaching refers to the use of effective teaching techniques for content coverage and teacher presentations, known as the SCREAM variables: structure, clarity, redundancy, enthusiasm, appropriate rate, and maximized engagement through questioning and feedback (Mastropieri & Scruggs, 2002, 2004; Scruggs & Mastropieri, 1995). If you implement differentiated instruction using these techniques and consider the specific needs of students with disabilities, all students may be more successfully included, and overall classroom achievement will improve. The *Research Highlight* later in the chapter describes investigations of teachers' understandings of evidence-based practice.

STRATEGIES FOR
IMPLEMENTING THE SCREAM VARIABLES

STRUCTURE YOUR LESSONS   Structure refers to the organization of the components of the lesson. Structure does not necessarily mean that the content of your lesson will be teacher-driven or that your students sit in rows doing worksheets. Rather, lessons are structured when you (1) communicate to students the overall organization and purpose of the lesson, (2) display outlines of the lesson and indicate transition points, (3) emphasize the critical points of the lesson, and (4) summarize and review throughout the lesson. Following is an example of structure in teacher dialogue, taken from a fourth-grade science lesson on ecosystems:

> The first thing—and Mrs. [name of special education teacher], if you would like to write this on the board—the first thing you're going to do is get your supplies and aquarium. . . . The second thing that I want you to do is put your gravel in, which is step number 2 . . . [repeats]. . . . The third thing that's going to happen is that you are going to fill out parts of your activity sheet. . . . (Mastropieri et al., 1998, p. 18)

Structure is particularly helpful for students who have difficulty sustaining attention or who exhibit difficulties in language comprehension. Structure refers not only to providing an overall organizational framework for the lesson but also to ensuring that students understand this organization.

Communicate Lesson Structure to Your Students   Carefully design your lessons with a clear idea of the structure, including stating the purpose, reviewing the main ideas, and making clear transitions between lesson elements (Good & Brophy, 2007). You will communicate structure best to your students if you yourself are very familiar with the structure and organization of your lessons.

Tell students the structure of the lesson. This can be done by announcing the components of the lesson directly, by writing the outline on the board or on an overhead projector, and by using illustrations or handouts to indicate the lesson's sequence.

Remind students about the structure throughout the lesson. Say, for example, "Remember, when you finish your group work, we are going to meet again as a class to review what we have learned about bird migration."

PROMOTE CLARITY IN YOUR PRESENTATIONS   A teacher exhibits clarity when he or she speaks clearly and directly to the point of the objective; avoids unclear or vague language or terminology; and provides concrete, explicit examples of the content being covered. Clear presentations address only one objective at a time and are directed explicitly to the lesson objective.

Select Vocabulary and Syntax That Are Familiar to All Students in the Class   If you use a word that is unfamiliar to some or all students, take a minute to explain the word's meaning. If English language learners are included in the class, use illustrations, physical modeling, or hand gestures to support verbally provided directions. These procedures are also beneficial for communicating with students with hearing impairments who have language difficulties and students with learning disabilities who have language comprehension difficulties. When employing co-teaching, the special education teacher can assume the role of promoting clarity and understanding where needed.

Eliminate Vague Language in Your Presentations   Smith and Land (1981) reported that vague terms added to teacher presentations consistently lowered achievement. Vague terms are in italics in the following teacher presentation:

> This mathematics lesson *might* enable you to understand *a little more* about *some things* we *usually call* number patterns. *Maybe* before we get to *probably* the main idea of the lesson, you should review *a few* prerequisite concepts. *Actually,* the first concept you need to review is positive integers. *As you know,* a positive integer is any whole number greater than zero. (Smith & Land, 1981, p. 38)

Clarity is also impeded by *mazes,* which include confusing word patterns ("we don't know it can't be done without . . ."), false starts ("facilit . . . I mean, make it better to . . ."), and unnecessary or irrelevant repetition ("This is, this is . . . it's true that this is the most important . . ."). Smith (1977) reported that lower student achievement was found in classrooms where teachers said "uh" frequently. Also avoid vague language such as "kind of," "you know," "sort of," and "pretty much." Avoid *negated intensifiers* ("not a lot," "not much," "not very"), *indeterminate quantification* ("a number," "a few of," "several"), and *ambiguous designation* ("some kind of," "somewhere"). Instead, use clear, direct, and precise language (Good & Brophy, 2007; Smith & Land, 1981). Clarity can be particularly important when restating comments made by individual students so that they will be more understandable to all students.

EMPLOY REDUNDANCY EFFECTIVELY   Redundancy increases learning by emphasizing and reinforcing the most important aspects of lessons. Unlike unnecessary and irrelevant repetition of words, continued emphasis on key concepts, procedures, and rules is critical to the success of the lesson. Many students with disabilities require additional opportunities to hear, see, and practice lessons before mastering the objectives. It is unnecessary for components of the lesson to be identical to provide redundancy for students (Archer & Hughes, 2011).

Embed redundancy in your presentations. Discuss the main points of the lesson, and then be sure to refer to the key concepts throughout the lesson. Question students directly on these key concepts to reinforce their learning.

Create opportunities for extra practice to help provide redundancy for selected students. For example, supplemental practice times can be arranged for students either before or after school or during lunch and study hall periods. Peers who have mastered the topics can be asked to provide assistance during these additional practice periods. Focus on the most important content, and provide many opportunities for responding.

Create opportunities to apply and generalize learned information to novel situations. For example, prompt students to use newly learned arithmetic to compute the cost of a single slice of a whole pizza or to use a reading-comprehension strategy to study a social studies book.

TEACH WITH ENTHUSIASM!   Students consistently learn more and appreciate the content more when teachers display enthusiasm in their teaching. Enthusiasm also creates higher levels of student engagement with the lesson, increasing academic learning time. Enthusiastic teachers create exciting learning environments, in which students perceive that learning is fun, challenges are great, curiosity is enhanced, and thinking is encouraged (Good & Brophy, 2007). Enthusiastic teaching can be especially helpful for students who have histories of academic failure and are poorly motivated to succeed in school. For example, some students with disabilities are used to performing poorly in classes and have little motivation to attempt to succeed; however, an enthusiastic teaching style can provide the necessary excitement and encouragement to motivate such students to be successful (Wentzel & Brophy, 2014).

Teaching with enthusiasm can be used to stimulate student interest and attention, and it involves the use of several techniques that have been described by researchers, including the following:

- Varying speaking rates and using an upbeat tone of voice
- Using physical gestures to emphasize important points
- Using facial expressions and eye movements that convey positive interest
- Choosing a variety of expressive words
- Exhibiting a high overall energy level (e.g., Brigham, Scruggs, & Mastropieri, 1992; Kunter, Frenzel, Nagy, Baumert, & Pekrun, 2010).

These techniques demonstrate that enthusiasm is something that teachers *do,* not something that teachers *are*. It is clear that teachers can change the amount of enthusiasm they display and improve student motivation and affect when they do so.

Enthusiasm is an attribute that you can vary within your own teaching (Brigham et al., 1992). And although it may make you a little self-conscious at first, you can practice being enthusiastic simply by raising and lowering the intonation of your voice and by using your hands and arms when you talk to students to explain or elaborate on a point. Statements made enthusiastically can gain students' attention. For example, one fourth-grade teacher used the following statement to gain attention and to control transitions within her classroom during an ecosystems science activity: "Class, when I say 'ecosystems are a *blast*,' everyone go to your science groups!"

Enthusiastic teaching also involves open acceptance of student contributions. This is of critical importance for students with special needs, who may believe their contributions are not welcome. In the case of disabilities such as communication disorders or hearing impairments, it may take longer for students to communicate ideas to the class. In other cases, the ideas, answers, or suggestions offered may seem less sophisticated than those of some other students. In these instances, it is particularly important for teachers to demonstrate enthusiastically that ideas and input from all students are welcome.

Can enthusiasm be overdone? Possibly. But one essential element of enthusiasm is that it must be (or appear to be) sincere. If students regard teachers' enthusiasm as genuine, they will probably welcome and appreciate very high levels of enthusiasm. On the other hand, if the enthusiasm seems forced or insincere, students will be less likely to appreciate it. Overall, however, our experiences (and research evidence) have convinced us that teacher enthusiasm promotes motivation and positive affect and that enthusiasm is often underused but rarely overused.

USE AN APPROPRIATE RATE OF PRESENTATION Effective teachers deliver instruction at the optimal rate. Generally, a brisk rate of presentation throughout the lesson and a brisk rate of interacting with students work well with enthusiasm variables and help keep lessons interesting and motivating. During basic skills instruction, a fast pace may be important in increasing learning (Carnine, 1976; Gleason, Carnine, & Vala, 1991). However, an excessively rapid rate of presentation may not be related to increased learning. When learning outcomes are not being met, changing the overall rate of presentation may allow information to be better understood by all students.

Begin with a brisk presentation rate, and frequently question students. Students' answers to your questions will tell you whether you are proceeding too rapidly. Record yourself, and evaluate your rate of presentation. Perhaps your rate of presentation is good, but other presentation elements (speaking directly and clearly and with sufficient volume) are inhibiting understanding and need to be modified.

Some teachers begin lessons with a brisk rate of presentation, but they later slow down and lose student attention by overly focusing on minor issues or by questioning some students repetitively while the rest of the class waits. If some individual students, but not others, need additional practice, provide differentiated instruction by working with them individually, in small groups, or with peer tutors (Good & Brophy, 2007).

Jimmy

Jimmy is a 10-year-old fifth grader who was having trouble succeeding academically in school. His teacher, Ms. Marshak, believed that Jimmy had the overall ability to succeed in her classroom, but he rarely completed his work. As a result, he was falling far behind the other students in the class.

Ms. Marshak began to pay more attention to how Jimmy was spending his time. She found that he was often the last student to take his books, paper, and pencil from his desk and begin working. During this period, he also spent more time than other students going to the pencil sharpener, asking to get a drink of water, daydreaming, or playing with pencils or rulers in his desk. When Ms. Marshak recorded his behavior at the end of every minute over a 30-minute period, she found that Jimmy was actually working on his assignment only 10 of the 30 times she sampled his behavior. Clearly, Jimmy needed to increase the amount of time he put into his schoolwork.

QUESTIONS FOR REFLECTION

1. Why is Jimmy off-task so often? How could you find out?
2. Why doesn't concern about poor grades motivate Jimmy to work harder?
3. What are some simple things Ms. Marshak could do to help Jimmy?

MAXIMIZE ACADEMIC ENGAGEMENT Research has consistently supported the idea that the more time students devote to a particular subject or skill, the more likely they are to master it. This is true whether the area is reading, science, creative writing, archery, music, or debate: more time effectively engaged in learning leads to more (and better) learning outcomes. Maximizing student engagement and time-on-task is the single best way of increasing your students' learning.

In the previous scenario, it seems clear that Jimmy's learning will not improve until he can increase the amount of time spent on his work. Although most teachers **allocate** appropriate time for learning a certain subject (by, for example, scheduling a specific amount of time per day to reading instruction), a far smaller number of teachers will ensure that students are actually **engaged** in learning, to the greatest extent possible, during this allocated time. This distinction between allocated and engaged academic time is critical for student learning. In some cases, teachers may be able to greatly increase classroom learning simply by increasing student engagement rates (Seo, Brownell, Bishop, & Dingle, 2008).

But what are the specific techniques you can use to maximize academic engaged time? In a broad sense, teachers need to maximize student learning by maximizing student engagement with instruction and instructional materials. Selecting materials that are at the correct level of difficulty and that are motivating and interesting for students will help with this. Additionally, teachers need to carefully plan, monitor, and reward high rates of engagement, such as in the scenario about Jimmy, and carefully implement questioning, praise, and feedback. However, the first step is to understand what is meant by academic engaged time, or "on-task" behavior.

On-task behaviors of students vary depending on the grade level of the students, the curriculum, the type of lesson, the learning activities, and the behavior of the teacher. However, in general, students are considered on-task when they are doing such things as actively looking at or otherwise attending to the teacher, instructional materials, or other students who are actively engaged. Giving direct answers to relevant teacher questions or asking relevant questions are also considered on-task behaviors. During teacher presentations, examples of on-task student behavior include actively listening, taking notes, outlining, and asking for clarification. Likewise, being appropriately engaged in science experiments or math manipulatives and engaging in relevant debate in social studies can also be considered on-task behaviors. Overall, student behavior is usually considered on-task if it is logically related to instructional activities.

Some students with disabilities may be engaged in different ways. For example, some students, including students with visual impairments, with emotional handicaps, or with autism, may not be actively watching the teacher but may nonetheless provide other signs that

Beliefs versus Knowledge of Effective Teachers

Urbach et al. (2014) studied the beliefs of more and less accomplished special education teachers regarding teacher roles and responsibilities and how those beliefs influenced their practice. Beliefs versus knowledge can impact teachers' practice and determine whether practice is evidence based or not. Beliefs can be conscious or unconscious expectations about teaching and students but may be derived from experiences, whereas knowledge is based on truths agreed upon by experts (e.g., Richardson, 2003). Use of evidence-based practices is based on knowledge, whereas the generation of idiosyncratic teaching practices is more likely derived from personal experiences. Guckert, Mastropieri, and Scruggs (2016) reported that highly competent teachers reported more knowledge about and use of evidence-based practices, whereas less qualified teachers relied on personalized experiences to guide their teaching practices. Ruiz, Rueda, Figueroa, and Boothroyd (1995) reported that teacher beliefs can be modified through effective training.

Urbach et al. (2014) used the RISE rating scale to identify more and less accomplished teachers. The RISE instrument consisted of 22 items addressing reading instruction, classroom management, and instructional practice and intended to evaluate effective reading instruction. Teachers were observed, and those with higher versus lower scores were classified as more or less accomplished. All teachers were then interviewed on such topics as teacher efficacy, teaching influences, teacher roles and responsibilities, and effective teaching. Interviews were recorded, coded, and analyzed using methodologies for qualitative data analysis.

Urbach et al. (2014) identified themes related to beliefs that were shared and that differentiated these more versus less accomplished teachers: (a) providing instruction, (b) being resourceful, (c) communicating and collaborating with general educators and parents, and (d) building relationships. The more accomplished teachers were relatively consistent in addressing these themes; however, less accomplished teachers were not. For example, more accomplished teachers linked their responses to student learning outcomes, identified the need for intensity of instruction, and determined what they could do to improve instruction, including adapting instruction to improve outcomes. More accomplished teachers also reported better self-efficacy and use of problem-solving techniques focusing on what they could implement to improve academic performance. In addition, more accomplished teachers adopted an attitude of teaching all students regardless of barriers. Relationship building with students was reported differently across groups. More accomplished teachers viewed relationship building as part of the academic learning process and never lost sight of the academic outcomes. In contrast, less accomplished teachers focused more on building relationships with their students at the expense of academic outcomes. This suggests that teachers who are more accomplished have beliefs related to knowledge, have higher self-efficacy, and are more likely to improve learning outcomes in their students.

QUESTIONS FOR REFLECTION

1. Why do you think a teacher's beliefs can play such an important role in instruction?
2. What could teachers do to become more knowledgeable and alter their beliefs?
3. Would strategies for changing teacher beliefs differ between elementary and secondary grade levels?

---

they are attending. Students with physical disabilities may interact differently with educational materials, but they nonetheless can be observed to be interacting. Students with hearing impairments may need to watch the interpreter rather than the teacher. Some students with learning disabilities are unable to listen and take notes simultaneously, but they may be on-task. Careful consideration of the special needs and abilities of different learners will reveal how different students may display appropriate on-task behavior.

On the other hand, off-task behavior is not logically related to academic learning. Off-task behavior can include tardiness, daydreaming, attending to inappropriate material, asking irrelevant questions or making irrelevant statements, or interacting inappropriately with peers or instructional materials. These activities are negatively related to learning; in other words, the more off-task behavior that occurs in a classroom, the less learning takes place.

STRATEGIES FOR

MAXIMIZING ON-TASK BEHAVIOR

Your on-task behaviors as a teacher influence how much students learn. These include statements directly relevant to the lesson, questioning and feedback directly relevant to the lesson, and demonstrations and modeling directly relevant to the lesson.

MyEdLab:
Video Example 6.3.

In this video, a teacher uses the KWL procedure to engage her students' attention and to motivate them to learn.

USE EFFECTIVE QUESTIONING TECHNIQUES Teachers must be effective at questioning students. Generally, the more questions asked that are directly relevant to the lesson, the more students learn from the lesson. Questioning has several purposes. First, questioning allows teachers to monitor students' understanding of the content being presented. In inclusive classrooms, questioning can be particularly helpful in determining whether all students understand the content being presented and whether instruction should be differentiated further. When breakdowns in understanding are revealed through questioning, teachers can modify and adjust their instruction (considering such things as rate of presentation, choice of vocabulary, and use of examples) to address students' learning needs more effectively.

Second, questioning allows students to actively practice the information being covered. In this way, repeated questioning related to the same concept can provide the redundancy necessary for information to be learned and remembered. For example, consider the following dialogue:

TEACHER: In Boston in 1770, what was one of the major concerns of the colonists, Marcia?

MARCIA: Taxation without representation.

TEACHER: Taxation without representation. What's another way of saying that, Dan?

DAN: That, uh, you have to pay taxes, but you don't have someone to represent you in the government.

TEACHER: You pay taxes, but don't have a representative, good!

Questioning can be delivered to individuals or groups. When addressing questions to individuals, state the question first before calling on a particular student. If you give a student's name first, other students may be less likely to carefully consider an answer. For example, ask, "Why do you think Germany would strengthen its relations with Mexico during the first years of World War I? Frederick, why do you think this happened?" Rather than, "Frederick, why do you think Germany . . .?" (Archer & Hughes, 2011).

Be certain the question is clearly stated so that students will know what type of response is expected and so that instructional time will not be lost in subsequent clarification. For example, referring to a passage in a text, a teacher might ask, "What problem do you see with this statement?" Although the teacher may be expecting an answer regarding verb tense, students might not know what the teacher means by "problem." Instead, she might ask, "Is there a problem with verb tense in this statement?" or, more generally, "Is there a grammatical problem in this sentence?" (Good & Brophy, 2007).

When addressing the question to groups, it may be possible to promote "covert" responding on the part of all students, which will maximize student engagement. For example, "Now I want everyone to think about this problem and make a prediction: If I add weight to this pendulum, will it swing more rapidly? Everyone think [pause], now, thumbs up for yes, thumbs down for no." Alternatively, ask students to write down answers to questions individually to be read back later. For example, "Everybody, write down a definition of *metonymy,* and give an example. When you're done, we'll compare answers." These answers can provide insights into how your instruction can be further differentiated.

There are also different types of questioning, including lower-level questioning and higher-level questioning. Lower-level questioning usually involves repetition or restatement of previously covered information and is often used in basic skills instruction or in early stages of learning. For basic skills and basic facts, questioning should be fast paced and require simple, direct answers (examples: "What is the silent-*e* rule?"; "What is the Pythagorean theorem?"; "What are the three branches of government?"). For this type of questioning, teachers should aim for 80% to 100% correct responding. This type of questioning is frequently used when building fluency with responding, such as when practicing math facts or vocabulary definitions using flashcards.

Higher-Level Questioning   Higher-level questioning requires more in-depth thinking. For higher-level responses requiring thinking and reflection, questioning should proceed at a slower rate and may not require simple, direct answers. For example, "Why do you think a type of moss is often found on the north side of trees? Would this be true all over the world?" In this example, students could consider the general position of the sun in the northern hemisphere and conclude that the south side of trees may often be drier. Considering the characteristics of moss, students may conclude that it may more frequently—but not always—grow on the north side of trees. This, of course, would not generally be true in the southern hemisphere. With such questioning, you should consider that students will need more time for reflection and may need additional questioning to direct their thinking (e.g., "What conditions are favorable for moss growth? When would moss not grow on the north side of a tree in the northern hemisphere? Is there a rule that would better predict where moss would grow on a tree?").

Research has documented that when students with mild disabilities have been "coached" to answer higher-level questions, they can be successful (Scruggs, Mastropieri, & Sullivan, 1994; Sullivan, Mastropieri, & Scruggs, 1995). For example, consider the coaching dialogue in Figure 6.1 used with students with learning disabilities and mild intellectual disabilities to promote thinking about animals. This type of explicit coaching provides the structure and support students need to promote reasoning, but it still allows them to come up with their own answers.

Some questions—some may say the most important questions—do not have simple answers with which everyone would agree. These include such questions as, "Who was the United States' most important president?"; "Should the Ten Commandments be displayed in schools?"; and "Does life exist on other planets?" Some students may have difficulty answering questions like these. When presenting these types of questions, inform students that a specific answer is not required and that, instead, the answer should reflect both knowledge of the subject and careful thought about the answer. Give students models of good possible answers. Ask students to consider subquestions, such as, "What qualities are considered important in a president?"; "What is the relevance of the 'establishment of religion' clause in the 1st Amendment?"; or "What conditions appear necessary for life to develop? What is the likelihood that these conditions exist elsewhere in the universe?"

Figure 6.1   Coaching Dialogue
Note: From "L'instruzione Mnemonica e L'interrogazione Elaborativa: Strategie per Ricordarsie per Pensare," by M. A. Mastropieri, 1995, in C. Cornoldi & R. Vianello (Eds.), *Handicap e Apprendimento: Ricerche e Proposte di Intervento* (pp. 117–124), Bergamo, Italy: Juvenilia. Copyright 1995 by Juvenilia. Reprinted with permission.

Experimenter: Anteaters have long claws on their front feet. Why does this make sense?

Student: I don't know.

Experimenter: Well, let's think. What do you know about anteaters? For example, what do they eat?

Student: Anteaters eat ants.

Experimenter: Good. And where do ants live?

Student: They live in holes in the ground.

Experimenter: Now, if anteaters eat ants, and ants live in holes in the ground, why do you think that anteaters have long claws on their front feet?

Student: To dig for ants.

Experimenter: Good. To dig for ants.

Good and Brophy (2007) suggested that teachers generally should avoid four types of questions:

1. Questions that require yes-or-no answers
2. "Tugging" questions ("What else?"; "Tell me more . . .")
3. "Guessing" questions, that is, asking students to guess when they do not have relevant information
4. Leading questions ("Isn't that so?")

Overall, the best questions are clear, purposeful, brief, phrased in simple language, sequenced, and thought provoking. This is true for all students but particularly for those with special needs.

PROVIDE HELPFUL FEEDBACK   How teachers respond to student answers is as important as how the questions are asked. Appropriate feedback can be helpful in informing students of their level of understanding, providing redundancy, and encouraging students to continue to learn (Burnett, 2003). Feedback should be clear and overt so that there is no ambiguity about the teacher's evaluation of the answer. When appropriate, it should provide the entire class with information on the correctness of the response of an individual student.

During rapid questioning, drill and practice of skills, or review of previously learned material, feedback may be simple and brief. In some cases, the fact that the teacher has continued with the lesson imparts the information that the previous answer was correct (e.g., multiplication facts prompted by flashcards). At other times, feedback may be more substantive.

The type of feedback delivered depends to some extent on the response that has been given. If a student does not respond right away, you should try to elicit some type of response to determine the level of student understanding. It is important to consider whether the question is a lower-level question that should require only a short "wait time" (the amount of time the teacher waits for a response) or a higher-level question that may require a longer wait time for the student to develop a more thoughtful answer. Research has shown that longer wait times (when appropriate to the question) are associated with better and longer student responses and an increase in voluntary student contributions (Good & Brophy, 2007).

When students do not respond correctly, it is important to determine whether the answer is unknown, whether the question was unclear, or whether the student simply did not hear the question. You should also determine whether students can answer the question with additional coaching or prompting. Teachers should not appear to "badger" students who clearly do not know how to respond. However, it is important to retest students later in the lesson.

For completely incorrect responses, a simple, tactful statement that the answer was incorrect may be sufficient. Simply state the correct answer, provide the student with a prompt or additional information and restate the question, or call on another student for the answer.

If an answer is partially correct, first acknowledge the part of the answer that is correct, and then provide additional prompts or restate the question to elicit the rest of the answer, or call on another student. For any question that was incorrectly answered, partially or completely, teachers should make an effort to return to the question with individual students later in the lesson to ensure that the material was learned.

If the question was correctly answered, acknowledge the correctness of the answer and move on in the lesson, as in the following example:

TEACHER: Now, which astronomer first determined that the planets travel in an elliptical pattern? Juanita?

JUANITA: Kepler.

TEACHER: Kepler, correct.

PRAISE STUDENTS FREQUENTLY   Praise can be an important motivator for students. When the situation warrants it, actively praise your students for paying attention to the lesson, carefully considering teacher questions, and providing answers that are correct, or at least reasonable and thoughtful. Effusive or overly elaborate praise may not be helpful in many instances because it may interrupt the flow of the lesson or embarrass students (particularly students at the secondary level). However, most teachers deliver too little praise to students. Praise may be particularly important to help students with disabilities or special learning needs persist in their efforts to learn.

Managing Time with the Time Timer™

Many students have difficulties with understanding the concept of time, especially when told they need to keep working for a specified amount of time. Other students have difficulties with transition periods and changing from one activity to the next. A technological device called the Time Timer can help students visually see the amount of time left as they work and help them comprehend in a more concrete fashion the amount of time left for work or the amount of time left for one activity before moving to the next activity. The visual timer is a clock that comes in various sizes. One standard version is approximately 8 inches square and has a 60-minute timer. A smaller, 3-inch-square version is also available that can be clipped to a student's belt. When setting a specified amount of time, say, 15 minutes, that amount of time appears in red. A red disk shows on the timer when a time is set. As the time passes, the red disk disappears bit by bit, such that when time is up, the red disk is gone. As this happens, students can visually see the red disk disappearing as time passes and obtain a better picture of the amount of time left. Such a device may help students feel more comfortable with the concept of time because it makes the concept more concrete for them.

An app version of Time Timer, the *iPad Edition* (Time Timer LLC), is available that functions similarly but is designed for use with an iPad. Again, the visual counting down of the minutes provides students with immediate cues about remaining time. Many additional timer apps are also available, including Timer⁺ (Minima Software LLC) and *Easy Stop Watch&Timer* (BND Co., Ltd.), which include similar features for counting down time; some also include stopwatch features.

From Time Timer LLC. Reprinted with permission.

Other apps help teachers track student behaviors. For example, *Teacher's Assistant: Track Student Behavior* (Lesson Portal, LLC) and *TeacherKit* (ITWorx Egypt) organize students by class, enable note taking for comments, allow storage of grades, interface with e-mail for contacting parents, and interface with Dropbox for backing up files.

STRATEGIES FOR

MAXIMIZING TIME FOR LEARNING

MAXIMIZE ON-TASK TEACHER BEHAVIOR   Teachers also may be off-task, and this behavior can impede student achievement. One example of off-task behavior is making unnecessary digressions, such as talking about personal experiences or current events that are irrelevant to the lesson. Students with special learning needs may find it especially difficult to follow teachers when they are making irrelevant digressions. During practice activities, teachers can be off-task by being unprepared with student materials or by speaking loudly to an individual student and disrupting other students. Teachers can also be off-task by not returning promptly after breaks, allowing longer-than-necessary transition times, and being unprepared for teacher presentations. The *Apps for Education* feature describes a helpful timer for class use.

Cultural diversity may also influence classroom interactions. The *Diversity in the Classroom* feature describes culturally responsive teaching for English language learners.

Research suggests that much **academic engaged time** is lost for a number of reasons, including inefficient transition activities, inappropriate verbalizations, and inappropriate social behavior.

STREAMLINE TRANSITION ACTIVITIES   Transition activities involve students moving from one location, subject, or group to another. Academic engaged time can be lost during transitions through such activities as going to the restroom, sharpening pencils, and unnecessary socializing. Students with disabilities can lose time going between the regular classroom and the resource room.

One way to maximize transition efficiency is to set time limits and reinforce adherence to those limits. For example, if classes begin at the sound of a bell, let students know exactly what is expected of them when the bell rings. Typically, students should be in their places and prepared with their materials at this time. Any time lost after the bell—for example, sharpening pencils or finding workbooks or other materials—takes away from instructional time. Likewise, at the end of the class, if materials are not put away before students leave, time may be lost at some other point in the day. If your students are transitioning to a resource room, you should document the time they left the classroom and report the time to the resource teacher. Similarly, the resource teacher should inform you when students have left the resource room to return to your class.

One obvious way to promote efficient transitions is to inform students that time lost in transition will be made up during free time, in after-school detention, or during other student activities. However, teachers can also reinforce prompt transitioning more positively by awarding points, stickers, or tokens or simply by responding positively to students when they make smooth transitions.

As the teacher, you can facilitate efficient transitions by being prepared ahead of time with materials for the next activity and not losing time looking for instructional materials, organizing supplies, or inefficiently passing out student materials. By setting a good model for transitions, you can promote good transitions in your students.

REDUCE INAPPROPRIATE VERBALIZATIONS Academic engaged time is lost when class discussions drift away from the point of the lesson. Teachers may find themselves wandering off-topic, and students may also wander by raising irrelevant issues. Some students deliberately attempt to keep teachers off-task to avoid getting to homework, tests, or other undesired activities. Monitor inappropriate verbalizations with video or audio recordings of individual lessons, and review them in reference to the purpose of the lesson and the appropriateness of teacher and student verbalizations.

At times, however, digressions may reflect genuine curiosity or interest on the part of students or a developing understanding of the concepts. When this happens, acknowledge that the lesson objective has changed, and evaluate it with respect to the changes that were made. Alternatively, you can inform students that the class can talk about those other important ideas after finishing the present activity.

REDUCE INAPPROPRIATE SOCIAL BEHAVIOR Inappropriate social behavior—including passing notes or electronic messages, teasing, arguing, and fighting—is one of the greatest threats to academic engaged time. Handle inappropriate social behavior quickly and efficiently so that as little instructional time as possible is lost. Punitive classroom environments that include long-winded lectures on social behavior are not as effective (or as time efficient) as positive learning environments where good behavior is expected and rewarded, and misbehavior is dealt with efficiently (Scheuermann & Hall, 2016). More information on reducing inappropriate social behavior is provided in Chapter 8.

USE STRATEGIES FOR INDIVIDUAL CASES Many inclusive classrooms contain one or more students who seem to spend far less time on schoolwork than other students. Frequently, these are the very students who need to spend more time on their schoolwork, such as Jimmy in the earlier scenario. In such cases, try to increase the students' amount of engaged time-on-task. Following are some procedures that may be helpful:

1. *Be certain the student can do the work.* Many students become off-task if they cannot (or believe they cannot) do the assigned work. If you find that the work is too difficult, assign more appropriate work or modify assignments. Also, consider enlisting support from special education teachers, paraprofessionals, or classroom peers.

2. *Try simple strategies, such as direct appeal and proximity.* Tell individual students that you would like to see them working harder on schoolwork. Tell them that you will send a signal when they are getting off-task by approaching their desks. When students return to work, walk away.

3. *Provide simple rewards or consequences.* Students can be offered stickers, free time for a preferred activity, or other rewards for completing all work in a specified time period. Alternately, students can be required to make up work they have not completed.

Culturally Responsive Teaching for English Language Learners

Diversity in schools has increased significantly as more students and families from various cultural and linguistic backgrounds move to the United States and enroll their children in local schools (Banks, 2015). With these increasing numbers, there is a need for educators to gain more information and skills for creating culturally inclusive classes and schools. Many of these students and their families lack facility with English and have not yet mastered speaking, understanding, reading, or writing English (Echevarria & Graves, 2015). In addition, some of these English language learners (ELLs) may be at risk for learning disabilities or have disabilities that may compound any difficulties encountered in school. By examining each student's and family's unique background, culture, ethnicity, and language, educators can begin to understand students' and their parents' needs. Improper placement of students in schools may result in deleterious effects on student academic and social-emotional well-being (e.g., Agirdag, 2009).

A promising approach for addressing these unique needs is the Sheltered Instruction Observation Protocol (SIOP) model used for assessing, planning, implementing, and monitoring instruction for ELLs (e.g., Echevarria, Richards-Tutor, Canges, & Francis, 2011). The SIOP model starts by evaluating and designing instruction with content-area and language objectives. Content objectives can be linked to the Common Core standards in English, math, science, or social studies. The lesson plan includes linking students' prior knowledge and learning experiences, developing meaningful activities and ordering them in a logical sequence, and planning for lesson review and informal assessment of objectives. Student activities are embedded within lessons with meaningfully designed content and language and vocabulary practice that students demonstrate at the end of lessons. Teachers are encouraged to use modeling and demonstrations and to provide corrective feedback as necessary throughout lessons. By combining language with content objectives, ELLs are provided more opportunities to learn and practice the new vocabulary typically encountered in their content-area classes. Echevarria and Graves (2015) provide numerous illustrations of how teachers of ELLs can incorporate the SIOP model within their instruction to accommodate students from various language and cultural backgrounds.

---

4. *Notify parents or guardians.* Contact parents or guardians to elicit their suggestions or support for increasing on-task behavior. Perhaps arrangements can be made to link home privileges or rewards to assignment completion in school. In some cases, simply communicating the idea that parents and teachers are interested in the student's academic progress can make an important difference.

> MyEdLab: **Self-Check 6.4**
>
> MyEdLab: **Application Exercise 6.2: Adapt Instruction**
>
>

S: SYSTEMATICALLY EVALUATE THE OUTCOMES OF YOUR INSTRUCTION

The last S in PASS stands for *systematic evaluation*. Systematic evaluation means frequently measuring students' progress toward meeting the instructional objectives of the class, as well as IEP objectives, using formative evaluation procedures. Teachers should continuously monitor and adjust instruction based on student progress as documented by formative evaluation measures. Formative evaluation measures can help identify which students may need differentiated instruction.

FORMATIVE EVALUATION   Formative evaluation refers to the frequent and systematic monitoring of learner progress toward prespecified goals and objectives. It is different from summative evaluation, in which, for example, tests are given at the end of a school year to determine how much was learned during the year. Teachers who use formative evaluation monitor student progress continuously throughout the school year and do not wait until the end of the year to determine whether learning took place.

Research has suggested that formative evaluation works best when it is used at least twice a week. In some cases, student learning (e.g., words read correctly per minute) can be recorded on a chart or graph so that rate of learning can be assessed. In other cases, student progress may be more difficult to place on a chart, but progress can still be monitored. For example, for evaluation of handwriting, weekly or monthly samples can be collected in student folders.

Systematic evaluation of student performance or products over time can provide teachers with important information regarding the adequacy of students' progress. This information is used, in turn, to make further adaptations in instruction to ensure learning is maximized for all students. When progress for one or more students is not acceptable, teachers can consider how to differentiate instruction to help students meet learning goals. For example, using the information from this chapter, a teacher could decide to increase academic engagement, increase review activities, improve teacher presentations, or make further adaptations in instructional materials. The Inclusion Checklist at the end of this chapter provides suggestions for improving instruction in specific areas in response to the outcomes of systematic evaluation of student performance.

Formative evaluation can be conducted on a variety of student outcomes, including regular "probes" of student skills and knowledge, evaluations of regularly implemented practice activities, and evaluation of homework products, as described in the following section.

STRATEGIES FOR
PROMOTING SYSTEMATIC EVALUATION OF INSTRUCTION

IMPLEMENT CURRICULUM-BASED MEASUREMENT
Curriculum-based measurement refers to regular assessment of student progress toward prespecified goals and objectives using frequently administered "probes" of student performance. For example, in reading instruction, Ms. Sánchez assigned Billy regular 1-minute timed readings of grade-appropriate text. For each timed reading, Ms. Sánchez calculated correct and incorrect words read per minute and placed the results on a chart that demonstrated Billy's progress over time. Teachers can evaluate progress on these measures to determine whether instructional modifications are necessary for the student to meet long-term goals. Curriculum-based measurement can also be used with a variety of student activities, as described next.

MONITOR AND EVALUATE PRACTICE ACTIVITIES
Practice activities are intended to reinforce memory and comprehension of information that was gained in the lesson. If the lesson involves the teaching of skills, such as how to write the letters *p*, *d*, and *q* in cursive, practice activities are used to promote application and skill development and to ensure that the skills learned will be remembered. If the lesson involves the acquisition of content information, such as the causes of the War of 1812, practice activities promote recall, comprehension, and application objectives. The products of practice activities can provide teachers with formative evaluation of student understandings of and progress within the curriculum.

Practice activities are particularly helpful for students with special needs because they provide more engaged time to ensure relevant concepts are fully understood. Often, practice activities are taken from worksheets or workbooks, but practice activities can take other forms as well, such as practice with tutors or classroom peers, flashcards, computer programs or apps, group problem solving, or application tasks using relevant materials. Table 6.4 provides examples of appropriate practice activities.

Practice activities can be divided into *guided* and *independent* practice (Archer & Hughes, 2011; Rosenshine & Stevens, 1986). Guided practice takes place under teacher supervision and is most appropriate immediately after presentation of the initial concept. Students' rates of correct responding may be lower in this type of practice, and more teacher supervision is needed than when students practice independently. Independent practice uses indirect teacher supervision (some activities can be done as homework) and is undertaken when students' rates of correct responding are very high and when students can correct themselves by proofreading and checking their work.

Both types of practice are necessary to ensure that concepts are mastered and remembered and that learning is complete for all students. Request assistance from special educators for devising supplemental practice activities, and determine when and where the extra practice can occur—for example, study hall, other school periods, or homeroom. Any successful practice activity must meet several criteria. First, it must be directly relevant to the objective of the

TABLE 6.4 Appropriate Practice Activities	
Lesson	**Practice Activity**
Writing words in cursive for handwriting practice	*Guided:* Teacher provides dictation; work is checked after every sentence. *Independent:* Students write from manuscript models, then check each other's work at the end of the period.
Solving quadratic equations from a formula	*Guided:* Students solve problems one at a time while the teacher monitors their execution of each step. *Independent:* Students solve problems independently, which are corrected by the teacher at the end of the activity.

lesson. Second, practice activities must be used to enhance learning that occurred during the earlier part of the lesson; practice activities usually are not intended to introduce new information or skills. Students with disabilities or other special learning needs are particularly unlikely to learn new information from worksheet-type activities. Therefore, select practice activities that enhance and augment learning that has already occurred.

Practice activities also must be at an appropriate level of difficulty. If they are too difficult, students will not be able to work on them independently. If they are too easy, student learning will not be enhanced. Finally, it must be remembered that students soon tire of repetitive, worksheet-type activities. Keep the pace and enthusiasm level as high as possible during guided practice (e.g., "Everyone who thinks they have the answer, put your thumbs up!"). During independent practice, teachers should reinforce prompt, accurate, and neat responding and should keep the activity moving at an efficient pace.

Homework can often be considered a type of independent practice activity, undertaken outside the classroom. Because teachers are less likely to be available to answer questions when homework assignments are being completed, it is necessary that students completely understand assignments before taking them home. It may be helpful to complete the first part of the homework assignment in class, as a guided practice activity, to be certain every student knows how to complete the assignment. Homework completion can be facilitated by having students meet in groups at the beginning of class, under the direction of rotating group leaders, to record and provide peer feedback on homework assignments (Jakulski & Mastropieri, 2004; Sheridan, 2009).

When using guided and independent practice activities in the form of classroom and homework activities, evaluate student products carefully, and use this information as a formative evaluation to determine whether students are making adequate progress, and if not, how instruction will be modified and adjusted to meet student goals and objectives. For example, satisfactory performance on independent practice and homework activities indicates that students have learned the material and are functioning satisfactorily. Difficulties in independent practice and homework activities suggest that students need further examples, explanation, and guided practice.

FREQUENTLY REVIEW IMPORTANT MATERIAL AND EVALUATE STUDENT PERFORMANCE Near the end of a lesson, it is important to summarize what has been learned and review this information with students. It is also important to review information weekly and monthly to ensure that previously learned information is not forgotten and that students understand the relation between previous and current learning. Information gained from regular review can provide formative data on student learning and retention over time, as well as important information for possible instructional modifications.

Although frequent review is helpful for all students, it is particularly so for students with disabilities, who may be more likely to forget or not understand the relevance of previously learned material. This extra review and evaluation may be especially helpful before exams. As discussed in the section on redundancy, students with disabilities not only benefit from review, but they may require more review to be successful. Additional review of successfully learned content can be helpful in "overlearning" information, which can help promote long-term retention, application, and generalization.

Special education teachers can assist in providing additional review for students with disabilities and in brainstorming ideas for review. For example, you could make video recordings of the class engaged in activities during the instructional unit, and then show them to students who may benefit from extra review of the information. Students can make "descriptive video scripts"

Daily Review
- Begins with a review of previous learning.
- Provides teacher with information on how much was learned and retained from previous lessons.
- An example of daily review:
  "We have been studying ecosystems. Hold up your hand if you can tell me what an ecosystem is [calls on individual students]. Yesterday, we said that ecosystems have nonliving and living parts. We listed several nonliving parts of ecosystems. Write down on your paper three nonliving parts of an ecosystem. [The teacher waits for a minute or two, walking around the classroom to encourage students to think and write answers.] Now, who can tell me what you wrote . . ."

Statement of Purpose
- State the main objective of the current lesson in language meaningful to students.
- An example stated clearly and simply is the following:
  "Today we are going to learn about the living parts of ecosystems, and how they may interact with the nonliving parts."

Presentation of Information
- Present the content of the lesson using a variety of instructional materials, depending on the purpose and objectives of the lesson.
- Use the teacher presentation or SCREAM variables. That is, deliver content or procedures with structure, clarity, redundancy, enthusiasm, appropriate rate, and maximized engagement using questioning, feedback, and praise.

Guided Practice
1. Practice newly acquired content, skills, or concepts with teacher guidance.
2. Carefully monitor students and provide corrective feedback, as necessary.

Independent Practice
- Provide opportunities for students to repeat, apply, and extend information from the lesson more independently.

Formative Evaluation
- Evaluate students' independent performance.
- An example could take the form of a brief quiz: "See if you can solve the following problems independently."
- Results provide the basis for decisions about the adequacy of student progress and can be considered in planning future lessons.

Figure 6.2 Putting the PASS Components into a Model Lesson

(narrations describing everything in the video) to accompany the videos, either on paper or using an audio recorder. Students with visual impairments may benefit from these descriptions. Photographs, student journals (including photo and vocabulary journals), and daily logs can also provide material for review.

Using a digital camera and scanner, you and your students can create websites that contain their journals and portfolios. Web Workshop, SchoolMessenger, and WordPress, for example, contain many easy-to-use templates to help students create websites. Student performance on these activities can also provide the basis for formative evaluation.

MyEdLab: **Self-Check 6.5**

MyEdLab: **Application Exercise 6.3: Systematically Teach Using SCREAM Variables**

PUTTING THE PASS VARIABLES TO WORK: INCLUDING MODEL LESSON COMPONENTS IN INSTRUCTION

The teacher effectiveness variables most closely related to high achievement have been described. But how do these variables appear in a real lesson? As you review the structure of a model lesson, observe how teacher effectiveness variables fit into a lesson sequence, as indicated in Figure 6.2.

6 Summary

- Differentiated instruction means making adjustments to meet the needs of all learners in an inclusive classroom.

- The PASS variables stand for: prioritize instruction; adapt instruction, materials, or the environment; systematically teach; and systematically evaluate the outcomes of instruction. The PASS variables provide a model for planning and delivering effective differentiated instruction in inclusive settings.

- *Prioritize* instruction to ensure that students are working on the most important objectives and that individual objectives reflect the characteristics of the student.

  — Planning for content coverage involves prioritizing instruction and is a critical component of teacher effectiveness. Teachers must carefully consider the role of prioritized objectives, scope and sequence, curriculum, and pacing of instruction over time.

- *Adapt* instruction, materials, and/or the environment to meet the specific characteristics of the student. Appropriately adapted instruction is a significant component of *differentiated instruction*.

  — Types of learning include discrimination, factual, procedural, rule, conceptual, and problem solving/critical thinking.

  — Levels of learning include acquisition, fluency, application, and generalization. Students can provide either identification or production responses.

  Consideration of types and levels of learning can be beneficial when planning appropriate differentiated instructional strategies.

- *Systematic teaching* refers to maximizing the effectiveness of your instruction and includes effective teacher presentations using the SCREAM variables.

  — Effective teaching strategies include maximizing academic time-on-task, developing effective teacher presentations, monitoring practice activities, providing opportunities for review, and completing formative evaluations. All are critical components of effective teaching for all students.

  — Effective teacher presentations use the SCREAM variables: structure, clarity, redundancy, enthusiasm, appropriate rate, and maximized engagement. Additionally, effectively used questioning, feedback, and praise are all important contributors to student learning.

- *Systematic evaluation* refers to the continuous measurement of student progress toward meeting the specific objectives. Teachers should continuously monitor and adjust instruction based on their students' progress on formative evaluation measures.

  — Curriculum-based measurement provides the basis for evaluating student progress in learning and determining whether student goals and objectives are being met.

  — Practice activities provide opportunities for students to solidify and apply their learning, and they provide more opportunities for formative evaluation of student progress over time. Practice activities can include guided practice, in which teachers closely monitor student responding, and independent practice, in which students work more independently. Homework can be considered a type of independent practice activity.

  — Frequent review promotes retention and long-term learning and provides teachers with opportunities to evaluate student learning. Students with disabilities may especially require frequent review of previously learned material.

PROFESSIONAL STANDARDS LINK:
Effective Differentiated Instruction for All Students

Information in this chapter links most directly to:

- CEC Standards: 1 (Learner Development and Individual Learning Differences), 4 (Assessment), 7 (Planning and Strategies)

- INTASC Standards: 2 (Learning Differences), 3 (Learning Environments), 6 (Assessment), 7 (Planning for Instruction), 8 (Instructional Strategies)

EFFECTIVE DIFFERENTIATED INSTRUCTION FOR ALL STUDENTS

If you are having problems with classroom or individual academic achievement, have you examined the following? If not, see the pages listed here.

STRATEGIES FOR PLANNING FOR CONTENT COVERAGE

STRATEGIES FOR MAKING ADAPTATIONS

STRATEGIES FOR IMPLEMENTING THE SCREAM VARIABLES

STRATEGIES FOR MAXIMIZING ON-TASK BEHAVIOR

STRATEGIES FOR MAXIMIZING TIME FOR LEARNING

STRATEGIES FOR PROMOTING SYSTEMATIC EVALUATION OF INSTRUCTION

7

Response to Intervention and Multi-Tiered Systems of Support

LEARNING OUTCOMES

After studying this chapter, you should be able to:

7.1 Describe the purpose and background of response to intervention (RTI) and multi-tiered systems of support (MTSS).

7.2 Define and describe schoolwide screening, progress monitoring, and data-based decision making.

7.3 Describe Tier 1: Effective instruction in general education.

7.4 Describe Tier 2: Interventions to remediate.

7.5 Describe Tier 3: Individualized, intensive instruction.

7.6 Describe fidelity of implementation.

7.7 Describe challenges with implementing RTI.

The 2004 Individuals with Disabilities Education Improvement Act (IDEA) regulations specified that states must not require discrepancy between ability and academic achievement as the means for determining learning disabilities (although individual schools may choose to use discrepancy). The regulations further specified that schools may use response to instructional intervention as part of the identification process. This means that schools may consider as part of an evaluation process the fact that students have not responded well to research-based instructional procedures. These regulations resulted in response-to-intervention (RTI) procedures that have been implemented throughout the country (O'Connor & Sanchez, 2011a; 2011b). Schools are now allowed to allocate up to 15% of their federal special education funding to implement RTI (IDEA, 2004).

In this chapter, we discuss the overall characteristics of RTI, followed by its components, including screening and progress monitoring, implementing the multiple tiers of intervention, and fidelity of implementation; we also present issues involving RTI. Although most attention on RTI to date has focused on early reading, RTI can be implemented in any academic or behavioral area at any grade level.

Some states prefer to use the term *multi-tiered system of support* (MTSS) rather than *RTI* because they regard this term as more inclusive in addressing the needs of all students, including social/behavioral areas in addition to academic issues. In this text, we use *RTI* and *MTSS* interchangeably to refer to all multi-tiered systems of support, keeping in mind that practice varies among different state and local education authorities and even within individual schools (Vaughn & Bos, 2015).

What Is RTI?

Response to intervention, or RTI, is a multilevel system of intervention designed to address different learning needs, reduce disability identification, and provide evidence for the appropriate identification of learning disabilities. It is intended to improve the overall quality of instructional offerings in schools and to integrate general education more completely with special education (Mellard & Johnson, 2008). It is also intended to provide appropriate services to students as soon as they are needed and prior to a formal referral to special education.

RTI is conceptually related to the Every Student Succeeds Act (ESSA) and the previous Elementary and Secondary Act (ESEA) and the No Child Left Behind Act (NCLB), particularly its Reading First component, as well as IDEA. Common components include use of evidence-based practice (instructional practices that have been validated by research evidence, see Stoiber & Gettinger, 2016), early intervention, and careful monitoring of progress. These common components are intended to integrate early identification and remediation with special education and to develop a more integrated framework to serve the interests of students with special learning needs (Mellard & Johnson, 2008).

As an alternative or supplement to discrepancy criteria for identifying learning disabilities, schools have been encouraged to employ an RTI approach in which general education teachers implement scientifically based practices and use curriculum-based measurement (see Chapter 12) to document student progress on a regular basis. Students who prove to be "treatment-resisters" (those who do not show adequate progress in spite of extra attention) may be eligible for more intensive interventions or referral to special education (Division for Learning Disabilities, 2007; Gresham, 2002; Scruggs & Mastropieri, 2002). These criteria are now specifically encouraged in the most recent IDEA amendments (Wright & Wright, 2005). More recent multi-tiered approaches address learning and behavioral needs more generally (Jimerson, Burns, & VanDerHayden, 2016).

RTI is intended to prevent school failure through early intervention, frequent progress monitoring, and a system of increasingly intensive evidence-based interventions (implemented in multiple levels, or *tiers*) for children who fail to respond sufficiently. In three-tiered systems, these have been referred to as Tier 1, Tier 2, and Tier 3, or the universal, targeted, and tertiary levels of intervention. Increasing intensity is usually associated with (a) more systematic and explicit instruction, (b) more frequently implemented instruction, (c) instruction of longer duration, (d) smaller and more homogeneous student groups, and (e) instructors with greater expertise (Fuchs & Fuchs, 2006). As noted, students who do not respond sufficiently to multiple tiers of intervention are considered treatment-resisters and are eligible for special education referral.

Different versions of RTI include a varying number of tiers of intervention, although three is the most common (Berkeley, Bender, Peaster, & Saunders, 2009; Fuchs, Fuchs, & Compton, 2012). In addition, RTI varies with respect to the approach employed. Most present RTI models employ either a ***problem-solving*** approach or a ***standard-treatment-protocol*** approach. For example, in the problem-solving approach, at Tier 1, the teacher may confer with the student's parents to help resolve the learning or behavioral problem. If the problem is not resolved, at Tier 2, the teacher may meet with the school-identified assistance team to identify the problem and plan an intervention. If the student does not succeed at this level, the agency staff may be called in to redesign and coordinate the implementation of Tier 3, which in many cases may include special education (Fuchs & Fuchs, 2006). However, because some schools employ more than three tiers of intervention, check with your own district regarding the specific number of tiers and how each is defined.

In the standard-treatment-protocol approach, Tier 1 could include some specific, evidence-based reading practice in the general education classroom, perhaps including classwide peer tutoring in reading, explicit instruction in reading skills and subskills where needed, and monitoring of student progress. For students who do not succeed in this program, Tier 2 might include standard small-group (four or five students) instruction in reading, perhaps for 30 minutes per day, 4 days per week, for 10 to 12 weeks. For students who do not succeed on this level, Tier 3 might include highly intensive, individualized instruction based on the student's individual needs, for example, 50 minutes of instruction 5 days per week with daily progress monitoring. In many cases, Tier 3 may include special education identification and placement (Mellard & Johnson, 2008). Special education referral can also be initiated by parents or school

MyEdLab:
Video Example 7.1.
The teacher in this video describes how RTI is used in her school.

personnel at any time. As with the problem-solving approach, there are presently many different versions of the standard-treatment-protocol approach (Fuchs & Fuchs, 2006). The *Diversity in the Classroom* feature describes the importance of culturally appropriate teaching practices throughout the implementation of RTI.

Multi-tiered systems of support may also focus on social behavior. Schoolwide behavior systems, such as **positive behavioral interventions and supports (PBIS)**, have been employed in multi-tiered prevention systems, or RTI for behavior management (Scheuermann & Hall, 2016). In this model, universal intervention (or Tier 1) for social skills might include schoolwide instruction of all students in positive social behaviors, targeted intervention (Tier 2) could be small-group instruction on specific social skills, and intensive (Tier 3) intervention could include individualized and comprehensive instruction in social skills.

Although not required by law, most states today are implementing some form of RTI or are developing models for its implementation (Berkeley et al., 2009). The RTI process employs multiple components, including screening and progress monitoring, data-based decision making, implementation of multiple tiers of intervention, and fidelity of implementation. Where appropriate, RTI procedures can facilitate meeting Common Core State Standards (Jimerson, Stein, Haddock, & Shahroozi, 2016).

In the following sections of this chapter, we discuss these components, considerations for the use of RTI at the secondary level, and challenges for implementation of RTI.

MyEdLab: **Self-Check 7.1**

MyEdLab: **Application Exercise 7.1: What is RTI?**

Schoolwide Screening, Progress Monitoring, and Data-Based Decision Making

In order to implement RTI efficiently, schools must identify and apply measures to identify students who may be at risk for academic failure. It is hoped that schools will be able to identify potential learning problems early, so they can be treated before more serious academic problems occur. It is also important that student progress is monitored over time in order to evaluate the rate of progress being made. Both schoolwide screening and progress monitoring use student performance data to make programming decisions (Deno, 2016).

STRATEGIES FOR
ADMINISTERING SCHOOLWIDE SCREENING

Schoolwide *screening* measures are intended to be easy to implement and score yet still provide a general picture of academic achievement in a particular area, such as reading. Screening measures may be brief and may be administered to all students at all grade levels. These screening measures should be used to indicate which students may require additional evaluation to determine if further assistance is needed. These may be administered approximately three times per year and may utilize district benchmark assessments or measures such as the Dynamic Indicators of Basic Early Literacy Skills (DIBELS, 2006), the Oral Reading Fluency Test (Kaminski & Good, 1998), or the Gates-MacGinitie Reading Tests (MacGinitie, MacGinitie, Maria, Dreyer, & Hughes, 2000).

SCREENING MEASURES For a screening measure to be effective, it must possess both *sensitivity* and *specificity*. **Sensitivity** means that it identifies students who are at risk for academic difficulties in the area being measured (that is, "true positives"), and **specificity** means that students who perform acceptably on the measure are unlikely to have academic problems in that area ("true negatives"). Screening measures are constructed to minimize both "false positives" (students inaccurately identified as having academic problems) and "false negatives" (students inaccurately identified as not having academic problems). These measures also must be implemented with fidelity, meaning they should be implemented exactly as intended.

It is important that schools identify the greatest number of students who truly are having learning difficulties so that they can receive appropriate services; however, if too many students are incorrectly identified, school resources can be misdirected to unnecessary treatments. Therefore, it is important for schools to determine optimal "cut scores" or "cut points" (which represent the line between adequate and inadequate performance) that reliably identify students in need of assistance but nevertheless do not overidentify. Some schools employ more than one instance of the same measure, for example, repeated administrations of the DIBELS for students who did not score adequately on the first administration, or use of multiple measures (Mellard & Johnson, 2008).

STRATEGIES FOR
PROGRESS MONITORING AND DATA-BASED DECISION MAKING

Screening measures are appropriate for identifying which students may be in need of additional attention, whereas *progress monitoring* is appropriate for assessing how individual students are progressing. **Progress monitoring** involves collecting multiple performance measures over time, in order to (a) determine whether progress is appropriate, and, if progress is not appropriate, (b) help identify more effective programs. Progress monitoring also can help determine whether individual students are not responding appropriately to different levels of instruction and may need to be evaluated for learning disabilities.

According to Mellard and Johnson (2008), progress monitoring must employ the following eight features to be effective within the context of RTI:

1. Progress monitoring is conducted in all tiers of instruction.

2. Progress-monitoring measures are based on and directly relevant to the curriculum, as well as the grade level and tier level of RTI.

3. In order to facilitate data collection, measures must be easy to administer and effective.

4. Results should be displayed in a manner that makes interpretation simple and efficient, for example, in charts or line graphs.

5. Rules for decision making must be determined for all aspects of progress-monitoring data, including cut scores for level (performance score), slope (change in performance over time), and percentage of mastery.

6. Cut scores and decision rules must have a clear rationale.

7. Progress-monitoring measures must be collected frequently enough to inform instructional and placement decisions. Frequency of administration may differ across different tiers, and guidelines for these should be specified.

8. Results of progress monitoring, although important, should be considered only one of several sources that inform instructional decision making.

Within the model of RTI, progress monitoring is undertaken at all tiers but in somewhat different ways. Each is described separately.

TIER 1 PROGRESS MONITORING The purpose of Tier 1 progress monitoring is to determine whether individual students are making adequate progress in the general education classroom. In some cases, students have been returned to the general education classroom from a higher-tier placement, and progress monitoring can help determine whether the general classroom is effectively meeting the student's needs.

Progress monitoring at Tier 1 differs from screening in its overall purpose and the frequency of administration. For example, an entire classroom may be given a general screening measure three times per year. After these measures are given, individual students may be determined to be in need of further evaluation. For example, Hasbrook and Tindal (2005) have determined that students read an average of 72 words per minute by the middle of second grade

MyEdLab:
Video Example 7.2.

In this video, a teacher describes the value of collecting and using data to enhance instruction for students with disabilities.

https://www.youtube.com/watch?v=bYurgW20Juw&list=UUQ2-KgUHhixii64uOQFEZUQ

Diversity in the Classroom

Cultural Considerations for RTI

 The RTI model holds promise for the achievement of all students by providing early attention and intervention programs to students from a diversity of backgrounds. Klingner and Edwards (2006) proposed a model of culturally responsive literacy instruction employing RTI with four tiers of intervention (rather than the three tiers described in most of this chapter), as follows:

Tier 1: Culturally Responsive Instruction in the General Education Classroom

This tier should be characterized not only by evidence-based interventions but also interventions that are implemented by teachers who are familiar with models of culturally responsive teaching and aware of methods for promoting academic growth for the particular groups of students in their classrooms (e.g., Gay, 2010; Harry & Klingner, 2014). Teachers with students who are English language learners should also be aware of evidence-based methods that are effective with these populations.

Tier 2: Intensive Supports

When students receiving culturally appropriate instruction are nevertheless still struggling to meet achievement expectations, culturally relevant Tier 2 instruction can provide intensive support to help promote student achievement. Because research support for culturally responsive Tier 2 interventions is less widely available, progress monitoring is of particular importance. Ongoing progress monitoring can be especially helpful in validating interventions when sufficient evidence-based practices are not available.

Tiers 2–3: Teacher Assistance Teams

This step, which can overlap as an additional component of Tier 2 interventions, involves the creation of a teacher assistance team or child study team. This team, which includes experts in the appropriate intervention area as well as experts in culturally responsive teaching, carefully considers the situation from the perspective of the individual student's academic, behavioral, and cultural needs; recommends appropriate treatments; and follows up on the effectiveness of these interventions.

Tier 3–4: Special Education

This tier (which is 3 in some districts, while 4 in other districts) is tailored to the individual needs of the student, does not have a specific ending date, consists of intensive interventions, and is for students with persistent below-grade-level performance. Given the problem of overrepresentation of some minority groups in special education (Harry & Klingner, 2014), it is of particular importance to determine that the evaluation for special education has been culturally fair and that all other possibilities for instructional supports have been implemented prior to referral.

Orosco and Klingner (2010) described the implementation of a three-tiered RTI model in one elementary school with a large proportion of enrolled English language learners. The results of their investigation suggested the need for teachers to implement culturally appropriate instruction and revealed the challenges that occur when teachers are not appropriately trained in these practices.

(see Table 7.1). A screening measure may identify some students who read below 42 words per minute, which is the 25th percentile according to Hasbrook and Tindal's (2005) norms (see also Mellard & Johnson, 2008). Students scoring below the 25th percentile may then be provided with more frequent progress monitoring (e.g., weekly; three times per week) in order to determine whether the lowered *level* of performance is also accompanied by a reduced *slope* of performance.

Consider an example in which screening identified that three students in a class (Tanya, Phil, and Joanie) scored below the 25th percentile (a lower level of performance) on oral reading fluency. These students were then provided with weekly progress monitoring. Performance data demonstrated that Tanya was responding well to instruction and making good progress (a positive performance slope), so current instruction was continued along with further progress monitoring. However, Phil's and Joanie's reduced levels of performance were also found to be associated over time with a reduced rate of progress (slope), so placement in a Tier 2 program was considered.

TABLE 7.1 Second-Grade Descriptive Statistics for Oral Reading Fluency Scores by Season

Season	Fall	Winter	Spring
Mean	55.49	72.75	89.28
Standard Deviation	37	40.62	41.95
10th Percentile	11	18	31
20th Percentile	20	33	54
25th Percentile	25	42	61
30th Percentile	30	49	68
40th Percentile	41	61	79
50th Percentile	51	72	89
60th Percentile	62	84	100
70th Percentile	72	94	111
75th Percentile	79	100	117
80th Percentile	86	107	124
90th Percentile	106	125	142

Source: Hasbrook and Tindal (2005, p. 8).

MyEdLab:
Video Example 7.3.

In this video, a teacher talks about using the DIBELS system and why she finds it to be so useful.

Performance monitoring can be conducted using **curriculum-based measurement** (CBM). Using CBM, skills from the entire year's curriculum are sampled in alternate forms. Web-based versions of CBM in reading and math include DIBELS (2006). Other CBM materials are shown in Table 7.2.

The Intervention Central website (interventioncentral.org) provides a system for generating CBM in reading, writing, and math. An area is identified (e.g., early reading measures such as letter and word reading; early math, math calculations and concepts; written expression), the parameters are set (e.g., grade level, number of items), and the calculators in the website generate CBM measures for individualized purposes. These calculators can be used for progress

TABLE 7.2 CBM Measures for Progress Monitoring

Measure	Areas	Publisher
DIBELS Data System	Early reading skills	University of Oregon dibels.uoregon.edu
Reading Fluency Progress Monitor (RFPM)	Reading fluency	Read Naturally readnaturally.com
AIMSweb	Reading, writing, math, social behavior	Pearson AIMSweb.com
EdCheckup	Reading, writing, math	EdCheckup edcheckup.com
Vanderbilt CBM Materials	Reading, math	Vanderbilt University Peabody #328 230 Appleton Place Nashville, TN 37203-5721
STAR Assessments	Reading, writing, math	Renaissance Learning renlearn.com
Test of Silent Word Reading Fluency (TOSWRF)	Word reading	ProEd proedinc.com
Test of Word Reading Efficiency (2nd ed.) (TOWRE-2)	Sight-word reading, phonetic decoding	Western Psychological Services wpspublish.com
Yearly ProgressPro	Reading, language arts, math	McGraw-Hill ctb.com

Computer-Based CBM for Progress Monitoring

Software has been developed to facilitate progress monitoring using curriculum-based measurement (CBM). Such software can increase accuracy and save time in implementing CBM, scoring and recording data, and making instructional decisions. Descriptions of some available programs follow.

The *EcoBehavioral Assessment Systems Software* was designed based on research at the Juniper Gardens Children's Project of the University of Kansas to assess the quality of core instruction. For example, student behaviors and academic instruction during Tier 1 classroom observations are analyzed to provide an overall assessment of core instruction relating to specific students.

The *DIBELS Data System* is a web-based database that can be used by schools and districts to enter the results of student assessments. The data system can also create reports based on these scores. Measures include the following:

- DIBELS® (*Dynamic Indicators of Basic Early Literacy Skills*) 6th edition
- IDEL (*Indicadores Dinámicos del Éxito en la Lectura*) for native Spanish speakers
- DIBELS® Next, a new version of reading assessments
- The easyCBM Math program
- One local or state outcome measure

The DIBELS Data System keeps track of progress on these measures for students, classes, schools, and school districts. Reports can be created as soon as scores are recorded, which can facilitate prompt decision making. The DIBELS Data System is operated by the Center on Teaching and Learning at the University of Oregon in Eugene.

monitoring for individual school purposes. This site also contains links to many CBM manuals, training materials, assessments, and scoring guides.

Apps are available to assist teachers with recording data. *BehaviorLENS* (SuperPsyched, LLC) provides options for recording interval, frequency, duration, and ABC (antecedent, behavior, consequence) data. *iBAA* (Future Help Designs) enables recording of qualitative and cumulative observations, interval and functional behavior, and environmental assessments, as well as summarizing of data in reports. The *Apps for Education* feature provides additional relevant resources.

Calculating Slopes How are slopes calculated for purposes of progress monitoring? One approach is Tukey's (1977) method of "tri-split slopes," as shown in Figure 7.1 (see also Fuchs, Fuchs, Hintze, & Lembke, 2007). Using this method, the number of total data points is divided into thirds (or the closest approximation when the number is not an exact multiple of 3). Examining the first third of the data points, the median value of the three is placed at the median (in this case, the second) observation point, where the "x" is placed (in the case of an even number of data points, the point halfway between the two "middle" values). In examining the final third of the data points, an "x" is also placed at the median value, at the median (in this case, eighth) observation point. Then a line is drawn between the two x's to indicate the slope. The numeric value of the slope can be calculated by subtracting the first median value from the third median value (in this case, 35 − 22) and dividing the difference by 1 less than the total number of data points (in this case, 9 − 1), to give a slope of 13/8, or 1.625. In the present case, it means that this student is increasing the number of words read correctly per minute by 1.625 words per week. Slope estimates obtained in this way then can be compared with published norms of progress in reading. They can also be compared with established goals. For example, Darcy is expected to read 80 words per minute by the end of the school year, as shown in Figure 7.2. The obtained slope of her actual reading progress (0.625) can be compared with the slope that would be necessary to reach the goal by the end of the year (1.80). If the obtained slope does not appear to be adequate for this purpose, a modification of methods or materials, or placement in a Tier 2 program, can be planned.

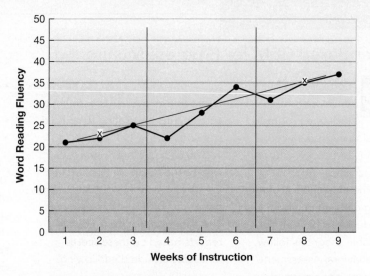

Steps in Calculating Slope According to the Tukey (1977) Method:

1. Divide graphed data points into three equal (or roughly equal) sections.
2. For each of the first and last sections, identify the median (middle) data value (in this case, 22 and 35), and the median time value (in this case, weeks 2 and 8). Draw an "x" at the median value at the median time.
3. Draw a line connecting the two "x"s, and extend the line through the data values.
4. Slope can then be calculated by subtracting the median data point of the third section from the median data point from the first section, and dividing the difference by one less than the total number of data points. In this case, subtract 22 from 35 (= 13), and divide 13 by 9 – 1, or 8, so 13/8 = 1.625. Therefore, slope equals:

$$\frac{\text{Median value from } 3^{rd} \text{ section} - \text{Median value from } 1^{st} \text{ section}}{\text{Total number of data points} - 1}$$

Figure 7.1   Calculating Slopes: An Example

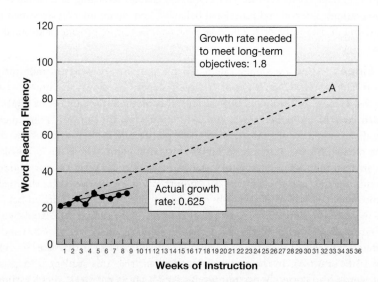

In the first 9 weeks of instruction, Darcy's reading fluency has grown from 22 to only 27 words per minute, a growth rate (slope) of 0.625. If Darcy's long-term goal (A) is to read grade level materials at 80 words per minute (wpm) by the end of the year, she will need to have a growth rate of 1.8.

Actual growth rate: 27 wpm – 22 wpm = 5 wpm, divided by 8 (9 weeks – 1) = 0.625

Projected growth rate (Goal Line): 85 wpm – 22 wpm = 63 wpm, divided by 35 weeks = 1.80

Figure 7.2   Growth Rate and Long-Term Goals

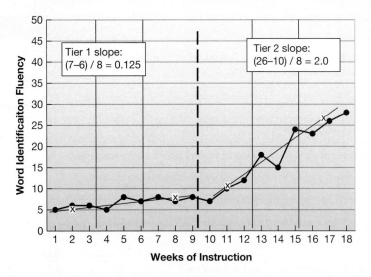

1. The slope for Tier 1 was calculated by dividing the first 9 data values into thirds, and identifying the median value and median week for the first and third, in this case 6 and 7. Subtract 6 from 7, and divide the difference by (9–1), or 8, to obtain (7–6)/8 = 1/8 = 0.125.

2. For the second set of 9 weeks (Tier 2 intervention), the median value/week of the third section is 26 and the median value/week of the first section is 10. Therefore, the slope is (26–10)/8 = 16/8 = 2.0.

Figure 7.3 Calculating Slopes Across Interventions

TIER 2 PROGRESS MONITORING When placed in Tier 2 programs, all students may be provided with frequent progress monitoring. Here, the purpose is a little different. Progress monitoring at this level can help determine whether the student has made adequate progress to resume placement in the Tier 1 setting (the general education classroom). If progress is not adequate, the information may be used to adapt the intervention. For example, progress monitoring at Tier 2 indicated that Phil was making adequate progress, so no instructional changes were made. Joanie, however, was making less progress, so it was decided to adapt her reading materials and provide more time for instruction. If progress monitoring reveals that Tier 2 instruction, after instructional modifications, is not resulting in adequate progress, evaluation for referral to Tier 3 (special education) may be appropriate. Figure 7.3 shows how progress-monitoring data can be calculated to indicate whether adequate progress is being made in Tier 2 interventions. After a period of ineffective Tier 1 instruction (slope = 0.125), a Tier 2 intervention was implemented; after this 9-week Tier 2 intervention, much greater progress was evident (slope = 2.0). These data can be compared with longer-term expectations to determine whether individual students should be returned to Tier 1, continued in Tier 2 interventions, or considered for special education placement in Tier 3.

Stecker, Fuchs, and Fuchs (2005) reviewed literature on the effectiveness of curriculum-based measurement and concluded that progress should be assessed twice per week during Tier 2 interventions. These data should be charted and reviewed regularly. These reviews should employ preexisting criteria to determine whether the intervention is adequate or whether further modifications are necessary.

Mellard and Johnson (2008, p. 50) described one use of the DIBELS (2006) and Read Naturally (readnaturally.com) reading and comprehension probes for a Tier 2 elementary-grade program. For first grade, the DIBELS weekly assessments included fluency measures of letter naming, phoneme segmentation, nonsense-word reading, and oral reading. For second grade, nonsense-word reading and oral reading fluency were assessed. In third through fifth grades, oral reading fluency was assessed. These progress data were compared with an "aim line" or "goal line" for each student, drawn on a chart from present performance to the student's longer-term aims. If the student had three consecutive weekly data points that were above this aim line, the goal was increased until the student was able to perform at the grade-level benchmarks. Conversely, if three consecutive weekly data points were below this line, instructional modifications were undertaken. If three additional weekly data points continued below the aim line, even after modifications, the student was considered for a Tier 3 placement.

TABLE 7.3 Standards for Evaluating Progress Monitoring

Directions: If the practice is implemented, indicate this with a checkmark (√); if the practice is being developed, rank by priority: 1 = highest priority; 2 = medium priority; 3 = lowest priority.

Practice	Priority
Progress monitoring occurs in all tiers (including general education).	
Scientifically based instruction includes the continuous progress monitoring of student performance across tiers.	
Teachers follow a designated procedure and schedule for progress monitoring and for regrouping students as needed.	
Measures are administered frequently to inform instruction and curricular placement decisions (in Tier 1, at least once every 3 weeks; in Tier 2 and beyond, 1–2 times per week; in special education, 3–5 times per week).	
Progress-monitoring measures are appropriate to the curriculum, grade level, and tier level.	
Data resulting from classroom-level progress monitoring are documented and analyzed.	
Teachers use progress-monitoring data to evaluate instructional effectiveness.	
An established data-management system allows ready access to students' progress-monitoring data.	
Progress-monitoring data are graphed to indicate percentages of students at varying levels of achievement.	
A graph is completed to display data for analysis and decision making to indicate percentages of students at risk, at some risk, and at low risk.	
Staff members receive training in the administration and interpretation of progress-monitoring measures.	
The school has designated reasonable *a priori* cut points and decision rules for the level, slope, or percentage of mastery to help determine responsiveness and distinguish adequate responsiveness from inadequate responsiveness.	
The efficacy of cut points is reviewed frequently; cut points are adjusted as necessary.	
A rationale is provided for the cut points and decision rules (e.g., normative or specific criteria reference).	

Source: Mellard and McKnight (2006, p. 6).

TIER 3 PROGRESS MONITORING   Progress monitoring at Tier 3 involves frequent measurement of learning outcomes and immediate and dynamic instructional decision making. In many cases, progress monitoring is undertaken after an individual student has been evaluated and found eligible for placement in special education, based on state and district standards. In this placement, progress monitoring is implemented in part to meet the requirements of IDEA, which mandates that progress toward students' short-term and annual goals must be assessed. In addition, progress monitoring continues to provide information about the adequacy of instruction and the possible need for modifications or adjustments in instructional programming. Progress-monitoring data may also be useful if student progress is considered sufficiently strong over time to justify consideration for placement in a less restrictive setting.

STANDARDS FOR EVALUATING PROGRESS MONITORING   Measures and procedures for progress monitoring must reflect specific requirements and therefore vary among states, districts, and schools. Nevertheless, it is important that progress monitoring be conducted efficiently and effectively. Table 7.3 (from Mellard & McKnight, 2006) displays standards for evaluating progress monitoring, and these criteria should be employed whenever progress monitoring is undertaken to maximize its effectiveness.

MyEdLab: **Self-Check 7.2**

MyEdLab: **Application Exercise 7.2: Schoolwide Screening**

Tier 1: Effective Instruction in General Education

As stated previously, RTI attempts to integrate special education with general education more effectively by providing a series of instructional interventions of increasing intensity, as needed, to deliver the most effective instruction based on students' individual needs. Although many different models have been proposed and implemented, here we discuss the three-tiered model most commonly employed in schools today (Berkeley et al., 2009). In this model, Tier 1 represents scientifically based instruction implemented in general education classrooms. Tier 2 is intended for those students for whom Tier 1 instruction is found to be insufficient, and it typically includes more intensive instruction delivered to smaller groups of students. Tier 3 is intended for those students for whom Tier 2 instruction is found to be insufficient, and it is represented by placement in special education. Across all tiers, specific features may be represented differentially, such as (a) instructional group size, (b) duration and frequency of the intervention, (c) instructor training and focus of content or skills being taught, and (d) performance standards and frequency of progress monitoring (Mellard & Johnson, 2008). Although the focus of RTI to date has been primarily on reading (and to a lesser extent, math and writing), effective Tier 1 instruction can include all relevant content and skill areas.

Tier 1 instruction occurs in general education classrooms and is delivered by general education teachers. The important principle regarding Tier 1 instruction is that it employs scientifically based instructional programs, as addressed in the ESSA and previously ESEA and its Reading First component. The term *scientifically based*, or *evidence based*, refers to research that employs rigorous and systematic procedures; that employs experimental or quasi-experimental research designs and reliable, valid measures; and that has been subjected to review by experts, for example, in peer-reviewed journals (Sugai, Horner, Fixen, & Blase, 2010). This research forms the foundation for evidence-based practice—instructional methods proven to be effective by such scientific methods. Evidence-based practice can be in the area of social behavior as well as academic skills (Ihlo & Nantais, 2010).

Although RTI could address any content or skill area, much of the emphasis in RTI treatments has been placed on reading. In that area, the National Reading Panel's report (National Institute of Child Health and Human Development, 2000) has focused on explicit and systematic instruction of five components of reading: phonemic awareness, phonics development, reading fluency, reading comprehension, and vocabulary development. In all content and skill areas, however, instruction should be scientifically based. This means that states, districts, and schools must identify evidence-based programs and instructional practices that can be implemented effectively in general education classrooms.

Differentiation of instruction can be employed as needed to address individual special needs within the general education classroom. This can take many forms but could include physical placement and arrangement of the classroom; classwide peer tutoring; individual assistance from teachers, paraprofessionals, or volunteers; modified instructional materials; or assistive instructional devices such as accessible keyboards or speech- and reading-recognition software. These instructional features can include universal design for learning (UDL) characteristics for assisting all students. Text with embedded text-to-speech capacity is a good UDL example because students can access the speech component when needed. Other examples involving UDL include visual presentations, Internet links to definitions, enlarged print, and multimedia presentations (Hall, Meyer, & Rose, 2012). The overall feature of Tier 1 instruction is that the teacher is leading the general education classroom, and all students are proceeding through a specified curriculum, using scientifically based practices.

In this book, we present instructional strategies and materials that are appropriate for addressing special needs in the general education classroom and that are supported by scientific research. To this extent, the entire book is devoted to effective instruction in general education classrooms, or Tier 1 instruction; however, many of the strategies are also appropriate for Tier 2 or Tier 3 instruction if employed in a different context.

FEATURES OF TIER 1 INSTRUCTION

According to Mellard and Johnson (2008, p. 64), interventions at the different tiers are distinguished by specific features at each, including the following:

1. Size of instructional group (e.g., whole class, small group, individualized)

2. Performance standards, including mastery requirements

MyEdLab:
Video Example 7.4.

This video gives an overview of the components of Tier 1 interventions.

3. Frequency of delivery of the intervention

4. Overall duration of the specific intervention

5. Frequency of progress monitoring, using screening measures

6. Training of the teacher or other specialist in the target content area

7. Focus of the content or skills

In the case of Tier 1 instruction, then, the instructional group size would be the entire classroom. Performance standards would be those benchmarks determined by the states and school districts to be appropriate indicators of grade-level performance. These indicators are screened frequently throughout instruction, and teachers make instructional modifications to accommodate individual students. Screening measures are implemented at least every week or two, with students at risk being monitored more frequently. Students remain in Tier 1, of course, throughout the school year, unless more intensive procedures are indicated; instruction is provided by general education teachers according to school schedules (e.g., daily). Instruction reflects the school's content standards for the full instructional program (Mellard & Johnson, 2008).

STRATEGIES FOR
IMPLEMENTATION OF TIER 1 INSTRUCTION

It is not true that Tier 1 is simply "general education as usual." Although Tier 1 instruction does involve general education teachers teaching the school's content standards in general education classrooms, it also requires substantial changes in school structure and staff roles. Instruction must include universal screening and progress monitoring, based on common standards and program coherence. In this case, all elements, including curriculum, instruction, intervention, and assessment, are aligned both horizontally (across curriculum) and vertically (across grade levels) throughout the schools. Schools, in turn, must work collaboratively to integrate all elements of this system coherently and to address the needs of both students and teaching staff (in terms of professional development).

TEACHER RESPONSIBILITIES   Teachers must be more oriented to scientifically based practices, must work to actively conduct screening and progress monitoring, and must systematically attend to the needs of individual students who may not be making adequate progress. Teachers will need to work collaboratively with others to ensure a seamless system of instructional delivery across tiers and, ultimately, with special educators when the need arises. Teacher responsibilities include timely administration of screening measures, charting and evaluating results over time, identifying students in need of additional assessments or accommodations, and providing information to parents when appropriate. Support staff and specialist responsibilities include assisting the general education teachers in implementation efforts, data collection, and identification of students in need of additional attention. Administrators will be responsible for leading the effort across the school; providing needed resources, including professional development activities; ensuring the program is being implemented faithfully; working with committees to identify screening tools; monitoring the performance of entire classrooms, reviewing data to inform decision making; and integrating this system with multiple requirements, such as those of the ESSA (Mellard & Johnson, 2008).

In some ways, Tier 1 is the most important tier—it is the most cost-effective, addresses all students, covers all relevant school content, and represents the first gate for more intensive levels of service, when needed (Denton & Vaughn, 2010; Mellard & Johnson, 2008). Tier 1 provides the broad foundation for all further educational interventions.

MyEdLab: **Self-Check 7.3**

Tier 2: Intervention to Remediate

Tier 1 instruction is intended to ensure that students are receiving high-quality instruction in general education classrooms. If progress monitoring reveals that individual students are not making adequate progress over time in the general education classroom, it may be appropriate to consider a more intensive level of instruction, represented by Tier 2. This instruction should be implemented as soon as it is determined that individual students are not progressing adequately. Tier 2 instruction includes several features parallel to those of Tier 1 instruction (Mellard & Johnson, 2008; see also Vaughn & Bos, 2015).

FEATURES OF TIER 2 INSTRUCTION

MyEdLab:
Video Example 7.5.
This video provides an overview of the components of Tier 2 interventions.

Tier 2 instruction may be delivered to small groups of students (e.g., two to five) who have demonstrated similar areas of difficulty. This instruction may take place in a separate area in the general education classroom or in a separate setting, and it is generally delivered by specialized instructional personnel (e.g., reading specialist, speech and language specialist). Like Tier 1 instruction, Tier 2 instruction employs scientifically based instructional programs oriented specifically to the students' areas of difficulty. Typically, specialized curriculum materials are used, instruction is more intensive and focused, and progress monitoring is conducted more frequently (e.g., one to three times per week).

Tier 2 instruction may be provided over an extended time period (e.g., 9 to 12 weeks in length), from three to four times a week, in 30- to 60-minute sessions. Longer time periods may be expected to help promote greater learning gains. Although Tier 2 instruction can take many forms, it is generally considered that it will include direct, systematic teaching to specific targeted objectives, including explicit presentation of information, modeling, provision of multiple examples, and direct, immediate feedback; multiple opportunities for student responding; relevant practice activities; appropriate pacing of instruction; and continuous monitoring of student performance.

It is generally considered that students in Tier 2 instruction will continue to receive Tier 1 instruction in the same content or skill area in general education classrooms. Therefore, Tier 2 instructors must ensure that their instruction is directly relevant to Tier 1 instruction and that continuous monitoring of Tier 1 performance is implemented to provide evidence of educational benefit.

STRATEGIES FOR
IMPLEMENTATION OF TIER 2 INSTRUCTION

Overall, two different approaches have been developed to implement Tier 2 instruction: the problem-solving and the standard-protocol approaches (Fuchs, Mock, Morgan, & Young, 2003; Marston, 2005). Although the differences between these two approaches are substantial, both aim to provide high-quality, specialized instruction intended to facilitate adequate achievement in general education classrooms.

PROBLEM-SOLVING APPROACHES   Most schools have teams of teachers and specialists referred to by various terms, such as *multidisciplinary teams*, *student instructional teams*, or *student study teams*. In problem-solving approaches, these teams meet, consider evidence regarding student academic progress, and, when needed, outline a plan to address learning challenges. According to Tilly (2003; see also Marston, 2005), the following questions are addressed:

- What is the problem?
- Why is the student having this problem?
- What can be done to address the problem?
- Has the intervention been effective?

States such as Nebraska and North Carolina have implemented problem-solving approaches (Berkeley et al., 2009). In Tilly's Heartland Early Literacy Project (Project HELP), some of the scientifically based strategies include curriculum-based measurement and evaluation, functional analysis of behavior and positive behavioral supports, direct instruction, peer-assisted learning strategies, and learning strategy instruction. Overall, the distinguishing feature of Tier 2 problem-solving approaches is in the individualized evaluation and planning for each student's specific needs. The approach is most likely to be effective if it combines scientifically based interventions, continuous progress monitoring with information from a variety of sources, effective collaborative relationships in the schools, and direct connection to

A Tier 2 Reading Intervention for Fourth-Grade Students

Ritchey, Silverman, Montanaro, Speece, and Schatschneider (2012) developed and implemented a multicomponent Tier 2 intervention in reading for fourth-grade students identified as being at risk for reading failure. They implemented this intervention with two cohorts of students over a 2-year period. The intervention employed science content-area texts to increase motivation and to ease scheduling demands when supplemental intervention required students to miss content-area instruction.

The intervention included 24 scripted lessons provided over 12- to 15-week periods and focused on expository text comprehension.

It included repeated reading to promote fluency, comprehension instruction, vocabulary instruction, and text instruction. Student choice and four hands-on science activities were included in the lessons to incorporate motivational components. After a 2-year implementation period, the performance scores of students in the Tier 2 intervention were compared with the scores of a no-treatment control condition. Intervention students performed significantly better on science knowledge as well as knowledge and use of comprehension strategies. However, students in the intervention did not perform better as a whole on word reading, fluency, or comprehension. Although some components of

this Tier 2 intervention were very successful, the limitations suggest that additional instructional time may be needed at the upper-elementary level and that further research is needed on RTI interventions at this level.

QUESTIONS FOR REFLECTION

1. Why do you think the researchers did not find performance differences on word reading, fluency, or comprehension?

2. What might you implement to obtain performance differences on word reading, fluency, and comprehension?

3. After training, what could you do to help students to continue to use the intervention independently or to generalize the intervention to social studies?

regular classroom instruction (Mellard & Johnson, 2008). The *Research Highlight* describes the implementation of a Tier 2 intervention with fourth-grade students at risk for reading failure.

STANDARD-PROTOCOL APPROACHES Using the standard-protocol approach, students are grouped according to instructional need and provided with interventions that have been validated through experimental research, for example, specific strategies for improving reading comprehension (e.g., Berkeley, Scruggs, & Mastropieri, 2010). These are intensive instructional interventions intended to remediate specific skill deficits. Schools implementing such approaches must indicate that their interventions replicate the intensity, duration, frequency, and procedures of interventions validated in previous research. They should also describe the skills addressed, the place of instruction, appropriate instructional materials, and means for assessing progress (Fuchs et al., 2003; Mellard & Johnson, 2008).

Most efforts to date to develop standard protocols of instruction have addressed reading, whereas other areas such as writing and math are continuing to be developed (Fuchs, Fuchs, & Malone, 2016). In the absence of specific standardized protocols, schools can implement practices that have been demonstrated to enhance performance in different areas. These practices include self-monitoring and questioning, direct instruction, strategy instruction, and appropriate feedback and are described in more detail throughout this text.

DECISION MAKING As stated previously, Tier 2 instruction can be implemented over a period of 9 to 12 weeks, during which student progress is monitored in both the Tier 2 setting and in the general education classroom. Near the end of the implementation period, a determination must be made regarding the effectiveness of the Tier 2 instruction. If the student's progress in the Tier 1 setting is now regarded as adequate, the student resumes being served in the general education classroom, and Tier 2 services are discontinued. If, however, progress is not regarded as adequate at the end of the instructional period, one of two decisions must be made. If the student is making progress but has not yet achieved at the level of the student's peers, additional Tier 2 instruction may be implemented. If, however, the level of functioning and progress is markedly different from that of the student's peers, referral for evaluation for Tier 3 (special education) may be warranted.

CONSIDERATIONS IN IMPLEMENTATION OF TIER 2 INSTRUCTION

Given the small group size and intensive procedures of Tier 2 instruction, appropriate allocation of resources may prove to be an important consideration. Additionally, challenges may be faced in the areas of implementation across the various grade and content areas represented in the schools. Although much progress has been made in the area of early reading, additional work needs to be done in other skill and content areas at other grade levels. In addition, appropriate implementation of Tier 2 instruction will require substantial efforts in professional development; recruiting and funding new staff; effective scheduling of Tier 2 instruction; implementing skill-monitoring procedures throughout Tiers 1 and 2; and coordinating all aspects of RTI across grade levels and teaching staff into a single, coherent program (Mellard & Johnson, 2008). Although the challenges of implementation are great, the results could bring increased achievement for all students throughout the grade levels.

MyEdLab: **Self-Check 7.4**

MyEdLab: **Application Exercise 7.3: Tier 2 Interventions**

Tier 3: Individualized, Intensive Instruction

If progress of students in Tier 2 is not satisfactory and additional Tier 2 instruction is not considered appropriate, students may be moved into an even more intensive level of instruction. Tier 3 typically involves intensive, individualized (or very small-group) instruction that is implemented more frequently and over a longer period of time than Tier 2 interventions and is focused directly on precise learning objectives (Powell & Fuchs, 2015; Vaughn, Denton, & Fletcher, 2010; Vaughn & Wanzek, 2014). Tier 3 may or may not involve referral to special education, depending on state and local guidelines. In some cases, referral to special education may be a component of Tier 3 in a three-tiered system; in others, referral may be part of a fourth or higher tier in schools where more than three tiers are employed.

In order to move into special education, however, special identification procedures need to be implemented, consistent with the requirements of IDEA. In the case of learning disabilities, the regulations specifically allow for RTI procedures to be included in the identification process and specify that states may not require an IQ–achievement discrepancy to be part of this process. IDEA specifies that the criteria adopted by states for identification of learning disabilities:

- Must not require the use of a severe discrepancy between intellectual ability and achievement for determining whether a child has a specific learning disability, as defined in 34 CFR 300.8(c)(10);

- Must permit the use of a process based on the child's response to scientific, research-based intervention; and

- May permit the use of other alternative research-based procedures for determining whether a child has a specific learning disability (IDEA, 2004, §1221e-3; §1401[30]; §1414[b][6]).

States, then, can use documented student failure to respond adequately to scientific, research-based interventions as one criterion for learning disabilities determination. Once this is implemented and the student is identified as having learning disabilities, an individualized education program (IEP) is developed, and the student is placed in special education. A variety

of placement options may be appropriate. Similar to Tier 1 and Tier 2 instruction, Tier 3 special education must include scientific, evidence-based practices and progress monitoring toward specific goals and objectives (Fuchs & Deshler, 2007).

STRATEGIES FOR

IMPLEMENTATION OF TIER 3 INSTRUCTION

Whereas Tier 1 instruction occurs in the general education class and Tier 2 instruction occurs in small groups, Tier 3 instruction is implemented individually or in small groups (or in inclusive classrooms) to meet specific goals and objectives. If students are placed in special education, instruction may address any number of skills and content areas, as well as social behavior (as identified on IEPs), and is usually associated with intensive instruction using specialized materials.

USE INTENSIVE, INDIVIDUALIZED INSTRUCTION Special education for students with learning disabilities and with other disabilities such as autism is typically associated with intensive, systematic, and explicit instruction (Mastropieri & Scruggs, 2002). This can include task analysis (breaking the task or skill down into teachable, sequential steps), direct instruction (explicit, direct drill and practice of target objectives), and strategy instruction (explicit provision of cognitive routines needed to execute a task) (Swanson, 2000). Special education can also include teacher modeling, frequent feedback, overlearning, generalization training, explicit reinforcement of appropriate behavior and/or skill mastery, and frequent monitoring of learner progress toward prespecified goals and objectives. Effective special education teachers monitor progress continuously and are prepared to modify and adjust instruction as needed when progress is insufficient.

REFERRAL TO SPECIAL EDUCATION Special education, which may include placement in general education classes for much or all of the school day with appropriate supports, may be part or all of the final tier in a three-tiered RTI system. Although there are usually no other placement options (special schools or other facilities may be appropriate in some limited cases), it is believed that many students placed in special education may make sufficient progress to be reintegrated into the general education class as regular education students. If that is not possible, students referred to special education should have as much access to general education classrooms and the general education curriculum as feasible (Fuchs et al., 2012).

> MyEdLab: **Self-Check 7.5**
>
> MyEdLab: **Application Exercise 7.4: Tier 3 Intervention**

Fidelity of Implementation

Although RTI models can be planned and developed skillfully, they cannot be effective unless they are implemented faithfully. *Fidelity of implementation* refers to the degree to which instruction is delivered in the way it was intended (Gresham, MacMillan, Beebe-Frankenberger, & Bocian, 2000) and is important because treatments, however effective on paper, will not be successful unless they are implemented correctly. It is important to ensure that both the school's procedures for RTI and instruction across the different tiers are implemented with fidelity.

The concept of treatment fidelity is predicated on the fact that instructional methods and interventions must use *evidence-based practice*, or practice that is supported by scientific evidence for its effectiveness when implemented as intended. That is, it is of little use to effectively implement a treatment or intervention that is not known to be effective in the first place. Criteria for evidence-based practice are explored in detail in Volume 71, Issue 2, of *Exceptional Children* (2005).

Mellard and Johnson (2008; see also Johnson, Mellard, Fuchs, & McKnight, 2006) have suggested that three elements, or "dimensions," are important to fidelity of implementation: (a) the *method* of evaluating fidelity, (b) the *frequency* of fidelity evaluations, and (c) the *support systems* needed to implement the program with fidelity. Each is discussed separately.

STRATEGIES FOR

DETERMINING FIDELITY OF IMPLEMENTATION

Gresham et al. (2000) described three types of fidelity assessments. The first is ***direct assessment* measures**, including checklists of intervention components, conducted by a person qualified to observe classroom procedures. The observer records the elements of effective implementation of the intervention and calculates the percentage of steps completed appropriately. For example, for a particular type of reading instruction, the checklist may include items such as the following:

- The classroom is well organized, including accessible materials, appropriate seating, and efficient transitions between activities.

- All parts of the lesson are covered.

- Appropriate pace and engagement of all students are maintained throughout the lesson.

- The teacher demonstrates enthusiasm and provides appropriate praise and feedback.

- Effective error correction is employed, according to the procedures outlined in the method.

- Both group and individual responses are solicited.

- Teacher ensures accurate responding before introducing new skills.

- Classroom behavior is effectively managed (students are motivated, expectations are clear, misbehavior is efficiently redirected).

- Reading checkouts (e.g., 1-minute reading timings) and evaluations are conducted efficiently and appropriately.

In most cases, items would also be specifically referenced to details of the method and curriculum being employed. Using a checklist prepared or approved by the district or school, a percent mastery score may be calculated by dividing the steps met adequately by the total number of steps in the checklist. For example, if the checklist contained 15 steps and the teacher was observed meeting 12 steps appropriately, the percent mastery could be calculated by dividing 12 by 15, for a total of 80%. Schools that employ standards for mastery also determine specifically what standard (e.g., 90%, 85%) constitutes fidelity. Many treatment-fidelity checklists can be found on the Internet; however, each school should determine that obtained checklists are appropriate for their own purposes.

INDIRECT ASSESSMENT **Indirect methods of fidelity assessment** include teacher self-reports of implementation, more general rating scales, teacher interviews, and permanent products of teacher and student work. Of these, permanent products are thought to be the most reliable (Mellard & Johnson, 2008) and may include, for example, products such as relevant completed student assignments or written teacher feedback that corresponds to components of the intervention. Other indirect assessments can also contribute to the overall picture of fidelity. Using rating scales, teachers can evaluate the extent to which they believe (e.g., 5 = *disagree* to 1 = *strongly agree*) that they implement components of the intervention. Similarly, observers could rate the observed lesson as a whole using such measures. Also, when direct measures of fidelity are not high, interviews and rating scales can help provide important information for improving fidelity.

TREATMENT MANUALS Some interventions have accompanying manuals detailing the components of their effective implementation. Some benefit may be obtained by providing teachers with manuals to accompany their treatments. However, unless these manuals are consulted frequently and supplemented with more direct measures, they are unlikely to ensure faithful implementation (Gresham et al., 2000).

FREQUENCY Schools must determine how frequently they will conduct fidelity evaluations, based on such considerations as the need for specific types of information and the availability of resources. Mellard and Johnson (2008) suggested that fidelity checks may depend in part on (a) the experience of the teacher, (b) teacher requests for support in implementation, (c) the performance of individual classes on screening and progress-monitoring measures, and (d) the number of special education referrals coming from individual classes.

Schools should determine how frequently (e.g., weekly, monthly, annually, as needed) they will check the fidelity of implementation for a number of tasks, and they should keep records of this information. Relevant tasks for which frequency should be established can include the following:

- Review of state and school district assessment results
- Implementation of screening measures
- Implementation and review of progress monitoring
- Completion of teacher fidelity evaluations
- Collection of input from teachers and staff
- Evaluation of new staff for treatment fidelity

Although frequency guidelines have been suggested for some measures (e.g., screening conducted three times yearly), schools should determine for themselves how frequently evaluations and fidelity checks should be conducted.

SUPPORT SYSTEMS Schools can always use fidelity-of-implementation data to help determine areas in need of remediation, as well as relative areas of strength. For example, fidelity-of-implementation data can be employed to identify teachers who are implementing their treatments with a high degree of fidelity. Newly hired teachers, as well as teachers who need additional support in implementing specific interventions, may need professional development and training. This may, in some cases, require reallocation of school resources. Overall, the purpose of fidelity-of-implementation evaluation should be to determine where additional supports are needed and then provide the necessary resources and training. Information from a variety of sources, including indirect and direct measures, teacher self-referral, and progress monitoring, can be employed to determine where to provide additional supports to assure optimal implementation of RTI.

Establishing fidelity of implementation involves several different steps. A task list for establishing fidelity-of-implementation procedures includes development of a timeline and assignment of individual responsibility for tasks. Staff professional development and schedules for continuous professional development are important. The data-collection system needs to include clear measures for data collection (e.g., observation checklists and products), the criteria for acceptable performance, and implementation schedules. Johnson et al. (2006) recommended developing plans for reviewing all the fidelity data and for providing ongoing professional development support as needed.

STRATEGIES FOR
IMPLEMENTING RTI AT THE SECONDARY LEVEL

The challenges of implementing RTI at the secondary level may in some ways be greater than those for RTI at the elementary level. Scheduling can be more complicated, a much greater and more varied number of subject areas are involved, and areas such as reading and basic math are in most cases no longer individual subjects of instruction. In addition, much less research has been conducted on RTI at the secondary level to date, although more attention has been directed to the secondary level more recently (e.g., Vaughn et al., 2011).

Shinn, Windram, and Bollman (2016) suggested that a confused or poorly articulated purpose is the major barrier to secondary RTI implementation. Clearly, RTI at the secondary level is no longer focused on early intervention as an important objective, as is RTI at the elementary level; however, at secondary levels, important goals include dropout prevention and development of skills and content knowledge sufficient to promote success and, ultimately, graduation from high school.

INTERVENTIONS FOR SECONDARY SKILLS AND CONTENT RTI in secondary schools may address various skills and content domains, as needed. Tier 1 would include evidence-based differentiated instruction in the content areas in the general education classroom, whereas Tier 2 interventions might include intensive instruction in reading, especially emphasizing reading fluency, word study, vocabulary, and passage comprehension (e.g., Vaughn et al., 2011). These Tier 2 interventions also may emphasize basic math, study skills, reading in the content areas, or supplemental subject-area instruction (Johnson, Smith, & Harris, 2009). For example, Vaughn et al. (2015) taught content reading skills to high school students in small groups over a period of 2 years. Skills taught addressed word study, vocabulary in content-area text, comprehension of content-area text, and engagement. Because the Common Core State Standards (CCSS) require students to read increasingly difficult texts to build content-specific knowledge in reading, it is important that supports for students are provided throughout (National Governors Association Center for Best Practices, Council of Chief State School Officers, 2010).

Another intervention that has been implemented in recent years is "double-dose" instruction, in which an elective class is replaced by a second, supporting class in the target area. For example, Cortes, Goodman, and Nomi (2013) described a program in which target students enrolled in two periods of ninth-grade algebra per day, with the second class providing support and additional practice. These courses were well coordinated, with 90% or more overlapping content. Cortes et al. concluded that the program had a facilitative effect on test scores and graduation rates. As with all RTI programs, formative evaluation is necessary to ensure that programs are leading to desired outcomes.

A system of positive behavioral supports may be implemented for problems with social behavior (Ihlo & Nantais, 2010). RTI procedures at the secondary level in these various areas are addressed in relevant chapters in this book.

Components of RTI that remain very similar between elementary and secondary levels include screening and progress monitoring, data-based decision making, fidelity of implementation, continuous improvement, and multi-tiered implementation. Although less attention has been paid to RTI at the secondary level, it nevertheless remains a very important component of a comprehensive program.

MyEdLab: **Self-Check 7.6**

Challenges with Implementing RTI

Although research and practice have developed greatly concerning RTI and its implementation, a number of challenges remain for the field. The role of RTI in evaluating students for placement in special education programs is not generally agreed upon, and the degree to which evaluations based on RTI discriminate between learning disabilities and other disabilities such as intellectual disabilities is not known. Presently, there are many different versions of RTI, and procedures for determining "success" in a given tier also vary widely. Many voices have called for more specific characterizations of each of the mechanisms of RTI in the future (Berkeley et al., 2009; Fuchs & Fuchs, 2006; Fuchs, Fuchs, & Stecker, 2010; Fuchs et al., 2003; Gerber, 2005).

When conducted by researchers using systematic protocols, Tier 2 instruction has resulted in substantial gains. Wanzek et al. (2015) conducted meta-analyses of 72 Tier 2 reading interventions with students from kindergarten through third grade and reported that, overall, students had benefited substantially from the intervention, in reading skills as well as comprehension. However, in a large-scale study of 146 schools in 13 states in which RTI was implemented by the schools themselves, Balu et al. (2015) reported that Tier 2 and Tier 3 instruction had no overall effect on reading outcomes in grades 1 through 3, although the effects varied significantly across schools. These findings help underscore the need for schools to implement treatments systematically and to collect and evaluate outcome data systematically, to ensure that the interventions are achieving their intended purpose.

A substantial amount of research has been conducted on RTI for early reading; however, effective and appropriate Tier 2 strategies for math, writing, and other content areas such as science and social studies await further development, particularly at the secondary level (Mastropieri & Scruggs, 2005; Vaughn & Bos, 2015). Some programs are under way in a number of different areas (e.g., Johnson et al., 2009); however, more information is needed on optimal RTI programs in these areas. Many of these issues may be addressed more satisfactorily in the future as schools develop more experience with RTI.

Although RTI was intended to implement needed services promptly, in some cases, extended exposure to RTI programs may delay the evaluation process for special education. Dr. Melody Musgrove, former director of the Office of Special Education Programs, communicated the following to the State Directors of Special Education:

> It has come to the attention of the Office of Special Education Programs (OSEP) that, in some instances, local education authorities (LEAs) may be using RTI strategies to delay or deny a timely initial evaluation of children suspected of having a disability. States and LEAs have an obligation to ensure that evaluation of children expected of having a disability are not delayed or denied because of implementation of an RTI strategy. (Musgrove, 2011, p. 1)

Fuchs et al. (2012) suggested future procedures for implementation of RTI, referred to as *Smart RTI*. These procedures include (a) collecting screening measures in multiple stages (e.g., two levels of assessment) to reduce the number of false positives referred to Tier 2 unnecessarily; (b) "fast tracking" those students whose failure to respond can be predicted (i.e., without implementing Tier 2) to special education; and (c) providing Tier 3 as intensive special education that features data-based individualized instruction, access to the general education curriculum, and movement across the different tiers of RTI as needed (see also Fuchs, Fuchs, Compton, Wehby, Schumacher, ...Jordan, 2015).

MyEdLab: **Self-Check 7.7**

---

7 Summary

- Response to intervention (RTI) is a multi-tiered system of support (MTSS) designed to address different learning needs and intended to improve instruction.

  — Much progress has been made to date in conceptualizing, implementing, and evaluating RTI (Glover, 2010), and additional progress continues to be made.

- Schoolwide screening, progress monitoring, and data-based decision making assist in identifying students at risk for academic failure, monitoring their progress, and making instructional decisions based on students' performance data.

  — At present, RTI holds considerable promise for identifying academic and behavioral problems in schools, providing appropriate intervention, and creating an integrated system of service delivery in general education and special education.

- Tier 1 instruction is scientifically based and delivered in the general education setting.

  — Teachers will benefit greatly by becoming well informed regarding their local school and district procedures for implementing RTI, and children with special needs will benefit from the implementation of a systematic, multi-tiered process for identifying and correcting learning and behavioral problems, beginning in the inclusive classroom.

- Tier 2 instruction provides more intensive interventions to identified smaller groups of students who still receive Tier 1 instruction.

- Tier 3 is more intensive and includes special education in many RTI models.

- Fidelity of implementation means that instruction is delivered as intended.

- Challenges exist with implementing RTI, but schools, teachers, and researchers are attempting to address these challenges.

PROFESSIONAL STANDARDS LINK:
Response to Intervention and Multi-Tiered Systems of Support

Information in this chapter links most directly to:

- CEC Standards: 2 (Learning Environments), 4 (Assessment), 5 (Instructional Planning and Strategies) 7 (Collaboration)
- INTASC Standards: 2 (Learning Differences), 3 (Learning Environments), 6 (Assessment), 7 (Planning for Instruction), 10 (Leadership and Collaboration)

STRATEGIES FOR IMPLEMENTING RESPONSE TO INTERVENTION

In considering implementing RTI, have you tried the following? If not, see the pages listed here.

8

Improving Motivation and Social Behavior

LEARNING OUTCOMES

After studying this chapter, you should be able to:

8.1 Identify preconditions and techniques for improving and enhancing student motivation and affect.

8.2 Describe how to manage classroom behaviors.

8.3 Describe techniques for teaching social skills.

Teachers often report that management of classroom behavior is of significant importance and is a significant influence on student learning (Tauber, 2007). Disciplined, well-managed classrooms are much more likely to promote learning for all students. However, classroom behavior is much more easily managed when students are motivated to learn and succeed in school (Wentzel & Brophy, 2014).

In this chapter, we discuss techniques for effective management of student behavior. First, however, we present motivational techniques that can be implemented to encourage students to work their hardest and to take control of their own learning. When students feel sufficiently motivated and empowered, classroom management techniques are much more likely to be implemented successfully.

Setting the Stage for Academic Success

Because of their combined effect on student learning, motivation and affect are among the most important topics in this book. Although motivation and affect overlap to some extent, they represent important, separate aspects of school functioning. **Motivation** refers to the degree to which students desire to succeed in school, whereas **affect** refers to the students' emotional mood and personal feelings. **Intrinsic motivation** refers to participation in an activity purely out of curiosity, desire to succeed, or desire to contribute. **Extrinsic motivation**, on the other hand, refers to participation in an activity in anticipation of an external reward (Wentzel & Brophy, 2014).

Given that instruction is adequate, high levels of motivation and positive affect provide students opportunities to master the learning tasks set before them. However, at one time or other, students—particularly those with disabilities and other special needs—can lack motivation and positive affect (e.g., Carlson, Booth, Shin, & Canu, 2002; Wolters, Denton, York, & Francis, 2014). Students who lack a life history of success may be more likely to quit working on a task because they believe they have little chance of succeeding (Nelson & Manset-Williamson, 2006).

Some students with disabilities may be more likely to fail at academic tasks and to attribute such failure to personal inadequacies rather than to lack of effort. Finally, students with disabilities and other special needs may be more at risk for affective problems such as anxiety (Nelson & Harwood, 2011), depression (Maag & Reid, 2006), and low self-esteem (Sideridis, 2007). The following scenario describes Danny's motivation problem in school.

Danny

Danny is enrolled in a ninth-grade mathematics class. In fifth grade, he was classified as having a learning disability in reading, and he attends the resource room for four 50-minute periods per week for help with his reading. He is interested in basketball and has many friends. In math class (pre-algebra), however, his manner is anything but cheerful. He received a failing grade the first semester, and he seems to be headed for another at the end of the next grading period. During lecture or class discussion, Danny seems to simply stare off into space. When given classroom assignments, he makes a modest effort to complete them, but it is clear from his manner that he is just waiting for the bell to ring. He turns in only about half of his homework assignments—and most of these are either incomplete or incorrect. Clearly, mathematics is neither an academic strength nor an interest area for Danny; nevertheless, it seems likely that he could produce work of a much higher quality if he applied himself more and developed a more positive attitude toward math. However, when his math teacher, Mr. Hamilton, spoke with him about his attitude, Danny seemed to believe his problem was hopeless. "What's the use?" he said. "You know I'll just fail anyway."

QUESTIONS FOR REFLECTION

1. Why do you think Danny feels this way about math?
2. When do you think simple statements of encouragement by his teacher would be likely to help? What kinds of statements would be best?
3. What are some ways his friends or peers could help?

The best way to handle the motivational and affective problems of all students, including those with disabilities, is to start by making the classroom a positive and motivating experience for all students.

STRATEGIES FOR
IMPROVING MOTIVATION AND AFFECT

Making decisions to create the most ideal conditions for motivating students and increasing positive affect is within your control as a teacher, and it can make an enormous difference in the classroom atmosphere and student achievement.

PRECONDITIONS Before any attempt to improve motivation and affect will succeed in inclusive classrooms, several preconditions must exist (Wentzel & Brophy, 2014). These are not motivational strategies in themselves, but they set the stage for the development of motivation and positive classroom affect. These preconditions include (a) supportive, organized classroom environment; (b) instructional materials that are at an appropriate difficulty level; (c) meaningful and relevant instructional tasks; and (d) task-oriented classrooms. Students are much more likely to become motivated in classrooms in which they feel welcome and important, for example, when teachers make supportive statements or enlist peer support. Another important consideration for creating a supportive atmosphere is ensuring your classroom is culturally responsive. The *Diversity in the Classroom* feature provides some suggestions. Students are more likely to maintain their motivation when tasks are relevant and meaningful to them and are neither too difficult nor too easy (Lavoie, 2007). Finally, students are more likely to feel motivated in "task-oriented" classrooms, where interest and effort are rewarded and where success is determined by a number of factors they can control. In contrast, in "ego-oriented" classrooms, students are evaluated more with respect to overall "capacity" and their performance as compared with other students (Nicholls, 1989). If students think they have low (or not sufficiently high) capacity for learning, they may be less likely to try their best in the future (see Anderman & Patrick, 2012). Table 8.1 provides comments characteristic of ego-oriented and task-oriented classrooms.

Once the important preconditions have been met to create a positive classroom atmosphere, you can turn to several general categories of techniques to enhance motivation and affect both in individual students and in your class as a whole: improving self-esteem and self-efficacy, increasing personal investment in learning, making learning fun and enjoyable, and using praise and rewards (Scruggs & Mastropieri, 1994).

Creating a Culturally Responsive Classroom

Culture influences all aspects of life and school. Students' cultures shape their language, behavior, emotions, customs, and traditions. Because of the importance of culture, students feel more motivated to learn if the classroom is responsive to their cultures. Gollnick and Chinn (2013) referred to students' cultures as microcultures consisting of interactions of race, ethnicity, language, gender, class, religion, age, geography, and disability. All of these characteristics merge to form an individual's culture, which in turn interacts with the dominant culture (see also Banks, 2015).

Gaining an understanding and an appreciation of these cultural influences will assist in developing culturally responsive education, which, in turn, should increase student motivation and investment in learning. For example, learn how education is viewed from the perspectives of your students and families. Find out how students and families perceive school visits, homework, school authority figures, and school activities. Learn about the cultural identities and strengths of your students and families. Design instruction and strategies to encourage involvement for members of all cultures in relevant school activities. Emphasize cooperation and motivation while relating educational goals to students and their families in culturally meaningful ways.

Set up or expand a literacy center at your school that emphasizes literacy for all and represents all cultural and linguistic groups. For example, King Middle School's literacy center began providing literacy assistance to adults and families in the evenings while supporting students during the school day (Ginsberg & Wlodkowski, 2009). Attendance at the center was encouraged for anyone requiring assistance with English. Community members from similar linguistic backgrounds might be available to help individuals feel more comfortable. The literacy center became a motivating focal point for the community and held events such as book discussions and folk art festivals sponsored by the local parent organization.

Demonstrate a sincere, caring, accepting attitude toward all individuals. Help students and families know that everyone, regardless of cultural or linguistic background, is an important member of your school's community.

TABLE 8.1 Ego-Oriented Versus Task-Oriented Classrooms

Classroom Orientation	Representative Teacher Comments
Ego-oriented	"Marcy, you're the smartest student in the class!"
	"Class, look at how smart Fredrica is, to have figured this out!"
	"Richard, why can't you be more like Bernie?"
Task-oriented	"Marcy, this is your best work yet!"
	"Fredrica must have worked very hard to have figured this out!"
	"Richard, I know you can do much better on this assignment if you use the strategies we practiced and put more effort into it."

RAISE STUDENTS' SELF-ESTEEM   Self-esteem is a general term for the regard in which individuals hold themselves. Generally, students who feel good about who they are and what they can do are more successful than students who do not feel good about themselves (Zheng, Erickson, Kingston, & Noonan, 2014). Self-esteem has been found to differ among boys and girls, students from different racial or ethnic groups, and students with and without disabilities. However, self-esteem has also been seen to be quite variable within all of these groups. That is, some students with disabilities exhibit very high self-esteem, and some high-achieving students exhibit low self-esteem. Some evidence suggests that students with milder disabilities may in some cases exhibit lower self-esteem than students with more significant disabilities (Harter, 2012).

Students with disabilities may be particularly vulnerable to beliefs that they do not compare favorably with their classmates (Ferro & Boyle, 2013). This suggests that students with disabilities should be carefully monitored for such affective characteristics as self-esteem and that the student's sense of worth and efficacy should be promoted wherever possible. This can be accomplished by providing students with tasks at which they can succeed and providing direct positive feedback and rewards for their success. Ensure that students with special needs know that they have an important role to play in the classroom by providing roles in which they can assume responsibility and ownership, such as taking care of classroom pets, distributing materials, or collecting papers. Such assignments, as well as public statements of support, can convince students with special needs that their presence is valued. Classroom peers can also assist in helping other students feel better about themselves.

PROMOTE SELF-EFFICACY   Students are motivated to persist on tasks at which they believe they will succeed. They are more apt to think they will succeed on future tasks if they have succeeded on similar previous tasks. In this situation, students believe they have the knowledge and the skills to ensure their attainment of the goal. This confidence in one's own abilities has been referred to as self-efficacy (Zimmerman & Kitsantas, 2007). You can improve self-efficacy by structuring academic tasks that can be accomplished with a reasonable effort and high rate of success and providing direct feedback when students are successful. Classroom activities benefit all students—especially students with disabilities—when they provide additional practice, continually assess understanding, make connections to prior learning, organize learning in advance of instruction, recognize good social models, and offer support for learning.

Other strategies that may improve self-efficacy include the following;

- **Provide additional practice to reinforce prior knowledge.** Initiate regular reviews and **overlearning** (additional practice after goals have been achieved) to reinforce any knowledge previously presented and increase student confidence. Additional practice could be provided by the special education teacher or by a parent, volunteer, or aide.

- **Use ongoing assessment strategies.** Monitor students' comprehension by asking frequent questions, and provide independent practice only after you are certain students can be successful independently so that students will learn to expect success in the classroom.

- **Point out appropriate social models.** Students may believe they can be successful—even if they have no experience with a task—if they observe students like themselves succeeding at the task. Say, for example, "Hey, last week, James couldn't do this either. James worked hard and learned to do this, so I'm sure you can learn to do it, too!"

- **Provide positive support.** Direct encouragement from teachers can help students' self-efficacy. Saying, "I really believe you will be able to do this if you give it a try!" provides positive support for effort, rather than criticism for failure, and can demonstrate your confidence in individual students.

Demonstration of genuine teacher interest at appropriate times can also improve student motivation and attitude toward schoolwork, as shown in the continuation of Danny's scenario.

Avoid Counterproductive Statements   One well-meaning strategy that is often counterproductive is characterizing a particular task as "easy" by saying, for example:

- "You can do this. It's easy!"
- "Anybody should be able to do this!"

Such statements are often intended to convince students that a task is doable and within their reach, but the effects of such statements can be very different. Because teachers rarely need to encourage a student to accomplish truly "easy" tasks, this strategy has often been used with tasks that the student considers difficult. However, the strategy can undermine motivation: little satisfaction is gained from accomplishing an "easy" task; shame and embarrassment result from failing at a task that is considered "easy."

Also, remember that if students express satisfaction in their performance by stating that a particular task was easy, use prudence in agreeing completely with such students. You could say something like, "It may have been easy for you because you worked hard to learn it, but I don't think it was really that easy!"

Danny

Mr. Hamilton arranged for a meeting with Danny. During this meeting, Mr. Hamilton expressed his concern about Danny's progress in math and his hope that he could improve. Danny seemed pleased with the extra attention from Mr. Hamilton but indicated his overall pessimistic attitude: "I appreciate you trying to help me, Mr. Hamilton, but it's no use. I'll never learn this math." Mr. Hamilton replied, "Danny, I think you're just not giving yourself a chance."

Mr. Hamilton arranged to edit Danny's homework assignments so that he could spend more time on a smaller number of problems within his current skill level. Mr. Hamilton would discuss the problems briefly with Danny in the few minutes before the class started; he would also arrange for a peer to help Danny during class exercises. Mr. Hamilton also began to privately praise Danny when he made an effort and completed his assignments: "You see? I told you that you would begin to catch on if you made this kind of effort!" When Danny's assignments were not completed, Mr. Hamilton displayed disappointment but expressed hope that the next assignment would be done correctly: "Danny, we both know from before that you can do better than this—I hope to see something really impressive on your next assignment!"

By the end of the second quarter, Danny's grade had improved from an F to a D+. On the last test of the semester, Danny earned a C+. Mr. Hamilton wrote a note to Danny's parents stating that he was the most improved student in his class. With additional prompting, Danny continued to perform successfully throughout the second semester. Danny concluded, "At first I thought I could never do it. But math's really not that bad if you put your mind to it!"

QUESTIONS FOR REFLECTION

1. Why do you think Mr. Hamilton was frustrated with Danny's performance in math?
2. What types of additional strategies might be helpful for Danny to use at home?
3. How can a monitoring system be established to determine whether the instructional interventions are working effectively?

TEACH STUDENTS TO SET GOALS Once students believe they are capable of accomplishing a task, involving them in goal setting can increase their motivation to complete that task. Research has found that students often increase their achievement when they help set their own goals (Konrad, Fowler, & Walker, 2007; Wentzel & Brophy, 2014). Students involved in setting their own goals and in monitoring their own progress will be more likely to see learning goals as meaningful and personal—more so than if they are simply imposed by the teacher. Motivation can be maximized when the goal is difficult for the student to attain but can be achieved with vigorous or persistent effort.

Establish realistic but challenging goals, and monitor progress on graphs or charts. For example, students can select goals for solving a certain number of math problems, reading a specific number of pages in a book daily, or getting 90% correct on weekly spelling tests. A sample goal sheet is depicted in Figure 8.1.

Parents are usually the primary advocates for their children and can be an invaluable source for promoting self-efficacy and supporting the continued efforts of students. Communicate frequently with parents to share your expectations for the student and ask for parents' help in meeting these goals. Parents often will agree to participate in a reinforcement system, through which the student is rewarded at home for positive efforts made during school.

TRAIN STUDENTS TO USE POSITIVE ATTRIBUTIONS With **attribution training,** students are taught to attribute success to their own efforts and academic strategies and to attribute failure to their lack of effort or failure to use appropriate strategies. Students who learn to attribute success and failure to things they control are more likely to try hard and succeed in the future than those who do not (Berkeley, Mastropieri, & Scruggs, 2011).

GOAL SHEET

Student name _____

Dates _____

Class _____

# of daily math problems	Monday	Tuesday	Wednesday	Thursday	Friday
Daily Goal	20	20	20	25	25
Accuracy Goal	18	19	20	20	22
Number Completed	16	19			
Number Correct	16	19			
Teacher Comment	Good work; try working faster	Super job!			

Figure 8.1   Sample Goal-Setting Sheet

Attributions that correctly attribute success or failure to student behavior—things a student does or could do—are called positive attributions. Negative attributions, on the other hand, attribute success or failure to such things as inherent ability or teacher prejudices. Examples of positive and negative attributions are given in Table 8.2.

As a teacher, you should be alert to the development of negative attributions, particularly for students with special needs. To counter these kinds of attributions, first, make certain that all assignments are within the ability of the student. Then simply do not accept negative statements such as "I'm stupid" or "I have a disability." These declarations should not be allowed to justify failure. You can reply to such attributions with statements such as, "No, the reason you failed is that you gave up too soon," or "No, the reason you failed is that you didn't use the strategies you practiced for that test."

When students succeed, be sure to reinforce the value of strategy use. For example, say, "The reason you did so well is that you used the strategy we have been learning" (Berkeley et al., 2011; Nelson & Manset-Williamson, 2006).

ARRANGE COUNSELING INTERVENTIONS WHEN NEEDED   Students with disabilities may experience problems of affect such as anxiety, depression, and low self-esteem. Counseling interventions have been designed to address affective problems of students and may involve a number of techniques (Sideridis, 2007; Thurneck, Warner, & Cobb, 2007).

TABLE 8.2   Student Attributions for Success and Failure

Positive Attributions	Negative Attributions
Success	**Success**
"I succeeded on the spelling test because I used the spelling strategy I learned."	"I succeeded on the spelling test because I got lucky."
"I got an A on my science project because I started early and used my time effectively."	"I got an A on my science project because my teacher likes me."
Failure	**Failure**
"I failed the math test because I put off studying until the last minute, and then I fell asleep. Next time, I'll start earlier."	"I failed the math test because I'm stupid at math."
"I didn't do as well as I could have on the test because I didn't study for an essay test. Next time, I'll practice writing essay answers when I study."	"I didn't do well on the test because the teacher doesn't grade fairly."

School counselors frequently use both individual and group counseling to work with students with disabilities and may provide self-esteem activities and social skills training; in addition, they can provide valuable feedback for multidisciplinary teams. Counseling interventions for students with disabilities have been found to increase relaxation, decrease school truancy, and increase self-esteem and general well-being (Leichtentritt & Shechtman, 2009). Although the training and activities of counselors may vary from school to school (Milsom & Akos, 2003), counselors should be considered potentially important participants in the lives of students with disabilities, and they should be consulted as appropriate in individual situations.

Exercise Care When Handling Serious Affective Disorders   Some disorders of affect are very serious and may not be substantially improved with the application of the strategies described in this chapter. If you encounter students with very serious affective problems, obtain professional assistance and contact the parents. Special education teachers, counselors, or school psychologists may help or refer you to other professionals if you have a student who appears to exhibit signs of severe depression, anxiety, or suicidal behavior.

INCREASE STUDENTS' PERSONAL INVESTMENT IN THE CLASSROOM

Students who believe they have some ownership in what is happening in your classroom are also more likely to make an effort to help the classroom be successful. If they have had some input in classroom decision making, students are also more likely to identify positively with classroom activities. Conversely, students who think they have no influence in how classroom business is conducted are more likely to lose motivation and interest.

MyEdLab:
Video Example 8.1.
The teacher in this video is eliciting procedures for working in the library from her students. Notice how the students participate and think about how they feel about the interaction.

Allow students to participate in decision making when possible, for example, in determining seating assignments or the sequence in which lessons and activities will be presented. Find out about your students' opinions with surveys and questionnaires, and implement suggestions when appropriate. If you are able to adapt the way you manage the classroom in response to student opinion, students are likely to feel that they are an important part of the classroom.

MAKE LEARNING MORE FUN AND ENJOYABLE

Motivation and positive affect will improve when students have enjoyable activities to look forward to each morning, rather than routine procedures that have become dull and stale.

Make Tasks More Interesting   Numerous strategies are at your disposal to utilize to make learning more interesting and fun (Wentzel & Brophy, 2014), such as the following.

1. *Prepare more concrete, meaningful lessons.* To increase motivation for learning, use personal examples, classroom exhibits and demonstrations, hands-on curriculum materials, and concrete models and illustrations.

2. *Create cognitive conflict.* Interest in learning can be aroused by discussion or demonstration of situations that promote **cognitive conflict**, situations that are not easily predictable or explainable at first. The presentation of discrepant events can create cognitive conflict in students. A discrepant event is an event (often in science) whereby things behave differently than expected (Gable, 2003; Kaya & Lundeen, 2010). An example of a discrepant event is "dancing" raisins, where raisins appear to move up and down independently in a soft drink. Further observation and deduction reveal that the raisins move because of the carbon dioxide in the soft drink. Discrepant events can enhance curiosity and interest and increase motivation to learn (Gonsalez-Spada, Bieeiel, & Birriel, 2010).

3. *Use novel ways to engage students.* Sometimes students begin to lose motivation simply because instruction has become stale and predictable. In this case, interest may be restored by incorporating novel ways of doing things. Changing the order of classroom routines, reallocating classroom responsibilities, and rearranging classroom seating are all ways to increase novelty.

    You also can provide variety in the way instruction is delivered by using different media, inviting guest speakers or student presenters, and using different applications of technology. Keep in mind that some students, for example, those with autism, may respond negatively to changes in classroom routine (Anckarsäter et al., 2010). However, in many cases, novelty can be useful in improving motivation and affect, especially when combined with other techniques described in this chapter.

4. *Develop competitive and gamelike activities.* Competition that pits students against one another and for which students may not perceive an equal chance of winning may be detrimental to motivation; such competition is more characteristic of ego-oriented classrooms. However, when students believe they have a fair chance of winning, and when the same small group of students does not always win, competition and gamelike activities can provide a high degree of motivation and interest in the class.

   The following is an example of small-group competition in a practice activity: First, divide students randomly into several small groups. Then direct one individual student from each group to take turns answering questions about the topic being studied. Allow the selected students to accept suggestions from other students in their groups, but let them know that they must decide on the answer individually. When an answer is correct, the group receives a point. At the end of the activity, the group with the most points is the "winner." In some cases, the winning group may be given a reward or privileges of some kind, but students may find it sufficiently rewarding simply to be on the winning team. Each time the game is played, assign students to different groups. Students with special needs can be included in activities such as this one because they are able to contribute to the activity.

5. *Make use of cooperative learning.* Cooperative learning strategies can also be used to enhance student interest, affect, and motivation. Group projects, group participation in science activities, group studying, guided-practice activities, and group competition in gamelike activities as described in the previous section are helpful in enhancing student interest. Chapter 9 provides additional examples for implementing cooperative learning. However, monitor group activity carefully to ensure that all students are being treated fairly and that all students are participating equally and learning adequately from the activities (McMaster & Fuchs, 2002).

6. *Be enthusiastic!* Enthusiasm is one of the teacher presentation variables that helps to develop student interest and make learning more fun. Enthusiastic teachers enhance motivation by modeling interest in the subject being learned and the amount of enjoyment that can be attained when learning occurs. Enthusiastic teachers also are more interesting presenters, so students are more likely to pay attention to what is being presented.

PRAISE STUDENTS AND REWARD THEIR EFFORTS   Praise and concrete rewards are often the first things people think of when considering ways to increase motivation and affect. Naturally, most people (including teachers) feel more valued and more motivated when they are praised and positively rewarded for their achievements.

Praise Student Effort   The effective use of praise is of paramount importance to enhancing motivation and affect, and when appropriately employed, use of praise closely conforms to the idea of a task-oriented classroom. Praise is highly motivating to students because it provides encouraging feedback for student efforts and demonstrates that their work is being appreciated. Unfortunately, teachers may sometimes provide the most praise to the highest-achieving students and withhold praise from lower-achieving students.

Praise should be linked to specific student actions and behaviors while specifying the criteria being met, such as "good work on your math problems—you had no errors!" rather than vague statements such as "good work." Praise must be genuine and sincere and not sound like repetitive, insincere statements ("good job," "good job," "good job") and should be given for especially noteworthy accomplishments. Indicate the relationship between student effort and achievement to promote personal satisfaction, such as, "You should be very proud of the hard work you did on this project!" Finally, suggest that similar efforts will result in the same future successes with statements such as, "If you keep working this well, you will earn As on all your math assignments this quarter!" (Wentzel & Brophy, 2014).

Henderlong and Lepper (2002) pointed out some areas where praise is not effective. Overall, praise that is vague or that describes general traits of students (e.g., "You are very bright") is not successful in promoting motivation and positive affect. Praise such as this—comments that give students the message that they are praiseworthy without making any particular effort—often does not motivate students. Conversely, praise that links accomplishment with effort, persistence, and effective study strategies is much more likely to be effective.

TABLE 8.3 Praise Statements and Explanations for Praise

Elementary-Level Examples	Secondary-Level Examples
• That's wonderful! You showed me how to write your name! • Super! I can tell you are trying your very best! • I like the way you are working! • Exactly right! You completed all the problems!	• That's a great observation! You understand how a pendulum works! • Terrific paper! Your writing has really improved. • Keep up the hard work! Your compositions are really improving! • Great sentences! Will you share your paper with the class?

Note: Many statements could be used with either elementary or secondary students.

Table 8.3 presents sample praise statements with corresponding explanations for both elementary- and secondary-level students. The *In the Classroom* feature provides some adjectives that can be used for praising students and corresponding behaviors that can be combined with them to create many alternatives to "Good job!"

USE REWARDS TO REINFORCE STUDENT SUCCESS   Rewards, when appropriately employed, can be very effective in promoting motivation to succeed. For example, Matson and Boisjoli (2009) described the powerful effect of extrinsic reward systems for individuals with autism and intellectual disabilities. Rewards can be intangible (privileges, free time) or tangible (stickers, pencils, snacks) and are discussed further in the classroom management section of this chapter. When employing rewards to increase motivation, apply them when intrinsic motivation is low, and be sure to link rewards to specific expectations, such as achieving a specific goal.

MyEdLab: **Self-Check 8.1**

MyEdLab: **Application Exercise 8.1: Improving Student Motivation and Affect**

MyEdLab:
Video Example 8.2.
This video shows a teacher providing a token economy for her students and rewarding students for being on task during group time. This is an example of students with special needs earning rewards.

In the Classroom

Example Alternative Statements for Praise

Use any of the following praise adjectives and match them with a variety of behavior words:

Adjectives:
Amazing, Astonishing, Fantastic, Super, Beautiful, Lovely, Fine, Gorgeous, Splendid, Wonderful, Terrific, I like the way you are _____, Fabulous, Incredible, Remarkable, Marvelous, Neat, Very impressive

Behaviors:
Work, Job, Performance, Thinking, Reflection, Judgment, Paper, Assignment, Reading, Homework, Exercise, Lesson, Practice activity, Sitting, Problem solving, Paying attention

Combinations of Adjectives and Behaviors:
Amazing work, Amazing job, Amazing performance, Astonishing thinking, Astonishing reflection, Fantastic judgment, Fantastic paper, Super assignment, Super reading, Beautiful homework, Lovely exercise, Fine lesson, Terrific practice activity, Splendid worksheet, Wonderful sitting, Wonderful problem solving, Terrific paying attention

Improving Classroom Behavior and Social Skills

All students must know how to interact with others appropriately in group learning experiences, how to engage in classroom discussion, and how to distinguish between classroom behavior that promotes learning and classroom behavior that disrupts learning. Classrooms are well managed when students stay on-task academically but also feel free to participate actively in classroom activities, take risks, and interact positively with others. By attending to two important components of the classroom social environment—classroom behavior and social skills—you can dramatically improve the success of your students.

MANAGING CLASSROOM BEHAVIOR

Student behavior is in many ways a response to the environment, which includes the teacher, peers, other school personnel, and even the physical environment (Kerr & Nelson, 2010). In all cases, an important key to effectively managing classroom behavior—and controlling the negative behaviors of some individual students—lies in establishing positive and caring relationships with all students in your class, implementing and consistently enforcing effective rules for classroom behavior, and helping students learn to make positive choices that increase their level of success in school (Sullivan, Johnson, Owens, & Conway, 2014).

One problem teachers frequently have is precisely describing the problem behavior that they would like the student to change. Although it may be true from the teacher's point of view that a student "misbehaves" or "has a bad attitude," such terms do not specify the behavior problem so that strategies for changing the behavior can be easily implemented and evaluated. Before effective interventions can be implemented, you must first carefully define classroom behavior so that it can be easily observed and recorded.

STRATEGIES FOR
OBSERVING AND RECORDING CLASSROOM BEHAVIOR

DEFINE BEHAVIOR   Before interventions on classroom behavior can be carried out, you must carefully observe and document the targeted behaviors. This process allows you to determine precisely what behaviors need to be changed and to evaluate whether progress is occurring after interventions. Several observation systems can be employed to accomplish this.

The first step in observing and recording behavior is to *operationally define* the behavior in question. This means that you describe the behavior so that another person knows exactly what is meant. For example, if you describe a student as "has a bad attitude," it may be difficult to know exactly what you mean. However, if you use specific behavioral descriptions, such as "late to class 70% of the time" or "takes at least 10 minutes after the assignment has been given to become actively engaged, 50% of the time," it is much easier to know what is meant. It is also much easier to specify how the behavior is to change and to know whether it has changed. For example, if "late to class less than 20% of the time" is specified as a behavioral objective, it will not be difficult to determine whether this objective has been met. Many students with disabilities have behavioral objectives such as these included on their individualized education programs (IEPs).

Following is an example of an **operational definition** of "on-task" behavior (other definitions are possible and may be more appropriate in particular situations):

- *On-task.* The student's eyes are directed toward the teacher (or classmate, if making a relevant contribution) or instructional materials (e.g., books, pencil, paper, laboratory materials), and the student is manually engaged with instructional materials in an appropriate way.

When you use operationalized behaviors, it is easier to create a behavioral objective specifying (a) the content of the objective, (b) the conditions under which a student's performance will be assessed, and (c) the criteria for acceptable performance. For example, an objective for on-task behavior could be: "The student will exhibit on-task behavior in social studies class, to a criterion of 85%, on 4 out of 5 consecutive days." This behavior can then be recorded, in baseline (preintervention) or intervention conditions, to determine whether it has improved.

TABLE 8.4 Observation and Recording Systems

Name	Description
Event recording	Observer tallies the number of times a particular behavior occurs. This procedure is best when documenting behaviors that are discrete, such as talk-outs, tardiness, or tantruming. If the duration of these behaviors is always similar, or irrelevant, the observer simply records the number of events.
Duration recording	Observer records (e.g., with a stopwatch) the cumulative amount of time during which the behavior occurs. This system is appropriate when the length, or duration, is of concern. For example, a teacher may wish to record the total amount of time a socially withdrawn student engages in solitary play activities during recess. The observer starts the stopwatch when the socially isolated play begins and stops it when the child begins interacting with others. The recording resumes when the child returns to isolated play.
Interval recording	The observer sets an interval, say, 1 minute, and documents whether a particular behavior has occurred at any time during that interval. For example, if talking to classmates is the target behavior, the observer records for each 1-minute interval whether the behavior has occurred. At the end of the period in question (e.g., a 50-minute class period), the number of intervals in which the behavior has occurred is divided by the total number of intervals (e.g., 50). Therefore, if talking to classmates was recorded for 10 intervals, then the amount of talking for the time period could be recorded as 10/50 = 20%.
Time sampling	At a specific point of time, the observer records whether a behavior is occurring. For example, a "beep" goes off in an observer's headset every 5-minute segment, and at that instant, the observer records whether the behavior (e.g., on-task) is being exhibited. At the end of the period, as with interval recording, the observer can divide the number of times a target behavior occurred by the total number of times sampled.

USE OBSERVATION AND RECORDING SYSTEMS   Table 8.4 provides some examples of observation and recording systems. These can be used to record specific behaviors, depending on the type of target behavior and the circumstances under which it is exhibited (Alberto & Troutman, 2012; Martin & Pear, 2014).

Observing and recording behaviors are much more difficult with large numbers of students. Some strategies for observing with large classes include enlisting the assistance of an aide, enlisting peer assistance, observing a small number of students at a time, and video recording the entire class and recording observations later. When observing the whole class, try using seating charts and time sampling at longer intervals. For example, at the end of every 10-minute interval, make a checkmark on the square representing the desk of every student who is off-task.

DETERMINE THE CONTEXT OF BEHAVIOR   One good strategy for determining the dynamics of classroom behavior is to use an "ABC" chart (Bijou, Peterson, & Ault, 1968; Kerr & Nelson, 2010). The teacher creates a chart with three columns: Antecedent, Behavior, and Consequence (see Figure 8.2 for an example). The target behavior to be observed is noted in the middle column (e.g., pushing, hitting), and the events that occurred immediately before the behavior (antecedent) are also noted, as well as the consequence, or what happened following the behavior.

In examining the ABC chart, you can ask, for example, when and where does the target behavior occur, who is present when it occurs, and what activities or events precede the target behavior? It is also important to note what happens after the target behavior occurs, what changes after the target behavior is exhibited, and what the student receives (or avoids) after the target behavior occurs (McDaniel & Flower, 2015). For example, you may find that peer attention was almost always a consequence of the behavior (verbal aggression toward teacher) or that independent work assignments usually were the antecedent. Such analysis can lead to a better understanding of where, when, and why the behavior is occurring (Crone & Horner, 2003).

Student's name: _Marcie_		Observer: _Mrs. Wilson_
Setting: _Cafeteria_		Date: _April 3, 2016_
Observation time period: _Lunch, 12:15 – 12:45_		

Antecedent Events	Behaviors Observed	Consequent Events
12:22: Marcie approaches a table in the lunchroom where several students are seated.	Shawna told Marcie, "You can't sit here!"	Marcie sits at another table.
12:28: Students seated at lunch table.	Shawna calls out to Marcie, "Marcie, you stay over there."	Marcie makes a face at Shawna.
12:45: Students are leaving the lunch area.	Shawna steps in front of Marcie, ostentatiously.	Marcie pushes Shawna, and says, "You get away from me!"

Figure 8.2   Example Record Form for an ABC Analysis

These insights are helpful in planning interventions. Consider a case in which Sean, a 10th-grade student, typically acts out in socially immature ways when given written assignments in English class. This gains the attention of some students, which appears to reinforce Sean. You may decide to examine the assignments to determine whether they are (or Sean perceives them to be) too difficult or uninteresting. If so, you could reduce the difficulty level of the assignments, increase the interest level, and provide some specific positive support for Sean's assignment completion. Further, you could arrange an intervention in which you support other students for ignoring Sean when he acts out. Although these strategies are likely to work, they may not—to be more certain of their effectiveness, graphically present data on Sean's behavior both before and after the intervention.

MAKE GRAPHIC PRESENTATIONS OF STUDENT BEHAVIOR   Behavior is much easier to evaluate over time if it is presented in some type of chart or other graphic display (Martin & Pear, 2014). For example, suppose the percent of time-on-task during math class is recorded for that week. Usually, the amount of behavior exhibited is recorded on the vertical axis, and the time (e.g., days) is recorded on the horizontal axis, as shown in Figure 8.3.

In Figure 8.3, the vertical axis records the percentage of on-task behavior for each day, and the horizontal axis records the days when the behavior was measured. In this example, on-task behavior is *stable* (does not appear to be going up or down over time) but is lower than desirable. If an intervention is planned, such as praise for on-task behavior and task completion, the effectiveness of this intervention can be evaluated, as illustrated in Figure 8.4. The vertical line represents the initiation of the intervention.

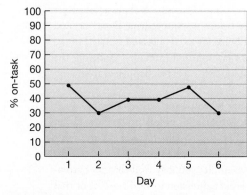

Figure 8.3   Recording On-Task Behavior

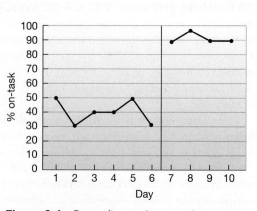

Figure 8.4   Recording an Intervention on On-Task Behavior

From the data in Figure 8.4, it appears that the intervention is having a positive effect on the behavior, at least initially (for more complex designs for establishing the validity of an intervention, such as the ABAB or reversal design, see Martin & Pear, 2014). For the most positive behavioral effects, use effective classroom management strategies.

STRATEGIES FOR
USING EFFECTIVE CLASSROOM MANAGEMENT METHODS

MyEdLab:
Video Example 8.3.
The teacher in this video discusses ways to establish a community in the classroom. Listen to some benefits of how she manages the classroom atmosphere.

ESTABLISH A POSITIVE CLASSROOM ATMOSPHERE   The first and most important step in effective classroom management is establishing and maintaining a positive, supportive classroom atmosphere. Students are more likely to follow directions, work hard, and exhibit positive classroom behavior when they feel wanted and appreciated by the teacher. This may be especially true of particularly difficult students, who may not trust adults and may feel that most teachers are "out to get them."

Project a feeling, caring persona. Convince students that you like them (even though you might not always appreciate their behaviors) and value them as individuals. Address students by name, and express an interest in their activities. Build up a store of positive comments to individual students so that if you must deliver negative feedback later, it is not the first evaluation you have made of the student. As described earlier in this chapter, teach with sincerity and enthusiasm, using interesting and motivational activities. If students enjoy your class and are interested in the subject, they will be less likely to misbehave. To build student confidence, try to maintain a very high rate of correct student responses to your questions.

If a student in your class exhibits hostile or aggressive behaviors, it is particularly important that you have established relations that are as positive as possible. This is true even if the student is rarely or never positive with you. You must enforce rules fairly and consistently, and you must not give in to student attempts to control the classroom agenda; nevertheless, you should always remain calm and polite, reminding difficult students that you simply wish to see them make good decisions.

STRATEGIES FOR
LESS-INTENSIVE CLASSROOM MANAGEMENT METHODS

As much as possible, keep your management strategies simple, low-key, direct, and practical. Low-intensity behavior management can be more effective for you in the long run and can reduce the danger of behavior escalating in the face of more intensive interventions. Such strategies include rules, praise and ignoring, proximity, direct appeals, and the judicious use of reprimands.

POST AND DISCUSS CLASSROOM RULES   An important early consideration for effective classroom management is familiarizing all students with your classroom rules. For younger students, post the classroom rules in a place where all students can observe them. Write them as positively as possible. When rules are first posted, describe them carefully to the class, model the behaviors covered by the rules, and ask students to give their own examples. Discuss instances and noninstances of following the rule. For example, a third-grade teacher might say about a rule, "If a student takes another student's eraser without asking to borrow it, is that respecting other people?" Refer to these rules often when discussing classroom behavior.

Providing rules is an important first step in classroom behavior management, but rules that are not enforced will soon lose their effectiveness. Several low-intensity strategies can help enforce your classroom rules.

PRAISE POSITIVE BEHAVIORS AND IGNORE INAPPROPRIATE BEHAVIORS   Although potentially dangerous disruptive behavior must be attended to immediately, many inappropriate behaviors can be effectively controlled by ignoring and pointing out positive models (Jones, Greenwood, & Dunn, 2016). For example, Sandra's fifth-grade teacher noticed that she was not getting her books and materials ready for a new lesson, so she acknowledged a positive example of a student seated near Sandra and said, "I like the way Melissa has put away her spelling book and taken out her reading book. She has all her materials ready and is ready to start class. Thank you, Melissa." Such comments show well-behaved students that their efforts are appreciated, and they provide a model for other students.

In the Classroom

A Summary of Research on Reprimands

_____ Reprimand students privately, not publicly, to avoid humiliating or embarrassing students.

_____ Stand near the student you are reprimanding. This allows you to use a more confidential tone of voice. However, remaining one-leg-length away respects the student's personal space.

_____ Use a normal tone of voice. Students can become desensitized over time to raised voices and may be less inclined to respond defensively to a calm tone.

_____ Look at the student while you are speaking, but do not insist that the student must return your eye contact. Forced eye contact can be viewed as hostile and aggressive, and in some cases, it can violate cultural norms.

_____ Do not point your finger at the student you are reprimanding because this conveys aggression and hostility.

_____ Do not insist on having the last word. This may be particularly true when dealing with adolescents. The final goal of your reprimand is increased student compliance with class rules, and if this goal is achieved in the long run (e.g., the student ultimately returns to work or stops bothering a classmate), a little face-saving posturing may be allowable.

Source: Adapted and reprinted with permission from _Strategies for managing behavior problems in the classroom_ (6th ed., p. 233), by M. M. Kerr & C. M. Nelson, 2010, Upper Saddle River, NJ: Merrill/Prentice Hall.

CONTROL BEHAVIOR WITH PROXIMITY Moving closer to students who are beginning to demonstrate off-task or disruptive behavior can, in many instances, help to minimize classroom behavior problems. Conroy, Asmus, Ladwig, Sellers, and Valcante (2004) found that teacher **proximity** generally increased appropriate behaviors of students with autism in general education settings (although a smaller number of students with autism did not respond positively to adult proximity). Additionally, be careful that your proximity does not become a reinforcer. Carey and Bourbon (2004) reported that a student with attention deficit hyperactivity disorder (ADHD) began to act out more frequently so that he could receive the reward (for him) of more teacher proximity.

MAKE DIRECT APPEALS Although they are often overlooked as a behavior management strategy, **direct appeals** can be effective. Students can simply be asked personally to follow class rules more carefully; alternately, a more systematic procedure can be used (Beck, Roblee, & Johns, 1982). Mary, an eighth grader in Ms. Simms's math class, frequently whispered and giggled with her neighboring classmate during whole-class activities. During an independent seatwork activity, Ms. Simms asked to speak to Mary privately. She asked Mary directly not to talk to her neighbor during class time. Ms. Simms also related that if she saw Mary talking again, she would prompt her to stop by moving toward Mary's desk (proximity). After this conversation, Mary's talking decreased substantially, and after a few prompts, it remained in control throughout the school year.

USE REPRIMANDS JUDICIOUSLY Although positive responses to positive behavior are among the best overall methods of classroom management, negative feedback in the form of reprimands is sometimes necessary to help students succeed in your class (Simonsen, Fairbanks, Briesch, Myers, & Sugai, 2008). Overall, reprimands are best viewed as direct feedback that the student's behavior is inappropriate. If they are provided in a way that indicates concern for the student's well-being, they can be effective in improving behavior. Reprimands are less effective when viewed as punishment—that is, when criticism and scorn or a negative, aggressive, or hostile tone of voice is expected to prevent the student from repeating the inappropriate behavior.

The *In the Classroom* feature offers a list of recommended guidelines for using reprimands (Kerr & Nelson, 2010). It is also important that teachers link reprimands directly to class rules and avoid warnings, threats, sarcasm, or ridicule that may further alienate the student. In addition, avoid allowing students to argue with you, by saying, for example:

- "For what? What'd I do?"
- "I didn't do anything!"
- "You let Fredericka do it!"
- "James started it!"

In some instances, excessive warnings have been known to increase the amount of inappropriate behavior (e.g., Twyman, Johnson, Buie, & Nelson, 1994). If your reprimand is ineffective and the behavior persists, avoid making additional reprimands. Instead, a more intensive, prearranged contingency should be enforced (e.g., the student loses a privilege, or a call is made to the student's home). If a student repeatedly argues with you, it may be helpful to set "arguing" as a personal target for that student to work on.

STRATEGIES FOR
MORE FORMAL CLASSROOM MANAGEMENT METHODS

Informal management systems can be helpful; however, when problems continue, more formal management systems may be necessary as a supplement to your ongoing informal management strategies.

SYSTEMATICALLY REINFORCE POSITIVE BEHAVIOR

Intangible rewards such as praise can be an effective method of promoting a positive classroom atmosphere and positive social behavior. However, sometimes more tangible reinforcement is required. Tangible reinforcement includes such things as stickers, stars, and **primary reinforcers** such as snacks or drinks. Positive reinforcement can be very effective with students with a variety of special needs in a variety of circumstances (Scheuermann & Hall, 2016; Watling & Schwartz, 2004). Some teachers disapprove of tangible reinforcers because they believe students should learn to work for the satisfaction of doing well in school. However, for some students, more tangible rewards may be necessary to help them succeed in the general education classroom. Survey students or keep personal records to determine what sort of reinforcers appeal to your students. Check out teacher stores that carry stickers, pencils, or other supplies that could be used as rewards. Rewards should be applied consistently for following specific rules or meeting specific academic or behavioral objectives.

Sometimes a student with special needs may require rewards for doing things for which other students in the classroom do not require rewards. For example, Larry is a student with intellectual disabilities who is newly enrolled in a general education sixth-grade classroom, and he exhibits a great deal of difficulty in sustaining attention on academic tasks. Larry does not respond well to reprimands, but he loves animal crackers. With the approval of Larry's mother, Ms. Irby made an arrangement with Larry that if he continued working on his assignments for 5 minutes, he would receive 1 point. After he collected 25 points, he could receive an animal cracker to eat at lunch. She made a point sheet and let Larry know after every 5-minute period whether he had earned a point.

Sometimes individual rewards can be combined with group rewards. If students feel "left out" because students with special needs are receiving rewards while they do not, allow the class to have some group reward if the students with special needs meet their goals. Emphasize that some students need to be treated a little differently to succeed in school, and that fairness has more to do with meeting people's needs than with everyone being treated exactly the same.

REWARD STUDENTS WITH TOKEN SYSTEMS

Token systems, or token economies, can be used with individual students, small groups of students, or entire classrooms (Scheuermann & Hall, 2016). In a token system, students who follow class rules are awarded points at the end

Class Rules

1. Always respect other people.
2. Raise your hand before speaking.
3. Remain in your seat.
4. Ask for help when you need it.
5. Complete all assignments.

Rule

Student	1	2	3	4	5
Marybeth	*	*	*	*	*
Bill	*	*	*	*	
Shawna		*	*		*
Michelle	*	*	*	*	*
Arnold	*	*	*	*	
James	*	*	*	*	*
Dustin	*	*	*	*	*
Chico		*	*	*	*
Kelly	*			*	*
Pam	*	*	*	*	*

Figure 8.5 Sample Recording Chart for Token System

of specified time periods, such as class periods. The positive benefits of token systems have long been observed (Jenkins & Gorrafa, 1974; McLaughlin & Malaby, 1976). Remember Larry and how points to be exchanged for animal crackers were used as a reward for increased on-task behavior? His points were offered in shorter increments of time because this met his special need. For other situations, however, you may want to award bonus points for unusually hard work or cooperative behavior. A sample chart that can be used to record tokens or points awarded to individual students is presented in Figure 8.5.

In the token system corresponding to the recording chart in Figure 8.5, students receive a star if they follow a classroom rule throughout a particular time period. In some cases, the period can be the entire school day. For younger students or students with special needs, it may be more appropriate to evaluate behavior after each period. Students can accumulate stars or points and exchange these later for small prizes (such as stickers or school supplies) or privileges. Entire classrooms can be awarded points after each period, depending on the behavior of all students, and thus accumulate points toward group rewards, such as a popcorn party or a longer recess break. Teachers can also post a "menu" of prizes or privileges that can be exchanged for tokens and the corresponding "price" of each. For older students, try holding an "auction" of possible prizes that students can bid on. Students can be surveyed ahead of time on their preferences for prizes.

Like all behavior management systems, token systems are most effective when they are used primarily to reward positive behavior. In many cases, not earning positive points can motivate students to exhibit appropriate behavior. However, when necessary, token systems can also be used as punishment for seriously inappropriate behavior. In a procedure also known as **response cost** (Buchard & Barrera, 1972; Simonsen et al., 2008), previously earned points are withdrawn for serious misbehavior. If using response cost, be certain that students have been informed of this possible consequence ahead of time and that the procedure produces the desired results.

TRAIN POSITIVE ATTRIBUTIONS FOR SOCIAL BEHAVIOR Attribution training can be effective as a motivational strategy, as described previously, but is also important in linking social behavior to things under students' control. For example, students with problem behaviors often make **negative attributions**—that is, they attribute things that happen to them to forces outside of their own control, for example, that they were picked on or treated unfairly, which caused them to misbehave.

The teacher's job is to help students learn to attribute social consequences to behavior that they control (Maag, 2006). Retraining in more appropriate attributions usually takes time and may require frequent review of appropriate attributions for positive outcomes:

The reason you got to come with us to the zoo today was that you tried very hard to control your talk-outs this week. Good job!

. . .as well as negative outcomes:

The reason you got detention today is that you chose not to do your work, and you argued with your teacher. Let's talk about some ways to keep out of detention in the future.

POST POSITIVE BEHAVIOR Public posting of students' behaviors has also been shown to reduce behavior problems (Troup, McLaughlin, Neyman, & Schuler, 2014). In one instance, public posting of daily quiz scores where behavior had been a problem improved both behavior and quiz scores (Jones & Van Houten, 1985). The daily quiz scores were displayed on laminated pieces of poster board and were recorded for 5-day periods. In other variations, students' behavior can be evaluated and recorded on a publicly posted chart. Students who follow all class rules can be given a star next to their names for each class period, day, or other appropriate length of time.

USE NEGATIVE CONSEQUENCES JUDICIOUSLY Punishment, in the form of negative consequences for inappropriate behavior, is less effective in the long run than positive reinforcement, and punishment should not be used when more positive alternatives are available (Maag, 2001; Wheeler & Richey, 2014). However, punishment is sometimes necessary to maintain order and provide a safe environment for all students. Canter and Canter (2010) recommended posting a "discipline hierarchy" so that students are informed about the consequences for violating a rule. Another advantage of posting rules and consequences is that the teacher can assume the role of enforcer or arbiter of class rules, rather than the role of a dictator who administers rewards and punishments at whim. If rules are consistently enforced, the teacher can merely state, "I'm sorry you broke the rules, too, but you were aware of the consequences. I will try to help you follow the rules better in the future."

A sample discipline hierarchy for grades 4 through 6, recommended by Canter and Canter (2010), lists consequences for rule infractions that progress as follows: "warning" (first time), sending a completed "think sheet" (described in the following paragraph) to parents (second time), brief amount of time away from the group (third time), calling parents (fourth time), and sending to the principal (fifth time). A "severe" clause refers to any severe breach of class rules, such as vandalism or fighting, and it replaces the routine sequence of the discipline hierarchy. That is, if a student disrupts the entire class or endangers the safety of other students, the student is sent directly to the principal, regardless of whether it is the first, second, or third violation of a rule.

A "think sheet" documents that the student understands the rule that was broken, why the rule was broken, and the consequences of breaking the rule and has a strategy for dealing with the same situation more appropriately in the future.

Other more substantial types of punishment are also sometimes used. **Suspension** involves not allowing the student to return to school for a specified time period. Some schools use **in-school suspension**, in which the student must attend a specific suspension room in the school and is not allowed in the regularly assigned classroom. Removing the student from school usually involves a group decision of teachers and administrators. Many states limit the number of days a student with disabilities may be suspended (e.g., 10 days) until it is considered a change of placement, which will then require a formal placement decision of the multidisciplinary team. It is also important to consider whether the behavior for which the student is being suspended is a consequence of the disability. If so, suspension may be considered a type of denial of school services because of the student's disability—which, of course, is inappropriate (Jones et al., 2016).

Some states also allow teachers or administrators to administer **corporal punishment**, such as paddling or some other method of inflicting physical pain. Professional organizations and others have long advocated against the use of corporal punishment because it is almost never more effective than alternatives and is almost certain to promote resentment and anger in the student (Council for Children with Behavioral Disorders, 1990; Scheuermann & Hall, 2016; U.S. Department of Education, 2017).

USE TIMEOUT FOR SPECIFIC BEHAVIOR PROBLEMS   Timeout refers to some type of separation of the student from the routine classroom environment, usually for a violation of class rules. It can include **contingent observation timeout**, where the student is seated nearby and can still observe group activities; **exclusionary timeout**, where the student is removed from the instructional activity; and **seclusionary timeout**, where the student is removed from the instructional setting to another setting, such as a timeout room.

Timeout can be useful to help students cool down after a volatile situation or provide them time to reflect quietly on their behavior. In other cases, timeout may serve as tangible feedback about their classroom behavior. Overall, timeout is most effective when the classroom activities the students are excluded from are enjoyable and rewarding (so they will not view timeout as an avoidance of undesirable schoolwork), and the students do not feel reinforced for the attention they receive when placed in timeout. It is also important that timeout periods be brief (e.g., 1 to 5 minutes) and that timeout is part of a larger behavior management plan that is mostly positive. Timeout should not be used if there is a possibility of self-injury. Student behavior should be monitored while in timeout, and timeout should never be considered a type of incarceration (Scheuermann & Hall, 2016). Behaviors that result in timeout, such as specific disruptive events, should be posted and discussed with the class before implementation of the procedure. Many states have specific policies regarding the use of timeout, so be certain to check with state as well as local policies when implementing this procedure.

Use Debriefing Procedures After Timeout   Regardless of the type of timeout, students need to be debriefed before returning to full status in the classroom. This is a form of attribution training and serves to ensure that students are aware of the behavior that resulted in the timeout and how they could handle a similar situation better in the future. Before returning to the classroom, students should be able to state clearly why they were placed in timeout (i.e., for which specific behaviors) and how such events can be avoided in the future. If, for example, a student's misbehavior was the apparent response to the perceived actions of another student ("Billy was teasing me"), the student should discuss how to respond appropriately to such behavior in the future.

PLAY THE GOOD-BEHAVIOR GAME   Researchers (e.g., Harris & Sherman, 1973; Leflot, van Lier, Onghena, & Colpin, 2010) have described a behavior management technique referred to as the Good-Behavior Game. Using this procedure, the teacher divides the class into two or more groups, alternating group members frequently. During an instructional period, each disruptive or noncompliant behavior counts as a point for the team of the offending student. Rules such as the following are set: "(a) raise your hand before talking; (b) sit in your seat properly; (c) pay attention; (d) keep your hands to yourself; and (e) stay in your seat" (Brigham, Bakken, Scruggs, & Mastropieri, 1992, p. 7). At the end of a designated time period, the team with the fewest points is declared the winner and may be provided with a group reward.

SET UP STUDENT CONTRACTING   Behavioral **contracting** involves the establishment of a written agreement that formalizes the behaviors a student agrees to exhibit and the positive consequences that will result from the fulfillment of the contract (Simonsen et al., 2008). Often, the negative consequences of not fulfilling the contract are also specified. Contracts can be a positive way to provide a role for families in improving classroom behavior. For example, Morris has been erratic in turning in his homework for math class. Sometimes he completes his homework assignments and turns them in promptly; other times, he does not turn in his homework and acts defensive and belligerent when questioned about it.

In a written, dated, and signed contract, Morris's parents agreed to take Morris to a popular amusement park for 2 days if he turns in all of his homework assignments in math for the next 2 months, with no more than two lapses. Conversely, if he misses more than two

Technology to Assist with Self-Monitoring of Attention and Apps for Recording and Praising Behavior

 Self-monitoring of attention can be successfully implemented with students of various ages with attention difficulties. Several types of self-monitoring procedures have proven effective. Key elements in the self-monitoring system include (a) precisely defined behaviors to be monitored, (b) a recording sheet or system that is easy to use, and (c) a predetermined system for knowing when to monitor the behaviors. Once these elements are established, many students can greatly improve their attention to school-related tasks.

Work closely with the student to describe exactly what is meant by "paying attention" or by "staying on-task during class." Specific examples of the behaviors using instances and noninstances are usually helpful at first. A simple recording sheet that contains two columns, one for on-task and one for off-task, on which students are taught to place a checkmark if they are on- or off-task is also a good starting place.

Systems can be employed to help students monitor their behaviors. Smartphones have timer applications that can produce a ringtone or vibration at specified intervals, such as *WatchMinder* (WatchMinder, Inc.). Watches that provide a vibrating sensation on the wrist can be used to self-monitor behaviors as well; for example, *VibraLITE* (Global Assistive Devices) makes several types of vibrating watches.

Additional types of vibrating devices have also been developed. The *MotivAider* is a small, pager-size device that can be programmed to vibrate at various intervals and at different duration and intensity levels (see habitchange.com). Similar devices that can be worn on a belt or in a pocket to produce vibrations or audible sounds include *Polder Digital Timer with Vibrating, Audible, and Illuminated Alarm* (Polder), the *Invisible Clock II Vibrating Reminder* (Time Now Corporation), and the *Multifunction Vibrating Timer* (TN Corporation).

Apps are also available to assist with recording, praising, and teaching student social behavior. *ABC Behavior Assessment* (Reticent Arts) allows recording of antecedents, behaviors, and consequences. Three additional apps are *Intervals, an ABA Interval Recording App; Duration, an ABA Duration Recording App;* and *Frequency, an ABA Frequency Recording App* (Christopher Mays); these provide the capacities to use duration, frequency, or interval recording of behavior. The *iPraiseU* (Pyramid Educational Consultants) app provides alternative praise statements randomly from a list of 100 to provide a variety of praise responses. The *Social Skills Sampler* (Conover Company) presents 62 functional social skills, and the *Social Skill Builder* (Social Skill Builder) presents many different problem-solving social situations to engage students in selecting correct social responses.

homework assignments in the next 2 months, he will lose some of his television privileges, according to the severity of his lapses.

PROMOTE SELF-MONITORING Self-monitoring strategies involve teaching students to monitor and evaluate their own classroom behavior (Jones et al., 2016; Maag, 2004). In some cases, students may be asked to monitor their general on-task behavior. In other cases, students may monitor themselves for a specific behavior, such as teasing. Before implementing self-monitoring interventions, meet individually and discuss with the students the purpose and importance of good classroom behavior and how they will benefit personally from better classroom behavior. The students should be made to understand that the intervention is in their best interest.

To implement a self-monitoring system for a target behavior, such as teasing, provide the student with a self-monitoring sheet for the target behavior. The behavior should be operationalized so that it is very clear what constitutes teasing and what does not. These definitions will depend on the particular student's behavior. For example, teasing could in some cases include making statements such as, "Cornelius is a stupid jerk." Teasing in other cases could involve making faces at another student, staring at another student, or scratching the head with the middle finger while looking at another student. Familiarize the student with the self-monitoring sheet and how to use it. After each specified time interval (e.g., 5 or 10 minutes), prompt the student, play a timed and audio-recorded "beep" (or, e.g., timer function on a smartphone), or ask the student to take responsibility for monitoring the clock. The student then checks the appropriate column for "teasing" or "not teasing" over the time interval. At the end of a class period or the end of a day, compare their results with your own observations. See the *Apps for Education* feature for some suggestions for self-recording. Students may not only receive rewards or consequences for behavior but also receive rewards for matching your recording of the behavior. The purpose is to make students conscious of their behavior so that they have more control of their actions. Self-monitoring sheets could be used with several students at a time to record several different target behaviors.

TEACH STUDENTS SELF-INSTRUCTION STRATEGIES Self-instruction or **self-regulation** training involves teaching students to employ self-directed statements that guide social problem solving and may be particularly useful at the upper-elementary or secondary level. Questions can involve defining the situation, thinking through possible solutions, and choosing the best option (see also Finch, Spirito, Imm, & Ott, 1993; Glago, Mastropieri, & Scruggs, 2009). Following is a possible example:

Check each step, and think before you act!

1. What happened?
2. What are all possible solutions?
3. What is my goal for right now?
4. What is the best thing for me to do?
5. Did I make the best choice?

Teachers should model and role-play these thought processes. For example, the teacher should provide an example by saying:

> **What happened** is that Kimberly is making faces at me. The **possible solutions** are that I could make faces back at her, I could tell the teacher, or I could try to ignore her and finish my work. **My goal for right now** is just to finish this assignment, so I think the **best thing to do** is try to ignore her and see if she stops. If she doesn't, I tell the teacher. Well, she stopped making faces at me (or if she didn't, I didn't notice), so I think I made the **best choice.**

TRAIN FOR GENERALIZATION Most positive social behaviors are of limited use unless they can be shown to generalize to appropriate situations outside the training context (Maag, 2004). It is particularly important that students in inclusive settings are able to generalize all the positive social behaviors they have learned in other settings; however, students with special needs often demonstrate problems in generalizing learned behavior (Kerr & Nelson, 2010). As important social behaviors are learned, make a list of all the settings and situations for which the behavior must generalize and all the individuals who will observe the generalized behavior. Then, create a plan to promote generalization across all of these settings and individuals.

Several strategies are available for promoting generalization, some of which have already been described. Self-monitoring and self-instruction are very relevant in promoting generalization through the use of cognitive routines. Students can use self-monitoring techniques to evaluate and modify their behavior in different contexts, as in the teasing example described previously. In addition, strive to teach behaviors that will be reinforced in natural settings, such as positive social responding. On other occasions, be sure that all relevant teachers and staff are aware of the behavior and reinforce it whenever it occurs. Classroom peers can also be very helpful in ensuring that target behavior is maintained over time and generalized by, for example, providing positive attention when students exhibit target behaviors. Train "loosely" so that students are provided with a variety of situations and a number of possible responses. Be ready to reinforce any unprompted generalization of a learned behavior. Finally, when needed, retrain positive behaviors in several appropriate contexts; for example, retrain appropriate sitting in all relevant contexts, such as in the classroom, in the resource room, in homeroom, during assemblies, and on the school bus. By using a variety of possible strategies and monitoring their effectiveness, students will be much more likely to generalize their positive behaviors.

STRATEGIES FOR
HANDLING CLASSROOM CONFRONTATIONS

One of the things that frightens teachers most is being directly confronted by students. Confrontations can constitute direct challenges to the authority of the teacher and can, depending on how they are handled, have a profound effect on the classroom environment.

The problems of confrontations can be seen in the dialogue in the following *Classroom Scenario* (see also Canter & Canter, 1993).

CLASSROOM SCENARIO

Marcus

Ms. Rothchild, the English teacher, has practiced brainstorming and organizing ideas with the class, and she has just directed them to start working on the first draft of their persuasive essays. Several minutes after giving the direction, she notices that Marcus has still not begun to write.

MS. ROTHCHILD:	Marcus, time to get started.
MARCUS:	I don't feel like it. Leave me alone, okay?
MS. ROTHCHILD:	Do you need some help getting started?
MARCUS:	I said I don't feel like it. Get out of my face.
MS. ROTHCHILD:	I don't appreciate your tone, young man. I gave you a direction, and I expect you to follow it.
MARCUS:	(*raising his voice*) Back off. I told you I don't feel like it!
MS. ROTHCHILD:	(*raising her voice*) Now you listen to me! I've had enough of your attitude. Now get started on your assignment or else!
MARCUS:	(*mumbling*) I'll tell you where you can put your assignment . . . . . .(*students laugh*)
MS. ROTHSCHILD:	That's it, Marcus. I've had enough of your backtalk. Apologize right now, or you'll be in detention for the rest of the year.
MARCUS:	Yeah? Well, I don't care what you think. I'm out of here. (*overturns desk and storms out of the classroom*)

Marcus has placed himself in a situation where his anger and anxiety can only escalate. By also being confrontational, the teacher has helped place Marcus in this position. The teacher has reacted emotionally, and this emotional reaction has fed into Marcus's desire to control the situation. A difficult situation has become more difficult, the teacher's relationship with Marcus has deteriorated, and now the entire class is off-task. Some students, such as Marcus, may not believe that teachers can be trusted to act in the students' best interest and may feel compelled to fight teachers in these situations.

QUESTIONS FOR REFLECTION

1. What factors could have prompted Marcus's strong response to such a reasonable teacher direction?
2. What contributions are made by both Marcus and the teacher that escalate this conflict?
3. What are some alternative responses by the teacher and by Marcus that could have improved this situation?

DIFFUSE CONFRONTATIONS WITH A CALM, MEASURED RESPONSE Canter and Canter (1993) recommended several steps for dealing with this type of confrontation. The most important thing to remember is to *remain calm*. Count to 3, 4, 5, or 10 if necessary. Control your breathing by taking long, slow breaths. Take yourself out of the situation by depersonalizing it. In Marcus's case, if you have been doing your job as a teacher, he is probably responding to his own past experiences, lack of trust, and his own needs at the moment. *Don't* *take it personally.* Remind yourself, "This is not about me!" If you are able to remain calm, you will have more control of the situation. Your calmness and task-orientation in the face of hostility can go far toward resolving the situation.

The most effective approach would be not to escalate the situation in the first place by making loud reprimands and threats. Remain calm, restate your desire privately to Marcus that he return to work, and restate your personal interest in his success in your classroom:

> MS. ROTHSCHILD: *(quietly and calmly)* I understand you're upset, Marcus, but I really need you to go back to work now. I know you can do well on this.

If necessary, move Marcus away from his peers, and speak to him privately—preferably with Marcus seated with his back to the class. Then, if Marcus is still upset, give him a little time and space to make a positive choice.

Speak to the student later if this seems a better solution. Ultimately, of course, your rules must be enforced. However, keep in mind the bigger picture of establishing trust and helping Marcus fit into the classroom environment. Do not behave in such a way that Marcus feels heroic by standing up to your raised voice and threatening manner. Make Marcus believe that you wish him to get started on his work simply because you want him to succeed in school and do not want to see him get a failing grade on the assignment. Do not feel that you must have the last word in the dialogue. As one principal said, "Teenagers need the last word a lot more than I do!" (Kerr & Nelson, 2010, p. 262). If Marcus returns to work, even while grumbling and rolling his eyes, you have achieved your purpose for the moment, and you have prevented an unpleasant situation from escalating.

If a student's behavior seems very much out of character, it may be wise to ignore the behavior for the moment and discuss the problem later when the student has calmed down somewhat. It may also be necessary to back off for a certain period of time if the student's behavior appears particularly volatile or threatening or if a student refuses to leave the peer group. If you believe that situations such as these are possible in your classroom, find out ahead of time how to call for support (Canter & Canter, 1993).

Kerr and Nelson (2010) provided several additional suggestions for de-escalating verbal confrontations, including the following:

- "Pick your battles" by declining to fight over inconsequential issues.
- Listen to what the student is saying to reduce hostility and help find a good solution.
- Avoid sarcasm, which often escalates tension.
- Allow students to save face by avoiding humiliating or embarrassing a student.
- Stay in control of your own emotions.

Kerr and Nelson (2010) emphasized that you should get to know your students, including their personal and cultural backgrounds and beliefs. Better awareness of your students can lead to better communication and better overall classroom management.

STRATEGIES FOR
IMPLEMENTING SCHOOLWIDE DISCIPLINE SYSTEMS

An obvious advantage of schoolwide discipline systems is that the same rules are enforced in the same way throughout the school, and the structured consistency can be beneficial to limit-seeking students, as well as to students who have difficulty adjusting to different standards or rules being enforced in different classrooms (Kerr & Nelson, 2010). Some disadvantages of schoolwide discipline systems are that, unless specifically programmed, they may not effectively address the needs of all individual students, and that, if misunderstood or misapplied, they can promote an overall punitive atmosphere throughout the school. Any behavior management system must be as positive toward and supportive of the needs of students as possible because schools that are perceived as punitive or oppressive will be resented and may actually encourage noncompliance and vandalism (Mayer, Nafpaktitis, Butterworth, & Hollingsworth, 1987; Rosenberg & Jackman, 2003). These concerns have led to the development and application of positive behavioral interventions and supports (PBIS).

IMPLEMENT POSITIVE BEHAVIORAL INTERVENTIONS AND SUPPORTS Previously, schoolwide discipline emphasized reacting to specific student misbehavior with the use of punishment-based strategies. However, teaching the behavioral expectations and rewarding students for following them is a much more positive approach than simply waiting for misbehavior to occur before responding. The overall purpose of schoolwide PBIS is to establish a positive climate in which appropriate behavior is the expectation for all students (OSEP Technical Assistance Center on PBIS, 2012). As such, PBIS employs, on a schoolwide level, principles very similar to those discussed previously in this chapter.

Positive behavioral interventions and supports rely on behavioral principles to produce socially important outcomes with procedures that are socially and culturally appropriate (Crone & Horner, 2003; Kerr & Nelson, 2010; Missouri Schoolwide Positive Behavior Support, 2011–2012). Behavioral support is not viewed simply as a way of reducing or eliminating inappropriate social behavior through punishment or extinction; rather, it is a process of assisting students in being successful within a social or educational context (Lewis-Palmer & Barrett, 2007). It involves a functional behavioral assessment (FBA) to determine the nature of problem behavior and how it is maintained within a social system (typically including ABC charts, such as the one shown in Figure 8.2). Based on the FBA, a behavioral support plan can be developed that focuses on (a) altering the environment so that problem behaviors become irrelevant, (b) teaching new skills to students to supplant previous counterproductive behaviors, and (c) establishing consequences that make inappropriate behaviors less effective and, ultimately, irrelevant (Crone & Horner, 2003; Lewis, Jones, Horner, & Sugai, 2010).

Nelson and Sugai (1999; see also Crone & Horner, 2003) described the schoolwide application of PBIS as a four-stage process that is undertaken by a rotating committee of eight (or fewer) members representative of the entire school staff (behavior support team). During stage 1, the committee defines and identifies the problems to be addressed by the schoolwide PBIS program. This can be accomplished with the use of surveys and interviews, direct observations, and archival school data. During stage 2, the committee undertakes a site analysis to determine that the necessary aspects of PBIS are in place. In stage 3, the committee works to develop and implement the PBIS programs in four systems: schoolwide, for all staff, students, and settings; specific settings or nonclassroom settings (e.g., restrooms, cafeterias); classroom systems; and systems for support of individual students, usually those with serious and chronic problem behavior. The program is developed and revised through a multistep consensus-building process. As the programs are implemented, progress is monitored in stage 4 with respect to baseline data collected during a needs assessment. Findings of the evaluation are shared with all staff members on a regular basis, and the programs are adjusted as needed, based on the results of the evaluation.

For example, office referral data could indicate that inappropriate behavior often occurs outside the music room during transitions. These instances could be further investigated with interviews of the relevant teachers and direct observations of the hallways at this time. It could be determined, for example, that much of the inappropriate behavior is involved with the unstructured milling about of many students in a relatively small area. Potential solutions could include announcing that students are to stay to the right when exiting the music room, ensuring that one class has exited the room before others enter, or having students exit by a different door. The selected interventions are then monitored to determine whether they have addressed the problem (Kerr & Nelson, 2010).

PBIS programs have produced positive results (Coffey & Horner, 2012; OSEP Technical Assistance Center on PBIS, 2012). PBIS programs try to solve significant behavior problems by examining behavior in the context of the entire social system and by devising overall positive alternatives to inappropriate behavior (Barnhill, 2005; Safran & Oswald, 2003). Because teachers and schools in many instances choose reactive, negative consequences to disruptive or noncompliant behavior (Crone, Hawkins, & Horner, 2010), PBIS provides significant positive alternatives for achieving success.

IMPLEMENT MULTI-TIERED SYSTEMS OF SUPPORT WITHIN A PBIS FRAMEWORK

Multi-tiered systems of support are designed to address different needs, reduce special education placement, and provide evidence for the appropriate identification of disabilities. They are intended to better integrate general education with special education and to provide appropriate services as soon as they are needed, prior to a formal referral to special education.

MyEdLab:
Video Example 8.4.
The principal in this video describes her school's schoolwide PBIS system that was implemented in response to problems with school tardiness. Think about how students might feel about interacting with their principal in such positive ways.

Scheuermann and Hall (2016) described appropriate procedures for Tier 1 (universal), Tier 2 (targeted), and Tier 3 (tertiary) levels of support. Universal levels of support include optimal classroom management strategies, such as those described in this chapter, that are provided in every classroom. These can include consistent enforcement of rules and explanation of the procedures for following these rules, classroom organization and management, and effective instructional planning and delivery. Also included are procedures for observing and recording behavior in order to determine whether the interventions and supports are effective for all students. This level of support is expected to be successful with 80% to 90% of students (Scheuermann & Hall, 2016).

If it is determined that individual students are not succeeding with the universal level of support, a PBIS leadership team (usually including administrators, general and special education teachers, and support staff) can help evaluate problem behaviors and recommend interventions and supports at the second tier. These targeted interventions can include social skills training, in which targeted social behaviors are directly taught (see the Social Skills section of this chapter), often through small-group instruction; or "check in, check out" (CICO) interventions (Hawken & Horner, 2003), in which individual students are presented with daily or weekly goals, feedback for meeting or not meeting these goals is provided throughout the day, and points for reinforcements are awarded. Students check in and check out at the beginning and end of the school day and receive a formal evaluation of their progress (Filter et al., 2007).

If individual interventions and supports are needed beyond the targeted level, students can be placed in Tier 3, or the tertiary level of support, which may or may not include placement in special education. Tertiary-level interventions can include individualized, formal systems of behavior monitoring and systems of positive reinforcement or negative consequences when necessary that are intended to promote positive growth in social behavior, as planned and monitored by a PBIS leadership team. For an application of a schoolwide behavior management program based on the response-to-intervention (RTI) model, see the *Research Highlight*.

STRATEGIES FOR

CONFRONTING BULLYING

IMPLEMENT A BULLYING-PREVENTION PROGRAM Bullying is a fact of life in all schools, and students with disabilities are frequently the targets of bullying (Council for Exceptional Children [CEC], 2011; Rose, Monda-Amaya, & Espelage, 2011), although in some cases they also may act as the aggressors. Sustained bullying can become a significant problem for schools and can contribute to an anxious and fearful environment (Davis & Davis, 2007). **Cyberbullying**, in which harassing messages or malicious rumors are sent through computers or cell phones, has been widely reported (Kowalski, Limber, & Agatston, 2012).

Heinrichs (2003) described characteristics of successful bullying-prevention programs, including the following:

- Increase the awareness and involvement of adults.
- Survey students about bullying.
- Supervise high-risk areas during breaks.
- Form teacher discussion groups and coordinating groups.
- Display class rules about bullying.
- Have class meetings on bullying with students.
- Talk seriously with bullies and targets.
- Have serious talks with the parents of all involved students.

Targets of bullying can be provided with specific strategies, for example, to recognize the signs of bullying, to not display behaviors that invite bullying, and to avoid high-risk areas. Bullies can be provided with appropriate social skills training and consequences for aggressive acts toward others. Communicate with parents or other family members of bullies and targets of bullying. Bystanders (almost always present when bullying occurs) can be encouraged not to support or reinforce such behavior. Finally, all parties can be encouraged to contact responsible adults when they see bullying occurring. Richard, Schneider, and Mallet (2011) identified

MyEdLab:
Video Example 8.5.
This video discusses the reasoning behind bullying-prevention programs and some strategies for implementation. Pay attention to the strategies presented for teachers.

Multi-Tiered Systems of Support for Problem Behaviors

 Multi-tiered systems of support seek to identify and treat behavior and learning problems within a multiple-tier system or response-to-intervention (RTI) framework. For example, all students are provided with evidence-based instruction in reading (Tier 1). For students who exhibit learning problems, a second tier of small-group, higher-intensity instruction is delivered (Tier 2). For students who fail to show adequate progress in this second tier, a third tier of services that are even more intensive (perhaps including assessment for special education services) is implemented.

Fairbanks, Sugai, Guardino, and Lathrop (2007) extended this multiple-tier system of support to classroom behavior problems. That is, the Tier 1 intervention could include a universal schoolwide behavior management system, where behavioral expectations are explicitly stated, consequences are consistently applied, and progress toward meeting schoolwide goals is regularly monitored. The Tier 2 intervention is targeted toward students who do not succeed in the Tier 1 program, and it could include "check in, check out" (CICO) interventions that include additional structure and feedback, as well as daily behavior report cards in some cases. If students still exhibit problem behaviors, a Tier 3 individualized intervention, such as a functional behavior assessment (FBA; see the Positive Behavioral Interventions and Supports section in this chapter) and appropriate, intensive individual interventions may be necessary.

In the first study, results indicated that 4 of the 10 students made significant behavioral improvements as a result of the targeted intervention. Two of the remaining students remained in the CICO intervention, and four of the remaining students received individually developed function-based supports (Tier 3), with specific individualized target behaviors and associated rewards and consequences as well as frequent monitoring of performance. These four students, whose behavior did not improve during the Tier 2 CICO intervention, exhibited substantial behavior improvement in the Tier 3 intervention. In contrast, the two students who did not succeed in the CICO intervention and were continued on that intervention did not improve their behaviors.

Algozzine et al. (2012) examined the combined effects of a multi-tier system of support for academic and behavior interventions for children who were difficult to teach in kindergarten through grade 3. Outcome measures included basic literacy skills for the academic interventions and decreases in discipline referrals for the behavior interventions. Several steps were implemented, including instituting screening procedures to identify children requiring Tier 2 and Tier 3 interventions, supporting and scheduling tier interventions, documenting the fidelity of implementation, and monitoring and adjusting the interventions as needed. Students identified as difficult to teach (sample = 768) from five schools participated in one of three cohorts.

Academic instruction supports included Open Court Reading (Bereiter et al., 2002) and fluency building using peer coaches for Tier 1; researcher-developed Practice Court (Algozzine et al., 2012) for Tier 2; and Reading Mastery Classic I and II for Tier 3 instruction (Engelmann & Bruner, 1995a, 1995b). Behavior supports included schoolwide positive behavioral interventions and support (PBIS) for Tier 1; small-group social skills instruction, student contracting, self-monitoring, and self-evaluation for Tier 2; and functional behavioral assessment and individual positive behavior support plans for Tier 3. Findings revealed significantly improved nonsense-word fluency and phonemic segmentation skills in reading and significantly fewer discipline referrals. These results, taken together, demonstrate the potential of implementing multi-tiered systems of support to improve classroom behavior in inclusive classes. See also Coffey and Horner (2012) for a description of the sustainability of PBIS.

QUESTIONS FOR REFLECTION

1. Could this model be effective in upper-elementary or secondary classes?
2. What other behavior and academic outcome measures would be helpful to convince your school administrators to implement this intervention?
3. What would you need to do prior to implementing this on a schoolwide basis?

school security and positive teacher–student relations to be very important factors in bullying prevention. Effective schoolwide bullying prevention programs have reduced bullying problems by more than 50% and have also been integrated within schoolwide PBIS programs (Good, McIntosh, & Gietz, 2011).

MyEdLab: **Self-Check 8.2**

MyEdLab: **Application Exercise 8.2: Classroom Management**

Teaching Social Skills

Appropriate behavior from students is often limited because some students lack adequate knowledge of certain **social skills**. Social skills are the behaviors we use to work and socialize with other people. Good, or at least adequate, social skills are necessary for successful functioning in school, in society, and on the job.

Many different types of behaviors or responses can qualify as social skills. In fact, it could be argued that specific social skills are required for any social act a person engages in throughout life. Some of the social skills described and studied by researchers are listed in Table 8.5.

It may be useful to distinguish among the factors that seem to control particular social skills deficits. For example, Dale is an affectionate boy with intellectual disabilities who is disposed to hug nearly anyone he encounters. Dale's behavior is apparently controlled by the social satisfaction he gains from hugging, as well as his seeming inability to distinguish when his hugging is welcome and when it is not. Kyle, conversely, is a student with emotional/behavioral disorders who is often verbally abusive to other students and teachers. Kyle is aware that his behavior is not appreciated by others; his behavior is apparently controlled by the attention and reinforcement he seems to receive from upsetting others with his speech.

TABLE 8.5 Specific Social Skills

Content Area	Example Component Skills
Conversation skills	Starting a conversation Maintaining a conversation Use of appropriate distance and eye contact
Assertiveness skills	Making requests Denying requests Negotiating requests
"Play" interaction skills (e.g., making friends)	Sharing with others Inviting others to play Encouraging others
Problem-solving and coping skills	Staying calm and relaxed Listing possible solutions Choosing the best solution
Self-help skills	Good grooming (clean, neat) Good dressing (wearing clothes that fit well) Good table manners
Classroom task-related behaviors	On-task behavior Following directions Trying your best
Job interview skills	Being prepared (dress, attitude, etc.) Being attentive Asking for clarification

Note: From *Effective instruction for special education* (3rd ed., p. 252), Austin, TX: Pro-Ed. Copyright 2002 by Pro-Ed. Reprinted with permission.

In both cases, students exhibit inappropriate social skills and seem unaware that it is in their own long-term interest to improve their social behavior. However, Dale does not seem to be fully aware of the effects of his social behavior, whereas Kyle does appear to be aware of the social consequences of his behavior. For both Dale and Kyle, intervention is necessary; for Dale, training of specific social skills may be helpful, whereas for Kyle, rearranging the environmental contingencies that control his behavior may be appropriate.

STRATEGIES FOR
SOCIAL SKILLS TRAINING

Several methods are available for assessing the social skills and social acceptance of students in your classroom, such as student surveys and teacher rating scales (e.g., Gresham & Elliot, 2008b). Probably the best overall method of assessing social skills is by direct observation of social behavior in naturalistic settings, using observational procedures such as event recording, described previously. These observations, based on operationalized behaviors, can determine the specific levels of the behavior being exhibited. For example, you could observe a particular student and record the number of positive versus negative comments made to others during a cooperative learning activity. Further observations could determine whether a chosen intervention was effective.

Many different interventions to improve social skills have been undertaken. These include commercially available curriculum materials, such as the *Social Skills Intervention Guide* (Gresham & Elliott, 2008a) and *Social Skills Solutions: A Hands-On Manual for Teaching Social Skills to Children with Autism* (Krempa & McKinnon, 2002). However, most social skills training procedures are classified into four categories: (1) modeling, (2) shaping, (3) coaching, and (4) modeling/reinforcement (Mastropieri & Scruggs, 2002; Matson, Matson, & Rivet, 2007). Modeling involves demonstrating the appropriate social behavior and allowing students to observe. Shaping involves the use of positive reinforcement to gradually promote the use of a social skill. Coaching requires the use of verbal cues to improve target behaviors, and modeling/reinforcement employs a combination of demonstration and reinforcement techniques. Peers have also been enlisted to help train social skills, such as social initiations and turn-taking, for students with autism (e.g., Harper, Symon, & Grea, 2008).

TRAIN SPECIFIC SOCIAL SKILLS Social skills training often begins with a definition and discussion of the target social skill. The teacher models positive and negative examples of the social skill (e.g., inviting others to play; using polite words in appropriate circumstances) and asks students to identify these examples. Then the teacher may describe some scenarios for role-playing guided practice activities, and students offer suggestions or demonstrate examples of appropriate behavior. Students may be given independent practice activities, in which they are asked to record their own social behavior in relevant social situations outside of class. Formative evaluation is used to determine whether the purposes of the lessons have been accomplished. In this way, social skills instruction parallels the components of academic instruction, including review, statement of objective, presentation of information, guided practice, independent practice, and formative evaluation.

Similar types of instruction have been employed with students with autism through the use of social stories that are developed for individual students to work on specific target behaviors, such as appropriate cafeteria behavior. The teacher reviews photographs of the student exhibiting appropriate behavior and shows others being pleased by this behavior (Graetz, Mastropieri, & Scruggs, 2009). Baker (2006) described procedures for teaching conversation skills, cooperative play skills, and friendship and conflict management skills for individuals with Asperger's syndrome and social communication problems. Leber (2002) provided lessons for critical social skills in the primary grades. When using curriculum materials, be sure the objectives of the materials parallel the objectives for your students, and include suggestions for evaluating the effectiveness of the training.

CONDUCT ON-THE-SPOT TRAINING It is also important to monitor appropriate social skills outside of your training situations. If specific social skills have been targeted and practiced with particular students, prompt and reinforce those skills throughout the day. For example, Colin has a habit of taking things that he needs from classmates and teachers without asking permission. Even though he has learned and practiced more appropriate ways of interacting with others, he may still benefit from additional practice whenever this behavior reoccurs. If he takes a pencil without asking during math class, you could correct his behavior by reminding him to "ask politely," as covered in social skills training.

TRAIN FOR GENERALIZATION   In most cases, trained social skills are of limited use if these skills do not generalize to other social situations. Generalization of social skills, as with the other behaviors described previously, must be specifically programmed (Alberto & Troutman, 2012) and may include the following strategies (see also Bellini, Peters, Benner, & Hopf, 2007; Smith & Gilles, 2003):

- Make sure that students have mastered the skills they are to generalize. For example, a conversation skill that is not completely learned is not likely to generalize to other settings.

- Make the training as meaningful and realistic as possible so that students can recognize situations for which generalization is appropriate. For example, when training for job interview skills, make the situation as much like a real job interview as possible.

- Teach behaviors that will maximize students' social success and minimize their failures. This will make students want to generalize and maintain their behavior.

- Promote the application of learned social skills in other settings. For example, have students apply their skills in maintaining a conversation outside of class and report on their success the next day.

- Enlist the help of peers, parents, and school personnel with prompting and reinforcing the social skills. Teach others what social skills to prompt or watch for and how they can be appropriately rewarded.

- When appropriate, initially accompany the student into the generalization setting or situation, and prompt and reinforce the student in that setting.

- Teach self-management skills so that students learn to recognize appropriate situations for generalizing a social skill, and monitor their success.

- Use periodic retraining and reminders of social skills (e.g., "Remember how we practiced accepting feedback?").

VALIDATE TREATMENTS   Comprehensive reviews of research on social skills training have concluded that although social skills training generally produces positive effects, these effects are often relatively modest (Bellini et al., 2007; Kauffman & Landrum, 2013). Nevertheless, there is no doubt that many students lack important social skills and that many students benefit from social skills training. Kerr and Nelson (2010) suggested that teachers implementing social skills training (a) directly assess and systematically treat specific behaviors for chosen environments, (b) determine that the student lacks the specific skill ("can't") rather than simply refusing to demonstrate the skill ("won't") when planning interventions, and (c) be certain the social skill being trained will achieve the desired social outcome. Carefully document the effectiveness of your training to ensure that social skills instruction is having a maximum impact in improving the social skills of your students.

MyEdLab: **Self-Check 8.3**

MyEdLab: **Application Exercise 8.3: Social Skills Training**

---

8 Summary

- Motivation and affect can be improved by meeting preconditions and by engaging in specific practices, including raising students' self-esteem; promoting goal-setting behaviors; training positive attributions; promoting ownership in the classroom; making learning fun and interesting; and using positive feedback, praise, and rewards whenever possible to acknowledge and promote student accomplishment.

- Classroom behavior can be managed effectively by several techniques.

  — Operationalize and monitor behavior with formal observation and recording systems, such as event recording, duration recording, time sampling, and interval recording.

  — Less-intensive strategies, such as establishing rules, praise and ignoring, proximity, direct appeals, and reprimands, are helpful in maintaining appropriate classroom behavior.

  — Formal management systems for effective behavior management include positive reinforcement, punishment, token systems, attribution training, public posting, timeout and level systems, the Good-Behavior Game, and contracting.

  — Self-monitoring and self-instruction training is helpful in allowing students to become more aware and take more control of their own behavior.

  — A variety of strategies can be used to deal with confrontations effectively and to prevent them from escalating.

  — Schoolwide discipline systems, such as positive behavioral interventions and supports (PBIS), have been effective in managing classroom behavior across entire school environments.

- Social skills are usually taught by modeling, reinforcement, shaping, and modeling/reinforcement. Several strategies can be effective in promoting generalization of social skills.

PROFESSIONAL STANDARDS LINK:
Improving Motivation and Social Behavior

Information in this chapter links most directly to:

- CEC Standards: 2 (Development and Characteristics of Learners), 3 (Individual Learning Differences), 4 (Instructional Strategies), 5 (Learning Environments and Social Interactions), 7 (Instructional Planning), 10 (Collaboration)

- INTASC Standards: 2 (Learning Differences), 3 (Learning Environments), 7 (Planning for Instruction), 8 (Instructional Strategies)

IMPROVING MOTIVATION AND SOCIAL BEHAVIOR

If you are having problems with student motivation or social behavior, have you considered the following? If not, see the pages listed here.

STRATEGIES FOR IMPROVING MOTIVATION AND AFFECT

STRATEGIES FOR OBSERVING AND RECORDING CLASSROOM BEHAVIOR

GENERAL STRATEGIES FOR USING EFFECTIVE CLASSROOM MANAGEMENT STRATEGIES

LESS-INTENSIVE CLASSROOM MANAGEMENT STRATEGIES

MORE FORMAL MANAGEMENT STRATEGIES

STRATEGIES FOR HANDLING CLASSROOM CONFRONTATIONS

☐ Diffuse confrontations with a calm, measured response, 195–196

STRATEGIES FOR IMPLEMENTING SCHOOLWIDE DISCIPLINE SYSTEMS

☐ Implement positive behavioral interventions and supports, 197, 199
☐ Implement multi-tiered systems of support within a PBIS Framework, 197–198

STRATEGIES FOR CONFRONTING BULLYING

☐ Implement a bullying-prevention program, 198–200

STRATEGIES FOR SOCIAL SKILLS TRAINING

☐ Train specific social skills, 201
☐ Conduct on-the-spot training, 201–202
☐ Train for generalization, 202
☐ Train for generalization: Validate Treatments, 202

Inclusion Checklist

9

Promoting Inclusion with Classroom Peers

LEARNING OUTCOMES

After studying this chapter, you should be able to:

9.1 Describe how to implement peer-supported social acceptance.

9.2 Describe how students can be employed as peer assistants, and describe different uses of peer assistance.

9.3 Describe peer tutoring, and discuss how peer tutoring programs can be implemented.

9.4 Describe cooperative learning, and discuss how cooperative learning can be implemented.

Your general education classroom students can play a critically important role in the successful inclusion of students with special needs. You and your students can set the stage for celebrating diversity within your class by openly accepting all students as equal members of the class and building a true community of learners. Within this community, an accepting atmosphere is established in which all students help and encourage one another to reach their own potential. You can assist your students by teaching them several strategies for working more effectively with classmates who have special needs. These strategies help promote acceptance of all students and teach students how to support one another using peer assistance, peer tutoring, and cooperative learning. All of these strategies can be implemented during academic and nonacademic situations and will help you and your students maintain a helpful, positive class environment.

Peer-Supported Social Acceptance

STRATEGIES FOR

PROMOTING SOCIAL ACCEPTANCE

Classroom peers can become involved in accepting students with special needs from their first placement in a general education classroom. Describe the new students before they arrive in class, remind the class what it feels like to enter a new classroom environment, and ask them to brainstorm strategies to help the new students feel more accepted. Then select one or more of these strategies that seem promising and ask for volunteers to implement them. For example, some students may volunteer to create a poster welcoming the new students into the classroom. Other students may volunteer to offer personal words of encouragement and support. Still other students may offer to help the new students orient to the new classroom or offer to telephone them at home. At the same time, introduce the new student to the materials, expectations, and tasks of the general education classroom, a procedure known as "priming" (Myles, 2007).

MyEdLab:
Video Example 9.1.

This video describes one way to integrate students with special needs into the classroom. There are a few strategies presented, as well as a demonstration in the classroom.

MyEdLab:
Video Example 9.2.

This video illustrates how teachers can capitalize on the use of informal peer buddies to help bring out the potential of a student with a disability.

When you help students with special needs become true members of your class, you will help prevent them from being ostracized or rejected by classroom peers (Manetti, Schneider, & Siperstein, 2001). In many ways, classroom peers are the key to social acceptance, and under the right circumstances, they can provide necessary assistance for helping students with disabilities be more accepted in the classroom (Frederickson & Furnham, 2004).

BUILD COMMUNITY WITH THE CIRCLE OF FRIENDS In the **Circle of Friends** activity (Forest & Lusthaus, 1989; Frederickson & Turner, 2003; Frederickson, Warren, & Turner, 2005), you distribute papers showing four concentric circles, with a stick figure in the middle. Students are told to write in the first circle the most important people in their lives, such as family members. In the second circle, they are to put their best friends, and in the third circle, they are to put other people they enjoy playing with or interacting with. In the fourth circle are people who are paid to be in their lives, such as doctors and dentists. When students have filled out the circles, ask the class how they would feel if they only had their mothers in the first circle and no one in the second and third circles. After students share their feelings (e.g., "I would be unhappy all the time"), inform the class that the new student might not have very many people in the second and third circles. The point of the activity is to demonstrate that everyone needs "circles" of friends, with people in every circle. Not everyone needs to be the student's best friend, but all can be friendly and interact well with the student.

Six to eight students are selected to form the Circle of Friends, and weekly meetings led by an outside facilitator (e.g., the classroom teacher) are held for 6 to 10 weeks. In these meetings, mutual support is emphasized, and target goals and strategies are developed and discussed. Previous successes are celebrated, and problem-solving strategies for the future are discussed. Role-play can be used to practice particular behaviors (e.g., a particular social skill target and students' suggested responses). Circle of Friends activities have been found to increase social acceptance (Frederickson & Turner, 2003; Frederickson et al., 2005).

PROMOTE ACCEPTANCE WITH SPECIAL FRIENDS Cole, Vandercook, and Rynders (1988) described a **Special Friends** program in which upper-elementary students were trained to interact with students with severe disabilities. The training sessions covered rules, procedures, and disability awareness. The students then interacted with their Special Friends two to four times per week, 15 minutes per session, for 8 weeks. Students enrolled in this program enjoyed the interactions with their Special Friends and maintained their contact with them after the sessions ended (see also Favazza, Phillipsen, & Kumar, 2000).

Another positive classroom activity to promote social acceptance involves dividing all students into pairs based on shared interest areas and asking them to complete a joint project on a subject in which they are both interested. Or, divide students into pairs and ask each student to complete a list of positive attributes of the other student (Mastropieri, Scruggs, & Bohs, 1994). These lists can then be read to the class.

MyEdLab: **Self-Check 9.1**

MyEdLab: **Application Exercise 9.1: Strategies for Promoting Social Acceptance**

Peer Assistance

Peer assistance, or peer support, refers to pairing students for the purpose of having one student available to assist another student when necessary (Carter, Moss, Hoffman, Chung, & Sisco, 2011; Chan et al., 2009). Peer assistance from a buddy can be helpful in promoting success in inclusive classrooms. However, peers should lend assistance only when help is required. For example, some students may need directions read to them, others may need assistance getting materials to their desks, and others may require help transcribing lecture notes. Peers can support students who might need a door opened or furniture moved to accommodate a wheelchair. But when help is unnecessary, students with disabilities should be encouraged to perform tasks as independently as possible (Cushing & Kennedy, 2003).

Peer assistance need not be arduous or time consuming for the helpers. Many of the activities are tasks the peer assistants would be performing anyway, and helping their buddies usually does not take much extra time. Peers can share responsibilities with peer assistants. Carter and colleagues (Carter, Cushing, & Kennedy, 2009; Carter et al., 2011) described peer-support strategies for assisting students with disabilities and reported increases in peer interactions for all students. Overall, however, it is important to consider that peer assistance can be beneficial for the student helper, promoting such positive attributes as awareness of the needs of others and social responsibility.

STRATEGIES FOR
ENLISTING PEER ASSISTANCE

TRAIN STUDENTS IN PEER ASSISTANCE   Peer-assistance programs should be set up in a systematic manner. The following *In the Classroom* feature offers a checklist for implementing peer-assistance programs. The first consideration is to determine the precise nature of the situation that requires peer assistance. It is insufficient, for example, to think, "Mario has a visual impairment. I must assign a peer assistant to help Mario." Rather, consider the specific need that you believe peer assistance can address and how it can be addressed. For example, you may think, "Mario has a visual impairment and sometimes needs someone to read information to him that is written on the blackboard."

Next, identify the student or students who can serve as peer assistants. In selecting peer assistants, teachers must exercise their best judgment based on their knowledge of the students in their class. In the past, teachers usually considered only the most responsible students, those who exhibited qualities of academic responsibility and conscientiousness as peer assistants. However, it may be as beneficial to consider less obvious students, such as those who are shy or who at times have minor difficulties themselves with classroom assignments. These students usually are not only very capable of assuming the responsibilities but also may flourish when given the opportunity to be a peer assistant.

Provide advanced training to both the peer assistant and peer before starting the peer assistance. Inform students exactly what the relationship will entail. When the procedures are clear to both participants, role-play a few practice sessions, and then implement the peer-assistance program. Finally, monitor the program to determine that it is meeting its objective.

TRAIN PEERS TO ASSIST STUDENTS WITH DIFFERENT TYPES OF DISABILITIES
Peers can assume the role of assistant with any student. Table 9.1 provides some tasks and strategies that peer assistants can engage in with students with disabilities. Although some tasks appear very disability-specific, others are more general and extend across disability areas. For example, during emergency situations, it is essential that specific students have been designated to assist students with disabilities who may require special assistance. Closely monitor all emergency-related procedures.

Peer assistants also can help address safety issues by assisting with the handling of potentially dangerous materials—such as those that are breakable, sharp, or hot—that may be used in laboratory activities. Peers can describe or assist with the proper handling of materials that may be dangerous for someone with vision or fine motor difficulties.

When classroom activities are to be undertaken, peer assistants can provide concrete visual models to demonstrate what students are to do. When extensive listening is required, such as during teacher presentations, peer assistants can make copies of their notes so that students with hearing impairments or writing difficulties can focus their attention on the speaker or interpreter. Peers can also assist with speaking tasks if students with communication difficulties lack the stamina to complete a classroom presentation. For any kind of oral assignment, a peer assistant could share some of the speaking responsibilities.

In the Classroom

Checklist for Peer-Assistance Programs

_____ Identify situations and students who may require assistance.

_____ Target students who may be able to serve as peer assistants.

_____ Pair each peer assistant with one student with disabilities.

_____ Teach important general procedures, such as social interactions and corrective feedback, for working with students with special needs. Ensure both students have been trained in social interaction skills.

_____ When appropriate, provide occasions for peer assistants to observe the student and discuss how assistance can be provided.

_____ Teach peer assistants any specialized need areas for particular students (e.g., specific needs for students with physical or sensory disabilities).

_____ Arrange for a meeting time between peers to explain the process.

_____ Observe the first few interactions carefully, and compare observations with the objectives of the peer-assistance program. Monitor progress and make adjustments if needed.

TABLE 9.1 Suggestions for Use of Peer Assistants by Specific Disability and Task/Situation Area

Disability Area	Tasks/Situations	Strategies for Peer Assistants
All disabilities	Classroom activities	Answer questions and provide examples.
All disabilities	Emergencies (fire or tornado drills)	Provide assistance in exiting rapidly and safely.
Visual impairments	Mobility in unfamiliar places or rearranged rooms	Verbally describe the layouts of the rooms; guide students around new places.
Visual impairments	Written materials that are not enlarged print or braille	Read orally.
Visual impairments	Videos that are not in descriptive video format	Provide additional verbal descriptions.
Hearing impairments	Lectures or films without closed-captioning	Provide supplemental verbal or written information.
Hearing impairments	Abstract materials or concepts	Provide concrete models or descriptions.
Physical disabilities	Mobility	Provide assistance as necessary.
Physical disabilities	Fine motor tasks such as writing	Turn book pages, hold objects, take notes, act as scribe, provide copies of own notes.
Attention deficit hyperactivity disabilities	Attending	Reward student for on-task behavior and prompt student to get back to task.
Behavioral disabilities	Social skills	Provide appropriate social model.
Learning and cognitive disabilities	Writing	Act as scribe, take notes, share copies of notes.
Learning and cognitive disabilities	Reading	Read orally and provide summaries of materials.

Peers can assist with physical mobility by moving obstructions or collecting classroom materials. Peers can also assist students with classroom organization skills, including locker organization, keeping track of homework assignments, and keeping notebooks organized. In some cases, peers can promote appropriate social behavior by providing explicit models of positive classroom behavior and subtle prompts when appropriate.

PROMOTE PEER SOCIAL INITIATION   Peer social initiation refers to procedures intended to enlist peer assistance in promoting social interaction with withdrawn students, including children with autism (Kamps et al., 2002; Kerr & Nelson, 2010). This is done by such acts as asking the student to play, giving or sharing a desired toy, or assisting the student in using a particular material. This technique has been used successfully with students (often, preschool or primary-grade students) from a variety of disability areas, including nondisabled students who exhibit some social withdrawal (e.g., Tsao et al., 2008). These procedures can also be used with any shy child. Very young peer assistants, and even assistants with autism, have been successfully trained in initiating social interactions (Shabani, Katz, & Wilder, 2002).

According to Kerr and Nelson (2002), teachers should choose peer assistants who (a) attend school regularly, (b) consistently exhibit appropriate social skills with peers, (c) follow instructions reliably, and (d) can maintain concentration on the task for at least 10 minutes per session.

The first step in training is to explain to the peer assistant what will be expected (e.g., "Try to get Chris to play a game with you"). Assistants should be prepared for rejection, and teachers can role-play ignoring a positive social gesture from the peer assistant. Tell the student not to give up and to keep trying. If toys are being used to initiate social interaction, point out the target student's favorite toys, or provide cue cards to prompt the peer assistant. Continue to role-play until the student becomes skilled at persisting to prompt appropriate interaction; this may require at least four 20-minute sessions. Be sure the peer assistant is reinforced and supported for his or her efforts and understands the importance of this intervention. Kerr and Nelson (2002) suggest setting aside at least 6 minutes per day, in the same setting, and reviewing with the peer trainer the activities that are most likely to succeed. Reward the peer trainer for persistence in initiating interaction with the withdrawn student.

Peer networks also can be beneficial in providing support for greater integration in inclusive social environments for students with significant social deficits, including autism spectrum disorders (ASD). These interventions involve adult facilitation and direct teaching with repeated exposure to social learning opportunities. Peer networks have been found to improve skills such as initiating, responding, and maintaining social interactions (Kamps et al., 2015).

Overall, classroom peers can be used in many ways to promote social acceptance. By considering the great potential of peer assistance in promoting social acceptance, assisting with academic tasks, and planning strategies, you and your students can create positive and accepting social environments.

Peers can also be employed to increase socialization skills, such as sharing ideas, correcting and praising others, and helping others, in students with autism. The *Research Highlight* feature describes a recent investigation into this area.

MyEdLab: Self-Check 9.2

Peer Tutoring

Peer tutoring is one of the most widely studied interventions in education. Many positive effects of tutoring have been noted, indicating that tutoring can be a powerful tool in improving performance in the inclusive classroom (Harris & Meltzer, 2015; Okilwa & Shelby, 2010). Figure 9.1 highlights some student and teacher reactions to tutoring programs, and the following scenario discusses an application of peer tutoring.

Using Peer Networks to Improve Social Communication for Young Children with Autism

 Students with autism frequently fail to exhibit age-appropriate social communication skills; they rarely interact with age peers and initiate social interactions even less frequently. Kamps et al. (2015) evaluated the effects of a peer-network intervention and direct instruction for kindergarten and first-grade children with autism that was intended to improve language, adaptive communication, and prosocial skills with their peers.

The peer-network intervention established social groups with typical peers and used games and activities to teach social and communication skills approximately 3 days a week. Specific skills taught included asking and sharing, telling about my toys or others' toys, giving compliments, saying please and thank you, and using play organizers (Kamps et al., 2015). Classroom and resource teachers, speech therapists, counselors, and assistants were trained to implement the 25- to 30-minute sessions.

In each session, the instructor provided a 10-minute teacher-led discussion on the targeted social skills, supervised a 10- to 15-minute play time with games and activities that included peer prompting, and provided 5 minutes of teacher feedback on and reinforcement of observed skill use. The social communication skills of the children with autism were evaluated using a randomized experimental design, and results indicated that all students in the peer-network condition made substantial improvements over students in comparison conditions in terms of total communication responses to peer initiations during the play periods. In terms of social probes and generalization probes, students with autism in the peer-network condition improved in initiations to peers over students in the comparison condition. These results show that peer networks can provide a simple way to increase the social interaction between students with autism and their peers. See also the review of evidence-based social skills interventions for children with autism by Wang and Spillane (2009).

QUESTIONS FOR REFLECTION

1. Why did the researchers choose games and activities to implement the social interaction intervention?

2. How could you implement this intervention in a different situation?

3. After training, what could you do to help students with autism to continue to improve their social interactions without prompting and reinforcement?

CLASSROOM SCENARIO

Peer Tutoring in Seventh-Grade History

This year Ms. Conners, the seventh-grade history teacher, found the overall performance of her students with learning disabilities on weekly quizzes to be very poor, and she was beginning to wonder whether some of the students belonged in her class.

"Why should they be in my class if they cannot keep up with the work?" she asked Ms. Cuenca-Sanchez, the seventh-grade special education teacher. Ms. Cuenca-Sanchez knew something had to be done soon. She believed that with additional practice, the students with learning disabilities could master the class content.

After meeting with Ms. Conners and examining the students' schedules, she decided that she could set up a 25-minute peer-tutoring program 3 days a week during seventh-period study hall so that most of the students could practice studying and reviewing history with one another. The steps in the program are described as follows:

Step 1: *Determine the Content for Tutoring Material*
Ms. Cuenca-Sanchez met with Ms. Conners weekly and generated a list of the most important information from each social studies chapter. For example, some of the information on the World War I chapter included the following:

- Woodrow Wilson was the president of the United States.
- William Jennings Bryan, a pacifist, was secretary of state.

- Definition of alliance system, and how military alliances contributed to the start of World War I.
- Names of countries in the Central Powers and in the Allied Powers.
- Initial U.S. position was neutrality.
- Incidents leading up to the U.S. involvement in World War I, including the Zimmermann Note and the sinking of the *Lusitania*.
- Famous individuals of the era and their accomplishments, including flying ace Eddie Rickenbacker and songwriter George M. Cohan.

Step 2: *Devise a Tutoring Plan*

Ms. Cuenca-Sanchez designed a plan for tutoring that included specific procedures for students to use while tutoring each other and rules for appropriate behavior during tutoring sessions. In her program, students would serve as both tutors and tutees during sessions because they all needed review and practice in history. She put the questions and answers on index cards, to be used as the tutoring materials. For example, one card read on one side: "Who was Eddie Rickenbacker, and what was he famous for?" The other side held the answer: "Eddie Rickenbacker was a flying 'ace' who shot down 26 enemy aircraft."

Ms. Cuenca-Sanchez established guidelines for the tutoring session, which she posted on the wall:

1. Be nice to your partner, and sit facing each other.
2. Decide who will be the tutor first. The first tutor will go through the cards, asking each question in order. When the tutee responds, the tutor will verify the answer. If it was answered correctly, the tutor will place it in the "correct" pile. If answered incorrectly, the tutor will correct the tutee, ask the question again, and after it is answered correctly, will place it in the "incorrect" pile. The cards in the "incorrect" pile are asked again after the set of cards is completed. After 10 minutes, a timer rings, and students reverse roles.
3. Speak in a pleasant tone when asking questions and when responding.
4. Encourage your partner by using statements like, "Great job, good answer," or "Can you think of anything else?" For incorrect answers, the tutor can state, "No, the answer is _____. What (who) is _____?"
5. At the end of the two tutoring periods, students should quiz each other on the entire list and record the number of correct answers.

Step 3: *Tutor Roles and Behaviors*

Next, Ms. Cuenca-Sanchez planned a couple of sessions to review the tutoring roles and behaviors. She presented the guidelines and modeled both the tutor and tutee roles for the students. She then provided them with opportunities to practice both roles and provided feedback. When students had mastered the tutoring behaviors and understood their roles, she began the tutoring sessions.

Step 4: *Monitor Performance*

During the tutoring sessions, Ms. Cuenca-Sanchez collected systematic data on the efficacy of the tutoring. She wanted to know whether tutoring improved students' scores on their weekly quizzes in Ms. Conners's history class and if students enjoyed the tutoring. She began to collect students' weekly quiz scores and charted them. She also devised a questionnaire for students to answer periodically regarding their opinions of tutoring.

After a month of tutoring and collecting data, Ms. Cuenca-Sanchez found that students' quiz scores had increased an average of 30 points and that nearly all students reported enjoying being both tutors and tutees. Nearly all students reported that they did better on the weekly quizzes as a result of the tutoring sessions.

Step 5: *Collaborate with the History Teacher*

Ms. Conners also observed that many of the students were doing much better on the weekly quizzes. She considered the tutoring program successful and believed that there were many other students in her class who could benefit from tutoring sessions. With Ms. Cuenca-Sanchez's help, she began implementing 15-minute sessions in her own class 3 days per week. Under this new tutoring program, all students in her class benefited. Ms. Cuenca-Sanchez was able to reduce the students' tutoring sessions to 1 day per week, arranging for additional tutoring sessions only before major tests.

QUESTIONS FOR REFLECTION

1. Why do you think Ms. Cuenca-Sanchez felt she needed to include directions such as, "be nice," and "speak in a pleasant tone"?
2. If tutoring has been found to be effective by research, why did Ms. Cuenca-Sanchez add Step 4?
3. In what other areas do you think tutoring would be helpful?

BENEFITS OF PEER TUTORING

Tutoring can be helpful in addressing diverse learning needs in inclusive classrooms, and it can be applied to a number of content and skill areas (Maheady & Gard, 2010). However, tutoring, just like any educational strategy, should not be considered a panacea. When using peer tutoring, monitor the effectiveness of the intervention, and be prepared to adjust the program as needed.

Reviews of research have emphasized the benefits of tutoring (Harris & Meltzer, 2015; Regan, Evmenova, Mastropieri, & Scruggs, 2015) and described the circumstances in which it is most effective. Overall, peer tutoring has been effective in improving academic skills in the subject tutored, particularly when compared with traditional, whole-class instruction. However, it may not always be more effective than other alternatives; for example, a well-implemented independent study strategy or high-intensity small-group, teacher-led instruction may be as effective as—or

---

I enjoy tutoring a lot. I really look forward to it. It's my favorite part of the day. Some mornings I'll wake up and not want to go to school. Then I'll remember, David gets to start a new book today, or something like that, and I'll be excited all day!
Karen Mylerberg, sixth-grade tutor, Franklin School.

Kara, a sixth-grader, tutored Michael, a third-grader, in reading. Kara's parents reported that she commented daily on Michael and his reading lesson. "She talks about her job all the time." Michael must also talk about Kara, for at Christmas, Michael made "candy sundaes" for Kara and his resource room teacher. Expressions of caring such as these are not uncommon.
LMJ, special education resource teacher.

My children like working with their tutors more than anything else! P.E., music, and other activities that are usually favorites with children don't have as much appeal for them as the one-to-one companionship with their tutors.
Mary Davis, second-grade teacher, Audubon School, Redmond, Washington.

Scott, a fourth-grade youngster 2½ years behind in reading, was being tutored by the special education resource room teacher. Due to scheduling problems he had to be tutored during his lunch recess two times a week. Scott was not terribly enthusiastic about missing lunch recess and his teacher had to "find" him on those days. Later, as part of a cross-age tutoring program, Scott was assigned a fifth-grade girl, Kelly. With Kelly as his tutor, Scott always came to the resource room voluntarily. Scott and Kelly formed a good relationship and both gave up more recess time to make a "sticker poster for good work," which was hung in the resource room. In fact, Scott enjoyed being tutored by Kelly more than by the teacher. His own involvement in planning his lesson, and his perception of Kelly's commitment toward his learning to read, made noon recess an acceptable sacrifice.
LMJ.

Figure 9.1 Comments About Tutoring Programs
Note: From *Cross age and peer tutoring: Help for students with learning problems,* by J. R. Jenkins & L. M. Jenkins, 1981, Reston, VA: Council for Exceptional Children. Copyright 1981 by CEC. Repriinted with permission.

even more effective than—peer tutoring (Higgins, 1982; Sindelar, 1982). However, tutoring is likely to be very useful when individual teacher assistance is not available and when students lack effective independent study skills.

Students serving as tutors also usually benefit from tutoring, where tutors serve as "experts" in the content being tutored. However, the benefits are not as reliable as those for tutees. Tutors usually benefit academically from tutoring in areas in which they have gained some initial competence but still need some fluency building and comprehension development. Although it is often maintained that students can improve in general, overall self-esteem from tutoring, these benefits are less reliable. Nevertheless, appropriately trained tutors frequently benefit in terms of a positive attitude toward their tutoring partners, a positive attitude toward the content being tutored, and, in some cases, a positive attitude toward school (Scruggs & Mastropieri, 1998). Tutoring may increase self-concept in the more specific areas being tutored, such as verbal self-concept or interpersonal skills self-concept (Leung, Marsh, Craven, Yeung, & Abduljabbar, 2013). Students with disabilities in tutoring programs often report making new friends and may enjoy higher levels of social acceptance (Fuchs, Fuchs, Mathes, & Martinez, 2002).

MyEdLab:
Video Example 9.3.
This video shows classwide peer tutoring in science content.

STRATEGIES FOR
IMPLEMENTING A TUTORING PROGRAM

Tutoring programs must be carefully planned and systematically implemented. The following *In the Classroom* feature presents some suggestions for planning and implementing tutoring programs. Remember also that students serving as tutors often model their teacher's behavior—so be sure that your own teaching style is a good model for your classroom tutors.

WORK ACROSS GRADE LEVELS TO IMPLEMENT CROSS-AGE TUTORING In **cross-age tutoring**, older students serve as tutors for younger, lower-functioning students. The roles of tutor and tutee are clearly established and do not alternate. An example of cross-age tutoring would be students from a nearby high school volunteering to tutor elementary school students who are having difficulty in school. The volunteers can schedule their time with the classroom teacher, be assigned a tutee, and be given explicit directions on their roles and responsibilities. It is also a good idea to have the tutors keep a notebook that details the dates and times of each session, the material tutored, and a report of the student's progress. Tutees can learn much from such partnerships, and volunteer tutors can gain valuable experiences, especially if they are considering a career in education or child care.

IMPLEMENT SAME-AGE TUTORING WITHIN YOUR CLASS Students can also tutor students of the same age. In some cases of **same-age tutoring**, students who are more skilled in a particular area can tutor less-skilled students. In other cases, pairs of students can alternate roles. This alternating-role tutoring can work particularly well when students drill one another with flashcards. In this way, the tutor does not need to know the correct answer because it is printed on the back of the card, as in the scenario with Ms. Cuenca-Sanchez.

STRATEGIES FOR
PROMOTING LEARNING WITH CLASSWIDE PEER TUTORING

One of the most highly recommended strategies for promoting achievement among diverse groups of learners is **classwide peer tutoring** (Kamps et al., 2008, 2015). All students in the class are divided into pairs of students, who then alternate roles of tutor and tutee to master basic academic skills. The most significant feature of classwide peer tutoring is the dramatic increase in engaged time-on-task and opportunities to respond. For example, consider a 45-minute fifth-grade reading class of 30 students, in which one student is called on to read aloud at a time. In this class, each student will read aloud for an average of no more than 1.5 minutes per class. In a classwide peer-tutoring program, however, students in this same class could read aloud for an average of as much as 22.5 minutes per class, an increase of 1,500%! As described in Chapter 6, increasing engaged time-on-task—or "maximizing engagement"—is closely linked to academic success. Although it is not successful in every case, research has documented the overall positive benefits of classwide peer tutoring (McMaster, Fuchs, & Fuchs, 2006). Successful classwide peer-tutoring

In the Classroom

Planning and Implementing a Tutoring Program

1. Clarify the specific objectives of the tutoring program, including both academic and social objectives when appropriate.

2. List objectives in a form that can be easily measured. For example:

   "Students serving as tutees will improve reading fluency by 30% on classroom reading materials in the next 12 weeks."

   "Performance of all students on weekly spelling tests will improve to an average of 85%; no student will score lower than 60%."

   "Within 8 weeks, students involved in tutoring will report that math is at least their third-favorite class."

3. Choose tutoring partners carefully. No firm conclusions can be drawn to direct tutoring choices; nevertheless, several considerations should be taken into account. Some teachers have recommended choosing students as tutors who are conscientious in class and who generally have to work for their grades. These teachers have believed that the brightest students may have less empathy for students who do not learn easily, although exceptions to this are commonly found. Other considerations include the compatibility of the tutoring pair. Teachers should find pairs who will work together well; however, they should also encourage pairing of students who are different in gender, race, or socioeconomic status whenever possible, rather than exclusively supporting established social groupings.

4. Establish rules and procedures for the tutoring program. These rules should cover how students are to interact with each other and specify the type of interactions that are not acceptable. Procedures should specify the times and dates of tutoring, the materials to be used, and the specific activities to be undertaken.

5. Implement the tutoring program, monitor it carefully, and be consistent in enforcing the rules and procedures. Modify rules and procedures as necessary.

6. Evaluate the program frequently, and do not wait for the end of the program to determine whether it was effective. Collect information throughout the program, and determine whether it is progressing satisfactorily. If progress is not being made, modify the program.

programs have been established in reading (Kearns, Fuchs, Fuchs, McMaster, & Sáenz, 2015; McMaster et al., 2006), elementary and secondary math (Calhoon & Fuchs, 2003; Powell & Fuchs, 2015), and spelling (Maheady, Mallette, & Harper, 2006), as well as secondary content areas such as social studies (Marshak, Mastropieri, & Scruggs, 2011; Scruggs, Mastropieri, & Marshak, 2012). It has also been found to be successful as a strategy for English language learners with learning disabilities (Richards-Tutor, Aceves, & Reutebuch, 2015; Sáenz, Fuchs, & Fuchs, 2005) and has been recommended as a Tier 1 response-to-intervention (RTI) approach (McMaster, Kung, Han, & Cao, 2008). Following are procedures for implementing classwide peer tutoring in reading (see Fuchs & Fuchs, 2005; Kearns et al., 2015).

IMPLEMENT CLASSWIDE PEER TUTORING IN READING To use the Peer-Assisted Learning Strategies (PALS) program (McMaster et al., 2006), first, pair each student with a partner. After the teacher announces the reading selection and tells the class to start, the stronger reader reads the passage aloud to the partner for 5 minutes. The roles are then reversed, and the weaker reader reads for 5 minutes. During oral reading, the partner follows along and corrects reading errors. After the 10-minute total reading session is a 2-minute "Retell" session, in which the weaker reader is prompted to answer the following questions:

- What did you learn first?
- What did you learn next?

The partner provides feedback on the answers. In the third segment, "Paragraph Shrinking," the weaker student is asked by the partner to provide the following information for each paragraph:

- Name the "who" or "what."
- State the most important thing about the "who" or "what."
- Say the main idea in 10 words or less.

When an error is made, tell partners to say, "No, that's not quite correct," and encourage the student to skim the passage for the answer. The last segment is the "Prediction Relay," and is composed of four segments:

Predict	_____	What do you predict will happen next?
Read	_____	Read half a page.
Check	_____	Did the prediction come true?
Summarize	_____	Name the who or what.
	_____	Tell the most important thing about the who or what.
	_____	Say the main idea in 10 words or less. (Mathes, Fuchs, Fuchs, Henley, & Sanders, 1994, p. 46)

Give students prompt cards that contain this information to assist them in questioning their partners.

Every 4 weeks, rearrange the tutoring pairs, and divide the entire class into two teams (e.g., a "Red" team and a "Blue" team). During classwide peer-tutoring sessions, give students a scorecard, on which points are tallied for good reading and good tutoring skills. At the end of a 4-week session, tally all individual scorecards, and encourage the entire class to congratulate the winning team. The second team is also congratulated. Then, two new teams are formed, and students again begin earning and accumulating points.

IMPLEMENT THE ELEMENTS OF CLASSWIDE PEER TUTORING SYSTEMATICALLY

Researchers have made several recommendations for implementing classwide peer tutoring, based on several years' experience in research and practice (Kearns et al., 2015; Maheady & Gard, 2010; Mathes et al., 1994; McMaster et al., 2006). These recommendations include the following.

Tutoring Materials   You can use a variety of reading materials in classwide peer-tutoring programs, including basal readers, novels, library books, and content-area textbooks. It is not necessary for all pairs to read from the same book; both members of a tutoring pair are encouraged to read from the less-capable reader's book to ensure that both students receive practice in reading. If a weaker reader is compelled to read from a text that is too difficult, the tutoring experience may become ineffective and frustrating.

Other helpful materials include a timer or stopwatch for timing sessions and a calculator for adding up team points. Student materials include, in addition to the reading materials, a prompt card, a scorecard, and pencils.

Scheduling   Schedule regular tutoring sessions, for example, 3 days per week, 35 minutes per day, for 15 weeks. Be sure to schedule the reading tutoring session when all members of the class are present (i.e., none, or as few as possible, are attending resource programs or other special services).

Training   Devote one 45-minute session to teach students how to use the materials correctly and how to be a helpful partner. Further, spend about two sessions for teaching each of the three reading activities, and teach only one activity at a time. That is, you could train and practice Retelling for the first week. The second week, train Paragraph Shrinking, and the third week, practice Retelling and Paragraph Shrinking together. The fourth week, add Prediction Relay, and then begin to practice all three activities together.

Students need time and practice to acquire the skills of sequencing, skimming, summarizing, stating the main idea, and predicting. Stating the main idea and summarizing may be the most difficult concepts to teach; it may be helpful to use pictures to promote the idea of the most important "who or what" before transferring the concept to reading.

Interpersonal Skills   Along with other researchers, Mathes et al. (1994) found that "many students left to their own devices may become bossy, impatient, or disrespectful toward their tutoring partner.... Giving positive feedback and rewards is not a natural behavior for most children" (p. 47). Teach students specific words and gestures for reinforcing partners, and emphasize good sportsmanship and cooperative behavior. Close monitoring of interpersonal skills is recommended in order to keep students positive toward one another.

USE CLASSWIDE PEER TUTORING ON THE SECONDARY LEVEL   Classwide peer tutoring has also been successfully implemented in middle school and high school settings in areas such as reading (Fuchs et al., 2002), social studies (Marshak et al., 2011), English (Mastropieri et al., 2001), and science (Mastropieri, Scruggs, & Graetz, 2005; McDuffie, Mastropieri, & Scruggs, 2009). In these investigations, students with a number of different types of disabilities were able to function effectively as tutors and tutees, and they improved in academic skills and classroom behavior when they did so. In addition, the tutoring content selected can be linked to Common Core State Standards.

Mastropieri, Scruggs, Spencer, and Fontana (2003) employed classwide peer tutoring in inclusive high school world history classes with students with learning disabilities, emotional disturbance, or mild intellectual disabilities. Students were divided into tutoring pairs, each including a stronger and a weaker reader. At the beginning of tutoring, "admirals" read one paragraph of the history text while "generals" listened, and then students reversed roles, reading the same paragraph a second time. Immediately after oral reading, students employed summarization strategies to promote reading comprehension. Students asked each other after reading each paragraph, "What is the most important what or who in the text?"; followed by, "What is the most important thing about the what or who in the text?"; and "What is the summary sentence?"; similar to the process explained for previous applications (e.g., Fuchs & Fuchs, 2005). After the tutoring session, the teacher provided whole-class review. Compared with students receiving more traditional instruction, students who participated in classwide peer tutoring scored much higher on chapter tests, unit tests, and an end-of-year cumulative exam.

Peer tutoring has also been employed in inclusive high school chemistry classes (Mastropieri et al., 2005). Student tutoring pairs used materials with which they questioned each other on important target content (e.g., "What is nonpolar covalent bonding?") as well as broader elaborations of that content ("What else is important to know about nonpolar covalent bonding?"). Tutoring was used as a supplement to regular instruction (about 15–20 minutes of a 90-minute class) to help ensure that students mastered basic facts and concepts in chemistry. Materials also included mnemonic (memory-enhancing) strategies (see Chapter 10) to be used when needed. Students who participated in classwide peer tutoring in chemistry outperformed students who did not use peer tutoring, and the learning gains were particularly strong for students with learning disabilities. In seventh-grade history classes, teachers divided students into tutoring pairs and had them question each other using teacher-made "fact sheets," which consisted of the most important content from the unit. Students—particularly those with special needs—scored higher on unit tests when classwide peer tutoring was implemented (Mastropieri, Scruggs, & Marshak, 2008).

Similarly, McDuffie et al. (2009) employed classwide peer tutoring using "fact sheets" of important target content to improve student learning of genetics content in middle school science classes (e.g., "List the four nitrogenous bases," "What are proteins used for?"). Students in tutoring conditions enjoyed tutoring each other and scored higher on content tests than students taught by more traditional methods.

CLASSWIDE PEER TUTORING, DIFFERENTIATED INSTRUCTION, AND UNIVERSAL DESIGN FOR LEARNING   Classwide peer tutoring is an ideal strategy for inclusive classrooms because it meets many of the criteria for differentiated instruction and universal design for learning (UDL). Tutoring is differentiated to the extent that learners receive instruction individually at the appropriate pace and level of redundancy and with the feedback that they need; classwide peer tutoring provides differentiation in the process of learning and in the

learning environment and the products (e.g., verbal vs. written responses) of learning (Tomlinson, 2014). UDL principles are addressed by classwide peer tutoring to the extent that peer tutoring can provide for multiple means of representation, action and expression, and engagement, especially as compared with traditional, whole-class instruction (Meyer, Rose, & Gordon, 2014).

MyEdLab: **Self-Check 9.3**

MyEdLab: **Application Exercise 9.2: Peer Tutoring**

MyEdLab: **Application Exercise 9.3: Classwide Peer Tutoring**

Cooperative Learning

Cooperative learning has been widely recommended as a technique to promote the inclusive education of diverse learners (Johnson & Johnson, 2009, 2013; Slavin, 2015). It has been found to result in increased achievement, improved attitude toward the subject matter, and increased cooperation among students from different ethnic backgrounds (Oortwijn, Boekaerts, & Vedder, 2008). In cooperative learning, students are assigned to small groups and work collaboratively to complete group activities. To this extent, cooperative learning addresses elements of differentiated instruction in a manner similar to classwide peer tutoring, for example, in providing different roles to different group members, and addresses elements of UDL in providing multiple means of representation, action and expression, and engagement with the curriculum (Meyer et al., 2014). Cooperative learning programs can be configured in many ways. Johnson and Johnson (1986, 2009) have described some important overall elements in implementing cooperative learning programs, as described next.

STRATEGIES FOR
IMPLEMENTING COOPERATIVE LEARNING

CREATE OBJECTIVES Carefully specify the academic objectives to be accomplished, as well as the collaborative skills objective, which includes the interpersonal skills and small-group skills that will be addressed. Whenever you implement a cooperative learning activity, you should specify the collaborative skills that will be necessary to complete the activity successfully and teach them as purposefully as the relevant academic skills.

DETERMINE GROUP PARAMETERS Cooperative learning groups usually range from two to six students. The groups should be larger when materials are scarce or when limited time is available to complete the activities. If students are younger or inexperienced with cooperative learning activities, the group size should be smaller. Students should not work in groups of four or more if they have not mastered the preskills of group work.

It is also important to plan carefully whether students should be in homogeneous or heterogeneous groupings. Although it is helpful to have groups that work well together, it is also important to mix groups by gender, race/ethnicity, and ability level. Sometimes random assignment to groups is effective. Teachers should also consider how long they want groups to operate together. For example, for a longer project on plant growth and development, it may be necessary for groups to remain intact throughout the activity. For other projects, groups can be changed more frequently. When absenteeism is a problem in the school, group assignments may need to be made daily.

Also consider the physical arrangement of the groups. Ideally, groups sit around a circular table that is small enough to provide close proximity and large enough to accommodate relevant materials. However, teachers usually must cope with the best furniture available. Just be sure that groups are arranged so that you can easily move from one to another. When distributing materials, try to arrange for cooperation. One way to do this is to provide only one set of materials that must be shared efficiently for the task to be completed.

It is also important to consider the roles that students will assume during the cooperative learning activity (Mastropieri & Scruggs, 1993). Usually, it is helpful to assign specific duties

Working with Peers on Computers, Tablets, and Mobile Devices

 Computers, tablets, and mobile devices provide ideal opportunities for peers to work collaboratively. Students enjoy the motivating aspects of working with electronic devices, and working collaboratively on projects involving technology can be a rewarding experience for all students. For example, students who are working on developing multimedia projects can assist one another in activities such as finding appropriate sources from the Internet, downloading multimedia files, developing podcasts, taking and editing pictures, and finding other multimedia items to include in their projects. One student can be designated as the official computer or mobile device operator and the other as a co-navigator. Roles can be reversed during the project after specified amounts of time. Before assigning partners, students can be ranked according to their computer expertise along a continuum of expert to novice. This information can be used to pair students so that computer experts are paired with novices. Once students gain more proficiency with the

electronic devices, different searching tasks can be assigned to everyone in the group. The models suggested for implementing peer tutoring and cooperative learning in other subject areas can be applied to the use of computers, tablets, and mobile devices during either peer-tutoring or cooperative learning scenarios.

Several researchers have successfully implemented collaborative group work for multimedia projects and in the use of computers to write essays. In an investigation by Ferretti, MacArthur, and Okolo (2001), students with learning disabilities and typically achieving partners worked collaboratively in small groups on developing multimedia technology-based projects in social studies. Students worked collaboratively, and all students gained in the social studies content being studied, although students with learning disabilities learned less than their typically achieving peers.

Consider pairing students to prepare presentations made on the computer. For example, many teachers have successfully taught students to use PowerPoint™

software to develop multimedia presentations. Some of the presentations can be simple, using only text, whereas more complex presentations can involve pictures, graphs, animation, and sounds. Pairing students to develop these projects can help all students gain the technological expertise necessary to function independently. See also Ferretti, MacArthur, and Okolo (2005) and Okolo, Englert, Bouck, Heutsche, and Wang (2011) for additional information.

Apps that help organize information can be useful for project-based learning activities. *CaptureNotes 2* (G&R Software, LLC) allows writing, taking notes, audio recording, inserting photos, importing PDF files, writing with a finger or stylus or typing notes, inserting notations, and creating notebooks to store similar documents. In addition, files can be exported to *Dropbox* for backup and accessed through any computer. Dropbox is another valuable app that functions as a storage place to hold copies of working files, pictures, and documents that can be synched and accessed among all of your various devices.

MyEdLab:
Video Example 9.4.
This video provides a short discussion of cooperative learning and illustrates its use in the classroom.

to individual students to promote teamwork and cooperation. These roles might include a summarizer (who restates the conclusions, consensus, or final products of the group), a checker (who ensures that all students understand the activity objectives), an accuracy coach (who corrects or verifies other students' responses), and an elaboration seeker (who attempts to relate learning of the present activity to other situations; Johnson & Johnson, 1986). Of course, individual students are also responsible for all other aspects of the assigned tasks. Another, more procedural set of roles that involves groups of four students is recommended in the *Full Option Science System* materials (available through Delta Education) and is described in Table 9.2.

Peers can also work cooperatively on computer activities, as described in the *Apps for Education* feature. Use of peers in these activities is particularly useful when there are more students than computers in a classroom, but the use of peers can also serve important learning objectives.

EXPLAIN GOALS, RULES, AND PROCEDURES Before group activities begin, be sure that all students understand both the assignment and the purpose of the activity. Group

In the Classroom

Evaluation Checklist for Cooperative Learning

Process Evaluation Component

_____ Is the student working with the group members?

_____ Does the student appear to understand what to do?

_____ Is the student capable of doing the assigned tasks?

_____ Do the group members encourage independent work when appropriate?

_____ Are all group members actively engaged in the activity?

_____ Do the group members appear to be getting along?

_____ Do the students exhibit appropriate social behavior?

_____ Do the group members share materials appropriately?

_____ Do the group members speak in a pleasant, quiet tone of voice?

_____ Does the group start and finish activities on time?

Product Evaluation Component

_____ Did the student complete the activity?

_____ Does it appear that the work completed meets the objective for the learning component of cooperative learning?

_____ When given a performance-based assessment covering the objectives, do students demonstrate mastery of their prioritized objectives?

_____ When questioned, can students with disabilities explain what they did or show you what they learned?

TABLE 9.2 Student Cooperative Learning Roles in the Full Option Science System

Role	Responsibility
Reader	**Readers** are responsible for reading all instructions, for checking that everyone understands the activity, and for summarizing the activity when everything is completed.
Recorder	**Recorders** record observations, predictions, and comparisons using such media as iPads, computers, audio recorders, camcorders, pens, and chart and graph paper. These observations can all be compiled in the final report.
Getter	**Getters** retrieve and return all materials at the beginning and end of activities, including iPads, cameras, microscopes, and trays. Getters can also keep track of materials during the course of the activity.
Starter	**Starters** initiate and supervise the interactions with materials, including assembling materials and providing all group members similar access to hands-on materials. Starters can also help monitor student engagement throughout the activity.

goals and rewards should be carefully explained to all group members, for example, bonus points for completing the task within a certain time period. Overall, students should be aware that they are responsible for (a) their own learning, (b) the learning of the group, and (c) the learning of the entire class, in that order. The criteria for success should be explained to the students. Individual accountability within the group structure is necessary and should

be clearly specified. Also, when appropriate, students could be informed that they can assist other groups if they have finished their own assignments first. Students trained appropriately in cooperative learning behaviors generally outperform students in less-structured cooperative learning activities (Johnson & Johnson, 2009, 2013).

Because cooperative learning activities are different from many other classroom activities, particularly independent seatwork, students need to be informed of what is and is not appropriate in cooperative learning exercises. One method of conveying expectations is by use of a **T-Chart** (Johnson, Johnson, & Holubec, 1991), which employs two columns in the shape of a T. The T-Chart specifies what the room will look like (e.g., "All students participating") and sound like (e.g., "Low voices from students in groups") if the rule is being followed. Other classroom rules for cooperative learning that could be displayed on a T-Chart include "Everyone shares with others" and "Students encourage each other."

MONITOR GROUP ACTIVITIES   When cooperative groups begin working, your role differs dramatically from that in more traditional instruction. Many teachers begin by presenting information to the class as a whole and then break students into their groups. Instead of directly presenting information or demonstrating procedures to the whole class for the entire period, the teacher's role involves moving around and monitoring group activities. Ensure that students remain on-task and interact appropriately. When necessary, you may assist with the task or demonstrate procedures. When students are interacting inappropriately, intervene to model, demonstrate, and teach the collaborative skills necessary for the task to be accomplished. Finally, when the activities are completed (or allocated time expires), you must provide closure to the lesson by restating the objectives, summarizing the major points, having students provide ideas or examples, and answering any final questions. Because cooperative learning activities are less formally structured than more traditional methods, summarizing and providing closure are critically important. Group activities can easily overrun the allotted time, so plan carefully to ensure that enough time remains for closure and summaries at the end of the activity.

EVALUATE INDIVIDUAL AND GROUP EFFORTS   Evaluation needs to occur throughout the cooperative learning process and include any individual and group products. You can evaluate the process for students with special needs by observing them while they are working in their groups. The *In the Classroom* feature lists some ideas for evaluating the process. Group efforts should be considered, and students should be individually evaluated for their own learning and their contributions to the group process. Finally, teachers and students should both evaluate how well the groups functioned and consider how the group could function better in the future.

INTEGRATE STUDENTS WITH SPECIAL NEEDS INTO COOPERATIVE LEARNING GROUPS   Students with special needs can benefit academically and socially from participating in cooperative learning. However, these benefits are not automatic. Take steps to ensure that students with special needs benefit as much as possible as well as interact positively and effectively with peers.

Prepare Students with Special Needs   Cooperative learning is frequently described as an important inclusion strategy because it enables students with special needs to receive additional attention and assistance from peers while making their own contributions to the group (Johnson & Johnson, 2009). Nevertheless, students with disabilities may be fearful or anxious about joining a cooperative learning group, and some may actually prefer to work independently (O'Connor & Jenkins, 2014). It is important to explain procedures and roles carefully so that students will understand the expectations. It may be helpful to role-play the roles the students will assume before the activity. Present them with roles in the group that are appropriate for their skill levels. For example, if a student does not read at the appropriate grade level, provide a role of organizing, summarizing, or restating what others have reported. If the student lacks some specific social or academic skill that is important for group functioning, see if the special education teacher can teach some of these skills before the student joins the group.

Prepare Students Without Disabilities   As stated earlier, classroom peers play an integral role in the integration of students with disabilities and other special needs into the general education classroom. However, students must be taught how to interact appropriately and how to accept individual differences in learning (Jenkins & O'Connor, 2003; O'Connor & Jenkins, 2014). Positive peer interactions should be prompted and carefully monitored. As an example of unproductive interactions on a group learning task, O'Connor and Jenkins (1996) provided the following observation:

> Toby, a fifth-grade boy with [learning disabilities], rarely received productive help from his partners, although he frequently requested it. By this point in our observation, Toby's partner had long since ceased to follow Toby's reading or correct his errors. Toby stopped reading and announced, "I need help." The partner supplied a word, but it was not the word in the text. Toby used it anyway, and they both laughed. This game escalated until each time Toby needed decoding help, his partner said, "I'm a dumbo," which Toby inserted into the sentence. . . . Eventually, Toby tired of the game. "I need help," he said again, but from this partner he would not receive it. (p. 36)

Some students may need particular types of assistance in cooperative group situations, such as help turning pages or understanding directions. The special education teacher may be able to meet with relevant cooperative groups and explain how best to interact with the student with special needs.

When students are working to earn group points or rewards, sometimes they are concerned that having a student with special needs will impair the group's chances to succeed. In these cases, consider varying the group criteria for different members or the amount of material each student is expected to master. For example, in a group spelling activity, an individual with learning disabilities may be expected to learn only certain targeted spelling words from the list. These students can also be evaluated with respect to how much they improved over the previous time period, rather than how much they learned in a particular activity. Individual students can be given different assignments, lists, or problems appropriate to their abilities and can be evaluated on the percentage correctly completed. Finally, consider awarding bonus points for groups that include students with disabilities. This may make group members more receptive to including students with special needs.

CREATE DIFFERENT TYPES OF COOPERATIVE GROUP ARRANGEMENTS

Cooperative learning activities can be arranged in many ways, and many types of tasks can be adapted for cooperative learning. Johnson et al. (1991) listed several ideas, including the following, intended to help teachers get started with cooperative group activities:

1. Students discuss a lesson with their neighbors for 3 to 5 minutes, asking questions and clarifying.

2. Students form reading groups, in which three students serve as reader, recorder, and checker, in reading material and answering questions.

3. Students meet in small groups and check homework assignments, discussing and resolving any questions that were answered differently.

4. Students meet in groups to proofread and critique each other's papers and meet again to respond to revisions.

5. Students work in small groups to prepare for specific tests.

Slavin (1991) described several types of more formal cooperative learning arrangements and activities:

1. *Student Teams-Achievement Divisions (STAD):* After the teacher has presented a lesson, students meet in heterogeneous groups to study the material. After the study session, students take a quiz and are graded with respect to how much improvement was made over the previous test. The winning group is recognized in a class newsletter.

2. *Team-Assisted Individualization (TAI):* In this procedure, students are given pretests in an academic area and are placed in a structured curriculum based on their scores. Students are then placed in heterogeneous groups and help each other complete their assignments. Rewards are based on the number of activities completed and on percentage correct.

3. *Cooperative Integrated Reading and Composition (CIRC):* Students work in cooperative groups on reading and writing assignments. For part of the instruction, teachers lead the instruction. Then students work cooperatively on decoding, vocabulary, writing, spelling, and comprehension activities and prepare each other for tests.

4. *Jigsaw:* This is a popular cooperative learning strategy in which each student learns a particular piece of information and then contributes it to the group. Students are tested individually on their learning of all the material. In another version of jigsaw, each student contributes a particular component of a larger task, and then the larger task is presented to the entire class. For instance, one group could be preparing a presentation on Dr. Martin Luther King. One student could prepare information on King's early life, another could prepare information on King and the civil rights movement, another could gather material from King's speeches, and a fourth could collect information about King's assassination. The group then meets and cooperatively compiles the entire presentation, with each student sharing what he or she has learned with the group. Souvignier and Kronenberger (2007) reported successful applications of jigsaw activities in math and science with students as young as third grade; however, overall learning was not always more effective than that for teacher-directed instruction.

5. *Group investigation:* Group investigation requires the most independence on the part of cooperative groups. In this method, students decide how they will learn the material, how they will go about organizing the group to best facilitate learning, and how they will communicate their results to the other students in the class.

Whereas some activities are intended to be undertaken throughout the year, for example, in science or mathematics, other cooperative group activities can be designed for a single lesson. Teachers should consider their own classroom needs to design the best arrangement for cooperative group learning.

USE PEER-MEDIATION STRATEGIES TO RESOLVE CONFLICTS In some cases, peer-mediation strategies have been used to manage conflict situations that occur among peers. Johnson, Johnson, Dudley, Ward, and Magnuson (1995) trained students in how to identify conflicts, how to negotiate, and how to mediate to better resolve peer conflicts. The negotiation procedure had five parts:

1. Jointly define the conflict (that is, both parties agree on the nature of the conflict).

2. Exchange positions and interests (each party describes his or her own position on the conflict).

3. Reverse perspectives (each party states the other party's point of view).

4. Invent at least three optional agreements for mutual gain (that is, solutions that benefit all parties).

5. Reach an integrative agreement (the optional agreement that seems best to all parties).

Johnson et al. (1995) reported that after 12 training sessions of 45 minutes each, the training had a significant effect on the strategies students used and the resulting resolutions of conflicts (see also Stevahn, Johnson, Johnson, & Schultz, 2002).

ADVANTAGES AND CHALLENGES OF COOPERATIVE LEARNING

ADVANTAGES It has been reported that cooperative learning is an effective strategy for improving achievement, group interactions, social learning, and the learning of students with disabilities and other special learning needs (Johnson et al., 1991; Slavin, 1991). With cooperative learning, students with disabilities can be included in—and contribute to—activities that they otherwise may not be able to participate in individually (Mastropieri et al., 1998). Johnson and Johnson (1986) concluded the following:

> In both competitive and individualistic learning situations teachers try to keep students away from each other. "Do not copy," "Move your desks apart," and "I want to see how well you can do, not your neighbor" are all phrases that teachers commonly use in their classrooms. Students are repeatedly told, "Do not care about the other students in this class. Take care of yourself!"... Cooperative learning, however, should be used whenever teachers want students to learn more, like school better, like each other better, have higher self-esteem, and learn more effective social skills. (p. 554)

CHALLENGES In spite of the benefits of cooperative learning, some potential limitations also exist that teachers should consider. Tateyama-Sniezek (1990) reviewed the literature on cooperative learning in research in which students with disabilities were participants and in which their achievement was examined separately from that of students without disabilities. She concluded that students with disabilities often did not learn significantly more than if they participated in alternative learning conditions. Stevens and Slavin (1991) responded that the effects for students with disabilities were generally positive, even if they were not always statistically significant. McMaster and Fuchs (2002) conducted a review of research and concluded that outcomes were variable for students with learning disabilities and overall not stronger than those of other types of peer mediation. However, cooperative learning programs appeared to be more successful when they combined individual accountability and group rewards. Jenkins and O'Connor (2003) concluded that teacher classroom behavior and student social skills were important to the success of cooperative learning. It should be noted that positive effects for students with disabilities are often, but not always, realized in cooperative learning interventions, and teachers should plan and monitor the interventions carefully to ensure they are having the desired effect (see also McMaster & Fuchs, 2005).

Overall, cooperative learning has been popular with participating teachers. Nevertheless, teachers have made several suggestions regarding cooperative learning, including the following: plan for increased teacher preparation and transition time, increase allocated time for lessons, and work to reduce any student anxieties about working together and teaching one another. Additionally, take care to ensure all students are working appropriately (and collaboratively) on the activities, ensure that assignments are at the appropriate level for all students, enforce individual accountability systems, and be prepared for higher noise levels (Jenkins & O'Connor, 2003).

Many of these potential concerns, however, may occur with other instructional arrangements, and strategies for dealing with several of these challenges have been presented earlier in the chapter. As with any educational intervention, teachers must ensure that they have maximized the positive benefits while addressing possible limitations. Gillies (2007) has described the concerns of some teachers in a time of high-stakes testing and has suggested that cooperative learning, when systematically employed and carefully monitored, can be successfully implemented to promote academic learning, especially when these procedures are employed over time.

Overall, cooperative learning can be an effective strategy for promoting inclusive instruction. For example, Mastropieri et al. (1998) employed cooperative learning to promote learning in a hands-on elementary science class that included five students with disabilities, including learning disabilities, emotional disturbance, mild intellectual disabilities, and physical disabilities. Not only did students in this class greatly outperform students in comparison classes, which employed traditional textbook-based instruction, but the students with disabilities overall achieved at about the middle level of their own class! Cooperative small-group work has also been found to be promising with English language learners and learners from other ethnic backgrounds, as described in the *Diversity in the Classroom* feature (Norland, 2005; Oortwijn et al., 2008). When appropriately employed, cooperative learning can be an important strategy for many classroom situations.

Cooperative Learning Activities in Multiethnic Classrooms

Many students prefer to work with peers for some school activities. Most students who have participated in peer tutoring or cooperative learning activities have reported enjoying working with partners. Sometimes students with disabilities have reported they have felt more comfortable reading with a single partner during peer tutoring than reading aloud in front of an entire class (see Mastropieri et al., 2001), and English learners have reported gaining confidence in their abilities (Norland, 2005). Similar, related findings have been found when students from various ethnic backgrounds have been placed in structured small-group cooperative learning situations. In some studies, students from diverse ethnic backgrounds were found to have increased popularity following multiple cooperative learning lessons. Oortwijn et al. (2008) implemented 11 cooperative learning lessons that included the rules for cooperative learning and authentic math assignments involving multiple possible solutions. Students who were placed in heterogeneous cooperative groups were informed that understanding—not completing the assignment—was the goal of each cooperative learning lesson. Improved cooperativeness and friendship among students from all ethnic groups was observed over time. These findings offer promise for using small-group activities when working with learners from various cultural and linguistic backgrounds.

MyEdLab: **Self-Check 9.4**

MyEdLab: **Application Exercise 9.4: Cooperative Learning**

9 Summary

- Peers can be employed to support social acceptance.
  - Circle of Friends and Special Friends are training programs that can promote classroom acceptance of students with disabilities or other special needs.

- Students can be employed as peer assistants by pairing students for the purpose of having one student available to assist another student when necessary.
  - It is important to identify the situations that require peer assistance, appropriately train students, match peer assistants and buddies carefully, and monitor progress and adapt as necessary.

- Peer tutoring can be a powerful tool in improving classroom performance, and it can also be very helpful in addressing diverse learning needs in inclusive classrooms.
  - Both tutors and tutees can gain academically and socially from tutoring interventions, although the procedures and outcomes should be carefully monitored.
  - Classwide peer tutoring, in which all students in a class are involved in peer tutoring, is one of the most highly recommended strategies for promoting achievement among diverse groups of learners.

- Cooperative learning involves the creation of cooperative learning groups of students and can improve achievement and social integration of diverse learners.
  - Cooperative learning interventions require specifying objectives, making placement decisions, explaining the task, monitoring effectiveness, and evaluating individual and group achievement.
  - A variety of formal and informal procedures for cooperative learning can be employed to address a variety of classroom situations.

PROFESSIONAL STANDARDS LINK:
Promoting Inclusion with Classroom Peers

Information in this chapter links most directly to:

- CEC Standards: 4 (Instructional Strategies), 5 (Learning Environments and Social Interactions), 7 (Instructional Planning)

- INTASC Standards: 2 (Learning Differences) 3 (Learning Environments) 7 (Planning for Instruction), 8 (Instructional Strategies)

PROMOTING INCLUSION WITH CLASSROOM PEERS

If you wish to increase cooperation and collaboration in your inclusive classroom and increase learning, have you considered the following? If not, see the pages listed here.

STRATEGIES FOR PROMOTING SOCIAL ACCEPTANCE

STRATEGIES FOR ENLISTING PEER ASSISTANCE

STRATEGIES FOR IMPLEMENTING A TUTORING PROGRAM

STRATEGIES FOR PROMOTING LEARNING WITH CLASSWIDE PEER TUTORING

STRATEGIES FOR IMPLEMENTING COOPERATIVE LEARNING

10

Improving Attention and Memory

LEARNING OUTCOMES

After studying this chapter, you should be able to:

10.1 Define attention difficulties, and describe preconditions and strategies for improving the school success of students with special needs.

10.2 Define memory difficulties, and describe preconditions and strategies for improving the school success of students with special needs.

Attention and memory are two fundamental psychological processes necessary for learning to occur. It is easy to understand that instruction, however well presented, is of little value if it is not remembered. Conversely, it is possible to remember only those things to which we have paid attention in the first place!

In this chapter, we describe the problems students may have with attention and memory, and we describe a number of strategies you can use to improve the attention and memory of your students. Given the significance of these important psychological processes to classroom learning, it is likely that careful application of the principles and strategies described in this chapter can make an important difference in the school success of all students, including those with special needs.

Attention

ATTENTION AND STUDENTS WITH SPECIAL NEEDS

All students exhibit occasional lapses in attention, either because of a lack of interest in a subject, boredom, fatigue, or being distracted by temporary anxieties or concerns. However, many students with special needs frequently exhibit difficulties with attention. For example, poor attention and concentration are commonly reported characteristics of students with learning disabilities (Lerner & Johns, 2012). Students with intellectual disabilities may fail to sustain attention in class and may exhibit difficulties attending to the appropriate stimulus in a lesson, such as focusing on the shape or color of the hands of a clock rather than the position of the hands in a lesson on telling time (Beirne-Smith, Patton, & Hill, in press).

Some students with physical or sensory impairments also have difficulty sustaining attention when attending to particular tasks that interact with disability areas. For example, some students with cerebral palsy have difficulty keeping their heads aligned and eyes focused on a class demonstration; some students with hearing impairments may tire from lengthy intervals of speech reading (Heward, 2013). For some students with attention deficit disorder (ADD) and attention deficit hyperactivity disorder (ADHD), attending is a significant problem. Some students with ADD or ADHD may qualify for services under the Individuals with Disabilities Education Act (IDEA) or Section 504.

MyEdLab:
Video Example 10.1.
This video shows a child with attention problems in the classroom. Notice the various strategies the teacher uses to redirect the student.

Serious problems with attention can severely impede learning (Barkley, 2015: Daley & Birchwood, 2010). Fortunately, many strategies are available for improving student attention, as described in the following section.

CLASSROOM SCENARIO

Ana

Ana is a fifth grader with average academic abilities and a positive disposition. However, she has difficulty sustaining her attention to school tasks for more than about 3 minutes at a time. When prompted, she returns to task, but within a few minutes, she is again off-task, looking out the window, playing with her pencils, or doodling on her paper. This happens during teacher presentations, seatwork activities, and sometimes during group activities. As a consequence, her grades have been falling, especially in math.

QUESTIONS FOR REFLECTION

1. Why do you think Ana is having problems sustaining attention?
2. What adaptations to the classroom environment might help Ana?
3. How could peers help Ana pay better attention?

STRATEGIES FOR
IMPROVING ATTENTION

ADDRESS THE PRECONDITIONS OF ATTENTION WITH TEACHER EFFECTIVENESS It is inappropriate for teachers to implement special interventions to improve attention without first making their classrooms as interesting and engaging as possible. For example, if you lecture day after day using the same presentation style or rely extensively on individual student worksheets, it would not be surprising if the attention of many of your students began to wander.

If getting and holding students' attention is a problem, first consider whether you are using effective teacher planning and presentation variables consistently. If each lesson does not contain elements such as structure, clarity, redundancy, and enthusiasm, it is unlikely to sustain student attention. Determine, for example, whether you have done as much as you can to teach enthusiastically (Reid & Johnson, 2012).

A huge part of teaching effectively—and thus maintaining student attention—is using interesting and motivating examples to enhance lessons. These examples allow teachers to personalize instruction and make the subject more meaningful and useful to students.

Finally, consider whether you are using attention-getting demonstrations. Demonstrations can include the use of "real" objects in teaching mathematical operations; showing artifacts in lessons on the Civil War; demonstrating, rather than describing, the effects of certain chemical interactions; or dressing in historical clothing and acting out scenes of life from different geographic regions and time periods. Pictures and illustrations can also be helpful when actual demonstrations are not possible.

However, if some students continue to have difficulty sustaining attention, try the following strategies.

PROVIDE ASSISTANCE WITH BASIC SKILLS PROBLEMS Many students with special needs do not read or write as well as other students in the class. These students may appear less attentive because paying attention requires reading from a text or writing notes that are beyond their skill level. For these students, find other means for them to acquire relevant information.

Some students do not complete assignments appropriately because they were not paying attention to directions. When giving directions, prompt student attending ("Listen carefully to what I'm going to say"), speak in a clear voice, and limit classroom distractions. Write the steps of the assignment so students can read as well as listen. Directions should include information about the content and format of the assignment, the reason it is being assigned, how students may receive assistance from others (e.g., adults, peers, and technology), how much time it should take to complete, and how it will be evaluated. Clear and specific directions can improve the performance of poor attenders (Jitendra, DuPaul, Someki, & Tresco, 2008).

In other cases, students may lose focus because they do not process oral language as fast as it is spoken. When this happens, try to find ways to reduce the rate of speaking, increase redundancy, provide "advance organizers," or find other means to present information. Mr. Davis, an eighth-grade social studies teacher, displayed charts containing the organizational framework of units during the entire month-long unit. Students said the charts helped them refer back to major points during classes and helped promote a better understanding of everything in the unit. Mrs. Fluke, a fourth-grade teacher, placed language cards containing pictures illustrating the concepts of new vocabulary on a bulletin board. She encouraged her students to make versions of the cards for their personal picture dictionaries.

USE DIRECT APPEAL   Direct appeal is a simple, sometimes overlooked strategy for improving attention and behavior problems (Gable, Hester, Rock, & Hughes, 2009; Redl, 1952; see also Chapter 8). To use direct appeal, find a quiet time and place to speak to students individually. Explain the problem as explicitly as possible, including the effect of the problem on you and other students as well as the target students. Then make a direct request to the students to improve their behavior. This strategy is likely to be effective when students recognize they are not paying attention and would like to succeed in school. An example of direct appeal is given in Figure 10.1.

USE PROXIMITY   Proximity is another simple strategy that can be effective in promoting attention (Conroy, Asmus, Ladwig, Sellers, & Valcante, 2004). Simply move physically toward or stand near a student who is beginning to lose attention. This can prompt the student to refocus attention. Once this strategy has been established, it may be possible to fade it over time to a direct glance or a gesture that the student can easily interpret as a prompt to refocus attention. It also may be helpful to move the student or rearrange the classroom to accommodate teacher proximity.

BREAK UP ACTIVITIES   Some students may be able to sit still and concentrate on a task for a certain number of minutes. Attention spans vary with the age and maturity of students. In general, however, rather than giving a younger student the full length of time to complete a

---

Teacher: Christine, may I speak with you privately for a minute?

Christine: OK.

Teacher: I think you're having a problem in my class. Do you know what I think it is?

Christine: No.

Teacher: Sometimes in class, I think you are having problems paying attention.

Christine: Oh.

Teacher: I think that because sometimes I see you just looking out the window, or doodling with your pencil, or wearing a blank expression on your face, as if you're daydreaming. Do you think that happens sometimes?

Christine: Yeah, I guess so. I guess I'm just not that interested in history.

Teacher: Well, I'm afraid that when that happens, it makes class harder for me, because I think I'm not getting through to you. Also, I think other students notice you and it makes them more likely to not pay attention.

Christine: Oh.

Teacher: But here's what I'd like to suggest. You daydream in class because you aren't interested in history. But if you think about what we're discussing a little more, and you raise your hand in class more often, I guarantee that you will begin to find class more interesting. You will also find that the time passes much more quickly. And most important—and this is what I want—you will find that you will get a much better grade in my class. So what do you say? Will you give it a try?

Christine: OK, I'll try.

Figure 10.1   Example of Direct Appeal

MyEdLab:
Video Example 10.2.
This video shows student teachers discussing their observations about teachers working with students with ADHD. Listen for strategies identified as effective.

relatively lengthy assignment, divide the task into 10 subtasks of, for example, 3 minutes each. At the end of each subtask, the student's progress could be checked, recorded, and praised by you or an assigned classroom peer. Dividing tasks into smaller segments is a great strategy for helping students with limited abilities to stay focused.

ALLOW SUFFICIENT MOVEMENT TO REDUCE RESTLESSNESS   In some cases, especially in the elementary grades, students begin to lose concentration if they have been made to sit still for a long time. Recording when student attention begins to fade is a way to determine when periods of student inactivity are too long. If students regularly begin to lose attention after extended periods of sitting, consider rearranging the classroom schedule (e.g., recess periods) to allow for more movement (Kerr & Nelson, 2010). Adjust the amount of time spent on each discipline and consider alternating between quiet sit-down activities and more actively involved learning activities. If your schedule cannot be easily changed, try giving students a minute to "stand, stretch, reach up to the ceiling, take a deep breath and let it out slowly, and march in place." Brief movement intervals are helpful in promoting student attention. Also, including student movement in lessons can be helpful.

PROVIDE STUDENT ACTIVITIES   Students are much more likely to pay attention when they are asked to engage in activities than when they are asked to listen to someone talk. Providing relevant activities can be an excellent way of promoting attention. For example, instead of asking students to listen to a verbal presentation on how a telegraph works, students could work in small groups to construct their own telegraphs and then send and decode messages to and from one another. Such activities help to focus student attention and make relevant concepts more meaningful.

Record any student's success at paying attention over a period of time and reinforce that behavior with positive recognition or rewards.

USE CLASSROOM PEERS TO PROMOTE ATTENTION   Classroom peers also can be effective in working with students who have attention problems (Watkins & Wentzel, 2008). Grauvogel-MacAleese and Wallace (2010) demonstrated that unsupervised peer attention can help maintain off-task behavior in students with ADHD. However, peers can be trained to prompt and reinforce attending behavior. Peer interventions can be set up through group activities or working one on one. Peers could be asked to work in pairs with students who have some difficulty sustaining attention. Such collaborative sharing of activities can help students with attention problems by providing ongoing prompts for students to attend only to relevant tasks.

Peers seated near target students can also prompt attention. Peers can be trained to provide subtle cues to students (e.g., lightly touching the student's back) when lapses in attention are observed; they can be asked to report inattention to you only when these more subtle prompts are disregarded. Before you use this kind of strategy, be sure everyone involved is amenable to trying to use peer-intervention strategies. Be sensitive to the needs of the students you are trying to help. Choose peer assistants wisely, using those students who appear to have strong interpersonal skills.

PROVIDE DIRECT CONSEQUENCES FOR ATTENTION   You can increase attention in individual students by measuring and reinforcing it (Crossairt, Hall, & Hopkins, 1973; Pfiffner & DuPaul, 2015). Set a timer, such as a wristwatch alarm, vibrating watch, audio recorder, iPod, or smartphone (with, for example, the Interval Timer app by Deltaworks) to sound or vibrate at random intervals (the length of the interval depends on the frequency of prompts the students need). Whenever the alarm sounds, determine whether the target students were paying attention at that instant. If so, they can be rewarded with verbal praise, points on a check sheet, or tokens that can be accumulated and exchanged at a later date for desired objects, privileges, or activities. For example, a student who earns 90% of possible tokens over a 2-week period might be entitled to take an extra recess with another class, go out for ice cream, or have a special break with you. If other students appear to resent this arrangement, consider including the rest of the class in some reward scheme for good behavior, such as a pizza party or game time. Allow the target student to work for a class reward or privilege, such as bonus recess time or a favored activity. In this way, the class can share responsibility for the target student's success or failure, as in the continuation of Ana's scenario.

Ana

Ana's teacher, Mrs. Lawson, asked a responsible student to sit behind Ana and prompt Ana when her attention wandered for more than a few seconds. This seemed to help, but Ana still seemed to need frequent reminders to maintain her concentration. Mrs. Lawson determined from talking to Ana and other students that Ana liked to please her classmates. Mrs. Lawson told Ana that she could help do something nice for the class. The peer who was monitoring Ana's inattention would tally each time Ana was prompted. If the number of prompts declined by half by the end of the week, Mrs. Lawson would allow her to distribute animal crackers to everyone in the class. Almost immediately, Ana began to pay more attention. After 3 weeks, Ana only required minimal prompting to stay attentive.

QUESTIONS FOR REFLECTION

1. Why do you think these strategies were successful for Ana?
2. What might be another way to use peers to assist?
3. How could a parent adapt these strategies for home use?

Mild corrections or reprimands have also been found effective for students with attention problems. Generally, short reprimands have been found to be more effective than long reprimands, and immediate reprimands have been found to be more effective than delayed reprimands (Gable et al., 2009). Saying something like, "When you pay attention in class, the teacher is very happy with you. When you don't pay attention, your grades will suffer," reminds students of the rule, their responsibilities, and the consequences, without placing too much emphasis on the reprimand component. Remember that reprimands lose their effectiveness if they are used too often (see Chapter 7), and that praise for appropriate behavior should be used far more frequently.

TEACH SELF-RECORDING STRATEGIES   Self-recording and self-regulation strategies are useful in teaching students how to monitor and evaluate their own attention (Joseph & Eveleigh, 2011). Special educators often teach self-monitoring strategies in their classrooms, and therefore many students with special needs may have already learned how to use self-recording strategies. Self-monitoring skills learned in a resource setting have been observed to improve student attention in the regular classroom (Reid, Trout, & Schartz, 2005; Slattery, Crosland, & Iovannone, 2015). With systematic communication between the regular and special education teachers, problems with attention can be improved.

To start a self-recording system, set up a procedure for delivering randomly spaced beeps, as described previously (see the *Apps for Education* feature in Chapter 8 for other suggestions). The cueing interval can be set at random between 10 and 90 seconds (average of about 45 seconds) at first and expanded as attention improves. This procedure could be used with several students at a time. If students have difficulty hearing an auditory cue, pair the sound with a vibrating or light stimulus, or provide the signal to a peer who then provides a visual or tactile cue to the target student.

When the cue sounds, the target students should indicate whether they were paying attention by placing a checkmark on a self-monitoring sheet. The self-monitoring sheet should have two columns. At the head of the first column is, "Was I paying attention?" including examples such as "Looking at teacher" and "Reading textbook." At the head of the second column is, "Was I **not** paying attention?" including examples such as "Looking out the window" and "Daydreaming." Under each column is a numbered underline (or box) where students can record their level of attending ("yes" or "no") after each cue.

At first, you should also make your own record of student attending and compare the two records at the end of the period. Students can be reinforced for recording at all appropriate times and for approximating the results obtained by you. For example, if you record 70% paying attention, the student should be rewarded for recording a similar level between 60% and 80%. As the recording becomes reliable, create a graph of student attending, and look for progress over time. Some investigators have demonstrated that it may not be necessary for teachers to verify the accuracy of attending for the procedure to be effective.

Self-Monitoring for Students with Autism

Attending to task is an important prerequisite for school success. Unfortunately, many students with autism exhibit difficulty sustaining attention in school, especially on independent seatwork. And although much research has been conducted on improving attention for students with mild disabilities such as ADHD (e.g., Harris, Danoff, Saddler, Frizzelle, & Graham, 2005), less research has involved students with autism. Holifield, Goodman, Hazelkorn, and Heflin (2010) examined the effectiveness of a self-monitoring intervention on the attention to task and academic success of two elementary-age students with autism, "Graham" and "Tony." Both students demonstrated significant attention and behavioral problems and were receiving speech and language services to help develop their communication skills.

Graham and Tony were each given the definition of "attending to task" and provided with a self-monitoring sheet showing two pictures of student attending, with the words "write," "count," and "work." Under these words, the phrases "attending to task—one" through "attending to task—four" were listed, followed in each case by "yes" and "no." The self-monitoring sheet was provided during the 20-minute periods of assigned independent seatwork in both language arts and math. As each period began, the teacher prompted each student every 5 minutes to record his attending, saying "attention to task" and indicating on the sheet for the student to circle "yes" or "no" for each of the four self-monitoring intervals. If the student was attending to task, the teacher provided verbal praise. The students accepted the task readily, and after a few days, they began to retrieve the self-monitoring sheets themselves from the teacher's desk.

Prior to the self-monitoring intervention, both students exhibited low levels (about 30%) of on-task behavior; for example, Tony was observed to be on task for 32% of the time during language arts. During the intervention, attention increased greatly, and accuracy increased along with the improved attention. Tony, for example, improved to 86% appropriate attending, with 90% accuracy on his assignments. Graham made similar improvements.

QUESTIONS FOR REFLECTION

1. Do you think this intervention could be implemented by paraprofessionals or classroom peers? Would any changes be needed?
2. What other areas could be addressed with self-monitoring techniques?
3. Do you think self-monitoring of academic performance (rather than attending to task) would also be effective? Why or why not?

Before beginning a self-recording intervention, meet individually with the students and discuss why paying attention in class is important and how the students will benefit from attending better. The students need to understand that the self-recording is in their best interest and that they will benefit as a result. It might be helpful to involve parents to support this intervention.

As students improve in monitoring their attention, you can set timers so that they sound less frequently. However, serious attending problems are unlikely to disappear in a short time. Consistency on your part is helpful in effecting long-term improvements in attention. Continue to give frequent and regular feedback to students on their ability to attend and on their consistent self-monitoring of their own attention. The *Research Highlight* describes a self-monitoring for attention intervention for students with autism.

As an alternative, students can be trained to record their performance—for example, the number of times a weekly spelling list was practiced correctly (Reid & Johnson, 2012). This method has also been shown to be effective, although not always more effective than self-recording of attention, and students may prefer this method.

STRATEGIES FOR
ADDRESSING EXTREME CASES OF ATTENTION DEFICITS

Some extreme cases of attention problems are challenging to address in a general education classroom without intensive assistance from special educators. Students with extreme attention problems may appear so distractible that they cannot reasonably be expected to attend appropriately for more than a few minutes at a time. In these cases, some special techniques may be helpful.

PROVIDE INTENSIVE TEACHER-LED INSTRUCTION   For students with extreme attention problems, brief, intensive teacher-led instructional sessions may be the most realistic teaching strategy. These sessions can be delivered either one to one or in small groups with a great deal of teacher–student interaction; novel, interesting, age-appropriate tasks; and frequent reinforcement, including preferred activities (Kerr & Nelson, 2010). Because your time for one-to-one instruction may be limited, this kind of intensive instruction may have to be accomplished by a closely supervised aide, an appropriate tier in a response-to-intervention (RTI) program, or the special education teacher.

CONSIDER STRENGTHS AND WEAKNESSES OF STIMULANT MEDICATION   Another alternative used more frequently in recent years is the administration (under medical supervision) of stimulant drugs to help students focus attention more appropriately. Although medication has certainly been helpful in many cases, often reducing the symptoms of ADHD, concern has been expressed that it has been overprescribed in recent years (Reid & Johnson, 2012; Ryan, Katsiyannis, Losinski, Reid, & Ellis, 2014). Stimulant medication generally affects behavior and attention more than higher-order skills, learning, or achievement. Side effects can include insomnia, decreased appetite, irritability, mood changes, weight loss, abdominal pain, and headaches; less common but more serious side effects include depression, agitation, and aggressive behavior (Reid & Johnson, 2012). If relevant and qualified medical professionals agree that stimulant medication is indicated for a specific student, your job as a teacher should be to collect formative data that identify how the medication affects the student's behavior both positively and negatively. It is also important for all participants to be aware that the long-term effects of stimulant medication have yet to be fully determined (Swanson, Baler, & Volkow, 2011).

In some cases, stimulant medication used in conjunction with cognitive/behavioral training can be effective (Ryan et al., 2014). In addition, parent training in cognitive/behavioral interventions and communication strategies has sometimes been effective in managing noncompliant behavior, reducing stress, and improving the quality of family relationships. Families can also be enlisted to provide consistency and support for school-based interventions (Jennifer, Mautone, Lefler, & Power, 2011).

PROVIDE BEHAVIORAL TECHNIQUES   Some students with autism have severe attention problems. Autistic students may attend little or not at all to teachers, even though they can be demonstrated to have adequate hearing (Zager, Wehmeyer, & Simpson, 2011). Students with such severe attention deficits may benefit from one-to-one instruction, specialized behavioral techniques, direct provision of tangible or edible reinforcers for attending and responding appropriately, and ongoing supervision. Parents and special educators may be able to provide more specific information on the needs of individual students. Educational placement in the general education classroom is possible if special educators or highly trained aides are available to provide individual attention.

PROMOTE JOINT ATTENTION   White et al. (2011) reviewed the problems of children with autism in the area of **joint attention**, which is the ability of an individual to coordinate attention between a desired object and a person in a social context, for example, to follow an adult's eye gaze directed to a specific object. Students with autism improved joint attention with intensive trial-based instruction, prompting, and reinforcement. Parents directed their gaze to a particular object (a desired toy); if the child followed the gaze, he or she was given a reinforcement (time to play with the toy). If not, the child was prompted and then reinforced for a shorter period.

Developmentally appropriate interventions may also increase the attending of students with autism. For younger children, child-directed play, reinforcement, prompting, and imitation have improved attending. Other approaches that focus instruction on the student's own specific interests may also improve attending (Patten & Watson, 2011). Older children have been seen to benefit from self-monitoring instruction (Holifield et al., 2010).

CLASSROOM SCENARIO

James

James was classified as having learning disabilities. With extra practice and resource room assistance, he was able to cope with the reading demands of his seventh-grade class; however, he continued to have difficulty remembering information for tests. A major concern of his was a test of states and capitals that was coming up in 4 weeks and was considered a test that all seventh graders must pass. He had studied on his own and even with classmates, but he had a difficult time remembering more than a few states and capitals at a time. He asked his resource teacher, Mr. Pearl, for help.

QUESTIONS FOR REFLECTION

1. What are some reasons James may be having trouble remembering states and capitals?
2. What are some other common facts that students may have difficulty remembering?
3. What would you recommend that Mr. Pearl do to help James?

MyEdLab: **Self-Check 10.1**

MyEdLab: **Application Exercise 10.1: Attention Difficulties**

Memory

Memory is a psychological process that is critically important for school learning. The great majority of items on classroom tests as well as statewide high-stakes tests require students to remember specific facts and concepts relevant to the content area (Overton, 2016). Even when teachers devote more of their test questions to such higher-order tasks as analysis, synthesis, and evaluation, students must first *remember* relevant information before they can reason effectively with this information. Effective memory therefore is a necessary requirement for school success.

Many different types of memory have been described (Radvansky, 2011). These include **semantic memory** (for facts and concepts about the world), **episodic memory** (of previous personal experience), and **everyday memory** (for information encountered in everyday experience). Memory researchers distinguish between relatively limitless **long-term memory** and **short-term memory**, which holds information only briefly (e.g., a telephone number) while it is used, until it is placed in long-term memory (e.g., by rehearsal), or until it is forgotten. Information actively processed in short-term memory (for example, in solving a two-part math problem) is referred to as **working memory** (Baddeley, Eysenck, & Anderson, 2015). Many students with special needs exhibit difficulties in one or more of these areas of memory (Henry & Winfield, 2010; Sheng, Byrd, McGregor, Zimmerman, & Bludau, 2015; Swanson, Zheng, & Jerman, 2009). However, specific strategies have been found to be effective in enhancing memory for all students, and these are described in the remainder of this chapter.

STRATEGIES FOR

IMPROVING MEMORY

ADDRESS MEMORY PRECONDITIONS   Before implementing memory strategies, consider the preconditions that must be in place for learning and memory to occur. One critical precondition is ensuring that all students are attending appropriately to instruction—students are unlikely to remember information they did not attend to in the first place. Increase attention by maintaining a well-organized and distraction-free classroom and by using the strategies discussed in the first part of this chapter.

Next, keep students motivated to learn. Even if they are paying attention, students will learn and recall little if they are not interested in or do not see the value of the content or do not believe they can succeed. Similarly, students are unlikely to remember information if they do not have a positive affective response to the content presented—that is, if they have indifferent or negative feelings toward the subject or if their morale is low (Ormrod, 2011). Finally, learning will be minimized if lessons seem boring and monotonous. Once the preconditions for good memory have been met, the following suggestions should improve students' memory.

DEVELOP "METAMEMORY"   **Metamemory** is the metacognitive process of knowing about memory. Specifically, metamemory is the process of knowing when, where, and how to remember (Dunlosky & Bjork, 2008). Many students, especially in the elementary grades, are unaware of the nature of memory and how they can learn to remember better. Activities and class discussions on memory and how it functions could help many students learn how to remember more efficiently. For example, help students understand some of the reasons we may forget, including the following:

- Fatigue when studying or when trying to remember
- Interference from such things as music, television, or distracting conversation
- Passing of time since the information was first learned
- Lack of effort when studying
- Unfamiliarity or difficulty of the content
- Failure to use an appropriate memory strategy

Likewise, memory improves with age, experience, prior knowledge, and use of memory strategies. For example, using stories and scenarios, discuss with students why children may remember, or forget, certain types of information. Discuss how memory could be improved. Training aspects of metamemory, through stories, examples, and activities, can help improve students' ability to remember (Ghetti, Mirandola, Angelini, Cornoldi, & Ciaramelli, 2011; Lucangeli, Galderisi, & Cornoldi, 1995).

USE EXTERNAL MEMORY External memory refers to the use of devices to increase memory (Dehn, 2010). In schools, external memory can be used to remember homework assignments, locker numbers, and important school dates and as a reminder to bring relevant materials home (or back to school). External memory examples include writing things down in notebooks, appointment books, smartphones, or language cards; placing things to be remembered in places where they will be seen (e.g., putting homework by the outside door); and physical prompts (e.g., attaching a note to clothing or backpack). Although external memory is not permissible in all situations (e.g., most written tests), students can be informed about appropriate times to use external memory to improve school functioning. The *Apps for Education* feature provides examples of devices for enhancing external memory.

MyEdLab:
Video Example 10.3.
This video shows an adolescent girl discussing her memory processes. Listen to the successful strategies she uses in school.

ENHANCE MEANINGFULNESS We remember meaningful information better than non-meaningful information (Baddeley et al., 2015). You can make learning more meaningful by providing specific examples that are directly relevant to your students' experiences. For example, in a presentation about how each of the three branches of government—legislative, executive, and judiciary—functions, use examples that are directly relevant to schools, and show how these examples affect students. That is, legislative bodies mandate specific laws for the establishment and operation of schools, the executive branch is responsible for enforcing these laws, and the judicial branch adjudicates and interprets these laws. Students can study and discuss how the actions of each of these branches affect their own lives personally with respect to school policy.

USE CONCRETE EXAMPLES, PICTURES, OR IMAGERY Concrete information is easier to remember than abstract information (Dunlosky & Bjork, 2008). You can enhance the concreteness of relevant content by bringing in examples of the topics being studied. For example, the study of trilobites (prehistoric marine animals) can be made more concrete by bringing in fossil specimens of trilobites, which can be used in discussions of the characteristics of trilobites. Such enriched thought, activity, and discussion can greatly improve memorization of the content.

Multimedia Presentations When specific examples cannot be brought to class, for example, because of their size, cost, or limited availability, consider enhancing visual imagery through the use of CDs, movies, or pictures. For example, DVDs and YouTube presentations provide excellent recordings of things students might not ordinarily have an opportunity to see, such as tornadoes, and can provide interesting visual coverage of such varied topics as Mayan architecture, insect life, and microorganisms. When selecting multimedia presentations, be certain that they assist directly in enhancing the concreteness of specific information to be remembered. View the presentation selectively, to focus specifically on instructional objectives (example: focusing on architecture—an instructional objective—in a media presentation on ancient Greece). Finally, do not be afraid to provide redundancy in viewing to help enhance the specific facts or concepts to be remembered. For students with visual impairments, descriptive video may be available or can be created.

Mobile Devices, Including Tablet Computers, Cell Phones, and Smartphones Improve Independence

 Students must remember many things to be successful in school, such as dates when projects are due and tests will be given, communications to be brought home for parents to read and sign, dates for field trips or special events, and class schedules. Remembering all these things may be particularly difficult for students who have difficulty with memory or organizational skills. To help these and other students, personal digital assistants (PDAs) may be useful.

Mobile devices include small handheld devices—iPads, Kindle Fire, iPods, e-readers, cell phones, and smartphones—that perform a multitude of tasks, from calendar functions, to-do lists, address books, and gaming to word processing, spreadsheets, and more. Devices range in size from very small handheld devices (palm size) to somewhat larger sizes (9.5 by 7.3 inches for the iPad). The screens also range from smaller black-and-white to larger color screens. Memory capacity also ranges from small to large. All mobile devices connect to larger computers to download and upload data, but many also have wireless capabilities. Newer devices contain cameras and cell phones and, when enabled with wireless capabilities, have the capacity to send pictures and movies via text and e-mail.

Mobile devices have enormous potential for assisting students with disabilities with organizational skills. To-do lists can contain homework assignments or tasks associated with before- and after-school activities. Ferguson, Myles, and Hagiwara (2005) successfully taught an adolescent with autism spectrum disorder to use a mobile device at home and school to monitor task-completion activities. For example, this boy experienced difficulties getting ready to leave for school in the mornings. Activities included getting dressed, washing up, taking medications, eating breakfast, getting school materials together, and leaving for school on time. Each task was associated with a time for completion, and columns were used to indicate whether tasks were completed independently or with prompts and the time of completion. All recording sheets were entered into a mobile device. Alarms were initially programmed into the mobile device to alert the boy to do an upcoming task. School-related tasks and evening home tasks were also eventually loaded into the mobile device. Either the boy's mother or school personnel checked his task completion during the intervention. Results indicated that this boy with autism learned to complete required tasks on time with the assistance of his mobile device reminders. Future

applications of mobile devices with school-aged students with disabilities appear limitless.

Apps allowing note taking, such as *Notes*, can also be written to include important content from the Common Core State Standards associated with specific memory strategies to help facilitate learning and memory for all students. As such, this type of note is an example of universal design for learning (UDL) allowing students to access the notes with strategies when needed. Many apps suitable for assisting with attention and memory have also been developed. *Best Sand Timer* (Smartphoneware) is a countdown digital sand timer that sounds alerts at prespecified intervals. This can be used to assist students with self-monitoring of attention. Other timers, including *Alarmed Reminders, Timers, and Alarm Clock* (David Mandell) and *Best Timer* (Smartphoneware), provide timers, clocks, and alarms to help with self-monitoring; in addition, numerous memory apps are available that range from *Memory Cards Lite*, a matching game by Libii; to *Memory Magic*, a twist on the concentration game by Funflip Studios; to more complex *BrainO*, a memory training game by Duolabs. All of these apps provide gamelike memory practice.

Illustrations   Using pictures, illustrations, or graphics enhances the concreteness and memorability of information and can promote memory more than animations when these images are more directly focused (Mayer, Hegarty, Mayer, & Campbell, 2005). Pictures are frequently provided in student textbooks or in PowerPoint presentations included in instructors' materials. Try to locate pictures that are directly relevant to instructional objectives—for example, illustrations that document clearly the physical characteristics of insects or the living conditions of American pioneers. The Internet is an excellent place to find all types of pictures. Ask your students to pay attention to specific aspects of the picture that are directly relevant to your instructional objectives (e.g., "Can you point out the thorax of the insect in the picture, Jackie?" or "Show me on the picture the things that make you know that it is a beetle, Bill"). Reading through diagrams carefully with students, and questioning them frequently, helps ensure that diagrams are understood (e.g., "Where is the switch in this electrical diagram, Darryl?"). After pictures and diagrams have been studied, question your students about the illustrations with their books closed, or the media turned off, so that they continue to practice studying the mental image of the illustration. Peers may assist students with visual impairments with the careful description of pictures, diagrams, or illustrations. Additionally, tactile representations of pictures can be created, as described in Chapter 4. Remember, however, that pictures may not promote learning if they are not directly relevant or if they distract students from the specific content to be learned (Uberti, Scruggs, & Mastropieri, 2003).

MyEdLab:
Video Example 10.4.
This video shows a classroom working in groups to generate memory strategies for an assignment. Listen for the different strategies from each group.

Imagery If you cannot locate relevant pictures and you feel unable to draw pictures yourself, you can encourage students to use their mental imagery to create pictures. For example, to help understand that whales are the largest animals on Earth, encourage students to imagine an enormous whale next to a much smaller elephant. Students should be encouraged to create details of the image and discuss them with the class for accuracy. For example, you could suggest that students imagine a very large whale and an elephant standing next to the whale that is only about as large as the whale is from its eye to the tip of its mouth. Students could then be asked other questions (example: "Which way is the elephant facing?") to make the image more permanent. Later, when students are asked this information ("What is the largest animal?"), they can also be asked to report how they remembered that fact. With practice, students can improve their ability to use and benefit from imagery (de la Iglesia, Bucete, & Campos, 2004).

Another way to improve the concreteness of a subject is through field trips to relevant zoos, museums, or nature areas. As with media presentations, focus your students' attention on the specific objectives to be met during field trips, and monitor that students are meeting these objectives. When appropriate, call ahead so that necessary preparations for specific students with disabilities can be made.

MINIMIZE INTERFERING INFORMATION Interference, in the form of competing or distracting stimuli, can inhibit memory (Re, De Franchis, & Cornoldi, 2010). Sometimes students forget information because interference was present or because the emphasis on the targeted content was insufficient to promote good memory. Be sure your presentation focuses directly on the content to be remembered, and avoid interfering or distracting information that is not directly relevant.

Teachers can inadvertently provide interfering information if they digress from the presentation, provide unnecessary elaboration or examples that are not directly relevant, or frequently interrupt presentations and lectures to address behavior management issues. In general, consider that information is more likely to be remembered when it is presented clearly, directly, and without unnecessary embellishment.

MyEdLab:
Video Example 10.5.
In this video, middle school students demonstrate using enactment in a science lesson. Notice what the teacher says about the process.

USE ENACTMENTS AND MANIPULATION We remember things we do better than things we hear and recite (Peterson & Mulligan, 2010). This may explain some of the positive effects typically found for hands-on science activities (Scruggs, Mastropieri, & Marshak, 2011). For example, students who have studied firsthand the effects of weak acid on the mineral calcite are more likely to remember these effects (the calcite begins to deteriorate) than if they simply read about the subject. Similarly, students are more likely to remember electric circuits they have constructed than electric circuits they have read about.

PROMOTE ACTIVE REASONING Information is better remembered if students actively participate in the learning process, particularly by actively reasoning through the content (Brigham, Scruggs, & Mastropieri, 2011; Craik & Lockhart, 1972). Answering any type of relevant question usually promotes better memory than passive listening to teacher lectures. Answering factual questions helps focus attention on the significant components of the content (e.g., "Who were the major U.S. novelists of the first half of the 19th century—Jeff?"). Answering questions that require reasoning can also help improve memory (e.g., "What do you think Hawthorne is trying to say about medical science in *Rappaccini's Daughter*—Marie?").

Provide additional coaching to assist students with disabilities when support is needed in thinking through information systematically and arriving at their own conclusions. Coach students to provide their own explanations about factual information, as in the following example:

TEACHER: The camel has a double row of eyelashes for each eye. Why does this make sense?

STUDENT: I don't know.

TEACHER: Well, let's think. What do you know about camels? For example, where do they live?

STUDENT: In the desert.

TEACHER: In the desert, good. And what is it like in the desert?

STUDENT: Hot and dry.

TEACHER: Good, what else can you think of about deserts?

STUDENT: Um, it's sandy. And windy.

TEACHER: Good, sandy and windy. So why would it make sense that camels would have two rows of eyelashes?

STUDENT: Oh! To keep the sand from blowing in their eyes.

TEACHER: To keep the sand out of their eyes, good!

Sullivan, Mastropieri, and Scruggs (1995) demonstrated that students taught with these questioning strategies remembered and understood more information than students who had been directly provided with the same information (e.g., "The camel has a double row of eyelashes for each eye to keep out the blowing sand").

INCREASE PRACTICE   Information is better remembered if it is practiced or rehearsed (Baddeley et al., 2015). Rehearsal or repetition has frequently been demonstrated to improve recall among students of all ages and ability groups. To increase the effects of practice, you should first target the information that is most important to be remembered. Then provide as much practice as possible in individual lessons by questioning. Questioning and practice after learning has been achieved is referred to as **overlearning**, and it can be an effective strategy for promoting long-term memory. Independent study skills can also promote recall and retention after content has been introduced and practiced. Review at home with family members is also an excellent way to increase recall of academic content. The *Diversity in the Classroom* feature describes involvement with families to help promote academic learning.

Increased practice can also be given as a classwide peer tutoring activity (Maheady & Gard, 2010). You might be surprised to discover how much information your students can learn in brief (e.g., 10–15 minutes), fast-paced daily sessions in which pairs of students question each other on the significant parts of lessons to be remembered, such as multiplication facts, spelling words, key facts and concepts in a geography unit, or parts of speech. You can feel even more confident about student success if you pair students with special needs with students who have demonstrated that they can be effective partners.

USE CLUSTERING AND ORGANIZATION   Information is better remembered if it is organized in some meaningful way (Baddeley et al., 2015). For example, products produced and exported by a country could be grouped as agricultural, industrial, and mining products before students practice remembering the list.

Another strategy is to incorporate content within graphic organizers, such as organizational charts, visual displays, **semantic maps**, and **relationship charts** (Dexter, Park, & Hughes, 2011). These displays present a spatially organized, as well as semantically organized, representation of the topic. For example, in a unit on Argentina, a visual display can be created that organizes the different areas of study in the unit, such as land features, natural resources, climate, history, and culture (see Figure 10.2).

Boundaries in Family and Professional Relationships

Regular practice at home is a key factor in memory of academic content. Parent and school relationships that improve communication and foster support for practice at home thus are critical to school success and may be of particular importance when working with culturally diverse families. In order to support school–family communication most effectively, it is important to be aware of boundaries. In this context, boundaries are the rules associated with the ways in which relationships function.

Nelson, Summers, and Turnbull (2004) examined the boundaries in family and professional relationships in special education. They held focus groups with parents and professionals in special education to help determine what types of boundaries were seen in their relationships.

Parents, professionals, and administrators from three states participated in individual interviews and focus groups to determine their opinions about optimal family and professional relationships. Participants represented culturally diverse groups, including 41% African American, 17% Hispanic, and 30% White, and represented a range of socioeconomic status, from lower to higher. Parents had children with a variety of disabilities of all ages, from preschool to high school and postsecondary. The participating professionals were mostly White and female (70% and 91%, respectively), most of whom (70%) were direct-service providers.

During the first of two focus-group interviews, participants were provided with guided questions to solicit information on successful and unsuccessful relationships between parents and professionals. In the second interview, participants were provided with a list of major themes from the first round and asked to respond, elaborate, or expand. Follow-up individual interviews were also held.

Findings revealed three major boundary themes: availability and accessibility, breadth of responsibility, and dual relationships. Parent responses included interest in the following:

- Flexibility for meeting times, including before- and after-school hours and weekends
- Defining responsibilities broadly to include home visits, evening phone calls, and assuming additional tasks
- Going beyond the job description to do things (e.g., visit child in hospital)
- Maintaining contact even after the child moves on to new teachers

Responses of professionals included:

- Belief that flexibility for meeting times was important, with acknowledgment of the challenges of meeting all needs with flexibility
- Support for going beyond the job description and increasing their breadth of responsibilities (Professionals reported participating in weddings, funerals, and birthday parties, but also acknowledged the challenges of "bringing the job home with them and going too far.")
- Expression of a need for setting limits with assistance or "friendships"

Both parents and professionals acknowledged the need for flexibility in meeting times and the desire to go beyond the simple job description to assist children and families. Professionals were cautiously aware of boundaries, and some expressed that they set limits for specific topics, including discussing religion and marital relationships with families. Teachers should consider the results of this study when discussing ways for improving parent–professional relationships.

PROMOTE ELABORATION Information is better remembered if it is elaborated (Bjorklund, 2012). You can provide simple elaborations to help students remember new words. For example, "To remember the meaning of *precipitation,* think of the 'sip' sound in 'precipitation': Animals can 'sip' from puddles left from precipitation." To promote elaboration, ask students to think of everything they can about a topic (e.g., "What else does buoyancy remind you of?" "How does a *buoy* remind you of *buoyancy?*"). Asking students simply to think about what a new word sounds like and how that links to its meaning can improve recall of the information. More formal forms of elaboration are known as *mnemonics,* as described in the following strategies.

Figure 10.2 Organizational Display

STRATEGIES FOR
IMPROVING MEMORY WITH MNEMONIC TECHNIQUES

Everyone remembers using specific mnemonic techniques to remember information. For example, most people remember using the acronym *HOMES* to remember the names of the Great Lakes. Many also remember the traditional rhyme "In fourteen hundred ninety-two, Columbus sailed the ocean blue" to remember the year that Columbus first sailed to America. What many people do not know is that mnemonic strategies are versatile and can be used in hundreds, even thousands, of situations to improve memory.

Another interesting research finding is that mnemonic strategies are powerful. Learning gains of as much as 2-to-1, or even 3-to-1, are common in mnemonic strategy research with a variety of students, including those with intellectual disabilities, learning disabilities, behavioral disorders or emotional disturbance, and even gifted and normally achieving students, and these gains have been found for students in the primary grades through high school (Scruggs & Mastropieri, 2013; Scruggs, Mastropieri, Berkeley, & Marshak, 2010; Wolgemuth, Cobb, & Alwell, 2008).

Nevertheless, mnemonic strategies, like any other teaching or learning strategies, have their limitations. Mnemonic techniques are most effective when they are

- used to reinforce objectives to remember specific content,
- directly taught and practiced,
- combined with comprehension instruction, and
- included with application activities.

Three specific types of mnemonic strategies—the **keyword method**, the **pegword method**, and **letter strategies**—have been successful in enhancing memory for students with memory difficulties (Scruggs et al., 2010).

USE THE KEYWORD METHOD FOR VERBAL ASSOCIATIONS The keyword method is used to strengthen the connection between a new word and its associated information. For example, *oxalis* is a *clover-like plant* (Figure 10.3). To strengthen this association, the learner is first provided a "keyword" for the new word, *oxalis*. A keyword is a word that is familiar to the learner but that sounds like the new word and is easily pictured. In the case of *oxalis*, a good keyword is *ox,* because it sounds like the first part of *oxalis* and is easy to picture. Next, a picture (or image) is created of the associates interacting together. Again

Oxalis (Ox)   Clover-like plant

Figure 10.3   Keyword Mnemonic Strategy for *Oxalis* = Clover-Like Plant

in the case of *oxalis,* the interactive picture could be a picture of an ox chewing on clover-like plants as in Figure 10.3. This picture then is shown to the student while the teacher describes the picture and strategy.

Sample teacher dialogue: *"Oxalis* is a clover-like plant. The keyword for *oxalis* is *ox* [show picture]. Remember this picture of an ox chewing clover-like plants. Remember this picture of what? Good, an ox chewing clover-like plants. Now, when I ask you for the meaning of *oxalis,* think first of the keyword, *ox.* Then think back to the picture with the ox in it, remember that the ox was chewing clover-like plants, and then retrieve the answer that *oxalis* is a clover-like plant. Now, what is *oxalis?* Good, *oxalis* is a clover-like plant. And, how did you remember that? Good, you thought of the keyword, *ox,* and remembered the picture of the ox chewing clover-like plants."

Keyword strategies have been successfully used to teach the following:

- Foreign-language vocabulary (e.g., to remember the Spanish word *pato* = duck, provide a picture of a duck with a pot—keyword for *pato*—on his head)
- Scientific terms such as *ranidae* (Figure 10.4)
- English vocabulary (e.g., for *barrister* = lawyer, provide a picture of a bear—keyword for *barrister*—pleading a case in a courtroom)
- People and their accomplishments, such as Zimmerman, the German foreign minister who sent the coded "Zimmerman Note" to Mexico that precipitated U.S. entry into World War I (e.g., show a swimmer—keyword for *Zimmerman*—carrying a note from Germany to Mexico)
- Map locations for Revolutionary War battles (e.g., a picture of a tiger—keyword for *Ticonderoga*—on a map showing where Ft. Ticonderoga is located)
- States and capitals (see the *In the Classroom* feature and Figure 10.5)

Ranidae (Rain)   Frog

Figure 10.4   Keyword Mnemonic Strategy for *Ranadae* = Common Frogs

Figure 10.5 Illustration of Mnemonic Strategy to Remember That Tallahassee (*Television*) Is the Capital of Florida (*Flower*). These strategies can be helpful for students who need assistance remembering long lists of information for school (see the *In the Classroom* feature).

Uberti et al. (2003) used mnemonic keyword strategies to improve learning and recall of new vocabulary words (e.g., *ionosphere, fjords, jettison*) prior to a story-reading activity in inclusive third-grade classes. Although the keyword strategies improved all students' recall of word meanings, students with learning disabilities benefited the most from the keyword method.

Terrill, Scruggs, and Mastropieri (2004) created keyword mnemonic strategies to help their high school students with learning disabilities learn important vocabulary words in preparation for the SAT. For example, for the vocabulary word *palatable,* the keyword was *table,* and a picture was shown of people sitting at a table enjoying a meal. A sentence under the picture stated, "All the food on the **table** tasted very good." Students learned and remembered 92% of the words they learned mnemonically and only 49% of the words they learned using more traditional activities, such as drill and worksheet activities.

Marshak, Mastropieri, and Scruggs (2011) employed mnemonic strategies with classwide peer tutoring in inclusive middle school history classes. For example, when students needed to remember that John D. Rockefeller controlled the oil industry in the 1920s, they were shown a picture of a rock (keyword for *Rockefeller*) with oil coming out of the rock. All students learned and remembered more information in the mnemonic tutoring condition; students with disabilities in the mnemonic condition remembered nearly twice as much information taught mnemonically, and overall performance was similar to that of normally achieving students.

CLASSROOM SCENARIO

James

Mr. Pearl, James's resource teacher, told James that he thought he had the solution to James's problem. He constructed keywords and simple pictures for all the states and capitals information, such as those in the *In the Classroom* feature. He spent one period with James in which he explained the keyword method and how it could be used to remember states and capitals. He demonstrated by teaching James capitals for six states. First, they practiced state names and their keywords (e.g., Arkansas—*ark*). Next, they practiced capital names and their keywords (e.g., Little Rock—*a little rock*). Then they went over the six pictures of states and capitals and practiced the strategies, as follows:

MR. PEARL: The capital of Arkansas is Little Rock. The keyword for Arkansas is...?

JAMES: Ark.

MR. PEARL: Good, and the keyword for Little Rock is...?

JAMES: A little rock.

MR. PEARL: Good! Now, remember this picture [shows picture] of Noah's ark landing on a little rock. Remember this picture of what?

JAMES: Noah's ark landing on a little rock.

MR. PEARL: [turns over the picture] And the capital of Arkansas is...?

JAMES: Little Rock.

MR. PEARL: Little Rock, good.

When James was certain he knew how the strategies worked, Mr. Pearl told him to study no more than six pictures at a time and to test himself frequently on the information he had accumulated. Mr. Pearl tested him periodically and encouraged him to keep studying.

When the time for the states and capitals test came, James received one of the highest scores in the class! The seventh-grade teacher, Mrs. Sullivan, was so impressed that she asked James how he was able to do so well. James showed her the mnemonic pictures, and Mrs. Sullivan asked Mr. Pearl if she could use the strategy with her entire class the following year.

Combine Mnemonic Strategies with Reconstructive Elaborations The term **reconstructive elaborations** refers to procedures for reconstructing information into more meaningful and memorable forms. Three types of reconstructions are acoustic (or keyword) reconstructions, symbolic reconstructions, and mimetic reconstructions (Scruggs et al., 2010; Scruggs & Mastropieri, 1992).

The keyword method (or **acoustic reconstructions**) is best used when the information to be learned is unfamiliar. Such terms as *nepenthe* and *carnelian* are excellent candidates for the keyword method because they are unfamiliar, and similar-sounding keywords (acoustic reconstructions) can be created, such as *Neptune* or *carnation*. Unfamiliar proper names (e.g., *Modigliani, Volga*) also fit into this category.

Some information is familiar to students but is more *abstract* and difficult to picture. In such cases, teachers can use **symbolic reconstructions**, in which the information is reconstructed into a symbolic picture, rather than a keyword (acoustic) picture. For example, to demonstrate the U.S. policy of neutrality before World War I, a picture could be shown of Uncle Sam (symbol for U.S. policy) watching the war in Europe and exclaiming, "It's not my fight!"

Some information is both familiar and concrete and does not need to be transformed into familiar forms. In these cases, **pictorial or mimetic reconstructions** work best. For example, a U.S. history text states that World War I soldiers stationed in unhealthy trenches were more likely to die from disease than from battle wounds. Because students probably are already familiar with *trench* and *disease*, it is not necessary to create keywords; rather, simply picture *sick soldiers* in *trenches* to demonstrate the relation. Students can simply think back to the picture and retrieve the answer (Scruggs et al., 2010). Similarly, to help students remember that sponges grow on the ocean floor, simply show a picture of sponges growing on the ocean floor.

Reconstructive elaborations are procedures for classifying important information in terms of familiarity and concreteness and developing appropriate strategies. This method can be useful in planning and developing mnemonic strategies across larger units of content.

USE THE PEGWORD METHOD FOR NUMBERED OR ORDERED INFORMATION

Pegwords are rhyming words for numbers, and they are useful in learning numbered or ordered information. Commonly used pegwords are provided in Figure 10.6 (see also Higbee, 2001). For example, to remember that insects have six legs, picture an insect crawling on sticks (pegword for *six*). To remember that spiders have eight legs, picture a spider spinning a web on a gate (pegword for *eight*).

In the Classroom

Mnemonic Strategies for Remembering the States and Their Capitals

Other strategies are possible; test these to see if they work well with your own students. Use your own artwork, student art, or clip art to create mnemonic pictures. Practice with students (or have students practice with partners) until recall is fluent and automatic. Practice recalling capitals ("What is the capital of Maryland?") as well as states ("Of what state is Bismarck the capital?").

State (Keyword)	Capital (Keyword)	Mnemonic Picture
Alabama (band)	Montgomery (monkey)	*Monkeys* playing in a *band.*
Alaska ("I'll ask her")	Juneau ("Do you know?")	Students talking: "*Do you know* the capital of Alaska?" "*I'll ask her!*"
Arizona (arid zone)	Phoenix (phone-x)	*Phone-x* (telephone) in an *arid zone* (desert).
Arkansas (ark)	Little Rock (little rock)	Noah's *ark* landing on a *little rock.*
California (calf horn)	Sacramento (sack of mint)	A *sack of mint* on a *calf's horn.*
Colorado (coloring)	Denver (den)	A child's "*coloring den.*"
Connecticut (convict)	Hartford (heart)	A *convict* in prison, with a broken *heart.*
Delaware (devil)	Dover (dove)	A *dove* on a *devil's* pitchfork.
Florida (flower)	Tallahassee (television)	A *flower* on a *television* set.
Georgia (George Washington)	Atlanta (Atlantic Ocean)	*George* Washington wading in the *Atlantic* Ocean.
Hawaii ("How are ya?")	Honolulu ("Honey, I'm Lou!")	A dialogue between two people: "*How are ya?*" "*Honey, I'm Lou!*"
Idaho ("I don't know")	Boise (boys)	Teacher and students: "What's the answer, *boys?*" "*I don't know!*"
Illinois (ill)	Springfield (spring)	A man who drank from a *spring* is feeling *ill.*
Indiana (Indian)	Indianapolis (Indianapolis 500)	An *Indian* driving a race car in the *Indianapolis* 500.
Iowa ("I owe ya!")	Des Moines (the mines)	A boss of the *mines* telling a worker, "*I owe ya!*" (his paycheck).
Kansas (can)	Topeka (top)	A *top* spinning on a *can.*
Kentucky (kennel)	Frankfort (frankfurter)	Dogs in a *kennel* eating *frankfurters.*
Louisiana (Louise and Anna)	Baton Rouge (batons and rouge)	Louise and Anna wearing *rouge* and twirling *batons.*
Maine (horse's mane)	Augusta (a gust of wind)	A *gust of* wind blowing a horse's *mane.*
Maryland (marry)	Annapolis (apple)	A couple getting *married* eating *apples.*
Massachusetts (mast)	Boston (boxer)	A *boxer* boxing in front of a ship's *mast.*
Michigan (pitch again)	Lansing (lamb)	A *lamb* at bat telling the pitcher, "*Pitch again!*"
Minnesota (mini-soda)	St. Paul (St. Paul)	*St. Paul* drinking a *mini-soda.*
Mississippi (misses)	Jackson (jacks)	Two girls (*misses*) playing with *jacks.*
Missouri (misery)	Jefferson City (chef)	A *chef* in *misery* because his cake fell.
Montana (mountain)	Helena (Helen of Troy)	*Helen of Troy* standing on a *mountain.*
Nebraska (new brass)	Lincoln (Abe Lincoln)	Abe *Lincoln* polishing *new brass.*
Nevada (new ladder)	Carson City (car city)	A man climbing a *ladder* to get to "*Car City.*"
New Hampshire (hamster)	Concord (conquer)	A *hamster* as a *conqueror.*

(continued)

Mnemonic Strategies for Remembering the States and Their Capitals—*continued*

State (Keyword)	Capital (Keyword)	Mnemonic Picture
New Jersey (jersey)	Trenton (tent)	A *tent* with a *jersey* on it.
New Mexico (Mexico)	Santa Fe (Santa Claus)	*Santa Claus* going to *Mexico*.
New York (new pork)	Albany (all baloney)	Man at deli counter: "Is this *new pork?*" Butcher: "It's *all baloney!*"
North Carolina (carolers)	Raleigh (trolley)	*Carolers* singing in a *trolley*.
North Dakota (northern coat)	Bismarck (businessman)	A *businessman* dressed in a *northern* (cold weather) *coat*.
Ohio ("Oh, hi!")	Columbus (Christopher Columbus)	A person saying, *"Oh, hi, Columbus!"*
Oklahoma (oak home)	Oklahoma City (Oak Home City)	Building an *oak home* in *"Oak Home"* City.
Oregon (ore)	Salem (sailboat)	A *sailboat* carrying *ore*.
Pennsylvania (pen)	Harrisburg (hairy)	A *hairy* (furry) *pen*.
Rhode Island (road to an island)	Providence (provide)	A builder says he will *provide a road* to the *island*.
South Carolina (southern carolers)	Columbia (column)	*Carolers* singing in front of a southern mansion with *columns*.
South Dakota (southern coat)	Pierre (pier)	A man wearing a *southern* (warm weather) *coat* standing at a *pier*.
Tennessee (tennis)	Nashville (cash)	Playing *tennis* for *cash*.
Texas (taxes)	Austin (ostrich)	An *ostrich* says, "I'll never be able to pay these *taxes!*"
Utah (you saw)	Salt Lake City (salt lake)	Dialogue: "What was it *you saw?*" "*Salt* in the *lake!*"
Vermont (Worm Mountain)	Montpelier (mountain pliers)	Removing worms from "Worm Mountain" with *mountain pliers*.
Virginia (fur)	Richmond (rich man)	A *rich man* buying a *fur* jacket.
Washington (wash a ton)	Olympia (Olympic)	An *Olympic* event: *Wash a ton* of laundry.
West Virginia (vest fur)	Charleston (King Charles)	King *Charles* wearing a *vest* made of *fur*.
Wisconsin (whisk broom)	Madison (maid)	A *maid* using a *whisk broom*.
Wyoming (Y-home)	Cheyenne (shy Anne)	*Shy Anne* lives in the *Y-home* (home shaped like a "Y").

Pegwords can be helpful in remembering the three classes of levers (based on the arrangement of fulcrum, load, and force). For example, a rake is an example of a third-class lever (with the fulcrum at one end and the force at the middle), so you can provide a picture of a rake leaning against a tree (pegword for *three*). Examples of each of the three classes of levers are shown in Figure 10.7.

Pegwords can also be used to remember lists of information, such as the following:

- The hardness levels of minerals (pegwords can also be combined with keywords for this; Scruggs, Mastropieri, McLoone, Levin, & Morrison, 1987)
- The order of U.S. presidents (Mastropieri, Scruggs, & Whedon, 1997)
- Multiplication tables (Greene, 1999; Zisimopoulos, 2010; see Chapter 14)

Number	Pegword	Number	Pegword
one	bun, sun, or gun	fourteen	forking
two	shoe	fifteen	fixing
three	tree	sixteen	sitting
four	door or floor	seventeen	severing
five	hive	eighteen	aiding
six	sticks	nineteen	knighting
seven	heaven	twenty	twin
eight	gate	thirty	dirty or thirsty
nine	vine or lion	forty	party
ten	hen	fifty	gifty
eleven	lever	sixty	witchy
twelve	elf	seventy	heavenly
thirteen	thirsting		

Figure 10.6 Pegwords

USE LETTER STRATEGIES FOR LISTS   Letter strategies can be useful for remembering lists of things (Reid, Lienemann, & Hagaman, 2013). For example, the HOMES strategy prompts recall of the names of the Great Lakes (H—Huron, O—Ontario, etc.). However, this strategy will only be effective if students are familiar enough with the names of the Great Lakes that thinking of a single letter will prompt the entire name. That is, if students are not familiar with the name *Ontario*, the letter O will not be enough to help them remember it. To ensure letter strategies are effective, ask students to rehearse the names represented by the letters.

The HOMES strategy is an example of an **acronym**. An acronym is a word formed from the first letters of the words to be remembered. Another example of an acronym is "FARM-B," which is used to remember the names of the classes of vertebrate animals (F—fish,

Figure 10.7   Pegword Mnemonic Strategy for Classes of Levers: Seesaw = First Class, Wheelbarrow = Second Class, Broom = Third Class

A—amphibian, R—reptile, M—mammal, B—bird). A picture showing vertebrate animals on a farm can help enforce this concept. In this strategy, the *B* serves no particular purpose—it is just left over after "farm" is spelled. Students need to practice this to remember it is FARM-B, and not some other letter.

Acronyms are also widely used to indicate the steps in cognitive strategies, such as the SNOW strategy for taking essay tests. Each letter in the acronym stands for a step in the cognitive procedure (S = Study the question; N = Note important points, etc.), as described in Chapter 13. Presentation of these strategies to students is usually accompanied with instruction in how to execute each of the steps indicated in the specific strategy.

In spite of their success and popularity, acronyms are not as versatile as other mnemonics. The reason for this is that many lists of things to be remembered do not contain first letters that can easily be combined into words. For example, the first letters of the planets in the solar system (M, V, E, M, J, S, U, N) cannot be easily combined into an acronym, mostly because the list contains six consonants and only two vowels. Also, it seems important to create a mnemonic that preserves the order of the planets in terms of their distance from the sun. To accomplish this, an **acrostic** can be used instead. To form an acrostic, a word is created from each first letter, and the words are arranged to make a sentence. To remember the planets, a good acrostic is, "My very educated mother just served us noodles." The first letter of each of the words in this sentence represents the planets in order of their distance from the sun. Another example of an acrostic is "My Dear Aunt Sally," which reminds students to *m*ultiply and *d*ivide before they *a*dd and *s*ubtract in a math sentence (see Chapter 15). Another version is "Please Excuse My Dear Aunt Sally," which includes *p*arenthetical expressions and *e*xponents, prior to the previously described sequence of operations. The elaborated sentence "King Philip's Class Ordered a Family of Gentile Spaniels" can promote memory of taxonomic ranks: kingdom, phylum, class, order, family, genus, and species. Both acronyms and acrostics must be practiced to ensure all aspects of the mnemonic have been mastered.

Finally, letter strategies can be combined with keywords or pegwords. For example, to promote recall of three countries in the Central Powers during World War I, provide a picture of children playing tag in Central Park. *Central Park* is a keyword for *Central Powers*, and *TAG* is an acronym for Turkey, Austria–Hungary, and Germany (Figure 10.8). To help students remember the freedoms guaranteed by the First Amendment to the Constitution, provide a picture of a rap singer who raps about buns. *Buns* is a pegword for *one*, or first, amendment, and *RAPS* is an acronym for the freedoms of religion, assembly, press, and speech.

CREATE MNEMONIC PICTURES   Although some mnemonic pictures are available commercially (e.g., see Burchers and Burchers [2007] for vocabulary materials), in most cases, teachers will have to develop their own materials. Some teachers feel that they cannot use mnemonic strategies because they are not artistically inclined and feel unable to draw

Figure 10.8   Mnemonic Strategy for Central Powers

good mnemonic pictures. However, it is not necessary that the pictures be "artistic"; rather, it is only important that they are recognizable. You can use stick figures or cutouts from magazines to create pictures. Some teachers have enlisted the assistance of an artistic student to help. However, clip art is probably the easiest way to create excellent mnemonic pictures. Software containing literally hundreds of thousands of clip-art pictures is available commercially, and clip art is sometimes included in word-processing and office software. As an alternative, a great deal of clip art is available on the Internet and can be located by typing in "clip art" followed by the picture being sought (e.g., "clip-art frog") on a search engine. Mnemonic pictures are not difficult to create, and once created, they can be used again and again to improve students' memory of important content. In some cases, as noted, materials have already been created.

COMBINE MNEMONIC STRATEGIES WITH OTHER CLASSROOM ACTIVITIES

Mnemonic strategies are not only powerful tools for improving memory, but they are also very versatile and can be incorporated with other means of instruction. For example, the keyword method was used to improve recall of important vocabulary (e.g., predator–prey; parasite–host) for hands-on science learning. Students used the keyword method to help remember important vocabulary while they engaged in hands-on activities to enhance their understanding of important scientific concepts relevant to ecosystems (Mastropieri et al., 1998).

Mnemonic strategies have also been employed in peer-tutoring configurations in high school chemistry classes. Mastropieri, Scruggs, and Graetz (2005) combined mnemonic strategies with peer tutoring to develop recall and comprehension of important science content. For example, to learn about *core* and *valence* electrons, students were shown a picture of an atom with apple cores (keyword for *core electrons*) closer to the nucleus and bridal veils (keyword for *valence*) farther away from the nucleus. Because students only used the mnemonic strategies when they were needed to enhance memory, the materials were relevant to UDL principles (Meyer, Rose, & Gordon, 2014). Students tutored each other on their recall of the fact and strategy. However, students also questioned each other on additional information about core and valence electrons, for instance, that valence electrons have higher energy levels than core electrons (see Figure 10.9; see also Marshak et al. [2011] for a social studies example).

Although mnemonic strategies have provided very powerful effects in experimental research in special and inclusive settings, they should not be considered a panacea for learning. Attend to all the strategies for improving memory, be sure to provide lots of practice, and monitor comprehension and application of learning to other domains. By using all of these strategies and evaluating progress, you can maximize each student's memory to aid in school success.

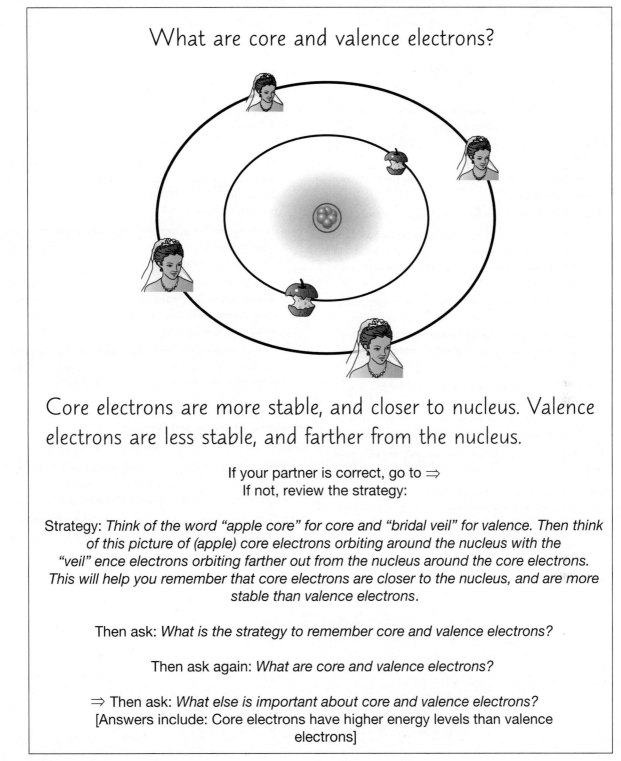

What are core and valence electrons?

Core electrons are more stable, and closer to nucleus. Valence electrons are less stable, and farther from the nucleus.

If your partner is correct, go to ⇒
If not, review the strategy:

Strategy: *Think of the word "apple core" for core and "bridal veil" for valence. Then think of this picture of (apple) core electrons orbiting around the nucleus with the "veil"ence electrons orbiting farther out from the nucleus around the core electrons. This will help you remember that core electrons are closer to the nucleus, and are more stable than valence electrons.*

Then ask: *What is the strategy to remember core and valence electrons?*

Then ask again: *What are core and valence electrons?*

⇒ Then ask: *What else is important about core and valence electrons?*
[Answers include: Core electrons have higher energy levels than valence electrons]

Figure 10.9 What Are Core and Valence Electrons?

MyEdLab: **Self-Check 10.2**

MyEdLab: **Application Exercise 10.2: Strategies to Improve Memory**

MyEdLab: **Application Exercise 10.3: Memory and Metamemory**

10 Summary

- Attention is important for success in school, and students with learning challenges often struggle with attention difficulties. Many strategies have helped students improve their attention.
  - Preconditions for improving attention in the classroom can be implemented.
  - Teach specific strategies for improving attention.
    - Simple strategies for increasing attention include asking students directly to try to pay attention better and moving closer to the student who struggles to attend.
    - Breaking activities into smaller segments, alternating among various types of class activities, allowing opportunities for movement, using reinforcement, and teaching self-recording may also help improve attention.
    - Peer assistance can be used to promote attention of students with a variety of special needs. Reinforcement of attention and instruction in self-recording strategies can also be effective.
  - Extreme cases of attention deficits and the effects of stimulant medications can be addressed.
  - Effective teaching, including the use of teacher planning and presentation variables, can help all students pay more attention in class.

- Memory is critical for success in school-related tasks. Strategies for improving the school success of students with special needs have been identified.
  - Meeting the preconditions for improving memory may help many students remember better. These preconditions include promoting attention, motivation, and positive attitudes.
  - Teaching students metacognitive awareness strategies ("metamemory") helps promote better memory strategies for all students.
  - Using pictures, enhancing meaningfulness, using activities, providing sufficient practice, and promoting active learning all help promote better memory for students with disabilities.
  - Use of mnemonic strategies such as the keyword method, the pegword method, and letter strategies helps promote learning of unfamiliar content.

PROFESSIONAL STANDARDS LINK:
Improving Attention and Memory

Information in this chapter links most directly to:

- CEC Standards: 1 (Learner Development and Individual Learning Differences), 2 (Learning Environments and Social Interactions), 5 (Instructional Planning and Strategies)
- INTASC Standards: 2 (Learning Differences), 3 (Learning Environments), 7 (Planning for Instruction), 8 (Instructional Strategies)

IMPROVING ATTENTION AND MEMORY

If students are having problems with attention, have you considered the following? If not, see the pages listed here.

STRATEGIES FOR IMPROVING ATTENTION

☐ Address the preconditions of attention with teacher effectiveness, 230

☐ Provide assistance with basic skills problems, 230–231

☐ Use direct appeal, 231

☐ Use proximity, 231

☐ Break up activities, 231–232

☐ Allow sufficient movement to reduce restlessness, 232

☐ Provide student activities, 232

☐ Use classroom peers to promote attention, 232

☐ Provide direct consequences for attention, 232–234

☐ Teach self-recording strategies, 234

STRATEGIES FOR ADDRESSING EXTREME CASES OF ATTENTION DEFICITS

☐ Provide intensive teacher-led instruction, 235

☐ Consider strengths and weaknesses of stimulant medication, 235

☐ Provide behavioral techniques, 235

☐ Promote joint attention, 235

If students are having problems with memory, have you considered the following? If not, see the pages listed here.

STRATEGIES FOR IMPROVING MEMORY

☐ Address memory preconditions, 236

☐ Develop "metamemory," 236–237

☐ Use external memory, 237

☐ Enhance meaningfulness, 237

☐ Use concrete examples, pictures, or imagery, 237–239

☐ Minimize interfering information, 239

☐ Use enactments and manipulation, 239

☐ Promote active reasoning, 239–240

☐ Increase practice, 240

☐ Use clustering and organization, 240

☐ Promote elaboration, 241

STRATEGIES FOR IMPROVING MEMORY WITH MNEMONIC TECHNIQUES

☐ Use the keyword method for verbal associations, 242–245

☐ Use the pegword method for numbered or ordered information, 245–248

☐ Use letter strategies for lists, 248–249

☐ Create mnemonic pictures, 249–250

☐ Combine mnemonic strategies with other classroom activities, 250–251

Inclusion Checklist

11

Teaching Study Skills

LEARNING OUTCOMES

After studying this chapter, you should be able to:

11.1 Demonstrate understanding of tools to develop independent learners, using personal organizational skills, and strategies for completing homework, for effective listening, and for note taking.

11.2 Demonstrate familiarity with various research and reference skills necessary for successfully completing reports or projects.

G ood study skills are necessary for success in school. Although some general education students appear to develop excellent organization and study skills independently, most students with disabilities and students at risk for failure in school can benefit from explicit instruction in organizing themselves for studying and completing assignments in a timely fashion. Research has demonstrated that individuals who are trained to use efficient study and organizational strategies perform better and are more likely to succeed in school (Dorminy, Luscre, & Gast, 2009).

CLASSROOM SCENARIO

Ravi

When Ravi, a ninth grader with learning disabilities, entered Mr. Ford's room, he was holding a stack of books with papers sticking out from all angles. Some of the papers were bent, some were folded, and some were slightly torn, but all books had been covered with brightly colored paper. As he approached the desks, his glasses were sliding down toward the end of his nose, and he slightly bumped the edge of one of the tables. Before you could blink your eyes, everything that had been in his arms was strewn all over the floor. Ravi smiled sheepishly as he began to pick up his belongings.

Somewhere in that pile of books and papers there was evidence of Ravi's attempts at completing his homework. When Mr. Ford asked him about it, Ravi said, "I've done some of the homework, but I can't seem to find it at the moment. . . ." This was a typical day for Ravi. Although he usually attempted his assignments, he either could not find them or he would forget about his homework and appear confused when asked about it—almost as if it were the first time he had heard of the assignment.

QUESTIONS FOR REFLECTION

1. Why is Ravi not able to improve his organizational skills?
2. Do you think external rewards would help Ravi? Why or why not?
3. What interventions might help Ravi?

Learning strategies help all students study more effectively, but they especially benefit students with disabilities such as those with autism, learning disabilities, and emotional disabilities. This chapter describes how to help your students become more personally organized and efficient at planning for homework, developing effective listening and note-taking skills, and learning to use outlining and guided notes. In addition, strategies are presented for using libraries, writing reports, completing long-term assignments and projects, and studying for later retrieval.

Tools for Developing Independent Learners

Study skills are tools for learning. Several study skills books are available (e.g., Carter, Bishop, & Kravits, 2011; Greene, 2004); many of these books present a number of study skills and strategies with the expectation that students will master all strategies with minimal instruction. Many students with disabilities, however, do not have good study and learning strategies and experience difficulties when trying to use these strategies independently. These students may require extensive explicit instruction in learning strategies, controlled practice, and feedback before they are able to execute them successfully and independently. Teaching students to become independent learners and thinkers includes providing "tools for learners" in self-instruction, self-monitoring, self-questioning, and self-reinforcement (Deshler & Schumaker, 2006; Reid, Lienemann, & Hagaman, 2013).

MyEdLab:
Video Example 11.1.
In this video, student expectations are clearly stated for students reviewing the morning routine.

STRATEGIES FOR

DEVELOPING PERSONAL ORGANIZATIONAL SKILLS

Personal organizational skills include using time schedules; understanding class and school schedules; using a daily, weekly, and monthly planner; and being organized for completing homework assignments. These skills are what some experts call good self-management skills. Other organizational skills include knowing how to analyze tasks required for assignments and optimizing performance and studying time (MacArthur, 2012). Provide general information about study skills to your entire class, and arrange small groups of students who need additional instruction in study skills. Special education teachers can work with you and provide instruction in these strategies for those who need it. Finally, you may decide to team-teach groups of students who need to learn these strategies. However you present them, study and organizational skills will reap huge benefits in student performance.

POST AND REVIEW CLASS AND TIME SCHEDULES   All grade levels follow systematic schedules. Present the schedules to students with disabilities in clear, comprehensible language to ensure they are prepared for each segment of the school day.

Many elementary teachers write daily agendas or schedules on the board that contain all daily class activities, such as the one shown in Figure 11.1. The list can include reminders to bring specific materials for various classes and brief descriptions of homework assignments.

8:00–8:10	Get ready for the school day (sharpen pencils, use restrooms)
8:10–8:15	Complete scrambled sentence activity
8:15–9:15	Reading
9:15–9:40	Recess and restroom breaks
9:40–10:40	Mathematics
10:40–11:15	Writing and Language Arts
11:15–12:15	Lunch and Recess
12:15–1:15	Science
1:15–2:15	Social Studies
2:15–2:45	Physical Education (Tues–Thurs)

BRING SHORTS and SNEAKERS for GYM Tomorrow!!!

Music (Mon)

Art (Wed–Fri)

Figure 11.1   Sample Elementary School Daily Agenda

Black Day Schedule	
Daily Order	Period
1. First	1. English, room 204
2. Second	2. Phys. Ed., gym
3. Third	3. Algebra I, room 105
4. Fourth	4. Study Hall, cafeteria

Red Day Schedule	
Daily Order	Period
1. First	5. Biology, room 209
2. Second	6. U.S. Government, room 115
3. Third	7. Band, music room
4. Fourth	8. Spanish, room 215

Figure 11.2 Sample Secondary School Schedule

Future events also can be highlighted. For example, highlighting special classes such as art, music, and physical education, can help students remember to bring sneakers and shorts for gym class or instruments for music class. Although many students may not require these reminders, students who do need them will not feel singled out when you make the information available to all.

Secondary schools require students to see many teachers throughout the school day. Some schools have a constant number of daily periods throughout the week, whereas other schools have rotating schedules—referred to as block scheduling—that alternate daily. Although they allow longer class periods, block systems can be confusing. You may need to review and re-review schedules with some students. Figure 11.2 shows an example of a block schedule containing eight periods, including black days (periods 1–4) and red days (periods 5–8).

How to Start At the beginning of a new year or semester, you may need to describe for students how to locate rooms within the school. This is especially important in very large buildings, where one floor looks similar to another. One idea might be to make yourself, a peer, or an aide available to meet students before or after school to go over their class schedules and walk the routes with them. Follow up by meeting students after each class when needed and walk with them to the next class until students demonstrate confidence about where they are and where they need to be at what time. All students wish to appear as competent as their peers seem to be, and although they might be confused about building layouts and schedules, they may not want to risk embarrassing themselves by asking for help. Your awareness and subtle ways of keying into students' needs can enhance students' self-perceptions.

Don't Forget Lockers As students move from class to class, they may need to visit their lockers for books or materials. This can be particularly challenging for some students with disabilities because the use of lockers requires extra time and mental and physical challenges. If students have trouble remembering the combination, practice with the students, or suggest they write the combination (secretly) on a wallet-size card or mobile device for easy access until they master the information.

Provide extra time and instructions for opening lockers. Some students have been known to carry everything (all books, notebooks, lunch, and coats) around all day simply because they could not open their lockers. Another student pretended she hated physical education and refused to participate in gym, when she actually did not know how to open her locker that contained her gym clothing. Finally, note the accessibility of lockers. Lockers or locks that are placed too high or low can cause unnecessary frustrations, especially for some students with physical limitations.

Clearly Post and Review Schedule Changes   Some students, such as those with autism, do not handle changes well, but if they are prepared ahead of time, they will be more likely to adjust to the changes (see also the IRIS Center module titled "Autism Spectrum Disorder: An Overview for Educators," at http://iris.peabody.vanderbilt.edu/). For example, explain what will happen if you are absent from school and a substitute teacher is assigned to take over the class. Believe it or not, some students with emotional disabilities may be very upset when you are absent! These changes may be particularly difficult for some students if you are gone for a long period of time, such as for an extended medical or maternity leave. When students are informed ahead of time, these transitions can be handled more smoothly.

At the middle and secondary levels, it is common for students to have different teachers for each subject. Each teacher may establish different class routines and expectations. Many students with disabilities require extra help learning the routines that are used in each teacher's classroom (Mastropieri & Scruggs, 2002). For example, some teachers may require students to be seated when the class bell rings, whereas others may require that students only be inside the room when the bell rings. Encourage students to write down any specific expectations and routines for each class and teacher. Take care to show students your own class expectations, schedules, and routines, and provide support for them while they are learning all of the new routines simultaneously. A little role-playing or memory game might help. For example, say the name of a teacher to a group of students and ask them to quickly tell you the unique expectations that teacher has.

USE STRATEGIES FOR DAILY, WEEKLY, AND MONTHLY PLANNING   Many adults use paper or electronic daily planner calendars that contain space for weekly and monthly entries. These planners are ideally suited to keeping track of both long- and short-term school assignments. Show students a variety of planner formats, and have them select one that meets their needs. Show them how most effective people in all disciplines use some type of planner to help keep organized. Ask other teachers, the principal, parents, and businesspeople from the community to visit your class and share the way they plan and schedule events.

Explain the differences between long- and short-term planning. Provide examples of how studying time needs to be divided among subject areas and across types of assignments (Rafoth, 2006). Provide examples of "to-do" lists, and show students how to prioritize them. Some people like to do the easiest thing on the list first; others prefer to get the hardest item out of the way first. Figure 11.3 shows a sample planner and to-do list that might work for individual content areas. Encourage students to discuss optimal ways of proceeding for themselves. Students with disabilities may need specific examples of each step spelled out for them. For example, general education students with good study habits:

1. review their assignment notebooks,

2. prioritize what needs to get accomplished,

Student _____				_____ Quarter	
Subject	To do	Assigned on	Due date	Turned in on	Parent initials

Figure 11.3   Sample Planner and To-Do List

3. set goals of finishing tasks for themselves, and

4. work hard to accomplish those goals.

Conversely, students with disabilities may be forgetful and may not deliberately plan their activities. Some may need teachers to complete sample planners for them and take them step by step through the thinking involved in figuring out what to do.

USE TASK ANALYSIS TO ORGANIZE ASSIGNMENTS   **Task analysis** is the process of taking a large task or assignment, breaking it into subcomponent smaller tasks, and estimating task completion time for each subcomponent. Teach students to write out the assignment, decide what must be done, sequence the steps of what must be done, and estimate the amount of time necessary to complete each step. For example, a biology teacher may make an assignment that students read pages 264–277 in the textbook, write a summary paragraph, and answer questions 13–21 at the end of the chapter. A task analysis may reveal that this requires the student to complete the following steps:

- Locate the textbook and a quiet area to work.
- Find the relevant text pages and read them carefully, while highlighting or taking notes.
- Write a summary paragraph based on reading and notes.
- Locate the relevant questions at the end of the chapter.
- Answer all questions, referring to text and notes.
- Check all work and be certain all components of the assignment are completed.

Figure 11.4 shows a planning task sequence for preparing a book report.

TEACH STRATEGIES FOR HOMEWORK COMPLETION   Homework is assigned at virtually all grade levels but increases in regularity and complexity with each grade level (Langberg, Epstein, Ginio-Herrera, Becker, Vaughn, & Altaye, 2011; Reid et al., 2013). Homework provides opportunities for students to develop fluency with the information being taught and to develop organizational and self-study skills.

Some homework assignments may need to be reduced in size and scope for students with disabilities, who may need more time to process and complete the same activities. Power, Werba, Watkins, Angelucci, and Eiraldi (2006) identified two main areas of homework problems: (a) homework inattention or avoidance and (b) not attending to rules or procedures. They also found that students with special needs exhibited significantly more homework problems. Because performance on homework is often included in computing semester grades, consider modifying the amount and type of homework or the grading procedures for students with disabilities (Bryan & Burstein, 2004). Figure 11.5 lists some assignments and possible adaptations.

Most students with disabilities find it helpful to record their assignments in an assignment notebook. Include spaces for teachers' and parents' signatures to help ensure that your students asked someone to verify whether assignments were completed accurately. This also keeps parents informed so that they can monitor homework progress daily. Most parents likely would appreciate a letter requesting their assistance in establishing homework procedures and arranging an environment conducive to studying at home (see Figure 11.6). Myles, Ferguson, and Hagiwara (2007) reported that an adolescent student with Asperger syndrome greatly improved in recording homework assignments by using a personal electronic device.

When assigning homework, provide clear instructions, and always explain the purpose of the assignment. Write assignments in the same location daily so that students can find them easily and copy them accurately into their assignment notebooks. Such predictable, consistent practices can help students establish patterns that promote success.

Several teaching practices can help students complete their homework successfully (see also Jakulski & Mastropieri, 2004; Vaughn & Bos, 2015):

- Give clear, concise directions for completing assignments; establish due dates that are reasonable and clearly communicated. Assignment boards and student recorders also may be helpful (see Ness, Sohlberg, & Albin, 2011).

	Sun	Mon	Tues	Wed	Thurs	Fri	Sat
Week 1							
Week 2							
Week 3							
Week 4							

Assigned Date _____ Due Date _____ Time Available _____ days

1. Go to library and select book. (1 day)
2. Count chapters or pages in book and determine the number of chapters or pages that should be read daily (e.g., 13 chapters or 208 pages). Adjust according to your reading rate and the number of days available. For example, if you can read 1 chapter per day you will need 13 days. If you can read 16 pages a day, you will need 13 days to read the book.
3. Brainstorm book report outline. (1 day)
4. Organize outline from brainstorming activity. (1 day)
5. Fill in details on outline. (1 day)
6. Write draft book report using outline. (2 days)
7. Proof and revise first and final draft of book report. (2 days)
8. Write final version and proof carefully. (2 days)

Total number of days necessary to complete assignment—20

	Sun	Mon	Tues	Wed	Thurs	Fri	Sat
Week 1		Go to library and select book	Count pages and chapters and figure out how much to read daily	Read	Read	Read	Read
Week 2		Read	Read	Read	Read	Read	Read
Week 3		Read	Read	Read	Brainstorm book report outline	Organize outline from brainstorming	Fill in outline details
Week 4		Write first draft	Write first draft	Proof and revise first draft	Proof and revise final draft	Write, edit, and proof final version	Write and proof final version

Figure 11.4 Task Planning for a Book Report

- Describe any materials necessary to complete each assignment. For example, will students need to take their textbooks home with them? Will they need to go to the library and sign out materials before they can complete the work? Will they need to bring materials to class?

- If you provide a sample of the homework assignment, complete it together as a class, be specific, and ensure that students understand what they are to do by asking two or three students to repeat or explain the directions.

- Anticipate any areas of difficulty with an assignment and attempt to provide extra clarification.

Subject	Assignment	Adapted Assignment
Spelling	Study 20 words.	Study 10 prioritized words.
Math	Complete 30 word problems.	Complete 15 prioritized word problems.
Reading	Read 2 chapters and write a summary.	Read 1 chapter and record a summary of the information; or listen to an audio recording of the 2 chapters and record a summary of both chapters.
Social Studies	Read section 3 in chapter 4 and answer the 20 questions at the end of the section.	Read section 3 in chapter 4 and answer the even-numbered questions at the end of the section (half the questions).
Science	Write a summary of the experiment completed during today's lab.	Record a summary of the experiment completed in today's lab (or use voice to text app).

Figure 11.5 Homework Assignments and Possible Adaptations

Date _____

Dear Parent,

As we begin this school year I want you to know how delighted I am to have your child, _____, in my class. I am looking forward to meeting you at our first Open House. Please try to come and bring any questions you may have about this school year with you.

I would like to explain to you some of the procedures and requirements of my class so you will have a better understanding of what is expected of your child. I usually assign homework nightly. Most nights the assignments are rather short and can be completed within 20 minutes. A few times throughout the year, however, I assign longer-term projects that will require your child to work a little bit each night over a period of about a month to complete the project. Examples of the longer-term projects include the following:

- Book reports
- Library research projects
- Models of inventions
- Science fair projects
- Interviews with business people from the community

I would like to request some assistance from you to ensure that your child successfully completes his or her assignments. Every afternoon or evening, **please ask your son or daughter to show you the assignment notebook.** Ideally your child should take the initiative and bring the notebook to you. Please initial and date that day's assignments. That will let me know that you have seen the assignment and ensure that it has been successfully completed or that an honest attempt was made to complete it. Some of you may want to see the assignment book and completed assignment, while others of you may wish to see only the assignment notebook.

Second, it would be most helpful if you could establish a **regular space** for your child to complete his or her assignments. That way, when he or she arrives home from school, all necessary school materials can be placed in a specific location and kept all together. Establishing a regular place also helps ensure that the materials are together and will not be forgotten when leaving for school the next morning.

Third, it would be beneficial to **establish a regular time for your child to do his or her homework.** I realize that this can be difficult because of extra-curricular activities. However, establishing regular homework times on Mondays, Tuesdays, Wednesdays, Thursdays, and Saturdays or Sundays can help illustrate the importance of maintaining responsibility for completing homework.

Finally, please feel free to add notes to the assignment notebook if you wish to communicate any information to me. If you have questions concerning your child's performance or understanding of the assignments, I will do my best to help.

If students don't complete or turn in assignments, they will lose points from their grade and be given after-school detention after missing three assignments.

Thanks so much for your help with this important matter. Please feel free to contact me by telephone or e-mail.

Regards,

Figure 11.6 Homework Procedures: Request for Home–School Cooperation

- Explain how students can get help if they confront problems. Perhaps some students could be trained as "homework assistants" who could be contacted in the evenings by telephone or text message until 8 o'clock. With permission, distribute a list of names and phone numbers of these homework assistants.

- Establish a regular time for collecting and distributing assignments. Establish special locations for dropping off and picking up completed and corrected assignments.

- Consistently collect, grade, and return assigned work. When teachers neglect to collect or return graded assignments, some students take away the message that homework is unimportant to them.

- Coordinate assignments with other teachers. Your students with disabilities will benefit greatly from any shared planning you do with your co-teachers to avoid scheduling several exams on a single day or overlapping longer-term assignments.

- Arrange classroom incentives for completing and turning in homework. Some teachers establish either individual or class rewards to encourage timely completion of homework. For example, Lynch, Theodore, Bray, and Kehle (2009) reported substantial improvement in the homework completion of students with disabilities when group rewards (e.g., stickers, extra recess, points toward a pizza party) were provided for homework completion.

- Remember to assign projects that are within the capability levels of all students. Homework is an opportunity to practice previously acquired skills, develop fluency, and practice applying these skills to new contexts.

MyEdLab:
Video Example 11.2.
Clearly stated expectations, both in the classroom and regarding homework, are needed for student success, as is demonstrated in this video.

Clearly State Class Expectations Provide students with specific expectations for completed work. Explain how you intend to evaluate work, and provide examples of what you consider to be "model" assignments and insufficiently completed assignments. Is it acceptable, for example, to turn in a page torn from a spiral notebook? May assignments be completed in pencil? Will you accept incomplete assignments, or will those be returned with the grade of "F"? Creating a checklist for students to keep in their notebooks would be helpful.

Cooperative Homework Teams O'Melia and Rosenberg (1994; see also Bryan & Burstein, 2004) created cooperative homework teams (CHTs) to help middle school students with learning and behavioral disabilities complete their mathematics homework more frequently and more accurately. Students in CHT classes were assigned to three- and four-member heterogeneous CHTs. During the first period of class, immediately after the opening activity, the teams met, and a "checker" who had been assigned to each team on a rotating basis graded the assignments for the day, using teacher-made answer sheets. The grades were recorded, and the assignments were returned to the students with corrections. Checkers then turned in all of the corrected homework. After 8 weeks of this intervention, results indicated that students who had participated in CHTs had a 74% rate of homework completion, compared with a 55% rate in comparison classes. Further, CHT students were 30% more accurate in the assignments they did complete.

Similarly, Houser, Maheady, Pomerantz, and Jabot (2015) described a "Radical Raceway" intervention using cooperative homework teams. Teams of five students matched overall for ability were created, which then met at the end of class to review and discuss homework. Teams with the highest completion or accuracy averages were allowed to advance their race cars two spaces ahead on the race track, whereas second-place teams advanced their cars ahead one space. The first team across the finish line was allowed to select a group reward. Houser et al. reported that when the intervention was in effect, students completed 86% of homework assignments, with an average of 78% correct. When the intervention was not in effect, student completion was just 57%, with 51% correct.

Assignment Completion Strategy Hughes, Ruhl, Schumaker, and Deshler (2002) successfully taught middle school students with learning disabilities an assignment completion strategy that was successfully used in their inclusive general education classes. The strategy was referred to as "PROJECT" and focused on the sequence of skills necessary for assignment completion. As students worked on the strategy, they completed three forms—a monthly planner, a weekly study schedule, and an assignment sheet—all of which were included in an assignment notebook. PROJECT was employed as a first-letter mnemonic device to represent the following steps:

- **P**repare your forms (fill in monthly planners and weekly study sheets).
- **R**ecord and ask (record the assignment on the assignment sheet, using abbreviations and circling appropriate words [e.g., "write"], and ask questions for clarification).
- **O**rganize (break assignment into parts, estimate number of study sessions, schedule sessions, and take materials home).
- **J**ump to it (overcome task avoidance; obtain needed materials).
- **E**ngage in the work (complete assignment and consult parents).
- **C**heck your work (evaluate quality of work and circle a "quality grade," e.g., A, B, C, on the assignment sheet).
- **T**urn in your work.

Students were trained in 30-minute sessions, four times per week, for 4 weeks. At the end of the training, it was observed that eight of the nine students mastered the strategy and improved significantly in homework completion rates, quality of completed assignments, and quarterly grades (see also Hampshire, Butera, & Hourcade, 2014).

Family involvement can also improve homework completion and improve study skills. The *Diversity in the Classroom* feature provides additional information on increasing family involvement.

STRATEGIES FOR
PROMOTING LISTENING SKILLS

Listening skills are critical for school success (Wong, 2015). Because teachers provide oral directions and instructions continually throughout the school day, students who have good listening skills can follow along, understand what is expected of them, and be successful in school. Many students, however, especially younger elementary-age children and students with disabilities and attention deficit disorders, lack good listening skills. This hinders their ability to succeed in classes (Deshler & Schumaker, 2006).

ADDRESS REQUISITE LISTENING SKILLS Verify whether students have the appropriate skills for listening by using the teacher checklist in the *In the Classroom* feature on page 265. First, determine if students can hear the speaker adequately. Judge whether a student's position in the classroom interferes with hearing abilities. For example, does the problem exist when information is presented over the loudspeaker or during multimedia presentations? Does it exist during teacher presentations in the classroom, in large-group sessions in auditoriums, or outdoors at recess? Difficulties in hearing in any of these environments may indicate that a referral is needed for a hearing test. Specific plans can be devised to assist students, providing them with various seating positions to meet their needs. Have students sit near audiovisual equipment or near the front of large auditoriums, or ask peer assistants to help by repeating directions given outdoors.

Second, determine whether an attention problem exists. To help students come to attention and to encourage active listening from the start, try pairing a visual cue with the beginning of the listening activity. For example, flip a light switch in the room or on the projector to alert students that the presentation is about to begin. Pair a teacher movement, such as walking and standing still in the front of the room for a few seconds, with the beginning of new lectures. Remember that attending may be a function of the degree to which you make your presentations interesting. Be sure to use interesting and engaging materials. Miller (2003), for example, explained how the listening skills of English language learners can be addressed by using culturally relevant, authentic materials.

Third, determine if students understand the speaker. Unfamiliar accents or dialects can be difficult to understand, or the vocabulary and sentence structure may be beyond the lexicon level of students with disabilities. Ask students to repeat what was just said in their own words.

Increasing Family Involvement

Communicating effectively with families can help promote the use of study skills at home. Create a climate of trust and mutual respect with families to increase the involvement of families representing diverse cultural and linguistic groups (see Banks, 2015). Ways to build and strengthen this relationship can be established by opening communication lines with all families. When families see that their partnerships and participation are valued in all aspects of school life, they will be more likely to feel that their cultural diversity is respected.

Learn about your students' sociocultural climates at home and in their local communities. Have students share information about their home lives to help familiarize you with their families. Create family-life history booklets using multimedia that students can print and share at school and home. Use this information to enhance instructional planning and to prepare for working with families representing diverse cultural backgrounds.

Determine optimal strategies for working with students and families for whom English is a second language. Effective strategies exist for easing communication challenges with individuals who may not use English at home. Use interpreters whenever possible, but also ask students for strategies for communicating with their families. Frequently, students can supply you with additional insights for communicating with their family members. For example, it may be beneficial to have the students with their family members at parent meetings. Students may be able to help bridge gaps in communication and help build family members' confidence in working with teachers. For additional information on working with dual-language learners and their families, see the 2015 IRIS Center Dual Language Learners in the Classroom module (http://iris.peabody.vanderbilt.edu/).

You may need to preteach difficult vocabulary and concepts before students can benefit from lecture activities.

Fourth, judge whether students can recognize and select important points from lectures or presentations. Can they follow the sequence of ideas? Do they understand organizational cues used during a lecture, such as *first*, *second*, *third*, *next,* and *then?* Teach students that important points are often introduced at the beginning of lectures and then explained and elaborated on separately after organizational cue statements.

TEACH LISTENING SKILLS   Some students require extra practice in learning how to listen. Design some fun lessons in which students are motivated to learn to listen (see also Spooner & Woodcock, 2010). Keep the activities short, and try the following:

- Explain the purpose of a listening activity, present information, and then have older students repeat what was presented in their own words. Have younger students act out the sequence of events.

- Model and demonstrate the use of key words and phrases, such as *first, second, third,* and *next.* Give students cards containing cue words, and direct them to raise the appropriate cards when they hear them.

- Have students identify important phrases, and ask them to tell you when they hear relevant sequences or specific details in the presentations.

- Demonstrate how certain verbal (e.g., "I want you to remember . . .") and nonverbal cues (e.g., extra-long pauses) can highlight important information. Have students act out or tell their neighbors the listening cues they hear during a presentation.

- Use topics that are interesting and motivating and include favorite characters from shows, musicians, words from songs, or interviews with famous athletes.

- Give students advance organizers of talks, and have them generate questions they would like answered about the upcoming talk.

In the Classroom

Checklist for Effective Listening Skills

Student must be able to:

_____ Hear the speaker

     _____ Teacher's voice

     _____ Loudspeaker

     _____ Multimedia presentations

     _____ Auditorium presentations

     _____ Outdoors at recess or field trips

_____ Attend to the speaker

     _____ Come to attention

     _____ Sustain attention

     _____ Understand the speaker

_____ Understand the vocabulary

_____ Recognize and select important points

_____ Follow a sequence of ideas

_____ Understand organizational cues (*first, then*)

_____ Attend to transitional statements ("Next I will")

_____ Understand verbal emphasis cues ("This is important")

_____ Understand nonverbal cues (teacher moves to the front of the room)

- Give students several questions before a presentation, and have them try to figure out answers to the questions during the talk.

- Ask students to relate a presentation to their own knowledge by asking them what else this talk reminded them of or what else they know about the topic.

- Give outlines or partially completed outlines and study guides to students before listening activities.

- Have students follow along, and instruct them to try to listen for "missing" information.

- Segment your presentation into three or four smaller parts. Stop after each segment, and have students summarize the major points from each segment and summarize the entire presentation at the conclusion.

When practicing listening skills, emphasize how it is necessary to try to remember the most important information and the sequence of events. Have students generate questions to use as listening guides. For example, "What is the purpose of this lecture?" or "What should I remember from this presentation?" These activities will prepare students for taking notes during lectures. There are, however, some ways you can adjust any lecture or use direct instruction for lower grade levels to effect better listening, as discussed next.

Adjust Lectures   You can include simple techniques during lectures to help facilitate listening and note taking for students (Carter et al., 2011):

- Begin presentations by stating the overall objectives, such as, "Today I will be talking about a, b, and c."

- Include key words, and emphasize their use during the presentations by saying in a louder voice, "This is *very* important," "Here are the three major points," "Listen to this and see if you can _____," or "There are five explanations for this event, and they are. . . ."

- Write key points on a PowerPoint slide, chalkboard, or dry-erase board while presenting.

- Adjust the pace of the presentation to accommodate students who are taking notes.

- Present schematic diagrams that explain complex concepts or use concrete manipulatives whenever possible to accompany verbal information.

- Stop frequently and encourage students to ask questions about the presented information, and have them summarize the content to peers.
- Ask students to predict what a test on the material might include.
- Include "errors" in your talk, and ask students to try to find the errors.

Finally, check with any students you suspect might need assistance to see if they obtained the necessary content or if they have any questions. Schedule extra help sessions, office hours, or study sessions when needed.

PLAN FOR SPECIAL LISTENING PROBLEMS   Sometimes there are special problems encountered by students with disabilities during oral presentations. Some of these include the following:

- The pace of the presenter is too rapid.
- The amount of information given is too great.
- Students lack prior knowledge on the presentation topic.
- The language is too difficult.
- Students have difficulties processing and organizing information.

Some presenters speak too rapidly for students with disabilities or students learning English as a second language to comprehend. When this occurs, ask lecturers to slow down and write major points on a PowerPoint slide or dry-erase board while speaking. The act of writing while speaking may slow the rate of presentation sufficiently for students. It is appropriate to ask presenters to repeat information to provide an additional opportunity for students to hear the same information. Record important presentations that are presented rapidly, place recordings on reserve or at a listening center, and encourage students to listen to the recordings again for review. If variable-speed audio recorders are available, students can play recordings at a comfortable speed for themselves.

The following scenario describes what Mrs. Goodwin does to help her students with disabilities become more familiar with new vocabulary in their general education classes.

CLASSROOM SCENARIO

Mrs. Goodwin

Mrs. Goodwin, a special education teacher, provides all her elementary students with lists of vocabulary that will be covered in future units. She passes the lists out a couple of weeks before the unit is introduced. All students read the words to her and to their parents daily. This familiarizes students with upcoming vocabulary so that when they hear the words in general education classes, they are already familiar with them. Knowing the vocabulary often puts students with special needs one jump ahead of general education students and thus builds self-esteem. The general education teachers tell Mrs. Goodwin that because of this extra practice, students with disabilities are better able to keep up with classwork in the new units. Students also seem to enjoy using the vocabulary lists.

QUESTIONS FOR REFLECTION
1. How would you decide which words should be targeted for practice?
2. What would be the best ways to communicate with parents about the vocabulary-learning task?
3. Could you employ a similar technique for material other than vocabulary?

Finally, some students have severe processing and organizing difficulties during listening activities. These students may require oral information to be repeated slowly before they are able to comprehend it. Handouts containing major points as well as assistance from special education teachers and speech and language specialists can provide students extra review and practice on the information covered. Also, enlist the help of peer assistants, siblings, and parents to provide additional review and practice at home. Don't forget to use the PASS variables to determine whether all information presented is essential for all students and that it is appropriately adapted, instructed, and evaluated.

STRATEGIES FOR

TEACHING NOTE-TAKING SKILLS

Note taking provides students with a greater depth of processing of information and can be used to review information presented orally (Carter et al., 2011). Note-taking skills become increasingly important as grade levels increase (Deshler & Schumaker, 2006), and secondary teachers expect students to have good note-taking skills. However, many students, particularly those with disabilities, are not skilled in taking good notes and can benefit from instruction on effective note taking (Boyle, 2010; Boyle & Forchelli, 2014; see also the *Research Highlight*). Several important skills are critical for successful note taking and are listed in the teacher checklist in Figure 11.7 (see also Boyle, 2007). Determine which skills students need help with and ensure that they acquire these skills.

MyEdLab:
Video Example 11.3.
This video describes a strategy for guided notes, which can be used in any type of classroom situation.

TEACH NOTE-TAKING SKILLS AND STRATEGIES Teach students that the purpose of notes is to facilitate recall and comprehension of information presented during lectures. Reviewing notes regularly, and particularly just before an exam, can increase a student's chances for success (Carter et al., 2011).

Be Prepared Helping students learn how they can be prepared to take notes will promote more self-sufficiency. Be sure they have the right type of paper and pencils or pens, or technology, to take notes. Encourage students to select the type of paper or pen that is best for them. Allowing students to select their own note-taking materials may help motivate them during note-taking activities. Tell students to write the date and topic of the lecture at the top of their papers (Boyle, 2007).

Teach How to Write Short Summaries Showing students how to write summary ideas rather than entire sentences assists them in becoming better at taking notes. Demonstrate with examples of good notes and poor notes. Good notes contain major ideas in students' own words and can be used for studying. Poor notes contain lots of unnecessary words, such as *the, if, and,* or *but,* or entire verbatim sentences. These practices may make it much more difficult to take notes efficiently, as well as result in notes that are difficult to study.

Does the student have:

_____ Listening skills?

_____ Handwriting skills?

    _____ Is the student's handwriting legible?

    _____ Can the student write rapidly enough?

_____ Keyboarding skills?

    _____ Can the student type fast enough?

    _____ Are computers and power sources readily available?

Can the student:

    _____ Determine the purpose of lectures?

    _____ Determine a plan of organization for notes?

    _____ Summarize and relate main ideas?

    _____ Write down main points?

    _____ Use abbreviations?

Does the student:

    _____ Read and revise notes?

    _____ Study notes?

Figure 11.7 Checklist for Prerequisite Skills for Note Taking

Note Taking Skills of Middle School Students

Success in content-area classes requires listening to lectures and recalling important content from those lectures. Teachers may emphasize important vocabulary, note critical points (e.g., Common Core content), and summarize content during lectures. Note taking can help organize and maintain permanent products from lectures while students process lecture content. Note taking, however, is not always an easy task for all students. Note taking requires metacognitive skills, attention, memory, and expressive writing skills. Boyle and Forchelli (2014) compared the note-taking skills of middle school students with learning disabilities, average achievers, and

high achievers. All students listened to and watched a science lecture video and were asked to take notes during the presentation. Following the presentation, notes were collected, and the students were given a 10-item quiz covering the content. In addition, all notes were scored to determine the number of total words, cued lecture points, all lecture points, and vocabulary words recorded by each student. The results indicated that students with learning disabilities struggled to complete notes containing key points and vocabulary compared with higher-achieving peers. For example, higher-achieving students recorded an average of 130.48 words, average-achieving students recorded 85.75 words, and students with learning

disabilities recorded an average of 44.97 words. The results from this research document the need to teach students with learning disabilities successful note-taking skills. Although this research was conducted with students with learning disabilities, the findings may be generalizable to other disability categories, such as individuals with autism and those with attention challenges.

QUESTIONS FOR REFLECTION

1. How do students normally learn how to take effective notes?
2. What can be done to improve note-taking skills for students who struggle?
3. What would be good ways to support students while they learn note-taking skills?

Ask Questions for Clarification   Encouraging students to ask you to repeat information or clarify the major purpose of lessons helps you monitor whether they know what to write in their notes. A good way to start is to have students ask what the purpose of the lecture is. You can help students with this process by explicitly stating the purpose of the lecture and describing an overall plan of organization before beginning a lecture.

Teach Abbreviations   Using abbreviations reduces the amount of writing and increases the speed of note taking. Teach commonly used abbreviations, and have students generate a list of words and possible abbreviations. For example, "w/" for *with,* "MD" for *doctor,* "<" for *less than,* and "ave." for *average* can easily be taught and are fairly easy to decipher later. Design practice activities containing common abbreviations, and have students practice using and interpreting the abbreviations.

Use Specific Formats for Note Taking   Different note-taking formats may be helpful in many cases (Kruse, 2010). Depending on the subject areas in which you teach, you may choose a particular format and encourage students to use it consistently. For example, notes can be written in one column, with key words, questions, or comments in another column. Summaries are sometimes included in a space at the bottom of the page. Distribute blank template sheets containing a specific format, explain how it works, and discuss why you consider it an effective note-taking format. Figure 11.8 displays a note-taking format that you might consider. Show students the importance of leaving spaces in their notes for additions or changes after the lecture, or writing on every other line.

Supplying guided notes to students helps decrease the amount of writing and increase the focus on major ideas. Guided notes are similar to partial outlines, but they usually contain more spaces for students to fill in important details during the lectures (Konrad, Joseph, & Itoi, 2011). Some teachers have students complete guided notes or partial outlines together as a class activity to ensure that students are obtaining critical information from lectures. Guided notes may be especially beneficial for topics that contain a great deal of new vocabulary and concepts

Class		Date	
New Information		Questions or Comments	

Figure 11.8   Sample Note-Taking Format

and that are directly linked to Common Core content. Figures 11.9 and 11.10 contain examples of partial outlines and guided notes.

Teach Speed and Accuracy Techniques   Start by demonstrating what good note-takers do. Have students share the ways they take notes. For example, some students never take extra time to erase mistakes in their notes; they simply draw a single line through errors. Encouraging students to develop methods and strategies with which they feel comfortable will help them be more effective.

Teach Students How to Study Using Notes   Don't forget to show students what to do with their notes. Many students take notes, close their notebooks after class, and never look at them again. Direct students to review notes after each class and make any corrections or clarifications (Boyle, 2007; Boyle, Rosen, & Forchelli, 2014). They should also jot down questions

Class: Social Studies   Topic: Products of Indiana   Date: 4/1

Major Ideas	Details	Questions
Agriculture	**Major Crops:** Corn _____ _____ _____	**Where within the state are the various crops grown?**
Industry	**Major Industries** Steel _____ _____ _____	**What are the products of the major industries?** **Where are the major industrial areas located and why?**

Figure 11.9   Guided Notes

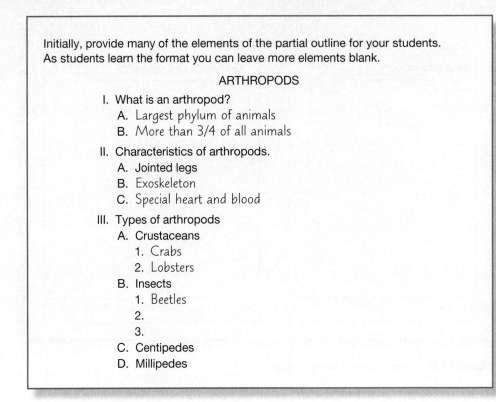

Initially, provide many of the elements of the partial outline for your students. As students learn the format you can leave more elements blank.

ARTHROPODS

I. What is an arthropod?
   A. Largest phylum of animals
   B. More than 3/4 of all animals

II. Characteristics of arthropods.
   A. Jointed legs
   B. Exoskeleton
   C. Special heart and blood

III. Types of arthropods
   A. Crustaceans
      1. Crabs
      2. Lobsters
   B. Insects
      1. Beetles
      2.
      3.
   C. Centipedes
   D. Millipedes

Figure 11.10 Partial Outline

they may need to clarify later. Show students how they can attach "sticky notes" to various pages in their notes to remind them of places with questions.

Finally, teach students how to study using their notes by helping them identify the most important information to study. Then show them how to generate study strategies to facilitate recall and understanding of that important information (e.g., Wong, 2015). Demonstrate strategies to help them remember information in their notes. Explain how they can use their notes to supplement their textbooks when studying for exams.

The AWARE Strategy   The AWARE strategy was developed for college students with learning disabilities, but it can be adapted for students in secondary settings (Boyle, Forchelli, & Cariss, 2015; Suritsky & Hughes, 1996). The five steps in AWARE are the following:

1. *A*rrange to take notes.
2. *W*rite quickly.
3. *A*pply cues.
4. *R*eview notes as soon as possible.
5. *E*dit notes. (Suritsky & Hughes, 1996, p. 308)

Each major strategy step can remind students of additional steps to implement. For example, "*A*rrange to take notes" refers to getting to class with all required materials, such as a notebook, writing materials, or even a tablet such as an iPad. Even if students are audio recording the lecture, it is a good idea to take some notes on verbal cues or highlighted content. The AWARE strategy can easily be adapted for students in secondary schools. You might try this strategy in your own college courses so you can teach it to students. Provide opportunities to review, and offer feedback during the initial phases of instruction.

Strategic Note Taking   Boyle and Weishaar (2001) provided students with mild disabilities a note-taking form to guide their note taking during class. The form prompted students, before the lecture began, to provide the name of the topic and their prior knowledge about the topic. During the lecture, they were prompted to write, on each page, three to seven points, including details and summaries. At the end of the lecture, they were directed to write and

TABLE 11.1 Special Problems with Note Taking and Possible Adaptations

Note-Taking Problem	Possible Solutions
Note-taker is too slow	• Provide basic outline as a handout. • Model outlining on the blackboard. • Use PowerPoint presentations during lectures. • Print slides for students.
Legibility	• Show how illegibility can affect the value of notes. • Use manuscript when needed. • Model "shorthand" and abbreviations. • Provide a variety of paper and pens, or tablets. • Use recording devices, and demonstrate their use.
Deciding what to write	• Organize lectures logically. • Present key points on board or slides as you lecture. • Provide guided notes as handouts or templates for students.
Deciding how to organize	• Provide a note-taking format, outlines, or guided notes. • Teach a particular note-taking strategy that suits your class.
Learning how to use notes	• Show how to review, correct, and elaborate on notes. • Model how to use notes for studying. • Schedule time for reviewing notes during class.

explain five summary points. Students who had used the note-taking form scored higher on immediate and long-term recall, comprehension, and the amount of notes taken.

Note-Taking Apps   Apps for note-taking assistance are available for personal tablets; one example is described in the *Apps for Education* feature. These applications can be very helpful for all students, particularly those who exhibit difficulty with note taking. However, many students with special needs will need assistance in implementing systematic use of the app. Practice applying the app in real classroom situations, and demonstrate to students how information collected in this way can be used to maximize learning and later test performance.

ADDRESS SPECIAL NOTE-TAKING PROBLEMS   Some students may experience great difficulties with note taking, in spite of attempts to teach skills to make all students successful. Table 11.1 lists some special problems that may be encountered by students when trying to take notes, as well as possible solutions that may help students overcome some of those problems.

MyEdLab: **Self-Check 11.1**

MyEdLab: **Application Exercise 11.1: Tools for Developing Independent Learners**

MyEdLab: **Application Exercise 11.2: Teaching Note-Taking Skills**

Research and Reference Skills

Although many general education students possess adequate knowledge of library and researching skills, students with special needs benefit from explicit instruction, practice, and feedback when learning and using the process (Hoover & Patton, 2006). Students need to know how to use reference materials such as reference books, indexes (e.g., periodical guides), computer-assisted literature and encyclopedia searches, and Internet search engines. You can increase your students' motivation for these activities by always encouraging students to ask questions and to search for the answers. Statements like, "That's an excellent question!" "What is a question we'd like to find the answer for?" and "How can we find the answer?" will show your students you value lifelong learning and library and research skills.

Assistive Technology Software and Apps for Help with Study Skills

 Computer programs to help students with mild disabilities at home and at school with their schoolwork have been developed. For example, KidTools™, KidSkills™, and StrategyTools™ were developed to provide elementary and secondary students with mild disabilities an assistive technological computer program to support self-regulation, learning strategy tools, and research-based tools that students, teachers, and parents can use to support school learning (Fitzgerald & Koury, 2001–2002, 2004–2005; Mitchem, Kight, Fitzgerald, Koury, & Boonseng, 2007). StrategyTools™, which was designed for secondary students, combines 39 computerized research-based tools organized into six major categories containing numerous templates that students, teachers, and parents can personalize. KidTools™ and KidSkills™ were developed for elementary-age students and then adapted for secondary students into the StrategyTools™ program. Both the elementary and secondary programs have positive preliminary data to support their use.

The StrategyTools™ categories include the following: Getting Organized, Learning New Information, Demonstrating Learning, Working on Projects, Solving Personal Problems, and Moving into the Future. Each category is located in a different section of the program. The "Getting Organized" category, which is located in the library section of the program,

contains tools for creating to-do lists, weekly planners, assignment cards, and job aids. The "Learning New Information" category, which is located in the study hall section, contains vocabulary cards, note-taking tools, compare-and-contrast tools, KWHL (What do I **K**now; what do I **W**ant to learn; how will I **F**ind information; what did I **L**earn) cards, and a chunker tool. The "Demonstrating Learning" category, which is located in the classroom section, contains tools such as composer tools, flashcards, memory cards, study guides, planning reports, self-tests, project review cards, and rubric tools. The "Working on Projects" category, which is located in the computer lab, contains source scanning, big-picture card, planning a report, project note cards, project review cards, and getting information tools. The "Solving Personal Problems" category, which is located in the conference room section, contains tools such as monitoring, making self- and two-party contracts, making choices, solving problems, and commitment cards. The "Moving into the Future" category, which is located in the information center, contains tools such as self-awareness, action planners, transition, budgeting, job search, and job-finding services. Mitchem et al. (2007) reported that secondary students and their teachers who used StrategyTools™ over an academic semester had positive views of the program. Students further indicated that the tools helped them to be more organized, to recognize

possible problematic areas, and to find more appropriate alternative responses.

Apps that greatly facilitate study skills are available. *Picture Scheduler* by Peter Jankuj is a scheduler that creates visual tasks with pictures and audio or video attachments that can be set with one of five sound-system alarms. Tasks can be categorized, and alarms can be preset daily, weekly, or monthly. An app for note taking and recording is *Soundnote* by David Estes, which can record the audio of lectures or meetings while the individual takes notes, including drawing pictures. After the lecture, the text, pictures, and audio can be e-mailed or transferred to a computer. *Note Taker HD* by Software Garden, Inc., is another note-taking app designed to allow handwritten notes, pictures, and diagrams to be input into a tablet or iPad using a finger or a stylus designed for a compatible device. Functions allow zooming in and out while taking notes. Pages of notes can be organized into relevant folders by date, by course, or by any other chosen system. Templates, clip art, and stickers can be added to notes, which can then be e-mailed or opened in other applications. Finally, PDF files can be opened and edited within Note Taker HD. The majority of these study-skills apps have embedded UDL features, such as text-to-speech capability, which eliminates handwriting and typing challenges and difficulties.

STRATEGIES FOR
TEACHING LIBRARY SKILLS

To get students started, provide maps of the interior of libraries that indicate where various sources are located, including computer stations and the reference librarians. Arrange meetings with reference librarians so that students become familiar with them and feel comfortable asking for assistance. Librarians can schedule special instructional sessions for classes and often will meet with smaller groups of students with special needs to provide extra guidance and practice in searching the library. Arrange to have special educators work with librarians to devise specialized training sessions for students with disabilities.

TEACH USE OF REFERENCE MATERIALS Familiarizing your students with the reference materials available in the school and public libraries can be made into a motivating activity by challenging teams of students to locate topics within all available sources. Typical materials include electronic and print versions of dictionaries, encyclopedias, biographical sources, almanacs, and various specific guide books, such as medical guides or natural history guides. Most reference materials are located together in libraries and usually cannot be checked out. Because print materials are often shelved in alphabetical order, provide practice or reference sheets containing the alphabet for younger students who have difficulty recalling alphabetical order. Summary guides listing reference books, types of information, and locations can serve as library guides for students. Many libraries provide their own guided tours and assistance with online reference sources. Setting up practice activities during which students are required to find and identify different pieces of information benefits all students. These activities can be made more exciting by arranging practice as part of a scavenger hunt game, conducted in the library or online. Grouping students into scavenger hunt teams may help inspire them, perhaps demonstrating how much fun it is to discover new information.

TEACH STUDENTS HOW TO USE DATABASES Many students will benefit from instruction on reference databases. Available databases may vary depending on whether the library is housed at an elementary, middle, or secondary school. High schools may have many more databases available than elementary schools. Subject areas may be identified, for example, biography, business, English/language arts, lifestyle, or science. By clicking on the appropriate subject, students can search for relevant references in a variety of areas. For example, consider a search for information about U.S. president Zachary Taylor. Clicking on a "biography" reveals a source such as the Gale Biography in Context™ database. This source provides a general entry on Taylor's life, followed by a featured article from the *Encyclopedia of World Biography*. Following these are a number of other sources, including news services, academic journals, websites, references, and magazines. Tools are also provided that allow students to bookmark, share, or e-mail entries. Dictionary access is also included for unfamiliar vocabulary. Basic facts about Taylor, images, and related people are also included. An accompanying text-reading device allows students to have the text read to them, at varying speeds, and highlights text as it is read. This may be particularly helpful for students with reading difficulties. Such databases are not difficult to use, although basic familiarity with computer screens, electronic devices, and use of the mouse, touchscreen, or voice-command device may be necessary for students to use them unassisted. It is also important to consider that any one individual database may not provide access to all relevant materials. The school librarian can provide specific information on the availability of various databases and how they can be used. Provide explicit practice for students with special needs, when necessary. Students should be able to locate relevant articles, copy down (or print out) identifying information, and know how to use this information to locate the articles. You can create library search activities in which you assign pairs or small groups of students to locate specific articles and identify where they can be found. If students learn to function independently with these skills, they will be able to write more thorough and informative research papers.

TEACH USE OF LIBRARY CATALOGS Library searches can also be conducted to identify print materials and e-books that are located in the library, although familiarity with particular computer systems is necessary. Searches can be completed by author, title, and subject area, and searches can be completed on books, multimedia materials, and various databases of journals by topical area. Resulting search information is displayed and can be printed out or copied by hand.

Search results contain several important pieces of information. First, Library of Congress or Dewey Decimal System call numbers of books are identified, along with author and publication information such as publisher, year, and city of publication. Longer formats are usually available and display abstracts of the materials. Model how reading abstracts and other displayed information helps students decide whether those materials should be included in their search. If materials appear relevant, students can print the screen information, copy it, or save it to a disk, and then locate the book in the library using the call number. Give your students self-monitoring sheets containing reminders about what information they should keep for looking up materials and for their reference lists.

Searching by author or title can be simpler than searching by topic. A title or author's name will yield all sources containing that title or name. Searching by subject topic is a little more complex, and guidance may be necessary to help narrow the descriptors. For example, if students select a broad descriptor like "pollution," several thousand entries might appear. Guide students in narrowing descriptors to focus their search efforts on a more restricted topic that yields a more realistic number of books or articles for them to scan. Divide the topic into smaller subtopics, such as air pollution, groundwater pollution, waste disposal, and agricultural pollution for the previous example. The resulting search will then be narrower and more focused on the student's interest area.

Making informed decisions about which entries should be examined more closely can be difficult. The selection process requires critical thinking, and students may need assistance to focus their thinking. Teach students to group potential sources into three categories: "Yes, definitely keep," "Maybe, look further and decide," and "No, do not keep." Be sure to review what they do to verify that they understand the process.

The next step is to obtain the "yes" and "maybe" materials and determine if they should be included. If students do not do this component of the task well, they may experience great difficulties completing the remaining steps of the project. Some of your students with disabilities may have difficulty with this component because it relies on reading and thinking skills. Model some samples for the class by speaking aloud the "thinking" you use for inclusion and exclusion of sources. Say, for example, "I will keep this abstract on the hazards of using too much fertilizer because it sounds as if it fits with my topic of agricultural pollution. But I will discard this article on toxic dumps because it doesn't seem to be related closely enough to agricultural pollution." You can divide students into small groups for practicing this task and require students to defend verbally their reasons for including or excluding abstracts.

TEACH USE OF INTERNET SEARCH ENGINES So much information can be accessed via the Internet that students should have practice in these search procedures as well. Most libraries have online access and numerous search engines to help students locate information on the Internet. Because some information from the Internet may be less reliable than information from printed sources, teach students to identify the source of the information and the reliability of that source, and teach them to verify information by comparing it with other source materials. Internet search engines on computers and tablets such as iPads have embedded universal design for learning (UDL) features such as voice-to-text capability, which can be used to eliminate writing and spelling difficulties while searching for relevant sources.

STRATEGIES FOR
PREPARING REPORTS AND PROJECTS

Assignments that involve writing papers are usually very challenging for students with disabilities as well as for other students in your classroom (Deshler & Schumaker, 2006). This writing process can be taught directly by practicing some of the subskills involved in writing a report. Ability to use the different skills of planning, reading, thinking, organizing, and writing is required for successful report writing (Muchnick, 2011).

DEFINE THE WRITING TASK SYSTEMATICALLY In defining the writing task, it is important to explain the following assignment details:

- Purpose of the writing assignment (e.g., inform, persuade, demonstrate)
- Audience for the assignment (e.g., teacher, classmates, general public)
- Format for the paper, in terms of both substance (book report, newspaper article, research report, other) and style (type, handwritten, font size and style)
- Required length in pages (or word count) and required scope and detail
- Date the assignment is due

This is also the time for students to estimate how long each step in the process will take and begin to plan a schedule for completing each step. Some of the steps may require additional subdividing. Have students record steps and due dates in their calendars. Finally, students can begin to work on the project according to their time schedules (Muchnick, 2011).

PROMOTE TOPIC SELECTION, DEVELOP A WRITING PLAN, AND BRAINSTORM IDEAS   Many students have difficulties selecting topics for their papers. Provide examples of topics that appear motivating and interesting to students and also are manageable in scope.

MyEdLab:
Video Example 11.4.
Several steps of the writing process are explored in this video.

Provide sample papers that address each purpose as models for students to see how the papers are constructed to answer the intended purpose. Maintain model papers from previous classes, and put them on reserve in the library. Seeing completed models helps students visualize the final product.

The development of a writing plan is crucial for students. This component requires additional subdividing: Will books be needed from the library? Will reading and taking notes from those books be required? Will students need to interview experts on the topic? Will visits to museums be necessary? This plan will vary depending on the topic and purpose of the assignment.

Show students sample writing plans from different types of written projects. Again model the development of plans during instruction. Have students complete partially developed plans before attempting to complete plans independently. During the actual writing of assignments, have students bring in their plans so that you can provide guidance and corrective feedback.

Once the writing topic has been selected, students need to brainstorm ideas for details. Model how, during the brainstorming process, all ideas are written down, and allow students opportunities to practice the brainstorming component. Then demonstrate how the brainstormed ideas are evaluated later for relevancy and how determinations are made as to whether to include them within the paper. After that, the relevant ideas are listed in order of importance for the project.

COLLECT AND ORGANIZE IDEAS AND INFORMATION   Lead students to collect and find the necessary information for writing their papers. As described previously, students may use the library, the Internet, other reference materials, or interviews depending on the paper topic and format required. Demonstrate how to find and collect information.

At this stage, students may write a more detailed outline for their papers. Notes from the obtained information can be included in the outline. Traditional outlines may or may not be used, but be sure to model how the use of an organizational framework facilitates the organization of the paper and assists students in completing the written product. A format may consist of titles, main ideas, supporting details under each main idea, and summary and conclusion sections. One key factor is to show students how to use the major purpose of the paper to guide the major subheadings for the paper.

WRITE FIRST DRAFT OF PAPER AND OBTAIN FEEDBACK   After completing the organizational outline or format, have students write the first draft of the paper. It should be relatively easy to write a first draft if note cards containing major points and outlines are used. Each organizational heading becomes a major section of the draft, and students put that information into sentences in their own words. Then, elaborations are added to those main ideas and details to complete the rough draft. At this point or earlier, you may need to explain why copying articles is illegal and that it is called plagiarism, and explain how you want your students to cite the information they are using for their papers. This may be especially important if students are downloading complete documents from the Internet.

Encourage students to obtain feedback from someone on their first drafts. The feedback provides them with information about what needs to be revised before completing their final versions. Teachers, parents, siblings, and peers can all be asked for feedback on draft versions. When possible, have students meet in pairs or small groups to provide constructive feedback on one another's draft reports.

REVISE AND REWRITE, PROOF, AND EDIT FINAL VERSION   Students should then incorporate the feedback into the revision of their drafts. Explain to students how a revision process may involve several changes to the draft. Most revisions employ grammatical, syntactical, semantic, and punctuation changes to improve the paper.

Even though you will probably hear your students groan, explain to them how important it is to edit the paper one final time. It is during this final editing and proofing stage that additional errors are often detected.

Writing papers or completing independent projects is difficult for many students, but it is critical for success in secondary schools and higher education (Englert et al., 2009). Without instruction in the entire process of writing papers and completing independent projects, many students may fail to achieve in this important area. However, by providing extra instruction in the process of writing, students may be better prepared to write papers, and they will be more likely to be successful in school.

> MyEdLab: **Self-Check 11.2**
>
> MyEdLab: **Application Exercise 11.3: Research and Reference Skills**

11 Summary

- Students with disabilities and those at risk for failure in school benefit from explicit instruction and practice with tools to develop as independent learners, using personal organizational skills, as well as strategies for completing homework and for effective listening, note-taking, and study skills.

  — Personal organization skills, such as knowing about class times and schedules, using assignment notebooks and monthly planners, and organizing homework, are important for success in school and can be effectively taught to students with special needs.

  — All students benefit from clearly stated expectations, such as those for the completion of homework.

  — Direct teaching of listening skills helps students with special needs be prepared to learn information presented orally in school.

  — Teaching students ways to take notes—including writing short summaries, using abbreviations, using specific note-taking formats and strategies, and applying appropriate technology—facilitates learning from lectures and presentations.

- Practice and instruction in using the library, including the use of reference materials and indices, online literature searches, and Internet search engines, assists students with special needs in learning how to search for and locate resources for schoolwork.

  — Direct instruction on how to write a research paper, including selecting topics, searching for information, organizing information, writing and editing first drafts, and preparing final versions, is essential for most students with special needs.

PROFESSIONAL STANDARDS LINK:
Teaching Study Skills

Information in this chapter links most directly to:

- CEC Standards: 1 (Learner Development and Individual Learning Differences), 5 (Instructional Planning and Strategies)

- INTASC Standards: 2 (Learning Differences), 7 (Planning for Instruction), 8 (Instructional Strategies)

TEACHING STUDY SKILLS

If a student is having difficulty with study skills—including organizational skills, listening skills, note-taking skills, and library skills—have you tried specific strategies for teaching? If not, see the pages listed here

STRATEGIES FOR DEVELOPING PERSONAL ORGANIZATIONAL SKILLS

- [ ] Post and review class and time schedules, 256–258
- [ ] Use strategies for daily, weekly, and monthly planning, 258–259
- [ ] Use task analysis to organize assignments, 259
- [ ] Teach strategies for homework completion, 259–263

STRATEGIES FOR PROMOTING LISTENING SKILLS

- [ ] Address requisite listening skills, 263–264
- [ ] Teach listening skills, 264–266
- [ ] Plan for special listening problems, 266–267

STRATEGIES FOR TEACHING NOTE-TAKING SKILLS

- [ ] Teach note-taking skills and strategies, 267–271
- [ ] Address special note-taking problems, 271

STRATEGIES FOR TEACHING LIBRARY SKILLS

- [ ] Teach use of reference materials, 273
- [ ] Teach students how to use databases, 273
- [ ] Teach use of library catalogs, 273–274
- [ ] Teach use of Internet search engines, 274

STRATEGIES FOR PREPARING REPORTS AND PROJECTS

- [ ] Define the writing task systematically, 274–275
- [ ] Promote topic selection, develop a writing plan, and brainstorm ideas, 275
- [ ] Collect and organize ideas and information, 275
- [ ] Write first draft of paper and obtain feedback, 275
- [ ] Revise and rewrite, proof, and edit final version, 275–276

12

Assessment

LEARNING OUTCOMES

After studying this chapter, you should be able to:

12.1 Identify and describe the uses of different types of tests, including norm-referenced tests, competency-based assessments, teacher-made tests, and criterion-referenced tests, in inclusive settings.

12.2 Describe how to adapt different types of tests for students with special needs.

12.3 Describe specific test-taking strategies for taking standardized tests and teacher-made tests, such as multiple-choice, true–false, matching, and essay tests.

12.4 Identify procedures and rationales for adjusting grading and scoring of tests for students with special needs.

Tests are a significant component of education because they provide information relevant to placement, instruction, and future career decisions. Tests are commonly being used to evaluate the performance of schools, and curriculum-based measurement is highly recommended for use in response-to-intervention (RTI) programming (Deno, 2016; Fuchs, Fuchs, & Compton, 2012). Tests, however, must be administered appropriately and interpreted correctly, or they can do more harm than good. It is also important to be able to describe the purposes of different tests to parents, as well as to be able to interpret for parents the information test results provide about their child. Teachers should be aware of different types of tests, the purposes they serve, how they can be used, and how their results can be interpreted. Skills for maximizing test performance and accommodating students with special needs are also necessary.

Types of Tests

In education, many different tests address many different, specific needs. One general type of test is no "better" than another because different tests serve different purposes. As a teacher, it is critical to understand what information specific tests provide and what information they do not provide.

One major distinction made in testing is between **norm-referenced** and **criterion-referenced** testing. In norm-referenced testing, student performance is compared with the performance of other students. Students receive scores such as "85th percentile," which means that the student scored higher than 85% of other students on that particular test. In criterion-referenced testing, student performance is compared with specific, specified criteria, usually considered as meeting minimal competency. A written test for a driver's license, in which individuals either pass or fail to meet a certain criterion, is a good example of a criterion-referenced test.

Nate

Mr. Montoya saw Nate in his middle school resource room for 45 minutes per day. Although much of the time was devoted to basic skills development, Mr. Montoya also allocated time to helping Nate prepare for upcoming tests. Nate had particular difficulty taking tests in his U.S. Constitution and government class, and Mr. Montoya also was having difficulty helping him. For 2 days before the test, he would work with Nate by reviewing the content and creating practice questions for Nate to answer. However, it seemed that no matter how well prepared Nate appeared to be, he did poorly on the test. When Mr. Montoya asked Nate why this was, he just shrugged his shoulders and said the test did not make any sense to him.

Both norm-referenced and criterion-referenced testing can be **standardized,** which means that all students take the test under the same, or standard, conditions. The information that comes from the test results, then, assumes standardized testing conditions were applied (Salvia, Ysseldyke, & Bolt, 2013). Standardized administration procedures are published in test manuals and are expected to be closely followed for the test scores to be meaningful.

Another important distinction is whether a test is **summative** or **formative** in nature. Summative testing usually refers to tests given at the end of a particular educational period. Achievement tests given at the end of a school year are good examples of summative evaluation. The results tell how much has been accomplished throughout the educational period and may provide implications for placement in the next educational period. Many norm-referenced tests are summative in nature, but criterion-referenced tests can also be summative if they are administered at the end of a particular educational experience.

Teachers use formative evaluation when they test at frequent intervals so that student progress can be evaluated. For example, students who are attempting to learn and remember 100 multiplication facts may take a weekly test on these facts so that the rate of growth can be evaluated and instructional modifications can be made (e.g., more time-on-task) when growth is unsatisfactory. Formative evaluation is most frequently used in basic-skills areas.

Evaluation can also be curriculum-based. This means that the tests are derived directly from the curriculum being taught (Hosp, Hosp, & Howell, 2016). Most teacher-made tests are intended to evaluate student learning of the curriculum, and therefore they are types of curriculum-based tests. Distinctions have been made between **curriculum-based assessment**—which could include any procedure that evaluates student performance in relation to the school curriculum, such as weekly spelling tests—and **curriculum-based measurement**—characterized by frequent, direct measurements of critical school behaviors, which could include timed (e.g., 1- to 5-minute) tests of performance on reading, math, and writing skills (Salvia et al., 2013). Curriculum-based measurement is formative in nature, and it allows teachers to make instructional decisions about teaching and curriculum while learning is taking place.

PERFORMANCE ASSESSMENTS AND PORTFOLIO ASSESSMENTS

Other types of tests include **performance assessments** and **portfolio assessments.** Performance assessments are usually curriculum-based, and they require students to engage in a process or construct some product, often on real-world tasks. Performance assessments can include such diverse outcomes as playing a piece on a piano, writing a persuasive essay, or conducting a science experiment (Johnson, Penny, & Gordon, 2009). Portfolio assessment is also usually curriculum-based, and it consists of student products and other relevant information collected over time and displayed in a portfolio. All of these types of tests have relevance to students with special needs.

Table 12.1 provides examples of these types of tests applied in the context of reading.

MyEdLab:
Video Example 12.1.
This video provides an overview of different types of assessments used in classroom settings.

TABLE 12.1 Examples of Reading Tests

Type of Test	Example Reading Test
Standardized, Norm-Referenced	Published reading achievement test administered under standardized conditions. Students may answer test questions on computerized answer sheets or give answers to an examiner in an individual administration. Student's score is compared with scores of a normative sample of students.
Criterion-Referenced	Students' test scores are compared with a certain predetermined criterion level to be considered competent in reading at their grade level.
Curriculum-Based Assessment	The test is based on the reading curriculum materials being used in class.
Curriculum-Based Measurement	Students take brief tests of reading speed, accuracy, and comprehension. These scores are monitored over time to determine whether progress is adequate.
Performance Assessment	Students could be asked to "perform" on a variety of reading-related tasks, such as summarizing a newspaper article, looking up a reference, or identifying a certain printed label in a store.
Portfolio Assessment	Various student products relevant to reading are collected, for example, list of books read, book reports written, or audio recordings of reading selections.

Regardless of the type of test, it must be demonstrated to have **reliability** and **validity** to be of value. All measures of reliability seek to determine that the test is consistent in what it measures. No less important, validity refers to the extent to which a particular test measures what it is intended to measure. Validity is often evaluated by comparing different tests of the same skills or abilities (Salvia et al., 2013). For example, students should receive similar scores on different standardized tests of reading achievement if both tests are valid.

Tests commonly used in special education are listed in Figure 12.1.

Intelligence Tests

   Kaufman Assessment Battery for Children II, 2nd ed. (Kaufman & Kaufman, 2006; Pearson/American Guidance Service)
   Stanford-Binet Intelligence Scale, 5th ed. (Roid, 2003; Psychological Corporation)
   Wechsler Intelligence Scale for Children—IV, 4th ed. (Wechsler, 2003; Psychological Corporation)

Achievement Tests

   Kaufman Test of Educational Achievement, 2nd ed. (KTEA – II) (Kaufman & Kaufman, 2004; Pearson/American Guidance Service)
   Key Math—3: Diagnostic Assessment (Pearson/American Guidance Service, 2007)
   Peabody Individual Achievement Test—Revised/Normative Update (PIAT—R) (Markwardt, 1997; Pearson/American Guidance Service)
   Test of Written Language—3 (TOWL) (Hammill & Larsen, 1996; PRO-ED)
   Wide Range Achievement Test—4 (Wilkenson & Robertson, 2006; Western Psychological Services)
   Woodcock-Johnson III: Tests of Achievement (Woodcock, Johnson, & Mather, 2001; Riverside)
   Woodcock Reading Mastery Test—Revised/Normative Update (Woodcock, 1998; Pearson/American Guidance Service)

Figure 12.1 Types of Tests

MyEdLab:
Video Example 12.2.

This video provides an overview of norm-referenced tests and standardized testing situations.

MyEdLab: **Self-Check 12.1**

MyEdLab: **Application Exercise 12.1: Types of Tests**

Adapting Tests for Students with Special Needs
STRATEGIES FOR

ADMINISTERING NORM-REFERENCED TESTS

Some students with special needs exhibit difficulties with norm-referenced tests that may limit the reliability and validity of their test scores. Problems may include language or communication styles (e.g., the need for a sign language interpreter or communication board), the length of the testing, attentional difficulties, or reading difficulties when reading competence is not being tested. Another threat to the validity of the individual scores of students with disabilities is that in some cases, individuals with disabilities are not included in the test's standardization sample (Shapiro, 2010). Further, some tests may not be fair for students from culturally diverse backgrounds (Baca & Cervantes, 2004; Harry & Klingner, 2006). Special considerations, including adjustments in the testing procedure, may be helpful and necessary (see also Gollnick & Chinn, 2009; Hoover & Klingner, 2011).

Unfortunately, substantive deviations from standardized administration procedures typically limit the usefulness of the test. If, for example, an individual student is provided with a calculator as an accommodation to assist with math computation on a problem-solving subtest, the resulting score cannot be fairly compared with the scores of students who did not have access to calculators. Even though it can be argued that problem solving, and not computation, is being evaluated, and the student in question has difficulty remembering math facts, it is unknown how the students in the standardization sample would have performed if they also had access to calculators. Therefore, the student's score cannot be easily interpreted with respect to the performance of the norm group (Salvia et al., 2013). Generally, it has been suggested that accommodations are appropriate when the benefit for students with disabilities is greater than that for students without disabilities (Fuchs, Fuchs, Eaton, Hamlett, & Karns, 2000; Laitusis, Buzick, Stone, Hansen, & Hakkinen, 2012). There are instances when standardized test accommodations are considered appropriate, and several states have published state-approved test accommodations (Lazarus, Thurlow, Lail, & Christensen, 2009; State of New Jersey, 2014).

USE TEST ACCOMMODATIONS   Many tests allow a variety of accommodations to be made, depending on individual needs and the testing situation. For example, students with visual impairments cannot be expected to perform appropriately on tests without accommodations such as larger print, braille versions of the test, or accommodations such as reading the test aloud. Where text-reading skill or reading of standard fonts is not being tested, accommodations seem appropriate, and even necessary, for obtaining a valid score. These accommodations include assistance before the test is administered, setting and time accommodations, assistance with directions or other assistance during test administration, use of assistive technology, revisions of test formats, and different response formats (Feldman, Kim, & Elliott, 2011; Fuchs, Fuchs, & Capizzi, 2006; Laitusis et al., 2012; Salvia et al., 2013), such as the following:

- Preparing the student with practice tests or teaching test-taking skills
- Altering the timing or scheduling of the test
- Extending time limits
- Spreading the test over several shorter time sessions
- Administering the test over several days
- Changing the setting, such as a smaller or distraction-free room
- Simplifying or reading directions; using sign language for directions

- Testing individually
- Altering the presentation of the test
- Simplifying the language of the test
- Providing prompts and feedback (including reinforcement)
- Allowing teachers to read the test and turn the test pages
- Providing assistive technology, such as a text-to-talk converter or visual magnification device
- Providing audio, large-print, or braille versions
- Changing the response formats
- Allowing verbal versus written responses or responses in a test booklet rather than answer sheet
- Allowing circling of answers versus filling in answer bubbles

MyEdLab:
Video Example 12.3.
Examples of accommodations can be seen in this video.

If students perform very differently under one or more reasonable accommodations, the standardized test may not have provided an accurate depiction of the student's ability. Research to date is somewhat equivocal regarding some of these accommodations; for example, extended time sometimes, but not always, has a differential benefit for students with disabilities (Gregg & Nelson, 2012; Lovett, 2010). Similarly, oral accommodations, such as reading tests aloud, sometimes, but not always, appears to benefit students with disabilities (Sireci, Scarpati, & Li, 2005). The variability observed in research findings on test accommodations suggests that schools and classrooms should ensure that accommodations as implemented are facilitating desired outcomes. More recent research has suggested that some accommodations may benefit all students, but students with disabilities may benefit more in some cases, particularly in the areas of self-efficacy and motivation (Feldman et al., 2011).

USE UNIVERSAL DESIGN FOR LEARNING (UDL)   Some features of UDL may have important implications for test design and development, ultimately limiting the need for separate accommodations (Meyer, Rose, & Gordon, 2014). For example, the state of Massachusetts mandated that state tests be administered without time limits (Sireci et al., 2005). Other considerations might include developing tests so that directions and content are edited for maximum readability and comprehensibility (Thompson, Johnstone, & Thurlow, 2002). On computer-based assessments, UDL features could include text-to-speech technology; electronic reading supports, such as navigation assistance, spoken voice, or visual highlighting; a variety of font and lighting choices and response formats; or a special mouse, trackball, or other alternate means of keyboard access. More of these features may be available on tests in the future.

USE INDIVIDUALLY ADMINISTERED TESTS   In addition to providing more detailed information about student performance in a particular area, individually administered tests avoid some potential problems associated with group administration, such as reading directions, working independently, and using machine-scored answer sheets. For example, in group-administered tests of reading, students may respond to more complicated formats to assess reading skills, whereas on an individually administered test, a student's individual reading can be directly assessed through interaction with the examiner. Therefore, it may be appropriate to rely more on individually administered tests for students who have difficulty taking group tests independently.

TEACH TEST-TAKING SKILLS   Some students may know much of the content being tested but do not understand how to apply that knowledge on the test. In these cases, students can be given specific training in **test-taking skills** appropriate to relevant tests, or they can be administered published practice tests and given feedback on their understanding of test formats (Elliott & Thurlow, 2006; Salend, 2009; Scruggs & Mastropieri, 1992). Training in test-taking skills, which is appropriate for many different types of tests, is discussed later in this chapter.

INCREASE MOTIVATION   In other cases, students may have relevant skills but not be sufficiently motivated to work their hardest during the test. This may be true for norm-referenced tests as well as all other types of tests. Although direct rewarding of test performance may violate standardization, other motivational strategies—such as including goal setting and attribution training, praising students' efforts, promoting self-efficacy and self-esteem, making the classroom atmosphere fun and enjoyable, and increasing students' personal investment—may be helpful in increasing the validity of the test performance of less-motivated test-takers.

IMPROVE EXAMINER FAMILIARITY   Some students score better on standardized tests if they are familiar with the examiner than if they are responding to an examiner they have not met before. This may be particularly true of African American and Latino students (Fuchs & Fuchs, 1989), students with learning disabilities (Fuchs, Fuchs, & Power, 1987), and students who speak English as a second language (Carey, Mannell, & Dunn, 2011). Try to arrange for an administrator who is well known by, or acquainted with, the student. If an outside examiner is used, he or she should first establish rapport with the student by introducing himself or herself, engaging the student in personal conversation, explaining the purpose of the testing, describing test activities, and encouraging student questions (Salvia et al., 2013). Such established familiarity may improve the validity of test responses.

REQUEST ACCOMMODATIONS FOR COLLEGE ENTRANCE EXAMS   Among the most frequently administered tests for college entrance are the SAT and the ACT. These are usually administered in a student's junior or senior year of high school. Both of these tests allow special accommodations to be made for students with disabilities (e.g., College Board, 2015).

Students with disabilities may be offered accommodations if they meet eligibility requirements. Accommodations that can be requested include extended time, small-group or private room setting, large type, alternative test form with accommodations required as noted on the student's individualized education program (IEP), a reader or recorder, audio recording with written form, dictated responding, a magnifying glass, or a four-function calculator.

STRATEGIES FOR
ADAPTING COMPETENCY-BASED LOCAL AND STATEWIDE ASSESSMENT

Many school districts employ "benchmarks" to determine standards for student achievement. The implementation of statewide competency testing, sometimes known as Common Core assessments, has helped develop common standards for educational attainment and establish educational accountability. In some states, performance on competency tests has become a requirement for graduation and other issues of school operation, and it has been referred to as "high-stakes" testing. Because of federal legislation, states today have statewide competency tests, although waivers of some of the federal requirements have been awarded to individual states (U.S. Department of Education, 2012).

Minimum competency tests share many characteristics with norm-referenced achievement tests. Although competency tests are oriented toward competencies students are expected to attain for promotion or graduation, they are also developed for comparative purposes. Therefore, allowing adaptations for special needs while still maintaining standardization is a concern of competency tests, and this can be determined through consultation with test developers or appropriate educational agencies (e.g., school district or state department of education).

USE TEST ACCOMMODATIONS   In many cases, testing accommodations are considered appropriate because they better allow some students to demonstrate what they know. Because many students with disabilities may need accommodations, the Individuals with Disabilities Education Act (IDEA) requires that individual student IEPs provide testing accommodations for state tests as well as district and teacher-made tests (Salend, 2008). Most states provide standard accommodations that are permissible on statewide competency tests (e.g., State of New Jersey, 2014). It is important that these accommodations do not change the nature of the test, for example, by reading passages to students on a test of reading comprehension (Salend, 2008).

Lazarus et al. (2009) studied state accommodation policies over time to determine how changes had occurred. They found that earlier reports focused on "leveling the playing field" (p. 67) for students with disabilities, whereas more recent reports focused on the test validity of the accommodations. More recent policies have generally supported the use of technology

MyEdLab:
Video Example 12.4.
This video gives several examples of how to adapt and accommodate assessment. Pay attention to the preparations teachers provide.

and extended time limits in appropriate cases; however, other accommodations, such as use of calculators, reading questions aloud, and use of spell checkers, have less consensus across states. Teachers should check with state policy when implementing accommodations for statewide assessments.

Salend (2008, p. 17) also described *linguistically based* accommodations, including using familiar language, repeating directions, teaching the language of testing, translating tests, allowing responses in different languages or dialects, providing translators, and use of bilingual materials. Cawthon (2008) surveyed professionals working with students who are deaf or hard of hearing and reported that accommodations for statewide testing most commonly reported included extra time, small-group administration, and test items and directions read or interpreted. The *Research Highlight* provides an example of using dictation and speech recognition as a test accommodation.

Some research has been conducted on the effectiveness of accommodations in statewide assessments. To date, the results of this research are somewhat inconsistent and equivocal (Lindstrom, 2011). Bolt and Thurlow (2004) suggested that the effects of accommodations should be evaluated for individual students, which can be done by monitoring performance with and without specific accommodations.

USE ALTERNATE ASSESSMENTS   Standard statewide assessments may not be appropriate for some students with disabilities, including those with significant cognitive disabilities or nonverbal students with autism. In these cases, it may be possible to arrange for *alternate assessment procedures based on alternate achievement standards*, or AA-AAS (Lazarus, Cormier, & Thurlow, 2010). All states have developed these assessments. In the state of Virginia, for example, students for whom the state competency tests are not considered appropriate may participate in the Virginia Alternate Assessment Program (VAAP). These assessments are administered at ages 8, 10, 13, and 1 year prior to the student's exit year. They consist of a "Collection of Evidence" that measures student performance relevant to IEP objectives that access Virginia's Standards of Learning. The assessment incorporates multiple forms of data collected over time and could include, for example, work samples; student observations; interviews with teachers, parents, or employers; videos of social skills or life skills; and journal entries (Training and Technical Assistance Center at the College of William and Mary, 2012). It is understood that students participating in alternate assessment are working on educational goals other than those prescribed for the traditional diplomas (modified standard, standard, or advanced studies), and they therefore would not be eligible for those diplomas (Virginia Department of Education, 2010).

In addition to the AA-AAS, states can develop *alternate assessments based upon modified achievement standards*, or AA-MAS, for any student unlikely to meet grade-level proficiency within the student's IEP year. Finally, *alternate assessments based upon grade-level assessments*, or AA-GLAS, can be developed to provide an alternate way for students to demonstrate grade-level skills and knowledge. However, to date, few states have developed these assessments (Thurlow & Quenemoen, 2011).

REQUEST ACCOMMODATIONS ON GED TESTS   Competency tests also include the Tests of General Educational Development (GED). GED tests evaluate the knowledge and skills that are intended to have been acquired from a 4-year high school program but that may have been acquired in a different manner, such as through independent study or tutoring. Students with special needs who have not graduated from high school but believe they have met high school graduation criteria can take the GED tests. Individuals wishing to take the GED must be a resident of the state in which the test is administered, and they usually must be older than 18 years of age. Also, students must not be enrolled in a public school; so, as a teacher, you may have little direct interaction with students taking the GED. However, you may be able to provide information about the GED to students who are about to leave school without graduating or to former students who may ask you for assistance in taking the GED.

Individuals with disabilities may apply for special testing accommodations at the nearest GED testing center, fill out the appropriate form, and sign a release-of-information form to have specific medical or psychological records sent to the GED center to be evaluated. Possible accommodations that may be obtained include an audio version of the test (with printed reference copy), a large-print version of the test, extended time for taking the test, use of a calculator, frequent breaks, and use of a private testing room (Learning Disabilities Association, 2011).

Test Accommodations Using Dictation and Speech Recognition

 Although testing accommodations are frequently recommended for students with disabilities, it is less certain whether all accommodations result in positive benefits. Accommodations are intended to remove performance barriers while maintaining the integrity and validity of the measure. The number of possible accommodations increases dramatically with the advancement of innovative technologies. MacArthur and Cavalier (2004) examined the effects of dictation using speech-recognition software compared with dictation using a scribe for a written exam taken by high school students with and without learning disabilities. Dictation with speech-recognition software has the potential advantages of allowing students to see and review developing text. All students participated in three testing conditions: handwriting, dictation using a scribe, and dictation using

speech software. All students were trained to use the speech software, *Dragon Naturally Speaking, Version 4* (Dragon Systems), to write persuasive essays. Students were taught to think of a sentence and dictate it one word at a time when using the software. All students were also taught a strategy to write persuasive essays. Strategic steps, which were consolidated into a graphic organizer, included writing their position, listing evidence points for position statements, noting reasons why some might disagree, and concluding with a strong statement. Students were then given three different essay prompts and required to complete the essays under one of the three conditions.

MacArthur and Cavalier (2004) reported that all students successfully learned to use the speech-to-text software, that students with learning disabilities created higher-quality written products when using dictation with a scribe rather than dictation

with speech-to-text software, and that both methods were superior to handwriting. The dictation methods did not result in superior essays for students without disabilities, indicating that use of dictation during essay writing may be a viable and valid test accommodation for students with learning disabilities.

QUESTIONS FOR REFLECTION

1. Why do you think dictation methods might work better for students with learning disabilities than for students without disabilities?

2. Why do you think effects were greater for dictation to a scribe than for speech-recognition software for students with learning disabilities?

3. How could you adapt the writing strategy for a lower-age-level group of students?

4. How could you design practice for learning to use the computer with students with disabilities?

STRATEGIES FOR

ADAPTING TEACHER-MADE AND CRITERION-REFERENCED TESTS

Classroom test scores represent a significant component of student grades (Boyle, 2013). In addition, the use of state high-stakes testing places added demands on students with disabilities. Clearly, helping students be successful in dealing with the challenges of testing is critical to promoting school success. The *Apps for Education* feature provides suggestions for collecting records and monitoring progress more efficiently.

Teachers can adapt their own tests in much the same way that other tests are adapted. However, be careful to ensure that your adaptations are having the desired effect of accommodating the student's disability. For example, Lewandowski, Lovett, Parolin, Gordon, and Codding (2007) reported that students with attention deficit hyperactivity disorder (ADHD) gained less than the students without ADHD from extended time limits on a math computation assessment.

REVISE TESTS In the earlier scenario, Nate performed well on answering questions on the chapter posed by the resource teacher, but he performed poorly on the actual test covering the U.S. Constitution and government. Because he apparently knew much of the required information, it is possible that Nate did not fully understand the format of the teacher-made test.

Software to Assist with Recordkeeping, Grading, Progress Monitoring, and Response to Intervention

 The need to maintain clear, accurate records of student performance and progress is important in education, especially when monitoring the progress of students with disabilities who are included in general education classes. Organized systems for creating and maintaining recordkeeping for students' assignments, homework, grades, attendance, portfolio assessment products, and progress monitoring will greatly reduce the amount of noninstructional time that teachers spend on these tasks. Recent advances in technology have led to the development of software that facilitates all recordkeeping and progress-monitoring activities.

Curriculum-based measurement (CBM) is one way to monitor student progress in academic areas. Curriculum-based measurement may be recommended as a way to help identify students with learning disabilities. As described in the text, teachers can develop their own CBM measures; however, software programs are available to facilitate the process of using CBM in basic skills such as reading, math, and spelling. The website of the National Center on Progress Monitoring (NCPM; http://www.rti4success.org) provides current sources on progress monitoring, including an analysis of available computer-assisted programs. Progress monitoring can be applied to the implementation of response to intervention (RTI) (e.g., Fuchs, 2008), and software developed specifically for RTI initiatives is analyzed on the NCPM site. NCPM standards for evaluating CBM materials include adequate reliability and validity, alternate forms, sensitivity to student improvement, academic-year benchmarks, student learning and/or teacher planning, and the specification of rates of improvement. Available materials including software are *RTIm Direct* (available from the Centris Group) and *aimsweb™Plus* (Pearson).

Software is also available to assist with managing students' assignments, homework, attendance, and grades, as well as both student and parent reports. *Grade Machine* (Misty City Software) contains features that allow teachers to upload student information from existing school database systems. In addition to tailoring systems to include a variety of recordkeeping formats, Grade Machine has features such as multilingual report writing (currently in Spanish, French, Russian, German, and English), electronic dissemination of reports to facilitate better home–school communication, and templates or customizing features for maintaining records of attendance, homework, assignments, behavior, and seating plans, as well as grading terms and scales.

Newer software enabling the use of multimedia is available that can assist with the maintenance of portfolio assessment materials. Teachers can manage their own as well as their students' portfolios using available software. Teachers can show their students how to compile their own portfolios using the available technology. With the use of scanners, digital cameras, digital videos, and available software, student products can be collected on a single CD rather than in a huge box.

Apps that manage data collection are also available. *Catalyst HD Compass Solutions for Autism* (Data Finch Technologies) is an app that enables data collection and management on iPads and has capabilities to synch to an online data-storage system. Features include sorting, graphing, and combining data in multiple formats. The *WhatISee* app (Tim Heuser) arranges a data-collection system, including a vibration or sound alarm to cue recorders for coding using interval, time sampling, or duration recording methods. The *Remember the Milk* app (Remember the Milk Pty. Ltd.) provides a system for organizing tasks by day and week. Priorities can be set, users can set up helpful reminders, and the program can be synched with an online system. The *Notes* app built into iPads, iPods, and iPhones records notes that can then be synched across devices.

Although training in test-taking skills may be important for Nate in this case, it is also possible that the social studies teacher could be encouraged to make some changes to the format of the test so that students will better understand what is required of them, as shown in the continuation of the scenario.

Most teachers view reasonable testing accommodations favorably, particularly if they are easy to make (Jayanthi, Epstein, Polloway, & Bursuck, 1996; Stufft, Bauman, & Ohlsen, 2009).

Nate

Mr. Montoya made an appointment to speak to Nate's social studies teacher, Ms. Leet. She acknowledged that Nate was not doing well on the tests and expressed a willingness to help solve the problem. Mr. Montoya and Ms. Leet examined the tests together, and Mr. Montoya noted that he believed Nate did know the answer to several of the questions that he had answered incorrectly. It appeared that Nate was more likely to answer questions incorrectly when the items contained double negatives, when items contained potentially confusing options such as "(e) all of the above except (b)," and when the test called for matching two columns of information. Mr. Montoya agreed to provide Nate with practice on test-taking skills and to provide practice tests that more closely resembled Ms. Leet's tests, and Ms. Leet agreed to make adjustments in her tests to make the individual items more understandable. She also asked her class to provide her with some sample items that they thought should be on the test.

With his training in test-taking skills and Ms. Leet's test revisions, Nate's scores increased from an average of D– to an average of C–. In addition, Ms. Leet found that the average score of her entire class seemed to improve.

QUESTIONS FOR REFLECTION

1. If test scores improve, how could you know if your revised tests are more easily understandable or simply easier?
2. What kind of students would you expect to benefit most from test revisions?
3. How could you determine what aspects of your tests need revision?

Salend (1995) surveyed the literature on test design and concluded that poorly or carelessly designed tests can negatively impact student performance. Well-designed tests, on the other hand, can be useful for all students.

Adjust Test Formats   Format adjustments that can be generally employed on teacher-made tests include the following (Gajria, Salend, & Hemrick, 1994, p. 238; Salend, 1995, 2009):

- Prepare typed rather than handwritten tests.
- Space items sufficiently to reduce interference.
- Provide space for students to respond on the test itself.
- Provide items in a predictable hierarchy.
- Administer more tests with fewer items, rather than fewer, longer tests.
- When not testing reading, adjust the reading level of the items, or provide assistance with reading when needed.
- Define unfamiliar or abstract words if their meanings are not directly being tested.
- Provide models of correctly answered items.
- Change the test setting for students with special needs (e.g., a quiet space where the student can work privately).
- Allow more time for test completion for students who are slower with reading, writing, or processing test requirements.
- Allow students to dictate responses or use communication boards to indicate their responses.

Specific Formats   Recommendations have also been made for specific types of tests (see Salend, 1995, 2009, 2011):

- For true–false items, write out the words *true* and *false* for clarity, and avoid double negatives or emphasize negatives with bold or underlining. Students may become confused when asked to choose "false" as the correct answer to a negative statement, such as, "The office of president is *not* described in the Constitution."

- For multiple-choice tests, reduce the number of options, and limit the number of confusing options, such as "(a) and (b) but not (c)." If possible, have students answer on the test itself rather than a separate answer sheet, particularly at the elementary grades.

- For matching items, reduce the overall number of items. Provide an example of a correctly answered item, and place the entire list on one page.

- For short-answer questions, consider providing a choice of answers for the student to circle, rather than filling in a blank.

- For essay questions, describe what you would like to see included in the essay (without providing too much information), and recommend how the answer should be organized.

ADJUST SCORING PROCEDURES In addition to adjusting the format of tests, you can also adjust the way you score the tests. If some students have particular difficulty in areas such as spelling and grammar, it probably is unnecessary to penalize these students in every class they take, particularly if they are doing all they can to improve in these areas. If it seems important to grade on spelling, grammar, and neatness, consider grading these areas separately from actual mastery of the content, and perhaps ascribing these areas less weight. It may also be helpful to consider giving partial credit for answers that are incorrect but nonetheless demonstrate some knowledge of the content covered. It seems reasonable that answers demonstrating even a little knowledge may be given more credit than answers reflecting no knowledge.

STRATEGIES FOR
USING CURRICULUM-BASED MEASUREMENT

Curriculum-based measurement (CBM) was developed to document student progress through the class curriculum and to assist teachers in creating more effective instructional environments for students. When teachers actively monitor instruction and make adjustments based on CBM, learning outcomes improve (Berkeley & Riccomini, 2011). Fuchs, Fuchs, Hamlett, Phillips, and Bentz (1994) described two major distinguishing features of CBM.

First, CBM entails a standardized (but probably not norm-referenced) set of procedures for administration. These standardized procedures include sampling test items from classroom curricula, administering the test under the same or similar conditions, summarizing the test information, and using the test information in instructional decision making.

The second distinguishing feature of CBM is its focus on a long-term curricular goal—for example, the goal that you wish students will achieve by the end of the year. To this extent, CBM differs from other types of continuous measurement (or formative evaluation), in which student progress is assessed directly through changing objectives and standards throughout the year. With CBM, the test domain remains constant from the beginning of the school year until the end.

APPLY CBM TO MONITOR LEARNING PROGRESS For an example of CBM, consider the curriculum area of spelling. The teacher examines the level of the curriculum for an entire domain of words that students are expected to be able to spell by the end of the year. Then the teacher samples from this list, creating, for example, 50 versions of a 20-item spelling test that include words that students will study throughout the year. The teacher administers one of these lists about twice a week under standardized administration procedures (e.g., words are read once every 7 seconds, and students write the words on lined, numbered paper). Student performance can be scored by means of measures that may be more sensitive than the number of words spelled correctly, such as the number of correct letter sequences (Berkeley & Riccomini, 2011).

Letter sequence scores can then be plotted over time, either for individual students or for the class as a whole (see Figure 12.2). Student progress can be plotted over time, and the teacher can estimate whether students will attain end-of-year goals if they continue to progress at the current rate. If progress seems inadequate, teachers can implement modifications, such as increased time-on-task or individual work with specific difficult letter patterns. Similarly, progress can be plotted on measures of reading (e.g., word reading fluency) or math (e.g., problem-solving fluency), and estimates can then be made of whether students are making adequate progress toward end-of-year goals. When progress is not adequate, instructional modifications are made (Stecker, Fuchs, & Fuchs, 2005).

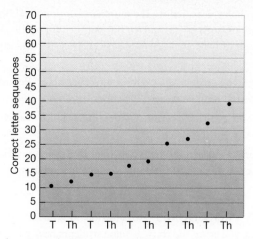

Figure 12.2 Curriculum-Based Measurement in Spelling Chart

Curriculum-based measurement also has been recommended for use in RTI programs (Fuchs & Fuchs, 2008). Students' responses to instruction can be measured formatively, based on the curriculum being used, as a guide to evaluation. Using CBM, adequate progress toward long-term objectives can be assessed to aid in placement decisions, for example, to determine placement eligibility for Tier 2 or Tier 3 RTI programs. CBM is also employed to inform instructional modifications in RTI programs.

STRATEGIES FOR
USING PERFORMANCE ASSESSMENT

Performance assessment addresses students' ability to interact (perform) appropriately with relevant instructional materials and the content of instruction. As such, this type of assessment relies much less on direct recall of verbal information than do more typical classroom tests, and it relies more on students' demonstration of understanding. Elements of performance assessment include (a) defined purpose, (b) performance tasks, (c) a direction for the student's performance, and (d) methods for assessment (Johnson et al., 2009). Performance assessment is also helpful when testing students who may have word-finding (retrieval) problems, communication disorders, or other skills that limit verbal communication. The state of California, for example, has established performance standards for alternate assessments in several content and skill areas (California Department of Education, 2015).

In an investigation by Scruggs, Mastropieri, Bakken, and Brigham (1993), students with learning disabilities performed relatively poorly on a more traditional test of their recall of vocabulary words after hands-on science instruction. However, they were much more able to demonstrate their knowledge in performance-based tests that required them to determine, for example, which of two minerals is harder or whether a mineral contains calcite. Performance assessment is an effective way of measuring all students' comprehension of academic content in at least part of virtually all school subjects, including science, math, social studies, music, art, vocational education, and physical education.

Although performance assessments may vary widely, they often have three key elements in common:

1. Students construct their own responses, rather than selecting or identifying correct responses.

2. Teachers can observe student performance on tasks reflecting real-world or authentic requirements.

3. Student responses can reveal patterns in students' thinking and learning, as well as whether the question was correctly answered. (Fuchs, 1994)

IMPLEMENT AND ADAPT PERFORMANCE ASSESSMENT To set up performance assessment measures, first determine exactly what you want students to be able to do after the instructional unit, and state it as a behavioral objective. The next step is to set up the materials and provide the opportunity for the student to perform on the test. Specific tasks can be placed at several stations around the classroom, and students can move from station to station individually, without observing another student's performance on the test.

Scoring is typically done by using a rubric that lists test items and scoring criteria. Performance assessments can be holistic (for the entire task) or analytic (for specific task components; Johnson et al., 2009).

For example, consider a performance assessment for a science unit on ecosystems (students had built their own "ecocolumns" using plants, animals, soil, water, and 2-liter bottles), which used the following test item:

- Draw a picture of an ecosystem. Label all parts.

To score this item objectively, a scoring rubric was constructed by which responses could be evaluated. For this item, the scoring criteria included the following:

MyEdLab:
Video Example 12.5.
This video exemplifies a performance assessment activity.

Scoring Rubric

Score	Scoring Criteria
3	Picture with living and nonliving things appearing to interact in some general way. Living and nonliving things labeled.
2	Picture of living and nonliving things not labeled, or labeled living, or labeled nonliving.
1	One of above or general relevant comment.
0	Nothing of relevance.

Using this key, then, a picture drawn by a student that included both living and nonliving things but did not have the items in the picture labeled would earn a score of 2 points. An example of a response to this particular item on a performance assessment is given in Figure 12.3. See if you can score number 2 in Figure 12.3.

Schirmer and Bailey (2000) described the development of a rubric for writing assessment that was employed successfully with middle school students who were deaf. They emphasized that the rubric should be a dynamic tool, capable of accommodating individual differences in student needs, content, assignments, and curriculum. That is, some students may benefit from a rubric that emphasizes word choice as a means for expanding vocabulary, whereas other students may benefit from a rubric that emphasizes organization of ideas. In creating a writing assessment rubric, teachers should:

- Identify the qualities of writing.
- Create a scale.
- Define each quality by listing the characteristics that describe performance at each point on the scale. (Schirmer & Bailey, 2000, p. 55)

These rubrics could include traits and their definitions, along with a scale for rating these traits. For example, Schirmer and Bailey (2000) created a rubric for writing assessment, adapted from a published English series, that listed traits, including topic, content, story development, organization, text structure, voice/audience, word choice, sentence structure, and mechanics. Specific definitions were provided for each trait. The *In the Classroom* feature on page 296 includes a math scoring rubric.

Accommodations in performance assessments may also be helpful for students with special needs. Crawford, Helwig, and Tindal (2004) reported some relative benefit from longer time limits on a performance assessment in writing, and Johnson, Kimball, Brown, and Anderson (2001) reported that reading math items to students with learning disabilities provided some benefit to test-takers.

STRATEGIES FOR
USING PORTFOLIO ASSESSMENT

DEVELOP PORTFOLIOS   A *portfolio* has been defined as a "systematic and organized collection of evidence used by the teacher and student to monitor the growth of the student's knowledge, skills, and attitudes" (Vavrus, 1990, p. 48). Using portfolios for assessment, teachers

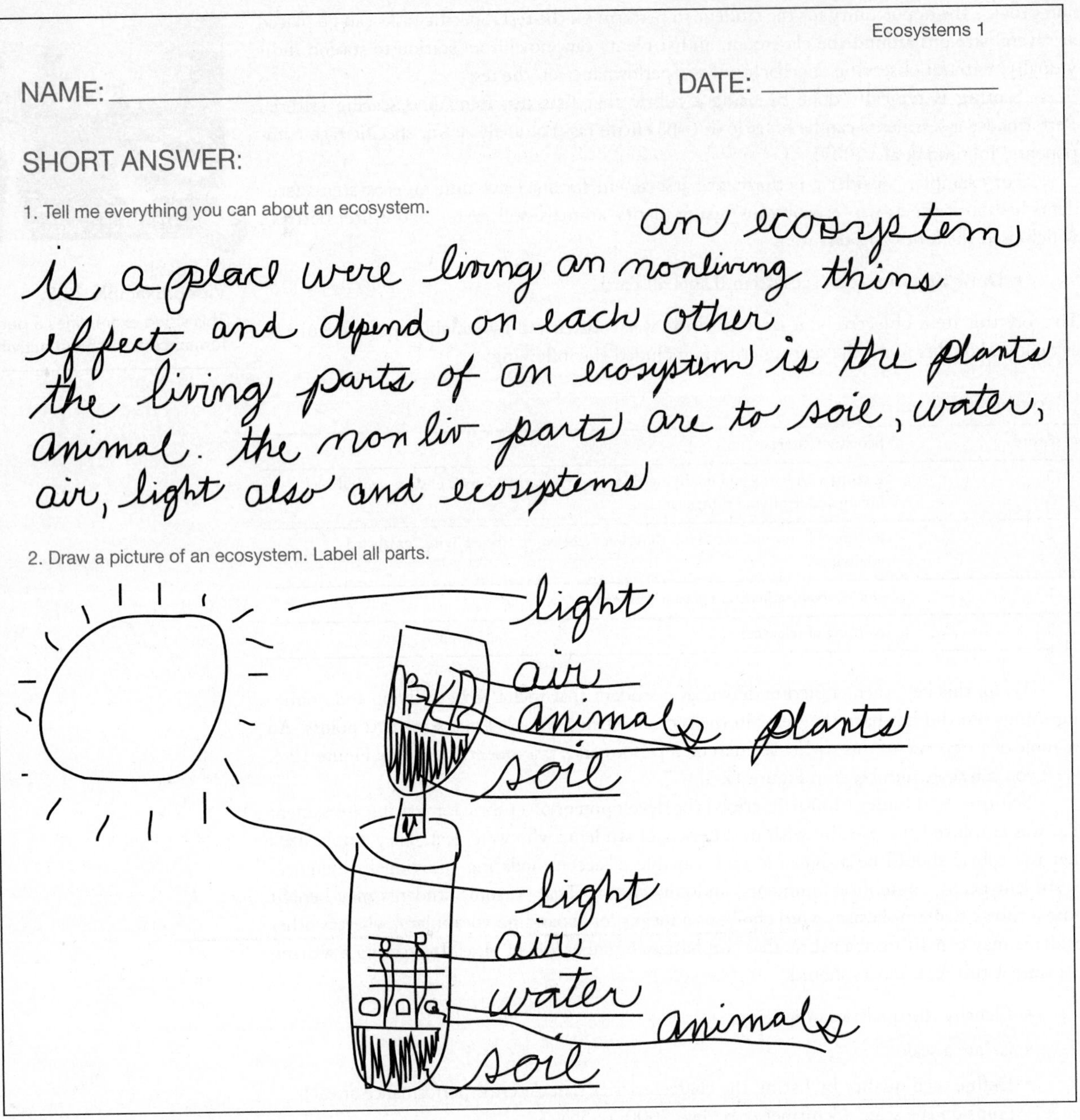

NAME: _____   DATE: _____

SHORT ANSWER:

1. Tell me everything you can about an ecosystem.

an ecosystem is a place were living an nonliving things effect and depend on each other the living parts of an ecosystem is the plants animal. the non liv parts are to soil, water, air, light also and ecosystems

2. Draw a picture of an ecosystem. Label all parts.

light
air
animals   *plants*
soil

light
air
water   *animals*
soil

Figure 12.3 Student Response on Ecosystem Item of Performance-Based Assessment

and students collect and organize relevant products to document performance and progress in different areas of academic and behavioral functioning (Wesson & King, 1996). These products can be collected in accordion folders or in three-ring notebooks with pocketed dividers. Portfolios can also be collected and stored electronically, including digital photos and videos and electronically scanned documents. Software is available for creating electronic and web-based portfolios (Barrett, 2000). You can refer to portfolios to document current functioning, to determine progress, to share information with parents and other teachers, and to plan appropriate interventions in the student's educational environment (Salend, 2009). Portfolios can be created in any area of student performance, including literacy, math, and science. Portfolios may also be useful in situations where more traditional standardized tests may not be appropriate, for example, for some students with autism.

Because student portfolios can be tailored to the specific needs of the classroom, the student, or the curriculum, they can be considered quite versatile. However, for these same reasons, portfolios may lack standardization and objectivity, and therefore teachers must ensure that judgments based on portfolio products are both reliable and valid (Salvia et al., 2013).

- Informal assessment samples
- Audio and video recordings of oral reading, comprehension think-alouds, descriptions, and story retells; interviews about performance and progress in reading over time and periodically throughout the school year
- Students' notebooks, logs of read books, written products
- Checklists
- Charts of curriculum-based measurement performance
- Teacher's notes, including error analysis
- Formal assessment samples
- Tests, such as teacher-made, criterion-referenced, and standardized

Figure 12.4   Potential Items to Include in a Literacy Portfolio

Helpful strategies include using multiple measures of the same skills or products, calculating interrater reliability (where different "experts" independently assess portfolio products), and making comparisons with more traditional measures (e.g., standardized tests or criterion-referenced measurement). Nevertheless, portfolios can provide authentic evidence of actual classroom performance that may be difficult to document by other methods. You can also use student portfolios to reflect on your own teaching. The *Diversity in the Classroom* feature on page 294 describes uses of portfolio assessment for English language learners.

MyEdLab:
Video Example 12.6.
This video clip reviews the process one teacher uses for portfolio assessment. Think about how to adjust this for students with special needs.

Figure 12.4 provides a list of items that could be included in a literacy portfolio, and Figure 12.5 provides a list of items that could be included in a science portfolio.

ADAPT PORTFOLIO ASSESSMENT   In addition to the "traditional" uses of portfolio assessment in education, portfolio assessment can also be used to document the performance of students who have been referred to special education. Portfolios are commonly used in developing alternate assessments (Salvia et al., 2013). Salend (2009) pointed out that portfolios could be linked with individual student IEPs by including work products that show growth on IEP objectives and by periodically completing summary sheets that link IEP objectives to documentation in the portfolio.

Wesson and King (1996) provided two case studies of the use of portfolios with students with disabilities. In the first study, a sixth-grade general education teacher used a portfolio to chronicle the progress of a student, Tom, classified as seriously emotionally/behaviorally disturbed. Tom was described as having difficulties getting along with peers and frequently fighting with them, being argumentative and noncompliant with teachers, being socially isolated, and making limited academic progress. Tom's portfolio included a video (updated regularly) of Tom's performance during cooperative group lessons, a description of Tom's outside-school social activities, and a list of narrative observations the teacher (or teacher's aide) had made as she watched Tom in social situations, including behavioral observations of Tom's problem behaviors.

- Authentic and performance assessment items
- Audio and video recordings of debates on climate change, science fair presentations, projects in the community such as recycling education programs
- Picture updates of longer-term projects such as building an ecosystem and conducting experiments on the ecosystem, including documentation of predictions and observations and a comparison of predictions with observations
- Samples of both formal and informal tests
- Teacher anecdotal records

Figure 12.5   Sample Portfolio Items for Science

Assessment Portfolios

With the increased accountability movement and the increased amount of standardized testing in schools, some have advocated the use of assessment portfolios for English language learners (ELLs; Gomez, 2001). Assessment portfolios are defined as the "systematic collection of student work measured against predetermined scoring criteria" (Gomez, 2001, p. 1). Student work includes various types of writing samples; different types of student reports from a variety of subject areas, such as social studies and science; samples of math problem solving; and copies of standardized test performance, such as results from statewide high-stakes tests and other norm-referenced standardized tests. Scoring criteria include scoring rubrics designed specifically for the contained assignments, checklists, and rating scales. Both the types of student work and the predetermined criteria for evaluating such work need to be established by the school or district.

The advantages of such a system are that it allows for breadth of evaluation of students who are English language learners, as well as inclusion of those students within the high-stakes testing of districts. In addition, the development of the assessment portfolio provides teachers and administrators opportunities to identify critical components of the curriculum, which can lead to a shared vision of teaching and learning for all students (see Rhodes, Ochoa, & Ortiz, 2005). District personnel can decide to include anything observable, along with its respective scoring criteria, in the portfolio. Such a process may represent a more authentic picture of what ELLs and all students have gained throughout a school year than simply a standardized score on a high-stakes test. The process may also yield information that is easier to communicate with parents. Sharing actual samples of student work and how it was evaluated during parent conferences might assist parents in understanding their child's level of performance better than a standardized test score. Suggestions for working with families of ELLs are provided at colorincolorado.org. Student portfolio progress and performance can also be used to help determine whether students need instructional and testing accommodations.

Banks (2015) suggests using multiple forms of assessment to evaluate students with cultural, ethnic, and linguistic diversity, including standardized and teacher-made summative and formative measures. A combination of measures provides students opportunities to demonstrate mastery learning (Kornhaber, 2012). Samples of all measures can be included in a student's portfolio.

Challenges associated with assessment portfolios also exist. As with any portfolio, there is a chance of more limited reliability and comparability across classes and grade levels compared with a single standardized test score. It also is a challenge to include standardized administration procedures for all works contained in the portfolio. For example, when including a long-term social studies project, it may be difficult to ensure that the student completed the work entirely independently. Overall, however, assessment portfolios can provide a rich and important complement to more traditional methods of assessment and may help to reveal relative strengths not documented with standardized tests.

In the second case study, a portfolio was created for the vocational experiences of Chris, a 16-year-old student with severe disabilities. This portfolio included a video showing Chris working in academic and vocational settings, a transcript of an interview the teacher conducted with Chris, a vocational skills checklist, and a list of Chris's circle of friends and their roles in her life. Chris's teacher hoped the portfolio would be useful when Chris began applying for jobs and working in the community (Wesson & King, 1996). Kearns, Burdge, and Clayton (2006) described the use of enhanced portfolio and performance assessments to document adapted grade-level content standards for statewide testing for students with significant cognitive disabilities. Teachers should consult individual state procedures for incorporating portfolio assessments within alternate state assessments.

Teach Test-Taking Skills

Tests are intended to measure knowledge and skill in specific areas; however, tests can also measure student "test-taking" skills. Many students with disabilities and at risk for failure in school perform poorly on tests in part because of poor test-taking skills (Deshler & Schumaker, 2006; Scruggs & Mastropieri, 1988, 1992).

Test-taking strategies help students with disabilities improve their performance on both standardized and teacher-made tests. Several researchers have described a number of test-taking strategies that have been helpful for all types of learners (Hughes, 1996; Hughes, Schumaker, Deshler, & Mercer, 1988; Kesselman-Turkel & Peterson, 2004; Salend, 2009, 2016; Scruggs & Mastropieri, 1992). This section describes test-taking strategies that are successful in increasing the test performance of students with special needs.

Anxiety reduction also can help. You can help students reduce anxieties during testing situations by encouraging their use of positive attributions—that is, by helping them focus on effort and strategies, rather than thinking about what their score will be or how others will do. Teach students to recognize signs of tension in themselves—such as grinding teeth, biting fingernails, and picking at hair or face—and to respond by consciously relaxing their muscles and controlling their breathing. Teaching test-taking and study skills can also help relieve anxiety (Lucangeli & Scruggs, 2003; Salend, 2011).

STRATEGIES FOR
TEACHING TEST-TAKING SKILLS

TEACH GENERAL TEST-PREPARATION STRATEGIES General preparation strategies refer to things students can do to help when preparing for any exam. Many students, but especially those with disabilities, will benefit from explicit instruction in each of these areas.

The first and most important general test strategy is academic preparation. The next general strategy is physical preparation, which includes getting enough rest and nourishment, particularly before studying and before taking the test. A positive attitude toward tests is also important. Improve test attitudes by helping students set realistic goals, providing practice tests, explaining the purpose of the particular test, rewarding effort, and providing training in test-taking skills.

TEACH GENERAL STRATEGIES FOR STANDARDIZED TESTS You can teach students general strategies that they can apply across a number of standardized tests and testing situations (Salend, 2009, 2016; Scruggs & Mastropieri, 1992). These strategies include using separate answer sheets, elimination strategies, guessing effectively, and using time wisely.

Separate Answer Sheets Most standardized tests require students to record their responses by filling a circle or "bubble" on separate answer sheets. Provide students with practice filling in the appropriate answer bubble "quick, dark, and inside the line." If practice tests are provided by the test publisher, provide instruction on the use of separate answer sheets (if not, make simulated answer sheets and test booklets when appropriate).

Use Elimination Strategies Teach students to eliminate response options they know are incorrect. For example, if there are four answer options and a test-taker can eliminate three of them, then the remaining option must be the correct response.

Guess When Appropriate Encourage guessing where appropriate, as many students with disabilities and at risk for school failure do not realize that guessing is better than leaving an item blank on most standardized tests (when there is not a penalty for guessing).

In the Classroom

Sample Mathematics Scoring Rubric

4 Exemplary Response
  4.1 Complete, with clear, coherent, unambiguous, and insightful explanation
  4.2 Shows understanding of underlying mathematical concepts, procedures, and structures
  4.3 Examines and satisfies all essential conditions of the problem
  4.4 Presents strong supporting arguments with examples and counterexamples as appropriate
  4.5 Solution and work is efficient and shows evidence of reflection and checking of work
  4.6 Appropriately applies mathematics to the situation

3 Competent Response
  3.1 Gives a fairly complete response with reasonably clear explanations
  3.2 Shows understanding of underlying mathematical concepts, procedures, and structures
  3.3 Examines and satisfies most essential conditions of the problem
  3.4 Presents adequate supporting arguments with examples and counterexamples as appropriate
  3.5 Solution and work show some evidence of reflection and checking of work
  3.6 Appropriately applies mathematics to the situation

2 Minimal Response
  2.1 Gives response, but explanations may be unclear or lack detail
  2.2 Exhibits minor flaws in underlying mathematical concepts, procedures, and structures
  2.3 Examines and satisfies some essential conditions of the problem
  2.4 Draws some accurate conclusions, but reasoning may be faulty or incomplete
  2.5 Shows little evidence of reflection and checking of work
  2.6 Some attempt to apply mathematics to the situation

1 Inadequate Response
  1.1 Response is incomplete, and explanation is insufficient or not understandable
  1.2 Exhibits major flaws in underlying mathematical concepts, procedures, and structures
  1.3 Fails to address essential conditions of the problem
  1.4 Uses faulty reasoning and draws incorrect conclusions
  1.5 Shows no evidence of reflection and checking of work
  1.6 Fails to apply mathematics to the situation

0 No attempt
  0.1 Provides irrelevant or no response
  0.2 Copies part of the problem but does not attempt a solution
  0.3 Illegible response

Note: To receive a particular score, a significant number of the associated criteria must be met.

Note: From *Connecting performance assessment to instruction* (p. 24), by L. S. Fuchs, 1994, Reston, VA: Council for Exceptional Children. Copyright 1994 by CEC. Reprinted with permission.

Use Time Wisely On timed tests, monitoring time while taking the test is important. Teach students to use time efficiently on familiar items and not to waste time on items they are unlikely to answer correctly. Teach students to monitor their time as they take the test. That is, when the testing period is half over, they should be finished with about half of the test. If they plan to have time at the end to review their answers, they should be finished with more than half of the test when the time period is half over.

TEACH SPECIFIC STRATEGIES FOR STANDARDIZED TESTS   Strategies can be employed for specific subtests of standardized tests.

Reading-Comprehension Subtests   Most standardized reading-comprehension subtests require students to read a specific passage and then answer questions about the passage. Teach students to read as much of the passage as possible because they can still answer many of the questions even if they have skipped some unfamiliar words. Encourage students to read the entire question and every stem option before selecting responses. Teach students to check back in the passage when possible to verify that their answer choice was correct. When reading selections contain information in tables, such as basketball schedules, teach students to quickly skim the information and then look to the questions and refer back to the table to identify answers.

Decoding Subtests   Because students do not respond orally and decode words, decoding subtests on group-administered standardized tests may have unusual formats. For example, students may be asked to match a word that contains the same sound as that underlined in the stem:

1. Which word contains the underlined sound?
   pl<u>ay</u>
   a. plan
   b. yard
   c. afraid
   d. drag

Teach students to say the underlined sound of the word to themselves, and be certain they have found an answer that matches this sound (c. "afraid"), not the appearance of the stem word (a. "plan").

Mathematics Computation Subtests   Mathematics computation subtests require students to look at test items, compute answers on scratch paper, and select the correct answer from the options provided. Provide students with practice in using scratch paper and identifying the correct answer from an array of choices. Teach students to rewrite the problem in the format that they are most comfortable with. Be sure students have sufficient practice with mathematics vocabulary that will be used in word problems. Review words such as *sum, product, difference, quotient,* and other words that may appear on the test.

Mathematics Concepts Subtests   Mathematics concepts subtests cover a range of skills in math and are presented in a variety of formats on standardized tests. Model examples in which you read the question, rephrase it, and then think aloud through to the solution. Some math problems may contain boxes to indicate missing values, as in the following example:

2. What number should be in the □ ?
   $524 - □ = 425 + 75$
   a. 500
   b. 75
   c. 24
   d. 425

Practice solving problems before the test using the types of boxes or other symbols that may be used on standardized tests. If specific formats that will be used are not known (and this is likely), practice solving problems throughout the year using different answering formats. Be sure students are aware of any specialized vocabulary (e.g., *quotient, subtrahend*) that is likely to be included on the test.

Math Problem-Solving Subtests   Tests of math problem solving require reading the problem, determining what is known, figuring out what operation is called for, generating a plan for a solution, computing the solution, selecting the correct answer from the options, and marking the selected response appropriately on the answer sheet. Provide students with practice using the scratch paper, which involves carefully matching the number of the problem on the scratch paper with the number in the test booklet, along with practice in executing all the other necessary steps in the procedure for solving word problems.

Tell students to practice requesting help with reading directions or word problems if they need it. If test administrators are not allowed to provide assistance in an area, they will simply say, "I cannot help you with that."

Some math problems do not contain all the necessary information to answer the question, and students are asked to furnish the missing, but necessary, information. For example:

3. Tyler is 66 inches tall. What else do you need to know to figure out how much he grew this year?
   a. How old he is this year
   b. How tall he was last year
   c. How tall his father is
   d. How much his brother grew last year

Practice with this type of format, and others, may be necessary for students with special needs to ensure successful performance. Model and demonstrate by thinking through the solution aloud. Have students practice using similar procedures.

Science and Social Studies Subtests   Formats for science and social studies exams typically parallel the formats employed in reading-comprehension and mathematics subtests. Many items require students to read expository passages and then answer questions about the passages. Other items require students to examine charts, diagrams, reference materials, or maps and interpret them before selecting correct answers. Provide practice using these various formats with students when teaching throughout the year.

TEACH STRATEGIES FOR TEACHER-MADE TESTS   Teachers sometimes use tests developed by textbook publishers to accompany adopted text materials. At other times, they develop their own tests. Both teacher-made and publisher-developed tests may include objective test formats such as multiple-choice, matching, and true–false items, as well as written formats that contain short-answer, fill-in-the-blank, essay, and performance-based items. The general preparation strategies, and many of the general strategies described for standardized tests, are also applicable to teacher-made tests. In addition, some specific strategies for teacher-made tests should be learned.

Objective Tests   Objective tests contain multiple-choice, true–false, and/or matching items. All strategies described so far may be applicable for helping students prepare for objective tests. However, students should be familiar with the content on teacher-made tests, and they can use this knowledge, or partial knowledge, to improve their test scores.

Written Tests   Written tests may contain sentence-completion, short-answer, or essay items. The following strategies can help students become better test-takers on these types of tests.

1. *Sentence-Completion Items and Short-Answer Items*. Sentence-completion items are usually short sentences containing blanks that must be filled in correctly ("The longest river in South America is _____"), whereas short-answer items ask questions requiring a brief response ("What were the causes of the War of 1812?").

Encourage students to provide some answer, even if it is only partially correct. Many teachers give partial credit for some answers, but they cannot provide any credit if the items are left blank. Have students guess if they are not completely sure, encourage them to use partial knowledge, and teach them to make the sentence sound logical in sentence-completion items. Sometimes lists of items are considered acceptable responses for short-answer items. Determine whether sentence fragments or lists will result in the same credit as complete sentences.

2. *Essay Questions*. Essay tests are difficult for students with disabilities, but strategies exist to facilitate essay test performance. One strategy is referred to as **SNOW**, which stands for the following:

Study the question

Note important points

Organize the information

Write directly to the point of the question. (Scruggs & Mastropieri, 1992, p. 89)

	Command Words on Test Items and Their Implications
Word	*Possible Implications*
Discuss	Provide reasoning behind; give different points of view.
Describe	Give an overall impression; give examples.
Compare	Show how two or more things are similar; provide examples of common characteristics.
Contrast	Show how two or more things are different; provide examples of differing characteristics.
Explain	Clarify or simplify; describe the rationale behind.
Justify	Argue in favor of; defend.
Critique	Argue in opposition of; find fault with.
List	Give a simple list of elements.
Outline	Give a list of elements organized into a system.

Figure 12.6 Command Words and Their Explanations

Note: From *Teaching test-taking skills: Helping students show what they know* (p. 90), by T. E. Scruggs & M. A. Mastropieri, 1992, Cambridge, MA: Brookline. Copyright 1992 by Brookline. Reprinted with permission.

Teach students how to implement each step of this strategy, and provide corrective feedback on their performance. Have them *study* the questions by underlining the specific words that tell them what to do, such as *describe, define, explain, compare, contrast, list, justify,* or *critique* (see Figure 12.6).

Next, students should *note* important points that come to mind. Then they should *organize* their notes by numbering the main and supporting points in logical order for discussion. Finally, they should *write* concisely and directly to the point of the question.

Performance Tests Performance tests are designed to parallel the exact format of what has been taught and practiced, and they are designed to provide better information about instruction (Baron, 1990). A practice test may be helpful for some students in preparing for the test. Teach students to read directions carefully and not to answer too quickly if something looks familiar. Show them how to talk through the steps of answers before responding.

TEACH OTHER TEST-TAKING STRATEGIES Other test-taking strategies may be helpful in preparing students to take tests. One strategy is called **SCORER** (Carman & Adams, 1972). Each letter in SCORER represents clue words to help students perform better during testing situations: **S**chedule time; **C**lue words (see Figure 12.6); **O**mit hard items; **R**ead carefully; **E**stimate answers; and **R**eview work. This strategy has been successfully used with students of middle school age (Ritter & Idol-Maestas, 1986).

Another strategy, **PIRATES**, is a seven-step strategy designed to help students perform better on teacher-made tests (Hughes, Rule, Deshler, & Schumaker, 1993). Each letter in PIRATES represents a step of the strategy: **P**repare to succeed; **I**nspect the instructions; **R**ead, remember, reduce; **A**nswer or abandon; **T**urn back; **E**stimate; **S**urvey. Although it is often used with students with learning disabilities and emotional/behavioral disorders (e.g., Banks & Eaton, 2014; Haynes, 2011), this strategy has also been employed successfully with high-functioning students with autism (Songlee, 2007).

Another test-taking strategy is called **ANSWER** (Hughes, 1996). Whereas PIRATES was originally designed for improving performance on objective tests, ANSWER is designed to assist students with essay-type exams. The steps in ANSWER can be summarized as follows:

- **A**nalyze the situation, by reading the item carefully, underlining important words, and estimating time needed.
- **N**otice requirements, by marking different parts of the question and committing to a quality answer.
- **S**et up an outline, including main ideas, and check outline ideas with the question.

- Work in details, remembering previous learning and applying it in appropriate order, using abbreviations.

- Engineer your answer, by writing an introductory paragraph, referring back to your outline, using topic sentences and additional details, and providing examples.

- Review your work, by checking the entire answer with all components of the question. (Hughes, 1996)

Remember that any learning strategy requires students to (a) identify when the strategy should be used, (b) retrieve the steps in the strategy, and (c) correctly apply the strategy steps to the task (Mastropieri & Scruggs, 2002). Students will need repeated exposure to, and practice with, each strategy in order to learn to use it effectively.

MyEdLab: **Self-Check 12.3**

MyEdLab: **Application Exercise 12.3: Test-Taking Skills**

MyEdLab:
Video Example 12.7.
This video clip provides an overview of how to structure grading for a student with special needs. This is done through a team meeting.

Grading
STRATEGIES FOR

ADAPTING REPORT CARD GRADING

Report card grading is an essential component of the U.S. educational system (Brookhart, 2004), and the importance of grades in our society cannot be denied. However, across the country, standards for grading appear to be somewhat variable. Polloway et al. (1994) reported that about 39% of the districts surveyed had a specific policy for adaptations in grading for students with disabilities (see also Munk & Bursuck, 2003). The most common responses involved adaptations reflected in the students' IEPs, decisions made by a committee, and notations of accommodations noted on the report card.

ADJUST GRADING PROCEDURES There appears to be no one "right" way to proceed when issuing report card grades to students with disabilities. However, following are some considerations that could be helpful in planning grading procedures (Brookhart, 2004; Christiansen & Vogel, 1998; Jung & Guskey, 2010; Munk & Bursuck, 1998):

1. *Consult school and district policy.* Some schools have established official policies on issuing report card grades to students with disabilities. Find out whether your school has such a policy, and, if so, follow its guidelines. Make recommendations when needed to appropriate school personnel.

2. *Follow recommendations on the IEP.* IEPs typically state explicit goals and objectives for the academic year. For example, an objective on an IEP may state that the student will score 70% correct on tests given in a general education science class. This goal can be taken into consideration when determining the student's grade in the class.

3. *Make no grading adjustments at all.* This approach is adopted by many regular classroom teachers, and there are some advantages to this approach. The grades the students earn directly reflect their success at performing in the regular classroom and can be a source of pride. However, many students may simply not be able to compete successfully in such an environment without supports, and grading without adjustments may doom some students to failure. Carefully consider the effect of adopting such a policy.

4. *Use a pass–fail system.* Consider carefully what the minimum standard for a passing grade would be, considering attendance, effort, and performance. Using the PASS variables, prioritize class objectives so that students with disabilities or other special needs receive as much appropriately adapted instruction on critical objectives as possible. At the end of the grading period, record performance with "pass" or "fail" (or "no pass").

5. *Use a double-standard approach.* With this approach, students with disabilities can be graded using different standards for letter grades. It may not be necessary simply to lower the standards, such that, for example, an "A" on the special education standard is equivalent to a "C" on the general education standard. It is also possible to consider the grade itself differently. For example, a grade on a special education standard could weight more heavily considerations such as effort, persistence, attitude, and progress (see Bursuck et al., 1996). Placing more importance on these areas also demonstrates to students that the grade they receive is more in their control than one that sets unrealistic academic standards and that may lead to resignation or quitting. A special education grading standard could also more carefully consider goals and objectives for the student documented on the student's IEP.

   Often when different grading standards are applied, some notation is included that acknowledges that the standard is different. This could be done by including a discreet note on the report card (e.g., "Special grading standard") or by circling the letter awarded. Use of different grading standards can make goals more realistic and achievable for students. However, it is important to first determine that the usual grading standards are not appropriate for particular students and that another standard is more appropriate (Jung & Guskey, 2010). If it seems that students may be able, with sufficient effort and support, to meet the same standards as the rest of the class, it may be best not to use a different standard.

6. *Contracting.* In some cases, it may be helpful to establish a formal contract with a student regarding report card grades. The contract can specify what the student will do to earn a particular grade in the class, with respect to, for example, attendance, punctuality, homework completion, participation, and test scores. Grades are then allocated according to the terms of the contract.

7. *Personal Grading Plans.* Munk and Bursuck (2001, 2003) described the development of Personal Grading Plans (PGPs) created by teams of general and special education teachers to provide more appropriate grading for individual students. For example, it was determined that the science grades of one eighth-grade student with learning disabilities were lower than expected because of the heavy weighting of tests and quiz scores. A PGP was developed that included specific objectives within each thematic unit, with specified criteria and an adjusted grading scale for each objective. With thoughtful adjustments and effective communication such as this, grading can be a useful and productive experience for everyone.

MyEdLab: **Self-Check 12.4**

MyEdLab: **Application Exercise 12.4: Portfolio Assessment**

12 Summary

- Many types of tests are used in education, including norm-referenced, criterion-referenced, competency-based, teacher-made, performance, portfolio, and curriculum-based tests. All tests must be reliable and valid to be useful.

- General strategies for adapting tests include using test accommodations, implementing individualized administration, teaching test-taking skills, and improving examiner familiarity. Other adaptation strategies can be applied to specific types of tests and test formats.

- Many students benefit from being taught test-taking skills, including general strategies such as elimination strategies, guessing, and efficient use of time; strategies for specific test formats; and strategies that can be applied to different types of tests.

- Adjustments can be made in grading and scoring the work of students with special needs. These adjustments can be applied to report card grades, homework, and seatwork.

PROFESSIONAL STANDARDS LINK: Assessment

Information in this chapter links most directly to:

- CEC Standards: 1 (Learning Development and Individual Learning Differences), 4 (Assessment), 5 (Instructional Planning and Strategies)

- INTASC Standards: 2 (Learning Differences), 6 (Assessment), 7 (Planning for Instruction), 8 (Instructional Strategies)

ASSESSMENT

When assessing students with disabilities, and other special needs, have you considered the following? If not, see the pages listed here.

STRATEGIES FOR ADMINISTERING NORM-REFERENCED TESTS

- ☐ Use test accommodations, 282–283
- ☐ Use universal design for learning, 283
- ☐ Use individually administered tests, 283
- ☐ Teach test-taking skills, 283
- ☐ Increase motivation, 283–284
- ☐ Improve examiner familiarity, 284
- ☐ Request accommodations for college entrance exams, 284

STRATEGIES FOR ADAPTING COMPETENCY-BASED LOCAL AND STATEWIDE ASSESSMENT

- ☐ Use test accommodations, 284–285
- ☐ Use alternate assessments, 285
- ☐ Request accommodations on GED tests, 285

STRATEGIES FOR ADAPTING TEACHER-MADE AND CRITERION-REFERENCED TESTS

- ☐ Revise tests, 286–289
- ☐ Adjust scoring procedures, 289

STRATEGIES FOR USING CURRICULUM-BASED MEASUREMENT

- ☐ Apply CBM to monitor learning progress, 289–290

STRATEGIES FOR USING PERFORMANCE ASSESSMENT

- ☐ Implement and adapt performance assessment, 290–291

STRATEGIES FOR USING PORTFOLIO ASSESSMENT

- ☐ Develop Portfolios, 291–293
- ☐ Adapt portfolio assessment, 293–294

STRATEGIES FOR TEACHING TEST-TAKING SKILLS

- ☐ Teach general test-preparation strategies, 295
- ☐ Teach general strategies for standardized tests, 295–296
- ☐ Teach specific strategies for standardized tests, 297–298
- ☐ Teach strategies for teacher-made tests, 298–299
- ☐ Teach other test-taking strategies, 299–300

STRATEGIES FOR ADAPTING REPORT CARD GRADING

- ☐ Adjust grading procedures, 300–301

13
14
15

Literacy

Mathematics

Science, Social Studies, and Transitions

13

Literacy

LEARNING OUTCOMES

After studying this chapter, you should be able to:

13.1 Understand considerations relevant to basal textbook, whole-language, Reading Recovery, direct-instruction, and code-emphasis approaches to reading.

13.2 Describe the Common Core State Standards for reading.

13.3 Describe strategies and adaptations for teaching basic reading skills, such as letter and word identification, phonemic awareness, phonics, and basic sight words; reading fluency; reading comprehension; and multi-tiered reading instruction with response to intervention.

13.4 Describe strategies and adaptations for teaching written expression, including handwriting, spelling, and written communication.

Reading is probably the most important academic skill students will learn in school. Most students acquire this skill with little apparent difficulty; however, for a smaller number, reading can represent a major stumbling block to school success (Pullen & Cash, 2011). The process of learning to read begins very early in life and extends well into adulthood.

Skills and understandings important for learning to read begin to develop in early infancy. These include recognizing books by the cover, pretending to read, listening to stories, attending to letters, and scribbling. Between the ages of 3 and 4, children begin to understand that it is print that is read in stories and that letters can be individually named. Pre-literate children learn to name some alphabet letters, attend to repeating (e.g., rhyming) sounds in language, and can connect information from a story to life experiences. Clearly, families can play a key role in promoting this important skill development (Paratore & Dougherty, 2011).

In school, children go through a sequence of levels of reading development, beginning with prereading skills such as sound segmentation and continuing through expert reading (Pressley, 2006; Pullen & Cash, 2011). After the early literacy or prereading stage, learners develop decoding skills (typically, grades 1–2), fluency and automaticity (grades 2–3), uses of reading for learning (grades 4–8), appreciation of multiple viewpoints and levels of comprehension (including literal, inferential, critical; grades 9–12), and construction and reconstruction of reading for one's own purposes (including personal, professional, and civic purposes; college and beyond). Common Core State Standards in English and language arts provide grade-appropriate reading standards in foundational skills, informational text, and literature across grades K–12 (National Governors Association Center for Best Practices & Council of Chief State School Officers, 2010).

Students with disabilities or other special needs may exhibit difficulties at any, or all, of these levels of learning to read. Some may have specific disabilities in reading, sometimes referred to as **dyslexia** (Lerner & Johns, 2015). In other cases, reading problems are a function of more general developmental or language delays or physical disabilities (Best, Heller, & Bigge, 2009). Students with hearing impairments often acquire reading skills at a slower rate (Stewart

& Kluwin, 2001), and students with visual impairments may require specialized materials. Students with emotional or behavioral disorders often read below grade level (Reid, Gonzalez, Nordness, Trout, & Epstein, 2004), and students with autism spectrum disorder also may read below grade level (Spector & Cavanaugh, 2015). However, in all cases, specific adaptations can significantly improve reading ability.

Approaches to Reading

There are several approaches to beginning reading instruction. It is important to understand these different approaches because they carry different implications for students who are having difficulty learning to read.

CLASSROOM SCENARIO

Markeisha

Markeisha is a sincere, likable seventh grader. However, she has struggled with reading since first grade. She marvels at how easily some of her peers are able to read. She can't figure out why it seems so easy for them and yet is so difficult for her. Sometimes when she looks at the printed page, the words make no sense at all. They don't look a bit familiar to her, even when her teacher has her repeat the words over and over. She does her best to get by in school by listening to other students read, by listening to her teachers, and by studying the illustrations in her books. She never raises her hand in class and sits quietly, hoping she will not be noticed. Markeisha really wants to learn to read better, but no one seems to be able to help her do so.

QUESTIONS FOR REFLECTION

1. Why does Markeisha not speak with her teacher about her reading problem?
2. What do you think might be the cause of this problem?
3. What could the teacher do to become more aware of reading problems in her classroom?

STRATEGIES FOR

IMPLEMENTING APPROACHES TO READING

IMPLEMENT AND ADAPT BASAL TEXTBOOK APPROACHES The most traditional approach to reading instruction involves the use of **basal textbooks**, with a different text assigned for each grade level from kindergarten through middle school (Temple, Ogle, Crawford, & Freppon, 2014). These textbooks contain short stories and comprehension questions designed to meet certain grade-level criteria. Some basal textbooks emphasize phonics; others highlight literature-based stories.

Most basal reading series include workbooks and worksheets that provide supplemental practice on comprehension and specific skills. In addition, the development of literacy is often supported by language arts classes, typically distinct from reading classes, whereby students are provided separate spelling and grammar textbooks.

Most students with reading difficulties have problems attending to the sounds in words and learning to decode (Pullen & Cash, 2011). If you have students with reading difficulties who are not making adequate progress in a particular basal series, determine whether your basal series offers a clear sequence of skills and sufficient review of these skills as they are learned. Consult with the special education teacher to determine whether a more structured phonetic approach might be more helpful, as a supplement or an alternative to the classroom materials. Some basal series provide a more balanced approach to literature and phonics instruction (e.g., Carnine, Silbert, Kameénui, Slocum, & Travers, 2016; Engelmann, Osborne, & Hanner, 2008).

IMPLEMENT AND ADAPT WHOLE-LANGUAGE APPROACHES The whole-language approach to reading emphasizes meaning and integrates all literacy tasks within reading instruction (Routman, 1991; Temple et al., 2014). A basic tenet of the approach is that the immersion of children in a literature-enriched environment promotes literacy. Many traditional skills, such as phonics, sounding out words, spelling, grammar, and comprehension strategies, are not directly taught (these are often addressed within the reading context), and there is an increased emphasis on meaning construction and use of context clues to figure out unknown words.

During whole-language instruction, students engage in reading **authentic literature** (e.g., trade books, real literature books) independently and maintain journals documenting their progress and comprehension of reading materials. Overall, the emphasis is placed on engaging students in literacy acts and promoting meaning (Goodman, 2006).

Unfortunately, as many as 25% of students do not discover sound–symbol relationships independently and without explicit instruction (Pullen & Cash, 2011). Students with serious reading difficulties frequently have deficits in **phonemic awareness** and need special training to learn that words are composed of smaller, individual speech sounds (phonemes)—for example, the word *pin* has three phonemes, /p/, /i/, and /n/. Phonemes can be added, subtracted, or rearranged to make new words (Pressley & Allington, 2015). In fact, foundational skills for reading, including phonemic awareness, phonics, word recognition, and fluency, are important components of early reading in the Common Core State Standards for English and language arts.

Most students with reading problems benefit from explicit training in phonological awareness, letter recognition and formation, sound–symbol relationships, decoding practice using controlled texts, comprehension strategies, and motivational techniques (Pressley & Allington, 2015; Pullen & Cash, 2011). Because whole-language approaches typically do not explicitly include such components, they may be less beneficial for students with serious reading difficulties unless additional instructional support is provided (Gersten & Dimino, 1993; Pressley & Rankin, 1994).

If you are using a whole-language approach to reading, collect reading performance data using curriculum-based measurement and audio recording of students' oral reading to ensure students are progressing satisfactorily. Fountas and Pinnell (2013) provide listings of thousands of trade books by graded reading level that can be used to support whole-language approaches to reading instruction (see also Wooten & Cullinan, 2015). Some students with severe reading deficits may benefit from whole-language instruction if they are also receiving specialized reading instruction from special educators (Rudenga, 1992). Finally, if you have the opportunity as a teacher to examine literature programs to make recommendations for adoption, review what considerations have been made to meet the reading needs of all students.

IMPLEMENT READING RECOVERY FOR STRUGGLING READERS Reading Recovery is a program that has been widely adopted in some states and school districts to help promote the early reading success of students at risk for reading failure (Slavin, 2005). Reading Recovery identifies primary-age students who are not learning to read and provides them with one-to-one tutorial instruction for 30 minutes daily. Sessions emphasize reading from familiar books, instruction in letter-identification strategies, writing and reading sentences and stories, assembling cut-up stories, and introducing the process of reading a new book. Teachers maintain daily records of students' reading progress, analyze children's problems, and devise appropriate instruction and feedback.

Reading Recovery has been considered effective for many young, struggling readers (D'Agostino & Murphy, 2004; Slavin, 2005). However, some findings suggest that the program may be less successful with students who have moderate to severe reading difficulties (Denton & Mathes, 2002; Hiebert, 1994; Reynolds & Wheldall, 2007), and others suggest that it lacks the carefully sequenced approach to skill development that is often recommended for such students (Bursuck & Damer, 2015). If Reading Recovery is used in your school with students with significant reading problems, be certain that their progress is carefully documented, and determine the steps that will be taken if acceptable progress is not being made.

IMPLEMENT AND ADAPT DIRECT-INSTRUCTION AND CODE-EMPHASIS APPROACHES **Direct instruction** is an instructional method that has proved successful with students with disabilities and those at risk for school failure (Carnine et al., 2016). Direct instruction involves a systematic, teacher-led approach using materials that contain a controlled vocabulary and emphasizing a **code-emphasis approach** to reading instruction. For example, students are taught the sound–symbol relationships among letters and are provided sufficient practice in decoding specific word patterns in reading passages before being presented with reading selections containing unfamiliar words. Individual sounds and words are introduced systematically and practiced in isolation and in word lists, sentences, paragraphs, short stories, and accompanying workbook activities. Frequently, students with serious reading difficulties benefit greatly from structured code-emphasis approaches (Shaywitz, 2003).

Curriculum materials are available that contain a code-emphasis approach to reading instruction. These materials include, for example, *Reading Mastery* (SRA/McGraw-Hill), a basal series intended for the entire general education classroom, and *Corrective Reading: Decoding Series* (SRA/McGraw-Hill), a series intended especially for students with reading problems. Both of these reading series promote an effective instruction model of delivery, including teacher modeling and demonstration, frequent student responding and feedback, and practice using controlled vocabulary materials to teach reading. Because students with reading disabilities frequently rely too much on context cues (Johnson, 1992; Pressley & Allington, 2015), the materials encourage use of word-attack skills, by, for example, not providing pictures or by providing pictures that can be seen only after reading and turning the page. In the *Corrective Reading Series*, students are given high-interest reading passages with controlled vocabulary that are introduced in a systematic sequence, with review following in subsequent passages.

Other commercially available structured reading programs include the *Merrill Reading Program* (SRA/McGraw-Hill) and *Read Well* (Voyager Sopris Learning) for early reading. These code-emphasis programs address all or nearly all of the Common Core State Standards relevant to reading (e.g., National Institute for Direct Instruction, 2015). The *Edmark Reading Program* (ProEd) is a sight-word program designed for students with few or no reading skills and those who have not benefited from an explicit phonics approach or other reading approaches. As with all programs, monitor progress carefully to be sure the methods and materials are having the desired effect.

Considerations and Adaptations Three commonly asked questions are whether students who are taught using a code-emphasis approach can transfer these reading skills to other, less-structured reading materials; whether they will lose motivation from all the structure; and whether they will learn comprehension skills. In fact, students with reading disabilities can transfer skills acquired from code-emphasis instruction to more literature-based programs (Snider, 1997). In addition, students can maintain their motivation if teachers use enthusiasm. Finally, teachers should ensure that any reading program is balanced and includes engaging text and sufficient comprehension instruction once students learn the necessary decoding skills (Adams, 1990; Klingner, Vaughn, & Boardman, 2007; Pressley & Allington, 2015). Ensure that your reading program provides all the elements necessary for students to become skilled and motivated readers.

MAKE ADAPTATIONS TO PROMOTE ACCESS TO TEXT For some students, physical and motor constraints can inhibit learning to read (Coleman & Heller, 2009). Regardless of the approach to reading, students must be able to stabilize reading materials and position themselves to facilitate efficient attending to the text. Ensure that students are positioned properly, with proper posture, in midline position, using supports when needed. Check to be sure the table and chair are at the right height and that the table is slanted when needed. Provide color contrasts—for example, with colored construction paper—for students with visual impairments.

For students who have difficulty turning pages, provide rubber fingertips (Swingline) or a pencil with an eraser end. Separate pages with notebook tabs, paper clips, or pieces of material such as sponge or weather stripping. Pages in electronic tablets can be easily turned with a touch of a finger.

For students who lose their place on the line, prepare a clear transparency with multicolored lines, composed of 1-inch strips of different colors. Place this transparency over pages as the student reads, and fade the use of the colored lines over time. Some students may become fatigued while reading, and the length of reading sessions may have to be adjusted (Heller & Alberto, 2010).

Some additional adaptations to promote access include modification of printed materials with braille or large print; use of magnifying devices; and use of optical character-recognition (OCR) systems, such as *Cicero Text Reader* (Dolphin Computer Access) and *Kurzweil 1000* and *Kurzweil 3000* (Kurzweil Education), that convert text to speech or braille. Other adaptations

MyEdLab:
Video Example 13.1.

In this video, an elementary school principal discusses the use of a "holistic" language-instruction approach (whole language) compared with a direct-instruction approach at a school with a large number of students for whom English is not their first language. Think about how their needs may be similar to those of some students with reading disabilities.

involve the use of audio-recording formats, including audio-recorded text, variable-speed cassettes and speech compressors, and listening centers. Apps such as *Voice Recorder* (TapMedia) allow for longer recordings on iPads or iPhones. Effective use of technology for students who are deaf includes use of hypertext to provide sign versions of printed text and use of word-processing software to integrate reading and writing (Schirmer & McGough, 2005). Apps for translating text to American Sign Language for iPhones and iPads include *ASL Translator* (Software Studios).

Employ Principles of Universal Design for Learning Universal design for learning (UDL) is a framework for designing instruction and learning activities to accommodate all learners (see cast.org; Hall, Meyer, & Rose, 2012; Meyer, Rose, & Gordon, 2014) that is similar in many ways to differentiated instruction. Many new technological advances are available to accommodate students with diverse learning needs in literacy instruction. For example, text-to-speech and speech-to-text software programs are widely available and even embedded into many existing programs, such as the Microsoft Office programs Word, Excel, and Outlook and the search engine Google Chrome. *Audible* is a program used to read aloud books that have recently been linked with Kindles, which are handheld devices containing downloaded electronic books. Students can begin reading a book and convert to listening to the book using Audible and revert back to reading or listening whenever desired. When starting up again, the program automatically syncs to the most recent stopping place, regardless of whether students were reading or listening. These applications, as well as the many other strategies described in this chapter, are consistent with UDL principles.

Common Core State Standards in Reading

Common Core State Standards for Reading (K–12) are found within the English Language Arts Standards and contain standards for reading in literature, informational text, and foundational skills. The grade-specific standards reflect end-of-year expectations and form, over all grade levels, a cumulative progression toward meeting college and career readiness in reading by the end of high school (National Governors Association Center for Best Practices & Council of Chief State School Officers, 2010). Foundational skills for reading at the fifth-grade level, for example, include the following:

- Phonics and Word Recognition:
  - Know and apply grade-level phonics and word analysis skills in decoding words.
  - Use combined knowledge of all letter–sound correspondences, syllabication patterns, and morphology (e.g., roots and affixes) to read accurately unfamiliar multisyllabic words in context and out of context.
- Fluency:
  - Read with sufficient accuracy and fluency to support comprehension.
  - Read grade-level text with purpose and understanding.
  - Read grade-level prose and poetry orally with accuracy, appropriate rate, and expression on successive readings.
  - Use context to confirm or self-correct word recognition and understanding, rereading as necessary. (© Copyright 2010. National Governors Association Center for Best Practices and Council of Chief State School Officers. All rights reserved.)

Informational text standards refer to understanding expository text, for example, science or history texts. Relevant skills include understanding relevant vocabulary, determining main ideas, summarizing text, identifying text structure, understanding how reasons and evidence are used to support points in a text, analyzing multiple accounts of the same topic, and integrating knowledge and ideas from multiple sources to write or speak knowledgeably about a given topic. Literature standards include quoting accurately from a text in explaining text content and drawing inferences, determining themes from details in the text, describing the role of a speaker's or narrator's point of view, and describing how different texts on the same topic address similar themes or topics (http://www.corestandards.org/ELA-Literacy/RF/5/; © Copyright 2010. National Governors Association Center for Best Practices and Council of Chief State School Officers. All rights reserved). For a detailed listing of all Common Core standards relevant to reading, refer to the Common Core website.

> MyEdLab: **Self-Check 13.1**
>
> MyEdLab: **Application Exercise 13.1: Approaches to Reading**

Teaching Reading Skills

Beyond the application of particular methods and materials reflecting different approaches to reading instruction, it is important for teachers to carefully attend to all aspects of the reading process to ensure that all students are receiving the instruction they need. It is also important that reading instruction is of high quality and based on research because, in many cases, it will represent the first tier of a school's response-to-intervention (RTI) approach to reading, as described later in this chapter.

STRATEGIES FOR

PROMOTING WORD IDENTIFICATION

Most students with reading difficulties require additional instruction and practice in identifying words. Readers need to become automatic and fluent at word reading so that they will be able to devote sufficient cognitive effort to comprehending what they read. However, before readers can acquire this automaticity, they must be able to read individual words. In order to do this, they must learn that words are composed of individual sounds, or phonemes.

PROVIDE PHONEMIC AWARENESS TRAINING   **Phonemes** are the smallest sound units, such as /t/ and /l/. Some students do not develop an understanding that words are composed of individual sounds as quickly as others, and therefore these students may find phonics instruction confusing. **Phonemic awareness** training includes activities to provide instruction and practice in listening and using sounds in isolation initially, followed by the use of words in context and in a reading passage. The purpose of phonemic (or phonological) awareness training is for students to learn that words are composed of individual sounds that can be combined and separated to create new words. Later, when they study phonics, they learn how these individual phonemes are represented by letters and letter combinations (Bursuck & Damer, 2015). Phonemic awareness is included prominently in foundational skills for grades K–1 in the Common Core State Standards for reading. Sample phonemic awareness activities include the following:

- Discriminating sounds, for example: "Tell me if these two words have the same, or different, first sound: *cap—cat.*"
- Sound blending or making individual sounds into words, for example: "What word am I saying: /k/–/a/–/t/?"
- Segmenting words into individual phonemes, for example: "How many sounds are in the word *fan?* What are the sounds?"
- Rhyming sounds, for example: "Tell me some words that rhyme with *fall.* Now, tell me some 'make-believe' words that rhyme with *fall.*"

Gamelike activities are available that emphasize phonological awareness training. For example, *Phonological Awareness Training for Reading* (Pro-Ed) includes a board game for skill development. In one game, Rocky the Robot "speaks" only in phonemes or **onset-rime** constructions, that is, the sounds that precede the first vowel in a syllable, followed by the remaining sounds. Students must create the words Rocky is trying to say. For example, a teacher could say, "Rocky says, 't-op.' What is he trying to say?" These materials provide instruction and practice with phonemic awareness skills over a 12- to 14-week period.

Phonemic awareness training may benefit your entire primary-grade classroom (Ehri et al., 2001; Suggate, 2016). For other grade levels, consult with special education teachers and speech and language specialists. These specialists can recommend specific practice activities to promote better phonemic awareness.

PROVIDE PHONICS INSTRUCTION Training in *phonics* follows phonemic awareness and refers to providing instruction in the sound–symbol associations among letters and symbols. Phonics skills are important components of Common Core State Standards in reading for grades K–5 (National Governors Association Center for Best Practices & Council of Chief State School Officers, 2010). Children who learn to read without any difficulties—and many do—may figure out this system independently. However, students without good phonics skills have to rely on visual memory, context clues, or picture clues to guess what the unfamiliar word is. Unfortunately, reliance on such clues is not always effective, especially when many letter–sound relationships are unknown (Pressley & Allington, 2015). These students can benefit from explicit phonics instruction. The National Reading Panel (2000) concluded that synthetic phonics—in which students are taught to convert letters into sounds or phonemes, then blend the sounds to form words—was associated with the largest overall positive effects in decoding, comprehension, and collateral skills such as spelling (Pullen & Lloyd, 2008).

According to Stahl (1992; see also Stahl, Duffy-Hester, & Dougherty-Stahl, 2006), an exemplary phonics program has the following characteristics:

- Builds on students' knowledge about how print works
- Builds on a phonemic awareness foundation
- Is explicit, clear, and direct
- Is integrated within a reading and language arts program
- Emphasizes reading words rather than memorizing rules
- Includes learning onsets and rimes
- Emphasizes development of independent word-recognition strategies
- Emphasizes development of fluency-building word-recognition skills

Instruction in phonics proceeds systematically; practice is provided using familiar words before new words are introduced. Usually, regular words are introduced before irregular words, and sufficient practice in reading and spelling is provided before introducing new vocabulary. In phonics-based programs, instruction follows a specific sequence of skills. Although variation exists, a possible sequence could include the following components (see also, for example, Bursuck & Damer, 2015; Mercer, Mercer, & Pullen, 2011):

1. Individual consonant and short vowel sounds (e.g., /s/, /a/)
2. Simple patterns such as *vc* (vowel–consonant, e.g., "at," "it") and *cvc* (consonant–vowel–consonant, e.g., "bat," "hit")
3. Consonant digraphs (e.g., *ch, sh, th*) and consonant blends (e.g., *bl, st, br*)
4. Long vowels, including final *e* (such as in *hope, tape*), and double vowels or vowel digraphs (such as in *keep, tail*)
5. *R*- and *l*-controlled vowels, such as in *car* and *call*
6. Diphthongs, such as *ow, oi, aw*

Once these skills and related skills are mastered, students can learn higher-level word-analysis skills, such as compound words, prefixes and suffixes, contractions, and syllabication. These skills should be integrated into the context of reading as they are acquired. As Stahl et al. (2006) emphasized, "Good phonics instruction should not teach rules, need not use worksheets, should not dominate instruction, and does not have to be boring" (p. 132).

Students with severe to profound hearing loss are typically far less proficient than other students in phonological skills. The reading skills of students with hearing impairments appear to be associated with language and vocabulary development (Marschark, 2009). During the elementary years, they appear to rely more on visual than acoustic cues for letters and words. In secondary school, and later in college, they may rely more on phonological information, particularly for words with regular spellings. Strategies recommended for teaching reading to students with

MyEdLab:
Video Example 13.2.

In this video, a teacher works with several children on a gamelike phonemic awareness activity.

severe hearing impairments include early access to language by means of signing and simultaneous exposure to written texts. Unfortunately, there is little research to demonstrate the effectiveness (or lack of effectiveness) of such techniques as phonemic awareness or phonics instruction, guided oral reading, and comprehension-monitoring strategies (see Hirshorn, Dye, Hauser, Supalla, & Bavelier, 2015). Instead, amount of time spent reading, greater background knowledge, language and vocabulary development, and word-recognition activities are associated with reading achievement (Schirmer & McGough, 2005). Most programs employ basal readers; however, consideration of a variety of alternatives is recommended (Stewart & Kluwin, 2001).

Software phonics programs are also available commercially. For example, *Reader Rabbit: Learn to Read with Phonics* (The Learning Company), *Lexia Reading Core5* (Lexia Learning), and *Fast ForWord* (Scientific Learning Corporation) are other approaches that emphasize phonemic awareness, phonics, and auditory discrimination. Mendez, Peltzman, and Frank (2016) used Reader Rabbit software in conjunction with *Reading Mastery* (SRA/McGraw-Hill) and concluded that it was effective as a Tier 2 intervention in promoting reading skills in elementary-grade struggling readers. Troia (2004) reported that Fast ForWord provided gains in sight-word reading, decoding, and expressive language for a sample of migrant students with limited English proficiency. A review of several interventions using Fast ForWord, however, suggested that the program may not always be effective (Strong, Torgerson, Torgerson, & Hulme, 2011); therefore, teachers should monitor student progress to ensure objectives are being met. For more information on software for promoting reading, see the *Apps for Education* feature.

TEACH STRUCTURAL ANALYSIS AS STUDENTS ACQUIRE PHONICS SKILLS

Older students begin to confront more complex words. **Structural analysis** refers to the ability to examine the structures of such words and break them into pronounceable syllables. Structural analysis involves examining a word by familiar word parts, such as the prefix, suffix, syllables, or smaller word parts. Teach basic syllabication rules to help students. The *Rewards* reading program (Voyager Sopris) provides an approach to teaching multisyllabic-word decoding that may be useful for upper elementary or secondary students.

The **DISSECT strategy** uses structural analysis as well as some other steps and provides a multiple-step procedure for figuring out unfamiliar words (Joseph & Schisler, 2009; Lenz & Hughes, 1990). Each letter in DISSECT stands for one of the steps in the procedure. The steps of the strategy are as follows:

- **D**iscover the context of the word.
- **I**solate the word's prefix.
- **S**eparate the word's suffix.
- **S**ay the word's stem.
- **E**xamine the word's stem using the following 3s and 2s rules, then segment into pronounceable parts:
  3s rule: underline 3 letters if stem begins with a consonant (example: re<u>new</u>al).
  2s rule: underline 2 letters if stem begins with a vowel (example: un<u>op</u>ened).

  Repeat for all letters in the stem.
- **C**heck with another person to see if you are correct.
- **T**ry finding the word in the dictionary.

Teaching students this strategy provides them with tools they can use independently when they encounter unfamiliar words.

Teach students other problem-solving strategies so that they will become more independent readers. For example, show them how to use context clues to guess what the word might be, based on the rest of the sentence or paragraph, the title, subheadings, charts, graphs, and accompanying illustrations (Deshler & Schumaker, 2006).

USE STRATEGIES FOR PROMOTING BASIC SIGHT VOCABULARY
Many words are used frequently at various grade levels; these words are often referred to as basic **sight words**. Some of these irregular words cannot be easily decoded using phonics skills, including words such as *the, a, is, to,* and *once.* Many word lists are available that contain graded sight-word lists (e.g., Dolch word lists). Students with reading difficulties may require additional practice in identifying and saying these words automatically.

MyEdLab:
Video Example 13.3.
In this video, the speaker discusses the importance of maximizing practice with decoding during instructional time.

Technology for Enhancing Literacy Instruction

 Technological advances have provided numerous opportunities to assist with teaching literacy for students with disabilities. Many of the devices are referred to as assistive technologies, in that students' access to the curriculum is increased either by enhancing the input or the output procedures, whereas others are referred to as software programs because they are materials designed to promote literacy. Both hardware and software devices are available that can be used to enhance literacy for students with disabilities.

IntelliKeys, an alternative to the traditional keyboard, is a device used to assist with keyboarding skills. IntelliKeys contains overlays consisting of large letters and numbers that are more accessible for some students with disabilities. IntelliKeys keyboards come in standard forms but are also programmable, using the *Overlay Maker* software program, to meet individual needs. The keyboards plug into USB ports.

Software is available that provides the ability to convert speech to computerized text. Such programs incorporate features of universal design for learning (UDL) by making text available to those who previously could not read or see the text. For example, some programs (e.g., *NaturalReader, Ivona,* and *TextSpeechPro*) can add the speech component to any computerized text, including text from word-processing programs, other computer programs, the Internet, scanned-in materials from classrooms, or any electronic text, so that the text can be read orally to students once the software is installed on a computer. Users can select the volume, speed, and pitch of the program and can alter the fonts and color of the text once it is imported into the program.

IntelliTalk (IntelliTools) adds speech components to word-processing texts in male or female voices. IntelliTalk's read-aloud feature can read each letter as it is typed into the program and can read back what has been written. It is also available in a Spanish version. These "talking" programs that provide speech output for highlighted words in word-processing programs are assistive technologies that enable struggling readers and writers to have more access to literacy tasks.

Write:Outloud (Don Johnston Incorporated) is another word-processing program that contains text-to-speech functions along with the typical word-processing functions such as spell checkers and search functions. This program was developed for children and is easy to learn to use. *Co:Writer* (Don Johnston Incorporated) contains word-prediction components that predict words based on the initial few letters that are typed. Students select the desired word from the word choices that are supplied.

Finally, *Draft:Builder* (Don Johnston Incorporated), another computerized program, provides students with visual support for organization, note taking, planning, writing drafts, and writing final products through the provision of templates and assistance.

Numerous software programs are available to provide assistance with literacy instruction. Examine the software to determine whether it meets the needs of your students.

Apps for literacy have the potential to provide students with supplemental practice in reading. For example, *ABC Expedition* (Meldmedia) provides an alphabet and animal learning environment for young children. *See Read Say HD* (28PM Software) contains all 220 Dolch sight words subdivided by preprimer, primer, and first- through third-grade word lists. A word is presented, learners read the word, and learners then click the word to have it spoken aloud. *Reading Remedies* (Needleworks Education) provides simple reading assessments in rhyming, blending, segmentation, sight words, fluency, and word-attack skills. *SentenceBuilder* and *StoryBuilder* (available from Mobil Education Store) are apps designed to facilitate written expression through gamelike formats. Both apps present options for improving sentences (SentenceBuilder) and paragraph organization (StoryBuilder) using visual and audio cues and reinforcement.

One suggestion for providing practice in developing basic sight-word vocabulary is to have students make and use flashcards containing their sight words. Some time each day can be devoted to saying the sight words with a partner. Cards containing words pronounced correctly and quickly can be stacked together, cards containing words said correctly but slowly in another stack, and cards containing words unknown in a third stack. Maintain records of the number of words in each stack. Gradually add new words as sight words are mastered.

a	came	her	look	people	too
after	can	here	looked	play	two
all	come	him	long	put	up
am	could	his	make	ran	us
an	day	house	man	run	very
and	did	how	me	said	was
are	do	I	mother	saw	we
as	don't	I'm	my	see	went
asked	down	if	no	she	were
at	for	in	not	so	what
away	from	into	now	some	when
back	get	is	of	that	where
be	go	it	old	the	will
because	going	just	on	then	with
before	good	keep	one	there	would
big	had	kind	or	they	you
boy	has	know	our	this	your
but	have	like	out	three	
by	he	little	over	to	

Figure 13.1 Wall Chart Containing Sight Words

Some teachers prepare checklists that contain new words or difficult words for students to learn, both at school and at home with their families. The checklists are practiced daily at school and at home, and teachers and parents simply put a checkmark next to words read correctly under the date.

Finally, some teachers prepare large wall charts and prominently display listings of words they want students to master. Figure 13.1 has an example of a word wall chart displaying many sight words. Charts can be changed as students master words.

Students with moderate and severe disabilities may benefit from being taught specific sight words (using, for example, the *Edmark* program) to enhance their classroom experience, daily living skills, and job skills (Browder, Wakeman, Spooner, Ahlgrim-Delzell, & Algozzine, 2006). These could include words for shopping, cooking, reading warning labels, and reading signs for community recreation and could be enhanced with pictures from *Boardmaker* (Mayer-Johnson) to create a readable text (Fossett, Smith, & Mirenda, 2003).

Fletcher and Abood (1988) found that students with mild intellectual disabilities who could read at nearly the fourth-grade level could not read the words on many warning labels, such as *inhale*, *flammable*, and *inaccessible*. Sight words have been taught using a variety of methods, including modeling, prompting, error correction, and feedback (Browder et al., 2006). Students' comprehension can be promoted by having them find the words in pictures or real settings or by having them give definitions. Try using classroom peers and sight-word cards to help promote sight-word recognition.

MyEdLab:
Video Example 13.4.
This video illustrates the importance of fluency and shows how it can be modeled by a teacher.

STRATEGIES FOR
PROMOTING READING FLUENCY

Reading fluency reflects not just accuracy but also rate. The Life Span Institute (2002) at the University of Kansas estimated that students should reach the following levels of fluency at each grade level, measured in correct words per minute (CWM) on grade-level passages: first grade—60; second—70; third—90; fourth—120; fifth—150. Behavioral Research and Teaching (2005), housed at the University of Oregon, published very similar norms: first—59; second—89; third—107; fourth—125; fifth—138; sixth—150; seventh—150; eighth—150.

Most students with reading difficulties require additional practice activities designed to help them read more fluently, even after they have mastered decoding skills. Several procedures are available to promote fluency (Chard, Vaughn, & Tyler, 2002; Kubina & Hughes, 2007).

USE REPEATED READINGS No one would expect students to learn to play the piano by continuously sight-reading new passages. Rather, students are expected to practice new pieces until they have become skilled and automatic before they move on to new and more difficult pieces (Anderson, Hiebert, Scott, & Wilkinson, 1985). Similarly, students who have struggled to learn to read a new passage should have the opportunity to reread the passage until fluent, effortless reading is achieved (Mercer et al., 2011). As their familiarity with the passage increases, their fluency and comprehension should also increase. Record reading rates on a graph, and indicate which passages are "repeated readings" and which are first-time readings. Set target rates (e.g., 140 words per minute), and reward students for reaching these targets. Provide extra practice on difficult words or phrases that slow students' rate. Research has suggested that repeated readings can improve fluency for individual passages as well as overall fluency and comprehension (Lee & Yoon, 2015; Staubitz, Cartledge, & Yurick, 2005; Therrien, 2004; Young, Moore, & Rasinski, 2014). However, research is equivocal regarding the effects of repeated reading. O'Connor, White, and Swanson (2007) implemented repeated reading and continuous reading with struggling readers in 15-minute sessions, three times per week for 14 weeks. They reported that repeated reading did not produce greater gains than continuous reading; however, each was effective compared with a control condition. At least in this case, what was most important was that students spent extra time in connected reading in order to develop their fluency skills.

USE CURRICULUM-BASED MEASUREMENT (CBM) Time students' oral reading rates on assigned texts several days a week, then chart their performance. Graphed reading rates will demonstrate to students the rate at which they are improving in reading fluency. For example, identify 100-word segments, and graph the amount of time taken to read the segment. Some teachers prefer to time students for a designated amount of time. For example, 1- or 2-minute time segments can be used, and teachers can graph the number of words read correctly (and incorrectly) in this time segment. To evaluate long-term progress, select several end-of-year passages and evaluate reading rate throughout the year. CBM can help you keep track of student progress and let you know when students are falling behind in their skill development (Berkeley & Riccomini, 2011).

USE CLASSWIDE PEER TUTORING More time spent in oral reading can help develop fluency over time. Classwide peer tutoring, in which pairs of students take turns reading to each other, is one good way of dramatically increasing the amount of time students spend actively engaged in reading (Fuchs & Fuchs, 2005). In classwide peer tutoring configurations, students can develop fluency using such other components as sustained or repeated readings, 1- or 2-minute timings, extra practice with difficult parts, and curriculum-based measurement.

USE SOFTWARE PROGRAMS Software designed for computers can provide an alternative means of practicing reading, decoding, and fluency-building activities. Students are usually highly motivated to use computers, and many programs contain gamelike formats to entice students to put forth extra effort. Computer software, for example, *Mindplay Reading Fluency* (Mindplay), is available to help promote reading fluency and promote reading comprehension.

MyEdLab: **Self-Check 13.2**

MyEdLab: **Application Exercise 13.2: Phonemic Awareness Training**

Reading Comprehension

Carmen

Carmen can read the words in the stories, but when someone asks him what the story is about, he can't remember. Ms. Simpson, his third-grade teacher, always has him read orally during class and consistently gives him praise for his word reading. However, whenever Ms. Simpson says, "Now tell me what the story is about in your own words," Carmen is lost. He is beginning to dislike reading class because more and more time is being devoted to questioning about the stories rather than just reading out loud.

QUESTIONS FOR REFLECTION

1. If a student can read the words, why might that student have difficulty comprehending what was read?
2. When is a good time to begin comprehension activities?
3. How can comprehension be encouraged across subject areas?

Reading comprehension is the process of extracting meaning from text, and it is a major consideration in the Common Core State Standards for reading (National Governors Association Center for Best Practices & Council of Chief State School Officers, 2010). Reading comprehension is the ultimate goal of reading; yet for many students, comprehension is a major problem. Fortunately, reading-comprehension research has uncovered some effective strategies for improving reading comprehension for students with disabilities and other special needs (Berkeley, Scruggs, & Mastropieri, 2010; Mastropieri & Scruggs, 1997; Pressley & Allington, 2015). Students with reading-comprehension difficulties often benefit from explicit instruction and practice using strategies that promote reading comprehension.

STRATEGIES FOR
TEACHING READING COMPREHENSION

Specific reading-comprehension strategies can be taught for use before, during, and after reading passages. These include basic skills approaches, text enhancements, and self-questioning strategies.

USE BASIC SKILLS AND REINFORCEMENT STRATEGIES

Reinforcement refers to providing rewards or positive comments to students to encourage and motivate them as they work and answer comprehension questions successfully. **Vocabulary instruction** refers to providing students with practice in learning specific vocabulary words that will be encountered in the readings (e.g., Coyne, Simmons, Kameénui, & Stoolmiller, 2004). **Corrective feedback** refers to providing students with immediate feedback when oral reading errors occur. The idea is that students' comprehension will improve when they are given immediate feedback on decoding errors. These strategies are often helpful; however, they may be more effective when combined with text enhancement or self-questioning strategies.

Repeated reading may also help increase comprehension of the material (Bursuck & Damer, 2015; O'Shea, Sindelar, & O'Shea, 1987; Vadasy & Sanders, 2008). However, use caution when assigning more than several repeated readings of the same passage because as the number of readings increases, students' motivation may decrease.

Direct instruction can refer to the use of published curriculum materials such as *Corrective Reading* and *Reading Mastery* (SRA/McGraw Hill). Research has indicated that this structured phonetic approach is effective in increasing comprehension as students become more skilled and fluent readers (Carnine et al., 2016; Shippen, Houchins, Steventon, & Sartor, 2005).

CREATE TEXT ENHANCEMENTS

Text enhancements can include illustrations, maps, diagrams, visual spatial displays, semantic-feature-analysis charts, mnemonic pictures, and other adjunct aids developed to accompany text materials to increase comprehension. Although publishers of curriculum materials frequently use text enhancements, they also may be developed by teachers or students, using drawings or materials found through Internet search engines.

Illustrations drawn to represent characters, events, places, and action in texts reinforce the sequence of events in the stories. Information can be organized into concept maps or spatially organized maps that show relationships among all events, people, and places. Mnemonic text enhancements can also be designed to promote memory of important concepts and features from reading materials.

Browder (2015) described the use of text illustrations to promote comprehension for students with moderate and severe cognitive disabilities. In one case, the student listened to the teacher read the book *Toy Story* and was able to point to symbols on her communication board to answer comprehension questions such as the following: "Who was the favorite toy first?"; "Who was the new toy?"; "When did the boy get the new toy?" (Browder, 2015, p. 56).

Imagery, the process of visualizing content from readings, may be a useful substitute when illustrations are unavailable. To assist students in using this strategy, model and demonstrate the imagery process. Break the strategy into three steps. First, tell students to read a passage. Second, have them think of a picture in their minds that represents important content in the story. Third, have students describe their "mental pictures" to you or a peer. Provide feedback on the quality of the images by adding any important features that may have been missing from their images. Although imagery has not yielded as powerful comprehension effects as some self-questioning strategies, actively picturing text content may be beneficial for some of your students.

Adjunct aids, including study guides, outlines, guided notes, partial outlines, and highlighting and underlining, are also examples of useful text enhancements.

TEACH SPECIFIC QUESTIONING STRATEGIES Asking students questions, and teaching them to ask themselves questions about readings, helps promote reading comprehension (Berkeley, Mastropieri, & Scruggs, 2011). Overall guidelines for teaching reading-comprehension strategies are given in Figure 13.2. Several questioning and self-questioning strategies that are particularly effective are listed in Figure 13.3. Most of these strategies were validated as being effective for students with learning disabilities (Brigham, Berkeley, Simpkins, & Brigham, 2007). However, they have also been shown to be effective for other students with reading-comprehension difficulties (e.g., Babyak, Koorland, & Mathes, 2000).

Activate Prior Knowledge Several strategies can help students activate their prior knowledge on topics before they begin reading. One strategy for **activating prior knowledge** is the **TELLS** fact-or-fiction strategy (Idol-Maestas, 1985; Ridge & Skinner, 2011). TELLS fact or fiction is an acronym for the following steps:

- Studying story Titles
- Examining pages for clue words

- Set clear objectives that are logically related to the use of each strategy for reading comprehension.
- Follow a specific instructional sequence:
  1. State the purpose of instruction.
  2. Provide instruction.
  3. Model use of the strategy.
  4. Prompt students to use the strategy following your model.
  5. Give corrective feedback.
  6. Provide guided practice of the strategy.
  7. Provide independent practice of the strategy.
- Inform students about the importance of the strategy.
- Monitor student performance.
- Encourage questioning that requires students to think about the strategies in relationship to the text.
- Encourage positive attributions.
- Teach for generalized use of the strategy.

Figure 13.2 Guidelines for Teaching Reading Comprehension

Activating Prior Knowledge Features:

- Teacher asks questions relevant to forthcoming readings
- Teacher teaches relevant vocabulary
- Teacher teaches using graphic organizers containing main ideas of forthcoming topic
- Students are taught to ask questions related to forthcoming topics
- Students complete activities containing relevant questions before reading

Summarization, Main Idea, Self-Monitoring, and Attribution Features:

- Students taught to ask questions about the reading material, such as "Who or what is the passage about?" "What is happening?"
- Students answer the questions they asked and summarize or paraphrase readings in their own words
- Students state what the whole passage is about in their own words
- Students initially use self-monitoring cards while learning strategy steps
- Teacher encourages independent monitoring of strategy use
- Teacher encourages appropriate strategy attributions
- Teacher encourages independent use of strategy

Text-Structure-Based:

- Teaches passage-specific strategies for different types of text structures, including main idea, list, order, compare–contrast, problem-solving passages, as well as narrative story grammar passages

Multicomponent Packages:*

- Incorporate all or many of the above features; students are taught to ask and answer questions about the reading materials
- Questioning typically includes summarizing, predicting, and clarifying
- Teacher has direct role in instruction first and students assume more independence gradually in most models

*In some models, students assume a more active role during initial phases of instruction

Figure 13.3 Features of Self-Questioning Research

- Looking for important words
- Looking for hard words
- Describing the Setting of the story
- Answering whether the story was **fact** or **fiction**

Before starting to read, students attempt to follow the steps in TELLS and decide whether the passage is fact or fiction, and then they check their answer after reading the passage.

Brainstorming with students is another strategy for activating prior knowledge. Before a lesson, present students with the major topic that will be introduced, and ask them to generate as many ideas as possible that are related or similar to that topic. Encourage participation from all students. Brainstorming can be a component of most questioning strategies, including those intended to activate prior knowledge.

K-W-L is another strategy used to access prior knowledge before reading (Ogle, 1986). During implementation of this strategy, students ask and answer three questions:

- "What do I **K**now about this topic?"
- "What do I **W**ant to know?"
- "What did I **L**earn?"

For the first question, teachers and students brainstorm ideas of related topics of which they have prior knowledge and categorize their ideas. For the second question, teachers and students discuss what they want to know from reading the information. For the final step, students write down information they learned after reading the passage. You can create worksheets containing columns for answering each of the K-W-L steps.

Promote Self-Generated Questions   Many reading-comprehension strategies require students to self-question before, during, and after reading. As such, these strategies promote **metacognition**, the awareness of one's own cognitive processes and how they can be enhanced (Montague, 1998). Although good readers may develop these skills independently, students with special needs (and many other students) can benefit from metacognitive training. Asking questions about reading material (e.g., "Why am I studying this passage?" "What is the main idea?" "What is a question about the main idea?") helps promote thinking about the information, which in turn facilitates recall and comprehension (Berkeley et al., 2010).

MyEdLab:
Video Example 13.5.
This video illustrates a teacher using K-W-L with her students. Pay attention as she follows the steps, and think about her evaluation of the strategy.

Summarize and Paraphrase   Several researchers have developed procedural steps for teaching students to summarize and paraphrase reading materials (see Gersten, Fuchs, Williams, & Baker, 2001, for a review). Although each approach varied somewhat, similar components included the following:

1. Read a passage or short segment from a book.
2. Ask yourself who or what the passage is about.
3. Ask yourself what was happening in the passage.
4. Make up a summary sentence in your own words using the answers to the questions asked.

For example, Ellis (1996) described the **RAP** strategy for paraphrasing reading passages. The letters of the acronym stand for the following steps:

- **R**ead a paragraph.
- **A**sk yourself what the paragraph was about.
- **P**ut the main idea and two details in your own words. (p. 73)

Teach students that the main idea tells what the whole story (or paragraph) is about in a short summary sentence (Berkeley et al., 2010).

Similarly, reading-comprehension strategies used in classwide peer-tutoring interventions (e.g., McMaster, Fuchs, & Fuchs, 2006) include the following questioning steps:

- What is the most important who or what in the text?
- What is the most important thing about the who or what?
- Write a summary sentence. (e.g., Mastropieri et al., 2001, p. 21)

Teach students to create concise summary sentences and to use their own words. Include self-monitoring instructions that list the selected procedures on cards or charts, and display them prominently during reading to help students master the strategy steps. In the early phases of instruction, ask students to answer the questions either verbally or in writing to verify whether all strategy steps have been implemented correctly.

Teach students to examine text structure as they study textbooks, including theme and main-idea identification (Williams, 2003). In expository text, some paragraphs contain a main idea—such as wind erosion—with supporting statements or examples. Some paragraphs present a list of information, such as chief exports of Guatemala. Others contain information presented as an ordered series, such as steps in the digestive process. Still others present cause–effect relations. Students trained to identify the text structure and create appropriate outlines have significantly outperformed other students on tests of recall and comprehension (Bakken & Whedon, 2002; Bursuck & Damer, 2015).

Story Maps   Story-mapping strategies demonstrate for students that most stories follow a particular pattern, or story grammar, including setting, problem, goals, action, and outcomes, as shown in Figure 13.4. Teaching students to use that pattern can promote comprehension (Boulineau, Fore, Hagan-Burke, & Burke, 2004). For example, Alves, Kennedy, Brown, and

The setting:

The characters:

The time:

The place:

The problem in the story:

The goals in the story:

The action in the story:

The outcomes of the story:

Figure 13.4 Story Grammar Training Card

Solis (2014) taught students to complete story-mapping worksheets while reading and found that these worksheets improved recall and comprehension.

Story-grammar training cards similar to those provided in Figure 13.4 can be designed. Provide instruction and practice using the sheets during reading activities. Encourage students to complete similar worksheets during independent reading.

Reciprocal Teaching Reciprocal teaching is a reading-comprehension strategy that contains four comprehension-fostering strategies: (1) summarizing, (2) predicting, (3) questioning, and (4) clarifying (Palincsar & Brown, 1984). In addition, during reciprocal teaching, students assume the role of teacher during instruction and take the lead on asking questions. Teachers can prompt students to create good comprehension questions, as in the following dialogue:

TEACHER: What do you think, Nell?

NELL: How can a doctor know that a person is dreaming?

TEACHER: Excellent question, Nell! That is perfect; that is an amazing, great question. What do you think, Andy?

ANDY: Why did the doctors need to learn about dreaming?

TEACHER: That is another excellent question! (Speece, MacDonald, Kilsheimer, & Krist, 1997, p. 183)

Reciprocal teaching incorporates the following elements:

- The teacher and the students silently read the reading selection.

- The teacher explains and demonstrates the four strategies using "talk-alouds," or talking aloud about thought processes used. For example, a teacher might say, "To *summarize,* I might think to myself, 'What is this entire passage about? What is the overall topic, and what is being said about it?'" The talk-aloud may then describe a summary of the passage being considered and why it is a good summary.

- Students then read another passage, and demonstrate out loud their strategy use for other students, while the teacher provides guidance and support (also known as "scaffolding"). Students construct their own comprehension questions.

- After practice, each student is expected to exhibit competence in the four strategies: summarizing, predicting, questioning, and clarifying (Palincsar & Brown, 1984; see also Bursuck & Damer, 2015).

Rosenshine and Meister (1994) concluded that reciprocal teaching is more effective when direct skills-based teaching (on, for example, summarizing or predicting) occurs before the model is implemented. As with all reading-comprehension instruction, provide students with sufficient modeling, support, and guidance during the early learning phases. Later, students can be more independent in their use of the strategies (Klingner et al., 2007).

Klingner, Vaughn, Arguelles, Hughes, and Leftwich (2004) implemented the Collaborative Strategic Reading (CSR) model, which incorporates elements of reciprocal teaching, in inclusive fourth-grade classrooms that also contained a substantial proportion of students limited in English proficiency. Students were taught strategies for brainstorming and predicting, monitoring understanding, generating questions, and reviewing key ideas, and they then implemented these strategies in cooperative groups. After a year's implementation, Klingner et al. concluded that CSR had resulted in a positive impact on students' reading skills (see Boardman et al., 2016; Klingner, Vaughn, Boardman, & Swanson, 2012).

ADAPT FORMATS OF READING-COMPREHENSION INSTRUCTION When needed, adapt the format of instructional materials. These adaptations may be required if students cannot read the materials, have limited writing abilities, or need more time to complete assignments. Possible adaptations are listed in Figure 13.5 and the following *In the Classroom* feature.

- Highlight text
- Alter font, spacing, and colors of text
- Magnify text
- Record text
- Use language masters for practice with difficult words
- Use talking computerized programs (scan texts)
- Use braille formats
- Rewrite text supplements using more familiar vocabulary
- Rewrite text supplements at a lower reading level
- Supplement with high-interest, low-vocabulary texts

Figure 13.5 Adapting Text Formats

In the Classroom

Alternative Teaching Suggestions

- Supplement texts with advance organizers:

illustrations	multimedia aids
graphic organizers	computer programs/apps
visual spatial displays	descriptive video
concrete manipulatives	study guides
summary charts	guided notes

- Preteach:

  difficult vocabulary

  new concepts

  organizational structure of text

  reading-comprehension strategies

- Provide sufficient practice activities
- Use teacher-effectiveness variables
- Use peers and cooperative groups
- Adapt assignments:

  reduce reading or writing requirements

  permit oral formats (e.g., audio-recorded answers)

  supply alternative materials such as multimedia or computer formats

In addition, promote culturally responsive literacy instruction to enhance the reading experience for all students. Suggestions are provided in the *Diversity in the Classroom* feature.

ADAPT INSTRUCTION FOR SECONDARY STUDENTS   Many students with special needs advance to secondary grade levels without completely mastering important reading skills. This is a particular problem because formal reading instruction ceases to be a part of the general education curriculum at secondary levels (Mastropieri, Scruggs, & Graetz, 2003). Nevertheless, there are actions that secondary-level teachers can take to promote reading skill development in their classes. First, they can support more intensive reading instruction in resource rooms, study periods, or Tier 2 RTI (see p. 326) programs by working with the special education teacher and emphasizing newly learned skills in the general education classroom. Secondary teachers can also teach and promote use of word-recognition strategies, such as the DISSECT strategy described previously (Ellis, 1996), to assist with independent reading skills, understanding of the text structure, and other strategies described previously to assist with text comprehension (Bakken & Whedon, 2002; Vaughn & Roberts, 2007). Additionally, secondary teachers can provide opportunities to practice reading skills in content-area instruction through classwide peer-tutoring interventions.

For example, Mastropieri et al. (2001) implemented classwide peer tutoring in middle school English classes that contained students with learning and behavior problems. Students worked in pairs, with the stronger reader reading first for 5 minutes, followed by the second reader reading the same passage for 5 minutes. At the end of each reading turn, the tutoring partner would ask the reader to provide story restatements or encourage summarization strategies. Prompts for story restatements included, "What is the first thing you learned?"; followed by, "What was the next thing you learned?"; with questions asked as often as needed to restate the story. Summarization strategies included, "What is the most important who or what in the text?"; followed by, "What is the most important thing about the who or what in the text?"; then, "What is the summary sentence?" After 5 weeks of the program, students who had participated in tutoring scored much higher than control students on a reading-comprehension test. Similar tutoring programs have helped improve reading skills as well as achievement in secondary content areas such as history, civics, and chemistry (Mastropieri et al., 2003; Spencer, Scruggs, & Mastropieri, 2003). These programs may be useful because they provide all students with additional practice on academic content and provide additional supervised reading practice for students with special needs.

Culturally Responsive Literacy Instruction

Literacy instruction is important for all students, but it is especially important to craft highly effective literacy instruction that is responsive to students representing all cultures (Callins, 2005). Graves (2010) described the longitudinal impact of beginning reading instruction on English learners. First-grade classes were selected if they contained English learners representing multiple languages, including Spanish, Vietnamese, Cambodian, French, Lao, a Cantonese dialect of Chinese, Hmong, Somalian, Sudanese, English, or Tagalog. Each teacher had a minimum of four languages in his or her respective classes, of which 80% to 100% of the English learners received free or reduced lunch. Students were tested at the beginning of first grade and at the end of second grade, then followed up every year through sixth grade. The *English Language Learners Classroom Observation Instrument* (ELCOI) was used during reading instruction to assess teacher practices and effectiveness along the dimensions of instructional practices, instruction for low performers, sheltered English techniques, interactive teaching, phonemic awareness, decoding, and vocabulary activities. In addition, students were assessed on English-language proficiency, reading fluency, and comprehension. By the end of year 2, students who had more effective teachers based on the ELCOI scores were performing higher on reading measures that those students who were enrolled in classes with teachers who were considered less effective. By the end of sixth grade, relationships between teacher effectiveness in first-grade reading maintained moderate correlations with reading performance. These findings highlight the importance of excellent beginning-reading instructional practices for promoting long-term reading growth for students who are English learners. Also see Echevarria and Graves (2015) for a description of sheltered instruction to assist English learners.

Vaughn et al. (2015) taught important reading skills to high school students with learning disabilities and behavior disorders with low comprehension scores. Over a 2-year period, they taught word-analysis skills (identifying affixes, vowels, and vowel combinations for segmenting multisyllabic words into decodable chunks) in combination with peer mediation through Collaborative Strategic Reading, described previously, to enhance their comprehension skills. Students received modeling, support, and practice time for a number of reading-comprehension strategies. These students made significant improvements over control students on a standardized reading-comprehension test.

USE ASSISTIVE TECHNOLOGY TO SUPPORT SECONDARY-LEVEL READERS

Many of the features of the Kurzweil 3000 program may be of particular benefit to secondary-level struggling readers. This program provides text-to-speech capabilities in seven languages and includes highlighters and sticky notes, vocabulary study guides, graphic organizers, and writing templates, as well as direct access to Bookshare and other online content providers. It also offers support for writing, comprehension, and test-taking and study skills. An app version is available for use on tablets and smartphones.

Digital highlighters such as the C-pen (C-pen) are pen-sized devices that allow students to scan sentences in text to transfer them into word-recognition software programs with translation, dictionary, and text-to-speech capabilities. Some employ Bluetooth technology for wireless connections. Digital pens such as the Livescribe 3 Smartpen (Livescribe) pair audio recording with note taking so that written notes are paired with audio and converted to text. Audio can be played wherever written notes are unclear or incomplete.

Low-tech applications can also be helpful. Dieker and Little (2005) recommended sticky notes for posting summaries over longer text, erasable highlighters that students can use to highlight or erase highlights as sentences are read and understood, magnetic printer paper or tape for categorizing or reviewing key vocabulary, and dry-erase boards and markers for outlining or summarizing points. These and similar adaptations can provide needed support for struggling readers.

STRATEGIES FOR

IMPLEMENTING MULTI-TIERED READING INSTRUCTION WITH RTI

Response-to-intervention (RTI) programs have been designed to prevent and treat academic failure, particularly in the area of reading (Division for Learning Disabilities, 2007). An RTI program employs multiple "tiers" of intervention—usually three or four—to monitor and adjust instruction to the specific needs of students, although a three-tier structure has been recommended (Fuchs, Fuchs, & Compton, 2012).

STRATEGIES FOR IMPLEMENTING PRIMARY (TIER 1) INTERVENTIONS   Tier 1 programs are usually considered evidence-based (or research-supported) instruction in the general education classroom (Foorman, 2007). Evidence-based approaches would include systematic instruction in reading skills and subskills such as phonemic awareness and phonics, lots of practice in building reading fluency, instruction in relevant reading vocabulary, use of a variety of texts, and effective comprehension-enhancing activities (Taylor, 2008; see also http://www.fcrr.org/essa/index.html). Academic engagement could be increased through the use of peer mediation, such as classwide peer tutoring. In addition, screening measures would be implemented to identify any students demonstrating problems in reading skills acquisition.

STRATEGIES FOR IMPLEMENTING SECONDARY (TIER 2) INTERVENTIONS   Secondary (Tier 2) interventions are "directed at students who are at risk for academic problems and for whom additional, more targeted instruction is provided to close the gap between their current performance and expected performance" (Vaughn & Roberts, 2007, p. 41). These interventions can take place with small groups of students who have not responded well to Tier 1 interventions. Tier 2 interventions should be more intensive and focused than those provided in Tier 1 and may include, for example, 20 to 30 minutes of homogeneous small-group (four or six students) instruction in addition to Tier 1 activities (Bursuck & Damer, 2015). During Tier 2 reading instruction, additional intensive instruction can be focused on phonemic awareness, phonics, spelling and writing, fluency development, vocabulary instruction, and comprehension enhancement, using many of the strategies described in this chapter. This can be implemented as a "standard protocol" approach (in which most students receive the same intervention) or a "problem-solving" approach (in which school personnel decide upon appropriate individualized interventions; Fuchs & Fuchs, 2007). Either way, the goal is to help students "catch up" with their classmates in a directed period of time (e.g., 10 to 20 weeks; Vaughn & Denton, 2008). If, after a specified time period, students still do not make acceptable progress (according to, for example, school benchmarks or failure to demonstrate adequate progress on curriculum-based measures), these data may be used, according to the Individuals with Disabilities Education Act (IDEA), in support of special education identification and placement decisions.

STRATEGIES FOR IMPLEMENTING TERTIARY (TIER 3 OR INTENSIVE) INTERVENTIONS   If students are still responding poorly to instruction after Tier 1 and Tier 2 interventions, they may be referred to Tier 3, which in many models includes special education referrals and treatments and may also be referred to as *intensive interventions*. Tier 3 intervention "is considered to be the most intensive and is focused on individual student need" (Stecker, 2007, p. 51), and it employs many of the strategies described in this chapter. In some models, special education referral is undertaken as a Tier 4 intervention when students do not respond positively to a separate Tier 3 intervention (Bursuck & Damer, 2015). The National Center on Intensive Intervention (2016) and Powell and Fuchs (2015) have provided intensive instruction activity guidelines that begin with explicit instruction and include modeling, guided practice, and feedback. Vaughn and Wanzek (2014) described longer-term (75–100 sessions) daily intensive instruction in reading for students with disabilities that included individualized or small-group instruction and direct teaching of a variety of specific reading skills. In addition to individualized instruction, these services could include (a) developing measurable shorter-term and annual goals, (b) using formative data to monitor progress and inform instruction, and (c) having special educators who have been trained to work effectively with students with disabilities serve as intervention agents (Fuchs et al., 2012; Stecker, 2007). Mastropieri and Scruggs (2014) described the importance of intensive instruction over longer periods of time to successfully promote essay writing achievement in a population of students with significant behavioral and learning disabilities.

MyEdLab: Self-Check 13.3

MyEdLab: Application Exercise 13.3: Strategies for Promoting Reading Fluency

MyEdLab: Application Exercise 13.4: Strategies for Reading Comprehension

Written Expression

Written language refers to handwriting, spelling, and composition. One or all of these may be especially problematic for students at risk for school failure. However, adaptations can be made in each area to promote success in inclusive classrooms. Although handwriting instruction has received less attention in recent years, evidence suggests that systematic handwriting instruction is an important component in preventing writing difficulties in the primary grades (Graham, Harris, & Fink, 2000).

STRATEGIES FOR
IMPROVING HANDWRITING

Competent handwriting is important for students at all grade levels in school; unfortunately, many students exhibit considerable difficulty with handwriting tasks. Students with physical disabilities can exhibit difficulty with the mechanical aspects of writing (Heller, 2010); other students have problems with fine motor skills. Some students with learning disabilities may exhibit what has been referred to as **dysgraphia**, or extreme difficulty with writing. Other students experience difficulty copying from the chalkboard or overhead projector, or what is referred to as "far-point copying." Still others have difficulty copying from models on or near their desks, or "near-point copying." Finally, forming letters from memory can present handwriting problems for some students (Lerner & Johns, 2015).

No matter what the difficulty, students need to acquire fluency with the mechanical aspects of handwriting, or they will experience difficulties composing written work. Illegible, dysfluent, and laborious handwriting interferes with students' abilities to complete written assignments in a timely fashion, take notes in classes, read and study materials they have written, and undertake writing tasks such as essay writing (Berninger & Amtmann, 2003; Gregg, Coleman, Davis, & Chalk, 2007). Some have suggested that illegibly written assignments receive lower grades and less careful consideration by teachers. Santangelo and Graham (2016) concluded that handwriting instruction is associated with higher quality, greater length, and increased fluency in students' writing.

For generations students were taught to use manuscript and cursive writing. Today some states require cursive writing instruction, while others do not. However, cursive writing may be useful for several aspects of literacy; for example, to be able to read cursive writing of others, to provide a signature, and to use cursive fonts in word processing programs.

Graham and Weintraub (1996) provided a thorough analysis of research on handwriting and concluded the following:

1. Handwriting problems are greatest among students who have academic difficulties.

2. Students develop their own style of writing regardless of script style taught.

3. Successful handwriting instruction for students with handwriting difficulties emphasizes the following:

   • Use paper with more space between the lines.

   • Provide models of the order, number, and direction of strokes.

   • Provide sufficient practice in tracing, copying, and writing from memory.

   • Use behavioral techniques such as cueing, shaping, and positive practice.

   • Teach self-regulation behaviors such as self-verbalizations during activities involving tracing, copying, and writing from memory.

- Use self-assessment as part of the handwriting instruction.
- Use self-instruction and self-correction as part of the handwriting instruction (see also Graham, 2010; Santangelo & Graham, 2016).

Berninger and Amtmann (2003) reported that studying visual cues (numbered arrow cues that show students the sequence of writing individual letters) and writing from memory improved both quality of handwriting and the amount written.

INCORPORATE SELF-REGULATION AND SELF-INSTRUCTIONAL STRATEGIES

It is important to model all the steps of the procedures and to provide practice opportunities for students to use self-regulation and self-instructional procedures. For example, a teacher might say the following while demonstrating the technique for writing *q*:

> I place my pen on a line of the paper and move up to the top of the "q." Without taking my pen off the paper, I make a *circle* around to the top again. Then, I go *down* below the line, then *loop* back to the top again. Finally, I *finish* on an upswing. Remember [repeats model], "Up, circle, down, loop, finish."

Some basic self-instructions include defining tasks to be undertaken (e.g., "I must write this sentence"), focusing attention on tasks, reviewing necessary strategic steps (e.g., "For a *t*, I go up and then down the same way, and later I come back to cross the *t*"), self-evaluating and self-correcting (e.g., "Did I write a *t* correctly?"), self-control, and self-reinforcement ("My writing was correct and legible"); see Graham and Harris (2005) for some examples.

USE MATERIALS TO DEVELOP MANUSCRIPT AND CURSIVE WRITING
Debate exists over whether manuscript (printing) or cursive (handwriting) both need to be taught, as well as which system for teaching each should be used (Graham, 2010; Graves, 2003). Some claim that manuscript resembles print more closely, that it is easier to learn, and that students with learning difficulties need to learn only one system. Others assert that children can write faster and are more motivated to learn to write when using a cursive system. Unfortunately, little convincing evidence supports one side over the other. You will need to decide what works best for your own individual students, within the context of district and state guidelines.

Some handwriting programs have been developed to teach handwriting skills efficiently and systematically. The *D'Nealian Handwriting* system (Pearson) teaches students a manuscript style that is said to lead more naturally into cursive writing. The *Cursive Writing Program* (SRA) provides a systematic introduction to handwriting letters, words, and then sentences. Zaner-Bloser's *Handwriting* series (2003) provides materials for handwriting instruction from kindergarten through eighth grade.

Although many script styles exist, the quality of handwriting can be evaluated according to legibility, shape, size, spacing, alignment, line quality, speed and ease of writing, slant, uppercase and lowercase letter formations, and manuscript and cursive script styles (Berninger & Amtmann, 2003). Set criteria for what your students should focus on first, and find an instructional system that will support students' efforts.

MAKE TECHNOLOGICAL ADAPTATIONS
Digital pens, described previously, can convert handwritten text to digital text. Computers and typewriters are effective alternatives for students who have persistent difficulties with handwriting. Keyboarding and typing skills need to be mastered and can be taught using one of several computerized programs, including *Typing Instructor for Kids* (Individual Software), *Mickey's Typing Adventure* (Individual Software), and *Type to Learn 4* (Sunburst Digital).

Advantages of using word processors include neatness, ease, increased fluency, availability of spelling and grammar checks, and increased motivation. In addition, use of the accessibility features on computers, tablets, and mobile devices can make it easier to use the mouse or keyboard, set up alternative input devices, optimize the visual display, or read text as it is typed. However, because students may not always have access to computers or related devices, supplement these programs with at least some basic handwriting skills for those with sufficient fine motor ability. For students who lack fine motor skills, voice-input devices can be added to computers, smartphones, and tablets, enabling the students to enter information orally and receive typed output. If technological adaptations are unavailable, assign scribes for students who cannot write independently.

Mario

Mario, a fourth grader with learning disabilities, is included in Ms. Wills's general education class for all subjects. Ms. Wills has weekly spelling tests every Friday. On Mondays, new spelling lists containing 20 words are distributed, and time is allocated throughout the week to study independently to prepare for Friday's test. But Mario is failing spelling. His recent weekly test scores were 50%, 45%, 30%, 40%, and 35% correct. He tries hard to learn the words, but he can't pronounce some of the words on the list. Both he and Ms. Wills are becoming frustrated with his spelling difficulties.

QUESTIONS FOR REFLECTION

1. What might be the cause of Mario's spelling problems?
2. What is happening in the classroom that may contribute to Mario's problem?
3. What changes can be made in the classroom routine to help Mario spell better?

STRATEGIES FOR
TEACHING SPELLING

Spelling can be a complex and difficult task for students with reading and writing difficulties. Efficient spellers rely on good memory, phonological awareness, phonemic awareness, orthographic skills, phonics skills, and self-checking skills, all of which are often deficit areas for many students with disabilities. Research has identified a number of effective spelling strategies that can be implemented in inclusive settings (Graham, 1999; Graham & Santangelo, 2014; McLaughlin, Weber, & Derby, 2013; Williams, Walker, Vaughn, & Wanzek, 2016).

First, ensure that all students can read all the words on their spelling lists. If students are unable to read spelling words, they will surely encounter difficulties in learning how to spell them. Systematic instruction in phonemic analysis and synthesis, as well as phonics, will prove helpful in promoting good spelling skills. Other general suggestions include the following:

- Teach common irregular spellings from the beginning of spelling instruction.
- Teach useful spelling rules.
- Teach students to use their prior knowledge about root words and the relationships among words to help them spell new words.
- Increase independent reading to increase exposure to words in print.
- Encourage students to use the spell-checking features on their computers and other electronic devices (Spear-Swerling, 2005).

You may also improve spelling performance by shortening the list length for students with spelling problems (Bryant, Drabin, & Gettinger, 1981). This means asking students to learn, for example, 10 rather than 20 words, or 5 rather than 10, in a week. Introduce a small number of words daily rather than providing a large list all at once. Introduce and practice three or four words on Monday; on Tuesday, review those words and introduce a few more words. However, simply shortening the list will be of little help if the words themselves are beyond the current abilities of the students.

SELECT WORDS FROM READING AND WRITING ACTIVITIES Spelling words that are relevant to students' reading and writing activities can be easier to learn, and students may be more likely to see the importance of learning to spell these words. Additionally, students can apply their reading decoding skills to the spelling lists.

PROVIDE DISTRIBUTED PRACTICE SESSIONS Distributed practice—providing shorter, more frequent periods for studying, rather than fewer, longer periods—may be beneficial for students with disabilities (Gettinger, Bryant, & Fayne, 1982). For example, several 15-minute spelling activity sessions scheduled throughout the school day could reinforce learning better than one 45-minute block.

MyEdLab:
Video Example 13.6.
The teacher in this video uses a word wall and repetition to reinforce spelling words with her students. Notice the elements of direct instruction used in her lesson as well.

USE PEER TUTORING   Peer-tutoring sessions also can help students with special needs (Bowman-Perrott, Burke, Zhang, & Zaini, 2014). Provide students with extra opportunities to practice spelling their new words (Maheady & Gard, 2010) after they have been trained in peer-tutoring procedures. Peer spelling sessions can be scheduled regularly. Flashcards can be used, and students can record their daily performance by stacking cards spelled correctly together. Keeping the stack of misspelled words to review several times within a single tutoring session or in multiple sessions can help students be more successful on tests. Alternatively, simple word lists can also be used as tutoring materials. Tutors can check off words spelled correctly. Students can be matched in almost any way for spelling tutoring sessions because the tutors can view the correct spellings on the word lists. Using tutoring for spelling can increase time-on-task, including increasing opportunities for responding and increasing feedback on spelling performance. Burks (2004) implemented classwide peer tutoring in spelling and reported that spelling performance improved for three fifth-grade students with disabilities, from an average of 73% to 91% correct, over scores after more traditional methods, such as independent seatwork.

MODIFY INSTRUCTION BASED ON ANALYSIS OF SPELLING ERRORS   Analyze the type of mistakes students are making in order to make instructional decisions. For example, if letters representing phonemes are deleted (e.g., *pince* rather than *prince*) or inserted (e.g., *subptract* rather than *subtract*), students may need phonics or phonemic awareness instruction. If spellings do not reflect conventional orthography (e.g., *wich* instead of *wish* or *hidn* instead of *hiding*), teach appropriate sound–spelling correspondences. If spelling errors reflect a lack of knowledge of spelling rules (e.g., doubling a consonant before adding a suffix), teach these rules. Directing instruction to individual error patterns is an efficient way of promoting good spelling (Berninger & Amtmann, 2003). For errors in parts of words that are not governed by conventional rules, teach mnemonic strategies.

TEACH MNEMONIC STRATEGIES FOR SPELLING   Show students mnemonic strategies to remember the difficult or unpredictable parts of words, for example, the *s* in *island* or the *d* in *Wednesday*. Create a sentence that contains the difficult word and another smaller word that includes the most difficult part of the word (Mastropieri & Scruggs, 1991). Focus on those parts and create strategies to promote learning the correct way to spell them. Shefter (1989) identified mnemonic strategies for some difficult words, for example:

- It is **VILE** to allow special pri**VILE**ge.
- Don't **MAR** your writing with bad gram**MAR**.
- You **GAIN** when you buy a bar**GAIN**.
- Draw **ALL** the lines par**ALL**el. (p. 19)

Notice that in each of these cases, there is no particular rule that governs the spelling of the word, so spelling mnemonics are appropriate. Similarly, teach distinctions between homonyms by making up sentences using the same procedures. For example:

- A princi**PAL** is your **PAL**; a princip**LE** is a ru**LE**.
- A lett**ER** is written on station**ER**y; the j**AR** is station**AR**y.

Sometimes an interactive illustration can be shown to help students remember the correct spelling, as in the mnemonic "She screamed **E-E-E** as she walked by the cemetery," to help remember the three *e*'s in *cemetery* (Figure 13.6). Dowling (1995) and Suid (1981) provide books of mnemonic spellings for difficult words. Additionally, a number of mnemonic spelling strategies can be found on the Internet. Generally, targeted elaborations of the type described here are more useful than acrostics that represent sentences, the first letters of which spell words (e.g., for *arithmetic*: "A rat in the house may eat the ice cream"; Wordplay, 2012).

TEACH SELF-INSTRUCTIONAL AND SELF-MONITORING STRATEGIES   Strategies are often taught so that students can use them independently. Self-monitoring strategies teach students to self-monitor their attention to task, their use of particular studying strategies, and their spelling performance. A recent review of spelling research concluded that explicit

Figure 13.6 Mnemonic Spelling Strategy

Note: From *Teaching students ways to remember: Strategies for learning mnemonically* (p. 84), by M. A. Mastropieri & T. E. Scruggs, 1991, Cambridge, MA: Brookline Books. Reprinted with permission.

instruction and self-correction were particularly effective for students with learning disabilities (Williams et al., 2016). The strategies are listed on a "self-monitoring" card and teach students the following steps:

- Say the spelling word.
- Write and say the spelling word.
- Check the spelling.
- Trace and say the word.
- Write the word without looking.
- Check the spelling.

Students repeat these steps as necessary (see Graham & Harris, 2006).

TEACH THE COVER–COPY–COMPARE STRATEGY   Teach students to say the word, look at the model, and study the spelling. Students then *cover* the model and try to *copy* the word from memory. Finally, students look at the model and *compare* their spelling with the model. Students repeat the steps until the spelling of the word is mastered.

Finally, include attributional and motivational components to help promote better spelling and overall studying habits (Fulk, 1997). This strategy has been shown to be effective for students with and without learning difficulties (Joseph et al., 2012).

USE SPECIALIZED SOFTWARE AND CURRICULUM MATERIALS   Technology can help improve spelling performance (Wissick & Gardner, 2011). Some software contains drill-and-practice formats in which students practice spelling new words. Other software resembles computer games, and students practice spelling words in more gamelike formats. *Ultimate Spelling* (eReflect Software), for example, provides access to classroom and other spelling lists, a variety of gamelike activities, and tools for evaluation and tracking progress. Numerous apps for tablets or smartphones also are available to support spelling objectives. Be sure to evaluate progress when using these apps.

Many curriculum materials also are available commercially to teach spelling, including SRA/McGraw-Hill's *Spelling Mastery* and *Spelling Through Morphographs* for older students. These programs emphasize systematic approaches using a direct-instruction format and spelling patterns. Both programs recommend daily lessons of 15 to 20 minutes and have supplemental activities to provide practice with the new words. *Spell It-Write* (Zaner-Bloser) is intended to teach spelling words in a way that will promote transition and application to student writing.

The *Directed Spelling List* (first through third grade) and the *Spelling for Writing List* (including word listings for students with disabilities; Graham, Harris, & Loynachan, 1994, 1996) are word lists based on analyses of commonly used words that are problematic for students. Using the *Directed Spelling Thinking Activity* (DSTA; Graham et al., 1996), students actively compare and contrast words that fit different, but related, patterns.

In a study by Graham, Harris, and Chorzempa (2002), pairs of second-grade poor spellers were tutored for three 20-minute sessions per week for 12 weeks. Students were presented with word categories, each represented by a master word card; for example, "**made**," "**maid**," and "**may**" represented three patterns for the long /A/ sound. Students sorted word cards into the categories, and the tutor corrected and explained as needed. The tutor also helped students state relevant rules and generate words of their own. Students then studied new spelling words they had previously misspelled that matched the word patterns. They also practiced sound–letter associations with flashcards and engaged in word-building spelling activities based on word patterns and spelling rules for consonants, blends, and digraphs. Students who participated in the training dramatically increased their spelling skills and transferred these skills to reading and writing.

ADAPT SPELLING OBJECTIVES   Spelling may not be as important during some written activities as it is during other activities, so consider prioritizing spelling objectives for your class. For example, during written essay exams, knowledge of the content, rather than spelling, is probably the major objective, so consider focusing the weight of the evaluation on content knowledge in this case.

Teach students compensation skills for spelling in their written work. Model how to use dictionaries to look up unknown words and how to use spell checkers on word-processing programs or apps on tablets or smartphones. The *Speaking Merriam-Webster's School Dictionary* (Franklin Electronics) can correct spellings of words and also includes a number of spelling-related word games.

APPLY SPELLING IN RTI PROGRAMS   Spelling can be included as a component of literacy interventions in Tier 2 programs. Spelling can be included within the teaching of reading skills such as phonemic analysis and phonics instruction. Direct teaching and practice, systematic skill development, and curriculum-based measurement can help enhance instruction in spelling skills in RTI programs (Gerber & Richards-Tutor, 2011).

STRATEGIES FOR
TEACHING WRITTEN COMMUNICATION

Written expression is a high level of communication that involves the integration of language, spelling, and reading skills. Students with special needs frequently experience problems with writing assignments due to their deficits in reading, spelling, or language. The Common Core State Standards include a sequence of standards for grades K–12 across multiple domains of writing. For example, for grade 6, standards are provided for writing persuasive, informative/explanatory, and narrative texts. Some standards for persuasive writing include the following: introduce claim(s) and organize the reasons and evidence clearly; support claim(s) with clear reasons and relevant evidence, using credible sources and demonstrating an understanding of the topic or text; and provide a concluding statement or section that follows from the argument presented (© Copyright 2010. National Governors Association Center for Best Practices and Council of Chief State School Officers. All rights reserved).

Research has demonstrated the effectiveness of planning, revising, and rewriting strategies designed to promote better writing (Gillespie & Graham, 2014; Graham & Harris, 2005, 2011). Involve students more actively in the writing process by having them write daily, choose their own topics, and revise their papers—often in collaboration with peers. Have students share their stories with classmates and answer questions from them. Such activities can help enforce the idea that writing is communication aimed at an audience and show students that peers can be helpful in expanding and improving that communication (Englert & Mariage, 1996). Peer groups can also be used in editing and revising activities (Englert & Mariage, 1996). Ask students to review and provide positive feedback on and suggestions for one another's written work and to collaborate in the revision process.

MyEdLab:
Video Example 13.7.

The teacher in this video describes the prewriting planning that goes into a biography-writing assignment. Notice the writing-process poster and how she addresses the purpose of the assignment and makes it clear to the students what criteria to follow.

TEACH STUDENTS TO PLAN FOR WRITING   According to Graham and Harris (2007), planning is an important component of skilled writing. However, students with writing difficulties often plan infrequently or ineffectively, writing the first thoughts that come to mind in order to finish the task. Efforts to enhance planning for writing, particularly for struggling writers, can have a positive impact. Before students undertake any writing task, be sure they understand the purpose of the writing assignment. They should then develop a plan that reflects careful thinking about the purpose, including the topic, how it will be developed, what information will be employed, and how the written product will be structured (Hauth, Mastropieri, Scruggs, & Regan, 2013). Discuss student plans, and provide feedback before they begin writing.

PROMOTE THINKING ABOUT WRITING   Students can be taught to use action words (verbs: *ran, drove, slept*), action helper words (adverbs: ran *fast,* drove *slowly,* slept *soundly*), and descriptive words (adjectives: *beautiful* scene, *delicious* meal, *enthusiastic* teacher) as they write (Graham & Harris, 2005). You can use pictures and have students describe the action they see taking place in the pictures. For example, brainstorm lists of words relevant to students' age and backgrounds and post them in the room.

IMPLEMENT SELF-REGULATION AND SELF-INSTRUCTIONAL WRITING STRATEGIES   The importance of teaching students effective strategies combined with self-regulation and self-instruction is emphasized generally in this text chapter and extends to teaching writing skills. As with all strategic instruction, model the self-instruction strategy before asking students to implement it.

Six basic types of self-instruction exist, which are presented with examples in Figure 13.7 (see also Harris, Graham, Mason, & Friedlander, 2008). Provide students with explanations of these types of self-instruction, and discuss how they can be helpful in completing writing tasks. With this background understanding, they may be more able to appreciate the value and purpose of more specific strategy instruction.

CHOOSE EFFECTIVE COMPOSITION STRATEGIES   Several strategies have been developed to help organize writing procedures. Story-grammar strategies were described in the reading-comprehension section of this chapter (see Figure 13.4), but they can also be applied effectively as composition strategies (De La Paz, 2007; Graham & Harris, 2005). Model all steps of the story-grammar strategy, and create smaller individual charts containing steps for students. For example, Graham and Harris (2005) described the **3-W, 2-What, 2-How** strategy for story writing:

- **Who** is in the story?
- **When** does the story take place?
- **Where** does the story take place?
- **What** happens in the story?
- **What** do the characters in the story do?
- **How** do the characters feel?
- **How** does the story end?

Discuss when the strategy is useful and how to use all the steps involved, and provide examples of how the strategy will benefit students in a variety of situations.

After modeling all the steps for self-regulation, have students practice the steps in the strategy with partners. Facilitate practice sessions during which students complete the self-talk of the regulation and self-instruction phases while completing the story grammar. Such practice sessions enable students to master both the strategy and the self-regulatory components.

The **SPACE** strategy is designed to help students think about more details that need to be included in their narrative stories and involves the following steps:

- Note **S**etting.
- Note **P**urpose.
- Note **A**ction.
- Note **C**onclusion.
- Note **E**motions. (Harris & Graham, 1992, p. 49)

Problem Definition
Sizing up the nature and demands of the task:
>"What is it I have to do here?"
>"What am I up to?"
>"What is my first step?"
>"I want to write a convincing essay."

Focusing of Attention and Planning
Focusing on the task at hand and generating a plan:
>"I have to concentrate, be careful . . . think of the steps."
>"To do this right I have to make a plan."
>"First I need to . . . then . . ."

Strategy
Engaging and implementing writing or self-regulating strategies:
>"First I will write down my essay writing reminder."
>"The first step in writing an essay is . . ."
>"My goals for this essay are . . .; I will self-record on . . ."

Self-Evaluating and Error Correcting
Evaluating performance, catching and correcting errors:
>"Have I used all of my story parts—let me check."
>"Oops, I missed one; that's okay, I can revise."
>"Am I following my plan?"

Coping and Self-Control
Subsuming difficulties or failures and dealing with forms of arousal:
>"Don't worry, worry doesn't help."
>"It's okay to feel a little anxious; a little anxiety can help."
>"I'm not going to get mad; mad makes me do bad."
>"I can handle this."
>"I need to go slow and take my time."

Self-Reinforcement
Providing reward:
>"I'm getting better at this."
>"I like this ending."
>"Wait 'til my teacher reads this!"
>"Hurray—I'm done!"

Figure 13.7 The Six Basic Types of Self-Instruction

Note: From *Helping young writers master the craft: Strategy instruction and self-regulation in the writing process* (p. 85), by K. R. Harris & S. Graham, 1992, Cambridge, MA: Brookline Books. Reprinted with permission.

Graham and Harris (2005) described the three-step strategy **THINK–STOP–DARE** for writing persuasive essays (De La Paz, 2007; De La Paz & Graham, 1997):

1. THINK—Who will read this? Why am I writing this?

2. STOP—**S**uspend judgment, **T**ake a side or position, **O**rganize ideas, and **P**lan more as you write.

3. DARE—**D**evelop your topic sentence, **A**dd supporting ideas, **R**eject opposing arguments, and **E**nd with a conclusion.

When teaching students these strategies, use effective instruction, and include models, demonstrations, and guided practice to promote independent and fluent strategy usage.

TEACH SELF-REGULATED STRATEGY DEVELOPMENT (SRSD) SRSD is a model for promoting higher-level cognitive skills and self-regulated use of cognitive strategies (Graham & Harris, 2005) and has provided some of the most positive effects of all writing interventions (Gillespie & Graham, 2014; Graham & Perin, 2007). The framework of SRSD consists of several instructional stages.

The first stage (Develop Background Knowledge) provides the pre-skills needed to acquire and use relevant writing strategies. In the second stage (Discuss It), students discuss their current writing performance and the strategies they use. In the third stage (Model It), the teacher models the process of the writing strategies using think-alouds that describe the steps:

- Problem definition (e.g., "I need to write a compare–contrast essay.")
- Planning ("How will I plan out the steps?")
- Strategy use ("Which strategies shall I use?")
- Self-evaluation ("How am I doing?")
- Error correction ("This part doesn't fit.")
- Self-reinforcement ("I did a good job on this!")

Students learn and use mnemonics to remember and practice the steps of strategies (e.g., THINK–STOP–DARE) in the fourth stage (Memorize It). In the fifth stage (Support It), teachers and students collaborate to use strategies and self-instructions to complete writing assignments. Graham and Harris (2011) summarized SRSD research and concluded that it led to improved writing performance across a variety of strategic writing tasks.

One strategy for persuasive writing that also has received much research attention is the **POW+TREE** strategy (Gillespie & Graham, 2014; Harris et al., 2008; Mastropieri et al., 2009, 2012). The strategy acronym represents the following steps:

Pick my idea

Organize my notes

Write and say more

    Topic sentence

    Reasons (three or more, with explanations)

    Ending (wrap it up)

    Examine (Do I have all the parts?)

When these strategies were implemented over time, combined with the general SRSD strategies, students with learning disabilities (Graham & Perin, 2007) and, more recently, students with emotional or behavioral disabilities were found to greatly improve their persuasive writing skills (Mastropieri et al., 2009, 2010, 2012, 2013, 2014). The *Research Highlight* describes this writing strategy implemented with middle school students with emotional disabilities.

PROVIDE SUPPORT FOR WRITTEN RESEARCH REPORTS Teachers frequently assign research reports as longer-term homework assignments. Such projects are often overwhelming for students with special needs, but teaching students specific strategies can help students to complete such assignments successfully. Several important skills are required for writing a research report, including the following:

- Brainstorming topics
- Selecting a topic
- Finding relevant sources
- Reading and note taking
- Organizing the paper's outline
- Filling in details in the outline
- Writing a rough draft
- Proofing and correcting the draft version
- Completing a final version

Determine which of these skills need to be taught to your students. For example, you may have covered brainstorming in previous classes and can simply review the procedures with students. Once you determine which skill areas need instruction, prepare explicit instruction, and provide plenty of opportunities for practice. For example, many students with disabilities require extensive instruction on how to find relevant sources. Determine the types of search procedures

Academic Instruction for Students with Emotional/Behavioral Disabilities

Challenges exist when meeting the academic needs of students with emotional and behavioral disabilities (EBDs) who have deficits in multiple academic areas, including expressive writing (Lane, 2004). Until recently, little research systematically addressed these students' academic needs. However, recent studies of written expression have been conducted using the self-regulation strategy development (SRSD) model and have yielded very promising findings (e.g., Cuenca-Sanchez, Mastropieri, Scruggs, & Kidd, 2012; Evmenova et al., 2016; Graham & Harris, 2005; Hauth et al., 2013; Mastropieri et al., 2015).

All studies taught middle school students with EBDs persuasive writing by using the SRSD model and the POW+TREE strategy described in the text (e.g., Mastropieri et al., 2015; Mastropieri et al., 2014). Some studies also taught students to include counterarguments in their persuasive essays (e.g., Mastropieri et al., 2012). Some studies included a fluency phase in which students learned to plan and write a single-paragraph response (Mastropieri et al.,

2009, 2012) after learning to write multiple-paragraph essays. Cuenca-Sanchez et al. (2012) embedded self-determination instruction within the writing instruction, and Hauth and colleagues (Hauth et al., 2013) taught students to use the strategy with social studies content. Cerar (2012) taught single paragraphs before teaching multiple paragraphs.

In all studies, students were taught in small groups, and the amount of instructional time required for students to master the strategy ranged from 7.5 hours to 25 hours. Findings revealed that all students successfully learned the strategy and significantly improved in their abilities to write high-quality persuasive essays. Students were able to learn to plan and write single-paragraph responses within a 10-minute timeframe for response. Students with more significant EBDs required substantially more intensity of instruction than students with EBDs in inclusive classes. Whenever specific instructional changes occurred, students were able to demonstrate successful learning of additional features, such as applying learning to social studies content and learning

basic self-determination skills. More recently, Evmenova et al. (2016) taught students with learning and behavioral disabilities a similar writing strategy that used a researcher-developed graphic organizer template created in Microsoft Office. In this strategy, students worked on iPads or computers to create their organizers and complete their essays.

Taken together, these findings indicate that students can learn and improve their writing but may require additional instruction and refresher "booster sessions" periodically throughout the school year.

QUESTIONS FOR REFLECTION

1. Why do you think students with EBDs perform well when taught using the SRSD writing strategy?
2. Why do you think students in self-contained settings might require more instructional time to learn the strategies?
3. What implications are associated with the need for greater instructional time for placement and instruction of students with EBDs?
4. What other extensions of this writing strategy instruction could be conducted?

---

students need to learn, design appropriate instructional strategies to promote the acquisition of the procedures, and provide ample practice opportunities. Encourage students to meet in pairs or small groups and proofread each other's work.

USE TECHNOLOGY TO HELP WITH THE WRITING PROCESS Computer technology is available to support writers on a number of writing tasks. Word-processing and related programs have been helpful in improving the writing of students with disabilities (Morphy & Graham, 2012). Keyboarding, voice-recognition, and word-prediction programs can accommodate students with slow or labored handwriting and those with physical disabilities. Spell checkers and grammar checkers can assist with proofreading if students are provided with instruction in their use. Software is available to assist with the steps in the writing process and provide prompts (Berninger & Amtmann, 2003). Evmenova et al. (2016) reported that a computer-based graphic organizer improved performance in essay planning and writing in a group of struggling writers. Applications for smartphones and tablets are also available to assist with writing tasks.

ADAPT INSTRUCTION TO OVERCOME MECHANICAL OBSTACLES TO WRITING

Many students become frustrated with writing assignments because they are overwhelmed with the mechanical obstacles of handwriting, spelling, and punctuation. Isaacson and Gleason (1997) proposed eight methods for helping students overcome those obstacles:

1. *Allow dictation instead of writing.* Provide students the flexibility of thinking without any writing impediments; however, a scribe or a speech-to-text program or app must be provided.

2. *Pre-cue spelling of difficult words.* Write difficult words on the board or prominently displayed chart cards.

3. *Teach a word-book strategy.* Have students maintain word books containing their own dictionaries of hard words, which they can refer to at any time to check their spelling.

4. *Ask for help.* Encourage students to ask others (teachers, aides, other students) for assistance, and ensure that someone is available to help them.

5. *Encourage invented spelling.* Sometimes students are reluctant to use interesting words simply because they do not know how to spell them. Encourage students to write their best guess of a word's spelling to encourage creativity and writing fluency. However, at some point, students must learn to identify and correct any misspellings. Invented spelling can facilitate writing by helping students focus on their ideas, but it is unlikely to improve their spelling.

6. *Encourage peer collaboration.* Peer collaboration establishes a cooperative approach to writing and may be beneficial during the brainstorming, preplanning, and revising stages.

7. *Encourage self-checking.* Teach students specific self-checking strategies. Some strategies include rereading to make sure sentences make logical sense, that capital letters are used appropriately, and that punctuation and spelling are accurate.

8. *Use technology.* Computers have become more available and more versatile for classroom use. Computer-assisted writing and dictation may prove to be a positive alternative for students with writing difficulties.

USE SPECIALIZED CURRICULUM MATERIALS AND SOFTWARE Some materials are commercially available to promote writing competencies for students with disabilities. *Reasoning and Writing* (SRA/McGraw-Hill) uses a direct-instruction format to provide practice in learning how to think through topics and write from beginning levels to more advanced levels. *Expressive Writing* (SRA/McGraw-Hill) is another resource using a direct-instruction approach that contains approximately 50 lessons for students who can read at the third-grade level or above; it teaches writing and editing skills.

Many computerized programs also are commercially available. *ACHIEVE! Writing & Language Arts* (Broderbund) promotes grammar, spelling, and creative writing with gamelike activities. *WordQ Writing Software* (Boundless Assistive Technology) offers word-prediction, spoken feedback, and proofreading assistance. *Paragraph Punch* (Merit Software) is intended to help older students with learning disabilities (grades 5–10) develop their paragraph-writing skills and includes prewriting, writing, organizing, revising, rewriting, and publishing steps. *Storybook Weaver Deluxe* (Riverdeep), a multimedia program, contains story starters, story ideas, and multicultural images to help improve students' writing skills. *StoryCraftPro*, story-development software from Writers Supercenter, walks older writers through the steps of the story-writing process. *Odyssey Writer* (Time 4 Learning) provides assistance with prewriting, writing, revising, and proofreading for elementary and middle school students. *Kurzweil 3000-firefly* (Kurzweil) contains many features to facilitate the writing process. In addition, several writing software programs address components of universal design for learning (Vue & Hall, 2012).

Carefully examine whether the programs' features are appropriate, and determine whether your students have the necessary skills to benefit from the software. Some programs also teach keyboarding skills so that students can make optimal use of computerized programs designed to improve written composition.

MyEdLab: **Self-Check 13.4**

13 Summary

- Many approaches exist for teaching students to read. Many students with reading disabilities lack phonemic awareness and phonics skills and overuse context cues when trying to read. Teachers should select reading programs that consider these areas of need.

- Common Core State Standards for reading address competencies in foundational skills, informational text, and literature and cover grades K–12.

- Teaching phonemic awareness, phonics, structural analysis, sight vocabulary, and reading fluency provides important basic skills for literacy. Reading-comprehension strategies can be employed before, during, or after reading. These strategies include basic skills instruction and text enhancements. Self-monitoring and self-questioning strategies are among the most effective reading-comprehension strategies.

- Written expression includes handwriting, spelling, and written communication. Problems in handwriting and spelling can be addressed by providing models and sufficient practice, using behavioral techniques, and teaching self-regulation and self-instructional strategies. Written communication problems can be addressed by using collaborative peer groups, teaching self-regulation and self-instructional strategies, and using story-grammar techniques and specific composition strategies.

PROFESSIONAL STANDARDS LINK:
Literacy

Information in this chapter links most directly to:

- CEC Standards: 1 (Learner Development and Individual Learning Differences), 2 (Learning Environments), 3 (Curricular Content Knowledge), and 5 (Instructional Planning and Strategies)

- INTASC Standards: 2 (Learning Differences), 3 (Learning Environments), 4 (Content Knowledge), 7 (Planning for Instruction), 8 (Instructional Strategies)

LITERACY

If any of your students are having difficulty in literacy, have you done the following? If not, see the pages listed here.

STRATEGIES FOR IMPLEMENTING APPROACHES TO READING

- ☐ Implement and adapt basal textbook approaches, 308
- ☐ Implement and adapt whole-language approaches, 308–309
- ☐ Implement Reading Recovery for struggling readers, 309
- ☐ Implement and adapt direct-instruction and code-emphasis approaches, 309–310
- ☐ Make adaptations to promote access to text, 310–311

STRATEGIES FOR PROMOTING WORD IDENTIFICATION

- ☐ Provide phonemic awareness training, 312–313
- ☐ Provide phonics instruction, 313–314
- ☐ Teach structural analysis as students acquire phonics skills, 314
- ☐ Use strategies for promoting basic-sight vocabulary, 314–316

STRATEGIES FOR PROMOTING READING FLUENCY

- ☐ Use repeated readings, 317
- ☐ Use curriculum-based measurement, 317
- ☐ Use classwide peer tutoring, 317
- ☐ Use software programs, 317

STRATEGIES FOR TEACHING READING COMPREHENSION

- ☐ Use basic skills and reinforcement strategies, 318
- ☐ Create text enhancements, 318–319
- ☐ Teach specific questioning strategies, 319–323
- ☐ Adapt formats of reading-comprehension instruction, 323–324
- ☐ Adapt instruction for secondary students, 324–325
- ☐ Use assistive technology to support secondary-level readers, 325

STRATEGIES FOR IMPLEMENTING MULTI-TIERED READING INSTRUCTION WITH RTI

- ☐ Strategies for implementing primary (Tier 1) interventions, 326
- ☐ Strategies for implementing secondary (Tier 2) interventions, 326
- ☐ Strategies for implementing tertiary (Tier 3) interventions, 326

STRATEGIES FOR IMPROVING HANDWRITING

- ☐ Incorporate self-regulation and self-instructional strategies, 328
- ☐ Use materials to develop manuscript and cursive writing, 328
- ☐ Make technological adaptations, 328

STRATEGIES FOR TEACHING SPELLING

- ☐ Select words from reading and writing activities, 329
- ☐ Provide distributed practice sessions, 329
- ☐ Use peer tutoring, 330

14

Mathematics

LEARNING OUTCOMES

After studying this chapter, you should be able to:

14.1 Describe reform movements in mathematics education, including the NCTM standards and the Common Core State Standards for Mathematics.

14.2 Describe difficulties in mathematics that may be experienced by students with disabilities.

14.3 Describe strategies for teaching mathematics in inclusive settings, including beginning math, addition and subtraction, multiplication and division, response-to-intervention strategies, problem solving, money and time, fractions and decimals, area and volume concepts, algebra, and functional math.

Mathematics is the academic discipline concerned with the solution of problems that involve quantity or number. Mathematics includes such branches as arithmetic, algebra, geometry, trigonometry, and calculus. Always an important field of study in education, mathematics has taken on increasing importance in modern society (Martin, 2007; National Council of Teachers of Mathematics, 2000; National Math Advisory Panel, 2008).

Students with disabilities need to gain proficiency in mathematics to fully participate in society (Sayeski & Paulsen, 2010). For this to occur, teachers must be fluent in a variety of instructional techniques that will allow students with diverse learning needs to meet their greatest potential in math.

Mathematics Education

Through much of U.S. history, mathematics was taught as a set of facts, rules, and procedures for dealing with numbers and quantitative concepts. Reform in mathematics education initiated by the National Council of Teachers of Mathematics (NCTM) resulted in the *Principles and Standards for School Mathematics* (Martin, 2007; NCTM, 2000). In this publication, six overarching principles are provided to describe features of high-quality mathematics education: equity, curriculum, teaching, learning, assessment, and technology. The Common Core State Standards (CCSS) Initiative provides standards in mathematics for kindergarten through high school levels in multiple areas, including arithmetic, algebra, functions, modeling, geometry, and statistics and probability (National Governors Association Center for Best Practices & Council of Chief State School Officers, 2010). For example, at the third-grade level, standards address numbers and operations in base 10; numbers and operations—fractions; measurement and data; and geometry. For numbers and operations in base 10, standards include the following: "Fluently add and subtract within 1000 using strategies and algorithms based on place value, properties of operations, and/or the relationship between addition and subtraction." (© Copyright 2010. National Governors Association Center for Best Practices and Council of Chief State School Officers. All rights reserved.)

The Common Core State Standards for Mathematics (CCSSM) have generally paralleled NCTM principles, particularly in the areas of the balance between mathematical concepts and

Multicultural Mathematics

 Many people assume that mathematics, as a subject area and a discipline, is universal and constant throughout the world. However, this is not the case. The study of the multicultural contributions to mathematics can help students understand the way different cultures throughout history have viewed mathematics and can lead to a deeper understanding of mathematics as a subject area.

For example, some African cultures use base-20 systems for counting. Learning these systems could contribute to a greater depth of understanding of Western base-10 systems. Babylonians created tables of reciprocals and used these tables to divide by multiplying by the reciprocals. Mathematics and music of different cultures can be combined in the study of polyrhythms, dividing beats in a measure in two or more ways at the same time. This is relevant to the study of fractions and least-common multiples.

Other examples of multicultural math include other African numeration and counting systems, the Arabic contribution to mathematics, Mayan calendars and numbering systems, ancient Chinese mathematics, and Egyptian and Babylonian mathematics. All of these topics are likely to be of interest to students and can help broaden their understanding of how different cultures have used mathematics. Samples and links to culturally relevant activities are available on the Internet (e.g., Math Forum at NCTM, 2016; McCoy, 2004).

Several relevant books on multicultural math are available and may be useful in including multicultural considerations in math class. These books include *Math Is a Verb: Activities and Lessons from Cultures Around the World* (Barta, Eglash, & Barkley, 2014); *Mathematics Lessons Learned from Across the World—PreK–8* (Lott & Lott, 2014); *Improving Access to Mathematics: Diversity and Equity in the Classroom* (Nasir & Cobb, 2007); *Africa Counts: Number and Pattern in African Cultures* (Zaslavsky, 1999); *The Crest of the Peacock: Non-European Roots of Mathematics* (Joseph, 2000); *Introduction to Cultural Mathematics: With Case Studies in the Otomies and Inca* (Gilsdorf, 2012); *The Multicultural Math Classroom: Bringing in the World* (Zaslavsky, 1995); and *Oral Storytelling and Teaching Mathematics: Pedagogical and Multicultural Perspectives* (Schiro, 2004).

procedural skills and an emphasis on mathematical process skills, referred to as Standards for Mathematical Practice in CCSS (NCTM, 2011).

The NCTM (2000) suggested that students with disabilities and other special needs may need accommodations in the form of language support, increased time, oral rather than written assignments, peer mentoring, and cross-age tutoring. This chapter presents a number of strategies that may be useful in teaching mathematics to students with special needs in inclusive settings. The *Diversity in the Classroom* feature presents information on the study of mathematics in other cultures.

Mathematics and Students with Disabilities

Some students with disabilities exhibit little difficulty in learning mathematics. For many others, however, math is an extremely challenging subject area. Many students with learning disabilities may exhibit difficulties in the areas of memory and general strategy use, literacy and communication, specific processes and strategies associated with solving math problems, and low motivation and affect (Mastropieri, Scruggs, Hauth, & Allen-Bronaugh, 2012; Montague & Jitendra, 2006).

Students with intellectual disabilities may exhibit many of these difficulties, as well as problems with acquiring math concepts, remembering and executing math facts and procedures, and mathematical reasoning (Butler, Miller, Lee, & Pierce, 2001). Students with emotional or behavioral disorders often score below grade level on tests of mathematics achievement (Reid, Gonzalez, Nordness, Trout, & Epstein, 2004), and students with attention problems may exhibit difficulties in organizing information in problem-solving tasks (Marzocchi, Lucangeli, De Meo, Fini, & Cornoldi, 2002).

For students with hearing impairments and communication disorders (as well as for students who are English language learners), math may be an area of relative strength. Nevertheless, many students may have difficulty with the English-language and communication aspects of mathematics (Lang & Pagliaro, 2007). Like many students with special needs, students with hearing impairments may benefit from authentic mathematic experiences, integration of vocabulary development, and classroom discourse about mathematics (Stewart & Kluwin, 2001). Students with visual impairments may also generally perform well on mathematics tasks if appropriate adaptations are made (Rosenblum & Amato, 2004). Finally, some students with physical disabilities may need specific assistance if concrete manipulative materials are used (Heller, 2010).

MyEdLab: Self-Check 14.1

Teaching Math in Inclusive Settings

Fuchs et al. (2011) described seven research-based principles for effective remediation in mathematics:

- *Explicit instruction*, in which the teacher directly provides important information and systematically supports student mastery
- *Instructional design* to minimize the learning challenge, including precise explanations and carefully sequenced instruction
- A *strong conceptual basis* for mathematical procedures to promote understanding, reduce confusion, and maintain and integrate previously mastered content
- *Drill and practice* to promote automaticity and overlearning
- *Cumulative review* to promote integration and retention of learning
- *Motivators* to promote effort, regulate attention, and address previous learning failures
- Systematic, ongoing *progress monitoring*

For all students, and particularly for those with cognitive or intellectual disabilities, development of mathematical understandings can be facilitated by progressing from concrete representations of quantity (e.g., beads or blocks) to semiconcrete (e.g., pictorial) representations, then finally to abstract (graphic) representations (Fuchs, Fuchs, & Courey, 2005; Mercer, Mercer, & Pullen, 2011). Concrete representations as well as "virtual" manipulatives have also been helpful for students with autism spectrum disorder (Barnett & Cleary, 2015). Mathematics functioning also has been improved by direct instruction, reinforcement, mnemonics, and cognitive strategy training (Jimenez & Staples, 2015; Mastropieri et al., 2012; Stein, Kinder, Silbert, & Carnine, 2006). Effective teaching strategies for different subject and skill areas are discussed in the upcoming sections.

David Rose and his colleagues at the Center for Universal Design for Learning (UDL) (cast .org) describe UDL as an approach to thinking about teaching and learning for all students, similar to differentiated instruction (see cast.org; Hall, Meyer, & Rose, 2012; Meyer, Rose, & Gordon, 2014). By applying UDL principles to mathematics, teachers make math instruction accessible to everyone. Examples include the use of manipulatives during instruction, provision of both verbal and written instructions, and use of technology with features such as font enlargement or text-to-voice and voice-to-text options that facilitate access to the material for all students. Other examples include allowing differentiated response formats for students based on their abilities, such as allowing the use of switch response formats for students with physical disabilities or severe disabilities and allowing oral or written responses. Most of the strategies in this chapter are consistent with UDL principles.

STRATEGIES FOR
TEACHING BEGINNING MATH

TEACH EARLY NUMBER CONCEPTS   Early number concepts are critically important for the development of later mathematical skill (Powell & Fuchs, 2012). Most children are already familiar with many elementary number concepts when they begin school (Berteletti, Lucangeli, Piazza, Dehaene, & Zorzi, 2010). These concepts are represented by words such as *more, less, any, none, none left, together, how many,* and *each.* Concepts such as these are necessary for the development of more complex understandings. It may become clear, however, from student responses to teacher questions (e.g., "Do you want more?" "Which container holds fewer pencils?") or by a student's statements that such concepts have not been mastered. Understanding of these concepts can be promoted by applying strategies for teaching language concepts. For example, during snack period, after a student eats one cracker, the teacher could say, "Do you want more?" When the student begins to reply correctly, the teacher could ask, "What do you want?" prompting the student to reply, "More crackers." Later, the teacher could hold two crackers in one hand and three in the other and ask, "Which hand has more crackers?"

TEACH STRATEGIES FOR COUNTING   Learning to count is a type of factual (serial list) learning and is best acquired with practice. Counting seems to be a very simple skill, but it can appear very complicated to those who have not yet mastered it. Be sure to address all the components of counting in early numeracy. *Acoustic counting* refers to saying numbers in sequence ("Everybody say with me, 'one, two, three...'"). *Point counting* refers to pointing to objects as each number name is said ("Let's count all the desks in the classroom. Point and count together..."); when done correctly, pointing and counting are *synchronized. Resultative counting* refers to the understanding that the order in which items are counted is irrelevant to obtaining the correct total ("Now let's count them in the other direction..."). *Counting on* is the ability to begin counting with a number other than 1 (and is a good way to introduce adding: "I've got five pencils in my left hand; let's count how many there are altogether: *"Five...* six, seven..."). *Skip counting* or "count by" is counting by groups of numbers, such as 2s and 5s. Finally, *subitizing* means totaling small numbers of objects (e.g., four pennies) without directly counting (Van Luit & Schopman, 2000).

Begin with just a few numbers, such as "one, two, three," and have students clap their hands each time they count. Students who are having more difficulty may benefit from practicing with a larger group of students. As number sequences are mastered, add a few numbers at a time. For additional time-on-task, ask peers to count with students who are still learning. Use of rhythms or regular emphasis may also help develop counting skills. Although group practice is helpful, it is also important to determine that individual students have mastered counting skills by asking them to count independently.

As the series of names of numbers is mastered, students should be introduced to the concept of counting *things.* Counting the students in the class or the pencils in a jar, for example, is an early means of demonstrating how similar objects can be counted. Again, practice, additional time-on-task, and use of peer assistance can help enforce the concept of numeration.

Jimenez and Staples (2015) taught early numeracy skills to students with significant intellectual disabilities, in alignment with Common Core State Standards for Mathematics. These skills included number identification, making sets of up to five items, and doing simple addition and used math stories, theme-based lessons, systematic prompting and feedback, and manipulatives and graphic organizers from the *Early Numeracy* materials developed by Jimenez, Browder, and Saunders (2012). The students made substantial progress toward meeting the standards on alternative assessments.

REINFORCE ONE-TO-ONE CORRESPONDENCE   *One-to-one correspondence* is the concept that sets of different objects (beads, blocks, and so on) can be matched according to quantity (Tucker, Singleton, & Weaver, 2006). That is, even though blocks are not the same as beads, a set of three blocks is equivalent to a set of three beads with respect to quantity. You can reinforce this correspondence by exhibiting two sets of objects and asking students to match them item for item, as shown in Figure 14.1. Before later concepts can be mastered effectively, it is important that students understand the concept of numerical equivalence.

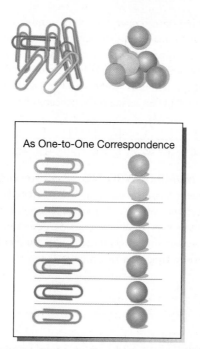

Figure 14.1 Understanding the Concept of Numerical Equivalence

INTRODUCE GEOMETRY CONCEPTS IN THE EARLY YEARS

It may be helpful to introduce the concept of shapes during the acquisition of early math concepts. Although precise rules that define particular geometric shapes can be provided later, you can teach students to identify simple shapes such as circles, squares, and triangles by the presentation of many examples and the use of teacher questioning.

Use different types of circles to enforce the relevant attributes of a circle—that shape is what matters, not other attributes such as color and size. Presenting noninstances also enforces the concept of *circle* ("Is this a circle?" [pointing to a square]). Also, give students different shapes, then ask them to hold up the shape that matches the teacher's shape.

STRATEGIES FOR
TEACHING ADDITION AND SUBTRACTION

USE MANIPULATIVES FOR TEACHING ADDITION AND SUBTRACTION CONCEPTS
Using such materials as beads, buttons, dried beans, or commercially available base-10 manipulatives (distributed by companies such as Delta Education), you can help students learn the concepts of addition and subtraction by counting. For example, show students 5 beans, and ask them to add 4 more. Demonstrate how to select 4 beans to add and employ a "counting-on" strategy, where they start at 5 and add the 4 beans, counting up to 9. You can also teach students to "take away" by starting with 9 beans and taking away 4, to leave the difference of 5. (Remember that small manipulatives can represent a choking hazard for very young children.)

USE NUMBER LINES TO PROMOTE OPERATIONS
A helpful intermediate step between counting actual objects and operating with numbers is the use of a **number line**. Number lines are lines with marks to represent quantity. Here is an example:

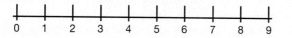

To add, have students place their pencils on the first addend on the number line and count forward using the second addend. For example, to add 2 + 3, students place their pencils on the 2 and then count forward: 1(3), 2(4), 3(5). Conversely, the subtraction problem 5 − 2 is solved by placing the pencil on the 5; counting two steps to the left, 1(4), 2(3); and noting the difference, 3. The relationship between operations with number lines and adding and subtracting beans and buttons should be made explicit. Also, number lines are useful when practicing "count-ons" and "count-backs" as precursors of learning addition and subtraction facts.

Provide physical assistance, enlarge or darken the number line, or use three-dimensional number lines to provide for special needs. Later, number lines that include negative numbers can be substituted to help students understand the concept of negative numbers:

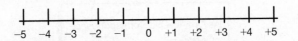

USE STRATEGIES FOR NUMBER WRITING
Some students have difficulty learning to write numbers and may benefit from the use of models or stencils, from copying over dashed-line numbers, or from additional practice. Some students may reverse numbers when they write. Although many reversals may be obvious (e.g., 3), other reversals may not. A reversed 2, for example, may look like a 6 and suggest a problem with number facts when the true problem is writing, as shown in the following illustration:

Bley and Thornton (2001) suggested a strategy for remembering the spatial orientation of 3, 5, 7, and 9. That is, the curved part of 3 and 5 can be represented with the right hand; the 7 and 9 can be represented with the right hand and right forearm. That is, if 3, 5, 7, and 9 are written correctly, they can be imitated with the right hand.

Some number writing reversals involve two digits. For example, 18 can be written as 81. Reversals such as this may arise because the names of both numbers begin with the same word sound (*eight*). Again, practice, feedback, and self-correction can be helpful in eliminating these reversals.

USE QUESTIONING TO PROMOTE UNDERSTANDING OF SYMBOLS
Ginsburg (1998a, 1998b) described the case of a first grader who could answer problems such as 3 + 4 = ? but could not explain what was meant by the "plus" and "equal" symbols:

TOBY:	. . . it tells you three plus four, three plus four, so it's telling you, that, um, I think, the, um, the end is coming up—the end.
INTERVIEWER:	The end is coming up—what do you mean, the end is coming up?
TOBY:	Like, if you have equals, and so you have seven, then. [She is gesturing to the problem on the table.] So if you do three plus four equals seven, that would be right. (Ginsburg, 1998a, p. 42)

Other children may state that = means "makes," as in "6 + 3 *makes* 9" (Ginsburg, 1998a). As students acquire skill in mathematics, question them to determine that they also understand concepts represented by mathematical symbols. If not, reemphasize previous concept-building activities, such as equivalence.

USE TOUCH MATH TO PROMOTE ADDITION AND SUBTRACTION COMPUTATION
Even when students have mastered the relevant concepts of addition and subtraction, they may not necessarily be able to calculate problems quickly and accurately. A method for assisting with calculating arithmetic problems is **Touch Math** materials (Innovative Learning Concepts). These materials represent quantity by dots on each of the numbers 1–9, as shown in Figure 14.2. Touch Math materials have been found to be effective with students with a variety of disabilities, including physical disabilities, intellectual or learning disabilities, and autism (e.g., Avant & Heller, 2011; Aydemir, 2015; Cihak & Foust, 2008; Simon & Hanrahan, 2004).

1 2 3 4 5 6 7 8 9

Figure 14.2 Touch Math Numbers

Note: Reprinted with permission of Innovative Learning Concepts.

Students learn that each number is associated with a certain number of dots ("touch points"), which can be counted forward or backward to compute sums and differences. Note that the numbers 1–5 have solid dots, the total representing the quantity of the number. After 5, Touch Math uses circled dots, or "double touch points," each of which represents the quantity 2. Students learn to touch each of the touch points once and to touch each double touch point twice with their pencil when counting. For example, to compute the quantity

students are taught to start with the larger number, 7, and count forward, touching each of the double touch points in the 6 twice. Students start with 7 and count "8–9, 10–11, 12–13" to arrive at the answer. To subtract, students are taught to start with the minuend and count backward on the subtrahend, using the touch points. A complete set of Touch Math materials has been developed, along with worksheets and teacher materials, and is available from Innovative Learning Concepts.

Individual students can be taught to use Touch Math methods if they are having particular difficulty remembering addition and subtraction facts and you want them to engage in computation problems with the rest of the class. Touch Math has been found to be effective with students with autism spectrum disorder (ASD; Barnett & Cleary, 2015). In some cases, particularly in the primary grades, teachers use Touch Math with the whole class. However, if remembering math facts is a classroom standard, it may be important to continue to teach these facts in later grades.

USE PRACTICE AND SPECIFIC STRATEGIES FOR ADDITION AND SUBTRACTION FACTS Many students, including those without disabilities, have difficulty remembering addition and subtraction facts (Geary, 2003). One way to ensure that math facts are learned is to spend enough time teaching them. Students can respond orally as a class to teacher questions ("Class, what is 4 plus 7?") or hold up numbers at their desks ("Class, hold up the answer to 6 plus 3"). Additionally, pairs of students can drill each other using flashcards. Assigning facts to be mastered at home with the help of parents or other family members can also provide additional time-on-task.

Students who appear to be learning at a slower rate may be able to practice difficult facts with a partner. You can provide opportunities for students to practice using flashcards independently. Additionally, students can also use calculator-type machines and computer software, such as *Math Blaster* (Knowledge Adventure), to practice math facts.

When teaching facts, it is important to stress commutativity, that is, 2 + 3 = 3 + 2. Students who understand commutativity must master only half as many facts. Bley and Thornton (2001) suggested that reversible cards be used to demonstrate the equivalence of, for example, 2 + 3 and 3 + 2. Use a card similar to the following, embedded with tags or paper clips:

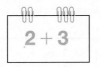

Teachers can reverse the card (3 + 2) to show that both sides represent the same fact. Bley and Thornton (2001) described several strategies to assist students with math facts. Looking at the matrix of 100 addition facts, they were able to demonstrate that most can be mastered with the following specific strategies:

1. Nineteen facts involve addition with zero (e.g., 3 + 0 = 3) and are easy to master.

2. Forty-five facts involve "count-ons," that is, addition with 1, 2, or 3 that can be "counted on" verbally to the other addend, for example, 8 + 2 or 6 + 3. Altogether, 64 of the 100 addition facts involve "zero facts" or "count-ons."

3. Of the remaining 36 facts (not covered by zero or count-ons), six facts involve "doubles" and can be represented by images or pictures of doubles. That is, $4 + 4$ is the "spider" fact, where the spider has four legs on each side; $5 + 5$ is the "fingers" fact (5 fingers on each hand); $6 + 6$ is the "egg carton" fact (6 eggs in each half dozen); $7 + 7$ is the "2-week fact (7 days in each of 2 weeks on a calendar); $8 + 8$ is the "crayon" fact (8 in each row); and $9 + 9$ is the "double 9 domino" fact (9 dots on each side of a domino). Double facts also exist for $2 + 2$ and $3 + 3$, but these are also covered by "count-ons."

4. In addition to the zero, count-on, and doubles facts, eight additional facts represent "doubles plus one," which means their sum is one more than the double. For example, $4 + 5$ is the same as the doubles fact (spider) $4 + 4 = 8$ plus one, or 9. The doubles and doubles-plus-one facts, together with the previously described facts, account for 78 facts in all.

5. Of the remaining 22 facts, 10 are referred to as "pattern 9" facts and can be learned by the following rule: the sum of a $+9$ fact can be obtained by subtracting one from the other addend and adding 10. For example, to add $9 + 5$, subtract 1 from the 5 ($= 4$) and add 10 to make 14.

6. Two additional facts ($6 + 4$ and $4 + 6$) are "other-10 sums," or other sums to 10, and two others ($7 + 4$ and $4 + 7$) are "10-plus-1" sums. Altogether, zero, count-ons, doubles, doubles plus one, pattern nine, other-10 sums, and 10-plus-1 sums account for 92 facts of the 100 addition facts, leaving only eight.

7. There is no specific rule for learning the remaining eight facts; however, commutativity reveals that these are actually only four facts, each of which can be expressed two ways: $5 + 7$ or $7 + 5$; $8 + 4$ or $4 + 8$; $8 + 5$ or $5 + 8$; and $8 + 6$ or $6 + 8$.

Use of the Bley and Thornton strategies is likely to prove helpful in assisting students who have difficulty recalling math facts.

Subtraction Facts Most students find it more difficult to learn subtraction facts than addition facts. One advantage, however, is that all subtraction facts are the inverse of particular addition facts and can be easily checked. That is, $9 - 5 = 4$ is the inverse fact of $4 + 5 = 9$. Use of base-10 blocks or other manipulatives can help enforce this concept. Some instructional materials (e.g., *Connecting Math Concepts,* published by SRA/McGraw-Hill) teach these facts together as number families. In this case, the number family would include $4 + 5 = 9$; $5 + 4 = 9$; $9 - 5 = 4$; and $9 - 4 = 5$.

Bley and Thornton (2001) provided several strategies to assist with subtraction facts. Of the 100 total subtraction facts, these include 27 "count-backs" when subtracting 1, 2, or 3 (e.g., for $11 - 2$, "10, 9").

There are also 19 "zero" facts, which involve subtracting zero from a number (e.g., $9 - 0$) or subtracting two identical numbers whose difference equals zero (e.g., $4 - 4$). An additional 15 facts are referred to as "count-ups," when the difference can be counted up by 1, 2, or 3. For example, for $12 - 9$, start at the subtrahend, 9, and count up to the minuend, 12, holding up fingers as you count, if needed: "9 – 10, 11, 12" (counting 3).

Bley and Thornton (2001) also list seven "10-frame" facts, where the student imagines a "frame" of two rows of five and calculates from these.

For example, for the fact $10 - 7$, subtracting 7 from the 10-frame removes all of the top row and two of the bottom row, leaving 3. Bley and Thornton (2001) also include $9 - 5$ and $9 - 4$ in this series, beginning with a frame of 9 (5 on top, 4 on the bottom).

Finally, Bley and Thornton (2001) list six facts as "new doubles," which means that when subtracted, doubles are revealed in the difference and subtrahend (e.g., $8 - 4 = 4$). Altogether, these strategies account for 74 subtraction facts, leaving 26 "harder facts" that must be learned through drill and practice and application of addition rules. These harder facts include the following:

- (17, 16, 15, 14, 13) − 9;
- (17, 15, 14, 13, 12) − 8;
- (16, 15, 13, 12, 11) − 7;
- (15, 14, 13, 11) − 6;
- (14, 13, 12, 11) − 5; and
- (13, 12, 11) − 4. (Bley & Thornton, 2001)

Use of tutoring pairs, computer software, apps such as *Math Fact Master* (TipTapTech), and homework can help promote mastery of these facts. Charts, such as the following, that demonstrate students' progress toward completion can help promote motivation and persistence of effort.

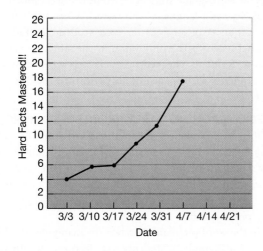

USE STRATEGIES FOR PLACE VALUE AND REGROUPING   Place value is a concept that is linked to our base-10 system, and students must learn this concept as they use numbers of more than one digit. Use of **base-10 blocks,** including base-10 place value charts (Delta Education), can be helpful in establishing this concept. First, students learn to count individual base-10 units. They next learn that units are combined as groups of 10, and then they learn that groups of 10 are combined as groups of 100. Therefore, the quantity 111 can be represented as follows:

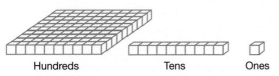

| Hundreds | Tens | Ones |

When students understand the concept of place value, they will be able to explain that the 1 in the quantity 123 represents 1 hundred, the 2 represents 2 tens, or 20, and the 3 represents 3 ones. You can practice place value by having students build, count, and record numbers from different values of ones, tens, and hundreds. Consider also virtual manipulatives, described later in the chapter.

Students can also learn to add and subtract with base-10 blocks. Making certain the appropriate values are lined up, students add or subtract within each column. Create a place value board with columns for hundreds, tens, and ones, with a picture of the appropriate base-10 block at the head of each column. Place the appropriate blocks on the place value board to represent the problem to be solved. For example, for 35 + 22, place 3 tens and 5 ones on the board in groups in the appropriate columns, and below these, place 2 tens and 2 ones. Addition is done by combining these quantities to 5 tens and 7 ones, or 57. Subtraction is done by removing the value of the base-10 blocks in the subtrahend from the minuend. In this same case, 2 tens and 2 ones are removed from 3 tens and 5 ones, leaving 1 ten and 3 ones, or 35 − 22 = 13.

Regrouping in addition occurs when the unit values of any column exceed 10. These units must then be combined and placed in the next higher value. For example, to add 35 + 18, first, represent the problem on the place value board with 3 tens and 5 ones above 1 ten and 8 ones. When these quantities are combined within their columns, the 5 ones added to the 8 ones result in 13 ones. Because this quantity exceeds 10, trade 10 ones for 1 ten, and place it in the tens column. The result is 5 tens and 3 ones, or 53. It is also important for students to see how numbers are used to represent these concepts by recording number values when the building and counting have been completed.

For regrouping in subtraction, students must learn to "trade up" for ten of a particular value in the higher column. For example, for the problem 14 − 6, students learn that the 1 ten must be traded for 10 ones and added to the 4 ones in the ones column. Subtracting 6 from the 14 ones, then, leaves 8, the difference.

Uberti, Mastropieri, and Scruggs (2004) described the use of a self-monitoring checklist to improve performance on regrouping algorithms. The teacher developed self-monitoring checklists for third-grade students with learning disabilities and some students for whom English was a second language who were having difficulties with regrouping. The checklists, based on an error analysis for each student, included steps for problem solution, including writing down the unit value in the sum and carrying the tens value above the tens columns. Students checked off each step when they completed it. After several practice tests, students with special needs performed the calculation at the level of the mean of the whole class.

USE STRATEGIES FOR TEACHING EARLY PROBLEM SOLVING WITH ADDITION AND SUBTRACTION

You can help promote the idea that mathematical operations have meaning by using manipulatives at the early stages of learning number concepts. As students move into the area of problem solving, these concepts can be enforced. Miller and Mercer (1993; see also Mercer et al., 2011) demonstrated the effectiveness of a graduated word-problem sequence strategy for teaching math problem solving, using concrete, semiconcrete, and abstract problem representations.

The word used in the word problems matched the manipulative objects in the concrete and semiconcrete levels. For example, if students were learning to subtract using cubes (concrete level), the word *cubes* was used in the problem (semiconcrete level):

$$
\begin{array}{r}
4 \text{ cubes} \\
-2 \text{ cubes} \\
\hline
\text{cubes}
\end{array}
$$

During the abstract level of instruction, the difficulty of word problems is increased gradually from simple words, phrases, and sentences, such as:

$$
\begin{array}{r}
8 \text{ pieces of candy} \\
-8 \text{ pieces of candy sold} \\
\hline
\underline{\quad} \text{ are left.}
\end{array}
$$

to more elaborate sentences:

Jennie had 4 pens.
She lost 2 of them.
She has _____ pens left.

Finally, students created their own word problems. This investigation demonstrated how students with learning problems in mathematics could learn to solve word problems by introducing increasing levels of complexity.

Students who have difficulty determining the operation for solving problems (e.g., addition, subtraction) can construct problems like this on their own. Bley and Thornton (2001) suggested several steps, summarized as follows:

1. Present a short problem that gives only the essential information (e.g., 3 apples, bought 2 more apples).

2. Tell what is missing. What is missing should be the solution of the problem (together, there are _____ apples).

3. Write in numerals (3) for number words (three).

4. Compute two-step problems separately. Color code each step.

5. Use picture choices; for example, show two picture representations of the problem—such as 3 apples being added to 3 more, or 2 apples being removed from a group of 3—and ask the student to choose the correct one.

MyEdLab: **Self-Check 14.2**

MyEdLab: **Application Exercise 14.1: Teaching Math in Inclusive Settings**

USE RESPONSE-TO-INTERVENTION STRATEGIES FOR EARLY PREVENTION AND IDENTIFICATION

Response to intervention (RTI) is a system of increasingly intensive interventions intended to prevent academic failure and provide evidence for identification for special education when necessary. In mathematics, Tier 1, or primary prevention, includes high-quality instructional procedures for the general education class with adaptations as needed, as described in this chapter. Students who do not demonstrate adequate progress in Tier 1 can be considered for Tier 2 interventions, which could include intensive small-group tutoring, and then Tier 3 interventions, which may include more intensive individual interventions or possible referral to special education (Fuchs, Fuchs, & Compton, 2012). Numerous procedures have been recommended for implementing RTI in mathematics (Riccomini & Witzel, 2010).

Dennis (2015) implemented Tier 2 instruction with second-grade students who were experiencing difficulties in learning mathematics. Students were taught in groups of three for 20 minutes, 4 times a week for a 10-week period. Topics included numerical order, quantity comparison, addition and subtraction facts, place value, and multiple-digit addition and subtraction and were aligned with the Common Core State Standards for Grade 2 Mathematics, Number and Operations in Base Ten (National Governors Association Center for Best Practices & Council of Chief State School Officers, 2010). Instructional procedures included direct modeling and teaching using scripted lessons, employing a concrete–representational–abstract strategy when appropriate; use of base-10 blocks, drawings, and numerals; and guided and independent practice. Overall, students improved substantially in their math scores. For three students who did not make adequate progress according to curriculum-based measurement, a Tier 3 intervention was implemented that included one-to-one instruction, additional practice and feedback, and 35-minute sessions rather than 20-minute sessions. This Tier 3 intervention was successful in promoting adequate progress in math. The *Research Highlight* describes another multi-tiered intervention in math calculation and problem solving.

Use Small-Group Tutoring as a Tier 2 Intervention Fuchs, Fuchs, and Hollenbeck (2007) described a model of intervention to identify students at risk for development of mathematics difficulty and a tier system for providing intervention. First-grade students who scored poorly during the third through fifth weeks of the school year (i.e., correctly answering an average of 11 or fewer of 25 problems on weekly tests) were provided with Tier 2 remedial help in the form of small-group tutoring using concrete, pictorial, and graphic materials, as well as practice on math facts with a software program. After 16 weeks of instruction, two or three times per week, 30 minutes per session, the proportion of students at risk for math difficulties was sharply reduced (e.g., from 9.75% to 5.14%). Students who failed to respond positively to the Tier 2 instruction could be considered for special education.

Fuchs et al. (2009) introduced "Pirate Math" with small-group tutoring to third-grade students having math difficulties in the general education class. They taught a strategy for developing number combination skills using number lines and finger counting (add = start with the bigger number and count up to the smaller number on your fingers, and the answer is the last number; subtract = start with the minus number—subtrahend—and count up to the number you started with, and the answer is the number of fingers you used to count up). When this approach was combined with other procedures, such as the RUN strategy for word

Multi-Tiered Support for Calculation and Word Problems

Students who struggle with calculation and word problem solving at the early elementary levels frequently develop more serious mathematics challenges in later years. In an attempt to assist these children at an early age, Powell et al. (2015) developed and compared the effects of two response-to-intervention (RTI) conditions with business-as-usual math instruction for struggling second graders who scored below the 40th percentile on calculation and word-problem-solving measures. One multi-tiered system focused on calculations, and the other taught word problem solving. Both interventions included two whole-class weekly sessions over 17 weeks (Tier 1 instruction) and 39 small-group tutoring sessions with two to three students (Tier 2 instruction), all delivered by research assistants. Explicit instruction was delivered during whole-class instruction, which also employed guided practice and feedback, partner practice, and then independent practice. The calculation intervention emphasized both conceptual and procedural instruction for addition and subtraction, including operational strategies, the commutative property, place value, and number families, using manipulatives and graphics. Intense review and practice were implemented for all skills. The word-problem-solving condition initially taught a generic strategy—read, underline labels, and identify the type of problem—followed by more

specific schema problem-solving strategies using graphics and examples. Mathematics language comprehension, such as comparing and relationships, was also taught. Across all units, foundational skills and relationships, as well as combine, compare, and change word problem types, were presented. Both intervention conditions also emphasized equivalence for solving equations, which is one of the prealgebraic skills (see Common Core State Standards for Mathematics for additional examples). The tutoring sessions were held outside the general education classroom, were supplemental to the whole-class instruction, and covered the more challenging content by providing gamelike practice activities, self-regulation strategies, scaffolded instruction, additional strategies, and reinforcement. The calculation condition included math addition and subtraction flashcards, number combinations, and double-digit flashcards. Tutoring in the word-problem-solving condition included various equation-solving games (e.g., finding x), equation completion, and the difference game (selecting inequality signs). The business-as-usual condition provided the adopted math curriculum and traditional instructional procedures.

Findings revealed that on both proximal and distal calculation measures, students in the multi-tiered calculation condition outperformed students in the multi-tiered word-problem-solving

condition and the business-as-usual condition. Students in the word-problem-solving condition also outperformed students in the business-as-usual condition on the distal calculation measures. On the proximal word-problem-solving measures, students in the multi-tiered word-problem-solving condition outperformed students in the calculation and business-as-usual conditions, but there were no significant differences on the distal measures. However, it was reported that the word-problem-solving condition produced better learning of prealgebraic concepts. These findings suggest that the calculation intervention produced important effects on calculation measures but did not transfer to problem-solving measures. In contrast, the word-problem-solving intervention produced some transfer effects to single-digit calculation measures. For additional information on tutoring, see Baker, Gersten, Dimino, and Griffiths (2004); Fuchs et al. (2005); and Fuchs et al. (2010). For tutoring implementation suggestions, see Kroeger and Kouche (2011).

QUESTIONS FOR REFLECTION

1. How could teachers, rather than research assistants, implement this model of instruction in math?
2. What additional resources might be needed for successful implementation by teachers?
3. How could you assist all teachers in effectively implementing this practice?

problems (Read the problem, Underline the question, Name the problem type—total, difference, or change), students made considerable gains in important math skills (see also Fuchs et al., 2010).

Bryant et al. (2011) implemented a Tier 2 math intervention with first-grade students who had exhibited difficulty in early math learning. They incorporated systematic small-group tutoring instruction along with visual representations of mathematical concepts, meaningful practice opportunities, and frequent progress monitoring to develop understanding in early numeracy skills and math concepts. These students made significant gains in curriculum-based measures and number computation.

Use Intensive Interventions as a Tier 3 Intervention   Students may be referred to special education for Tier 3 interventions in some districts. Tier 3 consists of very intensive interventions intended to help students who have not benefited from Tier 1 or 2 interventions and continue to perform well below grade level due to persistent difficulties. The National Center for Intensive Interventions (http://www.intensiveintervention.org/) developed sample activities for providing intensive interventions in math. These include general strategies for designing math interventions (National Center on Intensive Intervention, 2016b); considerations for teaching specific skills, for example, fractions; and lessons and activities to use for providing intensive interventions (National Center on Intensive Intervention, 2016a, 2016c). Powell and Fuchs (2015) provided a framework for designing intensive interventions that included focusing on critical content and skills; using explicit instruction, manipulatives, modeling, feedback, multiple opportunities for practice, and motivational strategies; developing fluency skills; connecting mathematical concepts with mathematical procedures; and monitoring and adjusting based on student performance data.

STRATEGIES FOR
TEACHING MULTIPLICATION AND DIVISION

USE MANIPULATIVES FOR TEACHING MULTIPLICATION AND DIVISION CONCEPTS   Multiplication and division concepts can be enforced through the use of manipulatives, such as base-10 blocks. Show students, for example, a set of 3 units, and ask them to put together four such sets. After this has been done, inform students that they have a set of 3, four *times.* By counting total units, it can be seen that 3 taken four times, or 4 times 3, is 12.

Students should come to understand that division is "the separation of a quantity into equal sized parts" (Tucker et al., 2006, p. 167). To enforce division concepts, show students a set of 12 units, and ask them how many separate groups of 3 they can make. It can then be shown that they can *divide* 12 units into 4 sets of 3. Therefore, 12 divided by 4 is 3. These concepts may not be acquired rapidly by all students, but repeated practice activities, such as those found in the *Building Understanding* series utilizing base-10 blocks (Activity Resources), can be helpful. It may also be important to extend the activities beyond base-10 blocks to enhance generalization of the concept, to, for example, beans, beads, or buttons.

TEACH "COUNT-BYS"   A useful bridge between learning multiplication concepts and learning multiplication facts is the use of count-bys. Students who have learned to count by 2 (2, 4, 6, 8, and so on) can use their fingers or pencil tallies to count up to 2 × 6 (2, 4, 6, 8, 10, *12*). Students also easily learn to count by 5s because all products end in 5 or 0.

It may be helpful to learn to count by other numbers as an introduction to fact learning with those numbers. Touch Math, described earlier, uses strategies involving count-bys to compute multiplication and division facts. In multiplication, students count by one number while touching the points on the other number. For example, for 5 × 4, students count by 5s while touching the four points on the 4: 5, 10, 15, *20.* Show students that it works the same if they count by 4s while touching the five points on the 5: 4, 8, 12, 16, *20.* Such procedures also enforce the concept of multiplication (e.g., 5, 4 times = 4, 5 times). For division, students make tally marks (/) while counting up to the divisor by units of the dividend. The number of tallies is the quotient. For example, for 12 ÷ 4, students count up by 4s while tallying, 4, 8, *12* (marking, / / /, or 3).

USE SPECIFIC STRATEGIES FOR TEACHING MULTIPLICATION AND DIVISION

FACTS Remember that the learning of multiplication and division facts is more of a verbal learning task than a mathematical reasoning task. That is, whereas understanding concepts relevant to multiplication and division (e.g., 6 groups of 4) involves mathematical reasoning, immediate recall of the fact ("What is 6 times 4?") requires verbal memory. Because that is the case, strategies for increasing verbal memory are appropriate. Use drill and practice with flash-cards, computer or tablet activities such as *Math Blaster* (Knowledge Adventure), peer tutoring, and homework assignments.

Target the Essential Facts First, identify exactly how many multiplication facts students actually need to learn so that students will not feel overwhelmed—they may already know more than they think they do. That is, students who understand relevant concepts already know the $\times 0$ and $\times 1$ facts (that is, any number multiplied by 0 is 0; any number multiplied by 1 is that same number). Students who know addition facts and understand relevant concepts already know the remaining $\times 2$ facts ($3 \times 2 = 3 + 3$). (Some students may also benefit from a $\times 4$ strategy; that is, a number times 4 is that number doubled, twice: $3 \times 4 = [3 \times 2] + [3 \times 2] = 12$.) Students who know how to count by 5s know or can easily determine the $\times 5$ facts.

Finally, students can use the **bent finger strategy** for calculating the $\times 9$ facts. Using this strategy, students hold their two hands, palms down, in front of them. They then count from left to right on their fingers by the number of the fact and bend down the relevant finger. That is, for 9×5, students count to 5 starting with the left little finger to the left thumb, then bend down that thumb. Then, the fingers to the left of the bent finger represent the tens and the fingers to the right of the bent finger represent the ones of the product. In the case of 9×5, there are 4 fingers to the left and 5 fingers to the right of the bent finger, so the answer is 45.

So, if students already know, or can cope with, the $\times 0$, $\times 1$, $\times 2$, $\times 5$, and $\times 9$ facts, and if they understand the principle of commutativity (e.g., $6 \times 4 = 4 \times 6$), you can show them that they only have 15 facts left to learn (and only 10 if they can use the $\times 4$ strategy)! Use charts, games, and software formats to monitor their progress toward remembering all 100 facts.

Division facts can be taught using similar versions of the same strategies used for teaching math facts. Division by 0 is impossible (or "undefined"), but the $\div 1$, $\div 2$, and $\div 5$ facts may be similarly derived using relevant concepts. A version of the bent finger strategy can also be applied to $\div 9$ facts: for example, for $45 \div 9 = ?$, students must first recognize that it is a $\div 9$ fact, then make the 45 with both palms down, 4 fingers on the left side, a bent finger (left thumb), and 5 fingers on the right side. The numbered finger bent down is the quotient, in this case, the fifth finger from the left (the left thumb), or 5. For $27 \div 9 = ?$, students make the 27 with their fingers; the bent finger is the third (or 3), the quotient.

Introduce students to three-number "fact families" to reinforce similarity with acquired multiplication facts (e.g., Stein et al., 2006). For example, consider the three-number fact family 3, 4, and 12. Within this family are the multiplication facts $3 \times 4 = 12$ and $4 \times 3 = 12$, as well the division facts $12 \div 4 = 3$ and $12 \div 3 = 4$. Students should refer to relevant fact families and relevant facts they already know when mastering division facts.

Use Mnemonic Strategies The remaining 15 multiplication facts still may not be easy for all students to learn, and many students may not automatically recognize the reverse (commutativity) of each fact. However, there is a mnemonic strategy that might be helpful in some cases. With the pegword strategy, rhyming words are developed for all numbers (e.g., *1* is *bun*, *2* is *shoe*, *3* is *tree*, *4* is *door*, *5* is *hive*, *6* is *sticks*, *7* is *heaven*, *8* is *gate*, *9* is *line* or *vine*). Pegwords for relevant numbers higher than 10 include the following: *12* is *elf,* *16* is *sitting,* and *18* is *aiding;* *20* is represented as *twin-ty,* so *21* is *twin buns;* *30* is *dirty* or *thirsty;* *40* is *party;* *50* is *gifty* (i.e., *gift-wrapped*); and *60* is *witchy.* Using these pegwords, sentences can be developed for each of the 15 remaining facts (see Mastropieri & Scruggs, 1991):

Fact	Pegword strategy
Three times three is nine.	Tree-to-tree vine.
Three times four is twelve.	Tree in door is elf.
Three times six is eighteen.	Tree losing sticks needs aiding.
Three times seven is twenty-one.	Tree in heaven has twin buns.
Three times eight is twenty-four.	Tree at a gate has twin doors.
Four times four is sixteen.	Door-by-door sitting.
Four times six is twenty-four.	Door with sticks has twin doors.
Four times seven is twenty-eight.	Door in heaven has twin gates.
Four times eight is thirty-two.	Door in gate has dirty shoe.
Six times six is thirty-six.	Sticks, sticks, and dirty sticks.
Six times seven is forty-two.	Sticks in heaven for party shoe.
Six times eight is forty-eight.	Sticks in gate is a party gate.
Seven times seven is forty-nine.	Heaven to heaven has party line.
Seven times eight is fifty-six.	Heaven's gate has gifty sticks.
Eight times eight is sixty-four.	Gate to gate is witchy door.

Some of these facts are easy to imagine; for example, *tree-to-tree vine* is simply a vine between two different (not twin) trees. Others, however, may be more difficult for students to imagine automatically. In these cases, a picture of the mnemonic may be helpful, such as the pictures for 4 × 4 = 16 and 6 × 6 = 36 shown in Figure 14.3.

Figure 14.3 Mnemonic Pictures of 6 × 6 = 36 and 4 × 4 = 16

Note: From *Mnemonic math facts,* © M. A. Mastropieri & T. E. Scruggs, 2014, Fairfax, VA: Graduate School of Education, George Mason University.

Guide students to learn to say the paired mnemonics together, such as "Heaven's gate has gifty sticks—seven times eight is fifty-six." Reserve these strategies for the facts students appear to be having the most difficulty with, rather than teaching all 15. These mnemonic pegword strategies have been shown to improve fact learning for students with learning disabilities (Greene, 1999), and a modified version of this strategy (students were shown the pegword for the answer only) was effective for students with intellectual disabilities (Zisimopoulos, 2010).

USE CALCULATORS WHEN APPROPRIATE   Although most schools remain committed to mastery of facts and computation procedures as important mathematics objectives, it is sometimes recommended that computers and calculators be used to replace memorization of math facts and computation exercises. Additionally, increasing use has been made of student groups that involve calculator use, invented or student-generated algorithms, and manipulatives to facilitate problem solving (Sayeski & Paulson, 2010). The Common Core State Standards in Mathematics also make reference to the use of calculators, although generally in the Standards for Mathematical Practice at the high school level when students are dealing with larger or more complicated data sets (National Governors Association Center for Best Practices & Council of Chief State School Officers, 2010).

When students are required to memorize math facts, it may become evident over time that some students are simply not succeeding and are beginning to lose valuable instructional time in other areas of math because of this problem. In such cases, it may be prudent to allow individual students to use calculators for help with computation while proceeding to other math objectives. If such a decision is made, however, make sure that those students have a documented failure to learn facts over time, that all known strategies and procedures have been attempted, and that the students are beginning to lose valuable instructional time in other areas of math.

If these conditions have been met, it may be sensible to allow students to use calculators. For example, Horton, Lovitt, and White (1992) found that junior high school students with mild intellectual disabilities performed similarly to nondisabled students in computation problems when they used calculators. Without calculators, however, their performance was lower. Bouck, Bouck, and Hunley (2015) reported that secondary students with disabilities solved more problems based on grade-level standards correctly when using calculators as an accommodation, although the size of the effect was not as large as anticipated. Do not assume all students will be able to use calculators without any training. When directing students to use calculators, provide modeling, prompting, and evaluation to ensure students are independent in calculator use.

Students should be retested periodically for their capacity to learn facts. It could be that with increasing age and cognitive development, or more familiarity with other aspects of math, fact learning can be attained at a future date.

REINFORCE ARITHMETIC VOCABULARY   In addition to number concepts, algorithms, and procedures, students in math classes are generally required to learn and apply many vocabulary words, such as *addend, sum, minuend, subtrahend, difference, product,* and *divisor.* For some students, this vocabulary can be confusing and difficult to learn. Prioritize your objectives so that you spend time teaching the most important vocabulary words.

To teach math vocabulary, provide additional time-on-task, use flashcards and peer tutors, and monitor progress toward mastery. Also consider using verbal elaboration strategies—for example, demonstrate to students how 3 is really the *difference* between 8 and 5; therefore, the term *difference* has some meaning. To help students remember that the *multiplier* is the number on the bottom of the multiplication problem, next to the multiplication sign (when presented vertically), draw the multiplication sign to represent an open pair of *pliers.* The *pliers* show which number is the multi*plier*. For another example, on a division problem, place *quotation marks* on the *quotient*:

$$8 \overline{)\ 24}^{\ \text{"}3\text{"}}$$

USE SPECIFIC STRATEGIES FOR TEACHING MULTIPLICATION AND DIVISION ALGORITHMS   Students must learn the order or sequence of arithmetic operations in more complex problems.

$$5 + 4 \times 3 - 2 =$$

To successfully solve this problem, students must know that the multiplication of the terms 4 and 3 must be done first, followed by the addition of 5 and subtraction of 2. A commonly used mnemonic to remember the order for math operations is as follows: *My Dear Aunt Sally*, who says, "*M*ultiply and *d*ivide before you *a*dd and *s*ubtract." In this case,

$$5 + (4 \times 3) - 2 =$$

where (4×3) is calculated first, followed by the addition and subtraction. An alternative strategy is "*P*lease *e*xcuse *my dear Aunt Sally*," where *p* and *e* stand for *p*arenthetical expression and *e*xponents, respectively, and are completed first. In this case,

$$5 + (4 + 3)^2 + 12 \times 6$$

where the parenthetical expression $(4 + 3)$ is calculated first, followed by the exponent $(7)^2$, which is followed by multiplication, 12×6, followed by addition, $5 + 49 + 72$.

   Another math procedure students need to learn is the sequence to follow when multiplying numbers of two or more digits. Learning how to do this kind of problem is often complicated because handwritten figures are not placed in proper relationship to one another. Try having students use graph paper, as shown in the illustration. Pro-Ed publishes *Guideline Math Paper,* specifically designed to assist students who have difficulty completing basic mathematics algorithms.

Demonstration Plus Permanent Model   For addressing problems in computational arithmetic skills, use the **Demonstration Plus Permanent Model** (Mercer & Miller, 1992; Rivera & Smith, 1987); demonstrate how to complete a particular type of problem, for example, subtraction with regrouping or long division, and provide a model, with steps, written on the student's page or somewhere easily accessible for future reference. The model can be written on a 3- × 5-inch index card for use when needed.

Long Division Strategies   Long division involves dividing beyond the 100 division facts. Some students exhibit difficulty learning the steps in long division. To facilitate memory of these steps, teach students to use the acrostic "**D**racula **M**ust **S**uck **B**lood" to remember the steps: divide, multiply, subtract, and bring down (Quintessential Education, 2016). For example:

$$13\overline{)143}$$ with quotient 1   **Divide**

then,

$$13\overline{)143}$$ quotient 1, with 13 below 14   **Multiply** (1 × 13)

then,

$$13\overline{)143}$$ quotient 1, −13, remainder 1   **Subtract** (14 − 13)

then,

$$13\overline{)143}$$ quotient 1, −13, bring down 3 to make 13   **Bring down (3 to make 13)**

Following the steps again provides 13 ÷ 13 (divide), 1 × 13 (multiply), and 13 − 13 = 0 (subtract), with no remaining numbers to bring down; therefore, 143 ÷ 13 = 11.

Modified Long Division   Some students exhibit extreme difficulty with long division (Montague, 2003). If other attempts have not been successful, it may be helpful to employ a simpler procedure for long division. This procedure lacks some of the precision of traditional long division, but it employs a simpler format that some students may find beneficial (see Pushparajan, 2011).

To use modified long division, construct the problem as usual, but draw a line straight down vertically from the end of the problem:

Now, ask students to guess the solution to the entire problem, "How many 23s are there in 4,859?" Even if students have difficulty estimating the answer closely, a good first guess might be 100. So, tell students to write the 100 to the right of the vertical line and multiply 23 by 100 and subtract from the dividend, like this:

$$
\begin{array}{r|l}
23\overline{)4859} & 100 \\
2300 & \\
\hline
2559 &
\end{array}
$$

Then, ask students the same question again, with respect to the difference, "How many 23s are there in 2,559?" Because 100 times 23 is 2,300, it makes sense to try 100 again. So, you write 100 again below the first 100, multiply 23 again by 100, and subtract from 2,559:

$$
\begin{array}{r|l}
23\overline{)4859} & 100 \\
-2300 & 100 \\
\hline
2559 & \\
-2300 & \\
\hline
259 &
\end{array}
$$

The remainder is now 259, so a good next guess would be 10:

$$
\begin{array}{r|l}
23\overline{)4859} & 100 \\
-2300 & 100 \\
\hline
2559 & 10 \\
-2300 & \\
\hline
259 & \\
-230 & \\
\hline
29 &
\end{array}
$$

Subtracting 230 from 259 leaves 29, so we subtract one more 23, then compute a remainder of 6. This number is smaller than the divisor, 23, so we cannot go any farther. Adding all estimates yields a sum of 211 with a remainder of 6 (or 6/23), the correct solution.

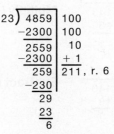

Error Examples	Possible Explanations	Suggested Interventions
$2 + 2 = 8$	1. Inadequate fact mastery. 2. Failure to apply learned strategies (e.g., "count-ons"). 3. Reversal ($2 = 6$).	1. Reteach facts. 2. Reteach strategies. 3. Teach strategies for writing orientation.
$22 - 9 = 27$	1. Inadequate fact mastery. 2. Regrouping error. 3. Reversed subtraction ($9 - 2 = 7$).	1. Reteach facts. 2. Reteach regrouping. 3. Reteach procedures.
$22 \times 12 = 66$	1. Place value error: $22 (1 \times 22) + 44 (2 \times 22) = 66$ 2. Algorithmic error (incorrect alignment of addends in problem solution): $$\begin{array}{r} 22 \\ \times 12 \\ \hline 44 \\ 22 \\ \hline 66 \end{array}$$	1. Reteach place value concepts. 2. Reteach algorithms, using Demonstration plus Permanent Model, graph paper.

Figure 14.4 Sample Error Analysis Procedures

One advantage of modified long division is that it allows students to view the entire problem at once. Because of this, they may be more able to focus on the problem and less likely to become entangled in a maze of algorithmic procedures. Nevertheless, students may still need much practice in learning and applying the steps of the modified long-division procedure.

Use Error Analysis to Inform Instruction When correcting student products, it is important to determine the *type* of error students consistently make and the type of remedial instruction that is indicated by these error patterns. Figure 14.4 lists common error types in arithmetic computation and possible explanations for them. Remember, before a firm conclusion can be drawn about a particular error type, it is best to obtain evidence that such errors occur repeatedly in a given student's work.

STRATEGIES FOR
TEACHING PROBLEM SOLVING

PROMOTE USE OF WORD MEANINGS Implied mathematical operations (e.g., add, multiply) are represented by the language of word problems. Some students have difficulty understanding how words are used in word problems and what specific operations are implied by these words. Some mathematics educators have criticized a strategy known as the *clue-word* or *key word* approach (not the same as the mnemonic keyword method) to solving word problems. In this approach, students are provided with key operation words and relevant operations, such as the following:

in all, together, total = add or multiply

left, remaining = subtract

each = divide

Students are encouraged to look in the problem for one of these words, then apply the associated operation. The concern is that students may use the method mindlessly, without carefully reasoning through problems (Cathcart, Poitier, Vance, & Bezuk, 2015; Kilpatrick, 1985).

However, words convey meanings, and to the extent that these meanings aid in problem solution, a careful analysis of words is appropriate. "In all" does, in fact, convey the idea of combining quantities (and thus, perhaps, addition or multiplication); "remaining" does suggest diminishing quantity (and thus, perhaps, subtraction). For students who have learning disabilities that involve language or language delays, it may be important to enforce the understanding of word meanings to solve word problems.

It is true that the mindless substitution of "each" for "divide," for example, may not be an appropriate strategy in most cases (it may be appropriate for a last-ditch effort during a timed math test). However, a problem that states a particular overall quantity and requests unstated information regarding "each" or "for one" certainly seems to be implying some type of division operation, and students should attend to the relevance of such cues.

In fact, the **"ask for one, tell for one"** strategy may be useful in helping students determine implied operations. That is, if a larger quantity and another quantity are given (10 cookies, 5 children), and the problem "asks for one (or each)" (e.g., "How many cookies does 1 child get?"), the operation is probably division. If a quantity associated with an individual unit ("tells for one") is given (e.g., 2 cookies for one or each child), and a larger number is requested ("How many cookies do 5 children get?"), the operation is probably multiplication. Encourage students to consider such linguistic information in addition to information gained from visualizing, using manipulatives, or drawing pictures of the problem.

TEACH COGNITIVE STRATEGIES FOR PROBLEM SOLVING   Montague (2008; Montague, Enders, & Dietz, 2011) successfully trained students to use *Solve It !,* a seven-step strategy to solve word problems:

1. *Read* the problem.
2. *Paraphrase* the problem.
3. *Visualize* (picture or diagram).
4. *Hypothesize* (a plan to solve the problem).
5. *Estimate* the answer.
6. *Compute.*
7. *Check* your answer.

Students were also given self-instructional training in implementing these cognitive processes, using SAY, ASK, and CHECK for each step. For example, for the *paraphrase* step, SAY indicates: "Underline the important information. Put the problem in my own words." ASK indicates: "Have I underlined the important information? What is the question?" CHECK indicates: Check "that the information goes with the question" (Montague, 2008, p. 41; see also Montague, 2003). Teachers provide think-alouds where they model the thinking process in solving problems as they employ the seven steps. Whitby (2013) used the *Solve It!* Strategy to increase the problem-solving abilities of a sample of middle school students with autistic spectrum disorder (ASD).

Similarly, Xin, Jitendra, and Deatline-Buchman (2005) taught students to identify the key problem and problem features and to map the information onto the diagram during instruction in problem schema analysis. Similar strategies have also been helpful for students with ASD (Barnett & Cleary, 2015). Shiah, Mastropieri, Scruggs, and Fulk (1994–1995) trained students with mathematics learning disabilities to use a computer program that included steps similar to *Solve It!*:

1. *Read* about the problem.
2. *Think* about the problem.
3. *Decide* the operation.
4. *Write* the math sentence.
5. *Do* the problem.
6. *Label* the answer.
7. *Check* every step.

Use of steps like these can help students solve word problems of the following type:

> There are 8 bookshelves in a library. Each bookshelf holds 26 books. How many books are in the library altogether?

Begin by providing students with a list of steps similar to that in Shiah et al. (1994–1995) so that they can check off the steps as they are completed. Be sure to train students on how to undertake each of the steps. For example, for step 2, "Think about the problem," students should be told to use visualization (Montague, 2008) and draw pictures and identify and circle cue words or phrases (Case, Harris, & Graham, 1992). For the current example, students could visualize or draw a library with 8 bookshelves; each one of the bookshelves holds 26 books. Alternately, to guide thinking, cue words such as *each* ("tells for one"), *bookshelf, books,* and *altogether* could be circled. Thinking about the problem should lead to making the operation decision and writing the math sentence (i.e., $8 \times 26 = \underline{\hspace{1cm}}$). After this step, students compute the answer, label the answer, and check every step. To enforce use of the systematic procedures, you could supply students with a self-monitoring sheet, on which they can check off each step as they complete it.

USE ENHANCED ANCHORED INSTRUCTION   Brian Bottge and colleagues (e.g., Bottge, Rueda, Grant, Stephens, & Laroque, 2010; Bottge et al., 2015) have implemented interventions they refer to as enhanced anchored instruction (EAI). EAI employs a problem-based learning approach, but it provides the problem in a video format; these researchers argue that the video provides for a more immediate experience than text. Students consider the "real-life" types of problems designed to motivate them, are engaged in learning through a variety of activities, and meet in groups to plan and execute problem solution, often involving fractions. The EAI strategy includes additional components to improve visualization of problems and help with calculation skills. In a number of investigations, students in inclusive classes taught problem solving with EAI outperformed control-condition students in business-as-usual conditions based on state standards in mathematics (Bottge et al., 2015).

USE TIER 2 PROBLEM-SOLVING INTERVENTIONS   Problem-solving strategies can also be provided in Tier 2 RTI interventions. Fuchs et al. (2007) implemented Hot Math for primary-grade students through small-group tutoring in specific problem-solving learning strategies combined with training in recognizing different problem types and transferring their skills to novel problem formats. During the first 3-week unit, students were taught basic problem-solving information, such as making sure answers make sense, aligning numbers correctly to perform math operations, and labeling work correctly with words and mathematics symbols. Each of the following units focused on one problem type, with solution processes, "buying bags" problems (e.g., "10 lemon drops to a bag, how many bags"), "shopping list" problems, "half" problems, and "pictograph" problems. After 16 weeks of tutoring sessions, two to three times per week, the proportion of nonresponsiveness to instruction (below the 16th percentile) dropped substantially.

STRATEGIES FOR

TEACHING ABOUT MONEY AND TIME

PRACTICE COIN RECOGNITION AND COUNTING MONEY WITH APPROPRIATE MATERIALS   One of the primary uses of mathematics in adult life is calculations involving money, and it is important to begin instruction in this area as soon as possible after students have mastered basic counting skills. An early concept students could learn is to identify coins of different values. This can be done through providing drill and practice and demonstrating instances and noninstances of coin values (simulated coins and bills and worksheets are available from Delta Education). *Learning Coins* (abcya.com) provides exercises on identifying coins and counting money.

Once students have learned to name coins, they need to learn the value of each coin. Again, direct teaching and drill and practice, perhaps using flashcards with the coin on one side and the value on the other, will help enforce these values. When values are mastered, students will be ready to learn to count change, as shown in the following *In the Classroom* feature. Additionally, the software programs *Making Change* (Attainment Company) and *Money Challenge* (GAMCO Educational Software) can provide useful practice, as can applications for smartphones and tablets. Touch Autism provides *Using and Saving Money: A Social Story About Basic Money Concepts* for iPad and other devices. *Money* (Delta Education) provides a wide variety of materials for teaching about money.

USE APPROPRIATE METHODS AND MATERIALS FOR TEACHING ABOUT TIME

Another important skill for all students is telling time. Materials such as student clocks that can be set to specific times and time worksheets are available from suppliers such as Delta

In the Classroom

Sequence of Coin Counting Skills

1. *Count numbers of the same coins.* Start with different numbers of pennies, and have students count by 1s (e.g., 7 pennies = 7 cents). Then move to higher values, and count by the relevant numbers. For example, count by 5s to calculate the value of 4 nickels = 20 cents, count by 10s to calculate the value of 6 dimes = 60 cents, and count by 25s to calculate the value of 3 quarters = 75 cents.

2. *Teach count-on strategies with same-coin values plus pennies.* That is, for 3 dimes and 3 pennies, count: "10, 20, 30 cents, 31, 32, 33 cents." For two quarters and four pennies, count: "25, 50 cents, 51, 52, 53, 54 cents."

3. *For more complex combinations of coins, teach students to first sort coins into groups containing multiples of 10. That is, two dimes is one group, and one quarter and one nickel is one group. So, for these groups, count: "10, 20 cents: [on fingers] 30, 40, 50 cents."*

4. *For making change, teach students to count up from the given value, counting first to a 10s or 25s value, then counting up to the dollar value. For example, for making change for one dollar for a 27-cent purchase, count up: "[in pennies] 28, 29, 30; [in dimes] 40, 50; [in quarters] 75, 1 dollar."*

Video Example 14.1.

In this video, students work with self-made fraction manipulatives cut from construction paper while the teacher demonstrates with plastic manipulatives on the overhead projector. Think about how the opportunity to work with their own set of manipulatives might benefit students.

Education. Generally, students are best taught by employing a specific set of subskills, as shown in the *In the Classroom* feature.

Teachers can model times or specific features of a clock on their own models and ask students to repeat the time on their own clock models. For example, for the subskill, "Recognize the hour hand," teachers can demonstrate 4 o'clock on their own clocks, then prompt students to set the hour hands on their own clocks to 4 o'clock.

Peer partners who are fluent in telling time can be assigned to students who need more practice. Use of the time-telling checklist provided in the *In the Classroom* feature may be helpful in targeting the exact skills students need to practice. Peers can also be helpful in promoting other students' knowledge of time throughout the day. Applications are also available on smartphones or tablets to promote telling time.

Finally, students who can recognize numbers but have difficulty learning to tell time may benefit from digital clocks and watches that display time in numerical formats that may be more easily recognizable. Use of digital timepieces can help improve students' knowledge of time while they are learning to tell time. *Tell Time!* (Horizon Business) provides practice in telling time on iPads, iPhones, and other devices.

STRATEGIES FOR

TEACHING FRACTIONS AND DECIMALS

USE APPROPRIATE METHODS AND MATERIALS FOR TEACHING FRACTIONS

As much as possible, the initial teaching of fractions should involve the students' own experiences. Most children know about sharing things, such as cookies, by breaking them into halves or other parts. Children are also usually aware that pizzas and pies are sliced into pieces. Use this knowledge to develop more advanced concepts of fractions. *Fraction Concepts* (Delta Education) provides many manipulative materials to promote understanding of fractions. One example is the *Fraction Burger* (Delta Education), in which the equally proportioned layers of a hamburger (e.g., meat, tomato, cheese, bun) are each made of different fractions (e.g., 3/3, 5/5) that total a circle of the same size. Demonstrate the different ways of creating a circle with different fraction pieces, and have students demonstrate their conceptual knowledge by posing simple problems, such as, "Show the whole burger in two halves," or "Show me a whole circle made of one-half (burger) and two-fourths (cheese)."

When students have learned relevant concepts, they must also learn how to represent fraction concepts in writing and to perform computations on fractions. These follow specific rules (e.g., for division, invert the divisor and multiply). One problem many students have with fractions is in reducing them to their lowest values. For students who have less of a mathematical "sense," fractions that need to be reduced may not appear as obvious as they may for other students. To help students determine whether a fraction can be reduced, a self-monitoring sheet may be helpful. For example, one teacher asked students who were having difficulty to ask themselves questions such as the following:

- Can the denominator be divided by the numerator?
- Do both numbers end in 5 or 0? (If so, divide by 5 or 10.)
- Can both numbers be divided by 2?
- Can both numbers be divided by 3?

If the answer is "yes" to any of the questions, students should execute the procedure. When they have gone through the whole list and reduced the fraction, they should go through it again to see if it can be reduced further. Although this routine will not effectively address all cases (e.g., 35/48), it does address most cases and can serve as a foundation for later understandings.

Shin and Bryant (2015) reviewed literature on fractions instruction for students with math difficulties and reported that the most effective techniques included concrete and visual representations; explicit, systematic instruction; a range and sequence of examples; cognitive strategies providing steps to problem solution; and the use of real-world problems.

MyEdLab:
Video Example 14.2.
This video shows cooperative learning while students figure out decimal placement. Listen carefully to how the students explain their work and the different strategies used.

USE APPROPRIATE METHODS AND MATERIALS FOR TEACHING DECIMALS If students have exhibited proficiency in aspects of arithmetic, procedures for using decimals should not be an overwhelming challenge. Procedures for adding and subtracting numbers with decimals involve keeping the decimal points aligned; again, graph paper may be useful for this purpose. For multiplication and division of decimals, additional practice and permanent models may be helpful.

Even if students learn to calculate with decimals, they may be less certain what decimal numbers mean. To enforce decimal concepts, Decimal Squares (ETA hand2mind) may be helpful. Decimal Squares represent decimal values on cards that have been divided into 100 or 1,000 smaller components. For example, to demonstrate a decimal value of 0.36, a card can be shown that represents a square divided into 100 equal parts, for which 36 squares are shaded. Students can also be shown that this proportion is equivalent to a square divided into 1,000 parts, for which 360 squares are shaded; therefore, 0.360 = 0.36. When 36 of 1,000 squares are shaded, this represents not 0.36, but 0.036 (see also Figure 14.5 for an illustration using base-10 blocks).

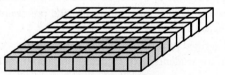

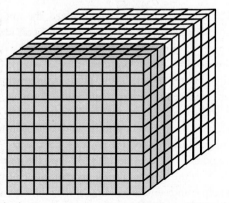

Figure 14.5   Base-10 Blocks Demonstrate Decimal Values (.36 and .360)

In the Classroom

Checklist of Subskills for Telling Time

___ 1. Identify the numbers on the clock face.

___ 2. Recognize the hour hand.

___ 3. Identify the hour indicated by the hour-hand position.

___ 4. Identify the minute hand.

___ 5. Identify the "o'clock" position with the minute hand on the 12 and the hour hand pointing to a specific hour.

___ 6. Identify the position of the minute hand on quarter-hours as 15-minute segments (e.g., 15, 30).

___ 7. Identify the position of 5-minute intervals on the clock face (e.g., 5, 10, 15, 20).

___ 8. Recognize the minute hand and identify the minute indicated by the minute-hand position, by counting by 1s past the previous 5-minute interval (e.g., for 23: "5, 10, 15, 20, 21, 22, 23").

___ 9. Identify the minute indicated by the minute-hand position, by counting by 15s, then 5s, then 1s (e.g., for 43: "15, 30, 35, 40, 41, 42, 43").

___10. Tell a specific time of day given the positions of the hour and minute hands, by first identifying the hour, then the minute.

___11. Identify time of day as a.m. or p.m.

STRATEGIES FOR

TEACHING AREA AND VOLUME CONCEPTS

PROVIDE VISUAL AND THREE-DIMENSIONAL REPRESENTATIONS Concepts of area and volume can be enhanced with visual and physical depictions. *Geometry* and *Measurement Supplies* (Delta Education) may be helpful in promoting understanding of area and volume. Three-dimensional representations of solids are also available from Delta Education. These figures are matched for height so that comparisons can be more easily made. Additionally, they can be filled with water to demonstrate relative volume measures. ETA hand2mind publishes physical models to support geometry concepts, including geoboards, geometric solids, and folding shapes. Experience with these models can provide important background for solving area and volume problems with formulas.

Browder (2015) described providing access to general education curriculum in a variety of areas, including math, for students with moderate and severe disabilities. With respect to area concepts, students were given a rectangle divided into 1-inch squares and asked to count the squares to determine the surface area of the rectangle.

TEACH "BIG IDEAS" Stein et al. (2006) emphasized the importance of teaching "big ideas" in mathematics so that students will have a more general idea of themes, rather than knowledge of a large number of unrelated formulas and problem solutions. For example, volume formulas could all proceed from the "big idea" that all represent the product of the area of the base and a multiple of the height. Then, rather than teaching separate formulas for rectangular prism, rectangular wedge, rectangular cylinder, triangular pyramid, rectangular pyramid, conic pyramid, and sphere, they can all be demonstrated to be functions of the products of base area and height. That is, for figures in which the sides go straight up, such as a rectangular prism (box) or cylinder, the volume is the area of the base times the height ($b \times h$). For figures that come to a point, such as pyramids and cones, the formula is the area of the base times 1/3 of the height ($b \times 1/3h$). Teaching students that different procedures can stem from a common principle can help enforce understanding of the relevant concept, as well as memory for a specific formula.

STRATEGIES FOR
TEACHING ALGEBRA

CLASSROOM SCENARIO

Brenda

Ever since Brenda started in algebra, she has exhibited problems with her attitude. Previously a hardworking, sincere student, she becomes angry and frustrated whenever she is confronted with an algebra problem. "This is stupid!" Brenda exclaims. "Why should I have to learn this? What difference does it make? I hate algebra!" Although other subjects also provide challenges, she doesn't seem to want to make an attempt to learn algebra. Her ninth-grade teacher, Ms. Moon, is considering placing her in a remedial math class.

QUESTIONS FOR REFLECTION

1. Why does Brenda single out algebra when other subjects also pose difficulties?

2. Do you think improving Brenda's skills or improving her attitude is of greater importance?

3. Based on your answer to question 2, what strategies would you recommend to Ms. Moon?

Algebra is required for more advanced problem solving, has been considered a gateway to expanded opportunities, and is increasingly required for high school graduation (Impecoven-Lind & Foegen, 2010). It is well represented in the Common Core State Standards for Mathematics, especially at the high school level. Algebra involves the use of letters, such as x and y, to represent unknown quantities in the solution of problems. Many students with disabilities and other special needs have problems with algebra, in part because of basic skill deficits, students' perception of self-efficacy, and the abstract nature of the content (Montague & Jitendra, 2006). General strategies for addressing achievement problems in secondary-level mathematics include organized, explicit teaching of important concepts; providing many examples of new concepts that address the overall range of the concept; direct teaching of relevant cognitive routines; and systematically teaching to prioritized, general objectives (Strickland & Maccini, 2010).

USE MANIPULATIVES TO TEACH NEGATIVE NUMBERS Many students with disabilities or other special needs have difficulty acquiring the concept of negative numbers, as in $-3 + 4 = 1$. One way of enhancing this concept is through the use of number lines, as described previously. In this instance, the student would be shown how to start at the -3, then count forward four numbers, through the 0, to 1. Another way of promoting the concept of negative numbers is by using the example of financial debt. One who owes $5, for example, must earn $5 before having 0 dollars (no surplus but no debt).

A third way of teaching about negative numbers is through the use of **algebra tiles** (ETA hand2mind). These manipulatives use dark-colored pieces to represent positive integers and lighter-colored pieces to represent negative numbers. The positive and negative tiles can be placed together to represent an equation, such as the following:

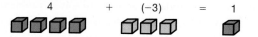

The three lighter-colored pieces "cancel out" three of the darker pieces, leaving only one positive integer, or 1. An alternative is to go to the website of the National Library of Virtual Manipulatives (www.nlvm.usu.edu), where you can find virtual representations of algebra tiles that can be manipulated online, as well as virtual manipulatives for number and operations, algebra, geometry, and measurement. See the *Apps for Education* feature for more ideas; for additional software for help with algebra, consider *Algebrator* (Softmath) or *Mighty Math*™ *Astro Algebra* (Riverdeep).

Virtual Manipulatives for Mathematics

Many mathematics skills and concepts are more concrete for students when manipulatives are used during instruction. Manipulatives give students experience with concrete representations of underlying concepts, which helps comprehension and understanding. Teachers, however, may have a limited supply of manipulatives. An inexpensive alternative to concrete manipulatives is the use of virtual manipulatives available on the Internet. The National Library of Virtual Manipulatives (NLVM) (http://nlvm.usu.edu) provides interactive online math lessons using virtual manipulatives in the areas of numbers and operations, algebra, geometry, measurement, data analysis, and probability (also available as an NLVM app). Within each general math category, the site contains multiple activities and problems using the virtual manipulatives. Problems can be reset to be computed again and again using different variations to provide additional practice of a general concept as necessary. In addition, all math areas are linked to grade-level standards and benchmarks and teacher and parent information on how to teach the concepts. For example, in the activity "Fractions—Parts of a Whole" for grades 3–5, practice with parts of a whole unit, using a written description and numeric fraction, is provided. In this activity, a picture is provided that can be divided into any number of parts. Students are taught that any whole can be divided into an equal number of parts and are asked to divide the whole picture into parts. They are then asked to highlight parts of the whole. When various fractions (parts) of the picture are highlighted, a corresponding fraction changes to reflect new values. Questions such as "How many ways can you describe parts of a unit?" are presented, and students are asked to discuss their answers with partners.

Mathematics activities are available on many other websites. The National Council of Teachers of Mathematics (NCTM) provides math activities, math standards, and web links on the site http://illuminations.nctm.org, which includes a virtual manipulatives link and online, interactive math activities designed to match NCTM principles and math standards. In addition, several indices of available virtual manipulatives web links provide links to a wealth of websites. Numerous mathematics apps are widely available and provide supplemental practice and assistance in learning math facts, skills, and problem solving. The *Khan Academy* app includes over 2,700 video lessons and practice exercises in multiple content areas, including the K–12 math content of basic arithmetic, algebra, geometry, probability, and calculus. Several apps are available that provide flashcard practice for basic math facts, including *My Flash Card* and *Math Flash Cards* (Power Math Apps). *Time, Money & Fractions On-Track* (School Zone Publishing) is a beginning-level math app that provides examples and practice in some basic math. Other problem-solving math apps include YourTeacher.com for algebra and other math areas (online math help), www.kahnacademy.org for all levels of math, and *Everyday Mathematics: Name that Number* (McGraw-Hill), which includes practice in learning the order of operations, building number sentences and equations, and solving problems. Many apps, such as *Motion Math: Hungry Fish* (Motion Math), are designed in gamelike formats that provide supplemental practice. Finally, the Tech Matrix (techmatrix.org) enables searching a database for assistive technology, tools, products, and resources, including research reports, across disability areas, age levels, and content areas, including math.

TEACH ALGEBRAIC REPRESENTATIONS EARLY Consistent with the Standards for Mathematical Practice, you can begin to teach algebraic representations at an early level of problem solving. For example, students can learn to solve a problem represented as $2 + 3 = \underline{\hspace{1cm}}$; or, $2 + 3 = ?$; or, $2 + 3 = x$. When students learn that x stands for an unknown quantity, they can also begin to solve equations such as $2 + x = 5$. Again, the concept of equivalence should be helpful in targeting the idea that both sides of the equation must represent the same quantity (Ginsburg, 1997). Using algebra tiles, a rectangular-shaped piece is used for the x value, so $2 + 3 = x$ is represented as follows:

The sets of two and three pieces can easily be combined to reveal the answer, $5 = x$; or, $x = 5$.

TEACH STRATEGIES FOR COMPUTATION   Some algebraic notation and conventions must be learned in order to compute algebraic equations. For example, the rule that like quantities, such as $2x + 3x$, can be summed to equal $5x$ can be practiced and conceptualized using algebra tiles. Manipulatives can also be employed to demonstrate that unlike quantities, such as $2a + 3b$, cannot be added.

Mnemonic strategies may be helpful for learning and remembering some of these algorithms. For example, consider the problem:

$$(x + 4)(x + 2) = x^2 + 6x + 8$$

Students should recognize that the parentheses mean that each "symbol and digit" in parentheses must be multiplied by one another. To expand the left side of the equation into the values of the right side, it is necessary to multiply in a specific order. The first step is to multiply the *first* terms, $(x)(x) = x^2$. The second steps are to sum the products of the *outer* $(x)(2)$ and the *inner* $(x)(4)$ terms, $2x + 4x = 6x$. The final step is to multiply the *last* terms, $(2)(4) = 8$. Added together, they provide the answer, $x^2 + 6x + 8$. To remember the sequence of this operation, it may be helpful to remember the mnemonic acronym **FOIL**, which stands for first terms, outer terms + inner terms, and last terms (Kilpatrick, 1985).

TEACH STRATEGIES FOR SOLVING QUADRATIC EQUATIONS   In a quadratic equation, the unknown variable is squared, and the equation can be written in the form:

$$ax^2 + bx + c = 0$$

There are several ways to solve quadratic equations, including completing the square and factoring the equation. Algebra tiles can be helpful in developing understanding of these concepts by using the square version of the x variable to represent x^2. To factor the equation, Strickland and Maccini (2010) recommended using a graphic organizer to represent steps in the solution. For example, for the equation

$$x^2 + 5x + 6 = 0$$

Strickland and Maccini presented a graphic organizer with the equation in a box at the top, two boxes in the middle, and one box on the bottom, with arrows connecting them. An arrow connects the top equation to the two middle boxes, and an arrow connects each middle box to the bottom box, where the answer will be placed. Follow the arrows from the top equation to the two middle boxes, and factor the equation in those two boxes. You can use the FOIL strategy in reverse to help arrive at these two equations: $x^2 = (x)(x)$, so x is the first element; $6 = 3 \times 2$, or 2×3, so these are the last elements; and the outer $(2x)$ and inner $(3x)$ terms sum to $5x$. The two factors $(x + 2 = 0$; and $x + 3 = 0)$ then go in each of the middle boxes below the equation. These two smaller equations can be solved by subtracting 2 and 3 from each side, respectively: $(x + 2) - 2 = 0 - 2$, so $x = -2$. The answer is written in the bottom box:

$$x = -2$$

$$x = -3$$

A third method for solving quadratic equations involves the use of an equation developed by mathematicians:

$$x = \frac{-b \pm \sqrt{b^2 - 4ac}}{2a}$$

If the numbers in the quadratic equation are used to replace a, b, and c (from the model $ax^2 + bx + c = 0$), the equation is relatively simple to solve. For example, if the quadratic equation is $x^2 + 8x + 15 = 0$, then $a = 1$, $b = 8$, and $c = 15$. Replacing these values in the formula results in the value

$$\frac{-8 \pm \sqrt{8^2 - 4(1 \cdot 15)}}{2 \cdot 1}$$

When calculated, then, x is shown to equal $\{-3, -5\}$. A problem with using this method is remembering the equation. One way to promote memory is to use a mnemonic strategy, using a bee with a minus sign for a stinger for $-b$, a "square" bee for b^2, four aces for $4ac$, and an American Airlines (AA) airplane for $2a$:

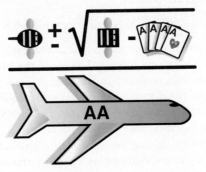

Such a strategy, of course, should be practiced many times, and particular attention must be paid to the elements that are *not* represented mnemonically ($+/-$; square root). Finally, students should have many opportunities to practice the application of this equation in the solution of problems. Remember, as with any academic strategy, students must be taught to *identify* the situation in which a particular strategy is called for, *remember* the steps of the strategy, and then correctly *apply* the strategy in the appropriate context.

TEACH PROBLEM-SOLVING STRATEGIES   Students can benefit from self-questioning strategies for solving algebra word problems (Impecoven-Lind & Foegen, 2010). Maccini and Hughes (2000) taught introductory algebra (e.g., operations with negative numbers) to secondary students with learning disabilities using concrete, semiconcrete, and abstract presentations, as discussed earlier. Again, the strategy considered problem representation and problem solution and employed the **STAR** strategy:

1. Search the word problem (read carefully, ask questions, look for facts).

2. Translate the problem into a pictured equation (choose a variable, identify the operation, and represent the problem in a concrete [manipulative, such as algebra tiles], semiconcrete [picture], or abstract [equation] application). (Students began with concrete representations and progressed to abstract representations.)

3. Answer the problem, attending to relevant signs.

4. Review the solution by reading the problem again and checking whether the answer is reasonable.

All students trained using this strategy improved in introductory algebra problem solving.

Hutchinson (1993) developed a strategy-based model that considered two separate phases: problem representation and problem solution (Janvier, 1987). Problem representation refers to an internal representation of the words of the problem. Problem solution refers to solution planning and solution execution to obtain the answer. Hutchinson employed different problem types: relational problems, proportion problems, problems that employed two variables, and problems that employed two equations. For example, for relational problems, students were required to identify the relational statement that provided information about one unknown quantity in terms of its relationship to another unknown quantity. Then, the solution focused on procedures and order of operations. One relational problem was as follows:

> A man walks 6 km farther than his son. If the total distance walked by both is 32 km, how far did each walk? (Hutchison, 1993, p. 38)

Students were then directed to use self-questioning for solving algebra problems by using a structured worksheet where they answer questions about the problem goal, known and unknown information, problem type, equation, solution, and checking the answer with the goal.

In this instance, you would prompt students to think through the fact that the man's son walked x km, and the man, who walked 6 km farther, walked $x + 6$ km. Using the worksheet questions, then, students could identify the goal, the unknowns, the knowns, the type of problem, and the equation. These two distances, x km and $x + 6$ km, totaled 32 km. Using the problem-solution strategy, students were able to obtain the correct answer, 13 km.

$$x + (x + 6) = 32$$

or,

$$2x + 6 = 32$$
$$(2x + 6) - 6 = 32 - 6$$
$$2x = 26$$
$$x = 13$$

so,

$$\text{man walked } x + 6 = 19 \text{ km}$$
$$\text{son walked } x = 13 \text{ km}$$

Students then compare their solution to the stated goal and check by replacing the obtained values in the original problem.

Similarly, Lang, Mastropieri, Scruggs, and Porter (2004) taught an algebra problem-solving strategy to students considered at risk for math failure. The following strategy steps were used in each example problem:

a. If I use this strategy, I will be successful.

b. What do we know?

c. What don't we know?

d. How can we represent the unknowns?

e. How can we represent the knowns?

f. Do we need more than one equation?

g. What is(are) the equation(s)?

h. Substitute the knowns into the equation(s).

i. Solve the equation(s).

j. Have I checked my answer?

Students went through each step of the strategy as they solved algebra problems and greatly improved their strategy use as they went through the training.

STRATEGIES FOR
TEACHING FUNCTIONAL MATH

USE APPROPRIATE METHODS AND MATERIALS FOR TEACHING FUNCTIONAL MATH
Many students do not take advanced math classes and instead take classes in which more emphasis is placed on basic skills and what is called **functional math** (Heller, 2010). Functional math includes aspects of mathematics that serve individuals in their daily living. These topics include using the calendar, writing checks and keeping checking and savings bank accounts, calculating household expenses, filling out income tax forms, and paying bills. These skills are important for all students to acquire, regardless of the program they are in (it is often assumed—perhaps incorrectly—that students already have these skills; Patton, Cronin, Bassett, & Koppel, 1998). A useful textbook reference on this subject is *The Pacemaker Curriculum: Practical Mathematics for Consumers* (Globe Fearon; reading level 3–4; Staudacher & Turner, 2003). Some materials from the *Essential Mathematics for Life* series (McGraw-Hill) also provide activities for functional math. Pro-Ed publishes the consumer math program *Real Life Math: Living on a Paycheck.* Because many of these topics may not be within the curriculum for other students, you many need to arrange some time for small-group teaching of these topics.

MyEdLab: Self-Check 14.3

MyEdLab: Application Exercise 14.2: Use Specific Strategies
for Teaching Multiplication and Division Facts

MyEdLab: Application Exercise 14.3: Teaching Fractions

MyEdLab: Application Exercise 14.4: Equations

14 Summary

- Reform movements in mathematics have included the *Principles and Standards for School Mathematics* by the National Council of Teachers of Mathematics (2000) and the Common Core State Standards for Mathematics (National Governors Association Center for Best Practices & Council of Chief State School Officers, 2010).

- Many students with disabilities encounter particular problems in learning mathematics, including acquiring math concepts, remembering and executing math facts and procedures, and mathematical reasoning. Students with sensory or physical disabilities may have problems with math in specific areas. Appropriate curriculum, effective teaching, and specific strategy instruction can help alleviate many of these problems.

- Math can be taught to students with disabilities in inclusive settings with the use of such principles as explicit instruction, appropriate instructional design, strong conceptual basis for mathematical procedures, drill and intensive practice, cumulative review, motivators, and ongoing progress monitoring. Many strategies are appropriate to the level and type of mathematics being taught.

  — Basic number and operation concepts (e.g., addition, subtraction) can be enforced by direct teaching, number lines, and manipulatives such as base-10 blocks. Learning of vocabulary concepts can be promoted by direct teaching, manipulatives, and verbal elaboration, including mnemonic strategies.

  — Learning of basic math facts can become a significant obstacle to many students with disabilities and other special needs. When possible, promote memory of basic facts through direct teaching, increased learning time, peer tutoring, specialized software, and independent study strategies. Additionally, use specific strategies for promoting recall of specific facts. If basic fact learning seems unproductive and frustrating for some students, consider allowing the use of calculators so that students can continue progressing in other areas of mathematics functioning. Return to fact learning when it appears it may be profitable.

  — Word problem solving can be facilitated by using a sequence of instruction that progresses from concrete to semiconcrete to abstract. In addition, use specific problem-solving strategies, such as the seven-step self-monitoring strategy, judicious use of clue words, highlighting, imagery, pictures, and others.

  — Important money and time concepts can be enforced by direct teaching, increased practice, use of manipulatives, and use of models, and by providing a careful sequence of skills.

  — Specific manipulative materials (commercially available or teacher made) can be helpful in promoting learning of fractions and decimals. Specific self-monitoring and other strategies can also be useful in promoting these concepts.

  — Promote concepts in algebra by providing early concept development, computation strategies, manipulatives such as algebra tiles, mnemonics, and self-monitoring strategies.

  — Ensure that students are acquiring sufficient "practical" mathematics skills for use in transition to community life and future employment. Curriculum materials are available that provide for instruction in these practical areas.

PROFESSIONAL STANDARDS LINK:
Mathematics

Information in this chapter links most directly to:

- CEC Standards: 1 (Learner Development and Individual Learning Differences), 2 (Learning Environments and Social Interactions), 3 (Curricular Content Knowledge), 4 (Assessment), 5 (Instructional Planning and Strategies)

- INTASC Standards: 2 (Learning Differences), 3 (Learning Environments), 4 (Content Knowledge), 5 (Application of Content), 7 (Planning for Instruction), 8 (Instructional Strategies)

MATHEMATICS

If the student is having difficulty in mathematics, have you tried the following strategies? If not, see the pages listed here.

STRATEGIES FOR TEACHING BEGINNING MATH

- [ ] Teach early number concepts, 346
- [ ] Teach strategies for counting, 346
- [ ] Reinforce one-to-one correspondence, 346–347
- [ ] Introduce geometry concepts in the early years, 347

STRATEGIES FOR TEACHING ADDITION AND SUBTRACTION

- [ ] Use manipulatives for teaching addition and subtraction concepts, 347
- [ ] Use number lines to promote operations, 347–348
- [ ] Use strategies for number writing, 348
- [ ] Use questioning to promote understanding of symbols, 348
- [ ] Use Touch Math to promote addition and subtraction computation, 348–349
- [ ] Use practice and specific strategies for addition and subtraction facts, 349–351
- [ ] Use strategies for place value and regrouping, 351–352
- [ ] Use strategies for teaching early problem solving with addition and subtraction, 352–353
- [ ] Use response-to-intervention strategies for early prevention and identification, 353–355

STRATEGIES FOR TEACHING MULTIPLICATION AND DIVISION

- [ ] Use manipulatives for teaching multiplication and division concepts, 355
- [ ] Teach "count-bys," 355
- [ ] Use specific strategies for teaching multiplication and division facts, 356–358,
- [ ] Use calculators when appropriate, 358
- [ ] Reinforce arithmetic vocabulary, 358
- [ ] Use specific strategies for teaching multiplication and division algorithms, 358–361

STRATEGIES FOR TEACHING PROBLEM SOLVING

- [ ] Promote use of word meanings, 361–362
- [ ] Teach cognitive strategies for problem solving, 362–363
- [ ] Use enhanced anchored instruction, 363
- [ ] Use Tier 2 problem-solving interventions, 363

STRATEGIES FOR TEACHING ABOUT MONEY AND TIME

- [ ] Practice coin recognition and counting money with appropriate materials, 363
- [ ] Use appropriate methods and materials for teaching about time, 363–364

STRATEGIES FOR TEACHING FRACTIONS AND DECIMALS

- [ ] Use appropriate methods and materials for teaching fractions, 364–365
- [ ] Use appropriate methods and materials for teaching decimals, 365

STRATEGIES FOR TEACHING AREA AND VOLUME CONCEPTS

- [ ] Provide visual and three-dimensional representations, 366
- [ ] Teach "big ideas," 366

STRATEGIES FOR TEACHING ALGEBRA

- [ ] Use manipulatives to teach negative numbers, 367
- [ ] Teach algebraic representations early, 368–369
- [ ] Teach strategies for computation, 369
- [ ] Teach strategies for solving quadratic equations, 369–370
- [ ] Teach problem-solving strategies, 370–371

STRATEGIES FOR TEACHING FUNCTIONAL MATH

- [ ] Use appropriate methods and materials for teaching functional math, 371

15

Science, Social Studies, and Transitions

LEARNING OUTCOMES

After studying this chapter, you should be able to:

15.1 Describe and apply strategies for adapting textbook- or content-oriented approaches in science and social studies, such as content enhancements and mnemonic strategies; evaluate and implement strategy instruction for using content-area textbooks; and describe and evaluate methods for selecting and adapting textbook materials to accommodate diverse learners in the classroom.

15.2 Discuss considerations and adaptations for science activities and ways to make appropriate adaptations for teaching science process skills and adapting science and social studies activities in specific science content areas, including life science, earth science, and physical science activities, for diverse learners.

15.3 Discuss ways for adapting inquiry-oriented approaches in science and social studies.

15.4 Identify the meaning of transition and the purpose of planning and designing transition programs for students with disabilities, including teaching self-advocacy and self-determination skills and planning and transitioning for graduation, future education, job opportunities, and independent living.

Science and social studies are academic disciplines concerned with concepts and knowledge of the physical and social world around us (Contant, Bass, & Carin, 2014; Parker & Beck, 2016), and as such, they are important subject areas for all students. Both subjects, however, present unique challenges to teachers who must adapt their instruction, materials, and procedures to accommodate students with special needs.

Adaptations for students with special needs must reflect the approach to instruction being used in the class (Scruggs & Mastropieri, 2007). That is, many schools employ a **textbook-oriented (or content-oriented) approach** in which students are taught and learn content information from textbooks about science and social studies. With this approach, adaptations may focus on teacher presentations and students' independent learning from textbooks. Other schools may embrace an **activities-oriented approach** to learning in which students undertake specific projects, experiments, or other activities to enhance their understanding of the subject. With this approach, adaptations may focus on physical activities as well as reading and writing requirements. In many schools, teachers may use features of both approaches.

Using either approach, teachers may emphasize an **inquiry-based model** of learning, in which students use their knowledge or experiences to invent, discover, or construct new knowledge. Adaptations for inquiry-based learning may focus on supports or enhancements to promote the thinking and reasoning process in students with special needs.

Adapting Textbook-Oriented Approaches in Science and Social Studies

CLASSROOM SCENARIO

Jeffrey

As Mr. Norland's sixth-grade science class enters the room on Monday of the second week of school, Mr. Norland booms, "Pick up your science lab materials on your way to your seat. Open up your textbooks to Activity 2–1 in Chapter 2 on page 26 and follow the instructions. If you have any problems with the steps, see me." After most of the class appears to have begun working, Mr. Norland notices that Jeffrey hasn't even started the activity. Mr. Norland speaks with Jeffrey and realizes Jeffrey can't follow through with the activity because he can't read what to do. Although embarrassed, Jeffrey agrees to work through the activity with one of his peers. At the end of the day, Mr. Norland approaches Jeffrey's special education teacher. "I know Jeffrey has a learning disability, but doing well in science this year is partly dependent on Jeffrey being able to read. We will do many of the activities in cooperative groups, but how will Jeffrey get the content background he needs unless he can read the text?"

QUESTIONS FOR REFLECTION

1. How do Mr. Norland's classroom routines affect Jeffrey's achievement in science?
2. Why doesn't Jeffrey ask for help?
3. What strategies might Mr. Norland use to help Jeffrey succeed?

Much instruction in social studies and science involves teaching and learning of content based on relevant textbook materials. Effective teacher presentations and specific strategies for studying textbooks can address a variety of special learning needs and enhance learning for all students.

COMMON CORE STATE STANDARDS RELEVANT TO SCIENCE AND SOCIAL STUDIES

The Common Core State Standards do not provide separate standards for science and social studies; beginning at the sixth grade, standards relevant to these subject areas are provided within the English language arts (ELA) standards. Standards for K–5 reading in subjects including history/social studies and science/technical subjects are integrated into the K–5 standards (National Governors Association Center for Best Practices, Council of Chief State School Officers, 2010). The standards for grades 6–12 in subject areas focus on four areas: *key ideas and details* (e.g., citing evidence from text to provide support for the analysis of primary and secondary sources); *craft and structure* (e.g., describing how text structure provides information, such as sequential, comparative, or causal); *integration of knowledge and ideas* (e.g., determining the degree to which the author's claims are supported by reasoning and evidence in a text); and *range of reading and level of text complexity* (by the end of 12th grade, read and comprehend texts in the grades 11–CCR [college and career anchor standard, text complexity band, grade 11] independently and proficiently). Similarly, standards for writing focus on communicating information from history/social studies and science and technical subjects (e.g., fairly developing claim[s] and counterclaims, including supporting data and evidence; providing a concluding statement drawn from or supporting the main argument). For a complete listing of ELA standards relevant to history/social studies, science, and technical subjects, see National Governors Association Center for Best Practices, Council of Chief State School Officers (2010). Many of the strategies described in the section are appropriate for addressing the Common Core State Standards.

STRATEGIES FOR
EFFECTIVE TEACHING IN SCIENCE AND SOCIAL STUDIES

You can enhance learning of science and social studies in inclusive classrooms by using the teacher-effectiveness variables (Good & Brophy, 2007), including the PASS and SCREAM variables, such as enthusiasm.

USE EFFECTIVE TEACHING STRATEGIES

Organizing your science or social studies content around "big ideas" will make subordinate concepts easier to understand (Slocum, 2004). For example, the model of convection, once clearly understood, can explain the behavior of water in a boiling pot, the movement of material in the Earth's mantle, and the movement of air masses, including atmospheric convection (Grossen & Burke, 1998; see also Okolo & Ferretti, 2013). Emphasize the organization of your presentations with outlines and important information highlighted on the board or slides, and refer frequently to this outline. Speak in a clear, direct manner, and avoid ambiguous language. Actively model excitement and enthusiasm about the content being covered. Repeat new or unfamiliar vocabulary or concepts, and provide multiple instances of new concepts (e.g., *saprophytic, nullification, hegemony*) to strengthen comprehension. Use mnemonics or other elaborations to promote recall of new vocabulary. Question students frequently, and adjust your instruction as needed. Promote the use of systematic note taking. At the end of presentations, be sure to summarize important lesson content, and monitor student understanding.

PROVIDE CONTENT-ENHANCEMENT STRATEGIES

Teachers can use **content-enhancement** strategies to further increase science and social studies learning. Content enhancements incorporate effective instructional design and make use of graphic organizers, including study guides, charts, diagrams, outlines, visual-spatial displays, mnemonics, and imagery, to promote learning and comprehension (Bulgren, 2004). Research has indicated that students with disabilities in inclusive classrooms have improved their performance when science and social studies teachers apply content-enhancement strategies in their teaching (Bulgren, Deshler, & Lenz, 2007).

SMARTER STRATEGY

Teachers can plan for instruction using the strategy cued by the acronym **SMARTER**. This includes **S**electing important content, **M**apping the organization of the content, **A**nalyzing learning problems, **R**eaching decisions about enhancement, **T**eaching according to decisions, **E**valuating, and **R**eteaching based upon the evaluation (Lenz, Bulgren, Kissam, & Taymans, 2004).

Lesson Organizer and Concept Mastery Routines

Two helpful content-enhancement strategies are the lesson organizer routine and the concept mastery routine. The *lesson organizer routine* is a visual advanced organizer frame to organize a lesson so students can see the main ideas, as well as how the main ideas relate to each other and to prior knowledge (Albert & Ammer, 2004; Lenz & Adams, 2006). The organizer does the following:

- Introduces the topic
- Changes difficult vocabulary to familiar vocabulary
- Teaches students relationships among concepts
- Identifies appropriate strategies for learning
- Graphically demonstrates relationships of lessons to an entire unit
- Graphically displays organization of the content
- Provides self-testing questions

As teachers present the visual displays and share information with students, they help show how the information is related to previously learned content. The organizer also functions as a teacher-planning device in that the sequences of content, concepts, and vocabulary are identified before instruction to ensure a developmentally appropriate lesson.

The *concept mastery routine* addresses the teaching of difficult concepts (King-Sears & Mooney, 2004; see also Bulgren, Graner, & Deshler, 2013). This content enhancement

MyEdLab:
Video Example 15.1.
Observe the students in this video as they complete a cooperative learning activity in science class with the use of a graphic organizer. Notice how the graphic organizer helps keep them on-task and helps to make their assignment clear to them.

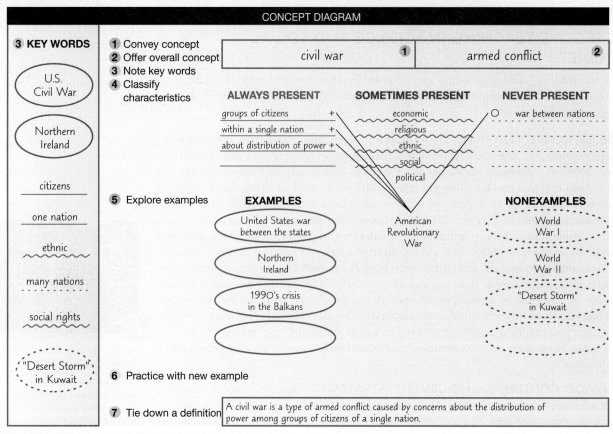

Figure 15.1 Sample Concept Diagram

Note: From *Teaching adolescents with learning disabilities: Strategies and methods* (2nd ed., p. 453), by D. D. Deshler, E. S. Ellis, & B. K. Lenz (Eds.), 1996, Denver, CO: Love Publishing. Reprinted with permission.

is designed around a concept diagram, a visual device that includes the following components:

- Concept name
- Class or category of concept
- Important information associated with concept
- Instances and noninstances of the concept
- Blank space for additions to the diagram
- Concept definition (Bulgren, Deshler, & Schumaker, 1993)

Specific instructional steps are provided for teachers to use when implementing the concept mastery routine. Figure 15.1 contains a sample concept diagram.

Bulgren (2004) emphasized that the graphic itself is not presented to students in its completed form; rather, the teacher may develop a graphic organizer before instruction begins, but the actual graphic organizer is developed interactively with students as they share their own ideas, knowledge, and questions.

USE MNEMONIC STRATEGIES Keyword, pegword, and letter strategies can be extremely useful for helping students remember vocabulary, terminology, and factual information involving science and social studies. Much information in science (e.g., *deciduous, thermic, trichina*) and social studies (e.g., *longitude, anarchy, Potawatomi*) is appropriate for mnemonic elaboration. These mnemonic strategies can be used whenever students exhibit difficulty remembering important content. For example, Mastropieri, Sweda, and Scruggs (2000) developed mnemonics to help fourth-grade students remember important information in a social studies unit (e.g., *Europe, charter*). Although the strategies helped the entire class, students with disabilities benefited the most. Marshak, Mastropieri, and Scruggs (2011) employed classroom peer tutoring with mnemonic strategies in middle school social studies classes and found that students significantly outperformed students in a traditional instruction condition (see the *Research Highlight* feature later in this chapter).

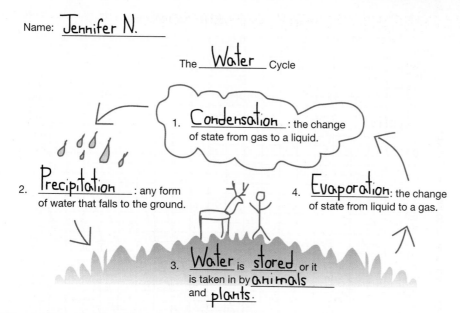

Name: Jennifer N.

The ___Water___ Cycle

1. ___Condensation___ : the change of state from gas to a liquid.

2. ___Precipitation___ : any form of water that falls to the ground.

4. ___Evaporation___: the change of state from liquid to a gas.

3. ___Water___ is ___stored___ or it is taken in by ___animals___ and ___plants___.

Figure 15.2 Modified Worksheet Assignment

Identify the most important content in science and social studies units that students have the most difficulty remembering. Create strategies for this information for class presentations, and ask students to develop their own strategies in group activities. For example, after information has been organized in a graphic organizer or relationship chart, ask students which important information seems most difficult to remember, and help them create effective mnemonic strategies.

ADAPT WORKSHEET ACTIVITIES Some students with special needs are able to address the content required in worksheet activities, but they may have difficulty with the mechanical aspects of writing necessary to complete the activity in the allotted time. Figure 15.2 includes a modified version of a science assignment for students with special needs. The modified assignment reduces the amount of reading and writing but covers the same major concepts (Mastropieri, Scruggs, Mantzicopoulos, Sturgeon, Goodwin, & Chung, 1988). This is an example of the concept of differentiated instruction (Tomlinson & Imbeau, 2010) applied to worksheet activities.

In addition to effective instruction and use of content enhancements to promote comprehension, another important area to consider is teaching students to learn independently from content-area textbooks.

STRATEGIES FOR
PROMOTING INDEPENDENT LEARNING FROM TEXTBOOKS

A large proportion of learning that takes place in science and social studies comes from independent studying of textbooks. For assignments, students are often required to read chapters and answer questions. Teachers often move rapidly from chapter to chapter because of pressures to cover a great deal of content. Science and social studies textbooks are often complex, contain high readability levels and many formats, and introduce a significant number of new vocabulary words and concepts (Best, Rowe, Ozuru, & McNamara, 2005; Scruggs & Mastropieri, 2015). Berkeley, King-Sears, Hott, and Bradley-Black (2014) investigated secondary history textbooks and found them to be frequently inconsiderate of poor readers and dense with factual information.

Given these analyses, it is not surprising that studying from textbooks can be frustrating for many students with disabilities and those at risk for school failure. When possible, select textbooks that effectively promote comprehension. Volunteer to be a member of your school district's textbook adoption committee. Carefully consider such features as readability, language, vocabulary, organization, and use of illustrations and diagrams. Your input on the selection of appropriate textbooks will benefit all students but especially those with special learning needs. One readability measure is provided in Figure 15.3.

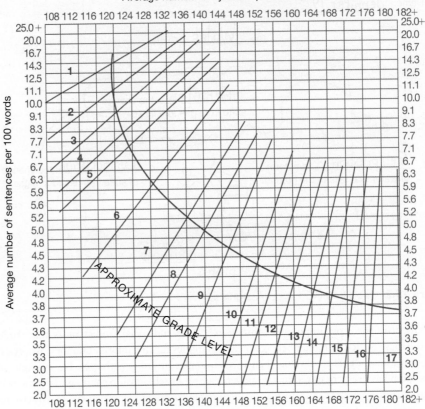

Average number of syllables per 100 words

Figure 15.3 graph

1. Randomly select three text samples of exactly 100 words, beginning with the beginning of a sentence. Count proper nouns, numerals, and initializations as words.

2. Count the number of sentences in each 100-word sample, estimating the length of the last sentence to the nearest one-tenth.

3. Count the total number of syllables in each 100-word sample. Count one syllable for each numeral or initial or symbol; for example, 1990 is one word and four syllables, LD is one word and two syllables, and "&" is one word and one syllable.

4. Average the number of sentences and number of syllables across the three samples.

5. Enter the average sentence length and average number of syllables on the graph. Put a dot where the two lines intersect. The area in which the dot is plotted will give you an approximate estimated readability.

6. If there is a great deal of variability in the syllable or sentence count across the three samples, more samples can be added.

Figure 15.3 Fry's Readability Graph and Formula
Note: From "Fry's readability graph: Clarifications, validity, and extension to Level 17," by E. Fry, 1977, *Journal of Reading, 21,* pp. 242–252.

MyEdLab:
Video Example 15.2.
This **video** illustrates the use of Power Outlining, in which students use an organizational strategy to help understand content-area reading. Notice how some students utilize shapes and colors in their outlines.

TEACH STUDY SKILLS STRATEGIES FOR CONTENT-AREA TEXTBOOKS Successful students develop their own effective study skills and strategies to use when studying textbooks independently. However, students with special needs may require explicit instruction in the use of these strategies. Learning how to predict text structures, how to highlight or outline essential information, and how to use text enhancements such as lesson organizers, graphic organizers, illustrations, charts, graphs, and diagrams are strategies for effectively using textbooks. Many of these strategies are appropriate for all expository text materials and therefore would be helpful for many other secondary-level classes, such as business education, foreign languages, home economics, and physical education.

TEACH STUDENTS TO IDENTIFY TEXT ORGANIZATION   Textbooks contain organizational features intended to help students learn academic content. Unfortunately, however, many students with special needs may not figure out text organization independently. Taking time to systematically teach students how the features of their textbooks are organized can help students learn more easily and make the use of textbooks more valuable. Point out to students how to use design features such as the following:

- The overall parts of the text (e.g., table of contents, index)
- The organizational system (sections, chapters)
- Specific features within chapters (objectives, outlines, boldface, vocabulary, illustrations, charts)
- Features associated with supplemental materials (workbooks, lab books, activity sheets)

Understanding the organization of a textbook can enhance students' comprehension of the content-area information presented. Use effective instruction principles when designing lessons to teach students about text features.

Train Students to Identify Text Structures   Expository science and social studies textbooks use several distinct types of structures (Cook & Mayer, 1988; Williams, 2003). These text structures include, for example, main idea, time–order, cause–effect, enumeration, and sequence.

All types of text structures may appear throughout a single science or social studies textbook. Therefore, students are likely to encounter many structures not only within a single textbook but also within a single chapter. Students should be taught to identify and understand these structures as a way to improve their comprehension of expository text (Bakken & Whedon, 2002; Bohaty, Hebert, Nelson, & Brown, 2014).

Once passage structures are identified, structure-specific reading-comprehension strategies can be used to improve understanding and recall. Bakken, Mastropieri, and Scruggs (1997) taught students with learning disabilities to recognize *main idea*, *list*, and *order* passage types and to apply structure-specific reading-comprehension strategies. For example, when studying main idea passages, students were taught to write down the main idea of the passage (e.g., in photosynthesis, plants convert light energy to carbohydrates) and then write supporting statements. For list passages (e.g., of a country's natural resources), students were taught to note items in the list. For order passages (e.g., the ordered steps in the digestive process), they were taught to write down the items in the appropriate sequence presented. These students greatly outperformed students who were given more general training, either to paraphrase information or to answer questions about the passages.

TEACH HIGHLIGHTING AND OUTLINING STRATEGIES   Highlighting and outlining are used to increase learning and memory of text by identifying the critical information in text or notes. Both of these techniques have been adapted to increase the learning of students with special needs (e.g., Horton, Boone, & Lovitt, 1990; Reid, Lienemann, & Hagaman, 2013). Information highlighted with bright colors, such as fluorescent yellow, stands out dramatically from the text, and such highlighting can be used to quickly find important information. Underlining is usually done in pencil or pen, but brightly colored highlighting pens can also be used. Brightly colored sticky notes can be used when students are not allowed to write in their textbooks. Electronic books have highlight features that allow the user to underline and add notes.

The most difficult aspect of highlighting or underlining for students is choosing which information is most important. Without training, many students may be unable to discern what is important to highlight or underline and may highlight or underline everything on a page. Obviously, this defeats the purpose of highlighting.

When using actual science or social studies text materials, proceed through a highlighting activity in which you describe to students why you are selecting certain sections to highlight, using a think-aloud protocol. Say, for example:

- "This looks like a new science concept, so I will highlight it. This next section just provides more information on the same concept, so I won't highlight it."

- "This looks like an important person in this history chapter, so I will highlight her, but this next paragraph just describes her background, so I won't highlight that."
- "This looks like an important vocabulary word, so I'll highlight it, but I already know what the next word means, so I won't highlight that."

Show students how to examine the features associated with their textbook. For example, organizational subheadings sometimes provide clues as to whether something is essential, and valuable information is often presented in maps, figures, charts, and diagrams within the text.

Finally, provide guided practice in which students work with partners or in small groups and practice identifying important information for highlighting. Stop occasionally and ask students whether they think some of the points meet the criteria for highlighting. Have students share with each other their rationale for the selections they highlighted.

Teach Outlining   Outlining is another study strategy that students can use while studying science and social studies textbooks independently. Before expecting students to outline, be sure they can identify different text structures. Point out how textbooks are organized under various levels of subheadings, which often can be used as levels in outlines. Then be sure to teach or review how to develop outlines. Demonstrate to students how determining the main idea is a first step, followed by selecting supporting ideas and details for each major idea. Before requiring students to create outlines independently, provide them with partially completed outlines in which they complete missing information as they study independently. Outlines set up like this are called **framed outlines**, and they have been used to promote the textbook learning of students with and without disabilities (Brigham, Scruggs, & Mastropieri, 2012). Figure 15.4 displays an example of a framed outline.

INTRODUCE STUDY GUIDES   Study guides take on a variety of forms and can be developed by teachers, students, or by both teachers and students using partially completed study guides similar to partially completed outlines. Lovitt and Horton and their colleagues studied

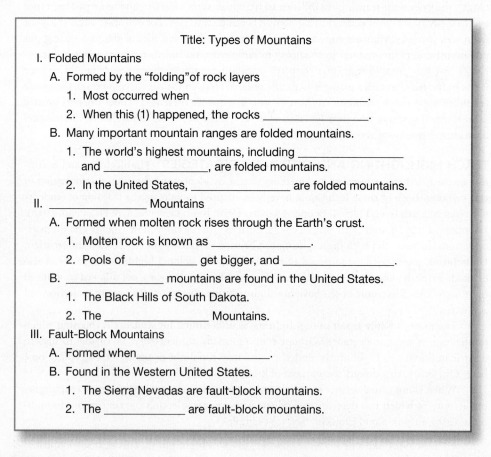

Title: Types of Mountains

I. Folded Mountains
    A. Formed by the "folding" of rock layers
        1. Most occurred when _____.
        2. When this (1) happened, the rocks _____.
    B. Many important mountain ranges are folded mountains.
        1. The world's highest mountains, including _____ and _____, are folded mountains.
        2. In the United States, _____ are folded mountains.
II. _____ Mountains
    A. Formed when molten rock rises through the Earth's crust.
        1. Molten rock is known as _____.
        2. Pools of _____ get bigger, and _____.
    B. _____ mountains are found in the United States.
        1. The Black Hills of South Dakota.
        2. The _____ Mountains.
III. Fault-Block Mountains
    A. Formed when _____.
    B. Found in the Western United States.
        1. The Sierra Nevadas are fault-block mountains.
        2. The _____ are fault-block mountains.

Figure 15.4   Sample Framed Outline

the effects of various study guides on the textbook comprehension of students with and without disabilities (e.g., Horton et al., 1990). Students used information in the science and social studies textbooks to complete short-answer questions on study guide forms. Students who used the study guides consistently outperformed students who did not have instruction using study guides. To create a study guide for your students, include critical features such as the formulation of questions, the use of vocabulary, the amount of content coverage, a predictable format for the guide, and time to review the study guide (Swanson et al., 2014). Consider such features as the amount of content covered, the type of study guide (question–answer, framed outline, schematic graph, graphic organizer), the difficulty level of the language, and the format of the questions (e.g., fill-in-the-blank, open-ended, or multiple-choice questions).

Try developing a few study guides annually to accompany your text. Save them or share them with another teacher who may also develop a few to share with you. Do not pressure yourself to complete the entire text at one time, or you may become overwhelmed. Over time, you will have accompanying study guides developed for entire textbooks in science and social studies.

TEACH LEARNING STRATEGIES Deshler and Schumaker and their colleagues at the University of Kansas Institute for Research in Learning Disabilities developed some excellent learning strategies, including an instructional model for optimal delivery of these strategies (see Deshler & Schumaker, 2006; Gildroy & Deshler, 2008; Lenz, Deshler, & Kissam, 2004; Schumaker & Deshler, 2003). Learning strategies should be implemented slowly over time to ensure that all students master all steps involved in learning and generalizing strategies. Key elements in the learning strategies model are listed in the following *In the Classroom* feature. The intent of instruction in learning strategies is for students to become independent at implementing the strategies in their own studying.

MultiPass A useful learning strategy for reading science and social studies textbooks is **MultiPass** (Schumaker, Deshler, Alley, Warner, & Denton, 1982). The steps in MultiPass are similar to those in the SQ3R strategy—Survey, Question, Read, Recite, and Review (Marchand-Martella, Martella, Modderman, Petersen, & Pan, 2013; McCormick & Cooper, 1991). With MultiPass, students are taught to review textbook reading materials three times, first to "survey," second to "size up," and third to "sort out" (O'Connor & Goodwin, 2011).

During the *survey* pass, students familiarize themselves with the organization of the text chapter, including the title, beginning paragraphs, subheadings, summary paragraphs, and the major ideas. Teach students to make associations with the information in this chapter and previously read chapters. Finally, teach students to summarize the information in the chapter in their own words.

For the *size-up* pass, teach students more study techniques to use when reviewing the chapter:

- Identify highlighted information.
- Read the questions at the end of the chapter.
- Make up questions from statements.
- Skim text to find answers to questions.
- Paraphrase answers without looking back at the chapter.

Finally, for the *sort-out* phase, teach students to test themselves on the information in the chapter. In addition, throughout all three phases of instruction, students can use self-monitoring procedures to ensure they have completed all necessary steps, including appropriate attribution. An example attribution statement to teach students is: "Using MultiPass should help me learn and do better on the next test."

IT FITS IT FITS was developed to help students with learning difficulties remember important information from science textbooks (King-Sears, Mercer, & Sindelar, 1992). IT FITS is an acronym for the steps in creating mnemonic keyword strategies. King-Sears et al. taught students with learning disabilities to use the IT FITS strategy as follows:

Identify the term (example: *ptero-*, as in *pterosaur* or *pteranodon*).

Tell the definition of the term ("winged").

Find a keyword (*tire*).

In the Classroom

Steps in Learning a Strategy Model

Step 1: Pretest learners, and have students make a commitment to learning.

Step 2: Present purpose and describe the learning strategy.

Step 3: Model strategy usage using think-alouds, and provide initial student practice with the strategy.

Step 4: Provide additional rehearsal and verbal elaboration practice with the strategy.

Step 5: Provide controlled practice and feedback with the strategy (guided practice).

Step 6: Provide advanced practice and feedback with the strategy (independent practice).

Step 7: Provide positive feedback for the learning strategy, and enlist support for generalization of self-use of the strategy.

Step 8: Provide generalization and maintenance training, support, and feedback.

Note: From "An instructional model for teaching students how to learn," by D. D. Deshler & J. B. Schumaker, 1988, in J. L. Graden, J. E. Zins, & M. J. Curtis (Eds.), *Alternative instructional delivery systems: Enhancing instructional options for all students*, Washington, DC: National Association of School Psychologists. (See also Gildroy and Deshler, 2008.)

Imagine the definition doing something with the keyword ("a tire with wings attached").

Think about the definition doing something with the keyword ("the attached wings lifting a tire into the air").

Study what you imagined until you know the definition (*ptero-* → tire → tire with wings → "winged"). (King-Sears et al., 1992; see also King-Sears & Mooney, 2004)

One student reported using the strategy to learn the meaning of *acoustic*. After *identifying* the term, he *told* the definition of the term ("having to do with hearing"), then *found* a keyword ("stick"). Next, he *imagined* the definition doing something with the keyword, by considering the stick (baton) that his bandleader used, which made a noise when it was tapped. He then *thought* about this definition and *studied* what he imagined until he remembered the keyword and the definition. Results indicated that students learned more science vocabulary when they used and implemented the IT FITS strategy.

TRAVEL Boyle and Weishaar (1997) taught students with learning disabilities to use the TRAVEL strategy for developing their own cognitive organizers to improve their comprehension and recall of text content:

Topic: Write down the topic and circle it.

Read: Read a paragraph.

Ask: Ask what the main idea and three details are and write them down.

Verify: Verify the main idea by circling it and linking its details.

Examine: Examine the next paragraph and ask and verify again.

Link: When finished with the story, link all circles. (p. 230)

Students who used the TRAVEL strategy outperformed control-condition students—as well as students who had studied an expert-generated cognitive organizer—on tests of literal and inferential recall.

Self-Monitoring Strategies   You can also teach students to use a self-monitoring strategy as they encounter headings and subheadings in content textbooks. For example, teach students to turn the heading, "The Election of 1976," into a question, such as, "Who won the election of 1976?" After reading the section, students should ask themselves, "Can I answer the question?" and then circle "yes" or "no" on a self-monitoring worksheet. If they circled "no," teach students to find the answer by, for example, (a) rereading the text; (b) checking their vocabulary understanding; (c) examining illustrations, tables, or figures; or (d) writing down questions to ask the teacher. Berkeley, Marshak, Mastropieri, and Scruggs (2011) taught middle school students to use this strategy in inclusive history classes and reported that students trained in this self-monitoring strategy scored much higher on content tests than students who were simply told to read the passages and remember as much as possible (see also O'Connor, Beach, Sanchez, Bocian, & Flynn, 2015).

STRATEGIES FOR
ADAPTING TEXTBOOK MATERIALS

Because textbooks are adopted for entire school districts, it is inevitable that the reading level of some books may be too difficult, and thus inaccessible, for some students. Some suggestions to help promote learning by adapting the use of textbooks are presented in Figure 15.5.

Provide alternative text formats.
- Use published recordings of texts or develop your own.
- Use digital text with audio components.
- Acquire enlarged-type versions of materials.
- As appropriate, use braille versions of materials.
- Assign peers to read text.

Develop or plan for use of alternative curricular materials.
- Revise or rewrite text, adapting higher-level concepts and vocabulary; insert guided questions to use with simplified text.
- Prepare and distribute study guides, outlines, or guided notes.
- Prepare and distribute mnemonic illustrations.
- Supplement with software or apps focused on simpler presentation of concepts.
- Use high-interest, low-vocabulary materials.
- Use activities-based materials (see next section).
- Shorten reading and writing assignments.
- Develop pictorial versions of text materials.

Modify teaching presentations.
- Preteach difficult concepts and vocabulary.
- Provide concrete examples.
- Activate prior knowledge.
- Reduce amount of new information.
- Provide illustrative aids and spatial organizers.
- Use study guides.
- Encourage active participation.
- Schedule regular meetings with special needs students.
- Require frequent verbal responses to check for understanding.
- Provide additional review sessions.
- Use trade books as supplements.
- Use multimedia supplements.
- Use flashcards for studying.
- Have students maintain journals containing new concepts and vocabulary.

Use peers (or parent volunteers) as assistants.
- To read or listen to reading.
- As study partners.
- To assist with writing tasks.

Figure 15.5   Suggestions for Adapting and Using Textbooks

Content-Area Instruction for Diverse Learners

Students from culturally diverse backgrounds, including English language learners, require additional supports in content-area classes. Students may require assistance with learning English while learning new content-area information, including the concepts and vocabulary of science, social studies, or math. The implementation of effective culturally responsive instructional procedures will be important. Some culturally responsive teaching approaches have been recommended, including collaborative teaching, problem solving, child-centered learning, use of appropriate assessments and materials, feedback-responsive teaching, modeling, and instructional scaffolding (Aceves & Orosco, 2014). Similarly,

Averill, Anderson, and Drake (2015) reported that coaching, rehearsal, and modeling can help improve culturally responsive teaching. Using multiple examples, including authentic culturally diverse examples, and connecting content-area learning to students' lives can help students make connections and relate the new content to their personal lives. However, it is also important to consider language objectives in addition to the content-area objectives when students are English language learners (Aceves & Orosco, 2014). Sheltered content instruction has many of the same components as effective instruction in general; in addition, it adds the following:

- identifying language proficiency levels;

- adapting speech, language, and vocabulary to proficiency levels;
- adapting content to students' language proficiency;
- providing sufficient response wait time;
- providing supplemental materials; and
- providing examples relevant to students' cultural and linguistic backgrounds (see Echevarria & Graves, 2015).

Other features shared with those of effective instruction include using clear language, providing consistent review, and using concrete, meaningful lessons with practice and multiple interaction opportunities.

Other students may have difficulties because they are learning to speak English at the same time they are learning academic content. Echevarria and Graves (2015) described a model of **sheltered content instruction** to support the content learning of English learners with diverse abilities. This model and culturally responsive teaching approaches are described in the *Diversity in the Classroom* feature.

PROMOTE PREREADING AND POSTREADING STRATEGIES   Before assigning independent textbook reading, explain the purpose of the assignment. For example, you could say, "When you finish reading the section of your U.S. history text tonight, you will all be able to tell me the causes of the Civil War tomorrow at the beginning of class."

Provide organizers as overviews of the text structures and the content students will be studying. Figure 15.6 provides an example of a spatially organized template from Inspiration Software that allows you or your students to create visual displays of historical events. Information from the visual display can be converted to and printed in an outline format.

Timelines can be constructed to demonstrate graphically the sequence of important events, for example, the events leading up to the Civil War. Timelines may or may not include pictures or symbols but always contain a chronological sequence in a graphic format. Design, develop, and show timelines that present detailed events that will be covered in the next social studies chapter.

Present difficult concepts or vocabulary words to students with disabilities in class before having them read about the information independently. Use some of the suggestions described in the MultiPass or mnemonic strategies sections to introduce and teach these concepts first. Demonstrate how students can use context clues, glossaries, and dictionaries to figure out new words they will encounter in the text. Have students practice these words at home and school to become familiar with the new words before hearing them for the first time in class. Figure 15.7 contains a partial vocabulary checklist.

Use Postreading Strategies   When textbook reading assignments have been completed, provide additional assistance to ensure content mastery, including reviewing major points in class, providing additional practice with peer tutors, providing extra help sessions, reviewing

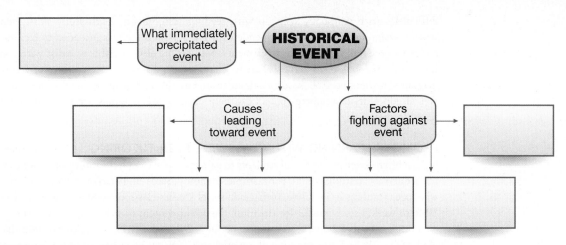

Figure 15.6 Template for Creating Visual Display for Historical Event
Note: Reprinted with permission from Inspiration Software, Portland, OR.

study guides, directing students to tell or write summaries, and providing practice tests. This additional review on the most important content can lead to greater academic success.

MAKE ADAPTATIONS FOR STUDENTS WITH VISUAL IMPAIRMENTS OR SEVERE READING PROBLEMS As Mr. Norland discovered of Jeffrey in the scenario at the beginning of this chapter, reading problems can significantly inhibit science learning. Students with visual impairments or severe reading problems will need to have written text available to them in alternative formats. Alternative formats include audio versions, computerized versions containing audio components, larger-print versions, or braille formats for students with very limited vision. The *Kurzweil Reader* (Kurzweil Educational Systems) is also useful for reading and interacting with text; the *Kurzweil 3000* is intended to help students who have

Vocabulary and Phrases

Direction: Place a checkmark in the box if the student reads and defines the word correctly.

Chapter 4: Ecosystems   S = At School   H = At Home

	S	H	S	H	S	H	S	H	S	H
Vocabulary Words & Phrases	Mon	Mon	Tues	Tues	Wed	Wed	Thur	Thur	Fri	Fri
ecosystem										
producer										
consumer										
decomposer										
community										
predator										
prey										
parasite										
host										

Figure 15.7 Sample Vocabulary Checklist
Note: From unpublished materials by M. A. Mastropieri & T. E. Scruggs, 1996, Fairfax, VA: Graduate School of Education, George Mason University. Reprinted with permission.

difficulties with textbooks keep up with reading assignments, learn study skills, complete written assignments, and test independently. The *Kurzweil 1000* is intended to facilitate text access for students with visual impairments. Services are also available to assist with completing braille versions of materials. Tactile graphics to improve understanding of figures and diagrams in science textbooks are available from American Printing House for the Blind. Some special educators or resource centers can help create class materials accessible in braille and raised formats.

PROMOTE LEARNING WITH CLASSWIDE PEER TUTORING   Classwide peer tutoring can be an excellent way for all students to gain extra practice on the most important content of science and social studies units. For example, Maheady, Sacca, and Harper (1988) employed classwide peer tutoring in inclusive 10th-grade social studies classrooms. Maheady et al. developed 30-item weekly study guides for the most important content of each chapter. Students tutored each other in pairs for about 30 minutes per day, 2 days per week, using items from the study guides (e.g., "What is the meaning of imperialism?"; "What is the governmental structure of the Communist Party?"). When participating in the peer-tutoring condition, students scored over 21 percentage points higher than they scored before the intervention began. Mastropieri, Scruggs, Spencer, and Fontana (2003) implemented classwide peer tutoring using reading-comprehension strategies ("Who or what is the section about?"; "What is happening to the who or what?"; "Write a summary sentence") and summary sheets in 10th-grade world history classes in units on the world wars. Students who had participated in tutoring performed better on chapter tests, unit tests, and end-of-year tests than students who had studied with guided notes.

Spencer, Scruggs, and Mastropieri (2003) implemented a similar reading-comprehension strategy using classwide peer tutoring with middle school students with emotional or behavioral disabilities studying social studies content (history and civics). Students read textbooks to each other in pairs and questioned each other about factual content (e.g., "What was the Teapot Dome scandal?"). Results revealed that students scored about 15 percentage points higher on weekly quizzes and chapter tests in the tutoring condition, and they were observed to have higher rates of academic on-task behavior. One teacher expressed surprise that the tutoring pairs generally interacted well but noted the value of careful student pairings.

Mastropieri, Scruggs, and Marshak (2008) implemented classwide peer tutoring in inclusive seventh-grade U.S. history classes. Teachers developed "fact sheets" of the most important textbook content to be remembered. On the fact sheets, questions (e.g., "What was the position of the United States at the beginning of World War I?"; "What was the *Lusitania,* and why was it important?") were printed in boxes on the left side of the page, with the corresponding answers on the right. Partners questioned each other on critical information using materials aligned with the high-stakes testing content and took practice tests covering the information. All parents were trained to use the web-based *Blackboard* program to access and use the same tutoring materials at home. Findings indicated that students scored higher in the peer-tutoring conditions than in control conditions, and the parents learned to use Blackboard and the tutoring materials effectively. Although the materials were the same for all students, instruction can be differentiated in that all students can practice until they reach mastery. All students in this and a related investigation (Scruggs, Mastropieri, & Marshak, 2012) benefited substantially from the tutoring intervention.

Peer tutoring has also been employed in secondary science with students with intellectual disabilities and more typically achieving peers (Jimenez, Browder, Spooner, & Dibiase, 2012). When matched with individual students with intellectual disabilities, peers taught important concepts in physical and earth science using a constant time-delay procedure, where intervals between questions and prompted responses were presented at a constant interval (initially, 0 seconds, then 4 seconds) systematically as students learned. In this case, also, students made use of a "KWHL" chart ("What do you **K**now?"; "What do you **W**ant to know?"; "**H**ow will you find out?"; and "What did you **L**earn?").

Classwide peer tutoring has also been used in inclusive high school chemistry classes with the use of mnemonic techniques (Mastropieri, Scruggs, & Graetz, 2005). Students were assigned to tutoring pairs and provided with materials containing relevant information (e.g., exothermic and endothermic reactions, enthalpy, the periodic table of elements, alkali metals, halogens, molarity, Avogadro's number). Students questioned each other on the information (e.g., "What is molarity?"). If the question was answered correctly, the tutor asked for further elaborations on the content to promote comprehension (e.g., "What else is important about

Peer Tutoring in Inclusive Social Studies Classes

 Secondary social studies courses contain a remarkable amount of factual information that students must assimilate in order to succeed in school and pass state high-stakes tests. Many students with disabilities have great difficulty mastering this content. Because many students with disabilities today receive social studies instruction in inclusive classes, strategies must be employed that accommodate all learners. Marshak et al. (2011) implemented a peer-tutoring intervention designed to deliver appropriate instruction to all students in inclusive history classes and maximize student engagement. Eight seventh-grade classrooms, containing 202 students without disabilities and 42 students with disabilities, were assigned at random to experimental and comparison conditions. The comparison classrooms received high-quality instruction in American history, with methods and materials including PowerPoint presentations, lecture, mapping activities, study guides for tests, graphic organizers, primary source documents, video clips, simulations, and fill-in-the-blank worksheets. The experimental classrooms included, in addition, classwide peer-tutoring methods.

Instructional time was equated for both conditions.

Teachers determined the most important content for the three units being taught (industrialization, progressive era, imperialism), and tutoring materials were developed for students to question each other on the content. Each item was associated with a mnemonic picture to help students remember, but these were only employed when students failed to recall the target content. When a student answered correctly, the tutor was instructed to provide positive feedback and move on to the next item. If an item was answered incorrectly, or there was no response in 3 seconds, the tutor showed the mnemonic picture and prompted the student to use the picture as a memory aid. For example, to remember that John D. Rockefeller controlled much of the oil business, a mnemonic picture was shown of oil being poured on a rock (keyword for *Rockefeller*). Tutees were taught, when asked about Rockefeller, to think of the picture of the rock, remember the oil being poured on the rock, and respond with the correct answer. This procedure was implemented about 2 days per week for about 20 minutes each day.

All students were pre- and posttested on the content of the three units. Results indicated that students in the experimental-condition classrooms retained substantially more social studies content than those in comparison-condition classrooms. Students with and without disabilities both gained similarly from the intervention. Survey data suggested that students and teachers alike enjoyed the intervention and felt it promoted learning for all students. This study demonstrated that classwide peer tutoring with differentiated mnemonic materials can significantly improve learning in middle school social studies classes. See also Regan, Evmenova, Mastropieri, and Scruggs (2015) and Scruggs and Mastropieri (2013a, 2013b).

QUESTIONS FOR REFLECTION

1. Why do you think students would enjoy classwide peer tutoring more than whole-class activities?
2. Do you think students should be allowed to choose their own tutoring partners? Why or why not?
3. Why do you think, in this investigation, that students with and without disabilities learned the same amount in the tutoring condition?

molarity?"). If the question was incorrectly answered, strategies such as the keyword method were provided, as shown in Figure 15.8. When the item was answered correctly, further elaboration was prompted. Results indicated that students in the tutoring condition outperformed comparison students in both recall and comprehension of chemistry content. In this case, instruction was differentiated in that students used elaborative strategies only when they were needed, although materials overall were the same for all students. For a similar example with social studies content (Marshak et al., 2011), see the *Research Highlight*.

Differentiated Curriculum Enhancements Peer-mediated interventions such as those just described, where all students proceed through the same classroom materials, which can be implemented differently depending on learner need (time to practice specific information, use of mnemonics), have been referred to as "differentiated curriculum enhancements" (Mastropieri et al., 2006). One advantage of this model is that it allows for differentiation without

What is molarity?

Concentration of a solute in a solution; moles per liter.

If your partner is correct, go to⇒
If your partner doesn't know the answer, review the strategy.

Strategy: Think of the word "moles" for mole, and remember the picture of a number of moles in solution, to remember molarity is the concentration of a solute in a solution, in moles per liter.

Then ask: *What is the strategy to remember molarity?*

Then ask again: *What does molarity mean?*

⇒ Then ask:
What else is important about molarity?

[Answers include: molarity is a ratio, moles of solute divided by liters of solution]

Figure 15.8 What Is Molarity?

Note: From "Teaching tutorial: Mnemonic instruction," by T. Scruggs & M. A. Mastropieri, 2002, TeachingLD.org, p. 19. Copyright 2002 by the Division for Learning Disabilities. Reprinted with permission.

providing qualitatively different materials for different students. Similarly, you can also implement differentiated instruction through the creation of activities of different difficulty levels, which are then completed by tutoring pairs. Mastropieri et al. (2006) developed materials for the "Scientific Method" unit for inclusive middle school science classes. For example, for the "Experimental Design" activity, students in small groups of two or three read research scenarios (e.g., an experiment involving plant growth) and matched independent (e.g., fertilizer) with dependent variables (e.g., plant height) for Level 1 activities. For Level 2, students independently produced the variables and hypotheses, with prompting when needed. Finally, students produced the names of variables and hypotheses without any prompting (Level 3). Various gamelike activities were employed for all levels. Because all students moved through all levels of all activities, there was no stigma associated with the lower-level materials. Students in classes employing these differentiated curriculum enhancements enjoyed learning scientific methods and significantly outperformed students in comparison conditions. Simpkins, Mastropieri, and Scruggs (2009) found that similar materials using gamelike formats (e.g., similar to Jeopardy, Concentration, Sorry) on two levels (Level 1: identification; Level 2: production) significantly increased learning of the content in the "Earth/Space" and "Light and Sound" units in an inclusive fifth-grade class.

MyEdLab: Self-Check 15.1

MyEdLab: Application Exercise 15.1: Textbook-Oriented
Approaches in Social Studies

Adapting Activities-Oriented Approaches in Science and Social Studies

Rather than relying primarily on textbooks, you can develop conceptual understanding of science and social studies with an activities-oriented approach to teaching. Research has indicated that activities-oriented approaches frequently produce superior learning in general education science and social studies classes (Chiappetta & Koballa, 2006; Parker & Beck, 2016). Some research indicates that activities-oriented approaches may be very beneficial for students with disabilities when sufficient support is provided (Brigham et al., 2012; Scruggs, Mastropieri, Bakken, & Brigham, 1993). Some of the advantages of activities-oriented approaches to science and social studies education are that they de-emphasize vocabulary learning and learning dependent on the reading of textbooks (areas of relative difficulty for many students with special needs). In addition, activities provide direct interaction with concrete, meaningful materials (areas of relative strength for many students with special needs) (Mastropieri, Scruggs, Mantzicopoulos, Sturgeon, Goodwin, & Chung, 1998). Two potential disadvantages to an activities approach are difficulty adjusting to the less-structured atmosphere of activities-oriented instruction and the fact that some students may exhibit difficulty with the inductive thinking often associated with such instruction (Scruggs & Mastropieri, 2013a).

Students who take alternate assessments based on alternate achievement standards (AA-AAAS) have also participated in science activities. Knight, Smith, Spooner, and Browder (2012) described how primary-grade students with autism spectrum disorder were taught relevant science content (e.g., *living, wet, rock*) using hands-on materials and direct teaching of instances and noninstances and were later able to generalize to novel objects. Browder (2015) described teaching students with moderate and severe disabilities early concepts in earth science (e.g., causes of earthquakes, properties of soil) using pictures and direct teaching and prompting (see also Jimenez, Lo, and Saunders [2014] for a science study with students with autism and intellectual disabilities).

Students with special needs may require adaptations and support when undertaking activities-oriented approaches to science and social studies learning (Melber & Heller, 2010). However, there are many different types of activities, and these different activities may require different adaptations. The following sections describe adaptations that may help you more effectively include your students with disabilities in science and social studies activities.

STRATEGIES FOR
ADAPTING SCIENCE ACTIVITIES

Students with disabilities can benefit greatly from the authentic learning experiences afforded by science activities, and many science activities can be adapted to accommodate special learning needs (Scruggs & Mastropieri, 2013a; 2013b). When planning activities-oriented instruction in science, consider both general accommodations as well as adaptations targeted to the specific disability area and the specific science activity. Both general and specific adaptations are described in the sections that follow. Many of these suggestions are described in more detail by the American Printing House for the Blind (2006); Melber and Heller (2010); Mastropieri and Scruggs (1993); Dion, Hoffman, and Matter (2000); Pence, Workman, and Riecke (2003); Rule, Stefanich, Boody, and Peiffer (2011); Scruggs and Mastropieri (1994, 1995a, 1995b, 2013a); and Scruggs, Mastropieri, and Marshak (2011).

EMPLOY PRINCIPLES OF UNIVERSAL DESIGN FOR LEARNING Burgstahler (2012) describes the application of universal design for learning (UDL) principles for making science labs accessible to students with disabilities. Arguing that UDL should be proactive when possible, she argues for science labs that already contain adjustable-height workstations, for example, so accommodations will not be needed for future students who use wheelchairs. Other UDL suggestions include providing both written and verbal instructions, demonstrations, and visual aids; using large-print, high-contrast materials for laboratory signs and equipment labels; maintaining wide aisles and uncluttered work areas; and acquiring lab products that can be used by students with a variety of abilities, such as nonslip mats, support stands, tactile models, and plastic rather than glass lab products.

Most of the methods and materials described in this section meet criteria for universal design because they provide assistance for a variety of student needs and abilities yet, in most cases, can be used by all students.

DEVELOP GENERAL LABORATORY PROCEDURES AND PRECAUTIONS Many adaptations can be implemented that enable students with all types of disabilities to be more active participants in science. As you think through the activity process, review the PASS variables: **P**rioritize all objectives and determine whether all objectives are necessary (for example, are lab activities such as slide-staining important objectives, or is observing cellular structure the most important objective?). Then, **A**dapt materials, the environment, instructional procedures, or assessment methods as needed to ensure success for all students. Next, use the SCREAM variables (e.g., **S**tructure, **C**larity, **R**edundancy) to maximize the effectiveness of your teaching. Finally, **S**ystematically evaluate whether your instruction has been successful. After considering these PASS variables, consider a number of general procedures to address diverse learning needs.

List Rules Explain, post, and strictly enforce laboratory rules. Speak privately with students when necessary. Have a "cooling-off" place in the room designated for any students who lose control of their behavior. Generously use praise to reinforce following of the science lab rules.

Ensure Safety Because safety is a major concern when using scientific equipment and materials, stabilize all scientific equipment and materials to avoid unnecessary spills. Velcro can be used to attach lighter objects to tables or trays, and string and trays can be used to hold larger and heavier objects. Use large, clear labels on all equipment and materials, including braille labels when needed for students with visual impairments. Be sure there is sufficient space for easy mobility and access to materials around the room and lab tables for all students, including those with physical and visual disabilities.

Give Clear Directions Be sure directions are clearly communicated, are parallel in construction, and follow a step-by-step process. List directions on the board or slides so students can refer to them easily. Color code tasks by order of importance. For instance, tasks written in red must be completed by all students, whereas tasks written in other colors may be less important. Provide adapted lab booklets that contain extra lines or spaces for writing or drawing examples of specimens. Make braille and textured versions of lab booklets, or use text enhancement or text-to-speech software when necessary. Furnish checklists of what needs to be accomplished in lab to assist students who have difficulties in completing longer tasks. Frequently check on student progress during lab activities. If students are working in cooperative groups, verify that students with disabilities are active participants rather than observers while their peers complete all activities.

Enhance Stimulus Value Implement closed-circuit television (CCTV) to ensure that students with vision problems can see all phenomena being observed in labs. CCTV can show enlarged versions of anything being studied. Acquire extra lighting and magnifying lenses to help visibility when needed during lab activities. For example, a "Big Eye Lamp" (Mattingly Low Vision) is available that consists of a high-intensity light with a large magnifying lens attached. Use of such a device can enhance viewing of small objects for all students but may be especially beneficial for students with low vision. It may also be helpful for students with less-well-developed fine motor skills, for example, when removing small animal bones from an owl pellet. Use video recordings to reinforce relevant concepts and provide redundancy; use or create descriptive video presentations that include audio descriptions of what's happening in the video for students who cannot see a television monitor clearly. Acquire extra microphones, stethoscopes, or tuning forks that can help students with hearing impairments hear or feel vibrations during various activities. For example, tuning forks can be placed in water, and students with hearing impairments can observe the sound waves in the water.

Prepare for Spills Prepare areas for spills by having plenty of cleanup materials handy. Place tarps on the floor before engaging in activities that may result in spills. This will save the floor or carpets and help keep custodians on your side. Have students bring in extra-large shirts that can be worn as "lab coats" that will protect their clothing in case of spills. Put felt on desk surfaces that are particularly slippery to help stabilize materials. Use trays, slatted trays, or small tubs to hold smaller items on students' desks. Anchor these trays or receptacles with bags of sand or marbles to reinforce and stabilize their positions. The trays and tubs will reduce the area of any potential spills.

MAKE ADAPTATIONS FOR TEACHING LAB SKILLS All students, including those with disabilities, benefit greatly from participating in lab activities. To ensure successful participation, prepare activity-specific adaptations, as discussed next.

Measuring and Pouring Obtain adaptive equipment for measuring and pouring activities. The Lawrence Hall of Science at the University of California at Berkeley developed many materials to help students with visual and physical disabilities. Some of these materials were included in the curriculum materials Science Activities for the Visually Impaired/Science Enrichment for the Learners with Physical Handicaps (SAVI/SELPH), which were later incorporated into the Full Option Science System for all students (FOSS Next Generation, available through Delta Education). All of their adapted materials include enlarged labels in print and braille formats. Some specific adapted materials include enlarged type and braille on enlarged rulers and number lines, enlarged syringe-like devices for measuring, enlarged graduated cylinders for measuring and pouring activities, and larger balance scales containing a plastic guide that students with visual or cognitive impairments can touch to determine whether the sides of the scale are equivalent. Have students use "scooper" devices, for example, a plastic quart bottle with the bottom removed, for obtaining water from larger receptacles, rather than obtaining it directly from the tap.

Balancing and Weighing Obtain simpler and larger scales and balances for weighing materials. The Vox-2 Talking Scale (Assistech Special Needs) weighs objects up to 11 lbs (about 5 kg) in one of four languages. Devise your own measuring adaptations to suit the activities in your class. For example, a spring scale with raised markers can be made suitable for students with visual impairments. When repeatedly using a specific measure on rulers, place a piece of tape or a rubber band on the exact measure required to help students with motor or cognitive difficulties be more precise with measuring. Substitute three-dimensional articles made of different textures so that students with visual impairments can feel objects that others are able to see to explore weight, texture, and simple measurements.

Charting/Graphing and Recording Data Most activities in science and social studies require students to record their observations on some type of chart, graph, or pictorial or in narrative format. Students with disabilities may require some preinstruction with the specific charting or recording procedures for your class. Prefamiliarize students with various types of charts and graphs, such as graph paper, bar charts, frequency charts, and histograms, using very concrete examples. Some of the materials in the Science and Technology for Children (STC; available from Carolina Biological Supply Company) and the Activities for Integrating Math and Science (AIMS; Education Foundation) curricula contain excellent lessons for use in teaching preskills in graphing, charting, and recording data. Try using some familiar topics to construct class graphs, such as students' favorite television programs.

Use larger graph paper for students with motor or visual difficulties. Label charts and graphs or use paper that has guidelines for students with reading and writing difficulties. Replace pencil or pen markings on charts or graphs with felt circles or squares or some other textured materials, such as Velcro, stickers, guide strips from computer paper, braille dots, or tactile dots, so students with visual and cognitive disabilities can feel the differences in the types of items charted and the quantities associated with each item. Make three-dimensional graphs using clay, tiles, golf tees, pushpins, yarn, chicken wire, and other materials to help students' comprehension. Three-dimensional graphs in larger formats can be more easily made by students with fine motor difficulties. Students with visual impairments may record observations by drawing on a screen board (crayon on paper over a screen), using clay models, or using braille numbers and raised lines.

Some computer software programs, such as Microsoft Word, have charting and graphing tools and may be especially helpful for students with disabilities. In addition, many computer programs collect, record, and graph data, as do graphing calculators and smartphone and tablet applications. Finally, consider grouping students with and without disabilities to record and graph data cooperatively (see Mastropieri et al., 2006). Peers may be able to assist with some of the more difficult components of the task. However, verify that all students are completing their share of the recording activities and comprehend the relevant concepts.

STRATEGIES FOR

ADAPTING LIFE SCIENCE ACTIVITIES

Life science strands include living things, ecology, cells, genetics, and evolution. Learning for all students, especially those with special needs, can be greatly enhanced with hands-on activities (Scruggs & Mastropieri, 2013a; 2013b). When teachers consider the following adaptations, students with special needs may become more actively involved during science activities.

ADAPT PLANT GROWTH AND DEVELOPMENT ACTIVITIES

- Because most household plants die from overwatering, and small fish are frequently overfed, set up a strict schedule for watering and feeding classroom plants and pets, using specific amounts of water or fish food. Water syringes may help students deliver the precise amount of water needed by the plant, and food portions can be prepared ahead of time.

- After planting seeds, plan other science activities to do while plants are growing. Because some students may have difficulty sustaining interest or attention over longer time periods, consider using plants that grow and develop quickly. For example, beans normally grow faster and flower sooner than peas. Further, consider acquiring Wisconsin Fast Plants (available from Carolina Biological Supply), which develop much faster than most plants.

- To help students plant seeds at a standard depth, wrap a rubber band around a dowel or pencil for use as a depth gauge.

- To help students directly observe root structure, grow plants in clear plastic baggies, or in hydroponic (all-water) containers. Students with visual impairments can also be encouraged to feel the sunlight in relation to a plant and feel the effect of the sunlight on the development of the plant.

ADAPT ACTIVITIES INVOLVING ANIMALS

- Carefully consider the purpose of acquiring classroom animals. Many schools have specific restrictions regarding animals, so it is important to first check out these policies before acquiring any animals.

- Any animals' characteristics or peculiarities need to be noted. For example, hamsters are largely nocturnal and may be less active during school hours. Reptiles must be kept warm (e.g., with special heaters), or they will not eat, and they may catch "colds" and die. Newts' water must be kept clean, or they may not be able to detect the presence of food placed in their tank. Crayfish are prone to diseases that may spread rapidly to other crayfish. Isolate crayfish for 5 days, check for any sign of red tinge to the underside, and quarantine affected crayfish.

- When ordering animals from supply houses, make sure the outdoor climate is appropriate for the animal being shipped, and be certain it will arrive at a time when it can be immediately attended to by an adult and at a time appropriate for the animals. For example, ordering a butterfly kit in the winter may mean releasing them when the weather is too cold for survival.

- Some animals (e.g., reptiles) require live food, so consider the effect this may have on students in your class. Some students with emotional or other handicaps may react strongly to some animals or to the behaviors of some animals. Finally, some students may be disposed to abuse animals in captivity, so be certain to promote an attitude of respect toward living things, and ensure that captive animals will be kept safe.

ADAPT ANATOMY ACTIVITIES

- Various three-dimensional models are available from supply companies, such as the Carolina Biological Supply Company. The *Visible Man/Visible Woman* (Craft House Corporation) also provides concrete information on anatomy. However, as with all models, be careful that too much valuable instructional time is not lost on assembling models versus learning relevant concepts. Anatomical models are also available from the American Printing House for the Blind.

- Students with hearing impairments who cannot use a stethoscope may be able to feel a pulse at the carotid or brachial arteries. Students with physical disabilities who cannot run in place can substitute another activity (such as raising or lowering the body from the arms of a wheelchair) to increase heartbeat.

- For students who do not have a good sense of their own bodies (e.g., younger students, students with cognitive or intellectual disabilities, or some students with emotional disturbance), use photographs, videos, and mirrors to reinforce body image.

ADAPT MICROSCOPE ACTIVITIES   Microscope activities can be interesting and accessible to a wide variety of learners. Browder (2015) described how students with moderate and severe disabilities were able to view microscopic images of a living leaf and a silk leaf, then make comparisons. When acquiring microscopes, consider the Brock Magiscope® (Brock Optical). This sturdy microscope is simple to use and maintains sufficient light even when it is moved around (see also the Wolfe® Wonderscope™, available from Carolina Biological Supply). Digital microscope images can also be displayed on large monitors for students with visual or physical impairments or can be printed from the screen and made into three-dimensional images. Projection microscopes (e.g., from Cosmo Laboratory Equipment) can project a large image from a slide onto a screen where they can be viewed by the whole class. Projected images can be copied on paper with a raised-line writing tool such as Hi-Marks (Lighthouse Guild) so that images can be experienced tactually. When microscopes are not available, or their use is not practical, acquire large color pictures or three-dimensional models of the microscopic objects being studied. For example, Carolina Biological Supply Company supplies three-dimensional plant and animal cells that present cross-sectional layers of cell structure. Many internet sites provide relevant photographs and video presentations of microscopic organisms, and many relevant science apps are available for smartphones and tablets. YouTube provides many videos of microscopic specimens that may be useful in enforcing relevant concepts.

CONSIDER HEALTH ISSUES   Students who have asthma or serious allergies may react negatively to dander in animal fur or to molds or pollens in plants. Consider the health needs of all students before including specific animals or plants in the classroom.

STRATEGIES FOR
ADAPTING EARTH SCIENCE ACTIVITIES

Earth science covers meteorology, astronomy, geology, and oceanography. Many relevant activities can be conducted in the classroom to enhance comprehension in these areas. Unlike in life sciences, students may be unfamiliar with many of the concepts and terms used, so be sure that relevant vocabulary is being learned.

ADAPT WEATHER ACTIVITIES

- Some concepts, such as humidity or air pressure, may be more difficult for younger students or students with intellectual impairments. Use students' prior knowledge of, for example, hot showers versus dry oven heat, and traveling in an airplane or a fast elevator, to make the concepts more meaningful.

- Place a barometer in a glass container with a rubber top to demonstrate changes as a function of pressure generated by pushing or pulling on the rubber top.

- The American Printing House for the Blind offers adapted and talking thermometers and tactile rulers and yardsticks to assist students with visual impairments.

ADAPT ROCKS AND MINERALS ACTIVITIES

- Some versions of the FOSS materials noted earlier feature an activity titled "Mock Rocks." The teacher creates "rocks" composed of such ingredients as water, flour, aquarium gravel, crushed oyster shells, and food coloring. These are mixed, formed into rock shapes, and allowed to dry; teachers could also acquire these or similar materials and create their own "rocks." In class, students physically disassemble these rocks into component parts, enforcing the concept that rocks are composed of many other components. Activities such as this may be particularly helpful for students with cognitive or intellectual impairments.

- Models of sedimentary rock can be created from differently colored layers of sand or gravel, in white glue and water, or plaster of Paris. Use of alternate layers can represent the layers of rock built up over time.

- Many specimens and models of rocks and minerals are available from supply companies. Generally, larger, loose specimens are preferable to smaller examples glued on a card. Students with visual impairments should be able to feel many properties of minerals, including heft, cleavage (see, especially, mica), fracture, and crystal faces. If students feel a specific place on a mineral before a scratch test, it may be possible to feel the scratch. It may be more difficult for students with visual impairments to detect color, luster, and streak, but students with some vision may detect these properties with enhanced illumination or magnification.

STRATEGIES FOR
ADAPTING PHYSICAL SCIENCE ACTIVITIES

Physical science activities can include sound, magnetism and electricity, force and motion, light, and powders, mixtures, and solutions.

ADAPT PHYSICS OF SOUND ACTIVITIES

- Students can observe and compare sounds made by different objects and conduct experiments on variations in the tension, thickness, and length of strings, cords, and rubber bands. Students may also examine the effect of sound-producing devices in vacuum chambers.

- Students with hearing impairments may have specific difficulties with this content area. For students with some hearing, amplification may be helpful. It may also be helpful to ensure that no other sound is detectable in the classroom other than the one being observed.

- In many cases, students with severe hearing loss may be able to feel the vibrations in different sound-producing objects. Carefully place tuning forks in water after being struck to demonstrate the vibrations in water. When using "waterphone bottle" (bottles filled with different levels of water) activities, indicate the level of the water with rubber bands placed around the bottles for students with visual impairments.

ADAPT MAGNETISM AND ELECTRICITY ACTIVITIES

- Students can make simple connections from batteries to small motors and light bulbs, identify conductors and insulators, and create series and parallel circuits, electromagnets, and telegraphs. Some science activities encourage students to find insulators and conductors by connecting circuits. Monitor these activities carefully, and be certain that classroom wiring and outlets are inaccessible.

- Adapt electricity boards with alligator clips and battery holders to make them easier to work with. These adapted boards may be beneficial for students with visual and physical disabilities, as well as any students who lack well-developed fine motor skills. For students with more severe physical disabilities, wires can be permanently attached to most connections.

- For students who cannot see whether light bulbs are lighted, substitute small electric motors, which can be heard when they are connected to a battery. When using electric motors with students with hearing impairments, attach a small paper flag to the rotor so that the movement can be observed when the power is connected.

- When constructing telegraphs, connect a light bulb to flash, so that the message can be observed by students with hearing impairments.

- Students with intellectual disabilities and younger students may have less-well-developed preconceptions about electricity—for example, the battery as a power source, the current that travels through a conductor, and the concept of a "circuit." Pretraining on some of these concepts may be helpful.

ADAPT FORCE AND MOTION ACTIVITIES

- Force and motion activities include investigations with simple machines (such as levers and pulleys), pendulum motion, and rubber-band-propelled airplanes. The concepts presented in force and motion activities are more abstract than they are in some other subjects; therefore, some concept-enhancement activities may be helpful for students with lower cognitive or intellectual functioning. Provide and practice many examples from students' experiences of new concepts as they are investigated.

- See-saws, hammers, rakes, and crowbars are good examples of levers; ramps and slides are good examples of inclined planes; playground swings and pendulum clocks are good examples of pendulums. Demonstrate how the principles learned in class generally apply to these more familiar objects.

ADAPT POWDERS, MIXTURES, AND SOLUTIONS ACTIVITIES

- An important first consideration for creating mixtures and solutions—and examining chemical properties and observing chemical changes such as saturation, concentration, and separation—is safety. Make certain that all students, including students with disabilities or other special needs, are familiar with specific rules about handling relevant materials. Such rules may include the following: never taste anything, clean up spilled substances immediately, avoid direct contact with the substances unless supervised, avoid blowing (or sneezing) into the powders, and use heat sources only with teacher supervision.

- Mixing substances together often produces some sound, such as fizzing. Encourage students to employ their hearing when making observations. Stethoscopes or microphones can be used to amplify the sound.

- Students with visual impairments can be encouraged to feel powders and substances that are not harmful to touch. Additionally, students can feel paper or other filters before and after mixtures and solutions have passed through them.

- For students with physical disabilities and fine or gross motor difficulties, determine whether measuring and pouring are essential parts of that particular activity. If not, perhaps these students can concentrate more on the more central aspects of the activity and rely on peers for measuring and pouring liquids. If measuring and pouring liquid are important and spilling is a concern, have students pour inside a sink or in a larger container, and practice with smaller quantities first.

STRATEGIES FOR
ADAPTING SOCIAL STUDIES ACTIVITIES

Social studies activities can address motivational problems and negative reactions to independent textbook-based assignments for students who have problems with reading or writing. These activities might include producing plays, reenacting historical events, creating maps, preparing foods from other cultures and historical periods, making historical or cultural dioramas, and interacting with experts on cultural events or historical periods. Students can also engage in discussion or debate about current issues or historical events and interact with virtual museums. Finally, students can participate in field trips to museums or historical sites. Overall, social studies activities ordinarily may not involve such a wide range of different materials and equipment as activities in science, and therefore fewer overall specific adaptations may be considered. General recommendations are noted in the following section and are also found in Scruggs, Mastropieri, and Okolo (2008); Okolo, Englert, Bouck, Heutsche, and Wang (2011); Okolo, Bouck, Heutsche, Courtad, and Englert (2011); Okolo and Ferretti (2013); Scruggs et al. (2011); and Parker and Beck (2016).

SUPPLEMENT TEXTBOOK-BASED INSTRUCTION As suggested throughout this book, whole-class teaching devoted solely to textbooks and worksheets is not an optimal way of addressing the diverse needs of students. Instead, use concrete activities, multimedia presentations, student projects, and technological applications whenever possible. For a description of technology that can supplement textbooks in science and social studies, see the *Apps for Education* feature.

Because disability awareness is very much a social issue, plan lesson content in this area as a component of the social studies curriculum. Many significant historical characters either had disabilities themselves or were very concerned with promoting the rights of individuals with disabilities—for example, Alexander Graham Bell, Franklin Roosevelt, Dorothy Dix, and Julia Ward Howe (see, for example, the website of the Disability Social History Project, disabilityhistory.org).

MAKE ADAPTATIONS FOR SPECIFIC SOCIAL STUDIES ACTIVITIES

- When planning meals from other cultures or historical periods, consider whether any of your students have specific food allergies.

- Role-play and reenactment activities can be supplemented with video recordings of the events being role-played to enhance understanding. Keep in mind students' special needs when assigning roles; for example, in reenactments, plan or adapt appropriate roles for students with mobility impairments.

- In geography, relief maps may be helpful not only for students with low vision but also for other students who may need assistance in understanding the representative function of maps. Braille maps, raised globes, and illuminated globes are also available to assist students with visual impairments.

- Prepare students for visitors who come into the classroom to demonstrate, for example, instruments, clothing, lifestyles, and habits from different countries. Some students may need additional preparation in appropriate attending skills and appropriate questions to ask.

MAKE ADAPTATIONS FOR SPECIAL NEEDS FOR FIELD TRIPS Field trips can often allow students to obtain firsthand exposure to people and things that they may not be able to experience in the classroom. In addition to museums and zoos, field trips can include visits to historical sites, living farms, archeological sites, weather stations, observatories, and public parks, to name only a few possibilities. Many students with special needs may benefit at least as much as other students, particularly if they have had fewer relevant background experiences or when they can benefit particularly from the enhanced stimulus value and added concreteness of the experience. Planning and supervision can ensure the field trip is a positive experience.

- Call the facility in advance and inform the staff that you will be attending, and inform them of any special needs your students may have. Advance visitation and planning will help you provide the necessary supports for students' needs.

- Students with visual impairments may require modifications or adaptations in lighting, printed materials, video presentations, seating arrangements, and any visually presented information.

- Considerations for students with hearing impairments may include the amount of background noise, seating, distance from speaker, interpreters, rate of speaker presentation, effective visual aids, and multisensory experiences, depending on the level of the hearing disability.

- Students with cognitive or intellectual impairments may need preparation or on-site support of teachers, aides, or peers to promote understanding of the information being presented.

- Students with attentional disorders may need assistance focusing attention on relevant exhibits and efficiently sequencing their visit.

Additional guidelines for teachers to consider for field trips are given in Figure 15.9.

Science, Social Studies, and Transition Apps

Spatial organizers help make content more concrete and more familiar to students when studying science and social studies. Graphic organizers can be used in almost any content area. Organizers can be used to teach sequences of events and cause-and-effect relationships, to compare and contrast ideas or concepts, or to illustrate hierarchies. Organizers can be used as story webs during the brainstorming phase of writing papers. Graphic organizers can be developed as story maps that include specific details to facilitate comprehension and learning about historical figures, major events, and historical themes. Organizers can be used to develop hierarchies of important to least-important content in science and social studies. Graphic organizers can also be used to design study guides to accompany content-area textbooks.

Organizers can take many forms. *Inspiration* and *Kidspiration* software provide assistance in developing graphic organizers, webs, brainstorming, diagramming, outlining, and prewriting strategies. Both programs contain numerous templates that can be adapted to suit needs and also offer the flexibility to allow users to create custom-made templates and designs. Directions for developing organizers are fairly clear, and students who have some facility with computer use and various software programs typically experience little difficulty in developing organizers independently.

Both Inspiration and Kidspiration have extensive libraries of graphics that can be integrated within diagrams to help make the information even more concrete and meaningful to students. Libraries of content areas, such as animals, foods, shapes, or plants, organize colored graphics. Users can also import graphics of their own from personal photos or from the Internet into Inspiration documents. The technology also offers a wide range of fonts and colors that can be changed during production of an organizer. Various fonts and colors can be used to highlight specific organized details within a single graphic organizer. Both programs have features that enable users to switch from diagrams to outlines and vice versa very easily and are printable in either format. Kidspiration has the unique feature of adding sound to the program such that words entered into the organizers can be "read aloud" for students. Both also have features that allow the versions to be saved into text documents or have applets that can be used with *AlphaSmarts* and then combined with the full-scale programs on computers.

Inspiration is listed as being appropriate from grades 6 through 12, and Kidspiration is appropriate for K–5. However, both may be adaptable up or down in grade levels depending on the individual ability levels of your students. Sample organizers from each are provided. Visit inspiration.com for additional information. A 30-day free trial version is available from the website.

Apps have been developed to assist in learning both science and social studies content. The *Kahn Academy* contains video lessons and exercises in both science and social studies content. *Kid Science* apps (Selectsoft) include separate apps for nature, chemistry, biology, and physics content and experiments. *Solar Walk—3D Solar System model* (Vito Technology Inc.) provides an interactive environment for traveling through the solar system. *OWL Pellet Activities* (Owl Brand Discovery Kits; Carolina Biological Supply) contains specific activities related to exploring owl pellets, and in Virtual Owl Pellet (Kidwing .com), students explore dissecting the owl pellet virtually. Social studies apps cover interactive maps (*History: Maps of the World*, Seung-Bin Cho); timelines (*US History Timeline*, DaolSoft Co., Ltd.); and apps designed for history and natural history units, such as *US History* (Sequens), 28 free U.S. history apps (elearningindustry .com), and *Dinosaurs: iPad: American Museum of Natural History Collections* (American Museum of Natural History and Mosaic Legends, LLC), or specific events in history, such as the Civil War (*History 3D: Civil War*, MIMA Studios).

Apps are available to help prepare students for transitions, including for students graduating with an individualized education program (IEP) diploma or heading to college. *Career Explorer 4-H* (Move Creative, LLC) uses a gamelike format to explore career options, including potential salaries, education, and positive and negative attributes of jobs. *Quick Cues* (Fraser) presents listening skills activities, talking on the phone, and conversation tips. *Chore Pad HD* (Nannek LLC) presents chores that can be customized for school, home, or transitions, which can be viewed in daily or weekly lists. *Checkbook HD* (iBear LLC) is an e-checkbook that calculates balances. *Google Maps* (Google, Inc.) displays maps, directions, points of interest, transit routes, and real-time traffic updates that can assist navigating unfamiliar areas. Monster has several apps that assist with searching for jobs. Monster.com *Job Search* and Monster .com *Interviews* (Monster Worldwide) provide comprehensive job-searching techniques and interviewing suggestions.

- Set learning objectives before the trip and discuss them with your students.
- Preview the field trip with students, including the procedures that will be involved and the behaviors they will be expected to exhibit. Obtain handouts of the facility, and preview them with the class.
- Practice any difficult or unusual vocabulary that students will encounter on the field trip, to maximize comprehension.
- Discuss the behavioral objectives for the trip, and describe your behavior management plan.
- Assign peer partners, buddies, or helpers when appropriate.
- During the trip, encourage active participation of all students.
- Use familiar and descriptive language whenever possible. Summarize information from the field trip to the students as they participate, and ask them to summarize what they have done.
- When it is not possible to touch or manipulate exhibits, describe sounds, odors, shapes, colors, and textures as much as possible.
- Emphasize multisensory presentations or examples whenever possible.
- Record the field trip, using photographs, video, or audio recorders. Edit the recordings, and review them with the students after the field trip, emphasizing important objectives.
- Make a book of the field trip for the class, or create a book as a class activity, and review it with students.

Figure 15.9 Teacher Guidelines for Field Trips

When certain field trips seem impractical, consider "virtual field trips" (e.g., virtual-fieldtrips.org). These may be useful when the particular location is inaccessible to the class overall, such as visiting different countries or cities. Other video presentations can help provide the class with a realistic experience and help enforce concepts learned in class.

MyEdLab: **Self-Check 15.2**

MyEdLab: **Application Exercise 15.2: Activities-Oriented Approaches in Science**

Inquiry Learning in Science and Social Studies

Many advocates of science and social studies instruction strongly endorse inquiry and problem-solving approaches to teaching. Inquiry approaches involve the presentation of questions and problems to students with less direct guidance during the problem-solution stages, and such approaches can be a significant component of both activities-oriented and textbook-based learning. Inquiry approaches promote critical thinking skills in addition to increasing content knowledge. In a recent review of inquiry-based science teaching, Furtak, Seidel, Iverson, and Briggs (2012) found that inquiry learning was effective in promoting science learning but more effective when teacher directed rather than student directed. For many students with disabilities, teacher-led inquiry could be particularly helpful (Scruggs & Mastropieri, 2011).

STRATEGIES FOR

ADAPTING INQUIRY LEARNING ACTIVITIES

PROMOTE ACTIVE THINKING WITH INQUIRY AND DEBATE   Ferretti, MacArthur, and Okolo (2001) directed an 8-week, project-based unit in American westward expansion.

Fifth-grade students were formed into groups of learners with diverse skills and prior knowledge. In these groups, students collected information and analyzed primary and secondary sources to create multimedia presentations. All of the group activities involved oral reading of the evidence and group discussion. Students were taught about perspectives and asked to provide supported answers for questions such as, "What is bias in evidence?"; "How do you know a piece of evidence is biased?"; and "Why do historians have different opinions about things that happened in the past?" All students gained in content knowledge as well as in their understanding of historical inquiry.

MacArthur, Ferretti, and Okolo (2002) formed cooperative groups of students in inclusive sixth-grade social studies classes and asked them to represent the historical views of immigrant groups versus nativists (anti-immigration groups) in class debates. Students collected information on these topics and used this information in debates. Results revealed that students with and without disabilities and boys and girls participated equally in the debates, and all students gained similarly in tests of content knowledge. However, MacArthur et al. reported that at times, debates seemed more like arguments, and guidance and modeling were necessary to shape the level of debate (see also Okolo & Ferretti, 2013).

PROMOTE REASONING WITH GUIDED QUESTIONING   Students with disabilities comprehend more and understand better when they actively reason through new information (e.g., Sullivan, Mastropieri, & Scruggs, 1995). For example, in a lesson about penguins, ask students to explain—rather than simply tell them—the fact that some penguins carry their eggs on top of their feet. If they cannot explain immediately, prompt them with directed questions, such as "Where do penguins live?"; "What is it like there?"; and "Why would that explain why penguins carry their eggs on top of their feet?"

In this case, students can be prompted to use information from their prior knowledge. In other cases ("Why do stars twinkle?"), additional relevant information may need to be provided.

Guided questioning can promote thinking in science classes containing students with cognitive or intellectual disabilities, as seen in this example of a discussion of the effects of capillary action when white flowers were placed in colored water:

> TEACHER: What do you think happened? I have a flower in blue water and a flower in green water, a white flower, right? How did I get the colors there?
>
> KEN: …Oh, you watered it with food coloring.
>
> TEACHER: But I didn't put any up here [the flower], did I?
>
> KEN: You put it in the dirt.
>
> TEACHER: But there's no dirt.
>
> KEN: Oh.
>
> TEACHER: How did it get from there to here?
>
> JIMMY: It went all the way up to here.
>
> TEACHER: Went all the way through water? The what, Mary?
>
> MARY: A stem.
>
> TEACHER: The stem. It went all the way through the stem—you're right.
> (Scruggs & Mastropieri, 1995b, p. 264)

In social studies subjects, teachers can describe the nature and characteristics of harbors and ask students why it makes sense that many cities are located on or near natural harbors. Or, describe the "fall line" where rivers near the coast are still navigable but move swiftly enough to power industry. Then, show students a physical map and ask them to predict where major cities probably would be located. They can then test their predictions on a political map. See Scruggs et al. (2011) for other suggestions.

ADAPT INSTRUCTION FOR DEVELOPMENTAL DIFFERENCES   Some students, especially those with intellectual disabilities, may have more difficulty with inductive reasoning tasks (Caffrey & Fuchs, 2007). For example, when a fourth grader with intellectual disabilities was questioned about the nature of air, he said it is cold, windy, and found outdoors (Scruggs, Mastropieri, & Wolfe, 1995, p. 228), a view commonly held by preschoolers (Driver, Asoko,

Leach, Mortimer, & Scott, 1994). Consider these possible differences in "preconceptions" or prior understandings when planning inquiry-oriented instruction, and provide additional instruction when needed.

Whereas many normally achieving students can answer higher-level questions with only subtle coaching, students with disabilities may require extensive levels of coaching to draw the same inference or to construct or discover scientific principles (e.g., buoyancy or pendulum movement; Scruggs & Mastropieri, 2007). However, more structured coaching can lead students to draw relevant inferences. For example, show students a number of pendulums with different weights attached, and ask them if they swing at different rates (they do not). Then show students a number of pendulums of different length, and ask them the same question (the longer pendulums swing more slowly). Then ask them to construct a general rule. Be sure all students have enough time to construct answers for themselves.

Promote deductive reasoning as well as inductive reasoning in students with special needs (see Mastropieri, Scruggs, Boon, & Carter, 2001). For example, rather than asking students to draw inductive conclusions about pendulum motion, directly provide the "rule" about pendulum motion (e.g., "The longer the string, the slower the swing"). Next, demonstrate different pendulums, and ask students to make predictions ("Which one do you think will swing faster, the short one or the long one?"). Finally, provide more divergent examples to further promote generalized knowledge of the concept ("What can I do to the bob of the pendulum [point to the bob] to make it run faster?").

Although inductive thinking activities have been widely promoted in education for many years, deductive thinking activities also are important, and in some cases, they may provide more realistic thinking activities for some students with special learning needs.

MyEdLab: **Self-Check 15.3**

MyEdLab: **Application Exercise 15.3: Inquiry Learning in Science**

Transitions

Transitions are natural passages in life that happen continually as we move to new schools, new jobs, and join new recreational organizations. Students with special needs typically have more difficulties than do students without disabilities in adjusting to new transitions. Planning for those transitions by making instructional accommodations can promote smoother and more successful transitions for students with disabilities (Morgan & Riesen, 2016). Planning, designing, and adapting appropriate programs for students with disabilities will allow many individuals to have successful careers and become self-sufficient.

PLANNING FOR TRANSITION

WHAT DOES TRANSITION MEAN? **Transition** is the process of planning for changes throughout a student's life. Most frequently, transition is referred to as the planning for a student's life after high school; however, planning for changes throughout life is a more accurate definition (Scanlon, 2011). **Transition programs** help prepare students for changes they will undertake throughout their school years and beyond. Examples of transitions can include changing grade levels or moving from kindergarten to elementary school to middle school to high school to college or vocational training; changing placement from special education to general education settings; obtaining a job; joining recreational activities; or moving to new living arrangements or to a new community (Clark & Patton, 2006).

Preparing students for transitions after high school may include career and technical education and directions for managing employment, supported living, or independent living arrangements.

Transitions, although exciting and challenging, can be traumatic events. Planning for transitions and preparing students with disabilities for those transitions can eliminate some of the difficult aspects of adjustment.

The Individuals with Disabilities Education Act (IDEA) defines transition services as coordinating services for students that promote the change from school to postschool. This means IDEA emphasizes only planning for transitions from high school to vocational education, postsecondary education, adult services, independent living, and community participation (Madaus, Banerjee, & Merchant, 2011). The coordination of transition services is based on student preferences, interests, and abilities and includes instruction, experiences in the community, and development of employment, postsecondary, daily living, and vocational objectives. However, it has been found that planning for transitions at all ages promotes the social and emotional well-being of students with disabilities (Bakken & Obiokor, 2008).

Planning for transitions helps prepare students for the expected changes that take place in their lives. The amount of planning for transitions and adaptations necessary varies depending on the type of transition and the severity level of disability. Planning includes involving all individuals who will be affected by the transition, including the student, parents, all teachers, transition coordinators, specialists, community representatives, employers, and support personnel (Griffin, Taylor, Urbano, & Hodapp, 2014). The Office of Special Education and Rehabilitative Services published a resource guide for transition planning which may be beneficial for students, teachers, schools and parents (U.S. Department Education, Office of Special Education and Rehabilitative Services, 2017).

Effective transition planning begins early, includes everyone who may be involved, provides an initial timeline, and involves continuous evaluation.

STRATEGIES FOR
PROMOTING TRANSITIONS

MAKE PREPARATIONS WITH STUDENTS TO PLAN FOR TRANSITIONS Many students have a difficult time going to school from home for the first time. Many young children with disabilities may not have been exposed to many different situations and people. It can also be frightening to move to a new school, teachers, and peers. The new school may be farther from home, which means leaving home earlier in the morning, riding a new school bus, and having a longer school day. Students may become more tired, frightened, and anxious until they feel accepted in the new environment. Preparatory actions can be undertaken to ease transitions where everything is so different; otherwise, students with disabilities may experience difficulties transitioning to the new site. Such actions include the following:

- Establishing a transition timeline
- Preparing all individuals involved
- Establishing communication procedures
- Visiting the new school with the student
- Planning activities to simulate the new environment to prepare the student
- Reviewing new procedures and explaining expectations
- Preparing new teachers and students for the new student
- Scheduling follow-up evaluation times

For example, Carter, Clark, Cushing, and Kennedy (2005) described a program for smoothing transitions from elementary to middle school for students with severe disabilities. They emphasized the importance of early planning and collaboration across schools, and recommended encouraging family involvement; addressing organizational issues such as lockers, books, schedules, assignments, and restrooms; developing programs of peer support that extend to unstructured times such as lunch and in the hallways; promoting school involvement; and fostering more independence through, for example, self-management strategies.

PLAN TRANSITIONS TO ADULTHOOD Planning transitions for adulthood is vitally important for students with disabilities. All students with disabilities who have IEPs are required to have individual transition plans (ITPs) when they reach the age of 14. Planning and instruction include teaching students self-advocacy and self-determination skills; planning for future education, such as college or other postsecondary training; planning for future employment opportunities; and preparing students for independent living situations (Morgan & Riesen, 2016).

Ricardo

Ricardo, an 18-year-old with learning disabilities, is preparing to move to the local university when the next fall semester begins. Ricardo has received special education services for his learning disabilities since third grade. He has particular difficulties with basic literacy tasks, especially reading and writing activities, which tend to require a great deal of time to complete. He has never lived away from home, and his parents have always been very supportive of anything he has tried to do. However, his parents have also had a tendency to help him with everything, including organizing his schoolwork and his homework schedule.

QUESTIONS FOR REFLECTION

1. How can you help prepare Ricardo for the transition to college, in all the areas of anticipated changes?
2. How can you help Ricardo develop self-advocacy and self-determination skills?
3. How can you prepare him for the changes from IDEA to the Americans with Disabilities Act (ADA) and describe what those changes will mean in terms of the responsibilities that he will have to assume?
4. What is a reasonable timeline for meeting Ricardo's transition needs?

PROMOTE SELF-ADVOCACY AND SELF-DETERMINATION Many students with special needs are overly dependent on others and are passive with respect to decision making. Although making decisions is difficult, students with disabilities will eventually be required to participate more actively in that process for themselves. Therefore, it is vital that opportunities, instruction, and practice in becoming more independent and in decision making are a part of a student's curriculum. Thus, training in **self-advocacy** and **self-determination** skills is a must (Cuenca-Sanchez, Mastropieri, Scruggs, & Kidd, 2012; Wehmeyer et al., 2012). This means that students may need assistance, instruction, and practice in learning how to become knowledgeable about themselves with respect to learning strengths, needs, preferences, interests, and rights and responsibilities. This knowledge can be used to request accommodations that promote more success in jobs, independent living, and postsecondary education. Sample self-advocacy skills include awareness of legal rights, requesting accommodations, requesting assistance from doctors and Social Security offices, having job-related social skills, planning for the future and making informed choices, and seeking assistance whenever needed.

Students with strong self-determination skills generally have better postschool outcomes. Nevertheless, self-determination skills are not always taught to students with disabilities, and in fact, overprotection in some cases by teachers, advocates, and parents may negatively affect the autonomy of students with disabilities. To be successful and independent in their lives after formal schooling, students need to have knowledge about their learning strengths and needs, to articulate those abilities and needs, and to participate actively in the IEP process. Konrad and Test (2007) successfully taught students with high-incidence disabilities how to write paragraphs related to their IEPs. Test, Fowler, Wood, Brewer, and Eddy (2005) developed a conceptual framework for self-advocacy, which included four components:

1. Knowledge of self (e.g., strengths, support needs, goals)
2. Knowledge of rights (e.g., personal rights, educational rights, steps to advocate for change)
3. Communication (e.g., assertiveness, negotiation, compromise)
4. Leadership (e.g., knowledge of group's rights, political action)

All of these components contribute to an overall sense of self-advocacy.

TEACH STRATEGIES FOR TRANSITIONS The I PLAN self-advocacy strategy includes several steps to assist students in acquiring skills for transition (Test & Neale, 2004; Van Reusen, Bos, Schumaker, & Deshler, 1994). Students evaluate and plan for transition to areas such as independent living, consumer skills, citizenship skills, employment skills, family-living skills, and recreational and leisure skills. Students describe their strengths, areas to improve, and preferred accommodations; share; actively listen and discuss; and identify goals.

The analysis also includes identifying strengths, such as math computation and social skills, and needs, such as skills in reading, reading comprehension, and written expression. Specific goals are identified, such as independent living and career employment goals. Choices for student learning preferences are also included on the inventory. For example, student preferences for certain activities and listings of helpful materials and testing procedures are identified. Finally, accommodations that are necessary to help students succeed are listed. After the inventory is completed, students are taught to use communication skills more effectively by using the **PLAN** and **SHARE** strategy prompts (Test & Neale, 2004):

Plan

Provide the inventory to teachers.

Listen and respond to the comments.

Ask relevant questions.

Name your goals.

Share

Sit up straight.

Have a nice tone of voice.

Activate your thinking.

Relax and remain calm.

Engage in eye contact. (Van Reusen et al., 1994)

TEACH ASSERTIVENESS SKILLS Many students require explicit social skills instruction in assertiveness, such as requesting assistance, asking for clarification, and negotiating changes.

Provide instruction and role-play situations during which students can practice developing and refining these skills in a safe environment. Finally, provide opportunities to practice generalizing the skills in a variety of situations with a number of different adults. During high school, teachers assume major responsibilities for ensuring that students with disabilities are given a free and appropriate education (FAPE) as required by IDEA. Remember that teachers are part of the IEP team and are legally bound to implement IEP objectives and classroom modifications. However, once students leave high schools and enroll in college, they are no longer covered by IDEA. They do have rights and responsibilities as identified in the Americans with Disabilities Act (ADA) and Section 504 of the Rehabilitation Act. Students, however, must meet any new classification criteria established at their respective institutions. Once student services are identified, usually with the assistance of personnel at a dean of students office, accommodations such as extended testing times, test administrations in a distraction-free environment, and provision of notes or copies of slide materials may be made available. However, according to ADA, students have to be more assertive and identify themselves as having disabilities to their professors before they are guaranteed modifications to their educational programs (Madaus et al., 2011). Then they need to notify professors of their learning needs. One method devised by some college students with disabilities is to compose a brief statement containing learning strengths and needs. Figure 15.10 contains a sample letter written by a college student, Toni, who has learning disabilities. Toni distributes the letter to all of her professors each semester during the first week of classes and then meets individually with them during the next week to discuss any follow-up questions or concerns.

Consider assisting students with disabilities while they are enrolled in middle and high school in developing statements similar to the one used by Toni. This activity familiarizes students with their learning needs, helps them communicate these needs whenever necessary, and provides them with practice for doing this when they no longer have the protective services of IDEA and must be independent.

PROMOTE TRANSITIONS WITH ASSESSMENT Assessment for transition consists of collecting information on students from all available sources (Sitlington, Neubert, & Clark, 2010). This includes the current IEPs, the school permanent records, school guidance counselors, formal and informal interviews with students and their families, and the answers to formal and informal transition-planning and **occupational surveys**. The collected information is compiled and evaluated by members of the transition team, who then make recommendations for the ITP.

Dear Professor:

I am Toni, a student enrolled in your class this semester. I have a learning disability. I learn best by seeing and hearing information rather than by reading. I can sit through lectures and not take any notes and do fairly well on exams. When I sit in lectures and try to take notes at the same time I usually do poorly on exams. I do not seem to be able to take notes and listen at the same time very well at all. When I have had the opportunity to have my textbooks provided on audio recordings I can perform even better.

I have also noticed that I have a very keen sense of hearing but have the inability to filter out unwanted noises. This causes a problem for me in some lectures. To cope with this I usually sit near the front of the room so I can see the lecturer's face and try to lip read. Lecture outlines are also very helpful for me to be able to keep up with the information being presented in class. I record all of my lectures so that I am able to listen more carefully later on when studying for exams. I use the recordings and the lecture outlines as review. At that time I usually insert additional important points into the outline to help with studying and remembering important information.

I also do better on exams if I can take them in a private, very quiet room. I know that the Dean of Students Office has testing facilities that can be used to take my exams, and I would prefer to be able to take all of my exams for this class there.

I work very hard in school and am willing to try to work as hard as possible in your class. I am looking forward to learning in your class this semester. I can be reached by phone or by e-mail, if you would like to communicate further on this issue.

Sincerely,

Toni Sanchez

Phone: 797-555-7346
E-mail: *toni@gmu.edu*

Figure 15.10 Self-Advocacy Letter to a College Professor from Toni, a Student with Learning Disabilities

One transition survey addresses the domains of instruction required by IDEA, including community experiences, employment, and postschool goals. The *Transition Planning Inventory–2nd Edition* (TPI-2, Pro-Ed) contains 57 transition planning statements organized around the four IDEA domains on several basic forms: the student interest forms, the home form, the school form, the profile and further assessment recommendations form, and a parent preferences and interest form. Raters indicate their level of agreement on a 5-point scale from strongly disagree to strongly agree with statements relevant to transition, such as knowing how to get a job, manage money, and set goals.

Occupational surveys are also commercially available. For example, the *Occupational Aptitude Survey and Interest Schedule* (OASIS-3; Parker, 2002) assesses whether students like, dislike, or have neutral feelings toward occupations and job activities using a pool of 240 items ranging across 12 vocational domains: artistic, scientific, nature, protective, mechanical, industrial, business detail, selling, accommodating, humanitarian, leading-influencing, and physical performing. Findings from this survey help develop a more comprehensive transition plan in the postsecondary vocational and educational areas.

IMPLEMENT TRANSITION CURRICULUM Commercially prepared curriculum resources are available that provide examples of life skills and **life-centered career objectives** and materials (Cronin, Patton, & Wood, 2007). Most curricula are designed around basic competencies that are subdivided according to the needs of targeted students. One curriculum, "Life Centered Career Education" (Council for Exceptional Children), for example, contains the following major areas: Daily Living Skills, Personal-Social Skills, and Occupational Guidance and

Preparation. Each area is then subdivided into more specific level competencies and objectives that also contain teaching suggestions to develop skills for successful living in maintaining a home and accepting responsibility for community living. Other suggestions for integrating a life skills curriculum within the general curriculum are provided by Cronin et al. (2007).

STRATEGIES FOR
TRANSITIONING FOR THE FUTURE

PLAN FOR GRADUATION   In many states, more demanding coursework (in, for example, algebra, geometry, or foreign languages) and competency exams such as Common Core State Standards are being required for graduation. At the same time, some of the more basic and career-oriented courses are being phased out in favor of more academically demanding courses. Some students with disabilities may find it extremely difficult, because of their disabilities, to pass one or more of these classes, even if modifications are made (Lindstrom, 2011). If a student's apparent inability to pass one or more particularly demanding courses appears to stand in the way of graduation, determine whether a substitute course could be included on the student's IEP that would be accepted toward the diploma.

States have variable policies toward awarding diplomas. Some states award what is known as differentiated or tiered diplomas, which may include certificates of attendance, standard diplomas, or advanced diplomas (Johnson, Stout, & Thurlow, 2009; "Rethinking the High School Diploma," 2015). For example, students meeting all requirements and who pass the state high-stakes tests or Common Core exams can be awarded an appropriate diploma; students who meet all requirements except passing the state high-stakes test could be awarded a general diploma. For individuals who have not been able to meet all the requirements for a standard diploma, an attendance certificate can be awarded for those who nonetheless have stayed in school and satisfactorily met attendance requirements throughout their school career. For students who have gone significantly beyond graduation requirements, advanced diplomas can be awarded to acknowledge this level of achievement. Any differentiated or tiered diploma may be associated with specific course and competency requirements. In your own school, find out what factors determine the type of diploma individual students will receive and how students' postsecondary futures (employment, vocational training, college entrance) will be affected by the type of diploma received.

In the attempt to ensure uniformly high standards, other states have begun to eliminate differentiated diplomas in favor of a single, more advanced diploma. Consultation with career counselors, vocational schools, parents, and community resources can help provide relevant information on how to best meet the needs of students with disabilities under these circumstances. Because IDEA allows students with disabilities to continue to attend school until age 22, some students with disabilities may be able to meet the higher requirements with additional years of schooling.

PLAN FOR FUTURE EDUCATION   Applying for colleges is an arduous task for all students but may be particularly overwhelming for students with disabilities. Provide additional assistance to those students to encourage them to pursue further education. Many resources are available commercially to help students learn more about colleges' and universities' programs and their services for students with disabilities. The Learning Disabilities Association of America provides one such listing. Another helpful resource is *The Complete Learning Disabilities Directory* (Grey House Publishing, Millerton, New York) and its online database, which contains information on products, resources, books, and services that are available to help individuals with learning disabilities. For example, names, addresses, and phone numbers are provided for government agencies and professional organizations, as well as listings of books and other materials for individuals with disabilities and their parents. Interested students and parents should contact their state chapter of the Council for Exceptional Children for additional information on services provided within their region at the higher education level. These and other resource guides may also be available at your local library or local bookstore.

Provide information on the standards necessary for admission to the college that students wish to attend. For example, some colleges require courses in foreign languages; others require specific units (high school credits) in math, science, and English; and most require submission of Scholastic Assessment Test (SAT) or American College Testing (ACT) scores with the completed applications by prespecified dates. This information can help students select appropriate

MyEdLab:
Video Example 15.3.
In this video, a coordinator for a vocational training program demonstrates the work skills that students with a range of disabilities are learning.

courses in high school. Additionally, they can prepare for taking the SAT or ACT by studying with pamphlets, commercially available books, and computer programs or by enrolling in classes designed to improve performance on the tests. SAT (collegeboard.org) and ACT (act.org) both offer practice materials on their websites. Some students may qualify for adapted testing procedures on the SAT or ACT, such as extended time or a larger-print format. Seek assistance from your local high school counselor to determine whether or not students qualify for testing adaptations, and help them obtain and submit the appropriate application forms.

Colleges have websites and application forms that can be submitted electronically. Provide opportunities for students to access this information so that they will be able to peruse the information independently. They can also practice completing their application forms prior to submission. Some universities offer postsecondary experiences for students with intellectual disabilities (e.g., the Mason LIFE program at George Mason University, masonlife.gmu.edu).

PLAN FOR FUTURE EMPLOYMENT OPPORTUNITIES   Planning for future employment can include internships, adult education, trade and technical schools, competitive employment, supported employment, sheltered workshops, and methods for searching for employment (Rojewski & Gregg, 2011). Provide opportunities to discuss future job options. Relate your class content to employment options and opportunities, and arrange for career and technical education when appropriate (Schloss & Gunter, 2011). Invite professionals from the community to discuss how their educational backgrounds assisted them in their vocations. Discuss what types of educational backgrounds are required for various professions. Plan field trips to community-based organizations so students can see firsthand the types of employment opportunities that are available. Use the expertise of your school guidance counselors to assist in disseminating job-related information. Whenever possible, integrate relevant job-related information within your regular curriculum. Use published curriculum materials for assessing and teaching employment-related skills.

PLAN FOR INDEPENDENT LIVING SITUATIONS   Many students require information on preparing for future independent living situations. One important issue is selecting, managing, and maintaining a home. Questions to consider include residential options—where to live, with whom, and with what degree of support (e.g., independent, residential group home, supported living situation, semi-independent living).

Provide information on the types of resources that will be required to go with each type of living arrangement. For example, if students select an independent living arrangement as their first choice, then they need to realize what financial resources will be necessary to accomplish this goal. Many teachers have included units on planning for independent living within their regular curriculum and have reported that students have enjoyed the opportunities to gain familiarity with what is required to own a car and live in an apartment. Preparing budgets allows students to examine expenses they will incur and help them examine employment opportunities that will enable them to realize their goals. Efforts to increase awareness of future needs helps students to be better planners and thus more successful later in life.

Other important living skills include caring for personal needs, getting around in the community, buying and preparing food, buying and maintaining clothing, engaging in community and civic activities, and selecting meaningful recreation and leisure activities (Scanlon, Patton, & Raskind, 2011). Individuals preparing for independent living also need to know about credit and how it can be used effectively.

Finally, vocational, personal, and social skills are important in independent living. Information provided by Cronin et al. (2007) can be helpful in planning and implementing programs to facilitate independent living, in school settings and beyond. It is important to note that supports for students with disabilities and other special needs do not need to stop at the end of schooling; all individuals should receive the needed preparation and necessary support to ensure quality and fulfillment in all of life's activities.

MyEdLab: Self-Check 15.4

MyEdLab: Application Exercise 15.4: Promote Self-Advocacy

15 Summary

- Much learning in science and social studies takes place in the context of textbook learning. Specific strategies can be employed to differentiate instruction for all in these content areas.

  — Content-enhancement devices are means for increasing recall and comprehension of content information and include the use of graphic organizers, study guides, diagrams, visual-spatial displays, and mnemonics.

  — Familiarization with text organization and structure can help students understand text content. Students can be taught to incorporate analysis of text structure into their study strategies. Highlighting, outlining, and study guides are also helpful.

  — Textbooks can be adapted for students with reading problems with such methods as audio-recorded texts, braille or enlarged-print versions, simplified texts, or modified presentations.

  — Before assigned readings, students can be familiarized with new vocabulary and provided with advance organizers such as visual-spatial displays, timelines, or concept maps. After assigned readings, students can be provided with reviews and summaries of the readings, practice with peers, and extra help sessions.

- Activities-oriented instruction can be helpful for students who do not learn as well from reading textbooks or who benefit from the enhanced concreteness and meaningfulness afforded by such instruction.

  — Many adaptations are available for accommodating special needs in such science activity areas as balancing and weighing, activities with plants and animals, anatomy, microscope activities, weather, rocks and minerals, and activities involving sound and light. These adaptations address specific need areas and also can enhance comprehension of the associated concepts.

  — Adaptations can also be incorporated into social studies areas, including role-play, simulation activities, and field trips.

- Inquiry-oriented approaches to science and social studies, found in both textbook and activities approaches, can also be adapted for students with special needs. These adaptations include using hands-on materials, implementing carefully structured questioning, redirecting attention, and reinforcing divergent, independent thinking.

- Transition planning is critical for students with disabilities. Prepare students of all ages for transitions, including transitions from home to preschool, to new schools, to new teachers, and, most important, to life after high school. Involve students, parents, teachers, counselors, transition coordinators, and community-based personnel as members of the transition team. All students with IEPs must have individual transition plans by the age of 14.

  — Students with disabilities may require instruction in self-advocacy and self-determination skills to provide them with skills to be more successful during and after high school. Provide ample practice in safe environments for the development of these skills.

  — Help prepare students for the appropriate high school graduation requirements necessary for their transition plans. Prepare students for life after high school by using appropriate transition assessment measures, carefully evaluating the results, and designing and implementing life skills programs.

  — Provide educational opportunities that prepare students with disabilities for future education, jobs, and independent or supported living arrangements.

PROFESSIONAL STANDARDS LINK:
Science, Social Studies, and Transitions

Information in this chapter links most directly to:

- CEC Standards: 1 (Learner Development and Individual Learning Differences), 2 (Learning Environments), 3 (Curricular Content Knowledge), 4 (Assessment), 5 (Instructional Planning and Strategies), 6 (Professional Learning and Ethical Practices), 7 (Collaboration)

- INTASC Standards: 2 (Learning Differences), 3 (Learning Environments), 4 (Content Knowledge), 5 (Application of Content), 7 (Planning for Instruction), 8 (Instructional Strategies)

SCIENCE AND SOCIAL STUDIES

If students are having difficulty learning from textbooks, have you tried the following? If not, see the pages listed here.

STRATEGIES FOR EFFECTIVE TEACHING IN SCIENCE AND SOCIAL STUDIES

STRATEGIES FOR PROMOTING INDEPENDENT LEARNING FROM TEXTBOOKS

STRATEGIES FOR ADAPTING TEXTBOOK MATERIALS

STRATEGIES FOR ADAPTING SCIENCE ACTIVITIES

STRATEGIES FOR ADAPTING LIFE SCIENCE ACTIVITIES

STRATEGIES FOR ADAPTING EARTH SCIENCE ACTIVITIES

STRATEGIES FOR ADAPTING PHYSICAL SCIENCE ACTIVITIES

STRATEGIES FOR ADAPTING SOCIAL STUDIES ACTIVITIES

STRATEGIES FOR ADAPTING INQUIRY LEARNING ACTIVITIES

TRANSITIONS

If you are promoting transitions, have you considered the following? If not, see the pages listed here.

STRATEGIES FOR PROMOTING TRANSITIONS

STRATEGIES FOR TRANSITIONING FOR THE FUTURE

Chapter 1

Alaska Statutes, Title 14, Chapter 30 (1971).

Andrews, J. F., Shaw, P. C., & Lomas, G. (2011). Deaf and hard of hearing students. In J. M. Kauffman & D. P. Hallahan (Eds.), *Handbook of special education* (pp. 233–246). New York, NY: Routledge.

Assistance to States for the Education of Children with Disabilities and Preschool Grants for Children with Disabilities; Final Rule, 34 C.F.R., § 300–301 (2006).

Beattie v. Board of Education of City of Antigo, 172 N.W. 153, 154 (1919).

Blankenship, C. (1981). *Mainstreaming students with learning and behavior problems.* Orlando, FL: Harcourt School.

Board of Education v. Rowley, 458 U.S. 176 (1982).

Brown v. Board of Education, 347 U.S. 483 (1954).

Chrismer, S., Hodge, S., & Saintil, D. (Eds.). (2006). Assessing NCLB: Perspectives and prescriptions. *Harvard Educational Review, 76,* 457–460.

Code of Virginia, § 22.275.3 (1973).

Cook, B. G., Tankersley, M., Cook, L., & Landrum, T. J. (2000). Teachers' attitudes toward their included students with disabilities. *Exceptional Children, 67,* 115–135.

Council for Exceptional Children (2002). No Child Left Behind has major implications for special education. *CEC Today, 9*(4), 4.

Crockett, J. (2011). Conceptual models for leading and administrating special education. In J. M. Kauffman & D. P. Hallahan (Eds.), *Handbook of special education* (pp. 351–362). New York, NY: Routledge.

Cullen, J. P., Gregory, J. P., & Noto, L. A. (2010, February). *The Teacher Attitudes Toward Inclusion Scale (TATIS): Technical report.* Paper presented at the Annual Meeting of the Eastern Educational Research Association, Savannah, GA. (ERIC Document Reproduction Service No. ED509930)

Davis, G. A., & Rimm, S. B. (2011). *Education of the gifted and talented* (6th ed.). Boston, MA: Allyn & Bacon.

deBettencourt, L. U. (2002). Understanding the differences between IDEA and Section 504. *Teaching Exceptional Children, 34*(3), 16–23.

Dettmer, P., Knackendoffel, A. P., & Thurston, L. P. (2013). *Consultation, collaboration, and teamwork for students with special needs* (7th ed.). Boston, MA: Allyn & Bacon.

Diana v. State Board of Education, Civ. No. C-70-37 RFP (N.D. Cal. 1970, 1973).

Downing, J. A. (2004). Related services for students with disabilities: Introduction to the special issue. *Intervention in School and Clinic, 39,* 195–208.

Educational Testing Service. (2002). *Special education: Core knowledge study guide.* Princeton, NJ: Author.

Frieman, B. B. (2001). *What teachers need to know about children at-risk.* New York, NY: Allyn & Bacon.

Fuchs, D., & Fuchs, L. S. (1994). Inclusive schools movement and the radicalization of special education reform. *Exceptional Children, 60,* 294–309.

Gollnick, D. M., & Chinn, P. C. (2013). *Multicultural education in a pluralistic society* (9th ed.). Boston, MA: Allyn & Bacon.

Honig v. Doe, 484 U.S. 305 S.Ct. 592, 98 L.Ed.2d 686, 43 Ed. Law Rep. 857 (1988).

Huefner, D. S. (2015). Placements for special education students: The promise and the peril. In B. Bateman, J. W. Lloyd, & M. Tankersley (Eds.), *Enduring issues in special education: Personal perspectives* (pp. 215–230). New York, NY: Routledge.

Individuals with Disabilities Education Improvement Act of 2004, Pub. L. No. 108-446, 20 U.S.C. §1400 *et seq.* (2004).

Johnson, T. P. (1986). *The principal's guide to the educational rights of handicapped students.* Reston, VA: National Association of Secondary School Principals.

Kauffman, J. M., Nelson, C. M., Simpson, R. L., & Mock, D. R. (2011). Contemporary issues. In J. M. Kauffman & D. P. Hallahan (Eds.), *Handbook of special education* (pp. 15–26). New York, NY: Routledge.

Larry P. v. Riles, 343 F. Supp. 1306 (N. D. Cal. 1972), *aff'd* 502 F.2d 963 (9th Cir. 1974), *further action* 495 F. Supp. 926 (N. D. Cal. 1979), *aff'd* 793 F. 2d 969 (9th Cir. 1984).

Lazarus, D., Thurlow, M., Lail, K., & Christensen, L. (2009). A longitudinal analysis of state accommodation policies. *Journal of Special Education, 43,* 67–80.

Lipsky, D. K., & Gartner, A. (1997). *Inclusion and school reform: Transforming America's classrooms.* Baltimore, MD: Paul H. Brookes.

Lipsky, D. K., & Gartner, A. (2008). *Inclusion: A service, not a place.* Port Chester, NY: Dude.

Majoko, T. (2016). Inclusion of children with autism spectrum disorders: Listening to and hearing voices from the grassroots. *Journal of Autism and Developmental Disorders, 46,* 1429–1440.

Mandlawitz, M. (2006). *What every teacher should know about IDEA 2004.* Boston, MA: Pearson.

Mills v. Board of Education, 348 F. Supp. 866 (D.D.C. 1972).

Murdick, N. L., Gartin, B. C., & Crabtree, T. L. (2014). *Special education law* (3rd ed.). Boston, MA: Pearson.

National Center for Technology Innovation (2011). Students with disabilities in charter schools. Arlington, VA: LD OnLine. Retrieved from http://www.ldonline.org/article/43436? theme=print).

National Governors Association Center for Best Practices, Council of Chief State School Officers. (2016). *Common Core State Standards initiative.* Washington, DC: Author. Retrieved from http://www.corestandards.org/

National School Boards Association. (2016). *Every Student Succeeds Act (ESSA).* Alexandria, VA: Author. Retrieved from https://www.nsba.org/advocacy/federal-legislative-priorities/every-student-succeeds-act-essa

Nevada Revised Statutes, § 39.050 (1963).

Oberti v. Board of Education of the Borough of Clementon School District, 995 F. 2d 1204 (3rd Cir. 1993).

Palmer, D. S., Fuller, K., Arora, T., & Nelson, M. (2001). Taking sides: Parent views on inclusion for their children with severe disabilities. *Exceptional Children, 67,* 467–484.

Pennsylvania Association for Retarded Children v. Commonwealth of Pennsylvania (PARC), 334 F. Supp. 1257 (E.D. Pa. 1972).

Rothstein, L. F., & Johnson, S. F. (2014). *Special education law* (5th ed.). Thousand Oaks, CA: Sage.

Rozalski, M., Miller, J., & Stewart, A. (2011). Least restrictive environment. In J. M. Kauffman & D. P. Hallahan (Eds.), *Handbook of special education* (pp. 107–120). New York, NY: Routledge.

Russell, C. L. (2008). How are your person-first skills? A self-assessment. *Teaching Exceptional Children, 40*(5), 40–43.

Scruggs, T. E. (2012). Differential facilitation of learning outcomes: What does it tell us about learning disabilities and instructional programming? *International Journal for Research in Learning Disabilities, 1*, 4–20.

Scruggs, T. E., Leins, P., & Mastropieri, M. A. (2011, April). *Teacher attitudes towards inclusion: A synthesis of survey, comparative, and qualitative research, 1958–2010.* Paper presented at the annual meeting of the Council for Exceptional Children, Washington, DC.

Scruggs, T. E., & Mastropieri, M. A. (1996). Teacher perceptions of mainstreaming/inclusion, 1958–1995: A research synthesis. *Exceptional Children, 63*, 59–74.

Siperstein, G., Parker, R., Norns Bardon, J., & Widerman, K. (2007). A national study of youth attitudes toward the inclusion of students with intellectual disabilities. *Exceptional Children, 73*, 435–455.

Smith, T. E. C. (2002). Section 504: What teachers need to know. *Intervention in School and Clinic, 37*, 259–266.

Staples, K., & Diliberto, J. (2010). Guidelines for successful parental involvement. *Teaching Exceptional Children, 42*(6), 58–63.

Tomlinson, C. A. (2014). *The differentiated classroom: Responding to the needs of all learners* (2nd ed.). Alexandria, VA: ASCD.

U.S. Department of Education. (2006). *Carl D. Perkins Career and Technical Education Act of 2006: Reauthorization of Perkins.* Washington, DC: Author. Retrieved from http://www.ed.gov/policy/sectech/leg/perkins/index.html

U.S. Department of Education, Office of Special Education and Rehabilitative Services. (2006). *Assistance to states for the education of children with disabilities and preschool grants for children with disabilities.* Final Regulations, 71 Fed. Reg. 46540 (30 C.F.R. Parts 300 and 301). Washington, DC: Author.

Watson v. City of Cambridge, 32 N.E. 864 (1893).

Will, M. (1986). Educating students with learning problems: A shared responsibility. *Exceptional Children, 52,* 411–415.

Wright, P. W. D., & Wright, P. D. (2005). *Wright's law IDEA 2004: Parts A & B.* Hartfield, VA: Harbor House Law Press.

Wright, P. W. D., & Wright, P. D. (2007). *Wrightslaw: Special education law* (2nd ed.). Hartfield, VA: Harbor House Law Press.

Wright, P. W. D., Wright, P. D., & Heath, S. W. (2004). *Wright's law: No child left behind.* Hartfield, VA: Harbor House Law Press.

Yell, M. (2016). *The law and special education* (4th ed.). Boston, MA: Pearson.

Yell, M. L., & Crockett, J. B. (2011). Free appropriate public education. In J. M. Kauffman & D. P. Hallahan (Eds.), *Handbook of special education* (pp. 77–90). New York, NY: Routledge.

Yell, M. L., Katsiyannis, A., & Bradley, R. (2011). The Individuals with Disabilities Education Act: The evolution of special education law. In J. M. Kauffman & D. P. Hallahan (Eds.), *The handbook of special education* (pp. 61–76). New York, NY: Routledge.

Yell, M. L., Shriner, J. G., & Katsiyannis, A. (2006). Individuals with Disabilities Education Improvement Act of 2004 and IDEA Regulations of 2006: Implications for educators, administrators, and teacher trainers. *Focus on Exceptional Children, 39,* 1–24.

Zigmond, N. (2015). Where should students with disabilities receive their education? In B. Bateman, J. W. Lloyd, & M. Tankersley (Eds.), *Enduring issues in special education: Personal perspectives* (pp. 198–214). New York, NY: Routledge.

Zigmond, N., & Kloo, A., (2008). General and special education are (and should be) different. In J. M. Kauffman & D. P. Hallahan (Eds.), *Handbook of special education* (pp. 160–172). New York, NY: Routledge.

Chapter 2

Bateman, B. D. (2011). Individual education programs for children with disabilities. In J. M. Kauffman & D. P. Hallahan (Eds.), *Handbook of special education* (pp. 91–106). New York, NY: Routledge.

Bennett, M. S., Erchul, W. P., Young, H. L., & Bartel, C. M. (2012). Exploring relational communication patterns in prereferral intervention teams. *Journal of Educational and Psychological Consultation, 22*, 187–207.

Berkeley, S., Bender, W. N., Peaster, L., & Saunders, L. (2009). Implementation of responsiveness to intervention: A snapshot of progress. *Remedial and Special Education, 42*, 85–95.

Buck, G. H., Polloway, E. A., Smith-Thomas, A., & Cook, K. W. (2003). Prereferral intervention processes: A survey of state practices. *Exceptional Children, 69*, 349–360.

Burns, M. K., & Symington, T. (2002). A meta-analysis of prereferral intervention teams: Student and systematic outcomes. *Journal of School Psychology, 40,* 437–447.

Capizzi, A. M. (2008). From assessment to annual goal: Engaging a decision-making process in writing measurable IEPs. *Teaching Exceptional Children, 41*, 18–25.

Carter, E., O'Rourke, L., & Sisco, L. (2009). Knowledge, responsibilities, and training needs of paraprofessionals in elementary and secondary schools. *Remedial and Special Education, 30,* 344–359.

Castro, V. E. (2007). *The effect of co-teaching on academic achievement of K–2 students with and without disabilities in inclusive and noninclusive classrooms* (Unpublished doctoral dissertation). Fordham University, New York, NY.

Conderman, G. (2011). Middle school co-teaching: Effective practices and student reflections. *Middle School Journal, 42*, 24–31.

Conners, N. A. (2008). *An in-depth study of expert middle school special educators* (Unpublished doctoral dissertation). George Mason University, Fairfax, VA.

Conroy, T., Yell, M., Katsiyannis, A., & Collins, T. (2010). The U.S. Supreme Court and parental rights under the Individuals with Disabilities Education Act. *Focus on Exceptional Children, 43*(2), 1–15.

Cook, B. G., McDuffie-Landrum, K. A., Oshita, L., & Cook, S. C. (2011). Co-teaching for students with disabilities. In J. M. Kauffman & D. P. Hallahan (Eds.), *Handbook of special education* (pp. 147–159). New York, NY: Routledge.

Davern, L. (2004). School-to-home notebooks: What parents have to say. *Teaching Exceptional Children, 36*(5), 22–27.

Division for Learning Disabilities. (2007). *Thinking about response to instruction and learning disabilities: A teacher's guide.* Arlington, VA: Author.

Friend, M., & Cook, L. (2013). *Interactions: Collaboration skills for school professionals* (7th ed.). Boston, MA: Allyn & Bacon.

Friend, M., Cook, L., Hurley-Chamberlain, D., & Shamberger, C. (2010). Co-teaching: An illustration of the complexity of collaboration in special education. *Journal of Educational and Psychological Consultation, 20*, 9–27.

Gartin, B., & Murdick, N. (2005). IDEA 2004: The IEP. *Remedial and Special Education, 26*, 327–331.

Giangreco, M. F., & Broer, S. M. (2007). School-based screening to determine overreliance on paraprofessionals. *Focus on Autism and Other Developmental Disabilities, 22*, 149–158.

Giangreco, M. F., Broer, S. M., & Suter, S. M. (2011). Guidelines for selecting alternatives to overreliance on paraprofessionals: Field-testing in inclusion-oriented schools. *Remedial and Special Education, 32,* 22–38.

Giangreco, M. F., Suter, S. M., & Doyle, M. (2010). Paraprofessionals in inclusive schools: A review of recent research. *Journal of Educational and Psychological Consultation, 20,* 41–57.

Ginott, H. (1998). *Teacher and child.* New York, NY: Touchstone.

Ginott, H. G., Ginott, A., & Goddard, H. W. (2003). *Between parent and child.* New York, NY: Three Rivers.

Gordon, T. (2003). *T.E.T.: Teacher effectiveness training.* New York, NY: Three Rivers.

Hoover, J. (2010). Special education eligibility decision making in response to intervention models. *Theory into Practice, 49,* 289–296.

Individuals with Disabilities Education Improvement Act of 2004, Pub. L. No. 108-446, 20 U.S.C. §1400 et seq. (2004).

Kamps, D., Abbott, M., Greenwood, C., Wills, H., Veerkamp, M., & Kaufman, J. (2008). Effects of small-group reading instruction and curriculum differences for students most at risk in kindergarten. *Journal of Learning Disabilities, 41,* 101–114.

Kampwirth, T. J., & Powers, K. M. (2016). *Collaborative consultation in the schools: Effective practices for students with learning and behavior problems* (5th ed.). Boston, MA: Pearson.

Magdalena, J., Kopechanski, L., Cameron, R., & Hughs, D. (2008). In transition: Experiences of parents of children with special needs at school entry. *Early Childhood Education Journal, 35,* 479–485.

Martin, J. E., Van Dyke, J. L., Greene, B. A., Gardner, J. E., Christensen, W. R., Woods, L. L., & Lovett, D. L. (2006). Direct observation of teacher-directed IEP meetings: Establishing the need for student IEP meeting instruction. *Exceptional Children, 72,* 187–200.

McDuffie, M. A., Mastropieri, M. A., & Scruggs, T. E. (2009). Differential effects of co-teaching and peer-mediated instruction: Results for content learning and student–teacher interactions. *Exceptional Children, 75,* 493–510.

McNaughton, D., Hamlin, D., McCarthy, J., Head-Reeves, D., & Schreiner, M. (2007). Learning to listen: An active listening strategy for preservice special education professionals. *Topics in Early Childhood Special Education, 27,* 223–231.

McNaughton, D., & Vostal, B. (2010). Using active listening to improve collaboration with parents: The LAFF don't CRY strategy. *Intervention in School and Clinic, 45,* 251–256.

Mueller, T. (2009). Alternative dispute resolution: A new agenda for special education policy. *Journal of Disability Policy Studies, 20,* 4–13.

Murawski, W. W. (2006). Student outcomes in co-taught secondary English classes: How can we improve? *Reading & Writing Quarterly: Overcoming Learning Difficulties, 22,* 227–247.

Murawski, W. W., & Dieker, L. (2004). Tips and strategies for co-teaching at the secondary level. *Teaching Exceptional Children, 36,* 52–58.

Murray, C. (2004). Clarifying collaborative roles in urban high schools: General educators' perspectives. *Teaching Exceptional Children, 36*(5), 44–51.

National Center on Response to Intervention. (2011). *Multi-level prevention system.* Washington, DC: Author. Retrieved from http://www.rti4success.org/

Pickett, A. L., & Gerlach, K. (Eds.). (2003). *Supervising paraeducators in educational settings: A team approach* (2nd ed.). Austin, TX: Pro-Ed.

Prewett, S., Mellard, D. F., Deshler, D. D., Allen, J., Alexander, R., & Stern, A. (2012). Response to intervention in middle schools: Practices and outcomes. *Learning Disabilities Research & Practice, 27,* 136–147.

Rock, M. L., & Zigmond, N. (2001). Intervention assistance: Is it substance or symbolism? *Preventing School Failure, 45,* 153–161.

Scruggs, T. E., Mastropieri, M. A., & McDuffie, K. A. (2007). Co-teaching in inclusive classrooms: A meta-synthesis of qualitative research. *Exceptional Children, 73,* 392–416.

Singer, G. H. S., Maul, C., Wang, M., & Ethridge, B. L. (2011). Resilience in families of children with disabilities. In J. M. Kauffman & D. P. Hallahan (Eds.), *Handbook of special education* (pp. 654–667). New York, NY: Routledge.

Solis, M., Vaughn, S., & Scammacca, N. (2015). The effects of an intensive reading intervention for ninth graders with very low reading comprehension. *Learning Disabilities Research & Practice, 30,* 104–113.

Steedman, W. (2012). *Independent educational evaluations.* In P. Wright & P. Wright (Eds.), *Wrightslaw.* Retrieved from http://www.wrightslaw.com/info/eval.iee.steedman.htm

Truscott, S., Celinae, E., Sams, D., Sanborn, K., & Frank, A. (2005). The current state(s) of pre-referral intervention teams: A report from two national surveys. *Remedial and Special Education, 26,* 130–140.

Turnbull, A., Turnbull, H. R., Erwin, E. J., Soodak, L. C., & Shogren, K. A. (2015). *Families, professionals, and exceptionality: Positive outcomes through partnerships and trust.* Boston, MA: Pearson.

Vaughn, S., & Roberts, G. (2007). Secondary interventions in reading: Providing additional instruction for students at risk. *Teaching Exceptional Children, 39*(5), 40–46.

Vostal, B. R., McNaughton, D. M., Benedik-Wood, E., & Hoffman, K. (2015). Preparing teachers for collaborative communication: Evaluation of instruction in an active listening strategy. *National Teacher Education Journal, 8,* 5–14.

Walker, V. L., & Smith, C. G. (2015). Training paraprofessionals to support students with disabilities: A literature review. *Exceptionality, 23,* 170–191.

Wanzek, J., & Vaughn, S. (2011). Is a three-tier intervention model associated with reduced placement in special education? *Remedial and Special Education, 32,* 167–175.

Weiss, M. P., & Lloyd, J. W. (2003). Conditions for co-teaching: Lessons from a case study. *Teacher Education and Special Education, 26,* 27–41.

Zhang, D., Hsu, H., Kwok, O., Benz, M., & Bowman-Perrott, L. (2011). The impact of basic-level parent engagements on student achievement: Patterns associated with race/ethnicity and socioeconomic status. *Journal of Disability Policy Studies, 22,* 28–39.

Chapter 3

Aceves, T. C., & Orosco, M. J. (2014). *Culturally responsive teaching* (Document No. IC-2). Gainesville, FL: University of Florida, Collaboration for Effective Educator, Development, Accountability, and Reform Center. Retrieved from http://ceedar.education.ufl.edu/tools/innovation-configurations/

Algozzine, B., Wang, C., & Violette, V. S. (2011). Reexamining the relationship between academic achievement and social behavior. *Journal of Positive Behavior Interventions, 13,* 3–16.

Al-Yagon, M., & Margalit, M. (2014). Social cognition of children and adolescents with learning disabilities: Intrapersonal and interpersonal perspectives. In H. L. Swanson, K. R. Harris, & S. Graham (Eds.), *Handbook of learning disabilities* (2nd ed., pp. 278–292). New York, NY: Guilford.

American Association on Intellectual and Developmental Disabilities (AAIDD). (2010). *Intellectual disability: Definition, classification, and systems of support* (11th ed.). Washington, DC: Author.

American Psychiatric Association. (2013). *Diagnostic and statistical manual of mental disorders: DSM V*. Washington, DC: Author.

Assistance to States for the Education of Children with Disabilities: A Child with a Disability, 34 C.F.R. § 300.7 (2002).

Assistance to States for Education of Handicapped Children: Procedures for Evaluating Specific Learning Disabilities, 42 C.F.R., § 121A (1977).

Astrom, R. L., Wadsworth, S. J., & DeFries, J. C. (2007). Etiology of the stability of reading difficulties: The longitudinal twin study of reading disabilities. *Twin Research and Human Genetics, 10*, 434–439.

Barkley, R. A. (2014). History of ADHD. In R. A. Barkley (Ed.), *Attention deficit hyperactivity disorder: A handbook for diagnosis and treatment* (4th ed., pp. 3–50). New York, NY: Guilford.

Bottge, B. A., Beukelman, D. R., & Mirenda, P. (2013). *Augmentative and alternative communication: Supporting children and adults with complex communication needs* (4th ed.). Baltimore, MD: Brookes.

Bottge, B. A., Heinrichs, M., Chan, S., & Serlin, R. (2001). Anchoring adolescents' understanding of math concepts in rich problem solving environments. *Remedial and Special Education, 22*, 299–314.

Bottge, B. A., Rueda, E., Grant, T. S., Stephens, A. C., & LaRoque, P. T. (2010). Anchoring problem-solving and computation instruction in context-rich learning environments. *Exceptional Children, 76*, 417–437.

Bottge, B. A., Toland, M. D., Gassaway, L., Butler, M., Choo, S., Griffen, A. K., & Ma, X. (2015). Impact of anchored enhanced instruction in inclusive math classrooms. *Exceptional Children, 81*, 158–175.

Camarota, S. A., & Zeigler, K. (2014). *One in five U.S. residents speaks foreign language at home, record 61.8 million*. Washington, DC: Center for Immigration Studies. Retrieved from http://cis.org//sites/cis.org/files/camarota-language.pdf

Carbone, D., Schmidt, L. A., Cunningham, C. C., McHolm, A. E., Edison, S., St. Pierre, J., & Boyle, M. H. (2010). Behavioral and socio-emotional functioning in children with selective mutism: A comparison with anxious and typically developing children across multiple informants. *Journal of Abnormal Child Psychology, 38*, 1057–1067.

Cascella, P. W. (2004). Receptive communication abilities among adults with significant intellectual disability. *Journal of Intellectual & Developmental Disability, 29*, 70–78.

Casteel, C. J., & Ballantyne, K. G. (Eds.). (2006). *Professional development in action: Improving teaching for English learners*. Washington, DC: National Clearinghouse for English Language Acquisition and Language Instruction Educational Programs. Retrieved from http://www.ncela.us/

Council for Exceptional Children (CEC). (2012). *Current special education topics: Identifying learning disabilities*. Arlington, VA: Author. Retrieved from http://www.cec.sped.org

Cronin, M. E., Patton, J. R., & Wood, S. J. (2007). *Life skills instruction* (2nd ed.). Austin, TX: Pro-Ed.

Denckla, M. B., Barquero, L. A., Lindstrom, E. R., Benedict, S. L., Wilson, L. M., & Cutting, L. E., (2014). Attention-deficit/hyperactivity disorder, executive function, and reading comprehension: Different but related. In H. L. Swanson, K. R. Harris, & S. Graham (Eds.), *Handbook of learning disabilities* (2nd ed., pp. 155–168). New York, NY: Guilford.

Division for Learning Disabilities. (2012). *DLD's views about response to intervention and learning disabilities*. Arlington, VA: Author. Retrieved from http://www.cec.sped.org/AM/Template.cfm?Section=Home&CAT=none&TEMPLATE=/CM/ContentDisplay.cfm&CONTENTID=8428

Duhaney, L. M. G. (2003). A practical approach to managing the behaviors of students with ADD. *Intervention in School and Clinic, 38,* 267–279.

Hoover, H. D., Dunbar, S. B., & Frisbie, D. A. (2007). *Iowa Tests of Basic Skills: Form C*. New York, NY: Houghton Mifflin Harcourt.

Echevarria, J., & Graves, A. (2011). *Sheltered content instruction: Teaching English language learners with diverse abilities* (4th ed.). Boston, MA: Pearson.

Echevarria, J., & Graves, A. (2015). *Sheltered content instruction: Teaching English language learners with diverse abilities* (5th ed.). Boston, PA: Pearson.

Epstein, M. H. (2004). *Behavioral and Emotional Rating Scale* (2nd ed.). Austin, TX: Pro-Ed.

Feingold, B. (1975). *Why your child is hyperactive*. New York, NY: Random House.

Fletcher, J. M., Lyon, G. R., Barnes, M., Stuebing, K. K., Francis, D. J., Olson, R. K., et al. (2002). Classification of learning disabilities: An evidence-based evaluation. In R. Bradley, L. Danielson, & D. P. Hallahan (Eds.), *Identification of learning disabilities: Research to practice* (pp. 185–250). Mahwah, NJ: Lawrence Erlbaum Associates.

Fletcher, J. M., Lyon, G. R., Fuchs, L. S., & Barnes, M. (2007). *Learning disabilities: From identification to intervention*. New York, NY: Guilford.

Ford, D. Y. (2012). Culturally different students in special education: Looking backward to move forward. *Exceptional Children, 78,* 391–405.

Fuchs, D., Fuchs, L. S., Mathes, P. G., Lipsey, M. L., & Roberts, P. H. (2002). Is "learning disabilities" just a fancy term for low achievement? A meta-analysis of reading differences between low achievers with and without the label. In R. Bradely, L. Danielson, & D. Hallahan (Eds.), *Identification of learning disabilities* (pp. 737–762). Mahwah, NJ: Erlbaum.

Furlong, M. J., Morrison, G. M., & Jimerson, S. (2004). Externalizing behaviors of aggression and violence. In R. B. Rutherford, M. M. Quinn, & S. R. Mathur (Eds.), *Handbook of research in emotional and behavioral disorders* (pp. 243–261). New York, NY: Guilford.

Geary, D. C. (2014). Learning disabilities in mathematics: Recent advances. In H. L. Swanson, K. R. Harris, & S. Graham (Eds.), *Handbook of learning disabilities* (pp. 239–255). New York, NY: Guilford.

Gerber, M. M. (2005). Teachers are still the test: Limitations of response to instruction strategies for identifying children with learning disabilities. *Journal of Learning Disabilities, 38,* 516–524.

Graham, S. (2004). Writing instruction. In B. Y. L. Wong (Ed.), *Learning about learning disabilities* (3rd ed., pp. 281–314). San Diego, CA: Elsevier Academic Press.

Graves, A. W. (2010). A longitudinal study of the impact of effective beginning reading instruction for English learners: Literacy, language, and learning disabilities. In T. E. Scruggs & M. A. Mastropieri (Eds.), *Literacy and learning: Advances in learning and behavioral disabilities* (Vol. 23, pp. 155–174). Oxford, UK: Emerald.

Grayson, G. L., Baird, W. D., Dearing, E., & Hamill, S. K. (2009). Cognitive self-regulation in youth with and without learning disabilities. *Journal of Social and Clinical Psychology, 28,* 881–908.

Gresham, F. M., & Kern, L. (2004). Internalizing behavior problems in children and adolescents. In R. B. Rutherford, M. M. Quinn, & S. R. Mathur (Eds.), *Handbook of research in emotional and behavioral disorders* (pp. 262–281). New York, NY: Guilford.

Hallahan, D. P., Pullen, P. C., & Ward, D. (2014). A brief history of the field of learning disabilities. In H. L. Swanson, K. R. Harris, & S. Graham (Eds.), *Handbook of learning disabilities* (2nd ed., pp. 15–32). New York, NY: Guilford.

Harris, J. C. (2010). *Intellectual disability: A guide for families and professionals.* New York, NY: Oxford University Press.

Harry, B. (2008). Family-professional collaboration with culturally and linguistically diverse families: Ideal vs. reality. *Exceptional Children, 72,* 372–388.

Hutchinson, N. L., Freeman, J. G., & Berg, D. H. (2004). Social competence of adolescents with learning disabilities: Interventions and issues. In B. Y. L. Wong (Ed.), *Learning about learning disabilities* (3rd ed., pp. 415–448). San Diego, CA: Elsevier Academic Press.

Jacobson, J. W., & Mulick, J. A. (1996). *Manual on diagnosis and professional practice in mental retardation.* Washington, DC: American Psychological Association.

Kauffman, J. M., & Landrum, T. (2013). *Characteristics of emotional and behavioral disorders of children and youth* (10th ed.). Upper Saddle River, NJ: Merrill/Pearson.

Kirkpatrick, R., Legrand, L., Iacono, W., & McGue, M. (2011). A twin and adoption study of reading achievement: Exploration of shared-environmental and gene-environment interaction effects. *Learning and Individual Differences, 21,* 368–375.

Landrum, T. (2011). Emotional and behavioral disorders. In J. M. Kauffman & D. P. Hallahan (Eds.), *Handbook of special education* (pp. 209–220). New York, NY: Routledge.

Lane, K. L. (2004). Academic instruction and tutoring interventions for students with emotional/behavioral disorders 1990 to present. In R. B. Rutherford, M. M. Quinn, & S. R. Mathur (Eds.), *Handbook of research in emotional and behavioral disorders* (pp. 462–486). New York, NY: Guilford.

Lyon, G. R., Fletcher, J. M., Shaywitz, S. E., Shaywitz, B. A., Torgesen, J. K., Wood, F. B.,... Olson, R. (2001). Rethinking learning disabilities. In C. E. Finn, Jr., A. J. Rotherham, & C. R. Hokanson, Jr. (Eds.), *Rethinking special education for a new century* (pp. 259–287). Washington, DC: Thomas B. Fordham Foundation.

Macmillan, D. L., & Siperstein, G. N. (2002). Learning disabilities as operationally defined by schools. In R. Bradley, L. Danielson, & D. P. Hallahan (Eds.), *Identification of learning disabilities* (pp. 287–333). Mahwah, NJ: Lawrence Erlbaum.

Mastropieri, M. A., & Scruggs, T. E. (2002). Discrepancy models in the identification of learning disabilities. In R. Bradley, L. Danielson, & D. P. Hallahan (Eds.), *Identification of learning disabilities* (pp. 449–466). Mahwah, NJ: Lawrence Erlbaum.

Mastropieri, M. A., & Scruggs, T. E. (2005). Feasibility and consequences of response to intervention (RTI): Examination of the issues and scientific evidence as a model for the identification of individuals with learning disabilities. *Journal of Learning Disabilities, 38,* 525–531.

Mastropieri, M. A., Scruggs, T. E., Boon, R., & Carter, K. B. (2001). Correlates of inquiry learning in science: Constructing concepts of density and buoyancy. *Remedial and Special Education, 22,* 130–138.

Mastropieri, M. A., Scruggs, T. E., Cerar, N. I., Allen-Bronaugh, D., Thompson, C., Guckert, M., . . . Cuenca-Sanchez, Y. (2012). Fluent persuasive writing with students with emotional disturbance: Developing arguments and counterarguments. *Journal of Special Education.* doi: 10.1177/0022466912440456

McDuffie, A., & Abbeduto, L. (2009). Language disorders in children with mental retardation of genetic origin: Down syndrome, fragile X syndrome, and Williams syndrome. In R. G. Schwartz (Ed.), *Handbook of child language disorders* (pp. 90–114). New York, NY: Psychology Press.

McGillivray, J. A., & Baker, K. L. (2009). Effects of comorbid ADHD with learning disabilities on anxiety, depression, and aggression in adults. *Journal of Learning Disabilities, 12,* 525–531.

Montague, M. (2011). Effective instruction in mathematics for students with learning disabilities. In C. Wyatt-Smith, J. Elkins, & S. Gunn (Eds.), *Multiple perspectives on difficulties in learning literacy and numeracy* (pp. 295–314). New York, NY: Springer.

National Center on Intensive Intervention at American Institutes for Research. (2016). Retrieved from http://www.intensiveintervention.org

National Center on Response to Intervention (2011). *Multi-level prevention system.* Washington, DC: Author. Retrieved from http://www.rti4success.org/

Oswald, D. P., Best, A. M., Coutinho, M. J., & Nagle, H. A. L. (2003). Trends in the special education identification rates of boys and girls: A call for research and change. *Exceptionality, 11,* 223–237.

Owens, R. E., Farinella, K. A., & Metz, D. E. (2015). *Introduction to communication disorders: A life span evidence-based perspective* (4th ed.). Boston, MA: Pearson.

Palson, K. (1986). *Essence of Kirstin.* Medfield, MA: Author.

Polloway, E. A., Patton, J. R., & Nelson, M. A. (2011). Intellectual and developmental disabilities. In J. M. Kauffman & D. P. Hallahan (Eds.), *Handbook of special education* (pp. 15–26). New York, NY: Routledge.

Polsgrove, L., & Smith, S. W. (2004). Informed practice in teaching self-control to children with emotional and behavioral disorders. In R. B. Rutherford, M. M. Quinn, & S. R. Mathur (Eds.), *Handbook of research in emotional and behavioral disorders* (pp. 399–425). New York, NY: Guilford.

Pullen, P. C., Lane, H. B., Ashworth, K. E., & Lovelace, S. P. (2011). Learning disabilities. In J. M. Kauffman & D. P. Hallahan (Eds.), *Handbook of special education* (pp. 187–197). New York, NY: Routledge.

Raymond, E. B. (2017). *Students with mild disabilities: A characteristics approach* (5th ed.). Boston, MA: Pearson.

Reynolds, C. R., & Kamphaus, C. W. (2004). *BASC-2: Behavior Assessment System for Children* (2nd ed.). San Antonio, TX: Psychological Corporation.

Rooney, K. J. (2011). Attention deficit hyperactivity disorder. In J. M. Kauffman & D. P. Hallahan (Eds.), *Handbook of special education* (pp. 198–208). New York, NY: Routledge.

Sailor, W., Doolittle, J., Bradley, R., & Danielson, L. (2009). Response to intervention and positive behavior support. In W. Sailor, G. Dunlap, G. Sugai, & R. Horner (Eds.), *Handbook of positive behaviour support* (pp. 729–753). New York, NY: Springer.

Schalock, R. L., Borthwick-Duffie, S., Bradley, V., Buntinx, W. H. E., Coulter, D. L., Craig, E. M., . . . Yeager, M. H. (2010). *Intellectual disability: Definition, classification, and systems of support.* Washington, DC: American Association on Intellectual and Developmental Disabilities.

Schalock, R. L., Luckasson, R. A., Shogren, K. A., Borthwick-Duffie, S., Bradley, V., Buntinx, W. H. E., et al. (2007). The renaming of mental retardation: Understanding the change to the term intellectual disability. *Intellectual and Developmental Disabilities, 45,* 116–124.

Scheuermann, B. K., & Hall, J. A. (2016). *Positive behavior supports for the classroom* (3rd ed.). Boston, MA: Pearson.

Schmitt, M. B., Justice, L. M., & Pentimonti, J. M. (2014). Language processes: Characterization and prevention of language-learning disabilities. In H. L. Swanson, K. R. Harris, & S. Graham (Eds.), *Handbook of learning disabilities* (2nd ed., pp. 256–277). New York, NY: Guilford.

Scott, L. (2010). *Stuttering: Straight talk for teachers* (3rd ed.). Memphis, TN: Stuttering Foundation of America.

Scruggs, T. E., & Marsing, L. (1988). Teaching test-taking skills to behaviorally disordered students. *Behavioral Disorders, 13,* 240–244.

Scruggs, T. E., Mastropieri, M. A., Berkeley, S., & Marshak, L. (2010). Mnemonic strategies: Evidence-based practice and practice-based evidence. *Intervention in School and Clinic, 46,* 79–86.

Shapiro, T. R. (2012). Number of Fairfax students who speak a foreign language at home to surpass 50 percent. *Washington Post,* September 8. Retrieved from https://www.washingtonpost.com/local/education/number-of-fairfax-students-who-speak-a-foreign-language-at-home-to-surpass-50-percent/2012/09/08/de47a92a-f84d-11e1-8253-3f495ae70650_story.html

Shriner, J. G., & Wehby, J. H. (2004). Accountability and assessment for students with emotional and behavioral disorders. In R. B. Rutherford, M. M. Quinn, & S. R. Mathur (Eds.), *Handbook of research in emotional and behavioral disorders* (pp. 216–234). New York, NY: Guilford.

Siegel, L. S., & Mazabel, S. (2014). Basic cognitive processes and learning disabilities. In H. L. Swanson, K. R. Harris, & S. Graham (Eds.), *Handbook of learning disabilities* (2nd ed., pp. 186–213). New York, NY: Guilford.

Smith, L. (1975). *Your child's behavior chemistry.* New York, NY: Random House.

Swanson, H. L., & Zheng, X. (2014). Memory and learning disabilities. In H. L. Swanson, K. R. Harris, & S. Graham (Eds.), *Handbook of learning disabilities* (2nd ed., pp. 214–238). New York, NY: Guilford.

Swendsen, J., Conway, K. P., Degenhardt, L., Glantz, M., Jin, R., Merikangas, K. R.,...Kessler, R. C. (2011). Mental disorders as risk factors for substance use, abuse and dependence: Results from the 10-year follow-up of the National Comorbidity Survey. *Addiction, 105,* 1117–1128.

U.S. Department of Education. (2014). *State nonfiscal public elementary/secondary education survey data.* Washington, DC: National Center for Education Statistics. Retrieved from http://nces.ed.gov/ccd/stnfis.asp

U.S. Department of Education. (2015). *Thirty-seventh annual report to Congress on the implementation of the Individuals with Disabilities Education Act.* Washington, DC: Author. Retrieved from http://www2.ed.gov/about/reports/annual/osep/2015/parts-b-c/37th-arc-for-idea.pdf

U.S. Department of Education, Office of Special Education and Rehabilitative Services, Office of Special Education Programs. (2008). *Identifying and treating attention deficit hyperactivity disorder: A resource for school and home.* Washington, DC: Author. Retrieved from https://www2.ed.gov/rschstat/research/pubs/adhd/adhd-identifying-2008.pdf

Vaughn, S. R., & Bos, C. S. (2015). *Strategies for teaching students with learning and behavior problems* (9th ed). Upper Saddle River, NJ: Pearson Education.

Vicari, S., Caselli, M. C., Gagliardi, C., Tonucci, F., & Volterra, V. (2002). Language acquisition in special populations: A comparison between Down and Williams syndrome. *Neuropsychologia, 40,* 2461–2470.

Wessendorp, M., Houwen, S., Hartman, E., & Visscher, C. (2011). Are gross motor skills and sports participation related in children with intellectual disabilities? *Research in Developmental Disabilities, 32,* 1147–1153.

Wolraich, M. L., DuPaul, G. J., & Stevens, S. W. (2010). *ADHD diagnosis and management: A practical guide for the clinic and the classroom.* Baltimore, MD: Brookes.

Wright, P. W. D., & Wright, P. D. (2005). *Wrightslaw: IDEA 2004.* Hartfield, VA: Harbor House Law Press.

Zhang, D., Hsu, H., Katsiyannis, A., Barrett, D. E., & Ju, S. (2011). Adolescents with disabilities in the juvenile justice system: Patterns of recidivism. *Exceptional Children, 77,* 283–296.

Chapter 4

American Association on Intellectual and Developmental Disabilities (AAIDD). (2010). *User's guide to intellectual disability: Definition, classification, and systems of support* (11th ed.). Washington, DC: Author.

American Psychiatric Association. (2013). *Diagnostic and statistical manual of mental disorders: DSM V.* Washington, DC: Author.

Andrews, J. F., Shaw, P. C., & Lomas, G. (2011). Deaf and hard of hearing students. In J. M. Kauffman & D. P. Hallahan (Eds.), *Handbook of special education* (pp. 247–261). New York, NY: Routledge.

Ayres, K. M., Lowrey, K. A., Douglas, K. H., & Sievers, C. (2011). I can identify Saturn but I can't brush my teeth: What happens when the curricular focus for students with severe disability shifts? *Education and Training in Autism and Developmental Disabilities, 46,* 28–35.

Barry, L. M., & Burlew, S. B. (2004). Using social stories to teach choice and play skills to children with autism. *Focus on Autism and Developmental Disabilities, 19,* 45–51.

Best, S. J. (2009). Coping with degenerative and terminal illness. In K. W. Heller, P. E. Forney, P. A. Alberto, S. J. Best, & M. N. Schwartzman (Eds.), *Understanding physical, health, and multiple disabilities* (pp. 281–292). Upper Saddle River, NJ: Merrill/Prentice Hall.

Best, S. J. (2010a). Health impairments and congenital infections. In S. J. Best, K. W. Heller, & J. L. Bigge (Eds.), *Teaching individuals with physical or multiple disabilities* (5th ed., pp. 59–85). Upper Saddle River, NJ: Merrill/Prentice Hall.

Best, S. J. (2010b). Physical disabilities. In S. J. Best, K. W. Heller, & J. L. Bigge (Eds.), *Teaching individuals with physical or multiple disabilities* (6th ed., pp. 32–58). Upper Saddle River, NJ: Merrill/Prentice Hall.

Best, S. J. (2010c). Understanding individuals with physical, health, and multiple disabilities. In S. J. Best, K. W. Heller, & J. L. Bigge (Eds.), *Teaching individuals with physical or multiple disabilities* (6th ed., pp. 3–31). Upper Saddle River, NJ: Merrill/Prentice Hall.

Best, S. J., & Bigge, J. L. (2010). Cerebral palsy. In S. J. Best, K. W. Heller, & J. L. Bigge (Eds.), *Teaching individuals with physical or multiple disabilities* (6th ed., pp. 59–81). Upper Saddle River, NJ: Merrill/Prentice Hall.

Best, S. J., & Heller, K. W. (2009). Acquired infections and AIDS. In K. W. Heller, P. E. Forney, P. A. Alberto, S. J. Best, & M. N. Schwartzman (Eds.), *Understanding physical, health, and multiple disabilities* (pp. 368–386). Upper Saddle River, NJ: Merrill/Prentice Hall.

Best, S. J., Heller, K. W., & Bigge, J. L. (Eds.). (2010). *Teaching individuals with physical or multiple disabilities* (6th ed.). Upper Saddle River, NJ: Merrill/Prentice Hall.

Best, S. J., Reed, P., & Bigge, J. L. (2010). Assistive technology. In S. J. Best, K. W. Heller, & J. L. Bigge (Eds.), *Teaching individuals with physical or multiple disabilities* (6th ed., pp. 175–220). Upper Saddle River, NJ: Merrill/Prentice Hall.

Bondy, A., & Frost, L. (2011). *A picture's worth: PECS and other visual communication strategies in autism* (2nd ed.). Bethesda, MD: Woodbine House.

Briggs, G. (2001). *Drugs in pregnancy and lactation* (6th ed.). Baltimore, MD: Williams and Wilkins.

Browder, D. M. (2015). What should we teach students with moderate and severe developmental disabilities? In B. Bateman, J. Lloyd, & M. Tankersley (Eds.), *Enduring issues in special education: Personal perspectives* (pp. 52–72). New York, NY: Routledge.

Brown, F., McDonnell, J., & Snell, M. E. (2016). *Instruction of students with severe disabilities* (8th ed.). Boston, MA: Pearson.

Bruce, S. M. (2011). Severe and multiple disabilities. In J. M. Kauffman & D. P. Hallahan (Eds.), *Handbook of special education* (pp. 291–303). New York, NY: Routledge.

Cardon, T. A. (2016). A look forward. In T. A. Cardon (Ed.), *Technology and the treatment of children with autism spectrum disorder* (pp. 151–154). New York, NY: Springer.

Carr, M. E., Moore, D. W., & Anderson, A. (2014). Self-management interventions on students with autism: A meta-analysis of single subject research. *Exceptional Children, 81,* 28–44.

Carroll, D. (2001). Considering paraeducator training, roles, and responsibilities. *Teaching Exceptional Children, 34,* 60–64.

Carter, E. W., Moss, C. K., Hoffman, A., Chung, Y., & Sisco, L. (2011). Efficacy and social validity of peer support arrangements for adolescents with disabilities. *Exceptional Children, 78,* 107–125.

Conroy, M., Stichter, J. P., & Gage, N. (2011). Current issues and trends in the education of children and youth with autism spectrum. In J. M. Kauffman & D. P. Hallahan (Eds.), *Handbook of special education* (pp. 277–290). New York, NY: Routledge.

Courtade, G., Spooner, F., Browder, D. M., & Jimenez, B. (2012). Seven reasons to promote standards-based instruction for students with severe disabilities. *Education and Training in Autism and Developmental Disabilities, 47,* 3–13.

Davis, P. (2003). *Including children with visual impairment in mainstream schools: A practical guide.* London, UK: David Fulton.

Definition; Child with a Disability; Specific Learning Disability, 20 U.S.C., § 1401(3); 1401(30) (2004).

Dunst, C. (2014). Meta-analysis of the effects of puppet shows on attitudes toward and knowledge of individuals with disabilities. *Exceptional Children, 80,* 136–148.

Flower, A., Burns, M. K., & Bottesford-Miller, N. A. (2007). Meta-analysis of disability simulation research. *Remedial and Special Education, 28,* 72–79.

Giangreco, M. F., & Broer, S. M. (2007). School-based screening to determine overreliance on paraprofessionals. *Focus on Autism and Other Developmental Disabilities, 22,* 149–158.

Giangreco, M. F., Broer, S. M., & Suter, J. C. (2011). Guidelines for selecting alternatives to overreliance on paraprofessionals: Field-testing in inclusion-oriented schools. *Remedial and Special Education, 32,* 22–28.

Giangreco, M. F., Doyle, S. M., & Suter, J. C. (2014). Teacher assistants in inclusive classes. In L. Florian (Ed.), *Sage handbook of special education* (vol. 2, pp. 691–702). Thousand Oaks, CA: Sage.

Goldstein, H., Lackey, K. C., & Schneider, N. J. (2014). A new framework for systematic reviews: Application to social skills interventions for preschoolers with autism. *Exceptional Children, 80,* 262–286.

Graetz, J. S., Mastropieri, M. A., & Scruggs, T. E. (2009). Promoting social behavior for adolescents with autism with social stories. *Education and Training in Developmental Disabilities, 44,* 91–104.

Grandinette, S., & Best, S. J. (2009). Traumatic brain injury. In K. W. Heller, P. E. Forney, P. A. Alberto, S. J. Best, & M. N. Schwartzman (Eds.), *Understanding physical, health, and multiple disabilities* (pp. 118–138). Upper Saddle River, NJ: Merrill/Prentice Hall.

Halgunseth, L. C., Peterson, A., Stark, D. R., & Moodie, S. (2009). *Family engagement, diverse families, and early childhood programs: An integrated review of the literature.* Washington, DC: National Association for the Education of Young Children, Pew Charitable Trusts.

Hall, L. J. (2013). *Autism spectrum disorders: From theory to practice* (2nd ed.). Upper Saddle River, NJ: Merrill/Pearson.

Hamill, A. C., & Stein, C. H. (2011). Culture and empowerment in the deaf community: An analysis of Internet weblogs. *Journal of Community and Applied Social Psychology, 21,* 388–406.

Harry, B. (2008). Family-professional collaboration with culturally and linguistically diverse families: Ideal vs. reality. *Exceptional Children, 72,* 372–388.

Heller, K. W. (2009). Traumatic spinal cord injury and spina bifida. In K. W. Heller, P. E. Forney, P. A. Alberto, S. J. Best, & M. N. Schwartzman (Eds.), *Understanding physical, health, and multiple disabilities* (pp. 94–117). Upper Saddle River, NJ: Merrill/Prentice Hall.

Heller, K. W., & Avant, M. J. T. (2009). Juvenile rheumatoid arthritis, arthrogryposis, and osteogenesis imperfecta. In K. W. Heller, P. E. Forney, P. A. Alberto, S. J. Best, & M. N. Schwartzman (Eds.), *Understanding physical, health, and multiple disabilities* (pp. 172–191). Upper Saddle River, NJ: Merrill/Prentice Hall.

Heller, K. W., Bigge, J. L., & Allgood, P. (2010). Adaptations for personal independence. In S. J. Best, K. W. Heller, & J. L. Bigge (Eds.), *Teaching individuals with physical or multiple disabilities* (6th ed., pp. 289–310). Upper Saddle River, NJ: Merrill/Prentice Hall.

Heller, K. W., & Cohen, E. T. (2009). Seizures and epilepsy. In K. W. Heller, P. E. Forney, P. A. Alberto, S. J. Best, & M. N. Schwartzman (Eds.), *Understanding physical, health, and multiple disabilities* (pp. 294–315). Upper Saddle River, NJ: Merrill/Prentice Hall.

Heller, K. W., Forney, P. E., Alberto, P. A., Best, S. J., & Schwartzman, M. N. (Eds.). (2009). *Understanding physical, health, and multiple disabilities* (2nd ed). Upper Saddle River, NJ: Merrill/Prentice Hall.

Heller, K. W., & Garrett, J. T. (2009). Cerebral palsy. In K. W. Heller, P. E. Forney, P. A. Alberto, S. J. Best, & M. N. Schwartzman (Eds.), *Understanding physical, health, and multiple disabilities* (pp. 72–93). Upper Saddle River, NJ: Merrill/Prentice Hall.

Heller, K. W., Mezei, P., & Schwartzman, M. (2009). Muscular dystrophies. In K. W. Heller, P. E. Forney, P. A. Alberto, S. J. Best, & M. N. Schwartzman (Eds.), *Understanding physical, health, and multiple disabilities* (pp. 232–249). Upper Saddle River, NJ: Merrill/Prentice Hall.

Hill, A. P., Zuckerman, K., & Fombonne, E. (2015). Epidemiology of autism spectrum disorders. In M. Robinson-Agramonte (Ed.), *Translational approaches to autism spectrum disorders* (pp. 13–38). New York, NY: Springer.

Hochman, J. M., Carter, E. W., Bottema-Beutel, K., Harvey, M. N., & Gustafson, J. R. (2015). Efficacy of peer networks to increase social connections among high school students with autism spectrum disorder. *Exceptional Children, 82,* 96–116.

Ioannou, D., Kelly, T. E., & Tempest, H. G. (2016). The role of genetic mechanisms in childhood disabilities. In R.H.A. Haslam & P. J. Valletutti (Eds.), *Medical and psychosocial problems in the classroom: The teacher's role in diagnosis and management* (5th ed., pp. 31–67). Austin, TX: Pro-Ed.

Ison, N., McIntyre, S., Rothery, S., Smithers-Sheedy, H., Goldsmith, S., Parsonage, S., & Foy, L. (2010). "Just like you": A disability awareness programme for children that enhanced knowledge, attitudes and acceptance: Pilot study findings. *Developmental Neurorehabilitation, 13,* 360–368.

Jacobson, J. W., & Mulick, J. A. (1996). *Manual of diagnosis and professional practice in mental retardation.* Washington, DC: American Psychological Association.

Jones, K. L., Smith, D. W., Ulleland, C. N., & Streissguth, A. P. (1973). Patterns of malformation in offspring of chronic alcoholic mothers. *The Lancet, 1*(1267), 1271.

Luckner, J. L., Slike, S. B., & Johnson, H. (2012). Helping students who are deaf or hard of hearing succeed. *Teaching Exceptional Children, 44*, 58–67.

Marshark, M., Lang, H. G., & Albertini, G. A. (2002). *Educating deaf students: From research to practice.* New York, NY: Oxford.

Martin, G., & Pear, J. (2015). *Behavior modification: What it is and how to do it* (10th ed.). Upper Saddle River, NJ: Merrill/Prentice Hall.

Mathews, J. (2008, March 31). New microphones are bringing crystal-clear changes. *Washington Post,* p. B2.

National Professional Development Center on Autism Spectrum Disorder. (2014). *Evidence-based practices.* Frank Porter Graham Center, University of North Carolina. Retrieved from http://autismpdc.fpg.unc.edu/evidence-based-practices?utm_source=Copy+of+Ready%2C+Set%2C+Go+%7C+April++2016&utm_campaign=Ready+Set+Go+April+2016&utm_medium=email

Obiakor, F. E., Utley, C. A., Smith, R., & Harris-Obiakor, P. (2002). The Comprehensive Support Model for culturally diverse exceptional learners: Intervention in an age of change. *Intervention in School and Clinic, 38,* 14–27.

Owens, R. E., Metz, D. E., & Farinella, K. A. (2011). *Introduction to communication disorders: A life span perspective* (4th ed.). Boston, MA: Allyn & Bacon.

Pakulski, L. A., & Kaderavek, J. N. (2002). Children with minimal hearing loss: Interventions in the classroom. *Intervention in School and Clinic, 38,* 96–103.

Polloway, E. A., Patton, J. R., & Nelson, M. A. (2011). Intellectual and developmental disabilities. In J. M. Kauffman & D. P. Hallahan (Eds.), *Handbook of special education* (pp. 15–26). New York, NY: Routledge.

Schalock, R. L., Borthwick-Duffie, S., Bradley, V., Buntinx, W. H. E., Coulter, D. L., Craig, E. M., . . . Yeager, M. H. (2010). *Intellectual disability: Definition, classification, and systems of support.* Washington, DC: American Association on Intellectual and Developmental Disabilities.

Scott, J., Clark, C., & Brady, M. (2000). *Students with autism: Characteristics and instructional programming for special educators.* San Diego, CA: Singular Press.

Stewart, D. A., & Kluwin, T. N. (2001). *Teaching deaf and hard of hearing students: Content, strategies, and curriculum.* Boston, MA: Allyn & Bacon.

Turnbull, A. P., Turnbull, H. R., Erwin, E., Soodak, L., & Shogren, K. (2015). *Families, professionals, and exceptionality: Positive outcomes through partnerships and trust.* Boston, MA: Pearson.

U.S. Department of Education. (2006). *The Individuals with Disabilities Act Amendments of 2004. Final regulations.* Washington, DC: Author. Retrieved from http://idea.ed.gov/explore/view/p/,root,regs,300,A,300%252E8

U.S. Department of Education. (2015). *Thirty-seventh annual report to Congress on the implementation of the Individuals with Disabilities Education Act.* Washington, DC: Author. Retrieved from https://www2.ed.gov/about/reports/annual/osep/2015/parts-b-c/37th-arc-for-idea.pdf

Westling, D. L., Fox, L., & Carter, E. (2015). *Teaching students with severe disabilities* (5th ed.). Boston, MA: Pearson.

Wheeler, J. J., Mayton, M. R., & Carter, S. L. (2015). *Methods for teaching students with autism spectrum disorders: Evidence-based practices.* Boston, MA: Pearson.

Wong, C., Odom, S. L., Hume, K. Cox., A. W., Fettig, A., Kucharczyk, S.,... Schultz, T. R. (2013). *Evidence-based practices for children, youth, and young adults with autism spectrum disorder.* Chapel Hill, NC: The University of North Carolina, Frank Porter Graham Child Development Institute, Autism Evidence-Based Practice Review Group. Retrieved from http://autismpdc.fpg.unc.edu/evidence-based-practices

Zhang, J., & Wheeler, J. J. (2011). A meta-analysis of peer-mediated interventions for young children with autism spectrum disorders. *Education and Training in Autism and Developmental Disabilities, 46,* 62–77.

Zimmerman, G. J., & Zebehazy, K. T. (2011). Blindness and low vision. In J. M. Kauffman & D. P. Hallahan (Eds.), *Handbook of special education* (pp. 247–261). New York, NY: Routledge.

Zirkel, P. A. (2009). What does the law say? New Section 504 student eligibility. *Teaching Exceptional Children, 41,* 68–71.

Chapter 5

Anastasiou, D., Gardner, R., & Michail, D. (2011). Ethnicity and exceptionality. In J. M. Kauffman & D. P. Hallahan (Eds.), *Handbook of special education* (pp. 745–758). New York, NY: Routledge.

Baca, L. M., Baca, E., & de Valenzuela, J. S. (2004a). Background and rationale for bilingual special education. In L. M. Baca & H. T. Cervantes (Eds.), *The bilingual special education interface* (4th ed., pp. 1–23). Upper Saddle River, NJ: Merrill/Prentice Hall.

Baca, L. M., Baca, E., & de Valenzuela, J. S. (2004b). Development of the bilingual special education interface. In L. M. Baca & H. T. Cervantes (Eds.), *The bilingual special education interface* (4th ed., pp. 101–123). Upper Saddle River, NJ: Merrill/Prentice Hall.

Baca, L. M., & Cervantes, H. T. (2004). *The bilingual special education interface* (4th ed.). Upper Saddle River, NJ: Merrill/Prentice Hall.

Baker, D. L., Al Otaiba, S., Ortiz, M., Correa, V., & Cole, R. (2014). Vocabulary development and intervention for English learners in the early grades. *Advances Child Development and Behavior, 46,* 281–338.

Banks, J. A. (2015). *Cultural diversity and education: Foundations, curriculum, and teaching* (6th ed.). Boston, MA: Pearson.

Beach, C. (2014). *At-risk students: Transforming student behavior.* Lanham, MD: Rowman & Littlefield Education.

Bireley, M. (1995). Identifying high ability/high achievement giftedness. In J. L. Genshaft, M. Bireley, & C. L. Hollinger (Eds.), *Serving gifted and talented students: A resource for school personnel* (pp. 49–65). Austin, TX: Pro-Ed.

Callahan, C. M. (2011). Special gifts and talents. In J. M. Kauffman & D. P. Hallahan (Eds.), *Handbook of special education* (pp. 304–317). New York, NY: Routledge.

Caplan, P., & Dinardo, L. (1986). Is there a relationship between child abuse and learning disability? *Canadian Journal of Behavioral Science, 18,* 367–380.

Cartledge, G., Gardner, R., & Ford, D. Y. (2008). *Diverse learners with exceptionalities: Culturally responsive teaching in the inclusive classroom.* Columbus, OH: Merrill Education.

Castellano, J. A., & Frazier, A. D. (Eds.). (2011). *Special populations in gifted education.* Waco, TX: Prufrock.

Child Welfare Information Gateway. (2011). *About CAPTA: A legislative history.* Washington, DC: U.S. Department of Health and Human Services, Children's Bureau.

Children's Defense Fund. (2011). *Each day in America.* Washington, DC: Author. Retrieved from http://www.childrensdefense.org/child-research-data-publications/each-day-in-america.html

Chinn, P. C., & Hughes, S. (1987). Representation of minority students in special education classes. *Remedial and Special Education, 8*(4), 41–46.

Clark, B. (2013). *Growing up gifted* (8th ed.). Boston, MA: Pearson.

Crosson-Tower, C. (2014). *Understanding child abuse and neglect* (9th ed.). Boston, MA: Allyn & Bacon.

Davis, G. A., Rimm, S. B., & Siegle, D. (2011). *Education of the gifted and talented* (6th ed.). Boston, MA: Allyn & Bacon.

Definitions; Gifted, Pub. L. No. 100-297, § 4103 (1998).

Diamond, L. J., & Jaudes, P. K. (1983). Child abuse in a cerebral-palsied population. *Developmental Medicine and Child Neurology, 25,* 169–174.

Donovan, S., & Cross, C. (Eds.). (2002). *Minority students in special and gifted education.* Washington, DC: National Research Council.

East, K., & Thomas, R. L. (2007). *Across cultures: A guide to multicultural literature for children.* Portsmouth, NH: Libraries Unlimited.

Echevarria, J. J., & Graves, A. (2015). *Sheltered content instruction: Teaching English learners with diverse abilities* (5th ed.). Boston, MA: Pearson.

Education Commission of the States. (2004). *State gifted and talented definitions.* Denver, CO: Author. Retrieved from http://www.ecs.org/state-and-federal-policy-gifted-and-talented-youth/

Ehlers-Zavala, F. P. (2011). History of bilingual special education. In A. F. Rotatori, F. E. Obiakor, & J. P. Bakken (Eds.), *History of special education* (pp. 343–362). Bingley, UK: Emerald.

Feldhusen, J. F., & Moon, S. (1995). The educational continuum and delivery of services. In J. L. Genshaft, M. Bireley, & C. L. Hollinger (Eds.), *Serving gifted and talented students: A resource for school personnel* (pp. 103–121). Austin, TX: Pro-Ed.

Ford, D. Y. (2011). *Reversing underachievement among gifted Black students.* Waco, TX: Prufrock.

Ford, D. Y. (2012). Culturally different students in special education: Looking backward to move forward. *Exceptional Children, 78,* 391–405.

Frieman, B. B. (2001). *What teachers need to know about children at risk.* Boston, MA: Allyn & Bacon.

Fuchs, L. S., & Vaughn, S. (2012). Responsiveness-to-intervention: A decade later. *Journal of Learning Disabilities, 45,* 195–203.

Gardner, H. (2006). *Multiple intelligences: New horizons in theory and practice.* New York, NY: Basic Books.

Gollnick, D. M., & Chinn, P. C. (2013). *Multicultural education in a pluralistic society* (9th ed.). Boston, MA: Allyn & Bacon.

Grandinette, S., & Best, S. J. (2009). Traumatic brain injury. In K. W. Heller, P. E. Forney, P. A. Alberto, S. J. Best, & M. N. Schwartzman (Eds.), *Understanding physical, health, and multiple disabilities* (pp. 118–138). Upper Saddle River, NJ: Merrill/Prentice Hall.

Grassi, E. A., & Barker, H. B. (2010). *Culturally and linguistically diverse exceptional students: Strategies for teaching and assessment.* Thousand Oaks, CA: Sage.

Gregory, D. A., Starnes, W. T., & Blaylock, A. W. (1988). Finding and nurturing potential giftedness among Black and Hispanic students. In A. A. Ortiz & B. A. Ramirez (Eds.), *Schools and the culturally diverse exceptional student: Promising practices and future directions* (pp. 76–85). Reston, VA: Council for Exceptional Children.

Grossman, R. (1997, July 6). What is an American? *Chicago Tribune Magazine,* pp. 11–16, 21.

Harry, B. (1992). *Cultural diversity, families, and the special education system.* New York, NY: Teachers College Press.

Harry, B. (1994). *The disproportionate representation of minority students in special education.* Alexandria, VA: National Association of State Directors of Special Education.

Harry, B., Arnaiz, P., Klingner, J., & Sturges, K. (2008). Schooling and the construction of identity in Spain and the United States. *Journal of Special Education, 42,* 15–25.

Harry, B., & Klingner, J. (2006). *Why are so many minority students in special education? Understanding race and disability in schools.* New York, NY: Teachers College Press.

Heflin, L. J., & Rudy, K. (1991). *Homeless and in need of special education.* Reston, VA: Council for Exceptional Children.

Hoffman, S. D., & Maynard, R. A. (2008). *Kids having kids: Economic costs and social consequences of teen pregnancy.* Washington, DC: Urban Institute Press.

Jensen, E. (2009). *Teaching with poverty in mind: What being poor does to kids' brains and what schools can do about it.* Alexandria, VA: ASCD.

Kalyanpur, M. (2008). The paradox of majority underrepresentation in special education in India: Constructions of difference in a developing country. *Journal of Special Education, 42,* 55–64.

Kauffman, J. M., & Landrum, T. (2013). *Characteristics of emotional and behavioral disorders of children and youth* (10th ed.). Upper Saddle River, NJ: Merrill/Pearson.

Klein, M., & Stern, L. (1971). Low birth weight and the battered child syndrome. *American Journal of Disabled Children, 122,* 15–18.

Klingner, J. K., & Edwards, P. A. (2006). Cultural considerations with response to intervention models. *Reading Research Quarterly, 41,* 108–117.

Lynch, E. W. (1992). Developing cross-cultural competence. In E. W. Lynch & M. J. Hanson (Eds.), *Developing cross-cultural competence* (pp. 35–59). Baltimore, MD: Brookes Publishing.

MacMillan, D. L., & Reschly, D. J. (1998). Overrepresentation of minority students: The case for greater specificity or reconsideration of the variables examined. *Journal of Special Education, 32,* 15–24.

Mellard, D., & Johnson, E. (2008). *RTI: A practitioner's guide to implementing response to intervention.* Thousand Oaks, CA: Corwin.

Miksic, S. (1987). Drug abuse management in adolescent special education. In M. M. Kerr, C. M. Nelson, & D. L. Lambert (Eds.), *Helping adolescents with learning and behavior problems* (pp. 226–253). Upper Saddle River, NJ: Merrill/Prentice Hall.

Mizerek, E. A., & Hinz, E. E. (2004). Helping homeless students. *Principal Leadership Magazine, 4*(8). Retrieved from http://www.naspcenter.org/principals/nassp_homeless.html

National Association of School Psychologists. (2012). *Preventing youth suicide–tips for parents and educators.* Washington, DC: Author. Retrieved from http://www.nasponline.org/resources/crisis_safety/suicideprevention.aspx

National Center on Addiction and Substance Abuse at Columbia University. (2011). *Adolescent substance use: America's #1 health problem.* New York, NY: Author. Retrieved http://www.casacolumbia.org/upload/2011/20110629adolescentsubstanceuse.pdf

National Coalition for the Homeless. (2007). *Education of homeless children and youth.* Washington, DC: Author. Retrieved from http://www.nationalhomeless.org/publications/facts/education.pdf

National Education Association. (2015). *50 multicultural books every child should read.* Washington, DC: Author. Retrieved from http://www.nea.org/grants/50-multicultural-books.html

Navan, J. (2008). *Nurturing the gifted female: A guide for educators and parents.* Thousand Oaks, CA: Corwin Press.

Norton, D. E. (2012). *Multicultural children's literature: Through the eyes of many children* (4th ed.). Boston, MA: Pearson.

Obiakor, F. E., & Roratori, A. (2014). *Multicultural education for learners with special needs in the twenty-first century.* Charlotte, NC: Information Age.

Ovando, C. J., & Combs, M. C. (2012). *Bilingual and ESL classroom: Teaching in multicultural contexts* (5th ed.). Boston, MA: McGraw-Hill.

Patton, J. M. (1998). The disproportionate representation of African Americans in special education: Looking behind the curtain for understanding and solutions. *Journal of Special Education, 32,* 25–31

Plucker, J., & Callahan, C. M. (Eds.). (2008). *Critical issues and practices in gifted education.* Waco, TX: Prufrock Press.

Plucker, J., & Callahan, C. M. (2014). Research on giftedness and gifted education: Status of the field and considerations for the future. *Exceptional Children, 80,* 390–406.

Renzulli, J. S. (2005). The three-ring conception of giftedness: A developmental model for promoting creative productivity. In R. J. Sternberg & J. E. Davidson (Eds.), *Conceptions of giftedness* (pp. 246–279). New York, NY: Cambridge University Press.

Richards-Tutor, C., Baker, D. L., Gersten, R., Baker, S. K., & Smith, J. M. (2016). The effectiveness of reading interventions for English learners: A research synthesis. *Exceptional Children, 82,* 144–169.

Salend, S. J., & Duhaney, L. M. G. (2005). Understanding and addressing the disproportionate representation of students of color in special education. *Intervention in School and Clinic, 40,* 213–221.

Sedlak, A. J., Mettenburg, J., Basena, M., Petta, I., McPherson, K., Greene, A., & Li, S. (2010). *Fourth National Incidence Study of Child Abuse and Neglect (NIS–4): Report to Congress.* Washington, DC: U.S. Department of Health and Human Services, Administration for Children and Families.

Shaahinfar, A., Whitelaw, K. D., & Mansour, K. M. (2015). Update on abusive head trauma. *Current Opinion in Pediatrics, 27,* 308–314.

Sternberg, R. J. (2005). The triarchic theory of successful intelligence. In D. P. Flanagan & P. L. Harrison (Eds.), *Contemporary intellectual assessment: Theories, tests, and issues* (pp. 103–119). New York, NY: Guilford.

Suicide Prevention Lifeline. (2005). *Suicide warning signs.* Washington, DC: U.S. Department of Health and Human Services. Retrieved from http://store.samhsa.gov/shin/content/SVP05-0126/SVP05-0126.pdf

Taormina-Weiss, W. (2012). Homeless children with disabilities in America. *Disabled World.* Retrieved from http://www.disabled-world.com/disability/children/homeless-kids.php

Taylor, L. S., & Whittaker, C. R. (2008). *Bridging multiple worlds: Case studies of diverse educational communities* (2nd ed.). Boston, MA: Allyn & Bacon.

Tornquist, E. H., Mastropieri, M. A., Scruggs, T. E., Berry, H. G., & Halloran, W. D. (2009). The impact of poverty on special education. In T. E. Scruggs & M. A. Mastropieri (Eds.), *Policy and practice: Advances in learning and behavioral disabilities* (Vol. 22, pp. 169–188). Bingley, UK: Emerald.

U.S. Census Bureau. (2010). *Language use in the United States: 2007.* Washington, DC: Author. Retrieved from http://www.census.gov/hhes/socdemo/language/data/acs/ACS-12.pdf

U.S. Census Bureau. (2011). *Overview of race and Hispanic origin: 2010.* Washington, DC: Author. Retrieved from http://www.census.gov/prod/cen2010/briefs/c2010br-02.pdf

U.S. Department of Education. (1993). *National excellence: A case for developing America's talent.* Washington, DC: Author. Retrieved from https://www.ocps.net/cs/ese/programs/gifted/Documents/National%20Excellence_%20A%20Case%20for%20Developing%20America%27s%20Talent_%20Introduction.pdf

U.S. Department of Education. (2015). *Thirtieth annual report to Congress on the implementation of the Individuals with Disabilities Education Act.* Washington, DC: Author.

Virginia Institute for Social Services Training Activities. (2016). *Child abuse and neglect: Recognition, reporting, and responding.*

Virginia Department of Social Services, Virginia Commonwealth University, Virginia Institute for Social Services Training Activities, and Virginia Department of Education. Richmond, VA: Author. Retrieved from http://www.dss.virginia.gov/family/cps/mandated_reporters/cwse5691/story.html

Yates, J. R., & Ortiz, A. A. (2004). Classification issues in special education for English language learners. In A. M. Sorrells, H. J. Rieth, & P. T. Sindelar (Eds.), *Critical issues in special education: Access, diversity, and accountability* (pp. 38–50). Boston, MA: Allyn & Bacon.

Chapter 6

Agirdag, O. (2009). All languages welcomed here. *Educational Leadership, 66*(7), 8–13.

Alberto, P. A., & Troutman, A. C. (2012). *Applied behavior analysis for teachers* (9th ed.). Upper Saddle River, NJ: Merrill/Prentice Hall.

Archer, A., & Hughes, C. A. (2011). *Explicit instruction: Effective and efficient teaching.* New York, NY: Guilford.

Banks, J. A. (2015). *Cultural diversity and education: Foundations, curriculum, and teaching* (6th ed.). Boston, MA: Pearson.

Brigham, F. J., Scruggs, T. E., & Mastropieri, M. A. (1992). The effect of teacher enthusiasm on the learning and behavior of learning disabled students. *Learning Disabilities Research & Practice, 7,* 68–73.

Burnett, P. C. (2003). The impact of teacher feedback on student self-talk and self-concept in reading and mathematics. *Journal of Classroom Interaction, 38,* 11–16.

Carnine, D. (1976). Effects of two teacher presentation rates on off-task behavior, answering correctly, and participation. *Journal of Applied Behavior Analysis, 9,* 199–206.

CAST. (2011). *Universal design for learning guidelines, version 2.0.* Wakefield, MA: Author.

CAST. (2012). *About UDL.* Cambridge, MA: Author. Retrieved from http://www.cast.org/udl/index.html

Center for Parent Information and Resources. (2016). *Supports, modifications, and accommodations for students.* Newark, NJ: Author. Retrieved from http://www.parentcenterhub.org/repository/accommodations/

Clare, S. K., Jenson, W. R., Kehle, T. J., & Bray, M. A. (2000). Self-modeling as a treatment for increasing on task behavior. *Psychology in the School, 37,* 517–523.

Danielson, C. (2010). *Implementing the framework for teaching in enhancing professional practice.* Alexandria, VA: ASCD.

Echevarria, J., & Graves, A. (2015). *Sheltered content instruction: Teaching English language learners with diverse abilities* (5th ed.). Boston, MA: Pearson.

Echevarria, J., Richards-Tutor, C., Canges, R., & Francis, D. (2011). Using the SIOP model to promote the acquisition of language and science concepts. *Bilingual Research Journal, 43,* 334–351.

Gartin, B. C., Murdick, N. L., Imbeau, M., & Perner, D. E. (2002). *How to use differentiated instruction with students with developmental disabilities in the general education classroom.* Reston, VA: Council for Exceptional Children.

Gleason, M., Carnine, D., & Vala, N. (1991). Cumulative versus rapid introduction of new information. *Exceptional Children, 57,* 353–358.

Good, T. L., & Brophy, J. E. (2007). *Looking in classrooms* (10th ed.). Boston, MA: Allyn & Bacon.

Guckert, M., Mastropieri, M. A., & Scruggs, T. E. (2016). Personalizing research: Special educators' awareness of evidence-based practice. *Exceptionality, 24,* 63–78.

Hall, T. E., Meyer, A., & Rose, D. H. (Eds.). (2012). *Universal design for learning in the classroom: Practical applications.* New York, NY: Guilford.

Individuals with Disabilities Education Improvement Act of 2004, Pub. L. No. 108-446, 20 U.S.C. §1400 *et seq.* (2004).

Jakulski, J., & Mastropieri, M. A. (2004). Homework for students with disabilities. In T. E. Scruggs & M. A. Mastropieri (Eds.), *Advances in learning and behavioral disabilities: Research in secondary settings* (Vol. 18, pp. 77–122). Oxford, UK: Elsevier.

Kunter, M., Frenzel, A., Nagy, G., Baumert, J., & Pekrun, R. (2010). Teacher enthusiasm: Dimensionality and context specificity. *Contemporary Educational Psychology, 36,* 289–301.

Larrivee, B. (1985). *Effective teaching for successful mainstreaming.* New York, NY: Longman.

Mastropieri, M. A., & Scruggs, T. E. (2002). *Effective instruction for special education* (3rd ed.). Columbus, OH: Merrill.

Mastropieri, M. A., & Scruggs, T. E. (2004). Effective classroom instruction. In C. Spielberger (Ed.), *Encyclopedia of applied psychology* (pp. 687–691). Oxford, UK: Elsevier.

Mastropieri, M. A., Scruggs, T. E., Mantzicopoulos, P. Y., Sturgeon, A., Goodwin, L., & Chung, S. (1998). "A place where living things affect and depend on each other": Qualitative and quantitative outcomes associated with inclusive science teaching. *Science Education, 82,* 163–179.

Meyer, A., Rose, D. M., & Gordon, D. (2014). *Universal design for learning: Theory and practice.* Wakefield, MA: CAST.

Moore, K. D. (2011). *Effective instructional strategies: From theory to practice.* Thousand Oaks, CA: Sage.

Rao, K., Ok, M. W., & Bryant, B. R. (2014). A review of research on universal design educational models. *Remedial and Special Education, 35,* 153–166.

Richardson, V. (2003). Preservice teachers' beliefs. In J. Raths & A. C. McAninch (Eds.), *Teacher beliefs and classroom performance: The impact of teacher education.* Greenwich, CT: Information Age Publishing.

Rosenshine, B., & Stevens, R. (1986). Teaching functions. In M. C. Wittrock (Ed.), *Handbook of research on teaching* (3rd ed., pp. 376–391). New York, NY: MacMillan.

Ruiz, N. T., Rueda, R., Figueroa, R. A., & Boothroyd, M. (1995). Bilingual special education teacher's shifting paradigms: Complex responses to educational reform. *Journal of Learning Disabilities, 28,* 622–635.

Sabornie, E. J., & deBettencourt, L. U. (2009). *Teaching students with mild and high-incidence disabilities at the secondary level* (3rd ed.). Upper Saddle River, NJ: Merrill/Prentice Hall.

Scheuermann, B. K., & Hall, J. A. (2016). *Positive behavior supports for the classroom* (3rd ed.). Boston, MA: Pearson.

Scruggs, T. E., & Mastropieri, M. A. (1994a). The effectiveness of generalization training: A quantitative synthesis of single subject research. In T. E. Scruggs & M. A. Mastropieri (Eds.), *Advances in learning and behavioral disabilities* (Vol. 8, pp. 259–280). Greenwich, CT: JAI Press.

Scruggs, T. E., & Mastropieri, M. A. (1994b). Successful mainstreaming in elementary science classes: A qualitative investigation of three reputational cases. *American Educational Research Journal, 31,* 785–811.

Scruggs, T. E., & Mastropieri, M. A. (1995). What makes special education special? An analysis of the PASS variables in inclusion settings. *Journal of Special Education, 29,* 224–233.

Scruggs, T. E., Mastropieri, M. A., & Brigham, F. J. (2013). Common core science standards: Implications for students with LD. *Learning Disabilities Research & Practice, 28,* 49–57.

Scruggs, T. E., Mastropieri, M. A., & Sullivan, G. S. (1994). Promoting relational thinking skills: Elaborative interrogation for mildly handicapped students. *Exceptional Children, 60,* 450–457.

Seo, S., Brownell, M. T., Bishop, A. G., & Dingle, M. (2008). An examination of beginning special education teachers' classroom practices that engage elementary students with learning disabilities in reading instruction. *Exceptional Children, 75,* 97–122.

Sheridan, S. M. (2009). Homework interventions for children with attention and learning problems: Where is the "home" in "homework"? *School Psychology Review, 38,* 334–337.

Smith, L. (1977). Aspects of teacher discourse and student achievement in mathematics. *Journal for Research in Mathematics Education, 8,* 195–204.

Smith, L., & Land, M. (1981). Low-inference verbal behaviors related to teacher clarity. *Journal of Classroom Interaction, 17,* 37–42.

Sullivan, G. S., Mastropieri, M. A., & Scruggs, T. E. (1995). Reasoning and remembering: Coaching thinking with students with learning disabilities. *Journal of Special Education, 29,* 310–322.

Tomlinson, C. A. (2014a). *Differentiation of instruction in the elementary grades.* (ERIC Document Reproduction Service No. ED 443 572)

Tomlinson, C. A. (2014b). *The differentiated classroom: Responding to the needs of all learners* (2nd ed.). Alexandria, VA: ASCD.

Urbach, J., Moore, B. A., Klingner, J. K., Galman, S., Haager, D., Brownell, M. T., & Dingle, M. (2014). "That's my job": Comparing the beliefs of more and less accomplished special educators related to their roles and responsibilities. *Teacher Education and Special Education, 38,* 323–336.

Wentzel, K. R., & Brophy, J. (2014). *Motivating students to learn* (4th ed.). New York, NY: Routledge.

Chapter 7

Balu, R., Zhu, P., Doolittle, F., Schiller, E., Jenkins, J., & Gersten, R. (2015). *Evaluation of response to intervention practices for elementary school reading.* Washington, DC: U.S. Department of Education, Institute of Education Sciences.

Berkeley, S., Bender, W. N., Peaster, L. G., & Saunders, L. (2009). Implementation of response to intervention: A snapshot of progress. *Journal of Learning Disabilities, 42,* 85–95.

Berkeley, S., Scruggs, T. E., & Mastropieri, M. A. (2010). Reading comprehension instruction for students with learning disabilities, 1995–2006: A meta-analysis. *Remedial and Special Education, 31,* 423–436.

Cortes, K., Goodman, J., & Nomi, T. (2013, Winter). A double dose of algebra. *Education Next, 71–76.* Retrieved from http://educationnext.org/files/ednext_20131_cortes.pdf

Deno, S. (2016). Data-based decision-making. In S. R. Jimerson, M. K. Burns, & A. M. VanDerHayden (Eds.), *Handbook of response to intervention: The science and practice of multi-tiered systems of support* (2nd ed., pp. 9–28). New York, NY: Springer.

Denton, C. A., & Vaughn, S. (2010). Preventing and remediating reading difficulties: Perspectives from research. In T. A. Glover & S. Vaughn (Eds.), *The promise of response to intervention: Evaluating current science and practice* (pp. 78–112). New York, NY: Guilford.

Division for Learning Disabilities. (2007). *Thinking about response to instruction and learning disabilities: A teacher's guide.* Arlington, VA: Author.

Dynamic Indicators of Basic Early Literacy Skills (DIBELS). (2006). Eugene, OR: University of Oregon, College of Education. Retrieved from http://dibels.uoregon.edu/

Fuchs, D., & Deshler, D. (2007). What we need to know about responsiveness to intervention (and shouldn't be afraid to ask). *Learning Disabilities Research and Practice, 22,* 129–136.

Fuchs, D., & Fuchs, L. S. (2006). Introduction to response to intervention: What, why, and how valid is it? *Reading Research Quarterly, 41,* 93–99.

Fuchs, D., Fuchs, L. S., & Compton, D. C. (2012). Smart RTI: A next-generation approach to multi-level prevention. *Exceptional Children, 78,* 263–279.

Fuchs, D., Fuchs, L. S., Compton, D. C., Wehby, J., Schumacher, R. F.,…. Jordan, N. C. (2015). Inclusion versus specialized intervention for very-low-performing students: What does *access* mean in an era of academic challenge? *Exceptional Children, 81,* 134–157.

Fuchs, D., Fuchs, L. S., & Stecker, P. M. (2010). The "blurring" of special education in a new continuum of placements and services. *Exceptional Children, 76,* 301–323.

Fuchs, D., Mock, D., Morgan, P. L., & Young, C. L. (2003). Responsiveness-to-intervention: Definitions, evidence, and implications for the learning disabilities construct. *Learning Disabilities Research and Practice, 18,* 157–171.

Fuchs, L. S., Fuchs, D., & Malone, A. S. (2016). Multilevel response-to-intervention prevention systems: Mathematics intervention at Tier 2. In S. R. Jimerson, M. K. Burns, & A. M. VanDerHayden (Eds.), *Handbook of response to intervention: The science and practice of multi-tiered systems of support* (2nd ed., pp. 3–28). New York, NY: Springer.

Gay, G. (2010). *Culturally responsive teaching: Theory, research, and practice* (2nd ed.). New York, NY: Teachers College Press.

Gerber, M. M. (2005). Teachers are still the test: Limitations of response to instruction strategies for identifying children with learning disabilities. *Journal of Learning Disabilities, 38,* 516–524.

Glover, T. A. (2010). Supporting all students: The promise of response to intervention. In T. A. Glover & S. Vaughn (Eds.), *The promise of response to intervention: Evaluating current science and practice* (pp. 1–6). New York, NY: Guilford.

Gresham, F. M. (2002). Responsiveness to intervention: An alternative approach to the identification of learning disabilities. In R. Bradley, L. Danielson, & D. P. Hallahan (Eds.), *Identification of learning disabilities* (pp. 467–519). Mahwah, NJ: Lawrence Erlbaum.

Gresham, F. M., MacMillan, D. L., Beebe-Frankenberger, M. E., & Bocian, K. M. (2000). Treatment integrity in learning disabilities intervention research: Do we really know how treatments are implemented? *Learning Disabilities Research and Practice, 15,* 198–205.

Hall, T. E., Meyer, A., & Rose, D. H. (Eds.). (2012). *Universal design for learning in the classroom: Practical applications.* New York, NY: Guilford.

Harry, B., & Klingner, J. K. (2014). *Why are so many minority students in special education? Understanding race and disability in schools* (2nd ed.). New York, NY: Teachers College Press.

Hasbrook, J., & Tindal, G. (2005). *Oral reading fluency: 90 years of measurement.* Technical Report #33, Behavioral Research and Teaching, University of Oregon, Eugene, OR. Retrieved from http://www.brtprojects.org/publications/dl/51

Ihlo, T., & Nantais, M. (2010). Evidence-based interventions within a multi-tier framework for positive behavioral supports. In T. A. Glover & S. Vaughn (Eds.), *The promise of response to intervention: Evaluating current science and practice* (pp. 239–266). New York, NY: Guilford.

Individuals with Disabilities Education Improvement Act of 2004, Pub. L. No. 108-446, 20 U.S.C. §1400 *et seq.* (2004).

Jimerson, S. R., Burns, M. K., & VanDerHayden A. M. (2016). From response to intervention to multi-tiered systems of support: Advances in the science and practice of assessment and intervention. In S. R. Jimerson, M. K. Burns, & A. M. VanDerHayden (Eds.), *Handbook of response to intervention: The science and practice of multi-tiered systems of support* (2nd ed., pp. 1–6). New York, NY: Springer.

Jimerson, S. R., Stein, R., Haddock, A., & Shahroozi, R. (2016). Common Core State Standards and response to intervention: The importance of assessment, intervention, and progress monitoring. In S. R. Jimerson, M. K. Burns, & A. M. VanDerHayden (Eds.), *Handbook of response to intervention: The science and practice of multi-tiered systems of support* (2nd ed., pp. 165–184). New York, NY: Springer.

Johnson, E., Mellard, D. F., Fuchs, D., & McKnight, M. A. (2006). *Responsiveness to intervention (RTI): How to do it.* Lawrence, KS: National Research Center on Learning Disabilities. Retrieved from https://eric.ed.gov/?id=ED496979

Johnson, E. S., Smith, L. A., & Harris, M. L. (2009). *How RTI works in secondary schools.* Thousand Oaks, CA: Corwin.

Kaminski, R. A., & Good, R. A. (1998). Use of curriculum-based measurement to assess early literacy: Dynamic indicators of basic early literacy skills. In M. R. Shinn (Ed.), *Advances in curriculum-based measurements and its use in a problem-solving model* (pp. 113–142). New York, NY: Guilford.

Klingner, J. K., & Edwards, P. A. (2006). Cultural considerations with response to intervention models. *Reading Research Quarterly, 41,* 108–117.

MacGinitie, W. H., MacGinitie, R. K., Maria, K., Dreyer, L. G., & Hughes, K. E. (2000). *Gates MacGinitie reading tests* (4th ed.). Rolling Meadows, IL: Riverside.

Marston, D. (2005). Tiers of intervention in responsiveness to intervention: Prevention outcomes and learning disabilities identification patterns. *Journal of Learning Disabilities, 38,* 539–544.

Mastropieri, M. A., & Scruggs, T. E. (2002). *Effective instruction for special education* (3rd ed.). Austin, TX: Pro-Ed.

Mastropieri, M. A., & Scruggs, T. E. (2005). Feasibility and consequences of response to intervention (RTI): Examination of the issues and scientific evidence as a model for the identification of individuals with learning disabilities. *Journal of Learning Disabilities, 38,* 525–531.

Mellard, D., & Johnson, E. (2008). *RTI: A practitioner's guide to implementing response to intervention.* Thousand Oaks, CA: Corwin.

Mellard, D. F., & McKnight, M. A. (2006). *RTI implementation tool for reading: Best practices.* [Brochure]. Lawrence, KS: National Research Center on Learning Disabilities. Retrieved from https://www.researchgate.net/profile/Daryl_Mellard/publication/265279115_RTI_Implementation_Tool_for_Reading_Best_Practices/links/5707e14908ae2eb9421bdbd9.pdf

Musgrove, M. (2011). *A response to instruction (RTI) process cannot be used to delay-deny an evaluation for disability under the Individuals with Disabilities Education Act (IDEA).* Memo sent to State Directors of Special Education. Washington, DC: Department of Education, Office of Special Education Programs.

National Governors Association Center for Best Practices, Council of Chief State School Officers. (2010). *Common Core State Standards for English language arts and literacy in history/social studies, science, and technical subjects.* Washington, DC: Author.

National Institute of Child Health and Human Development (NICHD). (2000). *Report to the National Reading Panel. Teaching children to read: An evidence-based assessment of the scientific research literature on reading and its implications for reading instruction.* NIH Publication No. 00-4769. Washington, DC: U.S. Government Printing Office.

O'Connor, R. E., & Sanchez, V. (2011a). Issues in assessment for intervention in implementation of responsiveness to intervention models. In T. E. Scruggs & M. A. Mastropieri (Eds.), *Assessment and intervention: Advances in learning and behavioral disabilities* (Vol. 24, pp. 149–170). Bingley, UK: Emerald.

O'Connor, R. E., & Sanchez, V. (2011b). Responsiveness to intervention models for reducing reading difficulties and identifying learning disability. In J. Kauffman, D. P. Hallahan, & J. Lloyd (Eds.), *Handbook of special education* (pp. 123–133). New York, NY: Routledge.

Orosco, M. J., & Klingner, J. (2010). One school's implementation of RTI with English language learners: "Referring into RTI." *Journal of Learning Disabilities, 43*, 269–288.

Powell, S. R., & Fuchs, L. S. (2015). Intensive interventions in mathematics. *Learning Disabilities Research and Practice, 30*, 182–192.

Richey, K., Silverman, R. D., Montanaro, E. A., Speece, D. L., & Schatschneider, C. (2012). Effects of a Tier 2 supplementary reading intervention for at-risk fourth grade students. *Exceptional Children, 78*, 318–334.

Scheuermann, B. K., & Hall, J. A. (2016). *Positive behavior supports for the classroom* (3rd ed.). Boston, MA: Pearson.

Scruggs, T. E., & Mastropieri, M. A. (2002). On babies and bathwater: Addressing the problems of assessment and identification of learning disabilities. *Learning Disability Quarterly, 25*, 155–168.

Shinn, M., Windram, H. S., & Bollman, K. A. (2016). Implementing response to intervention in secondary schools. In S. R. Jimerson, M. K. Burns, & A. M. VanDerHayden (Eds.), *Handbook of response to intervention: The science and practice of multi-tiered systems of support* (2nd ed., pp. 563–586). New York, NY: Springer.

Stecker, P. M., Fuchs, L. S., & Fuchs, D. (2005). Using curriculum-based measurement to improve student achievement: A review of research. *Psychology in the Schools, 42*, 795–819.

Stoiber, K. C., & Gettinger, M. (2016). Multi-tiered systems in evidence-based practices. In S. R. Jimerson, M. K. Burns, & A. M. VanDerHayden (Eds.), *Handbook of response to intervention: The science and practice of multi-tiered systems of support* (2nd ed., pp. 121–141). New York, NY: Springer.

Sugai, G., Horner, R. H., Fixen, D., & Blase, K. (2010). Developing systems-level capacity for RTI implementation: Current efforts and future directions. In T. A. Glover & S. Vaughn (Eds.), *The promise of response to intervention: Evaluating current science and practice* (pp. 286–309). New York, NY: Guilford.

Swanson, H. L. (2000). What instruction works for students with learning disabilities? Summarizing the results from a meta-analysis of intervention studies. In R. Gersten, E. P. Schiller, & S. Vaughn (Eds.), *Contemporary special education research: Syntheses of the knowledge base on critical instructional issues* (pp. 1–30). Mahwah, NJ: Erlbaum.

Tilly, W. D. (2003, December). *How many tiers are needed for successful prevention and early intervention? Heartland Area Education Agency's evolution from four to three tiers.* Paper presented at the NRCLD Responsiveness to Intervention Symposium, Kansas City, MO. Retrieved from http://citeseerx.ist.psu.edu/viewdoc/download?doi=10.1.1.520.4453&rep=rep1&type=pdf

Tukey, J. W. (1977). *Exploratory data analysis.* Reading, MA: Addison-Wesley-Longman.

Vaughn, S., & Bos, C. (2015). *Strategies for teaching students with learning and behavior problems* (9th ed.). Boston, MA: Pearson.

Vaughn, S., Denton, C. A., & Fletcher, J. M. (2010). Why intensive interventions are necessary for students with severe reading difficulties. *Psychology in the Schools, 47*, 432–444.

Vaughn, S., Roberts, G., Schnakenberg, J. B., Fall, A. M., Vaughn, M. G., & Wexler, J. (2015). Improving reading comprehension for high school students with disabilities: Effects for comprehension and school retention. *Exceptional Children, 82*, 117–137.

Vaughn, S., & Wanzek, J. (2014). Intensive intervention in reading for students with reading disabilities: Meaningful impacts. *Learning Disabilities Research and Practice, 29*, 46–53.

Vaughn, S., Wexler, J., Roberts, G., Barth, A. A., Cirino, P. T., Romain, M. A., … Denton, C. A. (2011). Effects of individualized and standardized interventions on middle school students with reading disabilities. *Exceptional Children, 77*, 391–407.

Wanzek, J., Vaughn, S., Scammacca, N., Gatlin, B., Walker, M. A., & Capin, P. (2015). Meta-analyses of the effects of Tier 2 type reading interventions in grades k–3. *Educational Psychology Review.* Advance online publication.

Wright, P. W. D., & Wright, P. D. (2005). *Wrightslaw: IDEA 2004.* Hartfield, VA: Harbor House Law Press.

Chapter 8

Alberto, P. A., & Troutman, A. C. (2012). *Applied behavior analysis for teachers* (9th ed.). Upper Saddle River, NJ: Merrill/Pearson.

Algozzine, B., Wang, C., White, R., Cooke, N., Marr, M. B., & Algozzine, K. (2012). Effects of multi-tiered academic and behavior instruction on difficult-to-teach students. *Exceptional Children, 79*, 45–64.

Anckarsäter, H., Stahlberg, O., Larson, T., Hakansson, C., Jutblad, S., Niklasson, L., et al. (2010). The impact of ADHD and autism spectrum disorders on temperament, character, and personality development. *Focus, 8*, 269–275.

Anderman, E. M., & Patrick, H. (2012). Achievement goal theory, conceptualization of ability/intelligence, and classroom climate. In S. L. Christenson, A. L. Reschly, & C. Wylie (Eds.), *Handbook of research on student engagement* (Part 2, pp. 173–191). New York, NY: Springer.

Baker, J. (2006). *The social skills picture book for high school and beyond.* Arlington, TX: Future Horizons.

Banks, J. A. (2015). *Cultural diversity and education: Foundations, curriculum, and teaching* (6th ed.). Upper Saddle River, NJ: Pearson.

Barnhill, G. P. (2005). Functional behavior assessment in schools. *Intervention in School and Clinic, 40*, 141–143.

Beck, M. A., Roblee, K., & Johns, C. (1982). The psychoeducational management of disturbed children. *Education, 102*, 232–235.

Bellini, S., Peters, J. K., Benner, L., & Hopf, A. (2007). A meta-analysis of school-based social skills interventions for children with autism spectrum disorders. *Remedial and Special Education, 28*, 153–162.

Bereiter, C., Brown, A., Campione, J., Carruthers, I., Case, R., Hirshberg, J.,… Treadway, G. H. (2002). *Open court reading.* Columbus, OH: SRA McGraw-Hill.

Berkeley, S., Mastropieri, M. A., & Scruggs, T. E. (2011). Reading comprehension strategy instruction and attribution retraining for secondary students with learning and other mild disabilities. *Journal of Learning Disabilities, 44*, 18–32.

Bijou, S. W., Peterson, R. F., & Ault, M. H. (1968). A method to integrate descriptive and experimental field studies at the level of data and empirical concepts. *Journal of Applied Behavior Analysis, 1*, 175–191.

Brigham, F. J., Bakken, J., Scruggs, T. E., & Mastropieri, M. A. (1992). Cooperative behavior management: A technique for improving classroom behavior. *Education and Training of the Mentally Retarded, 27*, 3–12.

Buchard, J. D., & Barrera, F. (1972). An analysis of time out and response cost in a programmed environment. *Journal of Applied Behavior Analysis, 5*, 271–282.

Canter, L., & Canter, M. (1993). *Succeeding with difficult students: New strategies for reaching your most challenging students.* Bloomington, IN: Solution Tree Press.

Canter, L., & Canter, M. (2010). *Assertive discipline: Positive behavior management for today's classroom* (4th ed.). Bloomington, IN: Solution Tree Press.

Carey, T. A., & Bourbon, W. T. (2004). Countercontrol: A new look at some old problems. *Intervention in School and Clinic, 40,* 3–9.

Carlson, C. L., Booth, J. E., Shin, M., & Canu, W. H. (2002). Parent-, teacher-, and self-rated motivational styles in ADHD subtypes. *Journal of Learning Disabilities, 35,* 104–113.

Coffey, J. H., & Horner, R. H. (2012). The sustainability of school-wide positive behavior interventions and supports. *Exceptional Children, 78,* 407–422.

Conroy, M. A., Asmus, J. M., Ladwig, C. N., Sellers, J. A., & Valcante, G. (2004). The effects of proximity on the classroom behaviors of students with autism in general education settings. *Behavioral Disorders, 29,* 119–129.

Council for Children with Behavioral Disorders. (1990). Position paper on behavior reduction strategies with children with behavioral disorders. *Behavioral Disorders, 15,* 243–260.

Council for Exceptional Children (CEC). (2011). *Bullying.* Arlington, VA: Author. Retrieved from http://www.cec.sped.org/

Crone, C. A., Hawkins, R., & Horner, R. (2010). *Responding to problem behavior in schools* (2nd ed.). New York, NY: Guilford.

Crone, C. A., & Horner, R. (2003). *Building positive behavior support systems in schools: Functional behavioral assessment.* New York, NY: Guilford.

Davis, S., & Davis, J. (2007). *Schools where everyone belongs: Practical strategies for reducing bullying* (2nd ed.). Champaign, IL: Research Press.

Engelmann, S., & Bruner, E. C. (1995a). *Reading mastery classic I.* Columbus, OH: SRA McGraw-Hill.

Engelmann, S., & Bruner, E. C. (1995b). *Reading mastery classic II.* Columbus, OH: SRA McGraw-Hill.

Fairbanks, S., Sugai, G., Guardino, D., & Lathrop, M. (2007). Response to intervention: Examining classroom behavior support in second grade. *Exceptional Children, 73,* 288–310.

Ferro, M. A., & Boyle, M. H. (2013). Testing measurement invariance and differences in self-concept between adolescents with and without physical illness or developmental disability. *Journal of Adolescence, 36,* 947–951.

Filter, K. J., McKenna, M. K., Benedict, E. A., Horner, R. H., Todd, A. W., & Watson, J. (2007). Check in/check out: A post-hoc evaluation of an efficient, secondary-level targeted intervention for reducing problem behaviors in schools. *Education and Treatment of Children, 30,* 69–84.

Finch, A. J., Jr., Spirito, A., Imm, P. S., & Ott, E. S. (1993). Cognitive self-instruction for impulse control in children. In A. J. Finch, W. M. Nelson, & E. S. Ott (Eds.), *Cognitive-behavioral procedures with children and adolescents: A practical guide* (pp. 233–256). Boston, MA: Allyn & Bacon.

Gable D. (2003). Enhancing the conceptual understanding of science. *Educational Horizons, 81,* 70–76.

Ginsberg, M. B., & Wlodkowski, R. J. (2009). Diversity and motivation: Culturally responsive teaching in college (2nd ed.). San Francisco: Jossey-Bass.

Glago, K., Mastropieri, M. A., & Scruggs, T. E. (2009). Improving problem solving of elementary students with mild disabilities. *Remedial and Special Education, 30,* 372–380.

Gollnick, D. M., & Chinn, P. C. (2013). *Multicultural education in a pluralistic society* (9th ed.). Upper Saddle River, NJ: Merrill/Prentice Hall.

Gonsalez-Spada, W. J., Bieeiel, J., & Birriel, I. (2010). Discrepant events: A challenge to students' intuition. *Physics Teacher, 48,* 508–511.

Good, C. P., McIntosh, K., & Gietz, C. (2011). Integration bullying prevention into schoolwide positive behavior support. *Teaching Exceptional Children, 44,* 48–56.

Graetz, J. S., Mastropieri, M. A., & Scruggs, T. E. (2009). Promoting social behavior for adolescents with autism with social stories. *Education and Training in Developmental Disabilities, 44,* 91–104.

Gresham, F. M., & Elliott, S. N. (2008a). *Social Skills Improvement System (SSIS) intervention guide.* Minneapolis, MN: Pearson.

Gresham, F. M., & Elliott, S. N. (2008b). *Social Skills Improvement System (SSIS) rating scales.* Minneapolis, MN: Pearson.

Harper, C. B., Symon, J. B. G., & Grea, W. D. (2008). Recess is timein: Using peers to improve social skills of children with autism. *Journal of Autism and Developmental Disorders, 38,* 815–826.

Harris, V. W., & Sherman, J. A. (1973). Use and analysis of the "Good Behavior Game" to reduce disruptive classroom behavior. *Journal of Applied Behavior Analysis, 6,* 405–417.

Harter, S. (2012). *The construction of the self: A developmental perspective* (2nd ed.). New York, NY: Guilford.

Hawken, L. H., & Horner, R. H. (2003). Evaluation of a targeted intervention within a schoolwide system of behavior support. *Journal of Behavioral Education, 12,* 225–240.

Heinrichs, R. R. (2003). A whole-school approach to bullying: Special considerations for children with exceptionalities. *Intervention in School and Clinic, 38,* 195–204.

Henderlong, J., & Lepper, M. R. (2002). The effects of praise on children's intrinsic motivation: A review and synthesis. *Psychological Bulletin, 128,* 774–795.

Jenkins, J. R., & Gorrafa, S. (1974). Academic performance of mentally handicapped children as a function of token economies and contingency contracts. *Education and Training of the Mentally Retarded, 9,* 183–186.

Jones, D. B., & Van Houten, R. (1985). The use of daily quizzes and public posting to decrease the disruptive behavior of secondary school students. *Education and Treatment of Children, 8,* 91–106.

Jones, V., Greenwood, A., & Dunn, C. (2016). *Effective supports for students with emotional and behavioral disorders.* Boston, MA: Pearson.

Kauffman, J., & Landrum, T. (2013). *Characteristics of emotional and behavioral disorders of children and youth* (10th ed.). Upper Saddle River, NJ: Prentice Hall.

Kaya, S., & Lundeen, C. (2010). Capturing parents' individual and instructional interest toward involvement in science education. *Journal of Science Teacher Education, 21,* 825–841.

Kerr, M. M., & Nelson, C. M. (2010). *Strategies for managing behavior problems in the classroom* (6th ed.). Upper Saddle River, NJ: Merrill/Prentice Hall.

Konrad, M., Fowler, C., & Walker, A. R. (2007). Effects of self-determination interventions on the academic skills of students with learning disabilities. *Learning Disability Quarterly, 30,* 89–113.

Kowalski, R. M., Limber, S. P., & Agatston, P. W. (2012). *Cyberbullying: Bullying in the digital age* (2nd ed.). Malden, MA: Blackwell.

Krempa, J., & McKinnon, K. (2002). *Social skills solutions: A hands-on manual for teaching social skills to students with autism.* New York: DRL Books.

Lavoie, R. (2007). *The motivation breakthrough: Six secrets to turning on the tuned-out child.* New York, NY: Simon and Schuster.

Leber, N. J. (2002). *Easy activities for building social skills.* New York, NY: Scholastic.

Leflot, G., van Lier, P., Onghena, P., & Colpin, H. (2010). The role of teacher behavior management in the development of disruptive behaviors: An intervention study with the Good Behavior Game. *Journal of Abnormal Child Psychology, 38,* 869–882.

Leichtentritt, J., & Shechtman, Z. (2009). Children with and without learning disabilities: A comparison of processes and outcomes following group counseling. *Journal of Learning Disabilities, 43,* 169–179.

Lewis, T. J., Jones, S. E. L., Horner, R. H., & Sugai, G. (2010). Schoolwide positive behavior support and students with emotional/behavioral disorders: Implications for prevention, identification, and intervention. *Exceptionality, 18,* 82–93.

Lewis-Palmer, T., & Barrett, S. (2007). Establishing and sustaining statewide positive behavior supports implementation: A description of Maryland's model. *Journal of Evidence-Based Practices for Schools, 8,* 45–62.

Maag, J. W. (2001). Rewarded by punishment: Reflections on the disuse of positive reinforcement in schools. *Exceptional Children, 67,* 173–186.

Maag, J. W. (2004). *Behavior management: From theoretical implications to practical applications* (2nd ed.). Florence, KY: Thompson/Wadsworth.

Maag, J. W. (2006). Social skills training for students with emotional and behavioral disorders: A review of reviews. *Behavioral Disorders, 32,* 5–17.

Maag, J. W., & Reid, R. (2006). Depression among students with learning disabilities: Assessing the risk. *Journal of Learning Disabilities, 39,* 3–10.

Martin, G., & Pear, J. (2014). *Behavior modification: What it is and how to do it* (10th ed.). Upper Saddle River, NJ: Prentice Hall.

Mastropieri, M. A., & Scruggs, T. E. (2002). *Effective instruction for special education* (3rd ed.). Austin, TX: Pro-Ed.

Mastropieri, M. A., Scruggs, T. E., & Ciccerelli, D. (2007). *Overcoming a significant challenge: Motivating students to learn!* Paper presented at the annual meeting of the Council for Exceptional Children, Louisville, KY.

Matson, J. L., & Boisjoli, J. A. (2009). The token economy for children with intellectual disability and/or autism: A review. *Research in Developmental Disabilities, 30,* 240–248.

Matson, J. L., Matson, M. L., & Rivet, T. T. (2007). Social-skills treatments for children with autism spectrum disorders: An overview. *Behavior Modification, 31,* 682–707.

Mayer, G. R., Nafpaktitis, M., Butterworth, T., & Hollingsworth, P. (1987). A search for the elusive setting events of school vandalism: A correlational study. *Education and Treatment of Children, 10,* 259–270.

McDaniel, S. C., & Flower, A. (2015). Use of a behavioral graphic organizer to reduce disruptive behavior. *Education and Treatment of Children, 38,* 505–522.

McLaughlin, T. F., & Malaby, J. E. (1976). An analysis of assignment completion and accuracy across time under fixed, variable, and extended token exchange periods in a classroom token economy. *Contemporary Educational Psychology, 1,* 346–355.

McMaster, K. N., & Fuchs, D. (2002). Effects of cooperative learning on the academic achievement of students with learning disabilities: An update of Tateyama-Sniezek's review. *Learning Disabilities Research & Practice, 17,* 107–117.

Milsom, A. S., & Akos, P. (2003). Counselor preparation: Preparing school counselors to work with students with disabilities. *Counselor Education and Supervision, 43,* 86–95.

Missouri Schoolwide Positive Behavior Support. (2011–2012). *Schoolwide positive behavior support team workbook.* Columbia, MO: University of Missouri. Retrieved from http://pbismissouri.org/wp-content/uploads/2013/04/MO-SW-PBS_13-14_Tier-1_Workbook.pdf

Nelson, J. M., & Harwood, H. (2011). Learning disabilities and anxiety: A meta-analysis. *Journal of Learning Disabilities, 44,* 3–17.

Nelson, J. M., & Manset-Williamson, G. (2006). The impact of explicit, self-regulatory reading comprehension strategy instruction on the reading-specific self-efficacy, attributions, and affect of students with reading disabilities. *Learning Disability Quarterly, 29,* 213–230.

Nelson, J. R., & Sugai, G. (1999). School-wide application of positive behavioral supports. In G. Sugai & T. Lewis (Eds.), *Developing positive behavioral support for students with challenging behaviors* (pp. 25–34). Arlington, VA: Council for Exceptional Children. (ERIC Document Reproduction Service No. 435155)

Nicholls, J. G. (1989). *The competitive ethos and democratic education.* Cambridge, MA: Harvard University Press.

OSEP Technical Assistance Center on Positive Behavioral Interventions and Supports (PBIS). (2012). *Effective schoolwide interventions.* Washington, DC: Office of Special Education Programs. Retrieved from http://www.pbis.org

Richard, J. F., Schneider, B. H., & Mallet, P. (2011). Revisiting the whole-school approach to bullying: Really looking at the whole school. *School Psychology International, 33,* 263–284.

Rose, C., Monda-Amaya, L. E., & Espelage, D. (2011). Bullying perpetration and victimization in special education: A review of the literature. *Remedial and Special Education, 32,* 114–130.

Rosenberg, M. S., & Jackman, L. A. (2003). Development, implementation, and sustainability of comprehensive schoolwide behavior management systems. *Intervention in School and Clinic, 39,* 10–21.

Safran, S. P., & Oswald, K. (2003). Positive behavior supports: Can schools reshape disciplinary practices? *Exceptional Children, 69,* 362–373.

Scheuermann, B. K., & Hall, J. A. (2016). *Positive behavioral supports for the classroom* (3rd ed.). Boston, MA: Pearson.

Scruggs, T. E., & Mastropieri, M. A. (1994). Successful mainstreaming in elementary science classes: A qualitative investigation of three reputational cases. *American Educational Research Journal, 31,* 785–811.

Sideridis, G. D. (2007). Why are students with LD depressed? A goal orientation model of depression vulnerability. *Journal of Learning Disabilities, 40,* 526–539.

Simonsen, B., Fairbanks, S., Briesch, A., Myers, D., & Sugai, G. (2008). Evidence-based practices in classroom management: Considerations for research to practice. *Education and Treatment of Children, 31,* 351–380.

Smith, S. W., & Gilles, D. L. (2003). Using key instructional elements to systematically promote social skill generalization for students with challenging behavior. *Intervention in School and Clinic, 39,* 30–37.

Sullivan, A. M., Johnson, B., Owens, L., & Conway, R. (2014). Punish them or engage them? Teachers' views of unproductive student behaviours in the classroom. *Australian Journal of Teacher Education, 39,* 43–56.

Tauber, R. T. (2007). *Classroom management: Sound theory and effective practice.* Westport, CT: Praeger.

Thurneck, D. A., Warner, P. J., & Cobb, H. C. (2007). Children and adolescents with disabilities and health care needs: Implications for intervention. In H. T. Prout & D. T. Brown (Eds.), *Counseling and psychotherapy with children and adolescents: Theory and practice for school and clinical settings* (4th ed., pp. 419–453). Hoboken, NJ: Wiley.

Troup, D. L., McLaughlin, T. F., Neyman, J., & Schuler, H. (2014). The use of online typing programs in combination with public posting with and without consequences to increase the typing fluency and accuracy for seven high school students with severe behavior disorders. *Journal of Education and Human Development, 3,* 181–201.

Twyman, J. S., Johnson, H., Buie, J. D., & Nelson, C. M. (1994). The use of a warning procedure to signal a more intrusive timeout contingency. *Behavioral Disorders, 19,* 243–253.

U.S. Department of Education (2017). *School climate and discipline.* Washington, DC: Author. Retrieved from https://ed.gov/policy/gen/guid/school-discipline/index.html

Watling, R., & Schwartz, I. S. (2004). Understanding and implementing positive reinforcement as an intervention strategy for children with disabilities. *American Journal of Occupational Therapy, 58,* 113–116.

Wentzel, K. R., & Brophy, J. (2014). *Motivating students to learn* (4th ed.). New York, NY: Routledge.

Wheeler, J. J., & Richey, D. D. (2014). *Behavior management: Principles and practices of positive behavior supports* (3rd ed.). Boston, MA: Pearson.

Wolters, C. A., Denton, C. A., York, M. J., & Francis, D. J. (2014). Adolescents' motivation for reading: Group differences and relation to standardized achievement. *Reading and Writing, 27,* 503–533.

Zheng, C., Erickson, A. G., Kingston, N. M., & Noonan, P. M. (2014). The relationship among self-determination, self-concept, and academic achievement for students with learning disabilities. *Journal of Learning Disabilities, 47,* 462–474.

Zimmerman, B., & Kitsantas, A. (2007). Reliability and validity of Self-Efficacy for Learning Form (SELF) scores of college students. *Journal of Psychology, 215,* 157–163.

Chapter 9

Calhoon, M. B., & Fuchs, L. S. (2003). The effects of peer-assisted learning strategies and curriculum-based measurement on the mathematics performance of secondary students with disabilities. *Remedial and Special Education, 24,* 235–245.

Carter, E. W., Cushing, L. S., & Kennedy, C. H. (2009). *Peer support strategies for improving all students' social lives and learning.* Baltimore, MD: Paul H. Brookes.

Carter, E. W., Moss, C. K., Hoffman, A., Chung, Y., & Sisco, L. (2011). Efficacy and social validity of peer support arrangements for adolescents with disabilities. *Exceptional Children, 78,* 107–125.

Chan, J. M., Lang, R., Rispoli, M., O'Reilly, M., Sigafoos, J., & Cole, H. (2009). Use of peer-mediated interventions in the treatment of autism spectrum disorders: A systematic review. *Research in Autism Spectrum Disorders, 3,* 876–889.

Cole, D. A., Vandercook, T., & Rynders, J. (1988). Comparison of two peer interaction programs: Children with and without severe disabilities. *American Educational Research Journal, 25,* 415–439.

Cushing, L. S., & Kennedy, C. H. (2003). Facilitating social relationships in general education settings. In D. L. Ryndak & S. Alper (Eds.), *Curriculum and instruction for students with significant disabilities in inclusive settings* (pp. 206–216). Boston, MA: Allyn & Bacon.

Favazza, P. C., Phillipsen, L., & Kumar, P. (2000). Measuring and promoting acceptance of young children with disabilities. *Exceptional Children, 66,* 491–508.

Ferretti, R. P., MacArthur, C. D., & Okolo, C. M. (2001). Teaching for historical understanding in inclusive classrooms. *Learning Disability Quarterly, 24,* 59–71.

Ferretti, R. P., MacArthur, C. D., & Okolo, C. M. (2005). Misconceptions about history: Reflections on teaching for historical understanding in a fifth-grade inclusive classroom. In T. E. Scruggs & M. A. Mastropieri (Eds.), *Cognition and learning in diverse settings: Advances in learning and behavioral disabilities* (pp. 275–313). Oxford, UK: Elsevier.

Forest, M., & Lusthaus, E. (1989). Promoting educational equity for all students. In S. Stainback, W. Stainback, & M. Forest (Eds.), *Educating all students in the mainstream of regular education* (pp. 47–49). Baltimore, MD: Paul Brookes.

Frederickson, N. L., & Furnham, A. F. (2004). Peer-assessed behavioural characteristics and sociometric rejection: Differences between pupils who have moderate learning difficulties and their mainstream peers. *British Journal of Educational Psychology, 74,* 391–410.

Frederickson, N. L., & Turner, J. (2003). Utilizing the classroom peer group to address children's social needs: An evaluation of the Circle of Friends intervention approach. *Journal of Special Education, 36,* 234–245.

Frederickson, N. L., Warner, J., & Turner, J. (2005). "Circle of Friends": An exploration of impact over time. *Educational Psychology in Practice, 21,* 197–217.

Fuchs, D., & Fuchs, L. S. (2005). Peer-assisted learning strategies: Promoting word recognition, fluency, and reading comprehension in young children. *Journal of Special Education, 39,* 34–44.

Fuchs, D., Fuchs, L., Mathes, P. G., & Martinez, E. A. (2002). Preliminary evidence on the social standing of students with learning disabilities in PALS and no-PALS classrooms. *Learning Disabilities Research & Practice, 17,* 205–215.

Gillies, R. M. (2007). *Cooperative learning: Integrating theory and practice.* Thousand Oaks, CA: Sage.

Harris, K. R., & Meltzer, L. (Eds.). (2015). *The power of peers in the classroom.* New York, NY: Guilford.

Higgins, T. S. (1982). *A comparison of two methods of practice on the spelling performance of learning disabled adolescents* (Unpublished doctoral dissertation). Georgia State University, Atlanta, GA.

Johnson, D. W., & Johnson, F. (2013). *Joining together: Group theory and group skills* (11th ed). Boston, MA: Allyn & Bacon.

Johnson, D. W., & Johnson, R. T. (1986). Mainstreaming and cooperative learning strategies. *Exceptional Children, 52,* 553–561.

Johnson, D. W., & Johnson, R. T. (2009). An educational psychology success story: Social interdependence theory: Cooperative learning. *Educational Researcher, 38,* 365–379.

Johnson, D. W., Johnson, R. T., Dudley, B., Ward, M., & Magnuson, D. (1995). The impact of peer mediation training on the management of school and home conflicts. *American Educational Research Journal, 32,* 829–844.

Johnson, D. W., Johnson, R. T., & Holubec, E. J. (1991). *Cooperation in the classroom.* Edina, MN: Interaction Book Company.

Kamps, D., Greenwood, C., Arreage-Mayer, C., Veerkamp, M. B., Utler, C., Tapia, Y.,… Bannister, H. (2008). The efficacy of classwide peer tutoring in middle schools. *Education and Treatment of Children, 31,* 119–152.

Kamps, D., Royer, J., Degan, E., Kravits, T., Gonzalez-Lopez, A., Garcia, J.,… Kane, L. G. (2002). Peer training to facilitate social interaction for elementary students with autism and their peers. *Exceptional Children, 68,* 173–187.

Kamps, D., Thiemann-Bourque, K., Heitzman-Powell, L., Schwartz, I., Rosenberg, N., Mason, R., & Cox, S. (2015). A comprehensive peer network intervention to improve social communication of children with autism spectrum disorders: A randomized trial in kindergarten and first grade. *Journal of Autism and Developmental Disorders, 45,* 1809–1824.

Kearns, D. M., Fuchs, D., Fuchs, L. S., McMaster, K. L., & Sáenz, L. (2015). Peer-assisted learning strategies to improve students' word recognition and reading comprehension. In K. R. Harris & L. Meltzer (Eds.), *The power of peers in the classroom* (pp. 143–187). New York, NY: Guilford.

Kerr, M. M., & Nelson, C. M. (2002). *Strategies for addressing behavior problems in the classroom* (4th ed.). Upper Saddle River, NJ: Merrill/Prentice Hall.

Kerr, M. M., & Nelson, C. M. (2010). *Strategies for addressing behavior problems in the classroom* (6th ed.). Upper Saddle River, NJ: Merrill/Prentice Hall.

Leung, K. C., Marsh, H. W., Craven, R. G., Yeung, A. S., & Abdul-Jabbar, A. S. (2013). Domain specificity between peer support and self-concept. *Journal of Early Adolescence, 33,* 227–244.

Maheady, L., & Gard, J. (2010). Classwide peer tutoring: Practice, theory, research, and personal narrative. *Intervention in School and Clinic, 46,* 71–78.

Maheady, L., Mallette, B., & Harper, G. F. (2006). Four classwide peer tutoring models: Similarities, differences, and implications for research and practice. *Reading & Writing Quarterly: Overcoming Learning Difficulties, 22*, 65–89.

Manetti, M., Schneider, B. H., & Siperstein, G. (2001). Social acceptance of children with mental retardation: Testing the contact hypothesis with an Italian sample. *International Journal of Behavioral Development, 25*, 279–286.

Marshak, L., Mastropieri, M. A., & Scruggs, T. E. (2011). Curriculum enhancements for inclusive secondary social studies classes. *Exceptionality, 19*, 61–74.

Mastropieri, M. A., & Scruggs, T. E. (1993). *A practical guide for teaching science to students with special needs in inclusive settings.* Austin, TX: Pro-Ed.

Mastropieri, M. A., Scruggs, T. E., & Bohs, K. (1994). Mainstreaming an emotionally handicapped student in science: A qualitative investigation. In T. E. Scruggs & M. A. Mastropieri (Eds.), *Advances in learning and behavioral disabilities* (Vol. 8, pp. 131–146). Greenwich, CT: JAI Press.

Mastropieri, M. A., Scruggs, T. E., & Graetz, J. (2005). Cognition and learning in inclusive high school chemistry classes. In T. E. Scruggs & M. A. Mastropieri (Eds.), *Cognition and learning in diverse settings: Advances in learning and behavioral disabilities* (Vol. 18, pp. 107–118). Oxford, UK: Elsevier.

Mastropieri, M. A., Scruggs, T. E., Mantzicopoulos, P. Y., Sturgeon, A., Goodwin, L., & Chung, S. (1998). "A place where living things affect and depend upon each other": Qualitative and quantitative outcomes associated with inclusive science teaching. *Science Education, 82*, 163–179.

Mastropieri, M. A., Scruggs, T. E., & Marshak, L. (2008). Training teachers, parents, and peers to implement effective teaching strategies for content area learning. In T. E. Scruggs & M. A. Mastropieri (Eds.), *Advances in learning and behavioral disabilities: Vol. 21. Personnel preparation.* Bingley, UK: Emerald.

Mastropieri, M. A., Scruggs, T. E., Mohler, L. J., Beranek, M. L., Spencer, V., Boon, R. T., & Talbott, E. (2001). Can middle school students with serious reading difficulties help each other and learn anything? *Learning Disabilities Research & Practice, 16*, 18–27.

Mastropieri, M. A., Scruggs, T. E., Spencer, V., & Fontana, J. (2003). Promoting success in high school world history: Peer tutoring versus guided notes. *Learning Disabilities Research & Practice, 18*, 52–65.

Mathes, P. G., Fuchs, D., Fuchs, L. S., Henley, A. M., & Sanders, A. (1994). Increasing strategic reading practice with Peabody Classwide Peer Tutoring. *Learning Disabilities Research & Practice, 9*, 44–48.

McDuffie, K. A., Mastropieri, M. A., & Scruggs, T. E. (2009). Differential effects of co-teaching and peer-mediated instruction: Results for content learning and student-teacher interactions. *Exceptional Children, 75*, 493–510.

McMaster, K. L., Fuchs, D., & Fuchs, L. S. (2006). Research on peer-assisted learning strategies: The promise and limitations of peer-mediated instruction. *Reading & Writing Quarterly: Overcoming Learning Difficulties, 22*, 5–25.

McMaster, K. L., Kung, S., Han, I., & Cao, M. (2008). Peer-assisted learning strategies: A "Tier 1" approach to promoting English learners' response to intervention. *Exceptional Children, 74*, 194–214.

McMaster, K. N., & Fuchs, D. (2002). Effects of cooperative learning on the academic achievement of students with learning disabilities: An update of Tateyama-Sniezek's review. *Learning Disabilities Research & Practice, 17*, 107–117.

McMaster, K. N., & Fuchs, D. (2005). *Cooperative learning: Use caution.* Current Practice Alerts, Division for Research and Division for Learning Disabilities, Council for Exceptional Children, Issue 11. Retrieved from http://s3.amazonaws.com/cmi-teaching-ld/alerts/8/uploaded_files/original_alert11.pdf?1301000897

Meyer, A., Rose, D. H., & Gordon, D. (2014). *Universal design for learning: Theory & practice.* Wakefield, MA: CAST Professional Publishing.

Myles, B. (2007). *Priming* [Council for Exceptional Children blog]. Retrieved from http://cecblog.typepad.com/cec/

Norland, J. J. (2005). *English language learners' interactions with various science curriculum features* (Unpublished doctoral dissertation). George Mason University, Fairfax, VA.

O'Connor, R. E., & Jenkins, J. R. (1996). Cooperative learning as an inclusion strategy: A closer look. *Exceptionality, 6*, 29–51.

O'Connor, R. E., & Jenkins, J. R. (2014). Cooperative learning for students with learning disabilities: Advice and caution derived from evidence. In H. L. Swanson, K. Harris, & S. Graham (Eds.), *Handbook of learning disabilities* (pp. 507–525). New York, NY: Guilford.

Okilwa, N. S. A., & Shelby, L. (2010). The effects of peer tutoring on academic performance of students with disabilities in grades 6 through 12: A synthesis of the literature. *Remedial and Special Education, 31*, 450–463.

Okolo, C. M., Englert, C. S., Bouck, E. C., Heutsche, A., & Wang, H. (2011). The Virtual History Museum: Learning American history in diverse eighth grade classrooms. *Remedial and Special Education, 32*, 417–428.

Oortwijn, M. B., Boekaerts, M., & Vedder, P. (2008). The impact of a cooperative learning experience on pupils' popularity, non-cooperativeness, and interethnic bias in multiethnic elementary schools. *Educational Psychology, 28*(2), 1–11.

Powell, S. R., & Fuchs, L. S. (2015). Peer-assisted learning strategies in mathematics. In K. R. Harris & L. Meltzer (Eds.). (2015). *The power of peers in the classroom* (pp. 188–223). New York, NY: Guilford.

Regan, K., Evmenova, A. S., Mastropieri, M. A., & Scruggs, T. E. (2015). Peer interactions in the content areas: Using differentiated instruction strategies. In K. R. Harris & L. Meltzer (Eds.), *The power of peers in the classroom* (pp. 33–68). New York, NY: Guilford.

Richards-Tutor, C., Aceves, T., & Reutebuch, C. (2015). Peer-supported instruction for English learners. In K. R. Harris & L. Meltzer (Eds.), *The power of peers in the classroom* (pp. 251–287). New York, NY: Guilford.

Sáenz, L. M., Fuchs, L. S., & Fuchs, D. (2005). Peer-assisted learning strategies for English language learners with learning disabilities. *Exceptional Children, 71*, 231–247.

Scruggs, T. E., & Mastropieri, M. A. (1998). Peer tutoring and students with special needs. In K. Topping & S. Ehly (Eds.), *Peer-assisted learning* (pp. 165–182). Mahwah, NJ: Lawrence Erlbaum.

Scruggs, T. E., Mastropieri, M. A., & Marshak, L. (2012). Peer-mediated instruction in inclusive secondary social studies learning: Direct and indirect learning effects. *Learning Disabilities Research and Practice, 27*, 12–20.

Shabani, D. B., Katz, R. C., & Wilder, D. A. (2002). Increasing social initiations in children with autism: Effects of a tactile prompt. *Journal of Applied Behavior Analysis, 35*, 79–83.

Sindelar, P. T. (1982). The effects of cross-age tutoring on the comprehension skills of remedial reading students. *Journal of Special Education, 16*, 199–206.

Slavin, R. E. (1991). Synthesis of research on cooperative learning. *Educational Leadership, 48*(5), 71–82.

Slavin, R. E. (2015). Cooperative learning in elementary schools. *Education 3-13: International Journal of Primary, Elementary and Early Years Education, 43*, 5–14.

Souvignier, E., & Kronenberger, J. (2007). Cooperative learning in third graders' jigsaw groups for mathematics and science with and without questioning training. *British Journal of Educational Psychology, 77*, 755–771.

Stevahn, L., Johnson, D. W., Johnson, R. T., & Schultz, R. (2002). Effects of conflict resolution training integrated into a high school social studies curriculum. *Journal of Social Psychology, 142*, 305–331.

Stevens, R. J., & Slavin, R. E. (1991). When cooperative learning improves the achievement of students with mild disabilities: A response to Tateyama-Sniezek. *Exceptional Children, 57*, 276–280.

Tateyama-Sniezek, K. M. (1990). Cooperative learning: Does it improve the academic achievement of students with handicaps? *Exceptional Children, 56*, 426–437.

Tomlinson, C. (2014). *The differentiated classroom: Responding to the needs of all learners* (2nd ed.). Alexandria, VA: ASCD.

Tsao, L., Odom, S. L., Vuysse, V., Skinner, M., West, T., & Vitztum-Komanecki, J. (2008). Social participation of children with disabilities in inclusive preschool programs: Program typology and ecological features. *Exceptionality, 16*, 125–140.

Wang, P., & Spillane, A. (2009). Evidence-based social skills interventions for children with autism: A meta-analysis. *Education and Training in Developmental Disabilities, 44*, 318–342.

Chapter 10

Baddeley, A., Eysenck, M. W., & Anderson, M. C. (2015). *Memory* (2nd ed.). New York, NY: Psychology Press.

Barkley, R. A. (Ed.). (2015). *Attention deficit hyperactivity disorder: A handbook of assessment and treatment*. New York, NY: Guilford.

Beirne-Smith, M., Patton, J. M., & Hill, S. (in press). *Introduction to intellectual disabilities* (8th ed.). Upper Saddle River, NJ: Prentice Hall.

Bjorklund, D. F. (2012). *Children's thinking: Cognitive development and developmental differences* (5th ed). Belmont, CA: Wadsworth.

Brigham, F. J., Scruggs, T. E., & Mastropieri, M. A. (2011). Science education and students with learning disabilities. *Learning Disabilities Research and Practice, 26*, 223–232.

Burchers, S., & Burchers, B. E. (2007). *Vocabulary cartoons II: SAT word power*. Punta Gorda, Florida: New Monic Books.

Conroy, M. A., Asmus, J. M., Ladwig, C. N., Sellers, J. A., & Valcante, G. (2004). The effects of proximity on the classroom behaviors of students with autism in general education settings. *Behavioral Disorders, 29*, 119–129.

Craik, F. I. M., & Lockhart, R. S. (1972). Levels of processing: A framework for memory research. *Journal of Verbal Learning and Verbal Behavior, 11*, 671–684.

Crossairt, A., Hall, R. V., & Hopkins, B. L. (1973). The effects of experimenter's instructions, feedback, and praise on teacher praise and student attending behavior. *Journal of Applied Behavior Analysis, 6*, 89–100.

Daley, D., & Birchwood, J. (2010). ADHD and academic performance: Why does ADHD impact on academic performance and what can be done to support ADHD children in the classroom? *Child: Care, Health and Development, 36*, 455–464.

de la Iglesia, J. C. F., Bucete, M. J., & Campos, A. (2004). The use of mental imagery in paired-associate learning in persons with Down syndrome. *The British Journal of Developmental Disabilities, 50*(98), 3–12.

Dehn, M. J. (2010). *Long-term memory problems in children and adolescents: Assessment, intervention, and effective instruction*. Hoboken, NJ: Wiley.

Dexter, D. D., Park, Y. J., & Hughes, C. A. (2011). A meta-analytic review of graphic organizers and science instruction for adolescents with learning disabilities: Implications for the intermediate and secondary science classroom. *Learning Disabilities Research and Practice, 26*, 204–213.

Dunlosky, J., & Bjork, R. A. (Eds.). (2008). *Handbook of metamemory and memory*. New York, NY: Taylor & Francis.

Ferguson, H., Myles, B. S., & Hagiwara, T. (2005). Using a personal digital assistant to enhance independence for an adolescent with autism. *Education and Training in Developmental Disabilities, 40*, 60–67.

Gable, R. A., Hester, P. H., Rock, M. L., & Hughes, K. G. (2009). Back to basics: Rules, praise, ignoring, and reprimands revisited. *Intervention in School and Clinic, 44*, 195–205.

Ghetti, S., Mirandola, C., Angelini, L., Cornoldi, C., & Ciaramelli, E. (2011). Development of subjective recollection: Understanding of and introspection on memory states. *Child Development, 82*, 1954–1969.

Grauvogel-MacAleese, A. N., & Wallace, M. D. (2010). Use of peer-mediated intervention in children with attention deficit hyperactivity disorder. *Journal of Applied Behavior Analysis, 43*, 547–551.

Greene, G. (1999). Mnemonic multiplication fact instruction for students with learning disabilities. *Learning Disabilities Research & Practice, 14*, 141–148.

Harris, K., Danoff, F., Saddler, B., Frizzelle, R., & Graham, S. (2005). Self-monitoring of attention versus self-monitoring of academic performance: Effects among students with ADHD in the general education classroom. *The Journal of Special Education, 39*, 145–156.

Henry, L., & Winfield, J. (2010). Working memory and educational achievement in children with intellectual disabilities. *Journal of Intellectual Disability Research, 54*, 354–365.

Heward, W. L. (2010). *Exceptional children: An introduction to special education* (10th ed.). Upper Saddle River, NJ: Prentice Hall.

Higbee, K. (2001). *Your memory: How it works and how to improve it*. New York, NY: Marlowe.

Holifield, C., Goodman, J., Hazelkorn, M., & Heflin, L. J. (2010). Using self-monitoring to increase attending to task and academic accuracy in children with autism. *Focus on Autism and Other Developmental Disabilities, 25*, 230–238.

Jennifer, A., Mautone, J. A., Lefler, E. K., & Power, T. J. (2011). Promoting family and school success for children with ADHD: Strengthening relationships while building skills. *Theory into Practice, 50*, 43–51.

Jitendra, A., DuPaul, G. J., Someki, F., & Tresco, K. E. (2008). Enhancing academic achievement for children with attention-deficit hyperactivity disorder: Evidence from school-based intervention research. *Developmental Disabilities Research Reviews, 14*, 325–330.

Joseph, L. M., & Eveleigh, E. L. (2011). A review of the effects of self-monitoring on reading performance of students with disabilities. *Journal of Special Education, 45*, 43–53.

Kerr, M. M., & Nelson, C. M. (2010). *Strategies for addressing behavior problems in the classroom* (6th ed.). Upper Saddle River, NJ: Merrill/Prentice Hall.

Lerner, J. W., & Johns, B. (2012). *Learning disabilities and related mild disabilities: Teaching strategies and new directions* (12th ed.). Belmont, CA: Wadsworth.

Lucangeli, D., Galderisi, D., & Cornoldi, C. (1995). Specific and general transfer effects following metamemory training. *Learning Disabilities Research and Practice, 10*, 11–21.

Maheady, L., & Gard, J. (2010). Classwide peer tutoring: Practice, theory, research, and personal narrative. *Intervention in School and Clinic, 46*, 71–78.

Marshak, L., Mastropieri, M. A., & Scruggs, T. E. (2011). Curriculum enhancements in inclusive secondary social studies classrooms. *Exceptionality, 19*, 61–74.

Mastropieri, M. A., Scruggs, T. E., & Graetz, J. (2005). Cognition and learning in inclusive high school chemistry classes. In T. E. Scruggs & M. A. Mastropieri (Eds.), *Cognition and learning in diverse settings: Advances in learning and behavioral disabilities* (Vol. 18, pp. 107–118). Oxford, UK: Elsevier.

Mastropieri, M. A., Scruggs, T. E., Mantzicopoulos, P., Sturgeon, A., Goodwin, L., & Chung, S. (1998). "A place where living things affect and depend on each other": Qualitative and quantitative outcomes associated with inclusive science teaching. *Science Education, 82*, 163–179.

Mastropieri, M. A., Scruggs, T. E., & Whedon, C. (1997). Using mnemonic strategies to teach information about U.S. presidents: A classroom-based investigation. *Learning Disability Quarterly, 20*, 13–21.

Mayer, R. E., Hegarty, M., Mayer, S. Y., & Campbell, J. (2005). When passive media promote active learning: Static diagrams versus animation in multimedia instruction. *Journal of Experimental Psychology: Applied, 11*, 256–265.

Meyer, A., Rose, D. H., & Gordon, D. (2014). *Universal design for learning: Theory and practice.* Wakefield, MA: CAST.

Nelson, L. G. L., Summers, J. A., & Turnbull, A. P. (2004). Boundaries in family-professional relationships: Implications for special education. *Remedial and Special Education, 25*, 153–165.

Ormrod, J. E. (2011). *Educational psychology: Developing learners* (7th ed.). Upper Saddle River, NJ: Prentice Hall.

Overton, T. (2016). *Assessing learners with special needs: An applied approach.* Boston, MA: Pearson.

Patten, E., & Watson, L. R. (2011). Interventions targeting attention in young children with autism. *American Journal of Speech-Language Pathology, 20*, 60–69.

Peterson, D. J., & Mulligan, N. W. (2010). Enactment and retrieval. *Memory and Cognition, 38*, 233–243.

Pfiffner, L. J., & DuPaul, G. J. (2015). Treatment of ADHD in school settings. In R. A. Barkley (Ed.), *Attention deficit hyperactivity disorder: A handbook of assessment and treatment* (pp. 596–629). New York, NY: Guilford.

Radvansky, G. A. (2011). *Human memory* (2nd ed.). New York, NY: Pearson.

Re, A., De Franchis, V., & Cornoldi, C. (2010). Working memory control deficit in kindergarten ADHD children. *Child Neuropsychology, 16*, 134–144.

Redl, F. (1952). *Controls from within: Techniques for the treatment of the aggressive child.* Glencoe, IL: Free Press.

Reid, R., & Johnson, J. (2012). *Teacher's guide to ADHD.* New York, NY: Guilford.

Reid, R., Lienemann, T. O., & Hagaman, J. L. (2013). *Strategy instruction for students with learning disabilities* (2nd ed.). New York, NY: Guilford.

Reid, R., Trout, A. L., & Schartz, M. (2005). Self-regulation interventions for children with attention deficit hyperactivity disorder. *Exceptional Children, 71*, 361–377.

Ryan, J. B., Katsiyannis, A., Losinski, L., Reid, R., & Ellis, C. (2014). Review of state medication policies/guidelines regarding psychotropic medications in public schools. *Journal of Child and Family Studies, 23*, 704–715.

Scruggs, T. E., & Mastropieri, M. A. (1992). Classroom applications of mnemonic instruction: Acquisition, maintenance, and generalization. *Exceptional Children, 58*, 219–229.

Scruggs, T. E., & Mastropieri, M. A. (2013). Teaching students with high-incidence disabilities. In B. G. Cook & M. Tankersley (Eds.), *Research-based practices in special education* (pp. 342–352). Boston, MA: Pearson.

Scruggs, T. E., Mastropieri, M. A., Berkeley, S. L., & Marshak, L. (2010). Mnemonic strategies: Evidence-based practice and practice-based evidence. *Intervention in School and Clinic, 46*, 79–86.

Scruggs, T. E., Mastropieri, M. A., & Marshak, M. (2011). Science and social studies. In J. M. Kauffman & D. P. Hallahan (Eds.), *Handbook of special education* (pp. 445–455). New York, NY: Routledge.

Scruggs, T. E., Mastropieri, M. A., McLoone, B. B., Levin, J. R., & Morrison, C. (1987). Mnemonic facilitation of learning disabled students' memory for expository prose. *Journal of Educational Psychology, 79*, 27–34.

Sheng, L., Byrd, C. T., McGregor, K. K., Zimmerman, H., & Bludau, K. (2015). List memory in young adults with language learning disability. *Journal of Speech, Language, and Hearing Research, 58*, 336–344.

Slattery, L., Crosland, K., & Iovannone, R. (2015). An evaluation of a self-management intervention to increase on-task behavior with individuals diagnosed with attention-deficit/hyperactivity disorder. *Journal of Positive Behavior Interventions.* Advance online publication. doi: 10.1177/1098300715588282

Sullivan, G. S., Mastropieri, M. A., & Scruggs, T. E. (1995). Reasoning and remembering: Coaching thinking with students with learning disabilities. *Journal of Special Education, 29*, 310–322.

Swanson, H. L., Zheng, X., & Jerman, O. (2009). Working memory, short term memory and reading disabilities: A selective meta-analysis of the literature. *Journal of Learning Disabilities, 42*, 260–287.

Swanson, J., Baler, R. D., & Volkow, N. D. (2011). Understanding the effects of stimulant medications on cognition in individuals with attention-deficit hyperactivity disorder: A decade of progress. *Neuropsychopharmacology, 36*, 207–226.

Terrill, C., Scruggs, T. E., & Mastropieri, M. A. (2004). SAT vocabulary instruction for high school students with learning disabilities. *Intervention in School and Clinic, 39*, 288–294.

Uberti, H. Z., Scruggs, T. E., & Mastropieri, M. A. (2003). Keywords make the difference! Mnemonic instruction in inclusive classrooms. A classroom application. *Teaching Exceptional Children, 35*(3), 56–61.

Watkins, D. E., & Wentzel, K. R. (2008). Training boys with ADHD to work collaboratively: Social and learning outcomes. *Contemporary Educational Psychology, 33*, 625–646.

White, P. J., O'Reilly, M., Streusand, W., Levine, A., Sigafoos, J., Lancioni, G.,... Aguilar, J. (2011). Best practices for teaching joint attention: A systematic review of the intervention literature. *Research in Autism Spectrum Disorders, 5*, 1283–1295.

Wolgemuth, J. R., Cobb, R. B., & Alwell, M. (2008). The effects of mnemonic interventions on academic outcomes for youth with disabilities: A systematic review. *Learning Disabilities Research & Practice, 23*, 1–10.

Zager, D., Wehmeyer, M. L., & Simpson, R. L. (Eds.). (2011). *Educating students with autism spectrum disorders: Research-based principles and practices.* London, UK: Routledge.

Zisimopoulos, D. A. (2010). Enhancing multiplication performance in students with moderate intellectual disabilities using pegword mnemonics paired with a picture fading technique. *Journal of Behavioral Education, 19*, 117–133.

Chapter 11

Banks, J. A. (2015). *Cultural diversity and teaching: Foundations, curriculum, and teaching* (6th ed.). Boston, MA: Pearson.

Boyle, J. R. (2007). The process of note taking: Implications for students with mild disabilities. *The Clearing House, 80*, 227–232.

Boyle, J. R. (2010). Note-taking skills of middle school students with and without learning disabilities. *Journal of Learning Disabilities, 43,* 530–542.

Boyle, J. R., & Forchelli, G. A. (2014). Differences in the note-taking skills of students with high achievement, average achievement, and learning disabilities. *Learning and Individual Differences, 35,* 9–14.

Boyle, J. R., Forchelli, G. A., & Cariss, K. (2015). Note taking interventions to assist students with disabilities in content area classes. *Intervention in School and Clinic, 59,* 186–195.

Boyle, J. R., Rosen, S. M., & Forchelli, G. (2014). Exploring metacognitive strategy use during note-taking for students with learning disabilities, *Education 3-13.* Advance online publication. doi: 10.1080/03004279.2014.929722

Boyle, J. R., & Weishaar, M. (2001). The effects of strategic note taking on the recall and comprehension of lecture information for high school students with learning disabilities. *Learning Disabilities Research and Practice, 16,* 133–141.

Bryan, T., & Burstein, K. (2004). Improving homework completion and academic performance: Lessons from special education. *Theory into Practice, 43,* 213–219.

Carter, C., Bishop, J., & Kravits, L. (2011). *Keys to effective learning: Study skills and habits for success* (6th ed.). Upper Saddle River, NJ: Merrill/Prentice Hall.

Deshler, D. D., & Schumaker, J. B. (2006). *Teaching adolescents with disabilities: Accessing the general education curriculum.* Thousand Oaks, CA: Corwin.

Dorminy, K. P., Luscre, D., & Gast, D. L. (2009). Teaching organizational skills to children with high functioning autism and Asperger's syndrome. *Education and Training in Developmental Disabilities, 44,* 538–550.

Englert, C. S., Mariage, T. V., Okolo, C. M., Shankland, R. K., Moxley, K. D., Courtad, C. A., ... Chen, H. Y. (2009). The learning-to-learn strategies of adolescents with disabilities: Highlighting, note taking, planning, and writing expository texts. *Assessment for Effective Intervention, 34,* 147–161.

Fitzgerald, G., & Koury, K. (2001–2002). *The KidTools support system* (Project #H327A000005). Washington, DC: United States Department of Education, Office of Special Education Programs.

Fitzgerald, G., & Koury, K. (2004–2005). *The Strategy Tools support system* (Project #H327A000005). Washington, DC: United States Department of Education, Office of Special Education Programs.

Greene, L. J. (2004). *Study max: Improving study skills in grades 9–12.* Thousand Oaks, CA: Corwin.

Hampshire, P. K., Butera, G. D., & Hourcade, J. J. (2014). Homework plans: A tool for promoting independence. *Teaching Exceptional Children, 46,* 158–168.

Hoover, J. J., & Patton, J. R. (2006). *Teaching study skills to students with learning problems: A teacher's guide for meeting diverse needs* (2nd ed.). Austin, TX: Pro-Ed.

Houser, D., Maheady, L., Pomerantz, D., & Jabot, M. (2015). The effects of the Radical Raceway on homework completion and accuracy of 9th grade social studies inclusion class. *Journal of Behavioral Education, 24* (4), 402–417.

Hughes, C. A., Ruhl, K. L., Schumaker, J. B., & Deshler, D. D. (2002). Effects of instruction in an assignment completion strategy on the homework performance of students with learning disabilities in general education classes. *Learning Disabilities Research & Practice, 17,* 1–18.

Jakulski, J., & Mastropieri, M. A. (2004). Homework for students with disabilities. In T. E. Scruggs & M. A. Mastropieri (Eds.), *Research in secondary schools: Advances in learning and behavioral disabilities* (Vol. 17, pp. 77–122). Oxford, UK: Elsevier.

Konrad, M., Joseph, L. M., & Itoi, M. (2011). Using guided notes to enhance instruction for all students. *Intervention in School and Clinic, 46,* 131–140.

Kruse, D. (2010). *Thinking tools for the inquiry classroom.* Carlton, Australia: Curriculum Corporation.

Langberg, J. M., Epstein, J. N., Ginio-Herrera E., Becker, S. P., Vaughn, A. J., & Altaye, M. (2011). Materials organization, planning, and homework completion in middle-school students with ADHD: Impact on academic performance. *School Mental Health, 3,* 93–101.

Lynch, A. M., Theodore, L. A., Bray, M. A., & Kehle, T. J. (2009). A comparison of group-oriented contingencies and randomized reinforcers to improve homework completion and accuracy for students with disabilities. *School Psychology Review, 38,* 307–324.

MacArthur, C. A. (2012). Strategies instruction. In K. R. Harris, S. Graham, T. Urdan, A. G. Bus, S. Major, & H. L. Swanson (Eds.), *APA educational psychology handbook* (Vol. 3, pp. 379–401). Washington, DC: American Psychological Association.

Mastropieri, M. A., & Scruggs, T. E. (2002). *Effective instruction for special education* (3rd ed.). Upper Saddle River, NJ: Prentice Hall/Merrill.

Miller, L. (2003). Developing listening skills with authentic materials. *ESL Magazine, 6*(2), 16–18.

Mitchem, K., Kight, J., Fitzgerald, G., Koury, K., & Boonseng, T. (2007). Electronic performance support systems: An assistive technology tool for secondary students with mild disabilities. *Journal of Special Education Technology, 22*(2), 1–14.

Muchnick, C. C. (2011). *The everything guide to study skills.* Avon, MA: F+WMedia.

Myles, B. S., Ferguson, H., & Hagiwara, T. (2007). Using a personal digital assistant to improve the recording homework assignments by an adolescent with Asperger syndrome. *Focus on Autism and Other Developmental Disabilities, 22,* 96–99.

Ness, B. M., Sohlberg, M. M., & Albin, R.W. (2011). Evaluation of a second-tier classroom-based assignment completion strategy for middle school students in a resource context. *Remedial and Special Education, 32,* 406–416.

O'Melia, M. C., & Rosenberg, M. S. (1994). Effects of cooperative homework teams on the acquisition of mathematics skills by secondary students with mild disabilities. *Exceptional Children, 60,* 538–548.

Power, T. J., Werba, B. E., Watkins, M. W., Angelucci, J. G., & Eiraldi, R. B. (2006). Patterns of parent-reported homework problems among ADHD: Referred and non-referred children. *School Psychology Quarterly, 21,* 13–33.

Rafoth, M. A. (2006). Strategic learning. In G. G. Bear & K. M. Minke (Eds.), *Children's needs III: Development prevention, and intervention* (pp. 473–483). Washington, DC: National Association of School Psychologists.

Reid, R., Lienemann, T. O., & Hagaman, J. L. (2013). *Strategy instruction for students with learning disabilities* (2nd ed.). New York, NY: Guilford.

Spooner, L., & Woodcock, J. (2010). *Teaching children to listen: A practical approach to developing children's listening skills.* New York, NY: Continuum.

Vaughn, S., & Bos, C. (2015). *Strategies for teaching students with learning and behavior problems* (9th ed.). Boston, MA: Pearson.

Wong, L. (2015). *Essential study skills* (8th ed.). Boston, MA: Wadsworth.

Chapter 12

Baca, L. M., & Cervantes, H. T. (2004). *The bilingual special education interface.* Upper Saddle River, NJ: Merrill/Prentice Hall.

Banks, J. A. (2015). *Cultural diversity and education: Foundations, curriculum, and teaching*. Upper Saddle River, NJ: Pearson Education.

Baron, J. B. (1990). Performance assessment: Blurring the edges among assessment, curriculum, and instruction. In A. B. Champaign, B. E. Lovitts, & B. J. Callinger (Eds.), *Assessment in the service of instruction* (pp. 127–148). Washington, DC: American Association for the Advancement of Science.

Barrett, H. C. (2000). Creating you own electronic portfolio: Using off the shelf software to showcase your own or student work. Retrieved from http://www.speakeasydesigns.com/SDSU/student/SAGE/compsprep/Create_your_own_Electronic_Portfolio.pdf

Berkeley, S., & Riccomini, P. J. (2011). Academic progress monitoring. In J. M. Kauffman & D. P. Hallahan (Eds.), *Handbook of special education* (pp. 334–339). New York, NY: Routledge.

Bolt, S. E., & Thurlow, M. L. (2004). Five of the most frequently allowed testing accommodations in state policy. *Remedial and Special Education, 25,* 141–152.

Boyle, J. R. (2013). Strategic note-taking for inclusive middle school science classrooms. *Remedial and Special Education, 34,* 78–90.

Brookhart, S. M. (2004). *Grading*. Upper Saddle River, NJ: Merrill/Prentice Hall.

Bursuck, W. D., Polloway, E. A., Plante, L., Epstein, M. H., Jayanthi, M., & McConeghy, J. (1996). Report card grading and adaptations: A national survey of classroom practices. *Exceptional Children, 62,* 301–318.

California Department of Education. (2015). *California alternate performance assessment*. Sacramento, CA: Author. Retrieved from http://www.cde.ca.gov/ta/tg/sr/capa.asp

Carey, M. D., Mannell, R. H., & Dunn, P. K. (2011). Does a rater's familiarity with a candidate's pronunciation affect the rating in oral proficiency interviews? *Language Testing, 28,* 201–219.

Carman, R. A., & Adams, W. R. (1972). *Study skills: A student's guide for survival*. New York, NY: Wiley.

Cawthon, S. W. (2008). Accommodations use for statewide standardized assessments: Prevalence and recommendations for students who are deaf or hard of hearing. *Journal of Deaf Studies and Deaf Education, 13,* 55–76.

Christiansen, J., & Vogel, J. R. (1998). A decision model for grading students with disabilities. *Teaching Exceptional Children, 31,* 30–35.

College Board. (2015). *Students with disabilities: The steps to receive test accommodations*. Retrieved from http://sat.collegeboard.org/register/for-students-with-disabilities

Connolly, A. J. (2007). *KeyMath 3 Diagnostic Assessment—revised*. San Antonio, TX: Pearson.

Crawford, L., Helwig, R., & Tindal, G. (2004). Writing performance assessments: How important is extended time? *Journal of Learning Disabilities, 37,* 132–142.

Deno, S. (2016). Data-based decision-making. In S. R. Jimerson, M. K. Burns, & A. M. VanDerHayden (Eds.), *Handbook of response to intervention: The science and practice of multi-tiered systems of support* (2nd ed., pp. 9–28). New York, NY: Springer.

Deshler, D. D., & Schumaker, J. B. (2006). *Teaching adolescents with disabilities: Accessing the general education curriculum*. Thousand Oaks, CA: Corwin.

Elliott, J., & Thurlow, M. (2006). *Improving test performance of students with disabilities on district and state assessments*. Thousand Oaks, CA: Corwin.

Feldman, E., Kim, J., & Elliott, S. N. (2011). The effects of accommodations on adolescents' self-efficacy and test performance. *Journal of Special Education, 45,* 77–88.

Fuchs, D., & Fuchs, L. S. (1989). Effects of examiner familiarity on Black, Caucasian, and Hispanic children: A meta-analysis. *Exceptional Children, 55,* 303–308.

Fuchs, D., Fuchs, L. S., & Compton, D. C. (2012). Smart RTI: A next-generation approach to multi-level prevention. *Exceptional Children, 78,* 263–279.

Fuchs, D., Fuchs, L. S., & Power, M. H. (1987). Effects of examiner familiarity of LD and MR students' language performance. *Remedial and Special Education, 8*(4), 47–52.

Fuchs, L. S. (1994). *Connecting performance assessment to instruction*. Reston, VA: Council for Exceptional Children.

Fuchs, L. S. (2008). *Progress monitoring within a multi-level prevention system*. Retrieved from http://www.rtinetwork.org/essential/assessment/progress/mutlilevelprevention

Fuchs, L. S., & Fuchs, D. (2008). The role of assessment within the RTI framework. In D. Fuchs, L. S. Fuchs, & S. Vaughn (Eds.), *Response to intervention: A framework for reading educators* (pp. 27–50). Newark, DE: International Reading Association.

Fuchs, L. S., Fuchs, D., & Capizzi, A. M. (2006). Identifying appropriate test accommodations for students with learning disabilities. *Focus on Exceptional Children, 37,* 1–8.

Fuchs, L. S., Fuchs, D., Eaton, S. B., Hamlett, C. L., & Karns, K. M. (2000). Supplementing teacher judgments of mathematics test accommodations with objective data sources. *School Psychology Review, 29,* 65–85.

Fuchs, L. S., Fuchs, D., Hamlett, C. L., Phillips, N. B., & Bentz, J. (1994). Classwide curriculum-based measurement: Helping general educators meet the challenge of student diversity. *Exceptional Children, 60,* 518–537.

Gajria, M., Salend, S. J., & Hemrick, M. A. (1994). Teacher acceptability of testing modifications for mainstreamed students. *Learning Disabilities Research & Practice, 9,* 236–243.

Gollnick, D. M., & Chinn, P. C. (2009). *Multicultural education in a pluralistic society* (8th ed.). Upper Saddle River, NJ: Merrill/Pearson.

Gomez, E. (2001). Assessment portfolios: Including English language learners in large-scale assessments. *ERIC Digest*. Washington, DC: ERIC Clearinghouse on Languages and Linguistics. (ERIC Document Reproduction Service No. ED447725)

Gregg, N., & Nelson, J. M. (2012). Meta-analysis on the effectiveness of extra time as a test accommodation for transitioning adolescents with learning disabilities: More questions than answers. *Journal of Learning Disabilities, 45,* 128–138.

Hammil, D. D., & Larsen S. C. (2009). *Test of Written Language—4 (TOWL-4)*. Austin, TX: Pro-Ed.

Harry, B., & Klingner, J. K. (2014). *Why are so many minority students in special education? Understanding race and disability in schools* (2nd ed.). New York, NY: Teachers College Press.

Haynes, P. (2011). *The effect of test-wiseness on self-efficacy and mathematic performance of middle school students with learning disabilities* (Unpublished doctoral dissertation). Virginia Commonwealth University, Richmond.

Hoover, J. J., & Klingner, J. (2011). Promoting cultural validity in the assessment of bilingual special education students. In M. Basterra, E. Trumbull, & G. Solano-Flores (Eds.), *Cultural validity in assessment* (pp. 143–167). New York, NY: Routledge.

Hosp, M. K., Hosp, J. L., & Howell, K. W. (2016). *The ABCs of CBM: A practical guide to curriculum-based measurement*. New York, NY: Guilford.

Hughes, C. (1996). Memory and test-taking strategies. In D. D. Deshler, E. S. Ellis, & B. K. Lenz (Eds.), *Teaching adolescents with learning disabilities: Strategies and methods* (2nd ed., pp. 209–266). Denver, CO: Love Publishing.

Hughes, C. A., Rule, K. L., Deshler, D., & Schumaker, J. B. (1993). Test-taking strategy instruction for adolescents with emotional and behavioral disorders. *Journal of Emotional and Behavioral Disorders, 1,* 189–198.

Hughes, C. A., Schumaker, J. B., Deshler, D. D., & Mercer, C. D. (1988). *The test-taking strategy*. Lawrence, KS: Edge Enterprises.

Jayanthi, M., Epstein, M. H., Polloway, E. A., & Bursuck, W. D. (1996). A national survey of general education teachers' perceptions of testing adaptations. *Journal of Special Education, 30*, 99–115.

Johnson, E., Kimball, L., Brown, S. O., & Anderson, D. (2001). A state-wide review of the use of accommodations in large-scale, high-scale, high-stakes assessments. *Exceptional Children, 67*, 251–264.

Johnson, R. L., Penny, J. A., & Gordon, B. (2009). *Assessing performance: Designing, scoring and validating performance tasks*. New York, NY: Guilford.

Jung, L. A., & Guskey, T. R. (2010). Grading exceptional learners. *Educational Leadership, 67*(5), 31–35.

Kaufman, A., & Kaufman, N. (2006). *The Kaufman Assessment Battery for Children–II*. San Antonio, TX: Pearson.

Kaufman, A. S., & Kaufman, N. L. (2004). *Kaufman Test of Educational Achievement* (2nd ed.). San Antonio, TX: Pearson.

Kearns, J., Burdge, M. D., & Clayton, J. (2006). How students demonstrate academic performance in portfolio assessment. In D. M. Browder & F. Spooner (Eds.), *Teaching language arts, math, & science to students with significant cognitive disabilities* (pp. 277–293). Baltimore, MD: Paul H. Brookes.

Kesselman-Turkel, J., & Peterson, F. (2004). *Test-taking strategies*. Madison, WI: University of Wisconsin Press.

Kornhaber, M. L. (2012). Standardized testing and standards. In J. A. Banks (Ed.), *Encyclopedia of diversity in education* (Vol. 4, pp. 2073–2076). Thousand Oaks, CA: Sage Publications.

Laitusis, C., Buzick, H., Stone, E., Hansen, E., & Hakkinen, M. (2012). *Smarter Balanced Assessment Consortium: Literature review of testing accommodations and accessibility tools for students with disabilities*. Princeton, NJ: Educational Testing Service.

Lazarus, S. S., Cormier, D. C., & Thurlow, M. L. (2010). States' accommodations policies and development of alternative assessments based on modified achievement standards: A discriminant analysis. *Remedial and Special Education, 32*, 301–308.

Lazarus, S. S., Thurlow, M. L., Lail, K. E., & Christensen, L. (2009). A longitudinal analysis of state accommodation policies: Twelve years of change. *Journal of Special Education, 43*, 67–80.

Learning Disabilities Association. (2011). *Graduation Equivalency Diploma: The GED. Accommodations for the GED*. Pittsburgh, PA: Author. Retrieved from https://ldaamerica.org/types-of-high-school-equivalency-exams/

Lewandowski, L. J., Lovett, B. J., Parolin, R., Gordon, M., & Codding, R. S. (2007). Extended time accommodations and the mathematics performance of students with and without ADHD. *Journal of Psychoeducational Assessment, 25*, 17–28.

Lindstrom, J. H. (2011). High stakes testing and accommodations. In J. M. Kauffman & D. P. Hallahan (Eds.), *Handbook of special education* (pp. 321–333). New York, NY: Routledge.

Lovett, B. J. (2010). Extended time testing accommodations for students with disabilities: Answers to five fundamental questions. *Review of Educational Research, 80*, 611–638.

Lucangeli, D., & Scruggs, T. E. (2003). Test anxiety, perceived competence, and academic achievement in secondary school students. In T. E. Scruggs & M. A. Mastropieri (Eds.), *Identification and assessment: Advances in learning and behavioral disabilities* (pp. 223–230). Oxford, UK: Elsevier Science.

MacArthur, C. A., & Cavalier, A. R. (2004). Dictation and speech recognition technology as test accommodations. *Exceptional Children, 71*, 43–58.

Markwardt, F. C. (1997). *Peabody Individual Achievement Test—normative update*. Upper Saddle River, NJ: Pearson.

Mastropieri, M. A., & Scruggs, T. E. (2002). *Effective instruction for special education* (3rd ed.). Austin, TX: Pro-Ed.

Meyer, A., Rose, D. H., & Gordon, D. (2014). *Universal design for learning: Theory and practice*. Wakefield, MA: CAST.

Munk, D., & Bursuck, W. D. (1998). Report card adaptations for students with disabilities: Types and acceptability. *Intervention in School and Clinic, 33*, 306–308.

Munk, D., & Bursuck, W. D. (2001). Preliminary findings on personalized grading plans for middle school students with learning disabilities. *Exceptional Children, 67*, 211–234.

Munk, D., & Bursuck, W. D. (2003). Grading students with disabilities. *Educational Leadership, 61*(2), 38–43.

Polloway, E. A., Epstein, M. H., Bursuck, W. D., Roderique, T. W., McConeky, J. L., & Jayanthi, M. (1994). Classroom grading: A national survey of policies. *Remedial and Special Education, 15*, 162–170.

Rhodes, R. L., Ochoa, S. H., & Ortiz, S. O. (2005). *Assessing culturally and linguistically diverse students*. New York, NY: Guilford.

Ritter, S., & Idol-Maestas, L. (1986). Teaching middle school students to use a test-taking strategy. *Journal of Educational Research, 79*, 350–357.

Roid, G. H. (2003). *Stanford-Binet Intelligence Scale* (5th ed.). Rolling Meadows, IL: Riverside Publishing.

Salend, S. J. (1995). Modifying tests for diverse learners. *Intervention in School and Clinic, 31*, 84–90.

Salend, S. J. (2008). Determining appropriate testing accommodations: Complying with NCLB and IDEA. *Teaching Exceptional Children, 40*(4), 14–22.

Salend, S. J. (2009). *Classroom testing and assessment for all students: Beyond standardization*. Thousand Oaks, CA: Corwin.

Salend, S. J. (2011a). Creating student-friendly tests. *Educational Leadership, 69*(3), 52–58.

Salend, S. J. (2011b). Addressing test anxiety. *Teaching Exceptional Children, 44*, 58–68.

Salend, S. J. (2016). *Creating inclusive classrooms: Effective, differentiated, and reflective practices*. Boston, MA: Pearson.

Salvia, J., Ysseldyke, J., & Bolt, S. (2013). *Assessment: In special and inclusive education* (11th ed.). Belmont, CA: Wadsworth.

Schirmer, B. R., & Bailey, J. (2000). Writing assessment rubric: An instructional approach with struggling writers. *Teaching Exceptional Children, 33*, 52–58.

Scruggs, T. E., & Mastropieri, M. A. (1988). Are learning disabled students "test-wise"? A review of recent research. *Learning Disabilities Focus, 3*, 87–97.

Scruggs, T. E., & Mastropieri, M. A. (1992). *Teaching test-taking skills: Helping students show what they know*. Cambridge, MA: Brookline Books.

Scruggs, T. E., Mastropieri, M. A., Bakken, J. P., & Brigham, F. J. (1993). Reading vs. doing: The relative effectiveness of textbook-based and inquiry-oriented approaches to science education. *Journal of Special Education, 27*, 1–15.

Shapiro, E. S. (2010). *Academic skills problems* (4th ed.). New York, NY: Guilford.

Sireci, S. G., Scarpati, S. E., & Li, S. (2005). Test accommodations for students with disabilities: An analysis of the interaction hypothesis. *Review of Educational Research, 75*, 457–490.

Songlee, D. H. (2007). *Effects of test-taking strategy instruction on high-functioning adolescents with autism spectrum disorder* (Unpublished doctoral dissertation). University of Nevada, Las Vegas, NV.

State of New Jersey, Department of Education. (2014). *Accommodations and modifications of test administration procedures for statewide assessments*. Trenton, NJ: Author. Retrieved from http://www.nj.gov/education/specialed/accom900.htm

Stecker, P. M., Fuchs, L. S., & Fuchs, D. (2005). Using curriculum-based measurement to improve student achievement: Review of research. *Psychology in the Schools, 42*, 795–819.

Stufft, D. L., Bauman, D., & Ohlsen, M. (2009). Preferences and attitudes toward accommodations of traditional assessment in secondary social studies classrooms. *Social Studies Research and Practice, 4*, 87–98.

Thompson, S. J., Johnstone, C. J., & Thurlow, M. L. (2002). *Universal design applied to large scale assessments* (Synthesis Report 44). Minneapolis, MN: University of Minnesota, National Center on Educational Outcomes. Retrieved from http://education.umn.edu/NCEO/OnlinePubs/Synthesis44.html

Thurlow, M., & Quenemoen, R. F. (2011). Standards-based reform and students with disabilities. In J. M. Kauffman & D. P. Hallahan (Eds.), *Handbook of special education* (pp. 134–146). New York, NY: Routledge.

Training and Technical Assistance Center at the College of William and Mary. (2005). *Virginia's alternate assessment program.* Williamsburg, VA: Author. Retrieved from http://education.wm.edu/centers/ttac/resources/articles/legalissues/vaalternate/index.php

U.S. Department of Education. (2012). *More local freedom: Flexibility and waivers.* Washington, DC: Author. Retrieved from http://www2.ed.gov/nclb/freedom/local/flexibility/index.html

Vavrus, L. (1990). Put portfolios to the test. *Instructor, 100*(1), 48–53.

Virginia Department of Education. (2010). *Virginia alternative and alternate assessment program.* Richmond, VA: Author. Retrieved from http://www.doe.virginia.gov/testing/alternative_assessments/vaap_va_alt_assessment_prog/index.shtml

Wechsler, D. (2003). *Wechsler Intelligence Scale for Children* (4th ed.). San Antonio, TX: Psychological Corporation.

Wesson, C. L., & King, R. P. (1996). Portfolio assessment and special education students. *Teaching Exceptional Children, 28*(2), 44–48.

Wilkenson, G. S., & Robertson, G. J. (2006). *Wide Range Achievement Test–4.* Lutz, FL: Psychological Assessment Resources.

Woodcock, R. W., Mather, N., & Schrank, F. (2001). *Woodcock-Johnson III, Diagnostic Reading Battery.* Rolling Meadows, IL: Riverside Publishing.

Woodcock, R. W., Johnson, M. B., & Mather, N. (2001). *Woodcock-Johnson III, Tests of Achievement.* Rolling Meadows, IL: Riverside Publishing.

Chapter 13

Adams, M. J. (1990). *Beginning to read.* Cambridge, MA: MIT Press.

Alves, K. D., Kennedy, M. J., Brown, T. S., & Solis, M. (2014). Story grammar instruction with third and fifth grade students with learning disabilities and other struggling readers. *Learning Disabilities: A Contemporary Journal, 13*, 73–93.

Anderson, R. C., Hiebert, E. H., Scott, J. A., & Wilkinson, I. A. G. (1985). *Becoming a nation of readers: The report of the commission on reading.* Washington, DC: National Academy of Education, Commission on Education and Public Policy.

Babyak, A. E., Koorland, M., & Mathes, P. G. (2000). The effects of story mapping instruction on the reading comprehension of students with behavioral disorders. *Behavioral Disorders, 25*, 239–258.

Bakken, J. P., & Whedon, C. K. (2002). Teaching text structure to improve reading comprehension. *Intervention in School and Clinic, 37*, 229–233.

Behavioral Research and Teaching. (2005). *Oral reading fluency: 90 years of measurement.* Eugene, OR: Author. Retrieved from http://brt.uoregon.edu

Berkeley, S., Mastropieri, M. A., & Scruggs, T. E. (2011). Reading comprehension strategy instruction and attribution retraining for secondary students with learning and other mild disabilities. *Journal of Learning Disabilities, 44*, 18–32.

Berkeley, S., & Riccomini, P. J. (2011). Academic progress monitoring. In J. M. Kauffman & D. P. Hallahan (Eds.), *Handbook of special education* (pp. 334–339). New York, NY: Routledge.

Berkeley, S., Scruggs, T. E., & Mastropieri, M. A. (2010). Reading comprehension instruction for students with learning disabilities, 1995–2006: A meta-analysis. *Remedial and Special Education, 31*, 423–436.

Berninger, V., & Amtmann, D. (2003). Preventing written expression disabilities through early and continuing assessment and intervention for handwriting and/or spelling problems: Research into practice. In H. L. Swanson, K. Harris, & S. Graham (Eds.), *Handbook of learning disabilities* (pp. 345–363). New York, NY: Guilford.

Best, S. J., Heller, K. W., & Bigge, J. L. (2009). *Teaching individuals with physical or multiple disabilities* (6th ed.). Upper Saddle River, NJ: Merrill/Prentice Hall.

Boardman, A., Vaughn, S., Buckley, P., Reutebuch, C., Roberts, G., & Klingner, J. (2016). Collaborative strategic reading for students with learning disabilities in upper elementary classrooms. *Exceptional Children, 82*, 409–427.

Bowman-Perrott, L., Burke, M.D., Zhang, D., & Zaini, S. (2014). Direct and collateral effects of peer tutoring on social and behavioral outcomes: A meta-analysis of single-case research. *School Psychology Review, 43*, 260–285.

Brigham, F. J., Berkeley, S. A., Simpkins, P., & Brigham, M. (2007). *Reading comprehension instruction* (DLD-DR Current Practice Alerts, Alert 12). Arlington, VA: Council for Exceptional Children, Division for Learning Disabilities.

Browder, D. M. (2015). What should we teach students with moderate and severe developmental disabilities? In B. Bateman, J. Lloyd, & M. Tankersley (Eds.), *Enduring issues in special education: Personal perspectives* (pp. 52–72). New York, NY: Routledge.

Browder, D. M., Wakeman, S. Y., Spooner, F., Ahlgrim-Delzell, L., & Algozzine, B. (2006). Research on reading instruction for individuals with significant cognitive disabilities. *Exceptional Children, 72*, 392–408.

Bryant, N. D., Drabin, I. R., & Gettinger, M. (1981). Effects of varying unit size on spelling achievement of learning disabled children. *Journal of Learning Disabilities, 14*, 200–203.

Burks, M. (2004). Effects of classwide peer tutoring on the number of words spelled correctly by students with LD. *Intervention in School and Clinic, 39*, 301–304.

Bursuck, W. D., & Damer, M. (2015). *Teaching reading to students who are at risk or have disabilities: A multi-tier, RTI approach* (3rd ed.). Boston, MA: Pearson.

Callins, T. (2005). *Culturally responsive literacy instruction* (Practitioner Brief Series: National Center for Culturally Responsive Educational Systems). Retrieved from http://www.niusileadscape.org/docs/FINAL_PRODUCTS/NCCRESt/practitioner_briefs/%95%20TEMPLATE/DRAFTS/AUTHOR%20revisions/annablis%20pracbrief%20templates/Literacy_Brief_highres.pdf

Carnine, D., Silbert, J., Kameénui, E. J., Slocum, T. A., & Travers, P. A. (2016). *Direct instruction reading* (6th ed.). Boston, MA: Pearson.

Cerar, N. (2012). *Students with emotional and behavior disorder learn how to write fluently persuasive essays and to write elaborated persuasive essays.* Unpublished doctoral dissertation, George Mason University, Fairfax, VA.

Chard, D. J., Vaughn, S., & Tyler, B. (2002). A synthesis of research on effective interventions for building reading fluency with elementary students with learning disabilities. *Journal of Learning Disabilities, 35,* 386–406.

Coleman, M. B., & Heller, K. W. (2009). Assistive technology considerations. In K. W. Heller, P. E. Forner, P. A. Alberto, S. J. Best, & M. N. Schwartzman (Eds.), *Understanding physical, health, and multiple disabilities* (2nd ed., pp. 139–155). Upper Saddle River, NJ: Prentice Hall.

Coyne, M. D., Simmons, D. C., Kameénui, E. J., & Stoolmiller, M. (2004). Teaching vocabulary during shared storybook readings: An examination of differential effects. *Exceptionality, 12,* 145–162.

Cuenca-Sanchez, Y., Mastropieri, M. A., Scruggs, T. E., & Kidd, J. (2012). Middle school students with emotional disorders: Determined to meet their needs through writing. *Exceptionality, 20,* 71–93.

D'Agostino, J. V., & Murphy, J. A. (2004). A meta-analysis of reading recovery in United States schools. *Educational Evaluation & Policy Analysis, 26,* 23–38.

De La Paz, S. (2007). Best practices in teaching writing to students with special needs. In S. Graham, C. MacArthur, & J. Fitzgerald (Eds.), *Best practices in writing instruction* (pp. 163–178). New York, NY: Guilford.

De La Paz, S., & Graham, S. (1997). Effects of dictation and advanced planning instruction on the composing of students with writing and learning problems. *Journal of Educational Psychology, 89,* 203–222.

Denton, C. A., & Mathes, P. G. (2002). *Reading Recovery* (DLD-DR Current Practice Alerts, Alert 7). Arlington, VA: Council for Exceptional Children, Division for Learning Disabilities.

Deshler, D. D., & Schumaker, J. (2006). *Teaching adolescents with disabilities: Accessing the general education curriculum.* Thousand Oaks, CA: Corwin.

Dieker, L. A., & Little, M. (2005). Secondary reading: Not just for reading teachers anymore. *Intervention in School and Clinic, 40,* 276–283.

Division for Learning Disabilities. (2007). *Thinking about response to intervention and learning disabilities: A teacher's guide.* Arlington, VA: Author.

Dowling, D. (1995). *303 dumb spelling mistakes and what you can do about them.* Lincolnwood, IL: National Textbook Company.

Echevarria, J. J., & Graves, A. (2015). *Sheltered content instruction: Teaching English learners with diverse abilities* (5th ed.). Boston, MA: Pearson.

Ehri, L. C., Nunes, S. R., Willows, D. M., Schuster, B. V., Yaghoub-Zadeh, Z., & Shanahan, T. (2001). Phonemic awareness instruction helps children learn to read: Evidence from the National Reading Panel's meta-analysis. *Reading Research Quarterly, 36,* 250–287.

Ellis, E. (1996). Reading strategy instruction. In D. Deshler, E. S. Ellis, & B. Lenz (Eds.), *Teaching adolescents with learning disabilities: Strategies and methods* (2nd ed., pp. 61–125). Denver, CO: Love.

Engelmann, S. E., Osborne, S., & Hanner, S. (2008). *Reading mastery signatures grade 4 and 5.* Columbus, OH: Science Research Associates.

Englert, C. S., & Mariage, T. V. (1996). A sociocultural perspective: Teaching ways-of-thinking and ways-of-talking in a literacy community. *Learning Disabilities Research & Practice, 11,* 157–167.

Evmenova, A. S., Regan, K., Boykin, A., Good, K., Hughes, M., MacVittie, N., … Chirinos, D. (2016). Emphasizing planning for essay writing with a computer-based graphic organizer. *Exceptional Children, 82,* 170–191.

Fletcher, D., & Abood, D. (1988). An analysis of the readability of product warning labels: Implications for curriculum development for persons with moderate and severe mental retardation. *Education and Training in Mental Retardation, 23,* 224–227.

Foorman, B. R. (2007). Primary prevention in classroom reading instruction. *Teaching Exceptional Children, 39*(5), 24–30.

Fossett, B., Smith, V., & Mirenda, P. (2003). Facilitating oral language and literacy development during general education activities. In D. L. Ryndak & S. Alper (Eds.), *Curriculum and instruction for students with significant disabilities in inclusive settings* (2nd ed., pp. 173–205). Boston, MA: Allyn & Bacon.

Fountas, I. C., & Pinnell, G. S. (2013). *The Fountas & Pinnell leveled book list, K–8+, 2013–2015 Edition.* Portsmouth, NH: Heinemann.

Fuchs, D., & Fuchs, L. S. (2005). Peer-assisted learning strategies: Promoting word recognition, fluency, and reading comprehension in young children. *Journal of Special Education, 39,* 34–44.

Fuchs, D., Fuchs, L. S., & Compton, D. C. (2012). Smart RTI: A next-generation approach to multi-level prevention. *Exceptional Children, 78,* 263–279.

Fuchs, L. S., & Fuchs, D. (2007). The role of assessment in the three-tier approach to reading instruction. In D. Haager, J. Klingner, & S. Vaughn (Eds.), *Evidence-based reading practices for response to intervention* (pp. 29–42). Baltimore, MD: Paul H Brookes.

Fulk, B. M. (1997). Think while you spell: A cognitive motivational approach to spelling instruction. *Teaching Exceptional Children, 29*(4), 70–71.

Gerber, M., & Richards-Tutor, M. M. (2011). Teaching spelling to students with learning disabilities. In R. O'Connor & P. Vadasy (Eds.), *Handbook of reading interventions* (pp. 113–137). New York, NY: Guilford.

Gersten, R., & Dimino, J. (1993). Visions and revisions: A special education perspective on the whole language controversy. *Remedial and Special Education, 14*(4), 5–13.

Gersten, R., Fuchs, L. S., Williams, J., & Baker, S. (2001). Teaching reading comprehension strategies to students with learning disabilities: A review of research. *Review of Educational Research, 71,* 279–320.

Gettinger, M., Bryant, N. D., & Fayne, H. R. (1982). Designing spelling instruction for learning disabled children: An emphasis on unit size, distributed practice, and training for transfer. *Journal of Special Education, 16,* 339–448.

Gillespie, A., & Graham, S. (2014). A meta-analysis of writing interventions for students with learning disabilities. *Exceptional Children, 80,* 454–473.

Goodman, K. (2006). *What's whole in whole language?* Muskegon, MI: RDR Books.

Graham, S. (1999). Handwriting and spelling instruction for students with learning disabilities: A review. *Learning Disability Quarterly, 22,* 78–98.

Graham, S. (2010). Want to improve children's writing? Don't neglect their handwriting. *American Educator, 33*(4), 20–40.

Graham, S., & Harris, K. R. (2005). *Writing better: Effective strategies for teaching students with learning difficulties.* Baltimore, MD: Brookes.

Graham, S., & Harris, K. R. (2006). Preventing writing difficulties: Providing additional handwriting and spelling instruction to at-risk children in first grade. *Teaching Exceptional Children, 38,* 64–66.

Graham, S., & Harris, K. (2007). Best practices in teaching planning. In S. Graham, C. MacArthur, & J. Fitzgerald (Eds.), *Best practices in writing instruction* (pp. 119–140). New York, NY: Guilford.

Graham, S., & Harris, K. (2011). Writing and students with disabilities. In J. M. Kauffman & D. P. Hallahan (Eds.), *Handbook of special education* (pp. 422–433). New York, NY: Routledge.

Graham, S., Harris, K. R., & Chorzempa, B. F. (2002). Contribution of spelling instruction to the spelling, writing, and reading of poor spellers. *Journal of Educational Psychology, 94,* 669–686.

Graham, S., Harris, K. R., & Fink, B. (2000). Is handwriting causally related to learning to write? Treatment of handwriting problems in beginning writers. *Journal of Educational Psychology, 92,* 620–633.

Graham, S., Harris, K. R., & Loynachan, C. (1994). The spelling for writing list. *Journal of Learning Disabilities, 27,* 210–214.

Graham, S., Harris, K. R., & Loynachan, C. (1996). The directed spelling thinking activity: Application with high-frequency words. *Learning Disabilities Research & Practice, 11,* 34–40.

Graham, S., & Perin, D. (2007). A meta-analysis of writing instruction for adolescent students. *Journal of Educational Psychology, 99,* 445–476.

Graham, S., & Santangelo, T. (2014). Does spelling instruction make students better spellers, readers, and writers? A meta-analytic review. *Reading & Writing: An Interdisciplinary Journal, 27,* 1703–1743.

Graham, S., & Weintraub, N. (1996). A review of handwriting research: Progress and prospects from 1980 to 1994. *Educational Psychology Review, 8,* 7–87.

Graves, A. W. (2010). A longitudinal study of the impact of effective beginning reading instruction for English learners: Literacy, language, and learning disabilities. In T. E. Scruggs & M. A. Mastropieri (Eds.), *Literacy and learning: Advances in learning and behavioral disabilities* (Vol. 23, pp. 155–174). Oxford, UK: Emerald.

Graves, D. H. (2003). *Writing: Teachers and children at work.* Portsmouth, NH: Heinemann.

Gregg, N. C., Coleman, C., Davis, M., & Chalk, J. C. (2007). Timed essay writing: Implications for high-stakes tests. *Journal of Learning Disabilities, 40,* 306–318.

Hall, T. E., Meyer, A., & Rose, D. H. (Eds.). (2012). *Universal design for learning in the classroom: Practical applications.* New York, NY: Guilford.

Harris, K. K., & Graham, S. (1992). *Helping young writers master the craft: Strategy instruction and self-regulation in the writing process.* Cambridge, MA: Brookline Books.

Harris, K. K., Graham, S., Mason, L. H., & Friedlander, B. (2008). *Powerful writing strategies for all students.* Baltimore, MD: Brookes.

Hauth, C., Mastropieri, M. A., Scruggs, T. E., & Regan, K. (2013). Can students with emotional and/or behavioral disabilities improve on planning and writing in the content areas of civics and mathematics? *Behavioral Disorders, 38,* 154–170.

Heller, K. W. (2010). Writing instruction and adaptations. In S. J. Best, K. W. Heller, & J. L. Bigge (Eds.), *Teaching individuals with physical or multiple disabilities* (6th ed., pp. 407–431). Upper Saddle River, NJ: Pearson.

Heller, K. W., & Alberto, P. A. (2010). Reading instruction and adaptations. In S. J. Best, K. W. Heller, & J. L. Bigge (Eds.), *Teaching individuals with physical or multiple disabilities* (6th ed., pp. 375–406). Upper Saddle River, NJ: Pearson.

Hiebert, E. H. (1994). Reading recovery in the United States: What difference does it make to an age cohort? *Educational Researcher, 23*(9), 15–25.

Hirshorn, E. A., Dye, M. W. G., Hauser, P., Supalla, T. R., & Bavelier, D. (2015). The contribution of phonological knowledge, memory, and language background to reading comprehension in deaf populations. *Frontiers in Psychology, 6,* 1153. Retrieved from http://www.ncbi.nlm.nih.gov/pmc/articles/PMC4548088/

Idol-Maestas, L. (1985). Getting ready to read: Guided probing for poor comprehenders. *Learning Disability Quarterly, 8,* 243–254.

Isaacson, S., & Gleason, M. M. (1997). Mechanical obstacles to writing: What can teachers do to help students with learning problems? *Learning Disabilities Research & Practice, 12,* 188–194.

Johnson, P. H. (1992). Understanding reading disability: A case study approach. In T. Heir & T. Latus (Eds.), *Special education at century's end: Evolution of theory and practice since 1970* (pp. 275–304). Reprint series No. 23, Harvard Educational Review. Cambridge, MA: President and Fellows of Harvard College.

Joseph, L. M., Konrad, M., Cates, G., Vajcner, T., Eveleigh, E., & Fishley, K. M. (2012). A meta-analytic review of the cover-copy-compare and variations of this self-management procedure. *Psychology in the Schools, 49,* 122–136.

Joseph, L. M., & Schisler, R. (2009). Should adolescents go back to the basics? A review of teaching word reading skills to middle and high school students. *Remedial and Special Education, 30,* 131–147.

Klingner, J. K., Vaughn, S., Arguelles, M. E., Hughes, M. T., & Leftwich, S. A. (2004). Collaborative strategic reading: "Real world" lessons from classroom teachers. *Remedial and Special Education, 25,* 291–302.

Klingner, J. K., Vaughn, S., & Boardman, A. (2007). *Teaching reading comprehension to students with reading difficulties.* New York, NY: Guilford.

Klingner, J. K., Vaughn, S. Boardman, A., & Swanson, E. (2012). *"Now I get it": Boosting comprehension with collaborative strategic reading.* San Francisco, CA: Jossey-Bass.

Kubina, R., & Hughes, C. A. (2007). *Fluency instruction* (DLD-DR Current Practice Alerts, Alert 15). Arlington, VA: Council for Exceptional Children, Division for Learning Disabilities.

Lane, K. L. (2004). Academic instruction and tutoring interventions for students with emotional/behavioral disorders 1990 to present. In R. B. Rutherford, M. M. Quinn, & S. R. Mathur (Eds.), *Handbook of research in emotional and behavioral disorders* (pp. 462–486). New York, NY: Guilford.

Lee, J., & Yoon, S. Y. (2015). The effects of repeated reading on reading fluency for students with reading disabilities: A meta-analysis. *Journal of Learning Disabilities.* Advance online publication. doi: 0022219415605194

Lenz, B. K., & Hughes, C. A. (1990). A word identification strategy for adolescents with learning disabilities. *Journal of Learning Disabilities, 23,* 149–163.

Lerner, J., & Johns, B. (2015). *Learning disabilities and related mild disabilities: Strategies for success* (13th ed.). Stamford, CT: Cengage.

Life Span Institute. (2002). *Reading fluency tables.* Lawrence, KS: University of Kansas.

Maheady, L., & Gard, J. (2010). Classwide peer tutoring: Practice, theory, research, and personal narrative. *Intervention in School and Clinic, 46,* 71–78.

Marschark, M. (2009). *Raising and educating a deaf child: A comprehensive guide to the choices, controversies, and decisions faced by parents and educators.* New York, NY: Oxford University Press.

Mastropieri, M. A., & Scruggs, T. E. (1991). *Teaching students ways to remember: Strategies for learning mnemonically.* Cambridge, MA: Brookline Books.

Mastropieri, M. A., & Scruggs, T. E. (1997). Best practices in promoting reading comprehension in students with learning disabilities: 1976 to 1996. *Remedial and Special Education, 18,* 197–213.

Mastropieri, M. A., & Scruggs, T. E. (2014). Intensive instruction to improve writing for students with emotional and behavioral disorders. *Behavioral Disorders, 48,* 78–83.

Mastropieri, M. A., Scruggs, T. E., Cerar, N. I., Allen-Bronaugh, D., Thompson, C., Guckert, M.,... Cuenca-Sanchez, Y. (2012). Fluent persuasive writing with students with emotional disturbance: Developing arguments and counterarguments. *Journal of Special Education*. Advance online publication. doi: 10.1177/0022466912440456

Mastropieri, M. A., Scruggs, T. E., Cerar, N. I., Allen-Bronaugh, D., Thompson, C., Guckert, M.,... Cuenca-Sanchez, Y. (2014). Fluent persuasive writing with counterarguments for students with emotional disturbance. *Journal of Special Education, 48*, 17–31.

Mastropieri, M. A., Scruggs, T. E., Cerar, N. I., Guckert, M., Thompson, C., Allen-Bronaugh, D.,... Cuenca-Carlino, Y. (2015). Strategic persuasive writing instruction for students with emotional and behavioral disabilities. *Exceptionality, 23*, 147–169.

Mastropieri, M. A., Scruggs, T. E., Cuenca-Sanchez, Y., Irby, N., Mills, S., Mason, L., & Kubina, R. (2010). Persuading students with emotional disabilities to write: A design study. In T. E. Scruggs & M. A. Mastropieri (Eds.), *Literacy and learning: Advances in learning and behavioral disabilities* (Vol. 23, pp. 237–268). Bingley, UK: Emerald.

Mastropieri, M. A., Scruggs, T. E., & Graetz, J. (2003). Reading comprehension for secondary students. *Learning Disability Quarterly, 26*, 103–116.

Mastropieri, M. A., Scruggs, T. E., Mills, S., Irby, N., Cuenca-Sanchez, Y., Bronaugh, D. A., ... Regan, K. (2009). Teaching students with emotional disabilities to write fluently. *Behavioral Disorders, 35*, 19–40.

Mastropieri, M. A., Scruggs, T. E., Mohler, L. J., Beranek, M. L., Spencer, V., Boon, R. T., & Talbott, E. (2001). Can middle school students with serious reading difficulties help each other and learn anything? *Learning Disabilities Research & Practice, 16*, 18–27.

McLaughlin, T. F., Weber, K. P., & Derby, K. M. (2013). Classroom spelling interventions for students with learning disabilities. In H. L. Swanson, K. R. Harris, & S. Graham (Eds.), *Handbook of research in learning disabilities* (2nd ed., pp. 439–447). New York, NY: Guilford.

McMaster, K. L., Fuchs, D., & Fuchs, L. S. (2006). Research on peer-assisted learning strategies: The promise and limitations of peer-mediated instruction. *Reading & Writing Quarterly: Overcoming Learning Difficulties, 22*, 5–25.

Mendez, L. M. R., Peltzman, C. A., & Frank, M. J. (2016). Engaging struggling early readers to promote reading success: A pilot study of reading by design. *Reading and Writing Quarterly, 32*, 273–297.

Mercer, C. D., Mercer, A. R., & Pullen, P. C. (2011). *Teaching students with learning problems.* Upper Saddle River, NJ: Pearson.

Meyer, A., Rose, D. M., & Gordon, D. (2014). *Universal design for learning: Theory and practice.* Wakefield, MA: CAST.

Montague, M. (1998). Research on metacognition in special education. In T. E. Scruggs & M. A. Mastropieri (Eds.), *Advances in learning and behavioral disabilities* (Vol. 12, pp. 151–184). Greenwich, CT: JAI.

Morphy, P., & Graham, S. (2012). Word processing programs and weaker writers/readers: A meta-analysis of research findings. *Reading and Writing, 25*, 641–678.

National Center for Intensive Intervention at American Institutes for Research. (2016). *Instructional support.* Retrieved from http://www.intensiveintervention.org/instructional-support

National Governors Association Center for Best Practices & Council of Chief State School Officers. (2010). *Common Core State Standards: English/language arts.* Washington, DC: Author.

National Institute for Direct Instruction. (2015). *Reading mastery signature edition.* Eugene, OR: Author. Retrieved from http://www.nifdi.org/programs/reading/reading-mastery

National Reading Panel. (2000). *Report of the National Reading Panel. Teaching children to read: An evidence-based assessment of the scientific research literature on reading and its implications for reading instruction.* Washington, DC: U.S. Department of Health and Human Services.

O'Connor, R. E., White, A., & Swanson, H. L. (2007). Repeated reading versus continuous reading: Influences on reading fluency and comprehension. *Exceptional Children, 74*, 31–46.

O'Shea, L. J., Sindelar, P. T., & O'Shea, D. (1987). The effects of repeated readings and attentional cues on the reading fluency and comprehension of learning disabled readers. *Learning Disabilities Research, 2*, 103–109.

Ogle, D. M. (1986). K-W-L: A teaching model that develops active reading of expository text. *The Reading Teacher, 39*, 564–570.

Palincsar, A. S., & Brown, A. L. (1984). Reciprocal teaching of comprehension fostering and comprehension monitoring activities. *Cognition and Instruction, 1*, 117–175.

Paratore, J. R., & Dougherty, S. (2011). Home differences and reading difficulty. In A. McGill-Franzen & R. L. Allington (Eds.), *Handbook of reading disability research* (pp. 93–109). New York, NY: Routledge.

Powell, S. R., & Fuchs, L. A. (2015). Intensive intervention in mathematics. *Learning Disabilities Research and Practice, 30*, 182–192.

Pressley, M. (2006). *Reading instruction that works: The case for balanced teaching* (3rd ed.). New York, NY: Guilford.

Pressley, M., & Allington, R. L. (2015). *Reading instruction that works: The case for balanced teaching* (4th ed.). New York, NY: Guilford.

Pressley, M., & Rankin, J. (1994). More about whole language methods of reading instruction for students at-risk for early reading failure. *Learning Disabilities Research & Practice, 9*, 156–168.

Pullen, P. C., & Cash, D. B. (2011). *Reading.* In J. M. Kauffman & D. P. Hallahan (Eds.), *Handbook of special education* (pp. 409–421). New York, NY: Routledge.

Pullen, P. C., & Lloyd, J. (2008). *Phonics instruction* (DLD-DR Current Practice Alerts, Alert 12). Arlington, VA: Council for Exceptional Children, Division for Learning Disabilities.

Reid, R., Gonzalez, J. E., Nordness, P. D., Trout, A., & Epstein, M. H. (2004). A meta-analysis of the academic status of students with emotional/behavioral disturbance. *Journal of Special Education, 38*, 130–143.

Reynolds, M., & Wheldall, K. (2007). Reading Recovery 20 years down the track: Looking forward, looking back. *International Journal of Disability, Development and Education, 54*, 199–223.

Ridge, A. D., & Skinner, C. H. (2011). Using the TELLS prereading procedure to enhance comprehension levels and rates in secondary students. *Psychology in the Schools, 48*, 46–58.

Rosenshine, B., & Meister, C. (1994). Reciprocal teaching: A review of the research. *Review of Educational Research, 64*, 479–530.

Routman, R. (1991). *Invitations: Changing as teachers and learners K–12.* Portsmouth, NH: Heinemann.

Rudenga, E. A. V. (1992). *Incompatibility? Ethnographic case studies of learning disabled students in a whole language classroom.* Unpublished doctoral dissertation, Purdue University, West Lafayette, IN.

Santangelo, T., & Graham, S. (2016). A comprehensive meta-analysis of handwriting instruction. *Educational Psychology Review, 28*, 225–265.

Schirmer, B. R., & McGough, S. M. (2005). Teaching reading to children who are deaf: Do the conclusions of the National Reading Panel apply? *Review of Educational Research, 75,* 83–117.

Shaywitz, S. (2003). *Overcoming dyslexia.* New York, NY: Knopf.

Shefter, H. (1989). *6 minutes a day to perfect spelling.* New York, NY: Pocket Books.

Shippen, M. E., Houchins, D. E., Steventon, C., & Sartor, D. (2005). A comparison of two direct instruction reading programs for urban middle school students. *Remedial and Special Education, 26,* 175–182.

Slavin, R. (2005). *Evidence-based reform: Advancing the education of students at risk.* Washington, DC: Center for American Progress.

Snider, V. E. (1997). Transfer of decoding skills to a literature basal. *Learning Disabilities Research & Practice, 12,* 54–62.

Spear-Swerling, L. (2005). *Spelling and students with learning disabilities.* Washington, DC: WETA. Retrieved from http://www.ldonline.org/article/5587/

Spector, J. E., & Cavanaugh, B. J. (2015). The conditions of beginning reading instruction for students with autism spectrum disorder. *Remedial and Special Education, 36,* 337–346.

Speece, D. L., MacDonald, V., Kilsheimer, L., & Krist, J. (1997). Research to practice: Preservice teachers reflect on reciprocal teaching. *Learning Disabilities Research & Practice, 12,* 177–187.

Spencer, V. G., Scruggs, T. E., & Mastropieri, M. A. (2003). Content area learning in middle school social studies classrooms and students with emotional or behavioral disorders: A comparison of strategies. *Behavioral Disorders, 28,* 77–93.

Stahl, S. A. (1992). Saying the "p" word: Nine guidelines for exemplary phonics instruction. *The Reading Teacher, 45,* 618–625.

Stahl, S. A., Duffy-Hester, A. M., & Dougherty-Stahl, K. A. (2006). Everything you wanted to know about phonics (and were afraid to ask). In L. M. Morrow, K. A. Dougherty-Stahl, & M. C. McKenna (Eds.), *Reading research at work: Foundations of effective practice* (pp. 126–156). New York, NY: Guilford.

Staubitz, J. E., Cartledge, G., & Yurick, A. L. (2005). Repeated reading for students with emotional or behavioral disorders: Peer- and trainer-mediated instruction. *Behavioral Disorders, 31,* 51–64.

Stecker, P. M. (2007). Tertiary intervention: Using progress monitoring with intensive services. *Teaching Exceptional Children, 39*(5), 50–57.

Stewart, D. A., & Kluwin, T. N. (2001). *Teaching deaf and hard of hearing students: Content, strategies, and curriculum.* Boston, MA: Allyn & Bacon.

Strong, G. K., Torgerson, C. J., Torgerson, D., & Hulme, C. (2011). A systematic meta-analytic review of evidence for the effectiveness of the 'Fast ForWord' language intervention program. *52,* 224–235.

Suggate, S. P. (2016). A meta-analysis of the long-term effects of phonemic awareness, phonics, fluency, and reading comprehension interventions. *Journal of Learning Disabilities, 49,* 77–96.

Suid, M. (1981). *Demonic mnemonics.* New York, NY: Dell Publishing.

Taylor, B. M. (2008). Tier 1: Effective classroom reading instruction in the elementary grades. In D. Fuchs, L. S. Fuchs, & S. Vaughn (Eds.), *Response to intervention: A framework for reading educators* (pp. 5–26). Newark, DE: International Reading Association.

Temple, C., Ogle, D., Crawford, A., & Freppon, P. (2014). *All children read: Teaching for literacy in today's diverse classrooms* (4th ed.). Boston, MA: Pearson.

Therrien, W. J. (2004). Fluency and comprehension gains as a result of repeated reading: A meta-analysis. *Remedial and Special Education, 25,* 252–261.

Troia, G. A. (2004). Migrant students with limited English proficiency: Can Fast ForWord Language make a difference in their language skills and academic achievement? *Remedial and Special Education, 25,* 353–366.

Vadasy, P., & Sanders, E. (2008). Benefits of repeated reading intervention for low-achieving fourth and fifth grade students. *Remedial and Special Education, 29,* 235–249.

Vaughn, S., & Denton, D. (2008). Tier 2: The role of intervention. In D. Fuchs, L. S. Fuchs, & S. Vaughn (Eds.), *Response to intervention: A framework for reading educators* (pp. 51–70). Newark, DE: International Reading Association.

Vaughn, S., & Roberts, G. (2007). Secondary interventions in reading: Providing additional instruction for students at risk. *Teaching Exceptional Children, 39*(5), 40–46.

Vaughn, S., Roberts, G., Schnakenberg, J. B., Fall, A-M., Vaughn, M. G., & Wexler, J. (2015). Improving reading comprehension for high school students with disabilities: Effects for comprehension and school retention. *Exceptional Children, 82,* 117–131.

Vaughn, S., & Wanzek, J. (2014). Intensive interventions in reading for students with reading disabilities: Meaningful impacts. *Learning Disabilities Research and Practice, 29,* 46–53.

Vue, G. E., & Hall, T. E. (2012). Transforming writing instruction with universal design for learning. In T. E. Hall, A. Meyer, & D. Rose (Eds.), *Universal design for learning in the classroom: Practical applications* (pp. 38–54). New York, NY: Guilford.

Williams, J. (2003). Teaching text structure to improve reading comprehension. In H. L. Swanson, K. Harris, & S. Graham (Eds.), *Handbook of learning disabilities* (pp. 293–305). New York, NY: Guilford.

Williams, K. A., Walker, M. A., Vaughn, S., & Wanzek, J. (2016). A synthesis of reading and spelling interventions and their effects on spelling outcomes for students with learning disabilities. *Journal of Learning Disabilities.* Advance online publication. doi: 10.1177/0022219415619753

Wissick, C. A., & Gardner, J. E. (2011). Technology and academic instruction: Considerations for students with high incidence cognitive disabilities. In J. M. Kauffman & D. P. Hallahan (Eds.), *Handbook of special education* (pp. 484–500). New York, NY: Routledge.

Wooten, D. A., & Cullinan, B. E. (Eds.). (2015). *Children's literature in the reading program: Engaging young readers in the 21st century.* Newark, DE: International Literacy Association.

Wordplay. (2012). *Some useful mnemonics.* Retrieved from http://www.fun-with-words.com

Young, C., Mohr, K. A. J., & Rasinski, T. (2014). Reading Together: A successful reading fluency intervention. *Literacy Research and Instruction, 54,* 67–81.

Zaner-Bloser handwriting. (2003). Columbus, OH: Zaner-Bloser.

Chapter 14

Avant, M. J. T., & Heller, K. W. (2011). Examining the effectiveness of Touch Math with students with physical disabilities. *Remedial and Special Education, 32,* 309–321.

Aydemir, T. (2015). A review of articles about Touch Math. *Procedia: Social and Behavioral Sciences, 174,* 1812–1819.

Baker, S., Gersten, R., Dimino, J. A., & Griffiths, R. (2004). The sustained use of research based instructional practice: A case study of peer-assisted learning strategies in math. *Remedial and Special Education, 25,* 5–24.

Barnett, J. E. H., & Cleary, S. (2015). Review of evidence-based mathematics interventions for students with autism. *Education and Training in Autism and Developmental Disabilities, 50,* 172–185.

Barth, J., Eglash, R., & Barkley, C. (2014). *Math is a verb: Activities and lessons from cultures around the world.* Reston, VA: National Council for Teachers of Mathematics.

Bouck, E. C., Bouck, M. K., & Hunley, M. (2015). The calculator effect: Understanding the impact of calculators as accommodations for secondary students with disabilities. *Journal of Special Education Technology, 30,* 77–88.

Berteletti, I., Lucangeli, D., Piazza, M., Dehaene, S., & Zorzi, M. (2010). Numerical estimation in preschoolers. *Developmental Psychology, 46,* 545–551.

Bley, N. S., & Thornton, C. A. (2001). *Teaching mathematics to students with learning disabilities* (4th ed.). Austin, TX: Pro-Ed.

Bottge, B. A., Rueda, E., Grant, T. S., Stephens, A. C., & LaRoque, P. T. (2010). Anchoring problem-solving and computation instruction in context-rich learning environments. *Exceptional Children, 4,* 417–437.

Bottge, B. A., Toland, M. D., Gassaway, L., Butler, M., Choo, S., Griffen, A. K., & Xin, M. (2015). Impact of enhanced anchored instruction in inclusive math classrooms. *Exceptional Children, 81,* 158–175.

Browder, D. (2015). What should we teach students with moderate and severe developmental disabilities? In B. Bateman, J. Lloyd, & M. Tankersley (Eds.), *Enduring issues in special education: Personal perspectives* (pp. 52–73). New York, NY: Routledge.

Bryant, D. P., Bryant, B. R., Roberts, G., Vaughn, S., Pfannenstiel, K. H., Porterfield, J., & Gersten, R. (2011). Early numeracy intervention for first grade students with math difficulties. *Exceptional Children, 78,* 7–23.

Butler, F. M., Miller, S. P., Lee, K., & Pierce, T. (2001). Teaching mathematics to students with mild-to-moderate mental retardation: A review of the literature. *Mental Retardation, 39,* 20–31.

Case, L. P., Harris, K. R., & Graham, S. (1992). Improving the mathematical problem-solving skills of students with learning disabilities: Self-regulated strategy development. *Journal of Special Education, 26,* 1–19.

Cathcart, W. G., Pothier, V. M., Vance, J. H., & Bezuk, N. S. (2015). *Learning mathematics in elementary and middle schools: A learner-centered approach.* Boston, MA: Pearson.

Cihak, D. F., & Foust, J. L. (2008). Comparing number lines and touch points to teach addition facts to students with autism. *Focus on Autism and Other Developmental Disabilities, 23,* 131–137.

Dennis, M. S. (2015). Effects of Tier 2 and Tier 3 mathematics interventions for 2nd graders with mathematics difficulties. *Learning Disabilities Research and Practice, 30,* 29–42.

Fuchs, D., Fuchs, L. S., & Compton, D. C. (2012). Smart RTI: A next-generation approach to multi-level prevention. *Exceptional Children, 78,* 263–279.

Fuchs, L., Fuchs, D., & Courey, S. (2005). Curriculum-based measurement of mathematics competence: From computation to concepts and applications to real-life problem solving. *Assessment for Effective Intervention, 30*(2), 33–46.

Fuchs, L. S., Fuchs, D., & Hollenbeck, K. N. (2007). Extending responsiveness to intervention to mathematics at first and third grades. *Learning Disabilities Research & Practice, 22,* 13–24.

Fuchs, L. S, Powell, S. R., Seethaler, P. M., Cirino, P. T., Fletcher, J. M., Fuchs, D., & Hamlet, C. (2010). The effects of strategic counting instruction, with and without deliberate practice, on number combination skill among students with math difficulties. *Learning and Individual Differences, 20,* 89–100.

Fuchs, L. S., Powell, S. R., Seethaler, P. M., Cirino, P. T., Fletcher, J. M., Fuchs, D., ... Zumeta, R. O. (2009). Remediating number combination and word problems deficits among students with math difficulties: A randomized control trial. *Journal of Educational Psychology, 101,* 561–576.

Fuchs, L. S., Powell, S. R., Seethaler, P. M., Cirino, P. T., Fletcher, J. M., Fuchs, D., & Hamlett, C. L. (2011). The development of arithmetic and word-problem skill among students with mathematics disability. In J. M. Kauffman & D. P. Hallahan (Eds.), *Handbook of special education* (pp. 434–444). New York, NY: Routledge.

Geary, D. C. (2003). Learning disabilities in arithmetic: Problem-solving differences and cognitive deficits. In H. L. Swanson, K. Harris, & S. Graham (Eds.), *Handbook of learning disabilities* (pp. 199–212). New York, NY: Guilford.

Gilsdorf, T. E. (2012). *Introduction to cultural mathematics: With case studies from the Otomies and Inca.* Hoboken, NJ: Wiley.

Ginsburg, H. P. (1997). Mathematics learning disabilities: A view from developmental psychology. *Journal of Learning Disabilities, 30,* 20–33.

Ginsburg, H. P. (1998a). Mathematics learning disabilities: A view from developmental psychology. In D. Rivera (Ed.), *Mathematics education for students with learning disabilities* (pp. 22–58). Austin, TX: Pro-Ed.

Ginsburg, H. P. (1998b). Toby's math. In R. J. Sternberg & T. Ben-Zeev (Eds.), *The nature of mathematical thinking* (pp. 175–202). Hillsdale, NJ: Lawrence Erlbaum.

Greene, G. (1999). Mnemonic multiplication fact instruction for students with learning disabilities. *Learning Disabilities Research and Practice, 14,* 141–148.

Hall, T. E., Meyer, A., & Rose, D. H. (Eds.). (2012). *Universal design for learning in the classroom: Practical applications.* New York, NY: Guilford.

Heller, K. W. (2010). Mathematics instruction and adaptations. In S. J. Best, K. W. Heller, & J. L. Bigge (Eds.), *Teaching individuals with physical or multiple disabilities* (6th ed., pp. 456–493). Upper Saddle River, NJ: Pearson.

Horton, S. V., Lovitt, T. C., & White, O. R. (1992). Teaching mathematics to adolescents classified as educable mentally handicapped: Using calculators to remove the computational onus. *Remedial and Special Education, 13*(3), 36–60.

Hutchinson, N. L. (1993). Effects of cognitive strategy instruction on algebra problem solving of adolescents with learning disabilities. *Learning Disability Quarterly, 16,* 34–63.

Impecoven-Lind, L. S., & Foegen, A. (2010). Teaching algebra to students with learning disabilities. *Intervention in School and Clinic September, 46,* 31–37.

Janvier, C. (1987). *Problems of representation in the teaching and learning of mathematics.* Mahwah, NJ: Lawrence Erlbaum.

Jimenez, B., Browder, D. M., & Saunders, A. (2012). *Early Numeracy: A skill building math program for students with moderate and severe disabilities.* Verona, WI: Attainment Company.

Jimenez, B. A., & Staples, K. (2015). Access to the Common Core State Standards in mathematics through early numeracy skill building for students with significant intellectual disability. *Education and Training in Autism and Developmental Disabilities, 50,* 17–30.

Joseph, G. G. (2000). *The crest of the peacock: Non-European roots of mathematics* (2nd ed.). Princeton, NJ: Princeton University Press.

Kilpatrick, J. (1985). Doing mathematics without understanding it: A commentary on Higbee and Kunihira. *Educational Psychologist, 20*(2), 65–68.

Kroeger, S. D., & Kouche, B. (2011). Using peer-assisted learning strategies to increase response to intervention in inclusive middle math settings. *Teaching Exceptional Children, 38*(5), 6–13.

Lang, C., Mastropieri, M. A., Scruggs, T. E., & Porter, M. (2004). The effects of self-instructional strategies on problem solving in algebra for students with special needs. In T. E. Scruggs & M. A. Mastropieri (Eds.), *Research in secondary schools: Advances in learning and behavioral disabilities* (Vol. 17, pp. 27–54). Oxford, UK: Elsevier.

Lang, H., & Pagliaro, C. (2007). Factors predicting recall of mathematics terms by deaf students: Implications for teaching. *Journal of Deaf Studies and Deaf Education, 12,* 449–460.

Lott, J. W., & Lott, C. J. (2014). *Mathematics lessons learned from across the world*. Reston, VA: National Council for Teachers of Mathematics.

Maccini, P., & Hughes, C. (2000). Effects of a problem-solving strategy on the introductory algebra performance of secondary students with learning disabilities. *Learning Disabilities Research & Practice, 15,* 10–21.

Martin, T. S. (2007). *Mathematics teaching today: Improving practice, improving student learning*. Reston, VA: National Council of Teachers of Mathematics.

Marzocchi, G. M., Lucangeli, D., De Meo, T., Fini, F., & Cornoldi, C. (2002). The disturbing effect of irrelevant information on arithmetic problem solving in inattentive children. *Developmental Neuropsychology, 21,* 73–92.

Mastropieri, M. A., & Scruggs, T. E. (1991). *Teaching students ways to remember: Strategies for learning mnemonically*. Cambridge, MA: Brookline Books.

Mastropieri, M. A., Scruggs, T. E., Hauth, C., & Allen-Bronaugh, D. (2012). Instructional interventions for students with mathematics learning disabilities. In B. Y. L. Wong (Ed.), *Learning about learning disabilities* (4th ed., pp. 217–241). New York, NY: Elsevier Science.

Math Forum at NCTM. (2016). Multicultural math fair, by the mathematics department, Frisbee Middle School. Retrieved from http://mathforum.org/alejandre/mathfair/

McCoy, L. P. (2004, April). *Mathematics activities from diverse cultures*. Paper presented at the annual meeting of the National Council of Teachers of Mathematics, Anaheim, CA. Retrieved from http://www.wfu.edu/~mccoy/mgames.pdf

Mercer, C. D., Mercer, A. R., & Pullen, P. C. (2011). *Teaching students with learning problems* (8th ed.). Upper Saddle River, NJ: Merrill/Prentice Hall.

Mercer, C. D., & Miller, S. P. (1992). Teaching students with learning problems in math to acquire, understand, and apply basic math facts. *Remedial and Special Education, 13,* 19–35.

Meyer, A., Rose, D. M., & Gordon, D. (2014). *Universal design for learning: Theory and practice*. Wakefield, MA: CAST.

Miller, S. P., & Mercer, C. D. (1993). Using a graduated word problem sequence to promote problem-solving skills. *Learning Disabilities Research & Practice, 8,* 169–174.

Montague, M. (2003). *Solve it! A practical approach to teaching mathematical problem solving skills*. Reston, VA: Exceptional Innovations.

Montague, M. (2008). Self-regulation strategies to improve mathematical problem solving for students with learning disabilities. *Learning Disability Quarterly, 31,* 37–44.

Montague, M., Enders, C., & Dietz, S. (2011). Effects of cognitive strategy instruction on math problem solving of middle school students with learning disabilities. *Learning Disability Quarterly, 34,* 262–272.

Montague, M., & Jitendra, A. (Eds.). (2006). *Teaching mathematics to middle school students with learning difficulties*. New York, NY: Guilford.

Nasir, N. A., & Cobb, P. (2007). *Improving access to mathematics: Diversity and equity in the classroom*. New York, NY: Teachers College Press.

National Center on Intensive Intervention. (2016a). *Computation of fractions: Considerations for instruction*. Washington, DC: Office of Special Education, U.S. Department of Education.

National Center on Intensive Intervention. (2016b). *Principles for designing intervention in mathematics*. Washington, DC: Office of Special Education, U.S. Department of Education.

National Center on Intensive Intervention. (2016c). *Sample fraction addition and subtraction concepts. Activities 1–3*. Washington, DC: Office of Special Education, U.S. Department of Education.

National Council of Teachers of Mathematics. (2000). *Principles and standards for school mathematics*. Reston, VA: Author.

National Council of Teachers of Mathematics. (2011). *Making it happen*. Reston, VA: Author.

National Governors Association Center for Best Practices & Council of Chief State School Officers. (2010). *Common Core State Standards: Mathematics*. Washington, DC: Author.

National Mathematics Advisory Panel. (2008). *Foundations for success: The final report of the National Mathematics Advisory Panel*. Washington, DC: U.S. Department of Education.

Patton, J. R., Cronin, M. E., Bassett, D. S., & Koppel, A. E. (1998). A life skills approach to mathematics instruction: Preparing students with learning disabilities for the real-life math demands of adulthood. In D. Rivera (Ed.), *Mathematics education for students with learning disabilities* (pp. 201–218). Austin, TX: Pro-Ed.

Powell, S. R., & Fuchs, L. S. (2012). Early numerical competencies and students with mathematics difficulty. *Focus on Exceptional Children, 44*(5), 1–16.

Powell, S. R., & Fuchs, L. S.. (2015). Intensive intervention in mathematics. *Learning Disabilities Research and Practice, 30,* 182–192.

Powell, S. R., Fuchs, L. S., Cirino, P. T., Fuchs, D., Compton, D. L., & Changas, P. C. (2015). Effects of a multitier support system on calculation, word problem, and prealgebraic performance among at-risk learners. *Exceptional Children, 81,* 443–470.

Pushparajan, V. (2011). *An algorithm a day*. Retrieved from http://analgorithmaday.blogspot.com/search?q=division

Quintessential Education. (2016). *A maths tuition pedagogy*. Singapore: Author. Retrieved from http://qeducation.sg/a-maths-tuition/

Reid, R., Gonzalez, J. E., Nordness, P. D., Trout, A., & Epstein, M. H. (2004). A meta-analysis of the academic status of students with emotional/behavioral disturbance. *Journal of Special Education, 38,* 130–143.

Riccomini, P. J., & Witzel, B. S. (2010). *Response to intervention in math*. Thousand Oaks, CA: Corwin.

Rivera, D. P., & Smith, D. D. (1987). Influence of modeling on acquisition and generalization of computational skills: A summary of research findings from three sites. *Learning Disability Quarterly, 10,* 69–80.

Rosenblum, L. P., & Amato, S. (2004). Preparation in and use of the Nemeth Braille Code for Mathematics by teachers of students with visual impairments. *Journal of Visual Impairment & Blindness, 98,* 484–495.

Sayeski, K. L., & Paulsen, K. J. (2010). Mathematics reform curricula and special education: Identifying intersections and implications for practice. *Intervention in School and Clinic, 46,* 13–21.

Schiro, M. S. (2004). *Oral storytelling and teaching mathematics: Pedagogical and multicultural perspectives*. Thousand Oaks, CA: Sage.

Shiah, R. L., Mastropieri, M. A., Scruggs, T. E., & Fulk, B. J. M. (1994–1995). The effects of computer assisted instruction on the mathematical problem solving of students with learning disabilities. *Exceptionality, 5,* 131–161.

Shin, M., & Bryant, D. P. (2015). Fraction interventions for students struggling to learn mathematics: A research synthesis. *Remedial and Special Education,* 374–387.

Simon, R., & Hanrahan, J. (2004). An evaluation of the Touch-Math method for teaching addition to students with learning disabilities in mathematics. *European Journal of Special Needs Education, 19,* 191–209.

Staudacher, C., & Turner, S. (1994). *Practical mathematics for consumers*. Paramus, NJ: Globe Fearon.

Stein, M., Kinder, D., Silbert, J., & Carnine, D. (2006). *Designing effective mathematics instruction* (4th ed.). Upper Saddle River, NJ: Merrill/Prentice Hall.

Stewart, D. A., & Kluwin, T. N. (2001). *Teaching deaf and hard of hearing students: Content, strategies, and curriculum.* Boston, MA: Allyn & Bacon.

Strickland, T. K., & Maccini, P. (2010). Strategies for teaching algebra to students with learning disabilities: Making research to practice connections. *Intervention in School and Clinic, 46,* 38–45.

Tucker, B. F., Singleton, A. H., & Weaver, T. L. (2006). *Teaching mathematics to all children: Designing and adapting instruction to meet the needs of diverse learners* (2nd ed.). Upper Saddle River, NJ: Merrill/Prentice Hall.

Uberti, H., Mastropieri, M. A., & Scruggs, T. E. (2004). Check it off: Individualizing a math algorithm for students with disabilities via self-monitoring checklists. *Intervention in School and Clinic, 39,* 269–275.

Van Luit, J. E. H., & Schopman, E. A. M. (2000). Improving early numeracy of young children with special educational needs. *Remedial and Special Education, 21,* 27–40.

Whitby, P. J. S. (2013). The effects of Solve It! on the mathematical word problem solving ability of adolescents with autism spectrum disorders. *Focus on Autism and Other Developmental Disabilities, 28,* 78–88.

Xin, Y. P., Jitendra, A. K., & Deatline-Buchman, A. (2005). Effects of mathematical word problem solving instruction on middle school students with learning problems. *Journal of Special Education, 39,* 181–192.

Zaslavsky, C. (1995). *The multicultural math classroom: Bringing in the world.* Portsmouth, NH: Heinemann.

Zaslavsky, C. (1999). *Africa counts: Number and pattern in African cultures* (3rd ed.). Chicago: Lawrence Hill.

Zisimopoulos, D. A. (2010). Enhancing multiplication performance in students with moderate intellectual disabilities using pegword mnemonics paired with a picture fading technique. *Journal of Behavioral Education, 19,* 117–133.

Chapter 15

Aceves, T. C., & Orosco, M. J. (2014). *Culturally responsive teaching* (Document No. IC-2). University of Florida, Collaboration for Effective Educator, Development, Accountability, and Reform Center. Retrieved from http://ceedar.education.ufl.edu/tools/innovation-configurations/

Albert, L. R., & Ammer, J. J. (2004). Lesson planning and delivery. In B. K. Lenz, D. D. Deshler, & B. R. Kissam (Eds.), *Teaching content to all: Evidence-based inclusive practices in middle and secondary schools* (pp. 195–220). Boston, MA: Allyn & Bacon.

American Printing House for the Blind. (2006). *Adapting science for students with visual impairments: Advance preparation checklist.* Louisville, KY: Author. Retrieved from https://www.aph.org/files/manuals/7-00001-00.pdf

Averill, R., Anderson, D., & Drake, M. (2015). Developing culturally responsive teaching through professional noticing within teacher educator modelling. *Mathematics Teacher Education and Development, 17,* 64–83.

Bakken, J. P., Mastropieri, M. A., & Scruggs, T. E. (1997). Reading comprehension of expository science material and students with learning disabilities: A comparison of strategies. *Journal of Special Education, 31,* 300–324.

Bakken, J. P., & Obiokor, F. E. (2008). *Transition planning for students with disabilities: What educators and service providers can do.* Springfield, IL: Charles C. Thomas.

Bakken, J. P., & Whedon, C. K. (2002). Teaching text structure to improve reading comprehension. *Intervention in School and Clinic, 37,* 229–233.

Berkeley, S., King-Sears, M. E., Hott, B. L., & Bradley-Black, K. (2014). Are history textbooks more "considerate" after 20 years? *Journal of Special Education, 47,* 217–230.

Berkeley, S., Marshak, L., Mastropieri, M. A., & Scruggs, T. E. (2011). Improving student comprehension of social studies text: A self-questioning strategy for inclusive middle school classes. *Remedial and Special Education, 32,* 105–113.

Best, R. M., Rowe, M., Ozuru, Y., & McNamara, D. S. (2005). Deep-level comprehension of science texts: The role of the reader and the text. *Topics in Language Disorders, 25,* 65–83.

Bohaty, J. J., Hebert, M. A., Nelson, J. R., & Brown, J. A. (2014). Methodological status and trends in expository text structure instruction efficacy research. *Reading Horizons, 34,* 35–55.

Boyle, J. R., & Weishaar, M. (1997). The effects of expert-generated versus student-generated cognitive organizers on the reading comprehension of students with learning disabilities. *Learning Disabilities Research & Practice, 12,* 228–251.

Brigham, F. J., Scruggs, T. E., & Mastropieri, M. A. (2012). Science education and students with learning disabilities. *Learning Disabilities Research and Practice, 26,* 223–232.

Browder, D. (2015). What should we teach students with moderate and severe disabilities? In B. Bateman, J. W. Lloyd, & M. Tankersley, (Eds.), *Enduring issues in special education.* (pp. 52–73). NY: Routledge Publishing Co.

Bulgren, J. A. (2004). Effective content area instruction for all students. In T. E. Scruggs & M. A. Mastropieri (Eds.), *Research in secondary schools: Advances in learning and behavioral disabilities* (Vol. 17, pp. 147–174). Oxford, UK: Elsevier.

Bulgren, J. A., Deshler, D. D., & Lenz, B. K. (2007). Engaging adolescents with LD in higher order thinking about history concepts using integrated content enhancement routines. *Journal of Learning Disabilities, 40,* 121–133.

Bulgren, J. A., Deshler, D. D., & Schumaker, J. B. (1993). *The content enhancement series: The concept mastery routine.* Lawrence, KS: Edge Enterprises.

Bulgren, J. A., Graner, P. S., & Deshler, D. D. (2013). Literacy challenges and opportunities for students with learning disabilities in social studies and history. *Learning Disabilities Research and Practice, 28,* 17–27.

Burgstahler, S. (2012). Equal access: Universal design of instruction. Seattle: DO-IT, University of Washington. Retrieved from www.uw.edu/doit/equal-access-universal-design-instruction

Caffrey, E., & Fuchs, D. (2007). Differences in performance between students with learning disabilities and mild mental retardation: Implications for categorical instruction. *Learning Disabilities Research & Practice, 22,* 119–128.

Carter, E. W., Clark, N. M., Cushing, L. S., & Kennedy, C. H. (2005). Moving from elementary to middle school: Supporting a smooth transition for students with severe disabilities. *Teaching Exceptional Children, 37*(3), 8–14.

Chiappetta, E. L., & Koballa, T. R. (2006). *Science instruction in the middle and secondary schools: Developing fundamental knowledge and skills for teachers* (6th ed.). Upper Saddle River, NJ: Merrill/Prentice Hall.

Clark, G. M., & Patton, J. R. (2006). *TPI-UV: Transition planning inventory: Updated version.* Austin, TX: Pro-Ed.

Contant, T. L., Bass, J. E., & Carin, A. A. (2014). *Teaching science through inquiry and investigation* (12th ed.). Boston, MA: Pearson.

Cook, L. K., & Mayer, R. E. (1988). Teaching readers about the structure of scientific text. *Journal of Educational Psychology, 80,* 448–456.

Cronin, M. E., Patton, J. R., & Wood, S. J. (2007). *Life skills instruction* (2nd ed.). Austin, TX: Pro-Ed.

Cuenca-Sanchez, Y., Mastropieri, M. A., Scruggs, T. E., & Kidd, J. (2012). Middle school students with emotional disorders: Determined to meet their needs through writing. *Exceptionality, 20,* 71–93.

Deshler, D. D., & Schumaker, J. B. (2006). *Teaching adolescents with disabilities: Accessing the general education curriculum.* Thousand Oaks, CA: Corwin.

Dion, M., Hoffman, K., & Matter, A. (2000). *Teacher's manual for adapting science experiments for blind and visually impaired students.* Worcester, MA: Worcester Polytechnic Institute and Visual Impairment Knowledge Center. Retrieved from http://www.perkinselearning.org/sites/elearning.perkinsdev1.org/files/teachers-manual.pdf

Driver, R., Asoko, H., Leach, J., Mortimer, E., & Scott, P. (1994). Constructing scientific knowledge in the classroom. *Educational Researcher, 23*(7), 5–12.

Echevarria, J., & Graves, A. (2015). *Sheltered content instruction: Teaching English Language Learners with diverse abilities* (5th ed.). Boston, MA: Pearson.

Ferretti, R. P., MacArthur, C. D., & Okolo, C. M. (2001). Teaching for historical understanding in inclusive classrooms. *Learning Disability Quarterly, 24,* 59–71.

Furtak, E. M., Seidel, T., Iverson, H., & Briggs, D. C. (2012). Experimental and quasi-experimental studies of inquiry-based science teaching: A meta-analysis. *Review of Educational Research, 82,* 300–329.

Gildroy, P., & Deshler, D. D. (2008). Effective learning strategy instruction. In R. Morris & N. Mather (Eds.), *Evidence-based practices for students with learning and behavioral challenges* (pp. 288–301). London, UK: Routledge.

Good, T. L., & Brophy, J. E. (2007). *Looking in classrooms* (10th ed.). Boston, MA: Allyn & Bacon.

Griffin, M. M., Taylor, J. L., Urbano, R. C., & Hodapp, R. M. (2014). Involvement in transition planning meetings among high school students with autism spectrum disorders. *Journal of Special Education, 47,* 256–264.

Grossen, B., & Burke, M. D. (1998). Instructional design that accommodates special learning needs in science. *Information Technology and Disabilities, 5,* 2.

Horton, S. V., Boone, R. A., & Lovitt, T. C. (1990). Teaching social studies to learning disabled high school students: Effects of a hypertext study guide. *British Journal of Educational Technology, 21,* 118–131.

Jimenez, B. A., Browder, D. M., Spooner, F., & Dibiase, W. (2012). Inclusive inquiry science using peer-mediated embedded instruction for students with moderate intellectual disability. *Exceptional Children, 78,* 301–317.

Jimenez, B. A., Lo, Y., & Saunders, A. F. (2014). The additive effects of scripted lessons plus guided notes on science quiz scores of students with intellectual disability and autism. *Journal of Special Education, 47,* 231–244.

Johnson, D. R., Stout, K. E., & Thurlow, M. L. (2009). Diploma options and perceived consequences for students with disabilities. *Exceptionality, 17,* 119–134.

King-Sears, M. E., Mercer, C. D., & Sindelar, P. T. (1992). Toward independence with keyword mnemonics: A strategy for science vocabulary instruction. *Remedial and Special Education, 13,* 22–33.

King-Sears, M. E., & Mooney, J. F. (2004). Teaching content in an academically diverse class. In B. K. Lenz, D. D. Deshler, & B. R. Kissam (Eds.), *Teaching content to all: Evidence-based inclusive practices in middle and secondary schools* (pp. 221–257). Boston, MA: Allyn & Bacon.

Knight, V. F., Smith, B. R., Spooner, F., & Browder, D. (2012). Using explicit instruction to teach science descriptors to students with autism spectrum disorder. *Journal of Autism and Developmental Disorders, 42,* 378–389.

Konrad, M., & Test, D. W. (2007). Effects of GO 4 IT…NOW! strategy instruction on the written IEP goal articulation and paragraph-writing skills of middle school students with disabilities. *Remedial and Special Education, 28,* 277–291.

Lenz, B. K., & Adams, G. (2006). Planning practices that optimize curriculum access. In D. D. Deshler & J. B. Schumaker (Eds.), *Teaching adolescents with disabilities: Accessing the general education curriculum* (pp. 35–78). Thousand Oaks, CA: Corwin Press.

Lenz, B. K., Bulgren, J., Kissam, B. R., & Taymans, J. (2004). SMARTER planning for academic diversity. In B. K. Lenz, D. D. Deshler, & B. R. Kissam (Eds.), *Teaching content to all: Evidence-based inclusive practices in middle and secondary schools* (pp. 47–77). Boston, MA: Allyn & Bacon.

Lenz, B. K., Deshler, D. D., & Kissam, B. R. (Eds.). (2004). *Teaching content to all: Evidence-based inclusive practices in middle and secondary schools.* Boston, MA: Allyn & Bacon.

Lindstrom, J. H. (2011). High stakes testing and accommodations. In J. M. Kauffman & D. P. Hallahan (Eds.), *Handbook of special education* (pp. 321–333). New York, NY: Routledge.

MacArthur, C. A., Ferretti, R. P., & Okolo, C. M. (2002). On defending controversial viewpoints: Debates of sixth graders about the desirability of early 20th century American immigration. *Learning Disabilities Research & Practice, 17,* 160–172.

Madaus, J. W., Banerjee, M., & Merchant, D. (2011). Transition to postsecondary education. In J. Kauffman, D. P. Hallahan, & J. Lloyd (Eds.), *Handbook of special education* (pp. 571–583). New York, NY: Routledge.

Maheady, L., Sacca, M. K., & Harper, G. F. (1988). Classwide peer tutoring with mildly handicapped high school students. *Exceptional Children, 55,* 52–59.

Marchand-Martella, N. E., Martella, R. C., Modderman, S. L., Petersen, H. M., & Pan, S. (2013). Key areas of effective adolescent literacy programs. *Education and Treatment of Children, 36,* 161–184.

Marshak, L., Mastropieri, M. A., & Scruggs, T. E. (2011). Curriculum enhancements for inclusive secondary social studies classes. *Exceptionality, 19,* 61–74.

Mastropieri, M. A., & Scruggs, T. E. (1993). *A practical guide for teaching science to students with special needs in inclusive settings.* Austin, TX: Pro-Ed.

Mastropieri, M. A., Scruggs, T. E., Boon, R., & Carter, K. B. (2001). Correlates of inquiry learning in science: Constructing concepts of density and buoyancy. *Remedial and Special Education, 22,* 130–138.

Mastropieri, M. A., Scruggs, T. E., & Graetz, J. (2005). Cognition and learning in inclusive high school chemistry classes. In T. E. Scruggs & M. A. Mastropieri (Eds.), *Cognition and learning in diverse settings: Advances in learning and behavioral disabilities* (Vol. 18, pp. 107–118). Oxford, UK: Elsevier Science.

Mastropieri, M. A., Scruggs, T. E., Mantzicopoulos, P. Y., Sturgeon, A., Goodwin, L., & Chung, S. (1998). "A place where living things affect and depend on each other": Qualitative and quantitative outcomes associated with inclusive science teaching. *Science Education, 82,* 163– 179.

Mastropieri, M. A., Scruggs, T. E., & Marshak, L. (2008). Training teachers, parents, and peers to implement effective teaching strategies for content area learning. In T. E. Scruggs & M. A. Mastropieri (Eds.), *Personal preparation: Advances in learning and behavioral disabilities* (Vol. 21, pp. 311–329). Bingley, UK: Emerald.

Mastropieri, M. A., Scruggs, T. E., Norland, J., Berkeley, S., McDuffie, K., Tornquist, E. H., & Conners, N. (2006). Differentiated curriculum enhancement in inclusive middle school science: Effects on classroom and high-stakes tests. *Journal of Special Education, 40*, 130–137.

Mastropieri, M. A., Scruggs, T. E., Spencer, V., & Fontana, J. (2003). Promoting success in high school world history: Peer tutoring versus guided notes. *Learning Disabilities Research & Practice, 18*, 52–65.

Mastropieri, M. A., Sweda, J., & Scruggs, T. E. (2000). Putting mnemonic strategies to work in an inclusive classroom. *Learning Disabilities Research & Practice, 15*, 69–74.

McCormick, S., & Cooper, J. O. (1991). Can SQ3R facilitate learning disabled students' literal comprehension of expository test? Three experiments. *Reading Psychology, 12*, 239–271.

Melber, L., & Heller, K. W. (2010). Science and social studies instruction and adaptations. In S. J. Best, K. W. Heller, & J. L. Bigge (Eds.), *Teaching individuals with physical or multiple disabilities* (6th ed., pp. 432–455). Upper Saddle River, NJ: Merrill/Prentice Hall.

Morgan, R. L., & Riesen, T. (2016). *Promoting successful transition to adulthood for students with disabilities*. New York, NY: Guilford.

National Governors Association Center for Best Practices & Council of Chief State School Officers. (2010). *Common Core State Standards: Mathematics*. Washington, DC: Author.

O'Connor, R., & Goodwin, V. (2011). Teaching older students to read. In R. O'Connor & P. Vadasy (Eds.), *Handbook of reading interventions* (pp. 380–412). New York, NY: Guilford.

O'Connor, R. E., Beach, K. D., Sanchez, V. M., Bocian, K. M., & Flynn, L. J. (2015). Building BRIDGES: A design experiment to improve reading and United States history knowledge of poor readers in eighth grade. *Exceptional Children, 81*, 399–425.

Okolo, C. M., Bouck, E., Heutsche, A., Courtad, C., & Englert, C. S. (2011). Technology in the social studies for students with disabilities. In T. Lintner & W. Schweder (Eds.), *Practical strategies for teaching K–12 social studies in inclusive classrooms* (pp. 67–87). Charlotte, NC: Information Age Publishers.

Okolo, C. M., Englert, C. S., Bouck, E. C., Heutsche, A., & Wang, H. (2011). The Virtual History Museum: Learning American history in diverse eighth grade classrooms. *Remedial and Special Education, 32*, 417–428.

Okolo, C. M., & Ferretti, R. P. (2013). History instruction for students with learning disabilities. In H. L. Swanson, K. Harris, & S. Graham (Eds.), *Handbook of learning disabilities* (2nd ed., pp. 463–488). New York, NY: Guilford.

Parker, R. M. (2002). *OASIS-3: Occupational aptitude survey and interest schedule* (3rd ed.). Austin, TX: Pro-Ed.

Parker, W. C., & Beck, T. A. (2016). *Social studies in elementary education* (15th ed.). Upper Saddle River, NJ: Merrill/Prentice Hall.

Pence, L. E., Workman, H. J., & Riecke, P. (2003). Effective laboratory experiences for students with disabilities: The role of a student laboratory assistant. *Journal of Chemical Education, 80*, 295–298.

Regan, K., Evmenova, A., Mastropieri, M. A., & Scruggs, T. E. (2015). Peer interactions in the content areas: Using differentiated instruction strategies. In K. R. Harris, & L. Meltzer (Eds.), *The power of peers: Enhancing learning, development and social skills* (pp. 33–68). New York, NY: Guilford.

Reid, R., Lienemann, T. O, & Hagaman, J. L. (2013). *Strategy instruction for students with learning disabilities*. New York, NY: Guilford.

"Rethinking the high school diploma." (2015). *Education Next*, 48–53. Retrieved from http://educationnext.org/files/ednext_XV_1_forum.pdf

Rojewski, J. W., & Gregg, N. (2011). Career choice patterns and behaviors of work-bound youth with high incidence disabilities. In J. Kauffman, D. P. Hallahan, & J. Lloyd (Eds.), *Handbook of special education* (pp. 584–593). New York, NY: Routledge.

Rule, A. C., Stefanich, G. P., Boody, R. M., & Peiffer, B. (2011). Impact of adaptive materials on teachers and their students with visual impairments in secondary science and mathematics classes. *International Journal of Science Education, 33*, 865–887.

Scanlon, D. (2011). Transition to adulthood and high incidence disabilities. In J. Kauffman, D. P. Hallahan, & J. Lloyd (Eds.), *Handbook of special education* (pp. 569–570). New York, NY: Routledge.

Scanlon, D., Patton, J. R., & Raskind, M. (2011). Transition to daily living for persons with high incidence disabilities. In J. Kauffman, D. P. Hallahan, & J. Lloyd (Eds.), *Handbook of special education* (pp. 594–607). New York, NY: Routledge.

Schloss, M. A., & Gunter, P. L. (2011). Career and technical education. In J. Kauffman, D. P. Hallahan, & J. Lloyd (Eds.), *Handbook of special education* (pp. 470–483). New York, NY: Routledge.

Schumaker, J., & Deshler, D. (2003). Can students with LD become competent writers? *Learning Disability Quarterly, 26*, 129–141.

Schumaker, J. B., Deshler, D. D., Alley, G. R., Warner, M. M., & Denton, P. H. (1982). Multipass: A learning strategy for improving reading comprehension. *Learning Disability Quarterly, 5*, 295–304.

Scruggs, T. E., & Mastropieri, M. A. (1994). Refocusing microscope activities for special students. *Science Scope, 17*, 74–78.

Scruggs, T. E., & Mastropieri, M. A. (1995a). Science education for students with behavior disorders. *Education and Treatment of Children, 3*, 322–334.

Scruggs, T. E., & Mastropieri, M. A. (1995b). Science and mental retardation: An analysis of curriculum features and learner characteristics. *Science Education, 79*, 251–271.

Scruggs, T. E., & Mastropieri, M. A. (2007). Science learning in special education: The case for constructed vs. instructed learning. *Exceptionality, 15*, 57–74.

Scruggs, T. E., & Mastropieri, M. A. (2011). Maximizing social studies learning for all with peer tutoring and learning strategies information. In T. Lintner (Ed.), *Practical strategies for teaching K–12 social studies in inclusive classrooms* (pp. 35–46). Charlotte, NC: Information Age.

Scruggs, T. E., & Mastropieri, M. A. (2013a). Science and social studies. In H. L. Swanson, K. Harris, & S. Graham (Eds.), *Handbook of learning disabilities* (2nd ed., pp. 448–462). New York, NY: Guilford.

Scruggs, T. E., & Mastropieri, M. A. (2013b). Teaching students with high incidence disabilities. In B. Cook & M. Tankersley (Eds.), *Research-based practices in special education* (pp. 342–352). Boston, MA: Pearson.

Scruggs, T. E., & Mastropieri, M. A. (2015). What makes special education special? In B. Bateman, J. Lloyd, & M. Tankersley (Eds.), *Enduring issues in special education: Personal perspectives* (pp. 22–36). New York, NY: Routledge.

Scruggs, T. E., Mastropieri, M. A., Bakken, J. P., & Brigham, F. J. (1993). Reading vs. doing. The relative effectiveness of textbook-based and inquiry-oriented approaches to science education. *Journal of Special Education, 27*, 1–15.

Scruggs, T. E., Mastropieri, M. A., & Marshak, L. (2011). Science and social studies. In J. Kauffman, D. P. Hallahan, & J. Lloyd (Eds.), *Handbook of special education* (pp. 445–455). New York, NY: Routledge.

Scruggs, T. E., Mastropieri, M. A., & Marshak, L. (2012). Peer-mediated instruction in inclusive secondary social studies learning: Direct and indirect learning effects. *Learning Disabilities Research and Practice, 27,* 12–20.

Scruggs, T. E., Mastropieri, M. A., & Okolo, C. (2008). Science and social studies for students with disabilities. *Focus on Exceptional Children, 41*(2), 1–24.

Scruggs, T. E., Mastropieri, M. A., & Wolfe, S. (1995). Scientific reasoning of students with mental retardation: Investigating preconceptions and conceptual change. *Exceptionality, 5,* 223–244.

Simpkins, P. M., Mastropieri, M. A., & Scruggs, T. E. (2009). Differentiated curriculum enhancements in inclusive 5th grade science classes. *Remedial and Special Education, 30,* 300–308.

Sitlington, P. L., Neubert, D. A., & Clark, G. M. (2010). *Transition education and services for students with disabilities* (5th ed.). Upper Saddle River, NJ: Prentice Hall.

Slocum, T. A. (2004). Direct instruction: The big ideas. In D. J. Moran & R. W. Malott (Eds.), *Evidence-based educational methods* (pp. 81–94). San Diego, CA: Elsevier Academic Press.

Spencer, V. G., Scruggs, T. E., & Mastropieri, M. A. (2003). Content area learning in middle school social studies classrooms and students with emotional or behavioral disorders: A comparison of strategies. *Behavioral Disorders, 28,* 77–93.

Sullivan, G. S., Mastropieri, M. A., & Scruggs, T. E. (1995). Reasoning and remembering: Coaching thinking with students with learning disabilities. *Journal of Special Education, 29,* 310–322.

Swanson, E., Hairrell, A., Kent, S., Ciullo, S., Wanzek, J. A., & Vaughn, S. (2014). A synthesis and meta-analysis of reading interventions using social studies content for students with learning disabilities. *Journal of Learning Disabilities, 47,* 178–195.

Test, D. W., Fowler, C. H., Wood, W. M., Brewer, D. M., & Eddy, S. (2005). A conceptual framework of self-advocacy for students with disabilities. *Remedial and Special Education, 26,* 43–54.

Test, D. W., & Neale, M. (2004). Using the self-advocacy strategy to increase middle graders' IEP participation. *Journal of Behavioral Education, 13,* 135–145.

Tomlinson, C. A., & Imbeau, M. B. (2010). *Leading and managing a differentiated classroom.* Alexandria, VA: Association for Supervision and Curriculum Development.

U.S. Department Education, Office of Special Education and Rehabilitative Services, (2017). *A transition guide to postsecondary education and employment for students and youth with disabilities,* Washington, DC.

Van Reusen, A. K., Bos, C. A., Schumaker, J. B., & Deshler, D. D. (1994). *The self-advocacy strategy for education and transition planning.* Lawrence, KS: Edge Enterprises.

Wehmeyer, M. L., Shogren, K. A., Palmer, S. B., Williams-Diehm, K. L., Little, T. D., & Boulton, A. (2012). The impact of the self-determined learning model of instruction on student self-determination. *Exceptional Children, 78,* 135–153.

Williams, J. P. (2003). Teaching text structure to improve reading comprehension. In H. L. Swanson, K. R. Harris, & S. Graham (Eds.), *Handbook of learning disabilities* (pp. 293–305). New York, NY: Guilford Press.

Classroom management and environment (*continued*)

severe or multiple disabilities, adaptation strategies, 93–97

speech and language impairment, adaptations for, 55–57

students at risk, adaptation strategies, 120–121

task- and ego-oriented classrooms, 176–177

time management strategies, 144–146

universal design for learning principles, 134–135

visual impairments, adaptation strategies, 98–99

Classwide peer tutoring, 215–219, 240

for reading skills, 317, 324

for science and social studies, 388–390

Cleft palate, 55

Clue-word, problem solving strategies, 361–363

Clustering, 240

Coaching, higher-level questions and, 142–143

Coaching, social skills training, 201

Cochlear implants, 100

Code-emphasis approach, 309–310

Cognitive-behavioral interventions, 74

Cognitive conflict, 181

Cognitive disability. *See* Intellectual disabilities

Collaboration

Classroom Scenario, 26

communication strategies, 27–30

cooperative learning, overview of, 219–226

co-teaching, 43–45

for culturally and linguistically diverse students, 113

defined, 27

homework assignments and, 262

for intervention, 30–34

with paraprofessionals, 44–45

with parents and families, 46–48

for referrals and placements, 34–42

school and parent responsibilities, 25–27

school personnel roles, 37

between special and general educators, 42

College, planning for, 407–408

College entrance exams, 284, 407–408

Coloboma, 97–98

Common Core State Standards (CCSS)

assessment strategies, 284–285

culturally responsive instruction and, 146

for English and language arts, 309, 310, 311–312

English learners, reading interventions for, 119

for mathematics, 61, 343–344, 358

overview of, 15–16

for science and social studies, 376

scope and sequence of instruction, 128

for written communication, 332

Communication. *See also* Autism; Language impairments; Linguistically diverse students; Speech impairments

active listening strategies, 27, 29

alternative and augmentative communication (AAC), 86

case conference committee meetings, 38, 39

clarity of presentations, 136–137

collaboration strategies, 27–30

counterproductive statements, 178

dialects and, 112

direct appeals, use of, 188

directions, giving of, 230–231

enthusiasm, teaching with, 137–138, 182

hearing impairments, education debate and, 100

of lesson structure, 136

listening skills, promotion of, 263–267

with paraprofessionals, 44–45

with parents and families, 46–48

praise, use of, 182–183, 187–188

reprimands, use of, 188–189

between special and general educators, 42

with students with emotional disturbance, 70–71

Communication boards, 86

Compensatory education programs, 120

Competency-based assessments, 284–285

Competition, motivation and, 182

Comprehensive Support Model, 95

Computers. *See* Apps for Education

Concept learning, 132, 133

Concept mastery routine, 377–378

Concepts, defined, 133, 134

Conductive hearing loss, 100. *See also* Hearing impairments

Conflict resolution, peer-mediations, 224

Confrontations, handling of, 195–196

Congenital disabilities, defined, 79

Congenital hearing loss, 99–100. *See also* Hearing impairments

Consequent events, 74

Consultant services, 17–18

Content-enhancement strategies, 377–378

Content-oriented approach, adaptations, 375. *See also* Adaptations

Contingent observation timeout, 192

Continuum of services, 16–21

Contracting, behavioral, 192–193

Contracting, grading strategies, 301

Cooperative homework teams (CHTs), 262

Cooperative Integrated Reading and Composition (CIRC), 224

Cooperative learning

advantages and challenges, 224–226

defined, 219

motivation and, 182

strategies for, 219–224

Corporal punishment, 192

Corrective feedback, defined, 318

Co-teaching models, 18, 19, 43–45

Council for Children with Behavioral Disorders, 48

Council for Exceptional Children (CEC), 16, 48

Counselors, 37, 180–181

Count-bys, math skills, 355

Counting, teaching of, 346, 364

Cover-copy-compare, spelling strategy, 331

Creative students. *See* Gifted, creative, and talented students

Criterion-referenced tests, 279–280, 281, 286–289. *See also* Assessment, academic skills

Critical thinking, learning types, 132, 133

Cross-age tutoring, 215

Culturally diverse students

adaptations, strategies for, 113–116

assessment for intervention, 109–110, 112–113

definitions and prevalence, 108–112

IDEA mandates and, 9

identification of disabilities and, 15

students from multiracial families, 111

Culturally responsive classrooms, creation of, 177

Culturally responsive instruction, 67, 110, 113–116, 157

Cultural pluralism, 110

Curriculum-based assessments, 280, 281, 287. *See also* Assessment, academic skills

Curriculum-based measurements. *See also* Assessment, academic skills

defined, 147, 280

performance monitoring and, 158–159

progress monitoring and, 147, 289–290

reading tests, 281, 317

Curriculum decisions, 128, 129

Cursive handwriting, 327, 328

Cyberbullying, 198, 200

Cystic fibrosis, 84

Databases, student use of, 273

Data collection, apps for, 287

Davidson Institute for Talent Development, 106

Deaf-blindness. *See also* Hearing impairments; Visual impairments

characteristics of, 7

prevalence rates by race and ethnicity, 108–109

Deafness. *See also* Hearing impairments

adaptations, strategies for, 101–102

characteristics of, 7

definitions and prevalence, 99–100

Debriefing procedures, 192

Decimals, teaching of, 364–365

Demonstration Plus Permanent Model, 359

Demonstrations, 230

Denial of services, 36, 37

Depersonalized conversations, 27–28

Depression, 180–181

Developmental delay, 6, 8, 63

Developmental Disabilities Assistance and Bill of Rights Acts (1984), 11

Developmental disability. *See* Intellectual disabilities

Dextroamphetamine, 74

Diabetes, 88

Diabetic retinopathy, 97

Diagnostician, role of, 37

Dialects, 112

Diana v. State Board of Education (1970), 9

DIBELS (Dynamic Indicators of Basic Early Literacy Skills), 155–156, 158–159

Differentiated instruction

adaptations for methods, materials, and environment, 129–136

classwide peer tutoring and, 218–219

cooperative learning and, 219

defined, 18, 96

feedback, providing, 143

overview of, 125–126

PASS variables, overview of, 127

praise, use of, 143

prioritizing instruction, 127–129

questioning techniques, 141–143

science and social studies, 389–390

systematic evaluation of instruction, 146–149